TRACKING NUCLEAR PROLIFERATION

A Guide in Maps and Charts, 1998

Rodney W. Jones
Mark G. McDonough
with Toby F. Dalton and
Gregory D. Koblentz

A CARNEGIE ENDOWMENT BOOK

© 1998 by the
Carnegie Endowment for International Peace
1779 Massachusetts Avenue, N.W.
Washington, D.C. 20036

Tracking Nuclear Proliferation: A Guide in Maps and Charts, 1998
may be ordered ($19.95) from the Carnegie Endowment's distributor:
The Brookings Institution Press
Department 029, Washington, D.C. 20042-0029, USA
Tel: 1-800-275-1447 or 202-797-6258
Fax: 202-797-6004, E-mail: bibooks@brook.edu

For permission to reproduce any part of *Tracking Nuclear Proliferation, 1998* for educational purposes, please contact the Non-Proliferation Project of the Carnegie Endowment (Tel: 202-939-2297, Fax: 202-483-1840, E-mail: nnp@ceip.org). Any updated figures available may also be obtained upon request. For a fuller description of the Project, including its Web site, see p. 329 of this volume.

Library of Congress Cataloging-in-Publication Data

Rodney W. Jones
     Tracking nuclear proliferation: a guide in maps and charts, 1998
/ Rodney W. Jones, Mark G. McDonough with Toby F. Dalton and Gregory D. Koblentz
          p.   cm.
     Rev. ed. of: Tracking nuclear proliferation / Leonard S. Spector, 1995.
     Includes bibliographical references.
     ISBN 0-87003-113-9 (pbk..)
     1. Nuclear weapons. 2. Nuclear weapons plants—Maps. 3. Nuclear weapons—Charts, diagrams, etc.
I. McDonough, Mark. G. II. Spector, Leonard S. Tracking nuclear proliferation. III. Title.
U264.J6623 1998   98-25810
355.02'17'0223—dc21   CIP

Printed by Automated Graphic Systems

CONTENTS

Foreword

Just as we were beginning to take some comfort in the nuclear non-proliferation successes of recent years, the May 1998 bomb blasts by India and Pakistan remind us that we are not out of the woods at all. There have been other signs, too, that proliferation problems are becoming much bigger. The end of the Cold War seemed at first to pave the way to wider cooperation against proliferation, but it also brought cash-starved defense firms from the former communist states into the global market place—with strong pressures to sell nuclear and missile technology and services to hostile actors and unstable regions. The Soviet collapse left unsecured bomb-grade materials in Russia, Kazakhstan, and Ukraine, and the fear that smugglers might feed these into a global black market. Even where progress has been visible in heading off dangerous nuclear transactions, the spread of missiles and of chemical and biological weapon capabilities is accelerating. The vivid demonstration of nuclear weapons in South Asia threatens not only the danger of nuclear war but the specter of corrosion in the regime and a chain reaction in proliferation to neighboring regions.

Tracking Nuclear Proliferation: A Guide in Maps and Charts, 1998 examines these problems as well as preventive measures in considerable detail. It is a major resource on the contemporary diplomatic history of the non-proliferation regime and a guide to U.S. policy and legislative efforts. It provides unique reference and university teaching materials on case histories of nuclear programs, technical activities, and import-export transactions. Its primers on nuclear technology and terminology make it exceptionally useful as an introduction to the nuclear policy field.

Tracking, 1998 is the latest volume in the nuclear proliferation series that Leonard S. Spector began in his former capacity as Senior Associate and Director of the Carnegie Endowment's Nuclear Non-Proliferation Project. Mr. Spector left the Endowment for a position in the U.S. Department of Energy in early September 1997, when this volume was under way but not yet complete. We are no less indebted to him, however, for his pioneering role in the series, and the vision and inspiration he brought to this vital subject over many years. Rodney W. Jones, an expert on nuclear arms control and non-proliferation who has published earlier

works, generously and skillfully took over the task of producing this volume, with the support of Carnegie's Non-Proliferation Project staff and contributions from selected outside authors and advisors, as detailed in the Preface.

Tracking, 1998 focuses primarily on nuclear proliferation. But it also covers key developments in the proliferation of missiles, and chemical and biological weapons. It places non-proliferation squarely in the complex, often fluid, post-Cold War security context of U.S.–Russian strategic arms control and the 1996 denuclearization of three post-Soviet states. The book traces China's step-by-step acceptance of non-proliferation norms, the continued dangers in Iraq and Iran, and the evolution of India's and Pakistan's nuclear weapons programs. It elucidates in each case the regime instruments and policy tools that have been developed to cope with proliferation.

Reining in the proliferation of nuclear weapons and of other weapons of mass destruction must remain at the top of our foreign policy priorities. Even if no final solution is close at hand, the record shows there are ways to contain proliferation through international vigilance and cooperation, buying time for diplomacy to work and to create improved security conditions. Barriers to proliferation could quickly give way, however, without sustained attention and energetic effort. Indeed, as this study makes clear, the nuclear tests in South Asia and the growing missile, chemical, and biological proliferation challenges stretch the existing regimes to their limits and demand fresh commitment, innovation, and resources to make them work.

We wish to express special thanks to the Carnegie Corporation of New York, the Ford Foundation, the W. Alton Jones Foundation, the John Merck Fund, the Prospect Hill Foundation, and the Ploughshares Fund for making this book possible through their programmatic support of the Carnegie Endowment's Non-Proliferation Project.

Jessica T. Mathews
President
Carnegie Endowment for
International Peace

Preface

Readers of *Tracking Nuclear Proliferation, 1998* who are already familiar with the 1995 version may benefit from a word on how this 1998 volume was produced. Most will recognize this book also reflects the spirit of Leonard S. Spector, the originator of the Carnegie series on nuclear non-proliferation. Sandy Spector accepted a position in the U.S. Department of Energy in September 1997, when he relinquished responsibility for this 1998 book, and ceased contributions to the manuscript. Carnegie turned to me to pull together the updating work already under way, and to produce the book. This meant updating preliminary chapter drafts and supporting materials, as well as authoring several that had not yet been produced.

This has been a challenging but rewarding task. The new version of *Tracking Nuclear Proliferation, 1998*, like its predecessor, is a factual and analytical treatment of the main features of the nuclear non-proliferation regime. It records regime successes and tracks continuing proliferation threats, country by country. It retains the easy-to-use format featuring maps and charts on the national nuclear programs of seventeen countries, appendices introducing newcomers to the basics of nuclear technology and multilateral nuclear controls, and detailed citations to help researchers and students who wish to go deeper. While the writing of each *Tracking, 1998* chapter was not completed at precisely the same time, the cutoff point for new material was generally December 1997. Selective updating continued until the book went to press in June 1998, primarily to cover the Indian and Pakistani nuclear tests of May 1998, but with some attention to developments in China, Russia, and Iraq as well.

This latest *Tracking* book has a number of new features. An Overview of Global Trends highlights the important changes and developments since April 1995—the cutoff date for the contents of the previous *Tracking* volume—and looks to the future. The complicated subject of U.S. legislative sanctions is given extensive coverage in several chapters, especially those on Iran, Iraq, Pakistan, China, and Russia. Each country chapter follows a basic two-part scheme. Material retained from the earlier book was placed in the Background section of each chapter, while material covering the period since April 1995 was placed in a Developments section. Instructors and scholars familiar with the previous book may find this demarcation of old and new helpful.

The International Nuclear Non-Proliferation Regime chapter is linked with new appendices on the outcomes of the 1995 NPT Review and Extension Conference, the negotiation and signature of the Comprehensive Test Ban Treaty, and the formation of Nuclear-Weapon-Free Zones (NWFZs). In this 1998 book, the subject of missile proliferation is covered in greater detail, both in several country chapters and in a chapter specifically dedicated to the subject, Missile Proliferation, 1995-97, along with charts of missile types, the countries that possess or export them, and an appendix describing the Missile Technology Control Regime (MTCR).

Like its predecessor, this book focuses primarily on the nuclear regime and nuclear proliferation, but it weaves in information on the proliferation of other weapons of mass destruction (WMD), particularly chemical- and biological-weapon capabilities and related export control issues. The formation of the Wassenaar Arrangement, touched on in several chapters, has its own new appendix. Wassenaar's export control guidelines focus on the transfer of conventional arms and dual-use technologies, and thereby reinforce the national and multilateral export control features of the nuclear non-proliferation regime as well as the MTCR. The maps and charts that track nuclear programs and weapons capabilities generally follow the format of the previous version of *Tracking Nuclear Proliferation*, but have been updated and, in several cases, modified, to reflect changed conditions or to make the presentation of detailed information more lucid.

As overall editor and co-author, I was pleased to share preparation of this book with Mark McDonough, who also co-authored the 1995 book with Leonard Spector. Mark's extraordinary attention to the detailed record and cogent analysis is evident in all the chapters on the Gulf and Middle East, as well as in the core International Nuclear Non-Proliferation Regime sections of the book. Richard Speier's primary contribution was the missile proliferation chapter and elucidation of the MTCR, but he also read, commented on, or improved the missile proliferation content of all of the country chapters. Toby Dalton, Gregory Koblentz, and Gregory Webb of the Carnegie Non-Proliferation Project staff each carried heavy loads, at different points, in doing primary periodical research, preliminary drafting of the updates of certain chapters, and the updating of maps and charts. Toby Dalton, who continues with the Project, worked intensively on the final assembly of the book. Anna Ivannakova and Antoine Duvauchelle, Project interns, provided vital research support, and Renate Seldon assisted with word-processing, clerical, and administrative tasks.

We are indebted for valuable chapter critiques and information from Carnegie colleagues and outside experts. Those who can be named include David Albright, Stephen P. Cohen, Rolf Ekeus, Jason Ellis, Dan Fenstermacher, Virginia Foran, Sherman Garnett, Arnold Horelick, David Kay, Michael Nacht, Robert S. Norris, Robert Oakley, George Perkovich, Alexander Pikayev, William Potter, John Redick, Randy Rydell, and Paul Stokes.

At the Carnegie Endowment, our thanks go to Jessica Mathews, President, and Thomas Carothers, Vice President for Global Policy, for their unflinching support in seeing this complicated project to completion; to Joseph Cirincione, Senior Associate in the Carnegie Non-Proliferation Project, for his promotional support of the final results; and to Valeriana Kallab, Carnegie Director of Publications, Sherry Pettie, Maria Sherzad, and Dixie Barlow for their graceful help with compression and style, meticulous attention to the detailed features of the book, and enormous effort in keeping the production timely.

While acknowledging appreciation to others who have contributed importantly to improving the quality of this book and to making it possible, including some who could not be named, the authors alone accept responsibility for the content and any errors that remain.

Rodney W. Jones

TRACKING NUCLEAR PROLIFERATION

1

AN OVERVIEW OF GLOBAL TRENDS 1998

An Overview of Global Trends

U ntil the Indian and Pakistani nuclear detonations of May 1998, international efforts to arrest the spread of nuclear arms in the 20th century's last decade seemed to be enjoying substantial success. The rate of nuclear proliferation appeared to be slowing, the geographic scope of proliferation was shrinking, and a landmark de-nuclearization was achieved in 1996 in part of the former Soviet Union. Three post-Soviet states with nuclear weapons left on their territory—Belarus, Kazakhstan, and Ukraine—cooperated in the removal of those weapons to Russia and joined the Nuclear Non-Proliferation Treaty (NPT) as non-nuclear-weapon states. The indefinite extension of the NPT itself in May 1995 showed that the norm of non-proliferation had become more deeply entrenched in international affairs than ever before. The positive trends were real, as this book shows in detail. Innovative diplomatic efforts, favorable political developments within potential proliferant states, and broader historical trends—especially the end of the Cold War and global economic expansion—contributed importantly to these accomplishments.

At the same time, one could see powerful countervailing currents that could place recent non-proliferation achievements at risk and even threaten to rupture the painstakingly built non-proliferation regime. Among these, the danger of leakage of nuclear weapons or weapons-usable materials from the former Soviet Union was rightly regarded as the most serious and came in for the lion's share of U.S. attention in the early 1990s. As for South Asia, it surely was known that the lid might suddenly blow off the ambiguous nuclear rivalry between India and Pakistan, but this scenario was too easily discounted in major-power official circles because of nuclear arms control successes, both in strategic arms reduction and in the 1996 conclusion of the Comprehensive Test Ban Treaty (CTBT). The CTBT was viewed as a crucial new global restraint on both nuclear proliferation and the strategic arms race. But the nuclear lid did blow in South Asia in May 1998. India's and Pakistan's nuclear explosive tests and self-declarations that they had become "nuclear weapon powers" could now give political cover to other proliferants that would be only too eager to follow suit.[1] These events certainly could spawn a geographically

continuous nuclear proliferation chain from Delhi to Baghdad.

While the sudden accrual of bombs in South Asia overshadowed almost everything else on the proliferation scene as this book went to press, it is important to note, also on the darker side, that nuclear proliferation threats in the 1990s became increasingly interwoven in the most hostile proliferant states with the spread of other "weapons of mass destruction" (WMD): chemical and biological weapons and missile delivery systems. Moreover, there are now increasing signs that the ability to manufacture portable WMD, especially chemical and germ weapons, is spreading among terrorist groups. Such weapons could be home-grown or smuggled past normal defenses to strike deep in domestic societies—imposing potentially unbearable stresses on democracies. Thus not only is it too early to declare a non-proliferation victory but newly emerging aspects of proliferation suggest it may be necessary to go back to the drawing board.

PROMISING TRENDS

Fewer States of Concern. The nuclear status chart at the end of this chapter shows that today only seven countries remain on the active nuclear proliferation "watch list": Israel, India, and Pakistan, all of which are deemed capable of deploying or launching nuclear arms; and Iran, Iraq, Libya, and North Korea, which are less advanced in their quest for nuclear arms but nevertheless remain states of significant proliferation concern. It is possible that Algeria also bears watching because of violent internal conflict and earlier, questionable nuclear technology cooperation with China. In addition, a late 1997 report of Syrian efforts to acquire nuclear research installations from Russia suggests that Syria may return to the nuclear watch list.[2]

Yet considerably fewer countries are currently attempting to acquire nuclear weapons (or the ability to make them) than were trying to do so during the 1980s. The seven states that are of greatest concern today were already then considered proliferation threats. Moreover, it is now known that Argentina, Brazil, Romania, and Taiwan all then took steps of one type or another to pursue nuclear arms but backed away or renounced their acquisition. South Africa—

which had secretly acquired a six-weapon undeclared nuclear arsenal in the late 1970s—actually eliminated the weapons it possessed in 1991, before disclosing it had done so in the process of formally renouncing nuclear arms in a dramatic move the following year.

De-Nuclearization of Former Soviet Republics. The presence of Soviet nuclear weapons on the territory of Belarus, Kazakhstan, and Ukraine following the dissolution of the Soviet Union raised the separate fear that one or more of these states might seize possession or assert political and military control over nuclear arms in order to become a *de facto* nuclear power overnight. Had this occurred, it would have had serious repercussions on the stability of Central Europe as well as on the viability of the traditional nuclear non-proliferation regime. All three states, however, have since cooperated with Russia and the United States in the removal to Russia of all the nuclear arms on their soil, and all have implemented earlier commitments to join the NPT as non-nuclear-weapon states. This de-nuclearization process had begun well before 1995, but de-nuclearization was not finally consummated in all three states until November 1996. Today, Russia is the only Soviet successor state with nuclear weapons.

Roll-backs and Renunciations. Significantly, most of the states that are no longer on the proliferation "watch list" did not merely cease the activities that had triggered concern. Rather, they took affirmative steps to dispel concerns through measures such as accepting new treaty restrictions on their nuclear affairs, disclosing and dismantling clandestine nuclear-weapon-related programs, and/or permitting wide-ranging international inspections to verify the cessation of offending activities. Moreover, South Africa's unprecedented elimination of its stock of six nuclear weapons demonstrated that the spread of nuclear weapons is not an irreversible process, a development that significantly bolstered the norm of non-proliferation.

Expansion of Export Controls. Beyond the roll-backs and renunciations, Argentina, Brazil, Romania, South Africa, and Ukraine have taken steps to halt proliferation elsewhere by joining the Nuclear Suppliers Group (NSG), the informal organization of states that have adopted parallel controls on their nuclear exports. Recently China joined the NPT's Nuclear Exporters (Zangger) Committee, which operates in parallel with the NSG to coordinate controls on exports of nuclear materials, equipment, and technology. In addition, Argentina, Brazil, and South Africa have become members of the Missile Technology Control Regime (MTCR), Israel has adhered through a memorandum of understanding, and Ukraine has agreed to abide by its standards—all thereby demonstrating a commitment to an important set of non-proliferation export control norms.

Robust Non-Proliferation Regime. In May 1995, the centerpiece of the regime, the NPT, was extended indefinitely by consensus. Adherence to the Treaty now is nearly universal. All five nuclear-weapon states (the United States, Russia, Great Britain, France, and China) and, as of late 1997, 180 non-nuclear-weapon states had become parties to the accord. Under the Treaty, all non-nuclear-weapon state parties agree to renounce nuclear arms and to accept inspection of all their nuclear installations by the International Atomic Energy Agency (IAEA) to verify that they are not being used for military purposes (a system known as "full-scope IAEA safeguards.") Today, apart from the five established nuclear powers, the only states with significant nuclear programs that are not subject to such full-scope IAEA inspections are India, Israel, and Pakistan.[3] The remarkable pervasiveness of the NPT/IAEA system has helped to create an increasingly powerful norm of nuclear weapons renunciation.[4]

Strengthened Safeguards. As detailed in the chapter on the International Non-Proliferation Regime and in Appendix D on IAEA Safeguards, other key elements of the non-proliferation regime also have been significantly strengthened in recent years. For example, IAEA safeguards inspectors now have the authority to demand special inspections of suspected (undeclared) nuclear sites in non-nuclear-weapon NPT state parties. Moreover, the export controls of the Nuclear Suppliers Group now extend not only to nuclear equipment, materials, and technology but also to dual-use commodities (those having nuclear as well as non-nuclear end uses).[5] Pressures to enhance both elements of the regime in large part sprang from the revelations regarding Iraq's clandestine nuclear weapons program that emerged during the inspections after the 1991 Gulf War. These inspections exposed weaknesses in the IAEA system as it had been implemented before and also highlighted gaps in Western nuclear export control systems.

Nuclear-Weapon-Free Zones. An additional regime component, regional nuclear-weapon-free zones, has also become more extensive geographically and has gained strength from wider adherence among the states concerned. These include the widely accepted nuclear-weapon-free-zone pacts in Latin America and the Caribbean (the 1967 Treaty of Tlatelolco) and the South Pacific (the 1985 Treaty of Rarotonga), as well as more recently initiated nuclear-weapon-free-zone accords in Southeast Asia (opened for signature on December 15, 1995) and Africa (the Treaty of Pelindaba, opened for signature on April 11, 1996).

Comprehensive Test Ban. A major new element was added in 1996 to reinforce the nuclear disarmament as well as non-proliferation objectives of the regime. This was the Comprehensive Test Ban Treaty (CTBT) prohibiting all nuclear explosive testing, which opened for signature in September 1996. Although it is technically possible that an emerging nuclear power could develop an early-generation fission (atomic) weapon without conducting an explosive test, the comprehensive test ban will present such states with a barrier to developing more sophisticated nuclear weapons, especially far more powerful thermonuclear weapons. The CTBT also could retard emerging nuclear powers from developing fission warheads for missiles. It also will stop each of the five nuclear powers, as long as it complies with the CTBT, from developing or producing nuclear weapons of "new design."

Nuclear Arms Reduction Agreements and Measures. Finally, though they are separate from the non-proliferation regime, the adoption by the nuclear-weapon states of additional nuclear arms reduction agreements such as the pending START II and anticipated START III, the unilateral reductions of the nuclear arsenals of these states, and the continuing dismantlement of nuclear weapons in Russia and the United States all reinforce the norm of nuclear non-proliferation. These measures have been accompanied by positive and negative assurances, undertaken by the nuclear-weapon states, to strengthen international security and the nuclear non-proliferation regime by restricting the use or threat of use of nuclear weapons against non-nuclear-weapon states that adhere to non-proliferation norms and are parties to the regime.

Ad Hoc Constraints. The strength of the consensus underlying international efforts to contain nuclear proliferation is also reflected in the fact that many of the states on today's proliferation watch list are under considerably greater constraints than they were as recently as five years ago.

- Iran's nuclear activities have become the target of intensive international scrutiny, leading to an embargo on all nuclear transfers to it by the West and to Iran's voluntary agreement to accept special IAEA "visits" at any location within its borders.

- Pursuant to U.N. mandates that followed the 1991 Gulf War, Iraq's nuclear infrastructure has been largely, if not totally, destroyed, and the country is now subject to an extraordinary U.N. Special Commission/IAEA monitoring regime.

- Under the 1994 "Agreed Framework" understanding with the United States, North Korea has ceased operating all of its facilities capable of producing weapons-usable nuclear material, and it has stopped the construction of several installations that could have greatly expanded this capability.

- Libya's bid for nuclear arms appears to be completely arrested as the result of a supplier-country embargo that has blocked its access to nuclear equipment and technology.

- Algeria, which in 1991 secretly purchased from China a large research reactor that was not under IAEA monitoring, was later persuaded to join the NPT and to place that unit and all of the country's nuclear activities under the Agency's monitoring system.

- The international reaction to India's and Pakistan's May 1998 tests was remarkably uniform in condemnation and desire to avoid rewarding them for defying the regime.

CONTINUING CHALLENGES

Leakage from the Former Soviet Union. The positive trends just outlined are predicated on an assumption that has underpinned the very concept of non-proliferation since the beginning of the nuclear age: namely, that a state seeking nuclear arms must produce the necessary weapons-usable nuclear material itself. This objective has usually taken any well-endowed state at least ten years to achieve through a dedicated program and has required the construction and operation of numerous, highly complex, and hard-to-disguise installations. The emergence of a black market putting such materials up for purchase would enable countries to sidestep the usual barriers and drastically alter this equation.[6]

Today, Russia possesses the vast bulk of the Soviet Union's weapons-grade materials—some 1,200 tons of weapons-grade uranium and 200 tons of plutonium, much of which is inadequately protected against theft or diversion.[7] Only about 15 kg of weapons-grade uranium, or 5 kg of plutonium, is needed for a nuclear device. Wholesale smuggling of these materials could vastly increase the capabilities of today's *de facto* nuclear powers and enable several aspiring nuclear states to emerge suddenly on the nuclear threshold—some perhaps within as little as a year's time, depending on preexisting technical and financial capabilities.

According to former CIA Director John Deutch, a number of states have been interested in Russian weapons material. Testifying in March 1996, Deutch stated, "We believe that several nations at one time or another have explored the possibility of purchasing strategic nuclear materials as the simplest and quickest and cheapest way to acquire nuclear weapons capability. Prominent examples include Iran and Iraq and, to a lesser extent, North Korea and Libya."[8] Iran is known to have inquired about the availability of nuclear material at one installation in Kazakhstan that at the time was holding considerable stocks of weapons-grade uranium.[9] A black market in nuclear weapons material could undermine the global non-proliferation verification system of the IAEA.[10] Indeed, it could destroy confidence in the traditional historical understanding of nuclear proliferation as a slow, potentially controllable process.

A number of confirmed episodes have already taken place in which very small quantities of weapons-usable nuclear material were stolen from Russian facilities and in some cases smuggled out of the country. None of the known episodes, however, has involved the quantity of material necessary to manufacture a nuclear explosive; nor has any involved successful delivery to a purchaser connected with a country of proliferation concern or with a terrorist organization. Moreover, the number of reported cases appears to be decreasing. It must be recognized, however, that other episodes may have taken place that have not come to the attention of law enforcement or intelligence officials.

With U.S. assistance, Russia and the other Soviet successor states are working to enhance security at the facilities where such material is processed and stored. Although significant security improvements are likely over the next two years, for now, especially in Russia, numerous facilities containing many tons of weapons-usable nuclear material remain highly vulnerable, as do key transportation links. Thus, whether a black market in such material will emerge or be suppressed is very much an open question—particularly given the social, political, and economic pressures on Russian society. It should be noted that security over nuclear weapons themselves is generally thought to be tighter, but even here, the picture is not altogether reassuring.[11]

India and Pakistan. As mentioned at the outset and also discussed in detail in the chapters on India and Pakistan, the May 1998 nuclear explosive tests opened a Pandora's box of pent-up nuclear competition on the Subcontinent, which will almost certainly precipitate a full-fledged nuclear arms and missile race. In India, where the pro-nuclear and Hindu nationalist Bharatiya Janata Party (BJP) had gained increasing influence and actually took power following the March 1998 elections, the preparations evidently had been made for conducting not just a second nuclear test, but a whole series of them, after a 24-year hiatus.[12] The preparations for such an Indian test series would seem, in retrospect, to date back to December 1995, when international disclosure and diplomatic pressure appeared to have forced cancellation but probably should have been viewed as only temporarily holding them back.[13]

Revelations in August 1996 that Pakistan was constructing a facility to manufacture nuclear-capable ballistic missiles (like the Chinese-origin M-11 and possibly M-9 systems), and 1997 reports that India had revived the nuclear-capable Agni medium-range missile program and intended to develop an intercontinental-range missile (ICBM) known as Surya, intensified the pressures on each government to step up the missile-development and testing activities and perhaps strengthened those circles that advocated openly deploying nuclear deterrent systems.

Once India conducted its nuclear explosive tests, it was almost certain that Pakistan would reciprocate by conducting one or more nuclear detonations itself—as it did within two weeks of India's tests in May. Pakistan may now also respond to the pressures of the Indian nuclear declarations and of sanctions by deploying the 30 Chinese-supplied M-11 missiles that Pakistan is believed to have in storage and by ending the informal freeze on the country's production of fissile material.

Apart from escalating the South Asian nuclear arms race, the Indian and Pakistani tests and each government's assertion that it had become a "nuclear weapons power" signify the arrival on the world scene of two self-declared nuclear states and challenge the non-proliferation regime in profound ways. On the one hand, the regime has no legal space for recognition of additional nuclear-weapon states, and its subscribing members will have to arrive at a consensus on how to treat this new situation. On the other, India's and Pakistan's actions will, unless offset by countervailing measures, tend to undermine confidence that proliferation can be contained. Especially if they are rewarded, the South Asian nuclear actions will be seized upon by other aspiring proliferators as political cover for their own efforts to move up the nuclear weapons ladder.

Other Counter-Currents. Despite significant gains in strengthening the non-proliferation regime in the 1990s, serious weaknesses remain. While the countries of principal proliferation concern today—India, Israel, and Pakistan apart—are all parties to the NPT, their commitments to the pact are in question, raising doubts about the effectiveness of the Treaty. North Korea, for one, is not yet in compliance with the full-scope safeguards requirements of the Treaty, and Iran, though apparently meeting its safeguards obligations, is thought to be pursuing activities inconsistent with the Treaty's prohibition against manufacturing nuclear weapons.

Developments in Iraq have highlighted the limits of the IAEA system. The defection of Iraqi General Hussein Kamal in August 1995 brought to light extensive new information unambiguously indicating that Iraq continued to conceal the full extent of its former nuclear program—despite the IAEA's extraordinary investigatory powers in that country under Security Council Resolutions 687, 707, and 715. Moreover, IAEA analysts assume that, notwithstanding the Agency's efforts, Iraq has continued to pursue work on nuclear weapon designs and to fabricate or acquire abroad key non-nuclear components for nuclear arms. These developments inevitably raise questions about the Agency's ability to detect clandestine activities using the more limited safeguards that it implements under the NPT—questions exacerbated by the hesitation of IAEA member states to endorse the complete set of new tools that the Agency has hoped to implement under its "93 + 2" program (see Appendix D on IAEA Safeguards). Late in 1997, efforts by the U.N. Special Commission (UNSCOM) to uncover and eradicate Iraq's chemical and biological weapons as well as nuclear and proscribed missile capabilities ran into intense resistance from Iraq and not only surfaced differences of approach between the United States and both Russia and France but also raised questions about whether Iraq's compliance with special inspections can be enforced by diplomatic means alone.

China's activities as a nuclear and missile supplier to Pakistan and Iran also have been special sources of concern in recent years. As a party to the NPT, China is required to ensure that exported nuclear equipment and materials are placed under IAEA inspection in the recipient state, but Beijing has not accepted all the additional Nuclear Suppliers Group restrictions. NSG guidelines prohibit nuclear sales to states such as Pakistan and India (which do not accept full-scope safe-guards), and regulate transfers of nuclear technology and dual-use commodities potentially useful in nuclear weapon programs. In 1989, China contracted with Pakistan to provide a nuclear power plant—still under construction at Chasma—that would be placed under safeguards anyway. Of far greater concern was past Chinese assistance to Pakistan's unsafeguarded program, specifically to the Kahuta enrichment plant connected with the country's nuclear weapons program. There has also been some evidence of past assistance by China to Pakistan's Khushab reactor, which appears to be designed as a plutonium-production reactor for the weapons program and thus would not be placed under safeguards. The United States was also concerned about China's nuclear assistance to Iran, which, although under IAEA safeguards, could indirectly contribute to Iran's apparent quest for nuclear weapons.[14]

Nevertheless, in 1996-97, China made significant progress in bringing its policies and practices into closer conformity with nuclear non-proliferation regime export control standards. In May 1996, after acknowledging that a Kahuta-related ring magnet transaction had gone forward, China pledged that it would "not provide assistance to unsafeguarded nuclear facilities."[15] In 1997, China promulgated stringent nuclear export control regulations that correspond to the guidelines of the Zangger Committee, actually joined the Zangger Committee and provided more explicit non-proliferation assurances to the United States at an October summit in Washington, and dropped virtually all nuclear cooperation with Iran. Although China's nuclear export policy actions in 1997 clearly represent a major step forward, the effectiveness of China's commitments remains to be determined by monitoring of its actual behavior and the behavior of its many semi-autonomous trading firms.

The growing threat of nuclear terrorism may also become a more potent counter-current to the regime. Two episodes in the 1990s highlighted the continuing interest of highly capable non-state actors in nuclear mischief. One was the 1993 effort of the Japanese Aum Shinrikyo—the cult responsible for releasing Sarin nerve gas in the Tokyo subway system—to acquire uranium mining property in Australia as part of its overall program to develop weapons of mass destruction. A second episode was the placement of some 30 pounds of radioactive cesium in a Moscow park by Chechen rebels, accompanied by the threat that an explosive device containing more of that material had been placed elsewhere in the city.[16] Although there was no risk of a nuclear detonation in either case, these episodes provide a taste of what the future may hold, particularly if weapons-usable nuclear materials begin to leak from the former Soviet Union.

Finally, the proliferation of other WMD—chemical and biological weapons—and of missile delivery systems for WMD has moved steadily ahead in the more hostile proliferant countries. Development or acquisition of these other deadly weapons often goes hand in hand with nuclear proliferation, or comes to

the forefront where efforts to arrest nuclear acquisition may have had a measure of success.

LOOKING TO THE FUTURE

Taking the brighter and darker trends together, the future priorities for non-proliferation will be threefold: repairing, sustaining, and broadening. These are overlapping, not mutually exclusive requirements. But the repairing category always tends to be the most urgent—frequently the result of a crisis that causes attrition or threatens a regime rupture. The Soviet collapse, the Gulf War aftermath, and the North Korean crisis fell in that category in the early 1990s, and the 1998 South Asian nuclear weaponization will take center field for a time.

Repairing and limiting further damage from South Asia means depriving India and Pakistan of symbolic, political, and material gains from their nuclear tests and declarations—to minimize the incentives for other proliferant states to follow suit. This task calls for close cooperation among the members of the non-proliferation regime, big and small powers alike. It does not mean cutting off India and Pakistan from normal diplomatic and trade relations, although the sanctions in law that were known beforehand and that automatically curtail taxpayer-funded "assistance" and "credit" programs to weaponizing countries are a legitimate response. Concessions should be made, if at all, only for tangible, measurable, and binding non-proliferation and international security gains.

The two regional security priorities that come up first—inhibiting the nuclear and missile arms races, and reducing the risk of an India-Pakistan nuclear war—cannot be promoted successfully without recognizing that the genuine defense needs of the two rivals (including those that are asymmetrical) must be recognized and balanced.

After reciprocal nuclear testing series were completed, the prime ministers of both India and Pakistan stopped short of ordering deployment of nuclear weapons and called for discussion of a testing moratorium. Diplomatic assistance in codifying this is warranted, but a mechanism worth considering is a U.N.–mandated special commission of representatives of seven countries, two nominated by India, two by Pakistan, and three by the Secretary-General in consultation with the permanent members of the Security Council. Such a commission, chaired by the Secretary-General or his designee, would start a diplomatic process that could dovetail international interests with those of the two South Asian states directly concerned by developing a binding constraint on nuclear testing (and possibly on nuclear weapons deployment) that would reflect, and be sensitive to, the realities of both the Subcontinent and neighboring regions. Should the commission find a solution acceptable to both sides that can be harmonized with the rights and obligations of parties to the CTBT, it could be a bridge to both countries adhering to the CTBT after all.

Sustaining the non-proliferation regime is a more familiar but still vital task of providing adequate support both for: (1) the relevant international law and institutions—such as the five-year reviews of the NPT, the replenishment of the IAEA, and the bolstering of the IAEA nuclear safeguards system—and (2) the consolidation of international cooperation in managing national nuclear export control functions, monitoring of dangerous trade, and reducing regional tensions and conflicts that create political or insecurity motives for proliferation. Preventing the development of a nuclear materials black market from the unsecured fissile material in the former Soviet Union has been a key recent priority on which progress has been made, although much remains to be done on this task. Ensuring that the U.N.–mandated monitoring of nuclear activities in Iraq continues and managing the Agreed Framework steps related to North Korea are other ongoing tasks indispensable to sustaining the regime. Successful efforts to scale back strategic and tactical nuclear weapons through negotiations between the nuclear-weapon states, the creation of security assurances for non-nuclear weapon states, the institutionalization of confidence-building measures through nuclear-weapon-free zones, and implementing the comprehensive nuclear test ban are also highly important elements of a strategy to sustain and strengthen the non-proliferation regime.

With only a very small number of states not accepting the NPT or equivalent IAEA controls on their nuclear activities, broadening the regime is in one sense a nearly accomplished fact. The unavoidable challenge for the future is inter-relating controls on nuclear weapons and materials with those on chemical and biological weapons and on delivery systems for weapons of mass destruction. While the magnitude of the nuclear dangers outweighs those from other forms of WMD, the very success of blocking the spread of nuclear weapons tends to give greater impetus to proliferation of the chemical and biological capabilities. The legal instruments for preventing the spread of chemical and biological weapons, and to check missile proliferation, are for the most part more recent in origin and have further to go before implementation than nuclear instruments such as the NPT and IAEA safeguards. But the severity of chemical and biological threats, and approaches to their international control (such as procedures for monitoring and compliance), have enough parallels to nuclear threats to lead authorities to address them together in security strategies. If we continue to make progress with non-proliferation, we are likely to see broader non-proliferation and security frameworks in the future.

NOTES

[1] The Nuclear Non-Proliferation Treaty (NPT) is the legal basis for the terminology that ascribes "nuclear-weapon state" exclusively to the five "established" (*de jure*) nuclear powers, each of which had detonated a nuclear device prior to 1967—an explicit cut-off date under Treaty provisions. Under the NPT, all other states are considered "non-nuclear-weapon states," irrespective of whether they are parties or not. It is considered highly unlikely that the NPT would be (or could be) amended to recognize *de facto* nuclear-weapon states as additional "nuclear-weapon states," whether such states have declared themselves nuclear-weapon states or not. The convention used in this book is to categorize such *de facto* nuclear-weapon states (e.g., Israel, India, and Pakistan) as "non-NPT nuclear-weapon states" in the NPT-related chart, and as "*de facto*," "threshold," or "self-declared" nuclear-weapon states in other contexts, as clarity may demand. Policy conventions on such terminology may evolve differently.

[2] According to the report, the Russian government has decided to allow negotiations with Syria on the sale of a nuclear research reactor. See David Makovsky, "Russia-Syria Nuclear Talks to Start," *Ha'aretz*, December 31, 1997.

[3] Brazil, though not a party to the NPT, accepts comparable IAEA monitoring and inspections under the Latin American and Caribbean Nuclear-Weapon Free Zone Treaty (Treaty of Tlatelolco), as well as through a quadripartite agreement with Argentina, the IAEA, and a bilateral inspection group called the Argentine-Brazilian Accounting and Control Commission (ABACC).

[4] The IAEA's unique discovery through inspection activities—undertaken in conjunction with the U.N. Special Commission (UNSCOM)—of the ambitious, variegated nuclear weapons program in Iraq is a *sui generis* element of the regime that plays a crucial role in suppressing Iraqi mass-destruction-weapon capabilities. The special inspections in Iraq have also served as a test bed for new IAEA verification measures that are now being integrated into the IAEA system as part of the 93 + 2 program. U.N. Security Council support for the IAEA in Iraq, which has included maintenance of economic sanctions and acceptance of the possible use of force to gain compliance with relevant Security Council resolutions, has also set a precedent that will encourage the involvement of this body in future nonproliferation crises.

[5] China is the only important nuclear-exporter state that is not a member of the Nuclear Suppliers Group. China did join the parallel NPT Nuclear Exporters (Zangger) Committee in the fall of 1997. As a party to the NPT, China is bound to ensure that all nuclear exports are placed under IAEA monitoring in the recipient state. In May 1996, Beijing pledged not to provide "assistance to any facility" that is not under IAEA inspection. "Foreign Ministry Spokesman on U.S. Decision Not to Impose Sanctions on China," *Xinhua News Service*, May 11, 1996. In the summer and fall of 1997, China issued stringent new export control regulations that conform to Zangger Committee guidelines, and it reaffirmed the 1996 pledge, along with additional assurances to the United States. See China chapter in this volume.

[6] An even more sudden form of nuclear proliferation would be acquisition of nuclear weapons themselves—directly, or by smuggling—from illicit sources in a nuclear-weapon state. Concerns that nuclear weapons might be smuggled out of Russia have been aired from time to time and cannot be totally put to rest. In 1997, there were reports initiated by Gen. Alexander Lebed, former Secretary of the Russian Security Council, who claimed to have attempted, without full success, to locate and make an accounting in Russian inventories of "portable" nuclear weapons (the press referred to "suitcase bombs," but Lebed probably meant atomic demolition munitions designed for use by special forces for sabotage behind enemy lines). Such weapons could easily be smuggled and probably made to operate by non-state actors as well as any recipient state.

[7] Carnegie Endowment for International Peace and Monterey Institute of International Studies, *Soviet Nuclear Successor States: Nuclear Weapon and Sensitive Export Status Report*, No. 4, May 1996; Graham T. Allison, Owen R. Coté, Jr., Richard A. Falkenrath, and Steven E. Miller, *Avoiding Nuclear Anarchy* (Cambridge, MA, and London: MIT Press, 1995), pp. 35 ff.

[8] Testimony of John Deutch, Director of the Central Intelligence Agency, before the Permanent Investigations Subcommittee of the Senate Governmental Affairs Committee, March 20, 1996.

[9] Kazakhstan released the bulk of this material, some 600 kg, to the United States in 1994, under Operation Sapphire. (See Kazakhstan chapter in this volume for more details.)

[10] The basic methodology of the global inspection system administered by the IAEA depends upon the careful accounting of nuclear materials as they are produced, processed, used, stored, and trans-

ferred. A widely available, clandestine source of weapons-usable nuclear material would wreak havoc with this system, making it impossible to be confident that all material within a state had been accounted for. Moreover, the IAEA's new special inspections, intended to ferret out clandestine weapons programs, depend in the first instance on the receipt of evidence of suspect activities. This evidence might be provided by the intelligence services of IAEA member states. But obtaining such evidence would be far more difficult where a black market in nuclear materials exists, since a proliferant state with access to that black market could avoid constructing the highly visible facilities normally needed to produce these materials.

[11]Allison et al., *Avoiding Nuclear Anarchy,* op. cit., pp. 35 ff.

[12]With the fall of the United Front government of I. K. Gujral in late 1997 and the continued decline of the Indian National Congress party, it was expected that the BJP would assume power in March 1998 elections—possibly even with a parliamentary majority. While the BJP failed to win an absolute majority by itself, it was able to form a governing coalition with small parties and independents—some having cooperated with the BJP in contesting the elections, and others becoming allied after the elections.

[13]Given the 1995 events and the BJP's assertion in its party platform of the intention to "induct nuclear weapons" in India's defense, the failure of the Clinton Administration to anticipate the 1998 tests is most remarkable; those events had been sufficient for "strategic warning" of a clear and present proliferation danger. There was, of course, a failure of instant intelligence recognition of signs at the test site, in the days or hours immediately before the Indian tests occurred, but only a more active White House interest would have kept those particular intelligence sections adequately staffed and at peak effort, or, more importantly, built the missing human intelligence capability that would have provided a longer warning lead-time. The biggest failure was not intelligence, however, but wishful thinking about India at the upper levels of the U.S. government, blinding officials to the deception being propagated after the BJP took power in Delhi. The objective after 1995 should have been to get the test equipment removed from the test site and to dissuade authorities from any desire to test—pressing for specific activities that could be verified by technical means.

[14]Responses of Tobi T. Gati, Assistant Secretary of State for Intelligence and Research, in the *Hearings on Current and Projected National Security Threats to the United States and Its Interests Abroad* before the Select Committee on Intelligence, U.S. Senate, February 22, 1996, p. 135.

[15]"Foreign Ministry Spokesman," *Xinhua,* op. cit.

[16]*Global Proliferation of Weapons of Mass Destruction,* Hearings before the Permanent Subcommittee on Investigations, U.S. Senate, October 31 and November 1, 1995, Part I, p. 75; Senator Richard G. Lugar, "Opening Statement on the Nunn-Lugar-Domenici Amendment to the 1997 Defense Authorization Bill," U.S. Senate, July 1996.

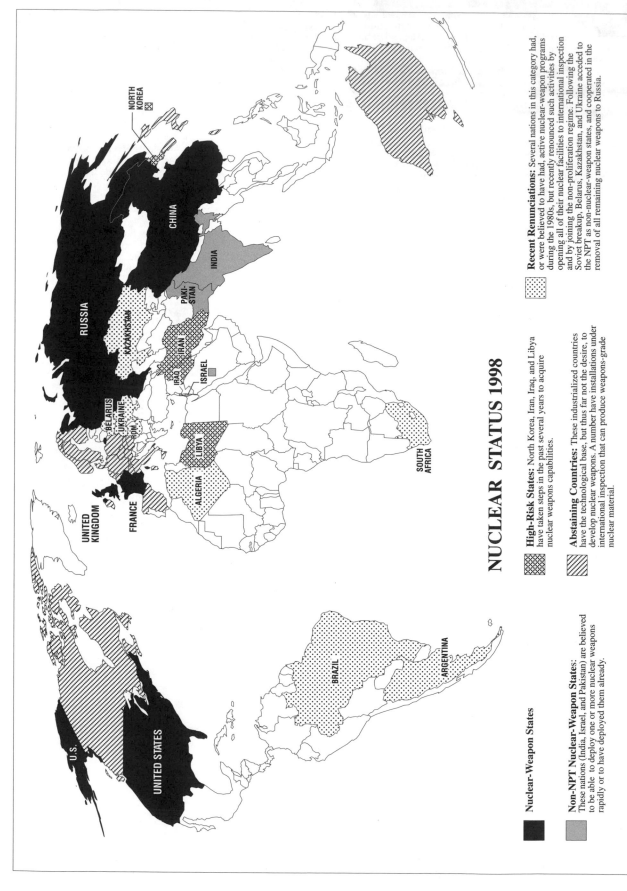

NUCLEAR STATUS 1998

Nuclear-Weapon States

Non-NPT Nuclear-Weapon States: These nations (India, Israel, and Pakistan) are believed to be able to deploy one or more nuclear weapons rapidly or to have deployed them already.

High-Risk States: North Korea, Iran, Iraq, and Libya have taken steps in the past several years to acquire nuclear weapons capabilities.

Abstaining Countries: These industrialized countries have the technological base, but thus far not the desire, to develop nuclear weapons. A number have installations under international inspection that can produce weapons-grade nuclear material.

Recent Renunciations: Several nations in this category had, or were believed to have had, active nuclear-weapon programs during the 1980s, but recently renounced such activities by opening all of their nuclear facilities to international inspection and by joining the non-proliferation regime. Following the Soviet breakup, Belarus, Kazakhstan, and Ukraine acceded to the NPT as non-nuclear-weapon states, and cooperated in the removal of all remaining nuclear weapons to Russia.

Carnegie Endowment for International Peace, *Tracking Nuclear Proliferation*, 1998

NUCLEAR STATUS, 1998

NUCLEAR-WEAPON STATES

China, France, Russia, United Kingdom, United States: Each of these five states originally declared its nuclear-weapons program and was recognized under the 1968 Nuclear Non-Proliferation Treaty (NPT) as a nuclear-weapon state because it had tested a nuclear weapon prior to Jan. 1, 1967. Estimated total nuclear warhead stockpiles: U.S., 12,070; Russia, 22,500; United Kingdom, 260; France, 450; China, 400.

When the Soviet Union collapsed in late 1991, nuclear weapons remained on the territory of many of the new independent states. Strategic nuclear weapons remained in three besides Russia: Belarus, Kazakhstan, and Ukraine. Russia was recognized as the Soviet Union's sole nuclear-weapon-state successor. All tactical nuclear weapons were withdrawn to Russia by June 1992. Russia assumed control over all Soviet nuclear weapons, and all strategic nuclear weapons were withdrawn to Russia by November 1996—completing an unprecedented de-nuclearization process (see Renunciations below).

NON-NPT NUCLEAR-WEAPON STATES

India, Israel, Pakistan: Both India and Pakistan conducted nuclear explosive tests in May 1998 and declared themselves nuclear-weapon states. Neither is an NPT member, and neither is recognized by the NPT or other international treaties as a nuclear-weapon state. Neither is believed to have deployed nuclear weapons as of June 1998, but India is considered to be able to assemble 60-70 weapons, and Pakistan about 15 weapons, on short notice. Israel, which also is not an NPT member, has not declared its nuclear-weapon capability but is believed to have an operational arsenal of over 100 weapons.

HIGH-RISK STATES

Iran, Iraq, Libya, North Korea: All are suspected of seeking nuclear weapons but are currently subject to international controls and technological constraints. Although these states are party to the NPT and have denied seeking nuclear weapons, their non-proliferation commitments are still considered suspect. North Korea is closest to having nuclear weapons; it agreed to freeze and ultimately dismantle its nuclear weapons program under the October 1994 U.S.–North Korean Agreed Framework; it may have separated enough weapons-grade material for a nuclear device. Iran is eight to ten years from nuclear weapons—but could accelerate its program if nuclear assets leaked from the former Soviet Union. Iraq's extensive nuclear program was dismantled by U.N. inspectors, but clandestine procurement efforts and nuclear-weapons-related research probably continue. Libya has an extremely limited nuclear infrastructure.

RENUNCIATIONS

Algeria, Argentina, Belarus, Brazil, Kazakhstan, Romania, South Africa, Ukraine: South Africa dismantled its arsenal of six nuclear weapons in the early 1990s and signed the NPT in 1991; the IAEA has verified complete dismantlement of all nuclear devices. Belarus, Kazakhstan, and Ukraine fulfilled earlier commitments to non-nuclear-weapon status and cooperated with Russia's removal of all strategic and tactical nuclear weapons located on their territory after the Soviet Union collapsed. The three joined the NPT as non-nuclear-weapon states and opened all of their nuclear facilities to IAEA inspections by the end of 1996. Argentina and Brazil each brought into force the Treaty of Tlatelolco and agreed to implement a system of comprehensive IAEA and bilateral inspections; Argentina acceded to the NPT in February 1995. Algeria acceded to the NPT in January 1995. Romania, under the Ceausescu regime, apparently pursued a nuclear-weapons development program, which included experimental plutonium extraction not subject to IAEA monitoring; after Ceausescu's overthrow in 1989, the Iliescu government terminated the program.

ABSTAINING COUNTRIES

Australia, Belgium, Bulgaria, Canada, the Czech Republic, Denmark, Finland, Germany, Hungary, Italy, Japan, Mexico, the Netherlands, Norway, Slovakia, South Korea, Spain, Sweden, Switzerland, and Taiwan: All are countries with a significant industrial base and at least one commercial-scale nuclear facility. Several had seriously explored a nuclear-weapons option in the 1960s or 1970s, but all have signed the NPT as non nuclear-weapon states, have accepted comprehensive IAEA inspections, and are believed to be in compliance with their NPT obligations.

2

THE INTERNATIONAL NUCLEAR NON-PROLIFERATION REGIME

The International Nuclear Non-Proliferation Regime

While the Treaty on the Non-Proliferation of Nuclear Weapons (NPT) is its centerpiece, the global nuclear non-proliferation regime consists of a series of interlocking international treaties, bilateral undertakings, and multilateral inspections aimed at halting the spread of nuclear weapons. Other major elements of the regime are the International Atomic Energy Agency (IAEA) and two closely connected export control systems implemented by the key nuclear supplier countries (for details on each of the regime elements, see Appendices A-F in this volume).

Nuclear Non-Proliferation Treaty (NPT). The NPT, which was opened for signature in 1968 and entered into force in 1970, divides the countries of the world into two categories, "nuclear-weapon states" and "non-nuclear-weapon states." It defines "nuclear-weapon states" as countries that detonated a nuclear explosion before January 1, 1967, namely the United States (first detonation in 1945), the Soviet Union (1949), Great Britain (1952), France (1960), and China (1964). Russia succeeded to the Soviet Union's status as a nuclear-weapon state under the Treaty in 1992. The NPT treats all other countries as non-nuclear-weapon states.[1]

Under the NPT:

- Non-nuclear-weapon states under the Treaty pledge not to manufacture or receive nuclear explosives. (Both nuclear weapons and "peaceful nuclear explosives" are prohibited.)

- To verify that they are living up to this pledge, non-nuclear-weapon states also agree to accept IAEA safeguards on *all* their peaceful nuclear activities, an arrangement known as "full-scope safeguards."[2]

- All countries accepting the Treaty agree not to export nuclear equipment or material to non-nuclear-weapon states except under IAEA safeguards, and nuclear-weapon states agree not to assist non-nuclear-weapon states in obtaining nuclear weapons.

- All countries accepting the Treaty agree to facilitate the fullest possible sharing of peaceful nuclear technology.

- All countries accepting the Treaty agree to pursue negotiations in good faith to end the nuclear-arms race and to achieve nuclear disarmament under international control. (In practice, this applies to the nuclear-weapon states.)

- A party may withdraw from the Treaty on ninety days' notice if "extraordinary events related to the subject matter of the Treaty" have "jeopardized its supreme interests."

All five established nuclear-weapon states are parties to the NPT. The United States, Russia, and Great Britain are the Treaty's depositary states; China and France did not join until 1992. As of the end of 1997, the Treaty had 180 non-nuclear-weapon state parties, for a total of 185 parties.

The NPT originally entered into force for 25 years, with periodic reviews of the Treaty occurring every 5 years. At the NPT Review and Extension Conference held in New York City in April-May 1995, the parties agreed to extend the Treaty indefinitely without conditions. In addition, they approved a set of principles and objectives to guide the parties during a strengthened review process in the future. The indefinite extension of the NPT was accomplished because many developing nations have come to recognize that nuclear proliferation threatens international peace and security.

Among the principal states of proliferation concern today, India, Israel, and Pakistan are not parties to the pact. Each has nuclear installations not subject to IAEA safeguards that contribute to its respective nuclear-weapons capability.[3] Iran, Iraq, and Libya are non-nuclear-weapon state parties to the Treaty, but their commitment to the accord is suspect because of their demonstrated interest in acquiring nuclear arms.[4]

North Korea became a party to the Treaty in 1985 but took until April 1992 to agree to IAEA inspections of its nuclear activities. During the interval, it produced a quantity of plutonium that may be sufficient for one or two nuclear weapons. North Korea has not satisfactorily accounted for this material and was not in compliance with its IAEA safeguards obligations under the Treaty because of its refusal to permit an IAEA "special inspection" of two nuclear-waste sites believed to contain information regarding past production of plutonium. Under an "Agreed Framework" signed with the United States in October 1994, North Korea agreed to resolve these issues at a future date; in the meantime, it has accepted restrictions on its nuclear activities that go beyond its obligations under the NPT, including a freeze on the operation and construction of a number of sensitive facilities.

International Atomic Energy Agency (IAEA). The IAEA is part of the foundation of the international non-proliferation regime. Created in 1957, the Vienna-based IAEA is an international organization with 126 member countries. Its principal missions are to facilitate the use of nuclear energy for peaceful purposes and to implement a system of audits and on-site inspections, collectively known as "safeguards," to verify that nuclear facilities and materials are not being diverted for nuclear explosive purposes.

In addition to monitoring all peaceful nuclear activities in non-nuclear-weapon state parties to the NPT, the Agency also monitors individual facilities and associated nuclear materials in non-NPT parties at the request of these states. Thus, even though India, Israel, and Pakistan are not parties to the NPT, several nuclear facilities in each of these countries are subject to IAEA monitoring, and these facilities cannot easily be used to support these nations' nuclear-weapons programs.

Until 1991, in non-nuclear-weapon state parties to the NPT, the IAEA monitored only those facilities declared by the inspected country and did not seek out possible undeclared nuclear installations. After the 1991 Gulf War, however, it was learned that Iraq had secretly developed a network of undeclared nuclear facilities as part of an extensive nuclear-weapons program. This led the IAEA to announce in late 1991 that it would begin to exercise its previously unused authority to conduct "special inspections," i.e., to demand access to undeclared sites where it suspected nuclear activities were being conducted. Subsequent measures were adopted under Program 93 + 2 in two installments. Part 1, implemented initially in 1996, consisted of measures that could be traced to existing legal authority. Part 2 consisted of measures whose implementation would require complementary legal authority. Part 2 measures were approved by the IAEA Board of Governors on May 15, 1997.

The Agency first attempted to conduct a special inspection in North Korea in 1992, but Pyongyang refused to comply with the IAEA's request, triggering a crisis that has yet to be fully resolved. However, the IAEA's new authority has indirectly provided added access for the Agency in Iran. Because an IAEA demand for special inspections carries the implied accusation that a country may be violating the NPT, Iran, anticipating that the Agency might seek special inspections within its territory, has sought to avert the stigma associated with such inspections by agreeing to permit the IAEA to visit any location in Iran on request. The Agency has visited undeclared sites in Iran several times but has not detected any activities in violation of Iran's NPT obligations.

Comprehensive Test Ban Treaty (CTBT). The newest element of the regime is the CTBT, a barrier to vertical as well as horizontal proliferation. The conclusion of this treaty fulfilled a preambular commitment of NPT parties to carry through with pledges made in the 1963 Partial Test Ban Treaty "to seek to achieve the discontinuance of all test explosions of nuclear weapons for all time." Opened for signature in New York on September 24, 1996, the CTBT prohibits nuclear test explosions of any size and establishes a rigorous verification system, including seismic monitoring and on-site inspections, to detect any violations.

The CTBT was negotiated at the Geneva Conference on Disarmament (CD), where decisions normally are made by consensus. India temporarily blocked approval of the treaty in mid-August 1996; it objected to the fact that the treaty did not include provisions demanded by India prescribing a "time-bound framework" for the global elimination of nuclear weapons. India also opposed the treaty's entry-into-force provision, which, in effect, would require India's ratification to bring the pact into force.[5] To circumvent India's veto, Australia introduced the treaty into the U.N. General Assembly, where decisions are made by majority rather than by consensus. The CTBT was adopted by the U.N. General Assembly on September 10, 1996, by a vote of 158 to 3 (the negative votes coming from India, Bhutan, and Libya). (For more details on the CTBT, see Appendix C.)

Supplier Control Mechanisms. Two informal coalitions of nations that voluntarily restrict the export of equipment and materials that could be used to develop nuclear weapons form a third major element of the non-proliferation regime.

Shortly after the NPT came into force in 1970, a number of Western and Soviet-bloc nuclear-supplier states began consultations concerning the procedures and standards that would apply to nuclear exports to non-nuclear-weapons states. The group, known as the NPT Exporters Committee (or the Zangger Committee, so named after its Swiss chairman), adopted a set of guidelines in August 1974, including a list of export items that would trigger the requirement for the application of IAEA safeguards in recipient states. These procedures and the "trigger list," updated in subsequent years, represent the first major agreement on uniform regulation of nuclear exports by actual and potential nuclear suppliers.

Following India's nuclear test in 1974, an overlapping group of nuclear supplier states—but in this case including France, which was not then a party to the NPT—met in London to elaborate export guidelines further. In January 1976, this London group—which became known as the Nuclear Suppliers Group (NSG)—adopted guidelines that were similar to those of the NPT Exporters Committee but also extended to transfers of technology and included agreement to "exercise restraint" in the transfer of uranium-enriched and plutonium-extraction equipment and facilities.

In April 1992, in the wake of the Gulf War, the NSG expanded its export control guidelines, which until then had covered only uniquely nuclear items, to cover 65 "dual-use" items as well. The group also added as a requirement for future exports that recipient states accept IAEA inspection on all of their peaceful nuclear activities. This rule, previously adopted by only some NSG members, effectively precludes nuclear commerce by NSG member states with India, Israel, and Pakistan.

In addition to agreeing to such full-scope safeguards, all nations importing regulated items from NSG member states must promise to furnish adequate physical security for transferred nuclear materials and facilities; pledge not to export nuclear materials and technologies to other nations without the permission of the original exporting nation or without a pledge from the recipient nation to abide by these same rules; and promise not to use any imports to build nuclear explosives. Similar rules—apart from the full-scope safeguards requirement—apply to exports regulated by the Zang-ger Committee, which continues to function, although it has been partially eclipsed by the Nuclear Suppliers Group, whose export controls have been more far-reaching. The members of the two supplier groups are listed, and more detailed discussion is provided, in Appendix F in this volume.

Nuclear-Weapon-Free Zones (NWFZs). NWFZs complement NPT arrangements because they can be geared to specific regional situations. The growing role of NWFZs as part of the non-proliferation regime was reflected in the draft review document of the 1995 NPT Review and Extension Conference: "the establishment of nuclear-weapon-free zones . . . constitutes an important disarmament measure which greatly strengthens the international non-proliferation regime in all its aspects" (see additional information on NWFZs in Appendix E in this volume). NWFZs have been established in Latin America (Treaty of Tlatelolco, 1967), the South Pacific (SPNFZ, 1996), and Africa (ANWFZ, 1996), and efforts have been made to establish one in Southeast Asia (SEANFWZ).

NOTES

[1] In this book, Israel, India, and Pakistan are described as *de facto*, non-NPT or "self declared" nuclear-weapon states. In May 1998, India and Pakistan each conducted nuclear weapon tests and declared themselves "nuclear powers." As a result, this book refers to the original five, NPT-recognized, nuclear-weapon states as the *de jure* or "established" nuclear-weapon states. The NPT and the non-proliferation regime have no legal category and no provision for additional nuclear-weapon states. Until a better term emerges, non-NPT or "self-declared" nuclear-weapon states may be acceptable as descriptive terminology.

[2] "Full-scope safeguards" were developed pursuant to the NPT and mean IAEA inspections and monitoring of all nuclear materials, and the facilities that contain those materials, within the jurisdiction of the state in question. The goal of IAEA inspections and monitoring under the NPT is to verify that nuclear materials are not being diverted by the state in question to nuclear weapons or nuclear explosive purposes of any kind. A state may declare and exempt nuclear materials from IAEA inspection for narrow military purposes, such as fueling naval nuclear reactors. To date, no non-nuclear-weapon state parties to the NPT have built nuclear submarines and obtained this exemption for naval nuclear propulsion. Since the IAEA monitors only activities connected with the production or use of nuclear materials, it does not have under its original charter (or even under the NPT) a basis for searching for and investigating nuclear-weapons-related activities, such as fabricating or testing the non-nuclear components of nuclear weapons, unless nuclear materials are present in these activities.

[3] Brazil also has a substantial nuclear infrastructure and a past interest in acquiring nuclear arms, and is not a party to the NPT. But Brazil has accepted equivalent restrictions on its nuclear activities pursuant to the Treaty of Tlatelolco, which establishes a nuclear-weapon-free zone in Latin America and the Caribbean, and pursuant to bilateral agreements with Argentina. Brazil's president has also urged the parliament to consider Brazil's joining the NPT.

[4] Iraq is also subject to a pervasive program of monitoring by the IAEA and the U.N. Special Commission on Iraq intended to eliminate its weapons of mass destruction and certain missile capabilities. These arrangements are being implemented pursuant to U.N. Security Council resolutions adopted in the aftermath of the 1991 Persian Gulf War.

[5] The CTBT's entry-into-force provision requires the ratification of 44 nations that possess either nuclear power or research reactors—a group that includes both the 5 established nuclear-weapon states and the *de facto* nuclear-weapon states (India, Israel, and Pakistan). If the treaty still has not entered into force by September 1999, three years after it was opened for signature, the nations that have ratified it may convene a conference to discuss ways to accelerate entry into force. As of October 1997, 148 nations (including the 5 established nuclear-weapon states and Israel) had signed the treaty. However, India and Pakistan, whose ratification of the treaty was seen as essential, had not signed.

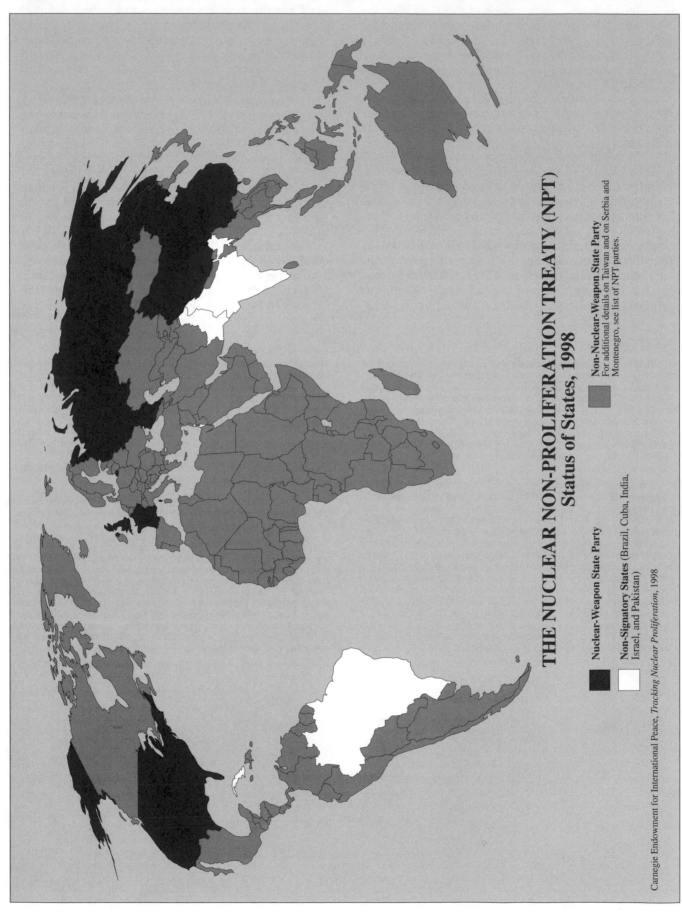

THE NUCLEAR NON-PROLIFERATION TREATY (NPT)
Status of States, 1998

Nuclear-Weapon State Party

Non-Signatory States (Brazil, Cuba, India, Israel, and Pakistan)

Non-Nuclear-Weapon State Party
For additional details on Taiwan and on Serbia and Montenegro, see list of NPT parties.

Carnegie Endowment for International Peace, *Tracking Nuclear Proliferation*, 1998

Nuclear Non-Proliferation Treaty (NPT) Parties, as of December 31, 1997[a,b]

COUNTRY	DATE SIGNED	DEPOSITED RATIFICATION	DEPOSITED ACCESSION
Afghanistan	7-01-68	2-04-70	
Albania			9-12-90
Algeria			1-12-95
Antigua & Barbuda			6-17-85
Andorra			6-07-96
Angola			10-14-96
Argentina			2-10-95
Armenia			7-15-93
Australia	2-27-70	1-23-73	
Austria	7-01-68	6-27-69	
Azerbaijan			9-22-92
Bahamas			8-11-76
Bahrain			11-03-88
Bangladesh			8-31-79
Barbados	7-01-68	2-21-80	
Belarus			7-22-93
Belgium	8-20-68	5-02-75	
Belize			8-09-85
Benin	7-01-68	10-31-72	
Bhutan			5-23-85
Bolivia	7-01-68	5-26-70	
Bosnia & Herzegovina			8-15-94
Botswana	7-01-68	4-28-69	
Brunei			3-26-85
Bulgaria	7-01-68	9-05-69	
Burkino Faso	11-25-68	3-03-70	
Burundi			3-19-71
Cambodia			6-02-72
Cameroon	7-17-68	1-08-69	
Canada	7-23-68	1-08-69	
Cape Verde			10-24-79
Central African Republic			10-25-70
Chad	7-01-68	3-10-71	
Chile			5-25-95
China, People's Republic[N]			3-09-92
Colombia	7-01-68	4-08-86	
Comoros			10-04-95
Congo, Democratic Republic	7-22-68	8-04-70	
Congo, People's Republic			10-23-78
Costa Rica	7-01-68	3-03-70	
Cote d'Ivoire	7-01-68	3-06-73	
Croatia			6-29-92
Cyprus	7-01-68	2-10-70	
Czech Republic			1-01-93
Denmark	7-01-68	1-03-69	
Djibouti			10-16-96
Dominica			8-10-84
Dominican Republic	7-01-68	7-24-71	
Ecuador	7-09-68	3-07-69	
Egypt	7-01-68	2-26-81	
El Salvador	7-01-68	7-11-72	
Equatorial Guinea			11-01-84
Eritrea			3-03-95

COUNTRY	DATE SIGNED	DEPOSITED RATIFICATION	DEPOSITED ACCESSION
Estonia			1-07-92
Ethiopia	9-05-68	2-05-70	
Fiji			7-14-72
Finland	7-01-68	2-05-69	
Former Yugoslav Republic of Macedonia			4-12-95
France[N]			8-03-92
Gabon			2-19-74
Gambia	9-04-68	5-12-75	
Georgia			3-07-94
Germany, Federal Republic	11-28-69	5-02-75	
Ghana	7-01-68	5-04-70	
Greece	7-01-68	3-11-70	
Grenada			9-02-75
Guatemala	7-26-68	9-22-70	
Guinea			4-29-85
Guinea-Bissau			8-20-76
Guyana	7-01-68		10-19-93
Haiti	7-01-68	6-02-70	
Holy See			2-25-71
Honduras	7-01-68	5-16-73	
Hungary	7-01-68	5-27-69	
Iceland	7-01-68	7-18-69	
Indonesia	3-02-70	7-12-79	
Iran	7-01-68	2-02-70	
Iraq	7-01-68	10-29-69	
Ireland	7-01-68	7-01-68	
Italy	1-28-69	5-02-75	
Jamaica	4-14-69	3-05-70	
Japan	2-03-70	6-08-76	
Jordan	7-10-68	2-11-70	
Kazakhstan			2-14-94
Kenya	7-01-68	6-11-70	
Kiribati			4-18-85
Korea, North			12-12-85
Korea, South	7-01-68	4-23-75	
Kuwait	8-15-68	11-17-89	
Kyrgyzstan			7-05-94
Laos	7-01-68	2-20-70	
Latvia			1-31-92
Lebanon	7-01-68	7-15-70	
Lesotho	7-09-68	5-20-70	
Liberia	7-01-68	3-05-70	
Libya	7-18-68	5-26-75	
Liechtenstein			4-20-78
Lithuania			9-23-91
Luxembourg	8-14-68	5-02-75	
Madagascar	8-22-68	10-08-70	
Malawi			2-18-86
Malaysia	7-01-68	3-05-70	
Maldive Islands	9-11-68	4-07-70	

Nuclear Non-Proliferation Treaty (NPT) Parties (cont'd.)

COUNTRY	DATE SIGNED	DEPOSITED RATIFICATION	DEPOSITED ACCESSION
Mali	7-14-69	2-10-70	
Malta	4-17-69	2-06-70	
Marshall Islands			1-30-95
Mauritania			10-23-93
Mauritius	7-01-68	4-08-69	
Mexico	7-26-68	1-21-69	
Micronesia			4-14-95
Moldova			10-11-94
Monaco			3-13-95
Mongolia	7-01-68	5-14-69	
Morocco	7-01-68	11-27-70	
Mozambique			9-04-90
Myanmar (Burma)			12-02-92
Namibia			10-02-92
Nauru			6-07-82
Nepal	7-01-68	1-05-70	
Netherlands	8-20-68	5-02-75	
New Zealand	7-01-68	9-10-69	
Nicaragua	7-01-68	3-06-73	
Niger			10-09-92
Nigeria	7-01-68	9-27-68	
Norway	7-01-68	2-05-69	
Oman			1-23-97
Palau			4-12-95
Panama	7-01-68	1-13-77	
Papua New Guinea			1-13-82
Paraguay	7-01-68	2-04-70	
Peru	7-01-68	3-03-70	
Philippines	7-01-68	10-05-72	
Poland	7-01-68	6-12-69	
Portugal			12-15-77
Qatar			4-03-89
Romania	7-01-68	2-04-70	
Russia*N	7-01-68	3-05-70	
Rwanda			5-20-75
Saint Kitts & Nevis			3-22-93
Saint Lucia			12-28-79
Saint Vincent & Grenadines			11-06-84
San Marino	7-01-68	8-10-70	
Sao Tome & Principe			7-20-83
Saudi Arabia			10-03-88
Senegal	7-01-68	12-17-70	
Seychelles			3-12-85
Sierra Leone			2-26-75
Singapore	2-05-70	3-10-76	
Slovakia			1-01-93
Slovenia			4-07-92
Solomon Islands			6-17-81
Somalia	7-01-68	3-05-70	
South Africa			7-10-91
Spain			11-05-87
Sri Lanka	7-01-68	3-05-79	
Sudan	12-24-68	10-31-73	
Suriname			6-30-76

COUNTRY	DATE SIGNED	DEPOSITED RATIFICATION	DEPOSITED ACCESSION
Swaziland	6-24-69	12-11-69	
Sweden	8-19-68	1-09-70	
Switzerland	11-27-69	3-09-77	
Syria	7-01-68	9-24-69	
Taiwan[c]	7-01-68	1-27-70	
Tajikistan			1-17-95
Tanzania			5-31-91
Thailand			12-02-72
Togo	7-01-68	2-26-70	
Tonga			7-07-71
Trinidad and Tobago	8-20-68	10-30-86	
Tunisia	7-01-68	2-26-70	
Turkey	1-28-69	4-17-80	
Turkmenistan			9-29-94
Tuvalu			1-19-79
Uganda			10-20-82
Ukraine			12-05-94
United Arab Emirates			9-26-95
United Kingdom*[N]	7-01-68	11-27-68	
United States*[N]	7-01-68	3-05-70	
Uruguay	7-01-68	8-31-70	
Uzbekistan			5-02-92
Vanuatu			8-26-95
Venezuela	7-01-68	9-25-75	
Vietnam			6-14-82
Western Samoa			3-17-75
Yemen	11-14-68	6-01-79	
Zambia			5-15-91
Zimbabwe			9-26-91

*Depositary States
N = Nuclear-Weapon States

NOTES

[a]Non-signatory states include Brazil, Cuba, India, Israel, and Pakistan.

[b]Serbia and Montenegro claims NPT membership as the sole successor state to Yugoslavia. Its NPT status remains in dispute.

[c]The United States recognizes the People's Republic of China as the sole legal government of China but regards Taiwan as bound by the terms of the NPT.

Sources: U.S. Arms Control and Disarmament Agency, "Signatories and Parties to the Treaty on the Non-Proliferation of Nuclear Weapons," Fact Sheet, January 23, 1997 (at http://www.acda.gov/treaties/npt3.txt; accessed November 7, 1997); The Arms Control Association, Washington, D.C.

3

NUCLEAR-WEAPON STATES

Russia

Six years after the collapse of the Soviet Union in December 1991, Russia alone—not two or three nuclear powers as feared—emerged as the nuclear-weapon-state successor to the Soviet Union. This outcome—a shared Russian and U.S. objective—was not a foregone conclusion in the circumstances of the Soviet breakup in 1997. By late 1996, however, it had materialized—as a result of Belarus, Kazakhstan, and Ukraine cooperating in the de-nuclearization process. Russia also succeeded to all of the Soviet Union's international legal obligations connected with nuclear-weapon state status.[1] In addition to the Nuclear Non-Proliferation Treaty (NPT), Russia thus succeeded to the Soviet Union's nuclear-weapons-related obligations under other important security agreements, including the Anti-Ballistic Missile (ABM) Treaty, the Strategic Arms Reduction Treaty (START), and the Intermediate-range Nuclear Forces (INF) Treaty.[2] Russia also assumed—almost immediately, on December 24, 1991—the Soviet Union's permanent seat on the U.N. Security Council.

Although some strategic and tactical nuclear weapons were dispersed in several other Soviet republics when the Soviet Union dissolved, the bulk of the Soviet nuclear arsenal and virtually all of its nuclear-weapons production infrastructure was concentrated on Russian territory. Russia essentially inherited the Soviet nuclear command structure, including key codes needed to target and launch the Soviet strategic nuclear systems, some of which were still deployed in Belarus, Kazakhstan, and Ukraine as late as 1996. Russian military personnel preserved control over all tactical and strategic nuclear weapons in the other new independent states. This prevented any of the other post-Soviet states from acquiring independent control or possession over nuclear weapons. Recognition of Russia as the sole nuclear-weapon-state successor to the Soviet Union prevented the creation of additional nuclear-weapon states, which would have generated severe instability in Central Europe and undermined the basic goal of the NPT.[3]

Russia now is a partner in a wide range of new non-proliferation activities, including the Missile Technology Control Regime (MTCR), the Comprehensive Test Ban Treaty (CTBT), the Nuclear Suppliers Group (NSG), the Chemical Weapons Convention (CWC), and the Wassenaar Arrangement for export controls over conventional military and dual-use technology. Close cooperation between Russia and the West continues in implementing arms control agreements and con-fidence-building measures; assuring the safety of stored nuclear weapons; achieving warhead dismantlement; and preventing the theft or diversion of fissile materials; as well as in finding civilian research alternatives for Russian weapons-related scientists (through the International Science and Technology Center, ISTC).

At the same time, Russia's space, missile, arms-production, and atomic energy establishments have revived international marketing efforts to survive in a changed political and economic environment. This has led to sensitive Russian nuclear trading relationships and arms sales—particularly with Syria, Iraq, Iran, India, and China—that appear to be inconsistent with rigorous non-proliferation controls and therefore with the regional stability needs of the Middle East, Gulf, South Asia, and the Pacific Rim. These commercial activities appear to go hand in hand with a perceptible hardening, recently, of Russian foreign and defense policy that has slowed the progress of strategic and nuclear arms reductions and inhibited new initiatives to broaden the areas of partnership and to solidify a non-adversarial post–Cold War environment.

BACKGROUND

De-Nuclearization Accords After Soviet Collapse. Russia took immediate steps in 1991 and 1992 to consolidate control over all of the former Soviet Union's nuclear arms, transporting those deployed or stored in other former Soviet states to Russian soil for redeployment, storage, or dismantling. The legal basis for Russia's sole custody of these weapons was agreed on December 21, 1991, at Alma-Ata (now Almaty), Kazakhstan, where leaders of eleven former Soviet republics signed a series of declarations establishing the Commonwealth of Independent States (CIS). In Article 6 of the Declaration on Nuclear Arms, a document signed only by the leaders of the four states with nuclear weapons on their territories, the four agreed that "[by] July 1, 1992, Belarus, Kazakhstan, and Ukraine will insure the withdrawal of tactical nuclear weapons to central factory premises for dismantling under joint supervision."[4] These three states also agreed not to transfer nuclear weapons on their territory to any state other than Russia—a proviso that anticipated the withdrawal of all Soviet nuclear weapons to Russia. At Alma-Ata, Belarus and Ukraine (but not Kazakhstan) committed themselves to join the NPT as non-nuclear-weapon states.

In a subsequent post-Soviet accord on nuclear command-and-control signed in Minsk on December 30, 1991, the leaders of the eleven CIS states agreed that a "decision on the need [to use nuclear weapons would be] made by the President of the Russian Federation in agreement with the heads of the Republic of Belarus, the Republic of Kazakhstan, and Ukraine, and in consultation with the heads of the other member states of the Commonwealth."[5] As a practical matter, however, control over the use of nuclear weapons remained under Russian authority. Arrangements for sharing authority in this area ended in June 1993, when Russia formally took full control over the use of all nuclear arms in post-Soviet states.[6] In the Minsk agreement, Ukraine also pledged that nuclear weapons on its territory would be dismantled by the end of 1994, with tactical nuclear weapons to be dismantled by July 1, 1992.[7]

START I and the Lisbon Protocol. The denuclearization framework was further elaborated in the Lisbon Protocol to the Strategic Arms Reduction Treaty (START I), signed on May 23, 1992, by Belarus, Kazakhstan, Russia, and Ukraine. Through the Protocol, the four states agreed to participate jointly in START I as successors to the former Soviet Union and to "implement the Treaty's limits and restrictions" (Article II of the Protocol). In addition, Belarus, Kazakhstan, and Ukraine agreed to "adhere to the Treaty on the Non-Proliferation of Nuclear Weapons" as non-nuclear-weapon state parties "in the shortest possible time" (Article V of the Protocol).[8] In separate letters to President George Bush, each of the three presidents also agreed to the elimination of all strategic nuclear arms on their territories within the seven-year START I implementation period. By this time, all tactical nuclear weapons already had been withdrawn to Russia from the three states.[9]

START I, the result of nine years of negotiations between the two superpowers, was signed in Moscow by the United States and the Soviet Union on July 31, 1991. It was the first strategic arms control treaty to actually cut levels of deployed strategic weapons as opposed to merely capping existing arsenals. Under START I (as modified by the Lisbon Protocol), the two sides must reduce their strategic nuclear forces to equal aggregate limits of 6,000 accountable warheads deployed on 1,600 strategic nuclear delivery vehicles—i.e., intercontinental ballistic missiles (ICBMs), submarine-launched ballistic missiles (SLBMs), and strategic bombers. Sublimits for warheads allow no more than 4,900 deployed on either side's ICBMs and SLBMs, and of this subtotal, no more than 1,100 warheads may be deployed on mobile ICBMs and no more than 1,540 warheads on heavy ICBMs (missiles armed with multiple, independently targetable reentry vehicles [MIRVs]).[10]

The entry into force of START I was considerably delayed by the need to secure ratification by each of the four successor states. In approving ratification on November 4, 1992, Russia's Supreme Soviet attached

a condition that Russia not exchange instruments of ratification until after the other three successor states had acceded to the NPT as non-nuclear-weapon states and carried out their other obligations under the Lisbon Protocol.[11] In Belarus and Kazakhstan, these NPT-related steps proved relatively uncontroversial. The Belarusian parliament ratified START I on February 4, 1993, and Belarus formally acceded to the NPT on July 22, 1993. The parliament of Kazakhstan ratified START I on July 2, 1992, and Kazakhstan formally acceded to the NPT on February 14, 1994. In Ukraine, however, where tensions with Russia intensified over a number of issues in 1993, acceptance of START I and the NPT proved more contentious.

Trilateral Accord with Ukraine. The Ukrainian parliament, or Rada, approved ratification of START I on November 18, 1993, but declared that a number of stiff conditions—which were unacceptable to Russia and the United States—would have to be met before ratification could be accomplished. Simultaneously, the Rada resolved that Ukraine was not bound by Article V of the Lisbon Protocol, calling for quick accession to the NPT as a non-nuclear-weapon state.[12]

After extensive negotiations, on January 14, 1994, Ukrainian President Leonid Kravchuk—together with President Bill Clinton and Russian President Boris Yeltsin—signed the Trilateral Statement, in which they agreed that all nuclear warheads would be withdrawn from the territory of Ukraine to Russia for the purpose of subsequent dismantling in the shortest possible time. Ukraine would in exchange receive a number of political, economic, and security benefits. As a result of this understanding, on February 3, 1994, the Rada approved a two-part resolution instructing President Kravchuk to exchange the instruments of ratification of START I and acknowledging that Article V of the Lisbon Protocol applied to Ukraine. The Rada also implicitly endorsed the Trilateral Statement but did not then approve accession to the NPT.[13]

The Ukrainian parliament finally approved the Trilateral Statement on November 16, 1994, but once again imposed conditions, making Ukraine's NPT accession contingent upon first receiving security assurances by the nuclear states. Security assurances, in the form of a multilateral memorandum signed by the United Kingdom, the United States, and Russia, were promised to Ukraine immediately prior to the November 16, 1994, parliamentary vote. At the Summit of the Conference on Security and Cooperation in Europe (CSCE), held in Budapest on December 5, 1994, the United Kingdom, the United States, and Russia provided this memorandum to Ukraine and initialed a document that also extended security assurances to Kazakhstan and Belarus. France also provided security assurances to Ukraine at the CSCE summit in a separate document. On the same occasion, Ukraine then presented its instruments of accession to the NPT.

This action, along with the earlier accessions by Belarus and Kazakhstan, satisfied Russia's conditions for ratifying START I. Consequently, at the same meeting, the United States, Russia, Belarus, Kazakhstan, and Ukraine exchanged their START I instruments of ratification, and formally brought the treaty into force.[14]

START II Landmark. Earlier, on January 3, 1993, Presidents Bush and Yeltsin had signed in Moscow the follow-on START II agreement, providing for even deeper strategic cuts than START I. START II provides for the elimination of all multiple-warhead ICBMs and for a two-phase reduction of nuclear warheads on deployed strategic delivery vehicles. At the end of the first phase—seven years after the entry into force of START I—the United States and Russia may not have more than 3,800 to 4,250 warheads on deployed delivery systems. In the second phase—by January 1, 2003 (or by December 31, 2000, if the United States is able to assist in financing the dismantlement and elimination of Russian nuclear weapons)—each of the two parties would reduce the overall total of deployed strategic warheads to between 3,000 and 3,500. This would represent a two-thirds reduction in strategic nuclear forces from peak Cold-War levels.[15] Because START II relied on the definitions, declarations, and verification provisions of START I, neither the U.S. Senate nor the Russian parliament would vote on ratification of START II until START I entered into force. (START II ratification delays and START III issues are discussed in Developments below.)

Confidence-Building: De-Targeting. On January 14, 1994, Russia and the United States agreed that they would no longer target strategic missiles at one another. Great Britain joined this agreement on February 15, 1994. The agreement stipulated that strategic missiles under the command of the countries party to the agreement were to be de-targeted no later than May 30, 1994. On September 2, 1994, Russia and China signed a similar de-targeting agreement, pledging that they would no longer aim missiles at each other.[16]

De-Activation of Systems Covered by START I. During the delay in START I entry into force, the United States and Russia took steps toward early de-activation of the strategic systems that were to be cut under the treaty. In early March 1995, U.S. Secretary of Defense William Perry reported to the Senate Foreign Relations Committee that the United States had "deactivated all of its forces to be eliminated under START I by removing over 3,900 warheads from ballistic missiles and retiring heavy bombers to elimination facilities." He also noted that the United States had "already eliminated about 290 missile launchers and over 230 heavy bombers, putting [the United States] below the first START I intermediate ceiling that will not come into effect until December 1997."[17] Earlier, Perry reported that Russia had already removed 2,600 warheads from missiles and bomber bases, taken 750 missiles off their launchers, and destroyed almost 600 launchers and bombers.[18]

Meanwhile, Russia concluded bilateral agreements with Belarus and Kazakhstan for the early de-activation and withdrawal of strategic systems to Russia. In the case of Belarus, 45 single-warhead SS-25

road-mobile ICBMs and their warheads were withdrawn to Russia by early December 1994.[19] The plan then was that all SS-25s and their warheads in Belarus would be removed by the end of July 1995. In Kazakhstan, by December 1994, 810 warheads—440 from 44 SS-18 ICBMs and 370 from air-launched cruise missiles (ALCMs)—had been removed from missiles. About 632 of these warheads had been returned to Russia by March 1995, including all 370 ALCM warheads and 260 SS-18 warheads. All 370 ALCMs and the associated strategic bombers were withdrawn to Russia, and reportedly twelve SS-18 missiles were moved to Russia as well.[20]

Ukraine's de-nuclearization process was guided by the Trilateral Statement noted earlier, which called for a phased de-activation and removal process. In the first phase, which was to be completed by mid-November 1994, all SS-24 ICBMs on Ukrainian territory were to be de-activated. In fact, by early December 1994, not only had Ukraine de-activated all its SS-24s, but it had also de-activated 40 of its 130 SS-19s. The Trilateral Statement also called for Ukraine to remove at least 200 warheads from its SS-19s and SS-24s to Russia by mid-November.[21] By February 1995, a total of 420 warheads (removed from SS-24 and SS-19 missiles, and from ALCMs deployed on heavy bombers) had been withdrawn to Russia.[22]

Disarmament Assistance. To ease the financial burden of dismantlement of nuclear weapons and delivery systems in Russia and the three other former Soviet states, the United States provided technical and financial assistance under the Cooperative Threat Reduction (CTR) program—also known as the Nunn-Lugar program (after its sponsors, Senators Sam Nunn and Richard Lugar). By late February 1995, the United States had proposed $503 million for projects in Russia. Most of the Nunn-Lugar projects are dedicated to assisting with the elimination of strategic offensive arms. Others, such as the project on Materials Protection, Control, and Accounting (MPC&A) were designed to curb the proliferation risks associated with stored fissile materials resulting from the drawdown of Russia's arsenal.[23] Of the funds authorized by Congress, $300 million had actually been obligated to projects in Russia by February 1995.

Other Initiatives. The United States agreed to purchase 500 metric tons of weapons-grade uranium from dismantled Russian nuclear weapons that is to be blended down to low-enriched uranium (LEU) suitable for use as nuclear power plant fuel. The LEU will be sold to the United States Enrichment Corporation (USEC) for eventual use in nuclear power reactors. American inspectors will be allowed to conduct limited inspections at two Russian material blending facilities in order to verify that the highly enriched uranium (HEU) actually comes from dismantled warheads.[24]

Another initiative is the International Science and Technology Center (ISTC), a Moscow-based multilateral organization that organizes peaceful employment opportunities for scientists and engineers in those new independent states that were previously involved in work on weapons of mass destruction and missile technology. The Center, which began operating in March 1994, was founded by the European Union, Japan, the Russian Federation, and the United States. In addition to the initial parties, by early 1995 Finland, Sweden, and Georgia had joined as members; and Belarus, Armenia, Kazakhstan, and Canada had taken steps to become members.[25]

Weaknesses in Non-Proliferation Control Measures. By 1994, despite the unprecedented progress in strategic arms reductions and the de-nuclearization of the other successor states, Russia had for several reasons emerged as a serious nuclear proliferation concern in the West. There were fears that Russia's severe political and economic difficulties, coupled with the collapse of the old Soviet personnel control system, could lead to a loss of central control over its large stockpiles of nuclear weapons and nuclear-weapons-grade materials. The problem seemed most severe for the nuclear materials.[26] The Soviet Union's regulatory mechanisms for the control of nuclear exports could prove inadequate for the changes that would occur with market-oriented economic reforms, and old border controls for the Soviet Union no longer fit the changes in the map of a down-sized Russia and its ties with the other former Soviet states. Russia's laudatory commitments to nuclear weapons dismantling programs meant that its stockpiles of weapons-grade materials and secure storage needs would actually increase. Without effective controls, Russian nuclear materials could find their way into a global black market in sensitive nuclear goods. This in turn could greatly accelerate the rate of proliferation by other states desiring nuclear arms while simultaneously undermining the International Atomic Energy Agency (IAEA) inspections and supplier-country export controls that form the backbone of the international nuclear non-proliferation regime.

Nuclear Theft and Smuggling. Prior to 1995, several episodes involving transport and theft of weapons-grade materials had been traced to Russia, including the "disappearance of an undisclosed quantity of HEU from the 'Luch' nuclear research facility at Podolsk, near Moscow"; the "theft of three fuel rods containing HEU from a naval base in Murmansk"; and a case involving the possible theft of some 2 kg or more of HEU from St. Petersburg.[27]

In 1994 there were at least five known instances involving the smuggling to Europe of weapons-usable materials that apparently originated in civilian research laboratories in Russia. German officials uncovered three distinct cases of the smuggling of weapons-grade plutonium: 6 grams of 99.75 percent Pu-39 were confiscated in Tengen, on May 10; 300 grams were seized on August 10 in a Munich airport on a flight from Moscow; and just under 2 grams were found in Bremen, on August 16.[28] In addition, there were two different seizures of HEU. One incident took place in Germany in mid-June 1994, when police in Landshut confiscated 800 milligrams of HEU enriched to 87.8

percent. The other incident occurred in Prague in mid-December 1994, when Czech police seized approximately 3 kg of HEU, the largest finding of weapons-grade nuclear material to date.[29]

In congressional testimony on June 27, 1994, former CIA Director R. James Woolsey said that Russian criminal organizations, which have established an extensive infrastructure consisting of front companies and international smuggling networks, may be facilitating the foreign transfer and sale of nuclear materials and possibly could acquire and sell nuclear weapons to foreign entities. He noted that the target of opportunity for these organized crime groups could be "hostile states such as Iran, Iraq, Libya, and North Korea [which] may try to accelerate or enhance their own weapons development programs" through the acquisition of weapons-usable nuclear materials, complete nuclear weapons, or other weapons of mass destruction.[30]

Political instability within the Russian Federation could lead not only to weakened controls over key nuclear assets but, in an extreme case, also to the emergence of new splinter states with nuclear assets located on their territory.[31] If the political factions comprising the leadership of new entities managed to obtain custody of deployed nuclear weapons, their ability to assume operational control would depend on their capability to bypass sensing devices and/or coded switches that control access to the arming and fusing circuitry of the weapons. As one panel of experts has noted, the existence of such devices "cannot provide reassurance that these weapons would be useless to mutinous custodians or political factions who had prolonged possession of the weapons, especially if they had technical expertise."[32]

DEVELOPMENTS

From early 1995 through 1997 Russia continued to experience considerable political turmoil and economic difficulties. Signs of economic stabilization emerged in late 1996 and 1997, feeding hopes that 1998 would finally show an upturn in economic growth (though economic crises in East Asia and Russia in the winter of 1997-98 postponed economic recovery). President Boris Yeltsin's relations with the State Duma (the lower house of Parliament) went from bad to worse with the December 1995 elections, which returned the Communist Party and its allies as the largest faction, albeit slightly short of an absolute majority. Liberals and reformers retained about a quarter of the Duma seats. The balance was held by various nationalist factions—often aligned with the Communists against President Yeltsin and in opposition to economic liberalization, political reform, and deeper cooperation with the West. Yeltsin, despite serious health problems, overcame a steep decline in popularity to narrowly win reelection over Gennady Zyuganov, the Communist Party candidate, in the mid-1996 presidential elections. Yeltsin underwent a successful cardiac operation the following winter and, as his health improved, sought to reassert presidential leadership in the spring and summer of 1997.

During the same period, Yeltsin's reform initiatives, foreign policy, and arms control efforts were increasingly buffeted by the resurgence of a more assertively nationalist outlook in Russia that constrained new opportunities for cooperation with the West. The nationalist mood, particularly among the foreign policy elite, was in part fueled by reactions to the gathering momentum of NATO enlargement but fundamentally driven by the dissatisfaction of the opposition factions in the Duma with Yeltsin's economic reform policies, the demoralization of the armed forces with internal war in Chechnya and general budgetary retrenchment, and the severe hardships that large sectors of the society suffered from the contraction of the economy and the decline of services, especially outside Moscow and St. Petersburg. Notwithstanding these difficulties, Russian political groups demonstrated broad acceptance of constitutional and democratic electoral procedures, and the administration managed to persist, unevenly, in steps toward a market economy. Western efforts to address the problems of nuclear arms reduction, defense conversion, and controls over nuclear materials through Russian cooperation continued to move forward, although more slowly than in the 1991-94 period.

De-Nuclearization.[33] The final steps in de-nuclearization—the removal of all strategic warheads from Belarus, Kazakhstan, and Ukraine—occurred in 1995 and 1996. All 1,410 strategic nuclear warheads attributable to strategic delivery systems located in Kazakhstan had left for Russia before the end of April 1995.[34] With respect to Ukraine, the 1,825 strategic warheads attributable to strategic delivery systems deployed on its soil in 1990 had all been withdrawn to Russia by May 1996.[35] The final batch of 81 road-mobile ICBMs and associated strategic warheads that had been deployed in Belarus was returned to Russia in late November 1996.[36]

Strategic Arms Reductions

START I Implementation: Implementation of the reductions prescribed for the successor states of the Soviet Union by START I proceeded rapidly after the treaty's entry into force on December 5, 1994. As of fall 1997, Russia, Belarus, Kazakhstan, and Ukraine collectively had eliminated or de-activated about 1,300 operational strategic launchers equipped with approximately 4,100 warheads and were almost two years ahead of schedule in meeting the first phase of START I reductions.[37] Although all strategic nuclear warheads had been removed from Belarus, Kazakhstan, and Ukraine by November 1996, cooperation and coordination between Russia and these three states was required to schedule reductions in the delivery systems and to declare periodic data to comply with the treaty's provisions. These provisions require the four countries collectively to meet the lower ceilings (stipulated in START I for the former Soviet Union as a whole) but allow Belarus,

Kazakhstan, and Ukraine to retain strategic launchers (silos and bombers) until the end of the seven-year reduction period. U.S. and Russian objectives nevertheless have been to facilitate acceleration in the dismantlement of missile silos and the removal to Russia of those missiles and bombers (that may not have to be physically eliminated under the ceilings) from the three other successor states.

As of December 1996, all 81 SS-25 road-mobile ICBMs deployed in Belarus before START I entry into force had been removed to Russia; the 104 SS-18 heavy ICBM silos deployed in Kazakhstan had been destroyed; all of the SS-18 missile airframes in Kazakhstan had been moved to Russia; and most of the 40 heavy bombers and approximately 370 associated air-launched cruise missiles (ALCMs) based in Kazakhstan had been moved to Russia (a few inoperable heavy bombers were still present in early 1997 at the Semipalatinsk air base in Kazakhstan, subject to an agreement to destroy them on site).[38] Of the 130 SS-19 silos present in Ukraine in 1991, 107 had been destroyed by December 1997, with the remainder to be destroyed in 1998; 44 SS-24 ICBM silos deployed in Ukraine are scheduled to be destroyed in 1998 with U.S. dismantlement assistance; and 44 heavy bombers remain in Ukraine, subject to elimination (Russia could have exercised the option to purchase some bombers from Ukraine, but in 1997 decided not to buy them because the aircraft had deteriorated, were generally not in flying condition, and would have been very costly to overhaul).[39]

By the end of 1997, the status of START I reductions of strategic offensive arms in Russia was as follows.

- ICBM launchers had been reduced from 1,064 to 751; and warheads accountable to deployed ICBMs, from 4,278 to 3,610.

- Deployed strategic submarine launchers had been reduced from 940 to 384, and the warheads attributable to the submarine-launched ballistic missiles (SLBMs) in these launchers had dropped from 2,804 to 1,824.

- The bomber force, affected by losses to Ukraine and the Russian decision to halt its own production of new strategic bombers, had been reduced to roughly half the number of bombers and to two-thirds the number of bomber-attributable warheads that the former Soviet Union had deployed as of 1990.[40]

With the de-nuclearization of the other three successor states, Russia could, in the absence of START II, retain forces up to the START I ceiling—a level of 6,000 accountable warheads, with the actual number somewhat higher; it is generally understood, however, that Russia cannot afford the high cost of maintaining this level.

In March 1997, Russia and the United States agreed to amend START I in order to give it permanent duration. This will resolve a concern that delays in implementing START II and negotiating START III could decouple them from START I, which contains the basic procedures for reductions and most of the verification rules for all the START treaties. Amending START I also needs the agreement of the other three parties—Belarus, Kazakhstan, and Ukraine—and will be codified by the START-implementing Joint Compliance and Inspection Commission (JCIC).

START II Ratification: START II had been signed in January 1993 by Russia and the United States as a bilateral, follow-on treaty (not involving Belarus, Kazakhstan, and Ukraine), but its ratification and implementation have been held up—first, by the three-and-a-half-year delay in bringing START I into force; and second, by the opposition to START II approval in the Russian parliament, especially in the State Duma.[41] In deference to Russia's early difficulties in ratifying START II, the U.S. Senate delayed its own advice and consent to START II ratification for two years but proceeded to approve START II formally on January 26, 1996.[42] President Yeltsin submitted START II to the Duma on June 20, 1995, stating that ratification was in Russia's interest but noting that "the START II treaty can be fulfilled only providing the United States preserves and strictly complies with the bilateral ABM Treaty of 1972."[43] This caveat reflected continuing Russian anxiety that U.S. plans to deploy theater missile defense (TMD) and Congressional pressures to build a national missile defense (NMD) could undercut the ABM Treaty and generate instability in the strategic relationship. Originally, the ABM Treaty was the primary concern of Russia's administration and defense establishment in hesitating to push for START II ratification. But by 1995, several other criticisms of START II had gained momentum among Russian defense experts and members of parliament.

Although START II called for equal warhead ceilings in the 3,000-3,500 range, and thus intended to achieve parity, it would in fact have distinct effects on the quite differently structured U.S. and Russian strategic forces. With respect to the treaty itself, one set of Russian criticisms focused on the high cost to Russia of implementing the treaty, and a second set alleged an unequal military result of the reductions for Russia, which would lose its most potent forces: MIRVed land-based missiles, the backbone of Russia's strategic arsenal.[44] As Russia's economy worsened, a related consideration loomed ever larger—the high cost for Russia of replacing MIRVed land-based missiles with new single-warhead missiles, as envisaged by earlier plans. The bulk of this future procurement cost could be avoided only if further reductions—in a START III agreement—lowered the ceilings on both sides to levels that Russia could afford. Finally, START II ratification languished in Moscow as most of Russia's political elite, irrespective of party affiliation, could not resist holding the treaty hostage to Western restraint in NATO expansion plans.[45]

These issues forced a U.S. strategic arms control review in the winter of 1996-97, producing substantially revised U.S. positions on START II and an outline for

START III that yielded agreements at the Helsinki Summit on March 20-21, 1997. Presidents Clinton and Yeltsin agreed to:

(1) Modify START II so as to postpone the deadline for START II reductions by five years—from January 1, 2003, to December 31, 2007 (easing the financial burden of reductions on Russia);

(2) Begin negotiations on a START III immediately after START II enters into force, agreeing in advance that that the lower ceilings for START III would be 2,000-2,500 warheads, with these reductions to occur by the same deadline of December 31, 2007 (removing from Russia the economic burden of building up single-warhead ICBMs to START II levels); and

(3) Remove the threat from missiles that would be eliminated under START II earlier, by de-activating them (either removing their nuclear warheads or taking other jointly agreed de-activation steps) no later than December 31, 2003.[46]

Also at Helsinki, the two presidents reaffirmed their commitments to the ABM Treaty and agreed on a formula that would allow their negotiators to finalize accords on the "demarcation" between strategic (ABM) and theater missile defenses (TMD)—clarifying the criteria that distinguish strategic and tactical missile defenses. ABM missile defenses are limited by the ABM Treaty, while theater (tactical) missile defenses are not. Agreement on demarcation had been under negotiation since 1993 and is viewed by the U.S. administration as a means of safeguarding the integrity of the ABM Treaty while modernizing it to deal with changes in technology, including those reflected in emerging missile proliferation threats.[47] According to U.S. officials, the Russian side indicated at the Helsinki Summit that the prospects for ratification of START II by the Russian parliament would greatly improve after the signing of the forthcoming NATO-Russia Founding Act and the completion of the ABM/TMD Demarcation Agreement. Once those hurdles had been crossed, President Yeltsin indicated, he would begin a major drive to gain parliamentary approval for the START II pact.

Shortly after the Helsinki Summit, Russian concerns regarding the enlargement of NATO were partially addressed with the signing in Paris of the NATO-Russia Founding Act on May 27, 1997. Among other initiatives, the Founding Act established a NATO-Russia Permanent Joint Council, giving Russia an additional channel for its voice on European security affairs.[48]

As envisaged at Helsinki in March, Russia and the United States signed the START II extension protocol in New York on September 26, 1997. Secretary of State Madeleine Albright and Foreign Minister Yevgeniy Primakov also exchanged letters in New York that codify the Helsinki commitment to "de-activate" those ICBMs that are to be eliminated under START II (Russian SS-18s and SS-24s, and the American MX) by December 31, 2003. De-activation will either entail removal of warheads or be carried out by other jointly agreed steps, which are yet to be negotiated. On Russia's behalf, Primakov issued a unilateral statement indicating that, once START II has entered into force, experts from both sides should immediately begin work on methods of de-activation and an appropriate program of U.S. assistance to implement them, and that Russia will proceed on the understanding that the START III treaty will be negotiated and in force well before the de-activation deadline. Also in September, the Russian government began new steps to win Duma approval of START II. But the Duma did not act on the treaty in 1997, and Russian ratification was postponed at least until the fall of 1998.

Unveiling START III: As noted above, Presidents Yeltsin and Clinton achieved an agreement in principle at the March 1997 Helsinki Summit on certain elements of START III, including lower ceilings on each side's forces in a range between 2,000 and 2,500 warheads, to be fulfilled by the end of 2007. They also agreed that START III would break new ground with provisions for the transparency of strategic nuclear warhead inventories and for irreversibility (i.e., destruction rather than stockpiling of strategic nuclear warheads removed from delivery systems eliminated under the START treaties).[49] In addition, the two presidents agreed to explore possible measures relating to long-range nuclear sea-launched cruise missiles and tactical nuclear systems. These discussions are to take place separately from, but in the context of, the START III negotiations.

Formal START III negotiations have awaited Russia's ratification of START II. Soon after the New York signature of the START II protocol in September 1997, however, U.S. and Russian experts began to meet informally to discuss issues that will need to be resolved in START III. These expert discussions continued through the winter of 1997-98, having been given impetus by October 1997 consultations between Deputy Foreign Minister Georgiy Mamedov and the new U.S. Ambassador in Moscow, James Collins; Foreign Minister Yevgeniy Primakov and Deputy Secretary of State Strobe Talbott; and Prime Minister Viktor Chernomyrdin and Vice President Albert Gore.

Disarmament Assistance. Substantial progress has been made with dismantlement projects in Russia since early 1995 under the CTR program. This program initially focused on securing nuclear weapons being withdrawn from service, including those removed from Belarus, Kazakhstan, and Ukraine. Under U.S. Department of Defense auspices, it continues to support activities related to the dismantlement or destruction of strategic delivery systems (e.g., ICBMs, SLBMs, missile launchers, and heavy bombers) and the dismantlement of nuclear warheads, as well as to help build secure storage facilities for fissile material derived from dismantled nuclear weapons.[50] The program also has been expanded in scope to provide assistance with the destruction of all weapons of mass destruction (WMD), especially chemical weapons. Related U.S. Department

of Energy initiatives will enable support for Russian commitments to shut down reactor facilities that have been important in the production of fissile material for nuclear weapons and to upgrade Russian methods of accounting for and securing or controlling fissile materials.

CTR program appropriations and expenditures for Russia, as well as for the other three successor states, have increased over time. By the end of 1997, aggregate totals of planned CTR assistance to the new independent states had reached over $1.8 billion. For Russia alone, U.S.–planned CTR assistance had reached a total of over $973 million.[51] Russia has been receiving roughly half the value of all the CTR programs, and the lion's share of that amount has been for eliminating strategic weapons and establishing more stringent fissile material controls. Other important expenditures include support for Russia's centralization and secure storage of fissile material from dismantled weapons (at the Mayak facility), and for Russia's destruction of chemical weapons at the Shchuchye facility.[52]

A clear picture of warhead dismantlement in Russia has yet to emerge. Russia has occasionally stated that it had a capacity to dismantle about 2,000 nuclear weapons a year; it has at the same time reported that the rate of dismantlement was slowed down by the lack of suitable storage space for dismantled components. The U.S. Department of Defense believes that Russia's large stockpile of tactical nuclear weapons is not being drawn down through dismantlement at the rate it could have been, and a November 1997 report states:

> If carried out, the Russian tactical warhead reduction initiatives, announced in 1991, could result in the elimination of a total of about 15,000 tactical warheads. Also, strategic arms agreements could result in the retirement and eventual disassembly of a total of more than 7,000 strategic warheads. The process of eliminating strategic warheads began in earnest in 1994. Russia is believed to be dismantling warheads, but Moscow has not divulged specific information on warhead reductions. The economic situation in the country probably has slowed the reduction effort; many retired warheads slated for elimination are awaiting dismantlement. However, the U.S. government assesses that strategic warheads constitute the majority of the warheads eliminated so far.[53]

This huge overhang of tactical nuclear warheads in Russia has been a concern of the United States as strategic arms reduction proposals point to ever deeper reduction of strategic nuclear weapons. Consequently, the U.S. position includes tactical nuclear weapon reductions among the issues that need to be addressed parallel to START III.

Defense Conversion and Domestic Nuclear Non-Proliferation Controls. In non-nuclear weapon states, the IAEA safeguards regime focuses on civilian nuclear facilities and nuclear material imports to detect or deter diversion of materials from civilian to military or weapons purposes. In Russia, which is a nuclear-weapon state and not obligated under the NPT to safeguard its nuclear facilities or materials, the basic fear of imminent proliferation risks is related to the breakdown of traditional physical security controls over nuclear weapons (especially those in storage), and over fissile materials, including those derived from the dismantling of nuclear weapons. The quantities of fissile material in storage must have grown significantly—since large numbers of nuclear weapons have been removed from service due to both unilateral measures and nuclear arms reduction agreements since 1990, and since a significant number of these weapons are reportedly dismantled every year. A number of CTR projects and programs, especially those supervised by the U.S. Department of Energy, have been designed to help Russia alleviate the proliferation risks from nuclear weapons dismantlement and storage.

Materials Protection, Control, and Accounting (MPC&A): In this category, the MPC&A program is one of the more recent and successful programs designed to assist Russian facility managers to control fissile materials, i.e., prevent theft or diversion of nuclear materials. Projects subsumed under MPC&A have spent over $300 million in the new independent states as a group, and $288 million in Russia alone. These projects have been developed through cooperation between the U.S. Department of Energy (DOE) and Russia's Ministry of Atomic Energy (Minatom) and through consultations and joint projects between managers at individual U.S. National Laboratories and their Russian counterparts, including those in the secret cities that harbored the weapons production complex. These projects involve the provision of U.S. assistance to Russian facilities for improved MPC&A as well as reciprocal visits by U.S. and Russian specialists to nuclear facilities handling fissile materials.

According to the MPC&A strategic plan, DOE is providing assistance to 53 facilities in the former Soviet Union.[54] By the end of 1997, physical security upgrades had been completed at 17 smaller sites, and DOE projects that upgrades will have been completed at 27 total sites by the end of 1998. In addition, DOE has helped establish training and education centers for Russian specialists at the Russian Methodological Training Center in Obninsk, the Moscow Engineering Physics Institute, and the Tomsk Polytechnic University; by January 1998, more than 2,000 individuals had received training under these programs. Recent developments include: expansion of the list of facilities to be covered under the program; conclusion of a comprehensive agreement with the Russian Navy for MPC&A at all naval sites, formalized in a protocol signed in December 1997; initiation of work with the Russian Navy to improve the security of highly enriched uranium fuel for submarine propulsion reactors; and new initiatives to improve nuclear materials transportation security. By the end of 1997, DOE was engaged in cooperative MPC&A projects at all sites in the former Soviet Union known to contain fissile material.

The Plutonium Production Reactor Agreement (PPRA): In May 1994, to support U.S. and Russian agreement on the goal of terminating the production of fissile material for nuclear weapons, Russia agreed to cease operating two plutonium production reactors at Seversk (Tomsk-7) and one at Zheleznogorsk (Krasnoyarsk-26) by December 31, 2000. Russia's condition was that U.S. assistance provide alternative sources of energy to these cities by that date to replace the district heating that the reactors provide. In addition, Russia agreed that, in the interim, no plutonium produced in these reactors would be used for nuclear arms and that the United States could verify this.

Russia later declared that it had, as of October 1, 1994, stopped using plutonium produced in the three production reactors for nuclear weapons.[55] It refused to bring the 1994 agreement into force, however, claiming that the United States was reneging on a pledge to finance the alternative power installations. Russia also declined U.S. access to the reprocessing (plutonium separation) facilities in the two cities, on grounds that this would divulge classified information. In June 1995, Russia agreed to allow the United States to monitor the operation of the three reactors and to monitor the plutonium separated from the spent fuel produced in these units—without, however, inspecting the reprocessing plants where the plutonium is separated.

In exchange, the United States agreed to assist Russia in conducting feasibility studies to assess possible energy alternatives to the reactors, including:

- Construction of conventional power plants;

- Construction of new nuclear power reactors whose spent fuel (unlike that of the existing reactors) could be stored without the need for reprocessing; and

- Conversion of the existing nuclear reactor cores to use fuel that would not produce weapons-grade plutonium and that would include uranium from dismantled nuclear weapons.

In May 1996, the reactor core-conversion option was selected. Following a detailed engineering study, the United States agreed to pay $10 million for a joint U.S.–Russian feasibility study on converting the reactors. The United States also agreed, in principle, to seek up to an additional $70 million to pay for the conversion of the three reactor cores, assuming a favorable result of the feasibility study and Russia's meeting certain agreed milestones.

In August 1996, negotiations began on a revised Plutonium Production Reactor Agreement for the conversion of the three reactors, and a new text was agreed upon in January 1997. Negotiations on a CTR Core Conversion Implementing Agreement began in June 1997 and concluded in September. Both agreements were signed on September 23, 1997, at the ninth meeting of the Gore-Chernomyrdin Commission in Moscow. The new text calls for the reactors to be modified by the year 2000 and provides for U.S. monitoring of all plutonium produced in the reactors and separated after January 1, 1995, to ensure that it is not used for weapons. (Russia will also be able to monitor former plutonium-producing reactors at Hanford and Savannah River to confirm that they are no longer operating.)[56] The agreement specifies that the Russian reactors will be shut down at the end of their normal lifetimes, approximately in 2009-2010.

Reciprocal Fissile Material Inspections: A March 16, 1994, initiative of U.S. Secretary of Energy Hazel O'Leary and Russian Minister of Atomic Energy Viktor Mikhailov was subsumed in the May 10, 1995, Moscow Summit commitment by Presidents Yeltsin and Clinton to pursue "a cooperative arrangement for reciprocal monitoring at storage facilities of fissile materials removed from nuclear warheads and declared to be excess to national security requirements to help confirm the irreversibility of the process of reducing nuclear weapons. . . ."[57] Development of reciprocal inspections has been stalled since late 1995, however, by Russian inability to exchange classified information. This reflects the difficult challenge of finding a way to avoid disclosing nuclear-weapon design information while verifying that fissile material subject to monitoring is in fact from dismantled nuclear weapons.[58] This issue must also be resolved for the transparency arrangements at the Mayak storage facility and to enable START III negotiations on the objective of irreversible warhead destruction.

Uranium Purchase Agreement: An important measure to reduce the risks of weapons-grade uranium from dismantled former Soviet nuclear weapons leaking into the nuclear black market was the U.S. agreement with Russia to pay nearly $12 billion for 500 metric tons of highly enriched uranium (HEU) over a 20-year period. Procured through the U.S. Enrichment Corporation (USEC), the HEU (over 90 percent U-235) is first blended in Russia with slightly enriched uranium to produce low-enriched uranium (LEU) suitable for use as power reactor fuel. After some delays during 1995, USEC received shipments containing the equivalent of 6 tons of HEU in 1995 and 12 tons in 1996. The deliveries were originally expected to average 10 tons of HEU per year for five years, and then 30 tons per year for the remaining fifteen years of the contract. But in November 1996, USEC and Minatom signed a revised contract providing for an accelerated payments and delivery schedule[59] for the subsequent five years; the equivalent of 7,500 nuclear warheads would be converted to nuclear fuel, with USEC paying $2 billion for the imported material. Transparency measures also have been developed and expanded to provide U.S. assurance that the material blended down actually comes from nuclear weapons, and reciprocal monitoring measures have been worked out for Russia to assure itself that the LEU is fabricated in American facilities as reactor fuel and does not reenter a weapons processing cycle.[60]

Other Fissile Material Monitoring Arrangements: A three-way U.S.–Russia–IAEA initiative launched on September 19, 1996, builds on separate U.S. and Russian pledges to place fissile materials that are no longer needed for defense purposes under IAEA safeguards.[61] A key objective of this initiative is to develop a new set of tools for international monitoring of excess fissile materials, especially those in sensitive forms, in the context of U.S. and Russian disarmament activities. To verify storage of nuclear weapon components (such as the plutonium "pits" that probably will be stored at Mayak) traditional IAEA safeguarding methods— which involve sampling, visual inspection, and various quantitative measurements—will have to be modified significantly to avoid the disclosure of sensitive nuclear-weapons design data.[62] After a negotiating pause in September 1997, U.S. and Russian officials issued a progress report to the IAEA General Conference on discussions regarding the trilateral initiative. In December, U.S., Russian, and IAEA experts met in the United States to examine possible methods for conducting IAEA monitoring under the initiative.

Nuclear Export Controls. Russia inherited the Soviet Union's adherence to the nuclear non-proliferation regime and commitment to export controls. Ironically, while the centralized communist political system lent itself to stringent export controls over nuclear items, the changes following the Soviet breakup weakened Russia's ability to enforce strict export control requirements. Russia's geographical boundaries were smaller. Customs arrangements had to be set up at new political borders. Some of Russia's laws and regulatory mechanisms had to be reconstructed for a new constitutional environment. Russia's deep post-Soviet economic difficulties—coupled with natural incentives to establish the international export competitiveness of its cash-starved arms and high technology industries—have created tremendous internal pressures to sidestep the export control regulations of the nuclear and missile non-proliferation regime. These pressures surfaced in the 1990s in strategic and conventional military exports to China, black market leakage of missile components to Iraq, nuclear and missile export deals with India and Iran, and the promotion of advanced conventional arms sales to Indonesia and elsewhere.[63]

Although Russia succeeded the Soviet Union as a key member of the Nuclear Suppliers Group (NSG), Russia and India reopened negotiations in the mid-1990s on a Soviet commitment to supply nuclear power reactors to India—despite the NSG's adoption in 1992 of guidelines barring such sales to countries like India that are not NPT adherents and are not covered by full-scope IAEA safeguards on their nuclear programs. With regard to Iran, which is subject to a comprehensive embargo on nuclear trade by the United States and other NSG members, Russia opened a nuclear cooperation channel in January 1995, offering not only to construct a nuclear reactor for Iran's Bushehr nuclear power plant for $800 million but also to assist Iran in developing nuclear technical proficiency in several areas of civil nuclear training, research, and development.[64] Reportedly, Russia even initially agreed to supply uranium enrichment (gas centrifuge) technology and heavy-water moderated reactors to Iran, although it dropped these militarily useful components of its offer after strong protest by the United States[65] (see Iran chapter in this volume for details).

Missile Technology Control Regime (MTCR). After earlier agreeing to abide by the MTCR guidelines, Russia announced in June 1995 that it would join the MTCR and issued an enabling decree in July. It was formally admitted into the regime in August, and participated in its first MTCR plenary meeting on October 10-12, 1995.[66] The MTCR prohibits or restricts transfers of missiles, components, and related production technology with respect to missiles able to carry nuclear, chemical, or biological warheads more than 300 km. Russia has adopted a detailed export control list of missile components and technologies. In 1995 and 1997, however, missile transactions originating in Russia have raised questions about its compliance with the aims if not the letter of the MTCR.

A shipment of Russian missile guidance components (from strategic missiles, then being dismantled under START I), en route to Iraq, was intercepted at the airport in Amman, Jordan, in November 1995, and U.N. inspectors fished out another shipment of Russian missile components from the Tigris River near Baghdad in Iraq in December. The Russian government denied knowledge of the shipments, indicating they had no official approval. Other sources in Russia indicated that the shipments had been exported by private businessmen who had circumvented the Russian customs by using false labeling.[67]

Beginning in early 1997, reports surfaced that SS-4 ballistic missile[68] technology had been transferred to Iran from Russian design institutes and companies and revealed the fact that Vice President Gore had notified Russian Prime Minister Chernomyrdin, ensuring that Moscow officials could not plead further ignorance.[69] The character of these transactions was unmistakably inconsistent with MTCR objectives. They encompassed missile-related equipment, special materials and technical information, as well as training of Iranian technicians at Russian institutes—all of which could assist Iran with developing and producing two planned ballistic missiles, the Shahab-3 and Shahab-4. Iran's Shahab-3 reportedly is based on North Korea's No Dong 1 missile and is expected to have a range of 1,300 km with a 700-kg payload—a range sufficient to reach Israel; by some estimates, it could be only a year from completion.[70] The Shahab-4, according to Israeli sources, is based on the Russian SS-4 medium-range ballistic missile (MRBM) design, would have a range of 2,000 km when carrying a payload of 1,000 kg and might be just three years from completion.[71]

U.S. officials at all levels have remonstrated with Russian counterparts against this missile assistance to Iran. Russian officials have disclaimed that there is any official Russian assistance of this kind to Tehran, or

that there is any significant missile-related technical assistance in private or educational channels. In July 1997, President Clinton assigned Ambassador Frank Wisner, a senior diplomat, to concentrate on this issue. President Yeltsin named Yuri Koptev, Russian Space Agency Director, as Wisner's counterpart. As of November 1997, Wisner and Koptev had held three rounds of talks. Russian officials have acknowledged that there have been Iranian efforts to acquire technology but have claimed that the Russian internal security service has thwarted all such attempts, including an Iranian attempt to have NPO Trud manufacture parts for a liquid-propellant missile.[72] In November, the security services caught and deported an Iranian diplomat who had been trying to buy missile design information from defense organizations.[73]

As of the end of 1997, U.S. officials remained highly concerned about Russia's propensity to trade in military goods with Iran but also believed at that time that Russia had not transferred any complete MRBMs to Iran. Iran apparently had not given priority to importing complete missiles of that kind, but rather had sought technical assistance and information that would enable it, eventually, to produce its own long-range missiles indigenously.[74] U.S. officials also believed that Russia urgently needed to improve its export controls but found Russia unreceptive to U.S. offers of help on export controls under the auspices of the Nunn-Lugar program.[75] The Clinton Administration's failure to get Russian cooperation in terminating missile-related activities with Iran has resulted in congressional pressure, including a Concurrent Resolution threatening sanctions on Russian entities[76] and restrictions on aid to Russia in the FY1998 Foreign Operations Appropriation Act.[77] The Act would withhold 50 percent of the aid to Russia unless the president certifies to Congress that the Russian government "has terminated implementation of arrangements to provide Iran with technical expertise, training, technology, or equipment necessary to develop a nuclear reactor, related nuclear research facilities or programs, or ballistic missile capability." The Act allows a presidential waiver of the restriction, subject to a notification to Congress that "making [the aid] available (A) is vital to the national security interest of the United States, and (B) that the Government of Russia is taking meaningful steps to limit major supply contracts and to curtail the transfer of . . . " nuclear and ballistic missile technology to Iran.[78]

Other Arms Control Measures

Chemical and Biological Weapons: Russia inherited the largest stockpile of chemical weapons in the world. It was therefore especially important that Russia's parliament ratified the Chemical Weapons Convention (CWC) by a large majority on November 5, 1997, in the first successful action on an international arms control treaty by Russia's State Duma and Federation Council. The CWC approval was conditioned on Western aid for chemical weapons destruction. The CTR program already is providing some assistance for this purpose, and a number of other Western nations have made commitments to help Russia eliminate its chemical weapons stockpile. Russia is a member of the Biological and Toxin Weapons Convention.

The U.S. Defense Department has stated in its annual report on proliferation that "Serious concerns remain about the status of Russian chemical and biological warfare programs, the accuracy of the information provided by Russia in its declarations, and the willingness of the Russian defense establishment to eliminate these capabilities."[79] The same report states that Russia's stockpile of chemical weapons agents measures about 40,000 metric tons and indicates that Russia may be developing new generations of chemical agents, has retained intact key components of the former Soviet Union's biological warfare program, and may be continuing some research related to biological warfare.[80] It also states that "the former Soviet offensive biological program was the world's largest" and expresses concern that "work outside the scope of legitimate biological defense activity may be occurring now at selected facilities within Russia."[81]

The Comprehensive Test Ban Treaty (CTBT): Russia has adhered to a moratorium against the testing of nuclear weapons since 1991. Once negotiation of the CTBT had progressed to the point of widespread acceptance of a zero-yield nuclear explosive test ban, Russia consistently supported a strict regime to inhibit advanced nuclear weapons development by undeclared nuclear-weapon states. Russia has not ratified the CTBT and is expected to await U.S. ratification before acting.

PROSPECTS

Arguably, no country's full participation in the global non-proliferation regime is more important than Russia's. Russia has been an effective partner in the peaceful de-nuclearization of the other Soviet-successor states and has continued to play a key leadership role in developing the nuclear non-proliferation regime— as a member of the Nuclear Suppliers Group, as a key supporter of the permanent extension of the NPT, and in voluntary cessation of nuclear weapons testing and strong support for the CTBT. As a U.N. Security Council Permanent Member, Russia was also an effective partner in devising the U.N. Special Commission (UNSCOM) inspection arrangements in Iraq after the Gulf War.

Russia has also enabled the implementation of START I, notwithstanding the unprecedented situation that had arisen with the breakup of the former Soviet Union and the complications Moscow faced with the Lisbon Protocol in coordinating its START I reduction and inspection obligations with Belarus, Kazakhstan, and Ukraine. The continued implementation of START-related nuclear arms reductions has been an important

underpinning of non-nuclear-weapon state confidence in the nuclear non-proliferation regime.

Russia has also worked closely with U.S. counterparts in developing post-Soviet controls over nuclear facilities and materials as well as the nuclear weapons infrastructure.[82] Among other things, this has included:

- A 500-metric-ton uranium deal—the blending down in Russia of weapons-grade uranium from dismantled nuclear weapons and delivery of the LEU for U.S. purchase as power reactor fuel;

- The utilization of U.S. assistance for materials protection, accounting, and control systems at Russian civilian nuclear facilities;

- Cooperation on devising the means for the eventual shut-down of Russian weapons-plutonium production reactors that also provide local heat and energy; and

- Consultation on approaches for transparency in, and the irreversible disposition of, plutonium extracted from dismantled weapons.

Russia has also joined the MTCR and the Wassenaar Arrangement, and it has recently ratified the CWC—thereby boosting confidence that cooperation in establishing common assumptions and ground rules for national export control laws and regulations, and their actual implementation, will proceed in the areas of advanced conventional arms and dual-use technologies, missiles, and chemical weapons. Progress in these areas is needed to strengthen several recent non-proliferation agreements that are evolving along with, and sometimes overlap, the long-established nuclear non-proliferation regime. Almost invariably this calls for close consultation about particular cases and thus must be a continuing process.

In looking to the future, however, it should be noted that challenges to close cooperation on certain aspects of non-proliferation have arisen with Russia and that others may emerge. As this chapter and those on Iran, Iraq, and India indicate, Russia does not see eye to eye with the United States on the best nuclear and arms export control lines to draw for non-proliferation purposes with troubled states and regions. Some of Russia's exports to China in the military and missile fields are also matters of concern. There have been politically costly delays in moving forward with strategic arms control as well: START II ratification and START III negotiations still hang in the balance, and discussions have yet to reach fruition in the difficult areas concerning the disposition of excess nuclear weapons and weapons-grade materials and the destruction of tactical nuclear weapons. Moreover, the 1997-98 financial crisis that held back Russia's hoped-for economic recovery increased the obstacles to implementing costly arms reduction measures in Russia.

NOTES

[1]For a review of international legal issues and the arms control ramifications of recognizing Russia as the successor to the Soviet Union's nuclear-weapon-state rights and obligations under international agreements, see George Bunn and John Rhinelander, "The Arms Control Obligations of the Former Soviet Union," *Virginia Journal of International Law*, Vol. 33, Winter 1993, pp. 323-350. Also, see "Message From Russian President Boris Yeltsin to Hans Blix, Director General of the International Atomic Energy Agency, January 17, 1992," Moscow, *Itar-Tass,* January 17, 1992, in *FBIS-SOV,* January 21, 1992, p. 38; also "The Written Statement by the Russian Side at the Signing of the Protocol to the START Treaty on 23 May 1992 in Lisbon," in which then Russian Foreign Minister Andrei Kozyrev noted "that Russia as the successor state of the USSR is a Party to the Non-Proliferation Treaty and acts as a depositary state of this Treaty," in "Documents," *Arms Control Today,* June 1992, p. 36; " 'Nonnuclear' States Join," *Itar-Tass,* May 24, 1992, in *FBIS-SOV-91-101,* May 26, 1992, p. 2.

[2]In certain cases, such as the INF, START, and ABM treaties, the treaties have been modified to name Russia as well as other post-Soviet states as successors to the rights and obligations of the Soviet Union under those treaties. In the case of the START treaty, as amended by the Lisbon Protocol of May 23, 1992, a distinction was made between Russia and the three other successor state parties, Russia being permitted to retain strategic and nuclear arms on its territory indefinitely, and the other three states obligated to eliminate them within seven years.

[3]Under the NPT, states that have nuclear weapons on their territory but do not control them are considered non-nuclear-weapon states. Thus states where U.S. nuclear weapons have been deployed at various times (including Germany and South Korea) have held this status after joining the NPT. The same has been true for Eastern European members of the Warsaw Pact on whose territory Soviet nuclear weapons had been deployed.

[4]See "Texts of Accords by Former Soviet Republics Forming Commonwealth of Independent States," *Facts on File,* 1991, p. 972. See also Eric Schmitt, "Soviet Nuclear Move Ahead of Schedule," *New York Times,* February 28, 1992. By May 7, 1992, both Belarus and Ukraine confirmed that the withdrawal of all tactical nuclear weapons to Russia was complete. Withdrawal of tactical nuclear weapons from Kazakhstan was complete by late January 1992. "Chronology of Commonwealth Security Issues," *Arms Control Today,* May 1992, p. 27.

[5]See "Minsk Agreement on Strategic Forces, December 30, 1991," *Arms Control Today,* January/February 1992, p. 39.

[6]In June 1993, CIS joint command was abolished and in July 1993 Marshall Evgenii Shaposhnikov, the commander of the CIS nuclear forces, handed his set of launch codes to Russian Defense Minister Pavel Grachev, ending any pretense that several independent nations would control these nuclear forces. See *Radio Free Europe/Radio Liberty Daily Report,* July 23, 1993.

[7]Ukraine's parliament refused to ratify the Alma-Ata and Minsk accords of 1991, however, and declared that Ukraine was not bound by its promise to return all nuclear arms to Russia (see note 5).

[8]See note 4 above. See "Documents: Protocol to the Treaty Between the United States of America and the Union of Soviet Socialist Republics on the Reduction and Limitation of Strategic Offensive Arms, *Arms Control Today,* June 1992, p. 33; "START I: Lisbon Protocol and the Nuclear Non-Proliferation Treaty," ACDA Fact Sheet, March 17, 1994.

[9]Initially, these weapons were deployed at more than 100 sites in Russia. Because of concerns over the stability of Russia's armed forces—highlighted in the refusal of certain units to follow orders during the internal Chechnya conflict—Washington urged the Russian government to consolidate these weapons in fewer locations with special security arrangements. Russia took such action in late 1994. (Interviews, Moscow, February 1995.)

[10]START I was signed by Presidents George Bush and Mikhail Gorbachev on July 31, 1991, in Moscow. For text of treaty, see *The Treaty Between the United States of America and the Union of Soviet Socialist Republics on the Reduction and Limitation of Strategic Offensive Arms, signed in Moscow on July 31, 1991*, U.S. Arms Control and Disarmament Agency, Washington, D.C. 1991. See also "Strategic Arms Reduction Treaty (START): Analysis, Summary, Text," *Arms Control Today,* November 1991, p. 17; "START I: Lisbon Protocol and the Nuclear Non-Proliferation Treaty," ACDA Fact Sheet, March

17, 1994; "START I Entry Into Force and Security Assurances," ACDA Fact Sheet, December 5, 1994.

At the time of the signing of the treaty, U.S. strategic forces comprised an estimated total of 9,680 warheads, 7,826 of which were deployed on ICBMs and SLBMs. Comparable figures for the Soviet Union were a total of 10,996 warheads, 10,181 of which were deployed on ballistic missiles. See International Institute for Strategic Studies, *The Military Balance 1990/91* (London: Oxford University Press for IISS, 1990), pp. 212-13.

[11]See "START I: Lisbon Protocol and the NPT," ACDA Fact Sheet, op. cit.

[12]The Rada's "resolution of ratification" declared that only 36 percent of delivery vehicles and 42 percent of warheads deployed on Ukrainian territory would be subject to elimination. It also made elimination of the remaining delivery vehicles and warheads conditional on receiving aid to cover dismantlement costs, compensation for nuclear materials to be extracted from the warheads, and complex security guarantees. See "Parliament Ratifies START I Treaty, Lisbon Protocol," *Interfax* (Moscow), November 18, 1993, in *FBIS-SOV-93-222,* November 19, 1993, p. 45; "Supreme Council START I Ratification Resolution," *UNIAR* (Kiev), November 18, 1993, in *FBIS-SOV-93-222,* November 19, 1993, p. 45.

[13]See the Ukraine chapter for more details.

[14]See "Text of Resolution Detailing NPT Reservations," *Kiev Radio Ukraine World Service in the Ukraine* in *FM-FBIS London UK,* November 16, 1994; "Ukraine Joins Treaty Curbing Nuclear Arms," *Washington Post,* November 17, 1994; "Ukraine Accedes to NPT Treaty," *United Press International,* December 5, 1994; "Remarks by President Clinton at Signing of Denuclearization Agreement," *Federal News Service,* December 5, 1994; "France Signs NPT Security Guarantee Document," *Interfax* (Moscow), December 5, 1994, in *FBIS-SOV-94-234,* December 6, 1994, p. 44; "START I Entry Into Force and Security Assurances," ACDA Fact Sheet, December 5, 1994; "START I Enters Into Force; Nuclear Arsenals to Be Reduced Dramatically," ACDA Press Release, December 5,1994.

[15]See *Treaty with the Russian Federation on Further Reduction and Limitation of Strategic Offensive Arms (The START II Treaty),* U.S. Senate, 103d Congress, 1st Session, Treaty Doc. 103-1 (Washington, DC: Government Printing Office, 1993); "START II: Analysis, Summary, Text," *Arms Control Today,* January/February 1993, p. 19; "Factfile: START II at a Glance," *Arms Control Today,* January/February 1993, p. 33; "Strategic Arms Reduction Treaty II Chronology," ACDA Fact Sheet, January 6, 1993.

[16]See "Russian Missiles No Longer Targeted on U.S., UK." *Interfax,* May 30, 1994, in *FBIS-SOV-94-104,* May 30, 1994; *Radio Free Europe/Radio Liberty Daily Report,* September 5. 1994.

[17]Testimony of U.S. Defense Secretary William Perry before the Senate Foreign Relations Committee, March 1, 1995.

[18]Speech by U.S. Defense Secretary William Perry, American Legion (Washington, D.C.), February 27, 1995.

[19]Dunbar Lockwood, "New Data from the Clinton Administration on the Status of Strategic Nuclear Weapons Deactivations," Memorandum, Arms Control Association, December 7, 1994; unclassified CIA report, September 1994, as cited in "Nuclear Weapons Deactivations Continue in FSU," *Arms Control Today,* November 1994, p. 27; General Roland LaJoie, Deputy Assistant to the Secretary of Defense for Cooperative Threat Reduction, special briefing on the Cooperative Threat Reduction Program for the Senate Foreign Relations Committee, February 23, 1995.

[20]LaJoie, special briefing on the CTR Program, op. cit; Lockwood, "New Data from the Clinton Administration," op. cit.; unclassified CIA report, September 1994, op. cit. In congressional testimony in April 1994, Assistant Secretary Carter stated that "12 SS-18s and 120 warheads had been removed from silos in Kazakhstan, and the process of dismantling SS-18 silos" was expected to begin later in the year. See Testimony of Ashton Carter, Assistant Secretary of Defense for International Security Policy, before the Senate Armed Services Committee, April 28, 1994. Press reports in February 1994 stated that the twelve SS-18s had already been sent to Russia for dismantlement. See *Radio Free Europe/Radio Liberty Daily Report,* February 14, 1994; "U.S. Reward Sought for Ceding A-Arms," *Washington Post,* February 14, 1994. According to the September 1994 CIA report noted earlier, an additional 32 SS-18s had been de-activated as of that date. See "Nuclear Weapons Deactivations Continue in FSU," *Arms Control Today,* op. cit. In May 1994 Russian press reports said

that all nuclear warheads in Kazakhstan would be withdrawn to Russia by mid-1995 and all missile silos would be dismantled by mid-1997 (see *Radio Free Europe/Radio Liberty Daily Report,* May 4, 1991). However, in his February 1995 briefing (cited above), General Lajoie projected that silo dismantlement would not be completed until the latter half of 1998.

[21]Although START I would have allowed up to seven years, after entry into force, as the timetable for the withdrawal (or elimination) of all the strategic systems, a protocol signed by Ukraine's Acting Prime Minister Yefim Zvyagilsky and Russian Prime Minister Viktor Chernomyrdin on May 16, 1994, obligated Ukraine to withdraw all nuclear warheads to Russia within three years of the signing of the Trilateral Statement. See "Ukraine Pledges to Double Speed of Disarmament," *Reuters,* May 19, 1994.

[22]See LaJoie, special briefing on the CTR Program, op. cit. In congressional testimony in October 1994, Ashton Carter reported that there were 1,731 warheads in Ukraine prior to the initiation of the dismantlement process in January 1994, as opposed to 1,564 accountable warheads as cited in the START I Memorandum of Understanding on Data (MOU), hereafter abbreviated to START I MOU. See Testimony of Assistant Secretary of Defense Ashton Carter before the Senate Foreign Relations Committee, October 4, 1994.

[23]Other projects include the provision of secure railcars for transporting warheads and assistance in strengthening export control measures. See "CTR Programs by Country" and "CTR Obligations by Country/Project," Department of Defense, Office of Cooperative Threat Reduction, February 20, 1995.

[24]Thomas W. Lippman, "Russia Aims to Unload Its Uranium in the U.S.; Deal Moves Slowly Through Thorny Issues," *Washington Post,* August 5, 1992; and *Nuclear Fuel,* March 28, 1994, pp. 6-8.

[25]By December 1994, 94 project proposals had been approved, representing a total funding commitment then of $48.5 million. See Joint Press Statement on International Science and Technology Center, Moscow, December 9, 1994; U.S. Department of State, Office of the Senior Coordinator for Nuclear Science and Science Centers, September 1994. Japan and several European states have provided funds for disarmament and for the ISTC. See Carnegie Endowment for International Peace and Monterey Institute of International Studies, *Nuclear Successor States of the Soviet Union: Nuclear Weapon and Sensitive Export Status Report,* No. 2, December 1994, pp. 26-29.

[26]In contrast to security arrangements for protecting deployed nuclear weapons, which are under exclusively military supervision and guarded by elite troops, security was relatively lax at facilities containing weapons-grade nuclear materials. This was particularly true at research institutes run by civilian organizations, which are guarded by non-elite Ministry of Interior forces or local militia/ police. Security applying to weapons-grade nuclear materials within the nuclear weapons production complex, under the control of the Ministry of Atomic Energy (Minatom) and guarded by Interior Ministry forces, is thought to be better than at the research institutes, but weaker than that covering nuclear weapons. See Testimony of Leonard Spector before the House Foreign Affairs Committee, Subcommittee on International Security, International Organizations, and Human Rights, June, 27, 1994.

[27]See prepared testimonies of William Potter and Leonard Spector before the House Foreign Affairs Committee, Subcommittee on International Security, International Organizations, and Human Rights, June 27, 1994.

[28]Mark Hibbs, "Pu-239 Stolen From Russian Lab Was Weapons-Enriched in Centrifuge Plant," *Nuclear Fuel,* July 18, 1994, p. 1; Ferdinand Protzman, "Germany Reaffirming Russian Origin of Seized Plutonium," *New York Times,* July 21, 1994; R. Jeffrey Smith and Steve Vogel, "Agencies Hunt Black-Market Plutonium," *Washington Post,* July 23, 1994; Craig R. Whitney, "Germans Seize 3d Atom Sample, Smuggled by Plane From Russia," *New York Times,* August 14, 1994; David Ljunggren, "Russia Disowns Plutonium Seized in Germany," *Reuters,* August 15, 1994; Steve Coll, "Stolen Plutonium Tied to Arms Labs; German Scientists Trace Origin of Nuclear Materials to Russia," *Washington Post,* August 17, 1994; Craig R. Whitney, "Germans Seize More Weapons Material," *New York Times,* August 17, 1994; Rick Atkinson, "Officials Say Contraband Not a Threat," *Washington Post,* August 28, 1994; R. Jeffrey Smith, "Anti-Smuggling Effort Largely in Disarray," *Washington Post,* August 28, 1994. See also Mark Hibbs, "Plutonium, Politics, and Panic," *Bulletin of the Atomic Scientists,* November/December 1994, pp. 24-31.

[29]Mark Hibbs, "German Police Find 800 Milligrams HEU. Say It May Be Sample of Larger Inventory," *Nuclear Fuel,* August 15, 1994,

p. 1; "Czechs Hold Three Suspects After Seizing Uranium," *New York Times,* December 20, 1994; Michael R. Gordon, "Czech Cache of Nuclear Material Being Tested for Bomb Potential," *New York Times,* December 21, 1994; Rick Atkinson, "Prague Says Uranium Found in Czech Auto Could Trigger Bomb," *Washington Post,* December 21, 1994; Mark Hibbs, "Czech Find May Be Re-Enriched REPU to Fuel Naval Research Reactors," *Nuclear Fuel,* January 2, 1995, p. 12.

[30]Testimony of R. James Woolsey, before the House Foreign Affairs Committee, Subcommittee on International Organizations, International Security and Human Rights, June 27, 1994.

[31]See Paul A. Goble, *Regions, Republics, and Russian Reform: Center-Periphery Relations in the Russian Federation* (Washington, DC: Carnegie Endowment for International Peace, 1994).

[32]Kurt M. Campbell, et al., "Soviet Nuclear Fission: Control of the Nuclear Arsenal in a Disintegrating Soviet Union," *CSIA Studies in International Security,* No. 1, Center for Science and International Affairs, Harvard University, November 1991, pp. 14-15. During a prolonged period of civil strife, components from dismantled nuclear weapons in storage—nuclear warheads, missile airframes, or ALCMs—would also be at risk of falling into the hands of parties not necessarily under central or national control (for example, extremists, smugglers). If a stored nuclear warhead came into the possession of such a party, the dangers would be great. Even if the warhead were equipped with sensing devices and/or coded switches or had been disabled by the removal of certain parts (for example tritium reservoir, electronic firing units), its disassembly by suitably trained individuals could provide "valuable first-hand information on its design, materials, and components" or access to the fissionable core for use in another weapon. See U.S. Congress, Office of Technology Assessment, *Technologies Underlying Weapons of Mass Destruction,* OTA-BP-ISC-I 15, December 1993, p. 128. It is also possible that a team with substantial technical expertise, with access to the weapon over an extended period, could recreate the missing parts and reactivate the weapon.

[33]For additional details and sources on de-nuclearization and the implementation of START I, see the series *Nuclear Successor States of the Soviet Union,* published jointly by the Monterey Institute of International Studies and the Carnegie Endowment for International Peace, Nos. 1-5 (May 1994, December 1994, July 1995, May 1996, and March 1998).

[34]See Doug Clarke, "Kazakhstan Free of Nuclear Weapons," *OMRI Daily Digest,* April 26, 1995, pp. 2-3; Doug Clarke, "Kazakhstan Confirms It Is Nuclear Free," *OMRI Daily Digest,* May 25, 1995, p. 3; prepared remarks of U.S. Undersecretary of Defense for Policy Walter B. Slocombe before the Senate Armed Services Committee, May 17, 1995.

[35]*Nuclear Successor States of the Soviet Union,* op. cit., No. 5, p. 20.

[36]Angela Charlton, "Belarus Marks Nuke Withdrawal," *Associated Press,* November 27, 1996.

[37]Office of the Secretary of Defense, *Proliferation: Threat and Response,* November 1997, p. 41.

[38]See Table I-C for Belarus and Kazakhstan (Nuclear Weapons Systems and Associated Warheads), and citations, in Carnegie Endowment for International Peace and Monterey Institute of International Studies, *Nuclear Successor States of the Soviet Union,* No. 5, March 1998.

[39]Ukraine has also agreed to physically eliminate the SS-19 missiles themselves; although not strictly required by the terms of START I (which merely requires the elimination of the silo launchers for missiles of this type), physical elimination has been encouraged by the U.S. dismantlement assistance (Nunn-Lugar) program. For details on both launchers and missiles destroyed, and on the status of strategic bombers in Ukraine (see *Nuclear Successor States,* No. 5, op. cit.).

[40]The Soviet Union had declared, as of September 1990, an aggregate of 162 deployed heavy bombers with 855 warheads under START I counting rules. (See original START I MOU, pp. 123-24, in *The Treaty Between the United States of America and the Union of Soviet Socialist Republics on the Reduction and Limitation of Strategic Offensive Arms, signed in Moscow on July 31, 1991,* U.S. Arms Control and Disarmament Agency, Washington, D.C. 1991.) Russia by itself had, by the end of July 1997, only 75 operationally deployed heavy bombers attributable with 565 START I-accountable warheads—having kept the more modern, higher-counting ALCM-carrying platforms. (See July 1997 START I MOU, pp. 84-89.) Using START II counting

rules, these heavy bombers would be attributed with 816 warheads. (Derived from data in Table I-C for Russia, Nuclear Weapons Systems and Associated Warheads, in *Nuclear Successor States of the Soviet Union*, No. 5, op. cit.)

[41]The Russian Constitution of 1993 created the Federal Assembly, in two bodies. The upper house is called the Federation Council (elected governors and heads of regional legislatures occupy seats in the Council); and the lower house, the State Duma (comprised of directly elected members and members selected from party lists). The ratification of an international treaty requires a law passed by a simple majority vote in each body. Consideration of a treaty usually begins in the State Duma.

[42]For the report on START II placed before the Senate for its consideration, prior to the vote on January 26, 1996, see *START II Treaty, Report Together With Additional Views,* U.S. Senate, Committee on Foreign Relations, 104th Congress, 1st Session, Exec. Report 104-10, December 15, 1995.

[43]Yuri K. Nazarkin and Rodney W. Jones, "Moscow's START II Ratification: Problems and Prospects," *Arms Control Today*, Vol. 25, No. 7, September 1995, p. 11.

[44]The Soviet Union traditionally concentrated the bulk of its nuclear strike forces in land-based missiles, rather than in bombers and submarines, while the United States has had a much larger proportion of its warheads carried by bombers and missiles on submarines. START II would alter the proportions of warheads in the three parts of the triad drastically for Russia, and much less for the United States.

Eliminating MIRVed ICBMs under START II had stronger appeal to Russian negotiators in 1992 because a consequence of the Soviet breakup was that the production plants for the heavily MIRVed SS-18 and SS-24 ICBMs were located in Ukraine, on which Russia no longer cared to be dependent. Russia's modernization plans were to rely on the SS-25 and its follow-on SS-27 (Topol M), deployed as single-warhead mobile and silo-based missiles. The financial cost to Russia of implementing the treaty became more apparent, however, as the economy declined and constraints on resources forced cutbacks not only in strategic modernization but in the maintenance of the strategic submarine and bomber forces.

[45]These Russian objections to START II and the differential impact of START II on either side's force structure are explained more fully in Nazarkin and Jones, "Moscow's START II Ratification," op. cit., pp. 8-14; and in Jack Mendelsohn, "START II and Beyond," *Arms Control Today*, Vol. 26, No. 8, October 1996, pp. 3-9.

[46]See Rodney W. Jones and Nikolai N. Sokov, "After Helsinki, the Hard Work," *The Bulletin of the Atomic Scientists*, July-August, 1997, pp. 26-30; Clinton-Yeltsin Summit, Helsinki, Finland, March 20-21, 1997, Joint Statement on Parameters of Future Reductions in Nuclear Forces.

[47]Clinton-Yeltsin Summit, Helsinki, Finland, March 20-21, 1997, Joint Statement Concerning the ABM Treaty.

[48]Founding Act on Mutual Relations, Cooperation and Security Between the Russian Federation and the North Atlantic Treaty Organization, Paris, May 27, 1997.

[49]Separate U.S.–Russian negotiations on warhead-related "safeguards, transparency, and irreversibility" (STI) had been pursued since the May 10, 1995, Moscow Summit, but had stalled since late 1995 over Russian unwillingness to complete an agreement for cooperation that would have allowed both sides to exchange classified information on their weapons stockpiles and practices. Incorporating these issues in the START negotiations reflects their growing importance as levels of strategic arms drop to much lower levels, in which cheating could change the strategic balance.

[50]For a concise review of the Department of Defense–supported CTR programs, see *Proliferation: Threat and Response,* op. cit., Section II, pp. 54-56.

[51]See Table 1-F, Department of Defense Cooperative Threat Reduction Program, in *Nuclear Successor States of the Soviet Union*, No. 5, op. cit.

[52]*Proliferation: Threat and Response,* op. cit., p. 55.

[53]Ibid., p. 43.

[54]U.S. Department of Energy, Office of Nonproliferation and National Security, "MPC&A Program Strategic Plan," January 1998. See page 11 for a comprehensive list of sites where DOE is engaged in MPC&A assistance.

[55]Russia has stated that it is retaining the plutonium produced at Zheleznogorsk (Krasnoyarsk-26) and Seversk (Tomsk-7) in oxide form and is not transforming it into the metallic form used in weapons.

[56]Mike Stafford, "Russian Plutonium Reactor Conversion," *Journal of Nuclear Materials Management,* June 1997, p. 60.

[57]Joint Statement on the Transparency and Irreversibility of the Process of Reducing Nuclear Weapons.

[58]As of early 1997, a draft "Mutual Reciprocal Inspection" demonstration agreement had been developed to allow the application of proposed verification measures to "classified forms," i.e., weapon components. Although a consensus exists regarding the use of certain measurements, there are continuing discussions on measuring the shape of inspected items. Guy Lunsford, "Mutual Reciprocal Inspections," *Journal of Nuclear Materials Management,* June 1997, p. 60. It is expected that inspection involving plutonium components will involve some disclosure of classified data, which can take place only after the adoption of the currently stalled intergovernmental agreement for cooperation authorizing the exchange of such information. Inspections of weapons-grade uranium from dismantled nuclear weapons may be possible on an unclassified basis.

[59]The amended agreement allows USEC to purchase the equivalent of 18 metric tons of weapons-grade uranium in 1997; 24 tons in 1998; 30 tons in 1999; 30 tons in 2000; and 30 tons in 2001. This will speed up the purchases over these years from previous goals by approximately 50 percent and will account for nearly one-third of the 500 metric tons covered by the original agreement.

[60]Agreements have been worked out for U.S. monitors to sample material entering and leaving Russian weapons-related plants, including two blending facilities—the Ural Electrochemical Integrated Enterprise in Novouralsk (Sverdlosk-44) and the Krasnoyarsk Electrochemical Plant—as well as the Seversk (Tomsk-7) plant, where Russian nuclear-weapon components are ground into chips and transformed from metallic HEU to oxide form, to verify with some confidence that the HEU was actually taken from dismantled nuclear weapons. The agreements provide for Russian reciprocal monitoring at USEC's Portsmouth Gaseous Diffusion Plant and at private contractor facilities that fabricate civilian power reactor fuel. For additional information on the "facility annexes" and verification procedures, see *Arms Control Reporter* (Cambridge, MA: Institute for Defense and Disarmament Studies, 1996), pp. 612.B-1.17 and 612B-1.33.

[61]The United States has declared 200 metric tons of fissile material to be excess to defense needs and has placed 12 tons of this total under IAEA inspection. At the September 1996 IAEA General Conference, U.S. Secretary of Energy Hazel O'Leary declared that the United States would place 26 additional tons of this material under IAEA oversight. Similarly, in an April 1996 address to the U.N. Security Council, President Boris Yeltsin, referring to the fissile material storage facility under construction at Mayak, declared that "After completion we propose to place it under IAEA control."

[62]For an analysis of the initiative from the perspective of the IAEA, see Bruno Pellaud, "International Verification of U.S. and Russian Materials Released for Storage and Disposition," *Journal of Nuclear Materials Management,* June 1997, p. 13.

[63]For a compilation of Russia's recent record on nuclear and missile export activities, see chapter on Russia in *The Proliferation Primer: A Majority Report of the Subcommittee on International Security, Proliferation, and Federal Services,* Committee on Governmental Affairs, U.S. Senate, January 1998, pp. 17-29.

[64]Russia contracted to provide nuclear fuel for the reactor for 20 years, to take back spent fuel for reprocessing, and to train Iranian nuclear technicians to operate the plant. Russia also offered, in principle, to build up to three additional power reactors at the site after finishing the first.

[65]Deputy Assistant Secretary of State Robert Einhorn made clear that the U.S. believes that assisting Iran even with civil nuclear power technology is dangerous because it will help Iranian technicians get up the "nuclear learning curve," potentially aiding a nuclear weapons program. See *Proliferation: Russian Case Studies,* Hearings of the Subcommittee on International Security, Proliferation, and Federal Services of Senate Governmental Affairs Committee, June 5, 1997, p. 11.

[66]"Russia: International Organizations and Treaties," *NIS Nuclear Profiles Database,* Center for Nonproliferation Studies, November 1997; Alexander Krasulin, "Decree on Missile Technology Export Controls," *Rossiyskaya Gazeta* (Moscow), August 18, 1995, p. 14; "MTCR Expands," *Arms Sales Monitor,* December 5, 1995, p. 4. In joining the MTCR, Russia undertook not to make future deals that

would conflict with the purposes and guidelines, but its agreement was on the condition that previous contracts could be fulfilled.

[67] David Hoffman, "Russian Missile Gyroscopes Were Sold to Iraq," *Washington Post,* September 12, 1997; R. Jeffrey Smith, "U.N. Is Said to Find Russian Markings on Iraq-Bound Military Equipment," *Washington Post,* December 15, 1995.
Private interviews in Moscow indicated that the guidance components that had been removed from dismantled missiles (relatively old SS-N-8 SLBMs that were being retired from service, quite apart from the START treaty) and, being considered as "trash" (of no military or commercial value), had been scavenged by private entrepreneurs, who happened to be familiar with the plant, and exported without any reference to the authorities. Whatever the military value of these old parts, that they had strategic missile origins and could be freely resold to Iraq clearly was an embarrassing symptom of breakdown in internal controls.

[68] Soviet SS-4 theater missiles were destroyed under the INF Treaty, but the usual procedure during elimination was to salvage guidance equipment, and design documentation would have been preserved. The SS-4 was a semi-mobile system (but normally deployed in fixed, surveyed sites) that became operational in the 1960s, probably the first Soviet missile type to use storable liquid propellants. It was replaced by the three-warhead, solid-fuel, mobile SS-20 IRBM, which was also eliminated under the INF Treaty. *The World's Missile Systems,* 7th ed. (Pomona, CA: General Dynamics, April 1982), pp. 205-206.

[69] Robin Wright, "Russia Warned on Helping Iran Missile Program," *Los Angeles Times,* February 12, 1997; Bill Gertz, "Gore Raises Sale to Iran with Chernomyrdin," *Washington Times,* February 13, 1997.

[70] Steven Erlanger, "U.S. Telling Russia to Bar Aid to Iran By Arms Experts," *New York Times,* August 22, 1997; Bill Gertz "Russia, China Aid Iran's Missile Program," *Washington Times,* September 10, 1997; Steve Rodan, "Secret Israeli Data Reveals Iran Can Make Missile in Year," *Defense News,* October 6-12, 1997; David Hoffman, "Gore Says Probe Shows Iran Seeks Technology to Build Nuclear Arms," *Washington Post,* September 24, 1997.

[71] Rodan, "Secret Israeli Data," ibid.

[72] Vladimir Isachenkov, "Russia Blocks Iran on Missiles, *Associated Press,* October 2, 1997; David Hoffman, "Russia Says It Thwarted Attempt by Iran to Get Missile Technology," *Washington Post,* October 3, 1997.

[73] Anatoly Verbin, "Russia Deports Iranian for Trying to Buy Missile Designs," *Reuters,* reprinted in *Washington Times,* November 15, 1997.

[74] *Proliferation: Russian Case Studies,* Senate hearings, op. cit., p. 5.

[75] Ibid.

[76] U.S. Congress, *Congressional Record,* 105th Cong., 1st Session, 1997, pp. S12064 and H10123.

[77] U.S. Congress, HR2159, November 13, 1997, signed into law by the President on November 26, 1997.

[78] Ibid.

[79] *Proliferation: Threat and Response,* op. cit., pp. 41-42, 45-46. The U.S. Defense Department estimates that the cost of destroying Russia's large chemical weapons (CW) stockpile in a safe and environmentally acceptable manner will be the equivalent of at least $5 billion, and notes that while Russia passed a law in May 1997 to authorize the destruction of CW stocks, no funds for this purpose have been authorized, nor are there yet facilities approved for this purpose. The CWC expects this destruction to be carried out in 10 years, or not more than 15, with an approved extension.

[80] Ibid., p. 42.

[81] The report adds that "The United States remains concerned at the threat of proliferation, both of biological warfare expertise and related hardware, from Russia. Russian scientists, many of whom either are unemployed or have not been paid for an extended period, may be vulnerable to recruitment by states trying to establish biological warfare programs. The availability of worldwide information exchange via the Internet or electronic mail facilitates this process." Ibid., p. 46.

[82] In April 1998, a new Russian government formed by Prime Minister Sergei Kiriyenko took office. It is expected that Kiriyenko will continue to meet with Vice President Gore in the Gore-Chernomyrdin Commission context.

Russia's Nuclear Weapons Infrastructure

Operational Strategic Nuclear Weapons Facilities

■ Silo-based Inter-Continental Ballistic Missiles (ICBMs)
⊠ Road-mobile ICBMs
⊡ Rail-mobile ICBMs
★ Anti-Ballistic Missiles (ABMs)
⬢ Submarine-Launched Ballistic Missiles (SLBMs)
▲ Heavy Bombers carrying Air-Launched Cruise Missiles (ALCMs) or Gravity Bombs

SOURCES: START Memorandum of Understanding on Data (MOU), September 1990–January 1998.

Locations with Weapons-Usable Fissile Material for One or More Nuclear Bombs

◖ Plutonium Production
⊗ Uranium Enrichment/Processing
▭ Warhead Assembly/Dismantlement
⊙ Research Institute/Research Reactor
◪ Fuel Storage

SOURCE: Monterey Institute of International Studies, Monterey, CA;
Natural Resources Defense Council, Washington, DC;
U.S. Department of Energy, Washington, DC.

FINLAND
ESTONIA
LATVIA
LITHUANIA
KALININGRAD
BELARUS
UKRAINE

Murmansk
Nerpich'ya
Yagel'naya
Ostrovnoy
Barents Sea

Novaya Zemlya
Nuclear test site

Arkhangel'sk
Severodvinsk

St. Petersburg
Vypolzovo
Dubna
Moscow
Obninsk
Kozel'sk
Kostroma
Teykovo
Podolsk
Ryazan
Sarov
Zarechniy
Tatishchevo
Dmitrovgrad
Engels
Kazan
Yur'ya
Yoshkar-Ola

Ural Mtns.

Lesnoy
Bershet
Yekaterinburg
Nizhniy Tagil
Novouralsk

RUSSIA

Ob River
Tobol River

Trekhgornyy
Kartaly
Dombaroskiy
Snezhinsk
Ozersk

Tomsk
Seversk
Uzhur

Novosibirsk

Barnaul
Aleysk

Black Sea
Caucasus Mtns.
Mozdok
GEORGIA
ARMENIA
AZERBAIJAN
Caspian Sea

KAZAKHSTAN

Aral Sea

IRAN
TURKMENISTAN
UZBEKISTAN

Volga River

0   500
Miles

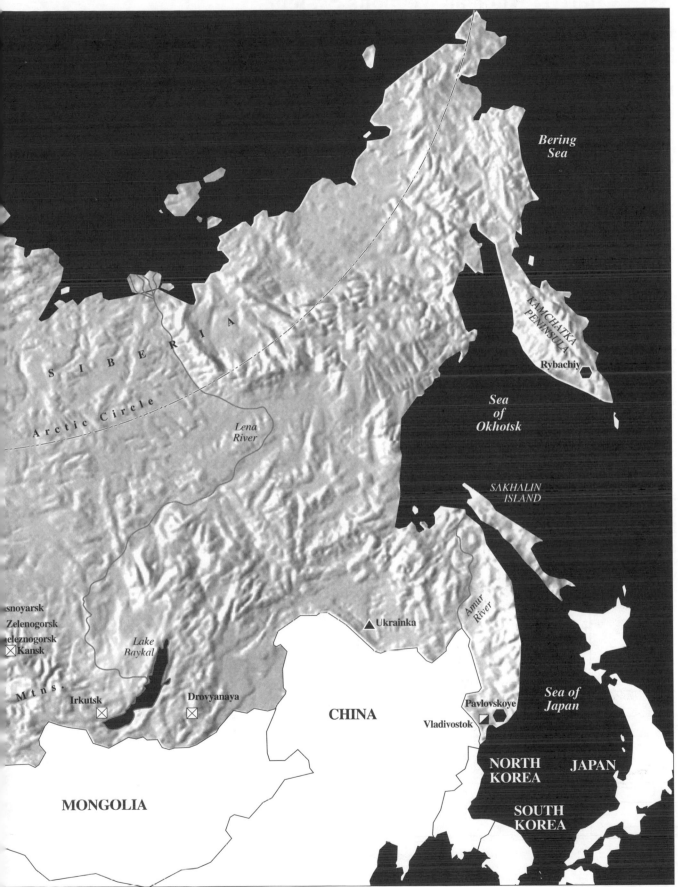

Bering
Sea

S I B E R I A

KAMCHATKA
PENINSULA

Rybachiy

Arctic Circle

Lena
River

Sea
of
Okhotsk

SAKHALIN
ISLAND

snoyarsk

Zelenogorsk

eleznogorsk

⊠Kansk

Lake
Baykal

▲Ukrainka

Amur
River

M t n s .

Irkutsk ⊠

Drovyanaya ⊠

CHINA

Pavlovskoye ⊠⬡

Vladivostok

Sea of
Japan

NORTH
KOREA

JAPAN

MONGOLIA

SOUTH
KOREA

Carnegie Endowment for International Peace, *Tracking Nuclear Proliferation*, 1998

RUSSIA Chart 1: Nuclear Weapons Systems[a]

TYPE	WEAPONS SYSTEMS (START I MOU/Current)	WARHEADS (START I MOU/Current)	CURRENT LOCATIONS	COMMENTS
ICBMs				
Total	**1064/751**	**4278/3610**		
SS-11	326/0	326/0		All SS-11s were dismantled by the end of 1995.
SS-13	40/0	40/0		All SS-13s have been dismantled.
SS-17	47/0	188/0		All SS-17s have been dismantled.
SS-18	204/180	2,040/1,800	Uzhur: 52 Aleysk: 30 Kartaly: 46 Dombaroskiy: 52	START I requires Russia to reduce its SS-18 deployment to 154 silos. START I attributes 10 warheads to each SS-18; some may carry fewer. START II requires elimination of all SS-18 ICBMs.
SS-19	170/165	1,020/990	Tatishchevo: 105 Kozel'sk: 60	START II would limit Russia to 105 deployed SS-19s, down-loaded to one warhead each.
SS-24	43/46	430/460	Bershet: 15 Kostroma: 12 Krasnoyarsk: 9 Tatishchevo: 10	Of the 46 SS-24s, 36 are rail-based and 10 are silo-based. Rail-based SS-24s were removed from alert status under the October 1991 Gorbachev initiative. START II requires elimination of these 10-warhead ICBMs.
SS-25	234/360	234/360	Irkutsk: 36 Kansk: 45 Novosibirsk: 45 Yoshkar-Ola: 36 Nizhniy Tagil: 45 Yur'ya: 45 Teykovo: 36 Vypolzovo: 18 Barnaul: 36 Drovyanaya: 18	To replace MIRVed ICBMs, whose elimination START II requires, Russia's land-based leg will rely more on single-warhead SS-25s, still being deployed, and on a new single-warhead ICBM, the Topol-M (SS-27), which was declared ready for deployment in July 1997; Russia expects to deploy 10 SS-27s by the end of 1998.[b]
BOMBERS[c]				
Total	**79/75**	**570/816**		
Bear-H	28/64	448/734	Mozdok: 21 Ukrainka: 43	40 Bear-H bombers were transferred from Kazakhstan to Russia.
Blackjack	2/6	24/72	Engels: 6	
Bear-G	49/5	98/10	Ryazan: 5	5 additional Bear-Gs are awaiting elimination at Engels.

TYPE	WEAPONS SYSTEMS (START I MOU/Current)	WARHEADS (START I MOU/Current)	CURRENT LOCATIONS	COMMENTS
S L B M s [d]				
Total	**940/384**	**2804/1824**		
SS-N-6	192/0	192/0	Rybachiy: 1 Yankee I sub	Although 16 SS-N-6s are accountable under START I, none are operationally deployed.[e]
SS-N-8	280/0	280/0	Ostrovnoy: 3 Delta I subs Rybachiy: 2 Delta I subs Yagel'naya: 2 Delta I subs 3 Delta II subs Pavlovskoye: 5 Delta I subs	Although 192 SS-N-8s are accountable under START I, none are operationally deployed.[f]
SS-N-17	12/0	12/0		All SS-N-17s have been destroyed.
SS-N-18	224/192	672/576	Rybachiy: 9 Delta III subs Yagel'naya 4 Delta III subs	Although 208 SS-N-18s are accountable under START I, only 192 are operational.[g]
SS-N-20	120/80	1,200/800	Nerpich'ya: 6 Typhoon subs	Although 120 SS-N-20s are accountable under START I, only 80 are operational.[h]
SS-N-23	112/112	448/448	Yagel'naya: 7 Delta IV subs	
O T H E R N U C L E A R W E A P O N S				
Tactical Nuclear Weapons		Estimates of the total number of tactical nuclear warheads in Russia range from 15,000 to upward of 20,000; the number deployed may be considerably lower.[i]	The number of tactical nuclear weapons deployment sites were reduced for security reasons in 1994.[j]	Approximately 4,000 tactical nuclear weapons were withdrawn to Russia from Belarus, Kazakhstan, and Ukraine.[k]
Strategic and Tactical Weapons in Storage and Dismantlement Facilities		The exact number of warheads in storage or dismantlement facilities is unknown.	Dismantlement Facilities: Sarov Zarechniy Lesnoy Trekhgornyy	Russia has told the U.S. Department of Defense that it is dismantling over 2,000 warheads per year.[l]
Anti-Ballistic Missiles	100	100	ABMs deployed within a 100-km radius of Moscow.	Nuclear warheads on ABM interceptors near Moscow may have been replaced with conventional ordnance.[m]

NOTES (Russia Chart 1)

[a]The original "START I" numbers for Russia in this chart are derived from the September 1990 START Memorandum of Understanding (MOU) on Data, an annex to the START treaty that declared "baseline" numbers and locations of the strategic offensive forces of the United States and the Soviet Union as of September 1990. See "START-Related Facilities by Republic as Declared in MOU Data Exchange, Sept. 1, 1990," *Hearings on the START Treaty*, Committee on Foreign Relations, U.S. Senate, 102nd Cong., 2nd Sess., February 6, 1992, p. 497. The MOU data were updated by the five START parties after the treaty entered into force in December 1994, and at six-month intervals thereafter.

"Current" numbers indicate the effects of reductions under the first phase of START I implementation (although, in some cases, the current numbers may increase due to Russia's ongoing ICBM modernization or the withdrawal to Russia of moveable strategic systems from Belarus and Kazakhstan). The current numbers reflect the status of deployed operational systems in Russia as of July 1997, but may exclude deactivated sytems, even if they have not yet been eliminated in treaty terms. The START I counting rules count deployed delivery systems and their attributable warheads as "deployed," until the systems have been eliminated (i.e., until missile launchers and heavy bombers slated for elimination are actually destroyed), even if the systems are known to be no longer operational. Current figures have been derived from subsequent START MOU updates, the latest available being that of January 1998, and various other open sources. See, for example, Carnegie Endowment for International Peace and Monterey Institute of International Studies, *Nuclear Successor States of the Soviet Union: Status Report on Nuclear Weapons, Fissile Materials, and Export Controls*, No. 5, March 1998; International Institute of Strategic Studies, *The Military Balance 1997/98* (London: Oxford University Press for IISS, 1997); "NRDC Nuclear Notebook," *The Bulletin of the Atomic Scientists*, March/April 1998, pp. 70-71.; and Thomas B. Cochran, et al., *Nuclear Weapons Databook—Volume IV: Soviet Nuclear Weapons,* (New York: Harper and Row, 1989).

The START I treaty parties were, as of December 1997, two full years ahead of the treaty reductions schedule, according to Robert Bell, the senior NSC official for defense and arms control, in his February 17, 1998 presentation to the Arms Control Association in Washington, D.C.

[b]Russia stationed two experimental Topol-Ms in refurbished SS-19 silos at Tatishchevo in December 1997. Neither missile is thought to be armed with a nuclear warhead. See "DOD sees only one Russian SS-X-27 missile potentially operational," *Aerospace Daily*, January 13, 1998; "Russia inaugurates first Topol-M ICBM in refurbished silo," *Aerospace Daily*, January 7, 1998, p. 25.

[c]Current totals reflect 64 Bear-H, 6 Blackjack, and 5 Bear-G bombers. Current bomber loadings are calculated using START II counting rules, and thus reflect the number of warheads for which the heavy bombers of a listed variant are actually equipped, rather than the number of warheads attributed to each aircraft by the START MOUs. The START MOUs intentionally undercount bomber loadings.

[d]The Yankee I, Delta II, Delta III, and Delta IV class submarines have 16 tubes each. The Delta I class submarine has 12 tubes and Typhoon class submarines have 20 tubes. Under START I counting rules, SLBMs are accountable until their associated launch tubes are destroyed.

[e]Robert S. Norris, "NRDC Nuclear Notebook," *The Bulletin of the Atomic Scientists*, March/April 1996, p. 62.

[f]Ibid., p. 62.

[g]"NRDC Nuclear Notebook," op. cit., pp. 70-71.

[h]Two Typhoon submarines with 20 tubes each are inoperable. Ibid.

[i]See Deputy Secretary of Defense John Deutch, U.S. Defense Department Briefing, September 22, 1994; and "Estimated Russian Nuclear Stockpile, September 1996," *The Bulletin of the Atomic Scientists*, September/October 1996, p. 17. Unfortunately, there is no authoritative baseline information on the number of tactical nuclear weapons deployed and stockpiled by the former Soviet Union as of 1991. Information released subsequently has been fragmentary and allows no reliable estimates either of the numbers or of the status of Russia's tactical nuclear weapons, whether deployed on launchers, stored but operationally ready for use by military units, retired from service but stored, or both retired and dismantled.

Alexei Arbatov, Russian Duma member, published a report listing the number of Soviet tactical nuclear weapons at 21,700 in 1991. Of these, 13,700 were, he suggested, subject to elimination under the 1991 reciprocal unilateral reductions declared by Presidents Gorbachev and Bush. An additional 4,200 from outside Russia would also have been subject to elimination. Arbatov claims that of the remaining weapons, perhaps 4,000, most are in storage. *Yadernye Vooruzheniya Rossii*, Alexei Arbatov, ed., (Moscow: IMEMO, 1997), p. 56. The U.S. Defense Department recently reported, however, that most Russian warhead dismantlement appears to have been of strategic rather than tactical nuclear warheads, and that relatively few of the 15,000 tactical warheads that were estimated to have been withdrawn from service under the 1991 unilateral initiative, and presumably subject to dismantlement, actually were dismantled. The report states that "Russia has not divulged specific information on warhead reductions." Office of the Secretary of Defense, *Proliferation: Threat and Response,* November 1997, p. 43.

[j]"Tactical Nuclear Arms Removed from Vessels," *ITAR-TASS*, February 4, 1994, in *FBIS-SOV-93-022*, February 4, 1994, p. 1.

[k]Testimony of Assistant Secretary of Defense Ashton Carter, before the Senate Armed Services Committee, April 28, 1994.

[l]Ashton Carter testimony, op. cit. These figures include the dismantlement of both tactical and strategic nuclear warheads. See note 9 above reflecting current Department of Defense skepticism that Russia's warhead dismantlement thus far has included a significant fraction of the tactical nuclear warhead inventory.

[m]In oral remarks, Col. Gen. Alexander Yesin, Deputy Secretary of the Security Council of the Russian Federation (and former chief of staff of the Strategic Rocket Forces) indicated at the Carnegie Endowment for International Peace, April 21, 1998, that Russia has been replacing nuclear with conventional warheads on the ABM system deployed around Moscow. This has not yet been confirmed publicly by official U.S. sources.

RUSSIA Chart 2: Locations with Weapons-Usable (Fissile) Material[a]

NAME/ LOCATION OF FACILITY	ACTIVITY	PLUTONIUM	WEAPONS-GRADE URANIUM	COMMENTS
Sarov (Arzamas-16)	Weapons R&D, warhead assembly/ dismantlement, research reactors.	Yes	Yes	4 research reactors and more than a ton of fissile material.
Baltiyskiy Zavod, St. Petersburg	Construction of nuclear icebreakers and other ships.		Yes	Fresh fuel in storage for up to a year.
Beloyarsk, near Yekaterinburg	BN-600 fast breeder reactor.	Yes	Yes	Spent fuel plutonium present.
A.A. Bochvar Institute, Moscow	Research on weapons-grade materials.	Yes	Yes	In early 1994, parts of the facility were closed due to lax plutonium protection arrangements.
Ozersk, Mayak Production Association (Chelyabinsk-65)	Plutonium and tritium production reactors, reprocessing, MOX fuel production, warhead component production.	Yes	Yes	All plutonium production reactors closed, but reprocessing and tritium production continue.
Snezhinsk (Chelyabinsk-70)	Warhead design, prototype warhead fabrication, research reactors.	Yes	Yes	More than a ton of weapons-usable material present.
Scientific Research Institute for Atomic Reactors, Dmitrovgrad	Research and plutonium production reactors, MOX fuel fabrication, reprocessing, hot cells.	Yes	Yes	More than a ton of weapons-usable material present.
Joint Institute of Nuclear Research, Dubna	Research reactors.	Yes	No	About 100 kg plutonium.
Elektrostal Machine-Building Plant, Moscow	Fuel fabrication for naval propulsion, fast breeder, VVER and RBMK reactors.	No	Yes	Produces fuel assemblies for VVER and RBMK nuclear power reactors.
Institute of Physics and Power Engineering, Obninsk	Research reactors, research on weapons-grade materials.	Yes	Yes	4 research reactors and up to 18 critical assemblies; approximately 1,000 kg plutonium and 7 tons of HEU present.
Karpov Institute of Physical Chemistry, Obninsk	Research reactor.	No	Yes	VVR-Ts tank reactor and "substantial amounts" of HEU.[b]
Khlopin Radium Institute, St. Petersburg	Research on reprocessing technologies.	Yes	Yes	Current research on using ex-weapon plutonium as fast reactor fuel.[c]

NAME/ LOCATION OF FACILITY	ACTIVITY	PLUTONIUM	WEAPONS-GRADE URANIUM	COMMENTS
Zheleznogorsk (Krasnoyarsk-26)	Plutonium production reactor, spent fuel reprocessing.	Yes	Yes	Russia will convert the core of the ADE-2 plutonium producing reactor by 2000 so that it no longer produces weapons-grade plutonium.[d]
Zelenogorsk (Krasnoyarsk-45)	Uranium enrichment, LEU production.	No	Yes	Former HEU producer for weapons, now blends down ex-weapon HEU into LEU reactor fuel.
Krylov Central Scientific Research Institute, St. Petersburg	Research reactor and critical assemblies.	No	Yes	Research and design of nuclear submarine reactors, and testing of other naval reactors.
Kurchatov Institute, Moscow	Research reactors, critical and subcritical assemblies.	Yes	Yes	Nuclear energy research facility; estimated to possess hundreds of kgs of HEU for the 6 operable research reactors.
Luch Scientific Production Association, Podolsk	HEU fuel fabrication for space-based reactors, research reactors.		Yes	More than a ton of weapons-usable material present.
Lytkarino Research Institute for Instruments, near Moscow	Research reactors.	Possible[e]	Yes	Five pulse research reactors and 90% enriched HEU.
Moscow Engineering Physics Institute	Research reactor.	No	Yes	Pond-type research reactor and kilograms of 90% enriched HEU.
Moscow Institute of Theoretical and Experimental Physics	Heavy-water research reactor and critical assembly.		Yes	Heavy-water research reactor shut down, but critical assembly still operating.
Novosibirsk Chemical Concentrates Plant	Fuel fabrication for VVER-1000 reactors, research reactors, and Pu-production reactors.	No	Yes	Produces LEU fuel for VVER civilian power reactors and HEU fuel for research, and plutonium and tritium production reactors.
Zarechniy (Penza-19)	Component fabrication, warhead assembly and disassembly.	Yes	Yes	Manufactures nuclear warheads components and has on-site storage.
Scientific Research and Design Institute of Power Technology, Moscow	Research reactors, subcritical assemblies.		Yes	Designs reactors for power generation, naval propulsion, heat production, research, and space-based applications.
Sverdlovsk Scientific Research and Design Institute of Power Technology, Yekaterinburg	Research reactor, critical assemblies, hot cells.		Yes	Designs RBMK reactors and conducts safety tests; 15 MW pool reactor fueled with 1.7 kg 90% enriched HEU.

RUSSIA Chart 2 (cont'd.)

NAME/ LOCATION OF FACILITY	ACTIVITY	PLUTONIUM	WEAPONS-GRADE URANIUM	COMMENTS
Nuclear Physics Institute (formerly Lenin Institute of Physics), St. Petersburg	Research reactors, critical assemblies.		Yes	18 MW pool reactor fueled with 90% HEU; a 100 MWt tank reactor is under construction.[f]
Novouralsk Urals Electrochemical Integrated Plant (Sverdlovsk-44), Yekaterinburg	Former HEU for weapons production site, LEU production.	No	Yes	Produces and exports blended down LEU for nuclear power reactors; converts former weapons HEU to 4% LEU.[g]
Elektrokhimpribor Combine (Sverdlovsk-45), Lesnoy	Final warhead assembly and dismantlement.	Yes	Yes	One of Russia's largest dismantlement and storage sites; dismantles approximately 1500 warheads per year.[h]
Siberian Chemical Combine (Tomsk-7), Seversk	Plutonium production, uranium enrichment, reprocessing, dismantled weapons storage.	Yes	Yes	Large quantities of fissile material including tens of tons of plutonium and HEU from dismantled weapons; 2 operating plutonium production reactor cores will be converted by 2000.[i]
Tomsk Polytechnic University	Research reactor.		Yes	6 MW tank research reactor and HEU fuel; 1 kg of 90% HEU was discovered missing in 1995, and was possibly diverted.[j]
Trekhgornyy Instrument Making Plant (Zlatoust-36)	Final warhead assembly and dismantlement.	Yes	Yes	In addition to warhead dismantlement and storage, also produces ballistic missile reentry vehicles.[k]
Northern Fleet Naval Shipyards, Murmansk	Fresh and spent fuel storage, submarine refueling, submarine construction and decommissioning.	No	Yes	Large stocks of fresh and spent naval reactor fuel, including HEU enriched up to 92%.
Pacific Fleet, Kamchatka Peninsula and Vladivostok	Fresh and spent fuel storage, naval reactor maintenance, submarine decommissioning.	No	Yes	Large stocks of naval reactor fuel, HEU enriched up to 90%.

Abbreviations:

HEU	=	highly enriched uranium
LEU	=	low-enriched uranium
nat. U	=	natural uranium
MWe	=	millions of watts of electrical output
MWt	=	millions of watts of thermal output
KWt	=	thousands of watts of thermal output

NOTES (Russia Chart 2)

[a]Weapons-usable fissile material includes uranium enriched to 90 percent or more in the isotope U-235 (referred to below as highly enriched uranium or HEU) and all forms of plutonium (Pu). About 15 kg of HEU or 5 kg of Pu are required for a nuclear weapon. None of these facilities are under IAEA safeguards.

Principal sources for this chart: Carnegie Endowment for International Peace and Monterey Institute of International Studies, *Nuclear Successor States of the Soviet Union: Status Report on Nuclear Weapons, Fissile Materials, and Export Controls*, No. 5, March 1998, Table I-E,; the NIS Nuclear Profiles Database, Center for Nonproliferation Studies, Monterey Institute of International Studies, 1997; *United States/Former Soviet Union: Program of Cooperation on Nuclear Material Protection, Control, and Accounting*, Department of Energy Nuclear Material Security Task Force, December 1996; and Department of Energy, Office of Nonproliferation and National Security, *MPC&A Program Strategic Plan*, January 1998.

[b]From an interview conducted by the Center for Nonproliferation Studies with a Russian nuclear official in August 1997 as reported in *Nuclear Successor States of the Soviet Union,* No. 5, op. cit.

[c]This project is funded by an ISTC award. "Summary of 26 New ISTC Awards," *Post-Soviet Nuclear & Defense Monitor,* July 7, 1995, pp. 7-10. See section I-F in *Nuclear Successor States of the Soviet Union,* No. 5, op. cit. for more on the ISTC.

[d]For more information on the terms and status of the reactor core conversion agreement, see the section on Cessation of Production of Plutonium at the Zheleznogorsk and Seversk Reactors in Table I-D, *Nuclear Successor States of the Soviet Union*, No. 5, op. cit.

[e]According to an article in *Nucleonics Week*, there may be an inventory of separated plutonium at the Lytkarino facility. Mark Hibbs, "Gosatomnadzor Warned U.S. of Insider Threat at Lytkarino Lab," *Nucleonics Week*, August 14, 1997, p. 5.

[f]Construction on the reactor is expected to be complete by the end of 1998. It will be fueled with about 30 kg of 90 percent HEU. U.S. General Accounting Office, *Nuclear Safety: Concerns With Nuclear Facilities and Other Sources of Radiation in the Former Soviet Union (Letter Report)*, GAO/RCED, November 7, 1995, Appendix II, pp. 23-25.

[g]Countries that have imported Russian LEU from Novouralsk include England, Belgium, Germany, Spain, France, Finland, and South Korea. "Uralskiy Elektrokhimicheskiy Krupniy Plan," *Atompressa*, Number 16, April 1997, pp. 2-3.

[h]According to Viktor Mikhailov, head of Minatom, in *Megaoplis-Ekspress*, July 22, 1992, p. 12.

[i]See note 4.

[j]Investigations by the Tomsk Polytechnic faculty and Gosatomnadzor were inconclusive. The missing HEU in the form of a fresh fuel assembly, may have been accidentally shipped to Tomsk-7, but it was deemed impossible to find there. See *Nuclear Successor States of the Soviet Union,* No. 5, op. cit., Table I-E note 256 for more detail.

[k]"Russia: Nuclear Weapons Facilities," NIS Nonproliferation Project, Center for Nonproliferation Studies, Monterey Institute of International Studies, August 1997.

China

China, a nuclear-weapon state since 1964, opened itself to wider international exchange and trade in the late 1970s and began to export arms and military technology on a significant scale. It also became a supplier of sensitive nuclear technology. China's exports posed major problems for the non-proliferation regime both because of their indiscriminate nature and because of China's failure to apply the safeguards and controls exercised by states compliant with the Nuclear Non-Proliferation Treaty (NPT). As a result, the United States and other countries began sustained efforts—through bilateral diplomatic and multilateral channels—to draw China into the international non-proliferation regime step by step. Over the more than two decades since China's "opening," these efforts have achieved incremental but important progress, although they remain incomplete. The non-proliferation stakes were important factors in U.S. revival of its "engagement" posture with China after the chilly interlude that followed the Chinese crackdown on democracy in the Tiananmen Square crisis of 1989.

A major focus of U.S. nuclear non-proliferation engagement with China after it joined the International Atomic Energy Agency (IAEA) in 1984 was the U.S.–China agreement on peaceful nuclear cooperation, signed in 1985 but held in abeyance through 1997 by congressional conditions that impose a certification requirement.[1] Efforts by a series of U.S. administrations to meet the congressional conditions have encouraged China, in steps, to apply controls on its nuclear exports that are closer to the standards of the major nuclear supplier countries. A critical peak in these efforts was triggered in 1996 by the disclosure of Chinese sales of ring magnets to Pakistan for use in Pakistan's nuclear weapons program to enrich uranium to weapons-grade levels.

In September 1997, China finally announced new steps to clarify and tighten up its nuclear export controls.[2] Just before and during the October 1997 summit in Washington, China provided further nuclear non-proliferation assurances, described later in this chapter. China thus satisfied the administration's certification requirements and Congress reviewed certification in February 1998 without overturning it. The U.S.–China agreement for cooperation took effect on March 18, 1998, paving the way for U.S. commercial sales to the civilian nuclear power program in China. Despite this progress, the effectiveness of China's new export control commitments and practices must be watched and measured in particular situations over the next few years. Efforts to win Chinese compliance with the guidelines of the Missile Technology Control Regime (MTCR) also have moved forward incrementally, but China's response is still incomplete. There is also some danger that the repercussions of India's and Pakistan's nuclear tests of May 1998 will retard China's non-proliferation progress.

BACKGROUND

Following its first nuclear test in 1964, China slowly developed a full-fledged nuclear weapons infrastructure and a strategic and tactical nuclear arsenal.[3] By NPT definition, China is one of the five *de jure* nuclear-weapon states because it declared and tested a nuclear weapon before 1967. Long disconnected from normal international relations after the communist revolution in 1947, China was also isolated from the evolving international framework of peaceful uses of nuclear energy as well as from the collaboration that produced the IAEA in the 1950s, the NPT in the late 1960s, and the development of nuclear export control guidelines in the 1970s. As a communist power during the Cold War, China was also excluded from the establishment of the MTCR, which originated in 1987 as a Western arrangement to restrain exports of nuclear-capable missiles and related technology.

During the years of isolation from the West, China's posture rhetorically *favored* nuclear weapons proliferation, particularly in the Third World, as a rallying point for anti-imperialism.[4] Through the 1970s, China's policy was *not to oppose* nuclear proliferation, which it still saw as limiting U.S. and Soviet power.[5] After China began to open to the West in the 1970s, its rhetorical position gradually shifted to one opposing nuclear proliferation, explicitly so after 1983.[6]

China's nuclear and arms trade practices did not, however, conform to international non-proliferation regime standards, and major efforts over two decades were required to persuade China to bring its nuclear trade practices into closer alignment with the policies of the other nuclear supplier states. There is still a gap that needs to be closed. To understand how far China has come on the non-proliferation path, two points should be made clear: China joined the IAEA in 1984, but it did not join the NPT until 1992. During this period, the non-proliferation regime, under U.S. urging, was itself raising the bar with stiffer export control requirements, making the standards applied to China today higher than those most Western states themselves lived by during the Cold War. That said, the higher standards are now indispensable for regime effectiveness, and the efforts to win full Chinese compliance must continue.

China's Challenges to the Non-Proliferation Regime. China has posed formidable challenges to the international non-proliferation regime. As a May 1996 Pentagon report points out, China has been a contributor to proliferation "primarily because of the role of Chinese companies in supplying a wide range of materials, equipment and technologies that could contribute to NBC [nuclear, biological, and chemical] weapons and missile programs in countries of proliferation concern."[7] China disregarded international norms during the 1980s by selling nuclear materials to countries such as South Africa, India, Pakistan, and Argentina, without requiring that the items be placed under IAEA safeguards.[8] Although China joined the NPT in 1992, and pledged to the United States in the same year and again in 1994 that it would abide by the MTCR, it was slow to adopt and publish nuclear export control laws.

China has posed a further challenge through the lack of transparency in its domestic nuclear safeguards and security measures; presumably these exist in some form to protect its nuclear arsenal and stockpile of fissile material from unauthorized use or theft. These internal measures might be too weak, however, to withstand the political instability and social upheaval of a major crisis in the country. After the 1989 Tiananmen crackdown on the student-led democracy movement, for example, observers feared that the post–Deng Xiaoping succession struggle could give rise to internal political disorder or even to state disintegration.[9]

Sensitive Nuclear Exports. China's nuclear exports to two particular countries, Pakistan and Iran, have been the leading causes of concern. Even though Pakistan is not a party to the NPT, has had a nuclear weapons program since 1972, and is believed to have had a small arsenal ready to assemble for a number of years, China has been its principal supplier of nuclear equipment and services since the late 1970s. Similarly, although Iran is a member of the NPT and is believed to have started a nuclear weapons program in the mid-1980s, China has been one of its principal suppliers of nuclear equipment and services.[10]

China's assistance to Pakistan's nuclear program over the last 15 years may have been crucial to Pakistan's nuclear weapons breakthroughs in the 1980s. It is widely believed that in the early 1980s China supplied Pakistan with design information for one of its own earlier atomic weapons, and there has also been speculation that China may have provided Pakistan with enough highly enriched uranium (HEU) for two such weapons.[11] According to an August 1997 report by the U.S. Arms Control and Disarmament Agency, "Prior to China's [1992] accession [to the NPT], the United States concluded that China had assisted Pakistan in developing nuclear explosives. . . . Questions remain about contacts between Chinese entities and elements associated with Pakistan's nuclear weapons program."[12]

China was also believed to have assisted Pakistan with building an unsafeguarded 50-70-MWt plutonium production reactor at Khushab[13] and to have helped Pakistan develop an unsafeguarded plutonium reprocessing facility at Chasma that was left unfinished when earlier French assistance was terminated in the late 1970s.[14] If these facilities were to come on line without safeguards, they would for the first time give Pakistan a source of plutonium for use in nuclear weapons.

China has also assisted Pakistan's civilian nuclear program—circumventing the nuclear trade embargo on Pakistan observed by members of the Nuclear Suppliers Group (NSG)—by helping build a 300-MWe power reactor at Chasma.[15] This reactor will be placed under IAEA safeguards as a condition of supply under the existing China-Pakistan agreement for peaceful nuclear cooperation. However, since Pakistan has not accepted full-scope safeguards, co-located facilities such as the partially completed Chasma reprocessing plant may remain inaccessible to IAEA inspection.

According to the Pentagon, China also has been a "principal supplier of nuclear technology to Iran."[16] It provided Iran three zero-power research reactors and one very small 30-KWt one, as well as two or three calutrons (electromagnetic isotope separation, or EMIS, machines). While calutrons in those numbers would not produce fissile uranium in significant quantity, they would serve to train personnel in a sensitive nuclear activity.[17] China and Iran signed a ten-year nuclear cooperation agreement in 1990, and Iran in 1992 agreed to purchase two 300-MWe pressurized water reactors (PWRs) from China.[18] In May 1995, Reza Amrollahi, head of Iran's Atomic Energy Organization, said that Iran had already made a down payment on the $600-$800 million power reactor contract.[19]

The United States has led an international effort to prevent the supply of nuclear technology to Iran and has placed pressure on China (and other suppliers) to cancel nuclear deals with Iran. With respect to China, by 1997 this U.S. pressure apparently had made a difference.

China has also pursued a continuing nuclear export relationship with Algeria. The first stage of this cooperation, under an agreement that dates back to 1983, involved the secret construction of the Es Salem 15-MWt research reactor at Ain Oussera.[20] Shortly after the reactor was discovered and publicized in April 1991,[21] Algeria agreed to place it under IAEA safeguards, and a safeguards agreement for this purpose was signed in February 1992. Thus the reactor has been subject to IAEA inspections since its inauguration in December 1993.[22] Although Algeria later acceded to the NPT, its interest in plutonium reprocessing and the possibility that China may have helped Algeria with this activity have kept Algeria on the watch-list.

Missile Export Activities. In the missile export field, China reportedly has aided the missile programs of Libya, Saudi Arabia, Syria, Iraq, Iran, Pakistan, and possibly North Korea. In Pakistan's case, China evidently transferred key components in the early 1990s for short-range, nuclear-capable M-11 surface-to-surface missiles. In June 1991, the United States imposed Missile Technology Control Regime (MTCR) Category II sanctions[23] against entities in Pakistan and China for missile technology transfers. These sanctions were lifted in March 1992 after the United States received written confirmation from China that it would abide by the MTCR "guidelines and parameters." Washington took this oral confirmation to mean China would not export either the M-9 or the M-11 missile.

Despite reports that China had transferred complete M-11s to Pakistan in late 1992 (which could trigger tougher Category I sanctions), the Clinton Administration again imposed the lighter Category II sanctions on Pakistan and China in August 1993 for the transfer of missile-related technology.[24] These sanctions were lifted in October 1994 after China promised not to export any "ground-to-ground" missiles "inherently capable" of delivering a 500-kg payload to at least 300 km—encompassing the M-11—and to abide by the "guidelines and parameters" of the MTCR. After these sanctions were lifted, however, reports persisted of Chinese aid to Pakistan's and Iran's missile programs.

Drawing China into the Non-Proliferation Regime. Drawing China into the nuclear and missile non-proliferation regimes has been a long-term process—part of a larger agenda of normalizing relations with a major regional power that had an independent civilization lasting thousands of years, experienced a communist revolution, made war against U.N. forces in Korea, and thereafter remained isolated for decades from normal international relations with the West. Taking the lead diplomatically with China in the 1970s, the United States has pressed for common understandings with China of stability and regional security. Drawing China into the sphere of multilateral problem-solving in the United Nations and into nuclear arms control fora has been an important part of a larger engagement process. To understand how U.S. sanctions laws and policies, as well as positive inducements, have helped draw China into the non-proliferation regime, it is important to see them in this larger context.

The engagement approach became feasible when China dropped its formerly close alignment with the Soviet Union and began looking for security alternatives. During the Cold War, the approach toward China was still heavily conditioned by other Western instruments of control, such as the Coordinating Committee on Multilateral Export Controls (COCOM), designed to keep state of the art military technologies out of the hands of communist adversaries.[25] This approach has been greatly relaxed since the end of the Cold War. The West's overhaul of technology transfer controls has been complicated by globalization and free trade principles. Related U.S. non-proliferation efforts have had to cope with not only the official behavior of the Chinese government but also the hidden activities of autonomous Chinese manufacturing and trading entities that have been encouraged to sell goods and services for profit in order to sustain themselves.

A "given" in this approach was that China was already a nuclear-weapon state. Hence, the objectives of drawing China into the non-proliferation regime were not to de-nuclearize China, but rather to elicit China's natural security interest and cooperation in preventing the spread of nuclear weapons to additional countries, including neighbors. The same logic applied later to winning China over to helping prevent the spread of missiles and chemical and biological weapons capabilities.

Having been a major adversary in Korea and Vietnam, as well as in the Cold War, China was not involved in one of the most important post–World War II and post–Cold War non-proliferation mechanisms: the central security alliances that were pivotal to winning deep non-proliferation commitments from such U.S. allies as Germany, Japan, and South Korea. Rather, the inducements offered China have consisted largely of recognition of its status as a major power by the world community and the access to international trade, capital, and technology that has supported rapid Chinese economic growth and modernization since 1983. Sanctions and penalties, as well as inducements, have played a significant role in shaping China's increasingly constructive role in international affairs.

The political ability of the United States and its non-proliferation partners to define and administer legal sanctions depends in part on target countries' legal undertakings and commitments. Sanctions devised for NPT or IAEA parties and those for non-parties may, for example, require different legal starting points. In the case of China, important legal standards had to be established—first, by China's joining the IAEA in 1984 (opening it to direct knowledge and familiarity with the international practice of nuclear facility and materials safeguards and inspections), and second, by China's joining the NPT in 1992.

The *fundamental* nuclear non-proliferation standards for China are those incurred by its adherence to the NPT after March 1992. As a nuclear-weapon state, China was then obligated for the first time, under NPT Article I, "not to transfer to any recipient whatsoever nuclear weapons or other nuclear explosive devices or control over such weapons or explosive devices directly, or indirectly; and *not in any way to assist, encourage, or induce* any non-nuclear weapon State to manufacture or otherwise acquire nuclear weapons or other nuclear explosive devices, or control over such weapons or explosive devices" (emphasis added). Under NPT Article III (2), China is obligated, along with all other parties, "not to provide: (a) source or special fissionable material, or (b) equipment or material especially designed or prepared for the processing, use or production of special fissionable material, to any non-nuclear weapon State for peaceful purposes, unless the source or special fissionable material shall be subject to the [IAEA] safeguards required by this article."

Bringing China to a common international understanding of the meaning of these provisions has also required that China be persuaded to embrace international nuclear export control guidelines and understandings, including those that cover dual-use materials and equipment. China only became part of the Zangger Committee at the end of 1997, but this implies that China now undertakes to understand the lists of controlled items, to consult on their meaning in particular cases, and to apply the same interpretation of IAEA safeguards requirements in regulating its own exports. This does not guarantee that differences of interpretation will not occur, but it guarantees that the other members can challenge Chinese practices that do not conform to a common understanding.

Under U.S. law, certain commercial sales and technology transfers to China are subject to conditions that China meet non-proliferation standards in its own policies and behavior. These conditions are often embodied in framework agreements and then applied in export licensing decisions. The most important areas of embargoed technology that the United States took steps to make available to China in the 1980s were: civilian nuclear equipment, technology and services, conventional weapons systems and military technology, military aviation technology, advanced computers, telecommunications technology, and the approvals needed for China to supply commercial space-launch services to American entities interested in launching satellites. These areas were opened to China in hope of China's commitment to satisfy certain conditions, usually based on U.S. national security and non-proliferation interests. Satisfying executive branch and congressional conditions for a nuclear trade agreement with China took nearly 15 years.

Certain U.S. statutes and legislative actions focus on nuclear non-proliferation criteria and related sanctions that are specifically applicable to China. One is the 1985 Congressional Resolution of Approval of the U.S.-China Agreement for Nuclear Cooperation, with its three broad conditions and requirement for presidential certification. Even though this agreement recently was certified, specific nuclear trade items will require licensing, case by case, and could be denied if China is not in compliance with its NPT obligations or with U.S. statutory requirements for non-proliferation practices.[26] Another is the Foreign Relations Authorization Act of 1990-91, which gathered the post-Tiananmen crisis sanctions governing U.S. foreign policy toward China into one statute, covering conventional arms, civil nuclear trade, cooperation related to outer space, and dual-use technology.[27]

In the domain of missile non-proliferation, the 1987 and 1993 MTCR guidelines are basic reference points for U.S. sanctions laws aimed at preventing transfers of nuclear-capable ballistic and cruise missiles, components, and production technology. The basic sanctions laws applicable to China's missile export behavior have been incorporated in the Arms Export Control Act and the Export Administration Act, as periodically updated and amended.[28]

DEVELOPMENTS

Apprehension that China might suffer major upheaval or disintegration pressures after the 1989 Tiananmen crisis—endangering controls against theft of weapons or diversion of fissile materials from facilities—persisted during the long period of Deng Xiaoping's physical decline in the mid-1990s. Uncertainty whether the leadership succession would be smooth or lead to an overt, divisive struggle for power remained until recently. Deng finally died on February 19, 1997, however, and his mantle passed in an orderly manner to Jiang Zemin, who remains president and Communist Party general secretary, as well as chairman of the Central Military Commission. Li Peng kept his position as prime minister and head of the government apparatus in 1997, but moved over to become head of the national legislature when his term as prime minister expired in March 1998. Zhu Rongji, who was elevated to the number three position in the Communist Party's inner circle, has succeeded Li Peng as premier.[29]

Continuity and political stability thus appear to have prevailed in China after Deng Xiaoping. The incumbent leaders face economic challenges as the remaining obstacles to reform are addressed, but they probably will succeed in maintaining a relatively high rate of economic growth. While the danger of structural disintegration over a struggle for power at the top in China thus appears to be receding, concern about the opaqueness and uncertain effectiveness of China's internal nuclear controls against penetration and diversion into illicit channels nevertheless remains high.[30]

Nuclear Exports to Pakistan. China's assistance to Pakistan's nuclear weapons program was brought into the spotlight again in 1996 by disclosure of China's controversial nuclear transfer of ring magnets for use in Pakistan's unsafeguarded uranium-enrichment program. China's export of ring magnets seemed to contradict its claims that it did not help other countries develop nuclear weapons and that it was tightening its nuclear export controls.

According to press reports, the Clinton Administration determined in August 1995 that China had sold 5,000 ring magnets valued at $70,000 to the Kahuta Research Laboratory between December 1994 and mid-1995.[31] This unsafeguarded gas-centrifuge facility had produced weapons-grade, highly enriched uranium until July 1991, when Pakistan agreed to an American demand to freeze its production of HEU.[32] The custom-built magnets, made of an advanced samarium-cobalt alloy, would enable Pakistan to upgrade and replace its enrichment centrifuges at the rate of 1,000 to 2,000 machines a year.[33] Although ring magnets are not on the nuclear trigger list, they are an integral part of magnetic suspension bearings, which are controlled, as dual-use items, by the Zangger Committee. While Pakistan denied that any such transfer occurred, China maintained that its nuclear cooperation with Pakistan was solely for peaceful purposes.[34]

China's sale of ring magnets to the unsafeguarded Kahuta facility set off a major controversy in Washington. Some believed the transfer should have triggered the 1994 Nuclear Proliferation Prevention Act sanctions, which require a cutoff of all U.S. Export-Import

Bank financing to any country which "has willfully aided and abetted any non-nuclear-weapon state" in acquiring unsafeguarded enriched uranium or plutonium.[35] The Export-Import Bank extends about $1 billion in credits each year to American companies doing business in China and a cutoff was widely estimated to endanger about $10 billion in proposed credits.[36] On February 28, 1996, the United States suspended the approval of new Export-Import Bank loan applications related to China.[37]

U.S.–Chinese discussions on the issue culminated on April 19 in a meeting between Secretary of State Warren Christopher and Chinese Foreign Minister Qian Qichen at The Hague, where the groundwork was laid for its resolution. The U.S. decision resulting from these discussions, announced on May 10, was not to impose sanctions against China, given three factors: (1) the finding that senior-level Chinese officials were unaware of the ring magnet transfer; (2) China's new public commitment not to "provide assistance to unsafeguarded nuclear facilities;" and (3) China's pledge to engage in a dialogue with the United States on improving export controls.[38] Later reports indicated that the Chinese government punished the official responsible for the ring magnet transfer.[39] Secretary Christopher explained that "Senior Chinese officials have explicitly confirmed our understanding that the Chinese policy of not assisting unsafeguarded nuclear facilities would prevent future sales . . . of ring magnets."[40]

Nuclear Exports to Iran. Iran has been the other major recipient of Chinese exports of nuclear and missile technology and expertise. By 1995, however, there were signs that China's nuclear cooperation with Iran was being scaled back. A factor in China's retrenchment of nuclear assistance to Iran may have been Russian competition as an alternative supplier.[41] Russia agreed to supply light-water nuclear reactors to Iran and to help Iran finish construction of the Bushehr nuclear power plant abandoned by German contractors during the Iran-Iraq war. U.S. opposition to China's contract to sell two 300-MWe pressurized water reactors to Iran probably also played a part.[42] Iranian shortages of capital may have been a third factor. At any rate in September 1995, China finally agreed to "suspend for the time being" its reactor sale to Iran.[43] A few months later, a Chinese Foreign Ministry spokesman acknowledged that "the implementation of the agreements between China and Iran on nuclear cooperation has ceased."[44]

China continued until 1997 to assist Iran in constructing a plant near Esfahan to produce uranium hexafluoride, the material fed into gas centrifuges for enrichment, and reports indicate that Chinese technicians are assisting Iran with other parts of the nuclear fuel cycle, such as uranium mining and processing and fuel fabrication.[45] These activities, however, appear to have been carried out in accordance with the NPT and under IAEA safeguards.

Nuclear Exports to Other Countries. Recently China signed agreements with Algeria covering the second and third stages of nuclear cooperation between the two countries.[46] China is apparently helping to construct the Algerian Center of Nuclear Energy Research, which will be placed under IAEA safeguards.[47] China's long-standing nuclear cooperation with Algeria remains sensitive today in light of Algeria's interest in reprocessing facilities. While Algeria formally acceded to the NPT in January 1995 and signed a safeguards agreement with the IAEA in May 1996, its reported "lack of candour" on the purposes of the hot-cell facility it has built—which is connected by a covered canal to the research reactor at Ain Oussera—created uncertainty.[48]

Algeria declared the hot-cell facility to the IAEA in 1992. If it were used in conjunction with a boosted output of the Es Salem reactor, which could produce up to 5 kg of plutonium a year, the hot-cell facility could separate weapons-grade plutonium. By the summer of 1997, IAEA inquiries appeared to satisfy U.S. officials that Algeria will operate the hot-cell facility under safeguards and allow IAEA environmental sampling, and that it will not build up an inventory of separated plutonium from spent fuel.[49] Of additional interest is a larger facility nearby that Algeria has not declared to the IAEA as a nuclear facility but that some Western officials believe may be intended as a large-scale reprocessing facility.[50]

Missile Exports to Pakistan. In the early 1990s, the United States twice imposed and lifted Category-II sanctions on Chinese and Pakistani organizations related to transfers of M-11 components or missiles—in return for Chinese assurances that such exports would not continue and that China would abide by the MTCR guidelines. After sanctions were lifted for the second time in October 1994, however, reports of continued Chinese assistance to Pakistan's missile program recurred.[51] This situation evidently was reflected in the Pentagon's April 1996 report, which stated, "China remains Pakistan's most important supplier of missile-related technologies."[52]

Accumulating evidence of Chinese transfer of complete M-11 missiles to Pakistan was revealed in press reports in the fall of 1996. One quoted a recent U.S. National Intelligence Estimate (a consensus document of U.S. intelligence agencies) indicating that Pakistan already had roughly three dozen M-11s stored in canisters at the Sargodha Air Force Base west of Lahore, along with maintenance facilities and missile launchers.[53] Although these missiles were not "operational," it was said they could be unpacked, mated with launchers, and made ready for launch in 48 hours. An even more disturbing conclusion of this report was that Pakistan, using blueprints and equipment supplied by China, began construction of a factory in late 1995 capable of producing short-range, solid-fuel missiles based on the Chinese-designed M-11. This factory, located near Rawalpindi, was then expected to be operational in one or two years.[54]

Chinese supply of complete missile systems or production technology covered by the MTCR would be a major violation of the guidelines and, according to U.S. law, should trigger Category I sanctions, which could block all trade between the United States and Chinese aerospace and electronics firms. China and Pakistan both have denied the existence of the missile plant.[55] In April 1997, State Department official Robert Einhorn reiterated the Clinton Administration's concerns about Chinese transfers of missile-related components, technology, and production technology to Pakistan.[56] However, he said that the United States could not make the determination that complete, operational missiles had been transferred; such a determination would require a "high evidentiary standard," since the consequences of sanctions on U.S. firms would be highly damaging.

Missile Exports to Iran. China has been a supplier to Iran of anti-ship cruise missiles (Silkworms, C-801s, and C-802s), since the Iran-Iraq war in the 1980s. More recently, China has also played a role in Iran's efforts to set up an indigenous ballistic missile development and production program. In June 1995, the CIA apparently concluded that China had delivered guidance systems, rocket fuel ingredients, and computerized machine tools to Iran to assist that country in improving imported ballistic missiles and producing its own missiles.[57] In August 1996, the China Precision Engineering Institute reportedly agreed to sell missile guidance equipment to Iran.[58] China has transferred short-range CSS-8 ballistic missiles to Iran.[59] In addition, China has sold ten fast-attack craft armed with C-802 anti-ship cruise missiles to Iran, and Iran is modifying additional fast-attack craft to launch the missile.[60]

Missile Exports to Other Countries. Syria also has received Chinese assistance for its ballistic missile program. A 1988 deal to sell Syria the M-9 missile was apparently canceled under U.S. pressure, but China has supplied Syria with technical expertise for its missile program and ingredients for solid rocket fuel.[61] Chinese assistance to Syria's missile program reportedly continued into 1996.[62] China has also sold Silkworm anti-ship cruise missiles to Iraq.

In 1988, China supplied Saudi Arabia with some 30 or more DF-3 (CSS-2) medium-range ballistic missiles (MRBMs). Although China had deployed these missiles earlier in its own arsenal with nuclear warheads, Chinese and Saudi officials insist that the missiles transferred to Saudi Arabia are equipped only with conventional warheads. Several hundred Chinese technicians maintain the missiles at their bases at Al-Sulayyil and Al-Leel. These missiles are nearing the end of their operational life and Saudi Arabia has begun looking for replacements.[63] U.S. missile sanctions laws could be triggered if China or Saudi Arabia "conspires or attempts to engage in" transfers of CSS-2 replacements.

China's Fissile Material Stockpile. A frequently overlooked proliferation threat posed by China is the large stockpile of weapons-usable fissile material it has produced over the past 30 years. Although the situation in China currently seems more stable than in Russia, increased political and economic instability could raise the risk of diversion of fissile material from China's nuclear complex. The possibilities run the spectrum from a breakup of China into multiple states, the breakdown of central authority and the rise of regional warlords, or a steady deterioration of central authority that would increase the opportunity for theft and smuggling of nuclear material or weapons.[64]

China produced weapons-usable enriched uranium from 1964 until 1987 at two sites, Lanzhou and Heping.[65] Plutonium was also produced at two sites, Jiuquan and Guangyuan, from 1968 until 1991.[66] There are several unofficial estimates on how much weapons-usable fissile material China has produced, but Beijing has not disclosed the size of either its nuclear weapon or fissile material stockpiles. Experts believe that China has tested about 45 nuclear explosive devices and built about 300 strategic warheads and 150 tactical warheads.[67] Together with materials used in the fuel for civil and military reactors, a considerable portion of the fissile materials produced must have been consumed or must be otherwise unavailable for weapons. According to the most recent estimates, it is believed that by the end of 1994, China's residual fissile material stockpiles may consist of as much as 4 metric tons of Pu and 23 metric tons of HEU—enough fissile material for approximately 2,700 nuclear weapons.[68]

China presumably has stored the residual fissile material stocks at various nuclear facilities. However, the locations and amounts of China's non-weaponized fissile material have not been declared and are not specifically known, nor is the degree of security at the storage sites known. The China National Nuclear Corporation (which has the status of a government ministry) "produces, stores, and controls all fissile material for civilian as well as military applications."[69] It is estimated that about 14 sites associated with the nuclear weapons program in China have significant quantities of weapons-usable fissile material. The primary locations of non-weaponized fissile material are believed to be China's plutonium-production and uranium-enrichment facilities as well as nuclear-weapons research institutes and other nuclear fuel-cycle facilities across the country.

China has conducted research and development on gas centrifuge technology for uranium enrichment as the likely technology choice to replace the gaseous-diffusion plants. Russia recently agreed to supply China with a gas-centrifuge plant to produce low-enriched uranium. The facility was expected to be in operation by 1997 and could be expanded.[70]

Information on China's material protection, control, and accounting (MPC&A) system is scarce, but the United States has been concerned enough to initiate discussions on MPC&A, among other issues, between the U.S. and Chinese national nuclear laboratories. There have been contacts between the nuclear weapons laboratories in the United States and China since 1994,[71] and five joint workshops were scheduled for 1996 with the Chinese Academy of Engineering Physics (CAEP), China's main nuclear weapons research center.[72] Although China's MPC&A system is modeled after the Soviet system, an expert at one of the U.S. national laboratories ranked China's MPC&A system as better than that of the Soviet Union before it collapsed.[73] In 1996, China commissioned a computerized "national nuclear materials accounting system" at about twelve nuclear facilities to improve its ability to prevent the illegal loss, theft or transfer of nuclear materials.[74]

China's Nuclear Weapons. China's nuclear arsenal of approximately 450 weapons would make it the third largest nuclear military power today.[75] China has only seven intercontinental ballistic missiles (ICBMs) capable of striking the continental United States (the DF-5s). It has a single nuclear submarine (SSBN), the Xia, based on the Shandong Peninsula.[76] China is currently modernizing its strategic missile force with three new solid-fuel ballistic missiles, including a submarine-launched missile.[77] A new generation of nuclear-powered submarines (Type 094) reportedly are scheduled for construction after the year 2000 and would carry 16 JL-2 missiles.[78] Some reports indicate that China's new DF-31 ICBMs, first tested in 1995, will be deployed with multiple warheads, but there has been no official confirmation that China has developed MIRV capability.[79] China's attempts to acquire advanced SS-18 missile-guidance technology from Russia and Ukraine may have been linked to the pursuit of MIRV capability.[80]

China has expressed concern that current U.S. missile defense programs could neutralize China's ICBMs, its principal strategic deterrent against the United States.[81] The combination of a national missile defense covering the United States and the sale of advanced theater missile defense systems to America's Asian allies would greatly complicate China's nuclear planning. China has reportedly tested intermediate-range ballistic missiles with penetration aids to foil missile defenses, and similar measures are expected to be added to China's new generation of long-range ballistic missiles.[82] Although the United States with Russia, and Russia with China, have agreed to strategic missile de-targeting measures between their respective sides, China has not agreed to de-targeting measures with the United States, and thus presumably still targets some of its long-range nuclear missiles at American cities.[83]

China would have been the last of the five nuclear powers to become familiar with and equip its nuclear weapons with modern permissive action links (PALs)—devices that prevent unauthorized arming of a weapon, or that may disable it if it is tampered with, and thus are important safeguards against unauthorized launch and accidental detonation.[84] It was not until after the 1989 Tiananmen Square incident, reportedly, that the leadership in Beijing began to think about how to ensure control over its nuclear arsenal during times of domestic crisis.[85] It is not known if Chinese tactical nuclear weapons are deployed in the field (along with their delivery systems) or kept in storage. China's means of providing physical security of warheads in transit or storage likewise is not known—nor is the extent to which PALs are actually used in different types of warhead, deployed or stored.

China's Non-Proliferation Commitments. With China an established nuclear-weapon state and permanent member of the U.N. Security Council, Beijing's nuclear policies, attitudes toward non-proliferation effectiveness of export controls, and quality of participation in global non-proliferation regimes naturally carry weight in the decision-making of other countries. Having been an outsider to most international arms control initiatives during the Cold War, China never signed the 1963 Partial Test Ban Treaty, only became a member of the IAEA in 1984, acceded to the NPT as recently as 1992, declined until 1997 to join the international Zangger Committee,[86] and still declines to join the Nuclear Suppliers Group. While it has agreed to observe the published MTCR guidelines of 1987, it still is not a full partner and may not be fully observant of the revised MTCR guidelines of 1993.[87] It also may have a unilateral interpretation of certain MTCR guidelines. It is clear that China shuns "informal" multilateral control arrangements such as the NSG, MTCR and, in the chemical weapons area, the Australia Group.

Nevertheless, China made notable strides to join formal arms control regimes in the 1990s—beginning with its accession to the NPT in 1992, its signature in 1993 and ratification in 1997 of the Chemical Weapons Convention (CWC),[88] and its cessation of nuclear weapon explosive testing and signature of the Comprehensive Test Ban Treaty (CTBT) in September, 1996.[89] China has supported the multilateral negotiations on a fissile-material production cutoff convention. China also acceded to the Biological Weapons Convention (BWC) in 1984.[90] Moreover, China has gradually clarified and upgraded the commitments it makes through export controls to nuclear and missile non-proliferation objectives.[91] These nuclear export control clarifications and practical improvements are worthy of note, as are the areas of continued divergence.

After joining the NPT in 1992, China enunciated three policy principles to guide its approach to nuclear exports:

> (1) All nuclear exports are for peaceful purposes only;
> (2) All recipients must accept IAEA safeguards on their nuclear imports from China; and
> (3) Recipients may not retransfer nuclear items imported from China without China's consent.[92]

In July 1993, China committed itself to report its trade in nuclear materials and its exports of nuclear equipment and related materials to the IAEA.[93] In the aftermath of the 1996 disclosure of its ring magnet export to Pakistan, China agreed not to provide assistance to unsafeguarded nuclear facilities and pledged to engage in a dialogue with the United States on improving export controls.

Clinton–Jiang Zemin Summit of October 1997. In preparing for the U.S.–China summit of October 1997, U.S. negotiators sought clear Chinese action on four major points needed for President Clinton to certify that China meets the congressional conditions attached to the 1985 agreement for nuclear cooperation:

(1) China's issuance of regulations on nuclear and nuclear-related exports that are consistent with international standards;

(2) China's formal membership in the Zangger Committee;

(3) China's strict adherence to its May 1996 pledge to export only to nuclear facilities that are under IAEA inspection; and

(4) China's cessation of nuclear assistance to Iran. [94]

China met these U.S. requirements shortly before or during the summit. On September 11, China adopted and published upgraded nuclear export control procedures, including:

(1) A centralized approval procedure, in the State Council or cabinet, of all its foreign sales of nuclear materials and equipment;

(2) A requirement for more explicit recipient "end-use" assurances, namely recipient guarantees that nuclear equipment and materials imported from China will not be used for the purpose of creating a nuclear explosive device; and

(3) A prohibition on export of nuclear and nuclear-related equipment to, or personnel exchange and technology cooperation with, nuclear facilities in any non-nuclear-weapon state that is not under IAEA inspection. [95]

Then, on September 30, China announced that it would join the Zangger Committee as a full member but would not alter its current policy of not imposing full-scope safeguards on its nuclear exports. [96] China formally joined the Zangger Committee on October 16 and published its own "nuclear exports control list" of controlled technologies and equipment, including nuclear-related, dual-use equipment and technology. U.S. officials recognized that China's list does essentially conform to the Zangger list. [97] During the summit, China also pledged in a confidential agreement to forego future nuclear cooperation as well as phase out existing nuclear cooperation with Iran, even under IAEA safeguards. [98] Two non-sensitive exceptions in existing China-Iran nuclear cooperation are grandfathered: one relating to completion of a zero-power research reactor and the other to a factory that makes zirconium cladding for power-plant fuel rods. [99]

With these Chinese steps established, President Clinton announced that he planned to certify China on the points contained in the congressional conditions attached to the 1985 U.S.–China agreement for nuclear

cooperation, and to send the required reports forward to Congress. Congress has 30 session days to evaluate the reports, and could block certification by a two-thirds vote during that period. While there was criticism of the summit outcome by members of Congress, President Clinton's certification was not overridden and the cooperation agreement took effect on March 18, 1998. [100]

Certification of the nuclear trade agreement was not tied by the Clinton Administration to objectionable Chinese practices in the missile export area. China did not forego its right to sell to Iran or other countries those missiles that are not controlled by the MTCR. However, it was reported that China had pledged, presumably confidentially, that it would halt "further sales" of anti-ship cruise missiles (e.g., the short-range C802s) to Iran—and therefore also would not sell to Iran the even more dangerous longer-range anti-ship cruise missiles. [101]

PROSPECTS

Compared with its past nuclear export practices, by the October 1997 U.S.–China summit, China appeared to have made decisive strides toward conforming its nuclear export policies, laws, and regulations to international standards. The primary remaining formal shortcomings are that:

(1) China still has not agreed to accept full-scope safeguards as an export requirement and has not agreed to join the Nuclear Suppliers Group (which goes further than the Zangger Committee by upholding that requirement); [102]

(2) China has not publicly adopted a "catch-all" obligation to deny nuclear or nuclear-related exports or assistance to a country that might satisfy formal IAEA and NPT criteria yet have a dubious non-proliferation record for other reasons; and

(3) China has not yet demonstrated its commitment to vigilantly follow up and monitor the end-use assurances on its nuclear and nuclear-related exports within recipient states and facilities. [103]

Moreover, formal adherence to legal standards is one thing, while effective enforcement of the underlying purposes is another. Past experience suggests that it will take some time to determine whether China's practices in nuclear exports and nuclear cooperation will meet international standards for nuclear-related and dual-use equipment, materials, and technology that could be used for nuclear weapon purposes. [104] In addition, it is one thing for the government of China to promulgate new export control regulations and another to ensure that they are effectively enforced by obtaining the compliance of all nuclear-related domestic manufacturing and trading firms—many of which are connected with the military yet operate as profit centers or revenue-raising mechanisms—as well as the compliance of the more typical, public-sector scientific and technical organizations and laboratories.

China is still on a learning curve, and endemic problems of a political, cultural, and organizational nature exist in China's decision-making and export control apparatus.[105] There may be, as the old adage goes, "more than a slip between the cup and the lip." Thus, continued vigilance and diplomatic interchange with China will almost certainly continue to be necessary on nuclear matters—as it has also been necessary in the past among culturally closer and more readily cooperative Western partners—to ensure that international nuclear non-proliferation standards are understood and observed.

The missile and chemical and biological areas will also require diligent attention. Up to 1994, China made progress on MTCR requirements. But it is still not clear that its professed restraint applies, as the MTCR requires, to missile components and technology—nor, indeed, that the restraint applies to more than complete "ground-to-ground" missiles. Compliance in this area, which is not defined by a treaty, is harder to nail down with standards that China can accept politically—and also entails more scope for ambiguities. The chemical area is defined by treaty, provides for declarations, and lists restricted items, but it covers a very large industrial domain. Considerable effort will be required to work out reliable non-proliferation standards in these areas. But progress with China in the nuclear areas should add confidence to such efforts in other areas.

In the lead-up to the U.S.–China summit of October 1997, the corporate sector made much of the potential—on the order of $50 billion—for large civilian nuclear sales by Western firms to China. Now that the agreement for cooperation is in force, such trade by U.S. firms presumably will go ahead. But proponents as well as critics of these transactions should keep in mind that they will require case-by-case approval and may run into difficulties if China's non-proliferation practices continue to raise difficult questions. This is an area where sanctions can be a natural part of the exchange process. It should also be recognized that the potential nuclear market in China may not be as lucrative as some imagine—not only because it will be divided, such as it is, among firms based in several supplier countries and spread over many years but also because China will almost certainly attempt to use this trade to build up its own civilian nuclear engineering self-sufficiency for domestic as well as export purposes. At the same time, if significant nuclear trade with China does materialize, the resulting cooperation could also contribute to greater Chinese understanding of its stakes in non-proliferation as well as in a culture of nuclear safety.

NOTES

[1]The Congressional joint resolution passed in 1985 makes implementation of the U.S.–PRC nuclear cooperation agreement contingent on presidential certification that the United States can: (1) verify the end use of all U.S. nuclear exports to China; (2) certify that China is not assisting other states to acquire nuclear weapons; and (3) satisfy itself that U.S. consent rights on reprocessing of U.S.–origin nuclear fuel in China, including such fuel retransferred elsewhere, will be met.

[2]China's new regulations announced on September 11, 1997, reportedly would: (1) require all of its sales of nuclear materials and equipment abroad to have the approval of the State Council (or cabinet); (2) require countries that import nuclear equipment and materials from China to guarantee that these will not be used with the aim of creating a nuclear explosive device; and (3) prohibit Chinese exports of nuclear equipment, personnel, and technology to nuclear facilities in any non-nuclear-weapon state that are not under IAEA inspection. *Reuters*, September 11, 1997.

[3]For the best published overview of Chinese nuclear weapons, see Robert S. Norris, Andrew S. Burrows, and Richard W. Fieldhouse, *Nuclear Weapons Databook, Vol. V: British, French, and Chinese Weapons* (Washington, DC: Natural Resources Defense Council, 1994).

[4]Two Chinese statements from 1963 illustrate the flavor of China's earlier attitude toward the spread of nuclear weapons. The first stated: "Nuclear weapons in the possession of a socialist country are always a means of defense against nuclear blackmail and nuclear war." The second, which is broader, stated: "It is absolutely impermissible for two or three countries to brandish their nuclear weapons at will, issue orders and commands, and lord it over in the world as self-ordained nuclear overlords, while the overwhelming majority of countries are expected to kneel and obey orders meekly, as if they were nuclear slaves. The time of power politics has gone forever, and major questions of the world can no longer be decided by a few big powers." Cited in John Wilson Lewis and Xue Litai, *China Builds the Bomb* (Stanford, CA: Stanford University Press, 1988), p. 36.

[5]Leonard S. Spector, *The Undeclared Bomb* (Cambridge, MA: Ballinger Publishing Company, 1988), p. 72.

[6]Spector notes that "in mid-1983, China began a dramatic shift in its posture," enabling the Reagan Administration to resume the bilateral talks on peaceful nuclear cooperation that had begun in mid-1981. Following China's joining the IAEA in January 1984 and assurance to the United States that in future it would require IAEA safeguards on its nuclear exports to non-nuclear-weapon states, and after a series of statements by top Chinese leaders declaring China's firm commitment to non-proliferation, the U.S.–Chinese talks on bilateral nuclear cooperation finally produced a nuclear trade agreement, initialed in Beijing during Reagan's April 1984 visit. Ibid., pp. 72-73. One such statement was that made by Premier Zhao Ziyang at a White House state dinner on January 10, 1984: "We are critical of the discriminatory treaty on the non-proliferation of nuclear weapons, but we do not advocate or encourage nuclear proliferation. We do not engage in nuclear proliferation ourselves, nor do we help other countries develop nuclear weapons." *Xinhua*, January 11, 1984.

[7]Office of the Secretary of Defense, *Proliferation: Threat and Response*, April 1996, p. 4.

[8]See Spector, *Undeclared Bomb*, op. cit., pp. 72-73, and related notes.

[9]For contrasting prognoses on the future of China, see Jack A. Goldstone, "The Coming Chinese Collapse," *Foreign Policy*, Summer 1995, pp. 35-52, and Yasheng Huang, "Why China Will Not Collapse," *Foreign Policy*, Summer 1995, pp. 54-68.

[10]For a recent evaluation of Iran's nuclear program efforts, see discussion in David Albright, Frans Berkhout, and William Walker, *Plutonium and Highly Enriched Uranium 1996: World Inventories, Capabilities and Policies,* (New York: Oxford University Press for Stockholm International Peace Research Institute, 1997), p. 359.

[11]Leslie Gelb, "Pakistan Link Perils U.S.-China Nuclear Pact," *New York Times*, June 22, 1984; Leslie Gelb, "Peking Said to Balk at Nuclear Pledges," *New York Times*, June 23, 1984; Gary Milhollin and Gerard White, "A New China Syndrome: Beijing's Atomic Bazaar," *Washington Post*, May 12, 1991. See also the recent treatment of these points in the estimate of Pakistan's inventory of fissile material in Albright, Berkhout, and Walker, *1996 World Inventories*, op. cit., p. 276.

[12]Arms Control and Disarmament Agency, *Adherence to and Compliance with Arms Control Agreements*, 1997, p. 80.

[13]Bill Gertz, "China Aids Pakistani Plutonium Plant," *Washington Times*, April 3, 1996. Sources differ on the form and extent of Chinese assistance to Pakistan for the Khusab reactor. If China supplied certain types of equipment or know-how to Pakistan for this reactor after China acceded to the NPT in 1992, China may be obliged to insist that IAEA safeguards be applied to Khusab. See discussions of both Khusab and the Chasma reprocessing plant (next note) in Albright, Berkhout, and Walker, *1996 World Inventories*, op. cit., p. 283.

[14]The reprocessing plant at Chasma was begun with French assistance in the early 1970s. France canceled the contract for this plant in 1977. Pakistan has been attempting to complete construction of the plant as an indigenous facility. In late 1997, however, U.S. officials described the Chasma reprocessing plant as "an empty shell." See also Pakistan chapter in this volume.

[15]Most of the foundation for the Chasma reactor has been completed and China has manufactured the reactor pressure vessel. *Reuters*, June 8, 1996; "'Nuclear Reactor Pressure Vessel' for Pakistan," *Heilongjiang People's Radio Network*, July 2, 1996, in *FBIS-CHI-96-140*, July 22, 1996.

[16]Office of the Secretary of Defense, *Proliferation: Threat and Response*, 1996, op cit., p. 14.

[17]See Albright, Berkhout, and Walker, *1996 World Inventories*, op. cit., pp. 359-60.

[18]Mark Hibbs, "Russian Industry May Be Key to Iran's Reactor Prospects," *Nucleonics Week*, September 17, 1992, p. 3.

[19]Elaine Sciolino, "Iran Says It Plans 10 Nuclear Plants But No Atom Arms," *New York Times*, May 14, 1995.

[20]Albright, Berkhout, and Walker, *1996 World Inventories*, op. cit., pp. 363-64.

[21]Bill Gertz, "China Helps Algeria Develop Nuclear Weapons," *Washington Times*, April 11, 1991.

[22]Albright, Berkhout, and Walker, *1996 World Inventories*, op. cit.

[23]See Appendix G in this volume for an explanation of the differences between MTCR Category I and II sanctions.

[24]If the Clinton Administration had firm knowledge of transfer of complete missiles, the appropriate sanctions to apply would have been those in Category I. It may be that the Administration had firm knowledge only of transfer of "missile-related technology," justifying lighter Category II sanctions.

[25]COCOM was a mechanism formed by the Allies after World War II to identify militarily sensitive technologies, products and information as well as to coordinate restrictions on exports of such items to the communist world. After the end of the Cold War and the collapse of the Soviet Union, the old COCOM structure has been replaced with a revamped technology transfer control mechanism that progressively removes trade barriers with the formerly communist countries that have undergone democratic reform and are themselves willing to adhere to the cooperative procedures of export control.

[26]For conditions in the congressional joint resolution passed in 1985, see note 1 above. The U.S. sanctions laws that focus generally on nuclear non-proliferation and that are also applicable to China in certain respects, especially to Chinese nuclear export practices or to nuclear exports by entities resident in China, are compiled in the Nuclear Non-Proliferation Act (NNPA) of 1978 and the Nuclear Proliferation Prevention Act (NPPA) of 1994.

[27]The "Tiananmen Square sanctions" initially suspended: (1) Overseas Private Investment Corporation financing for U.S. business with China; (2) Trade and Development Agency expenditures to support U.S. business with China; (3) munitions (conventional arms and military technology) export licenses; (4) cooperation in crime control; (5) export of satellites for launch by China; and (6) export to China of nuclear materials, equipment and services, and dual-use items that might be used for fissile material production or nuclear explosive device development.

[28]Relevant amendments may be found in the Foreign Relations Authorization Act of 1990-91, the National Defense Authorization Act of 1991, the Helms Amendment of 1992 (covering the applicability of the MTCR under U.S. law to non-market countries) and the Iran-Iraq Arms Non-Proliferation Act of 1992 (which specifies sanctions against countries or entities that transfer goods or technology to Iraq or Iran that could contribute to their efforts to acquire weapons of mass destruction—including "destabilizing numbers and types of advanced conventional weapons"—a term that includes cruise missiles).

[29]Steve Mufson, "Chinese Shake Up Leadership—Rival to President Ousted from Politburo," *Washington Post*, September 19, 1997.

[30]China's domestic nuclear control systems, like those of the former Soviet Union, "were designed to keep 'the outside out' rather than 'the inside in' and they relied heavily upon totalitarian instruments of social control." See discussion in Albright, Berkhout, and Walker, *1996 World Inventories*, op. cit., pp. 422-23.

[31]Bill Gertz, "China Nuclear Transfer Exposed," *Washington Times*, February 5, 1996; R. Jeffrey Smith, "U.S. Aides See Troubling Trend In China-Pakistan Nuclear Ties," *Washington Post*, April 1, 1996. One report indicates that the Administration first obtained evidence of the ring magnet transfer in August 1995. R. Jeffrey Smith, "U.S. Decides to Transfer Weapons That Pakistan Paid For in 1980s," *Washington Post*, March 20, 1996.

[32]See Pakistan chapter in this volume.

[33]Mark Hibbs, "China Said Aiding Kahuta Project," *Nucleonics Week*, February 8, 1996, p. 1. For a discussion of the likely scale of operations and centrifuge renovation issues in Pakistan's enrichment program, based on publicly available data, see Albright, Berkhout, and Walker, *1996 World Inventories*, op. cit., pp. 274-79.

[34]*Reuters* and *United Press International* reports, February 8, 1996.

[35]See Nuclear Proliferation Prevention Act of 1994 (Title VIII, Sec. 825, Foreign Relations Authorization Act, Fiscal Year 1994 and 1995, P.L. 103-236 [1994]).

[36]The $10 billion figure first appeared in R. Jeffrey Smith, "China Sent Nuclear Aid to Pakistan," *Washington Post*, February 7, 1996. However, according to an Export-Import Bank official, the bank currently extends only $1 billion worth of loan credits annually to support U.S. businesses in China. The $10 billion figure therefore probably represents applications for loans over a ten-year period.

[37]Bill Gertz, "U.S. Opts to Hold Up Fund After China's Nuclear Deal," *Washington Times*, February 28, 1996.

[38]U.S. Department of State, "Special Briefing on U.S.–China Discussions on Non-Proliferation and Nuclear-Related Exports," Washington, DC, May 10, 1996.

[39]Hearings on *Weapons Proliferation in China*, International Security, Proliferation and Federal Services Subcommittee of the Senate Governmental Affairs Committee, April 10, 1997.

[40]Testimony of Secretary of State Warren Christopher before the Commerce, Justice and Judiciary and Related Agencies Subcommittee of the House Appropriations Committee, May 15, 1996. However, due to the vague wording of the pledge, it is not clear what "assistance" actually means. The undefined scope of assistance was illustrated by a senior State Department official who led the negotiations with China on the ring magnet issue, when he stated, "We hope now that they've agreed not to provide assistance to unsafeguarded facilities they realize that that means not just items that are on the trigger list, but also dual-use items and any item that could contribute to a nuclear explosives program." Background briefing by senior State Department official, May 10, 1996.

[41]Mark Hibbs, "Russian Industry May Be Key to Iran's Reactor Prospects," *Nucleonics Week*, September 17, 1992, p. 3.

[42]Elaine Sciolino, "Iran Says It Plans 10 Nuclear Plants But No Atom Arms," *New York Times*, May 14, 1995.

[43]"China Softens Stance Against Iranian Reactors," *Washington Post*, September 30, 1995.

[44]"China-Iran," *Associated Press*, January 9, 1996.

[45]Bill Gertz, "Iran Gets China's Help on Nuclear Arms," *Washington Times*, April 17, 1996; R. Jeffrey Smith, "China Nuclear Deal With Iran Is Feared," *Washington Post*, April 17, 1995; David Albright, "An Iranian Bomb?" *Bulletin of Atomic Scientists*, July/August 1995, p. 25.

[46]"Algeria Signs Nuclear Draft Agreement With China," *Reuters*, June 2, 1996.

[47]"PRC, Algeria to Cooperate in Nuclear Energy Development," *Xinhua*, May 21, 1997 in *FBIS-CHI-97-141*, May 23, 1997.

[48]Albright, Berkhout, and Walker, *1996 World Inventories*, op. cit., pp. 363-64.

[49]Mark Hibbs, "Move to Block China Certification," *Nucleonics Week*, August 7, 1997, p. 11.

[50]Albright, Berkhout, and Walker, *1996 World Inventories*, op. cit., p. 364.

[51]R. Jeffrey Smith, "Spy Photos Suggest China Missile Trade," *Washington Post*, July 3, 1995; R. Jeffrey Smith, "An M-11 Missile Violation By Any Other Name . . . ," *Washington Post*, August 3, 1995; R. Jeffrey Smith, "Report Cites China-Pakistan Missile Links," *Washington Post*, June 13, 1996; Bill Gertz, "2 Lawmakers Say Pakistan Has Missiles," *Washington Times*, June 21, 1996.

[52]*Proliferation: Threat and Response, 1996,* op. cit., p. 39. The 1997 report said "China remains Pakistan's principal supplier of missile-related technology and assistance." Office of the Secretary of Defense, *Proliferation: Threat and Response,* November 1997, p. 20.

[53]R. Jeffrey Smith, "China Linked to Pakistani Missile Plant," *Washington Post*, August 25, 1996.

[54]Ibid.

[55]Aurang Zeb, "Pakistan Denies It's Building Missile Factory," *Reuters*, August 26, 1996.

[56]Senate Hearings on *Weapons Proliferation in China*, April 10, 1997, op. cit.

[57]Barbara Opall, "US Queries China on Iran," *Defense News*, June 14-25, 1995; Elaine Sciolino, "CIA Report Says Chinese Sent Iran Arms Components," *New York Times*, June 21, 1995. "Chinese Shipments Violate Controls," *Jane's Defence Weekly*, July 1, 1995, p. 3.

[58]Bill Gertz, "China Sold Iran Missile Technology," *Washington Times*, November 21, 1996.

[59]These missiles, which are not covered by the MTCR, are surface-to-air missiles modified for the surface-to-surface role. IISS estimates Iran's inventory to be 25 CSS-8 launchers and 210 missiles. International Institute for Strategic Studies, *The Military Balance 1995/96* (London: Oxford University Press for IISS, 1995), p. 133.

[60]The C-802 has a range of 60 miles and was first tested by Iran in January 1996. Barbara Starr, "Iran Adds New Threat with Cruise Missile Test," *Jane's Defence Weekly*, February 7, 1996, p. 14; "China Delivers More Cruise Missile Boats to Iran: US Official," *Korea Times*, April 12, 1996. The U.S. Department of State has decided that the C-802 missiles transferred to date have not triggered U.S. sanctions under the 1992 Iran-Iraq Arms Non-Proliferation Act. Bill Gertz, "China Sold Iran Missile Technology," *Washington Times*, November 21, 1996.

The Iran-Iraq Arms Non-Proliferation Act (P.L. 102-484, div. A, title XVI, Oct. 23, 1992, 106 Stat. 2571) expresses U.S. policy opposing transfer of "dual-use goods or technology [that] could materially contribute to either country's acquiring chemical, biological, nuclear, or destabilizing numbers and types of advanced conventional weapons," and authorizes a variety of sanctions against entities or governments that engage in such transfers.

[61]Elaine Sciolino, "China Said to Sell Parts for Missiles," *New York Times*, January 31, 1992, and William Safire, "China's 'Hama Rules'," *New York Times*, March 5, 1992.

[62]Bill Gertz, "CIA Suspects Chinese Firm of Syria Missile Aid," *Washington Times*, July 23, 1996.

[63]Philip Finnegan, "Saudis Study Missile Buy to Replace Aging Arsenal," *Defense News*, March 17-23, 1997, p. 3.

[64]An Islamic separatist movement has re-emerged in Xinjiang province, home of the Lop Nur nuclear test site and associated nuclear-weapon research facilities. "'Splittism' Tops Chinese Rulers' Security Concerns," *Washington Times*, July 6, 1996. Beijing's fear of social breakdown can be seen in the recent nationwide crackdown on crime called "Strike Hard." This campaign was motivated by the growth in violent crime and organized criminal groups, which grew from 500 in 1991 to an estimated 10,000 in 1995. See Patrick Tyler, "Crime (and Punishment) Rages Anew in China," *New York Times*, July 11, 1996.

[65]Ann MacLachlan and Mark Hibbs, "China Stops Production of Military HEU," *Nuclear Fuel*, November 13, 1989, p. 5. The 1987 date is based on a personal communication from Mark Hibbs, who was told this by the head of the China Nuclear Energy Industry Corporation. Cited in Albright, Berkhout, and Walker, *1996 World Inventories*, op. cit., p. 126.

[66]Robert Norris, Andrew Burrows, and Richard Fieldhouse, *Nuclear Weapons Databook Volume V: British, French and Chinese Nuclear Weapons* (Boulder, CO: Westview Press, 1994), p. 350.

[67]The warhead estimate is from Norris et al., *Nuclear Weapons Databook Volume V*, ibid., p. 358. This estimate is based on data available in 1994.

[68]Albright, Berkhout, and Walker, *1996 World Inventories*, op. cit., pp. 399-400. It should be noted that the plutonium inventory

estimate could be off by as much as 50 percent and the HEU inventory estimate off by 25 percent. These residual fissile-material inventory estimates have subtracted from larger fissile-material production estimates the quantities of fissile material probably "consumed" in nuclear weapon tests and as fuels irradiated in naval, civil, and production reactors, as well as materials probably tied up in the estimated inventory of nuclear weapons. The estimate of how many nuclear weapons could be derived from these residual fissile-material inventories assumes that a nuclear warhead nominally requires either 15 kg of HEU or 5 kg of plutonium.

[69]Wendy Frieman, "New Members of the Club: Chinese Participation in Arms Control Regimes 1980-1995," *Nonproliferation Review*, Spring-Summer 1996, p. 18.

[70]Albright, Berkhout, and Walker, *1996 World Inventories*, op. cit., p. 128.

[71]Steve Coll and David Ottaway, "Will the United States, Russia and China Be Nuclear Partners or Rivals in the 21st Century?" *Washington Post*, April 11, 1995.

[72]*Institute on Global Conflict and Cooperation Newsletter*, University of California at San Diego, Fall 1995, p. 9.

[73]Interview with a U.S. National Laboratory official, June 1996.

[74]Tang Bin, "Major Advances Realized in Nation's Nuclear Fuel Accounting System," *Zhongguo He Gongye Bao [China Nuclear Industry News]*, September 11, 1996 in *FBIS-CST-96 019*, November 26, 1996.

[75]In 1996, the Defense Intelligence Agency reported that China's "strategic nuclear force is expanding; we expect to see steady growth in this force." Testimony of Lieutenant General Patrick Hughes, DIA Director, before the Senate Select Committee on Intelligence, *Current and Projected National Security Threats to the United States and Its Interests Abroad,* (Washington, DC: GPO, February 22, 1996), p. 242.

[76]Admiral William Studeman, Senate Committee on Armed Services, *Worldwide Threat to the United States,* January 17, 1995. The Xia SSBN has an unsatisfactory operational history and does not go out on long voyages.

[77]See International Institute of Strategic Studies, *The Military Balance, 1997/98* (London: Oxford University Press for IISS, 1997), p. 176. China's strategic modernization program has actually proceeded at a slow pace, with technical results that typically are decades behind those of the United States and the former Soviet Union. For a careful analysis of what is publicly known about China's overall defense expenditures and technical efforts, including the strategic arsenal, see David Shambaugh, "China's Military: Real or Paper Tiger?" *Washington Quarterly*, Vol. 19, No. 2, pp. 19 ff.

[78]Office of Naval Intelligence, *Worldwide Submarine Challenges*, February 1997, p. 22. The JL-1 missile is a solid-fuel variant of the 1,700-1,800-km-range DF-21, far short of intercontinental reach.

[79]Multiple warheads on a ballistic missile that are released simultaneously to fall in a geographically compact cluster are referred to as MRV, or multiple reentry vehicle systems. China probably mastered this technology in recent years. The more modern system for sequentially dispensing multiple warheads from ballistic missiles allows each warhead to be delivered to widely separated targets. This is known as "multiple independently targeted reentry vehicle" or MIRV capability. China is presumed to be trying to master this capability (see next note).

[80]Steven Erlanger, "US Warns 3 Nations Against Sale of Soviet Missile Technology," *New York Times*, May 22, 1996.

[81]Since Russia is closer to China, China's intermediate-range missiles and medium-range bombers have also served as part of China's strategic deterrent against Russia. "Disarmament Envoy Urges End to Theater Missile Defense System," *Xinhua*, October 18, 1996 in *FBIS-CHI-96-204*, October 22, 1996; Theresa Hitchens and Naoaki Usui, "China Sees Japan's TMD as Threat to Nuclear Might," *Defense News*, April 22-28, 1996, p. 12.

[82]Bill Gertz, "Chinese ICBM Will Threaten U.S., Pacific by 2000," *Washington Times*, May 23, 1997.

[83]China rejected a U.S. proposal that both countries de-target their missiles against each other and instead proposed that both countries adopt no-first-use policies, which the United States is unwilling to do. Charles Hutzler, "US–China," *Reuters*, November 25, 1996. U.S. de-targeting procedures for strategic missiles have reprogrammed them to target open ocean areas, and thus they no longer routinely target Chinese territory.

[84]For a description of PAL applications in the U.S. arsenal, see Donald R. Cotter, "Peacetime Operations: Safety and Security," in Ashton B. Carter, John D. Steinbruner and Charles A. Zraket, eds., *Managing Nuclear Operations* (Washington, DC: The Brookings Institution, 1987), pp. 46-54.

[85]Steve Coll and David Ottaway, "Will the United States, Russia, and China Be Nuclear Partners or Rivals in the 21st Century?" *Washington Post*, April 11, 1995.

[86]China announced in 1997 that it would join the Zangger Committee, attended the May meeting as an observer, and attended its first meeting as a member in October 1997. The Zangger Committee, which decides policy by consensus, currently is considering shifting to the full-scope safeguards requirement in the year 2000. U.S. policymakers are concerned that China, which still objects to the full-scope safeguards requirement, may block this change after joining the Zangger Committee. *Proliferation: Threat and Response,* 1997, op. cit., p. 11.

[87]See Richard T. Cupitt and Yuzo Murayama, Center for International Trade and Security, *Export Controls in the People's Republic of China: Status Report, 1997* (Athens, GA: University of Georgia, 1997), p. 12.

[88]According to the Pentagon, China has a "mature chemical warfare capability" and has "produced and weaponized a wide variety of agents." See *Proliferation: Threat and Response,* 1996, op. cit., p. 9. Joining the CWC involves China's commitments not only to control exports of specified chemicals and technology that could be used to develop chemical weapons but to eliminate any stockpiles it may have of chemical weapons and chemical-weapon production facilities.

[89]Chinese adherence to the CTBT was both a major Chinese step toward the acceptance of constraints on its nuclear arsenal and a significant international arms control accomplishment. Being far behind the United States and the former Soviet Union in nuclear weapons development, China initially held back from full CTBT commitments in order to conduct a last nuclear explosive test series, completed with its 44th and 45th nuclear weapon test detonations on June 8, 1996, and July 29, 1996. See "China Stages Nuclear Test and Vows to Join Ban After One More," *New York Times,* June 9, 1996, and Mure Dickie, "Final China Nuclear Blast Heralds Test Moratorium," *Reuters,* July 29, 1996.

In the course of these tests, China dropped its insistence on allowing "peaceful nuclear explosions" under the CTBT, a loophole that would have seriously undermined the value of the treaty. See Steven Mufson, "China to Drop Its Demand on Nuclear Testing," *Washington Post,* June 7, 1996. China subsequently announced it would begin observing a nuclear test moratorium effective July 30, 1996, and it signed the treaty just under two months later.

[90]China is nonetheless believed to have maintained the offensive biological warfare program it had prior to its accession to the convention, including the manufacture of biological warfare agents, and ACDA recently reported that "it is highly probable that [China] remains noncompliant with [its BWC] obligations." See ACDA, *Report on Adherence to and Compliance with Arms Control Agreements,* August 1997, p. 87; and *Proliferation: Threat and Response,* 1996, op. cit., p. 9.

[91]Charles A. Goldman and Jonathan D. Pollack, *Engaging China in the International Export Control Process: Options for U.S. Policy* (Washington, DC: RAND Corporation, 1997).

[92]These points were reaffirmed recently at the 1997 IAEA General Conference by Jiang Xinxiong, Chairman of China's Atomic Energy Authority. See Mark Hibbs, "China to Join Zangger Committee, but Not with Full-Scope Safeguards," *Nucleonics Week,* October 2, 1997, pp. 1, 10.

[93]Cupitt and Murayama, *Export Controls in China,* op. cit., p. 6.

[94]R. Jeffrey Smith, "China to Purchase U.S. Reactors After Curbing Ties to Iran," *Washington Post,* October 25, 1997.

[95]See note 2. A translation of China's export control regulations may be found in "PRC Regulations on Nuclear Exports," *FBIS,* September 13, 1997, from *Beijing Xinhua Domestic Service,* September 11, 1997. Article 3 of the "Regulations of the People's Republic of China on Control of Nuclear Exports" (as translated) states, inter alia: "The state [China] prohibits assistance to nuclear facilities not subject to International Atomic Agency's guarantee and supervision, and does not engage in nuclear exports or personnel and technological exchanges and cooperation with them."

[96]Hibbs, "China to Join Zangger Committee," op. cit. In contrast to the Nuclear Suppliers Group, the Zangger Committee has thus far not adopted a full-scope safeguards requirement but does plan to introduce this in the year 2000. By joining the Committee, China could (and some observers believe will) pose an obstacle to the Committee's adoption of that requirement, since the Committee operates by consensus.

[97]Smith, "China to Purchase U.S. Reactors," op. cit.

[98]China's agreement to forego even safeguarded peaceful nuclear cooperation with Iran, which would be legal since Iran is an NPT party, is a concession that goes beyond the requirements of U.S. law and therefore, strictly speaking, exceeds the U.S. certification requirement.

[99]R. Jeffrey Smith, "China's Pledge to End Iran Nuclear Aid Yields U.S. Help," *Washington Post,* October 30, 1997.

[100]"Way Paved for U.S.–China Nuclear Cooperation: U.S. Officials," *Xinhua,* March 20, 1998.

[101]R. Jeffrey Smith, " China to Purchase U.S. Reactors," op. cit.

[102]China evidently resists the full-scope standard because this would oblige it to terminate peaceful nuclear cooperation with Pakistan and India. China has been a supplier of heavy-water as well has low-enriched uranium fuel to India—the latter needed for the U.S.–supplied Tarapur reactors (see also India chapter in this volume.) China currently is Pakistan's only nuclear supplier. In contrast to non-nuclear-weapon states that are NPT parties, India and Pakistan accept IAEA safeguards only on selected nuclear facilities (principally imported nuclear reactors), but not generally on so-called "indigenous" nuclear facilities.

[103]This is a new area of extra-territorial jurisdiction that is sensitive even among closely cooperating countries—and extremely difficult for a country like China to undertake in foreign countries, since it is itself extraordinarily suspicious of foreign intrusiveness and unaccustomed to any form of transparency in its own borders.

[104]The CIA acknowledged over a year ago that China's participation in international non-proliferation regimes such as the NPT and CWC, and its adherence to the MTCR guidelines, "have led to a moderate decline in its sensitive technology exports to other countries. In many cases, however, China is now selling dual-use technology, hardware, and expertise, which are not always explicitly controlled under these multilateral control regimes." Responses to questions for the record, dated May 10, 1996, from John Moseman, Director, Congressional Affairs, Central Intelligence Agency, in *Current and Projected National Security Threats to the United States and Its Interests Abroad* (Washington, DC: GPO, February 22, 1996), p. 75. Of continuing importance are questions regarding the treatment of "components" and "subcomponents" of sensitive equipment and technology in Chinese export policy and in the behavior of Chinese trading entities.

[105]Cupitt and Murayama, *Export Controls in China,* op. cit.

China:
Map and Charts

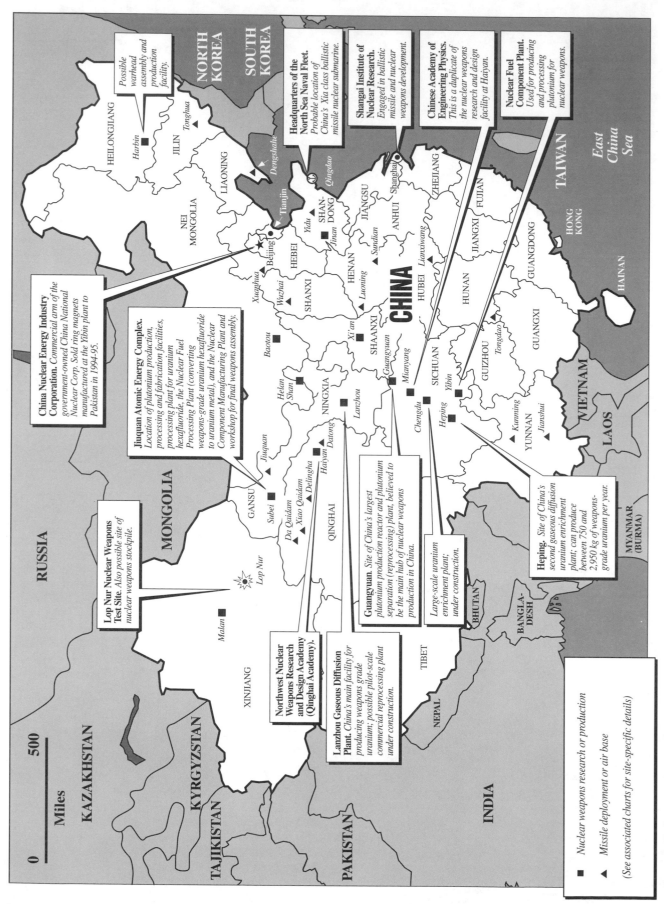

Possible warhead assembly and production facility.

NORTH KOREA

SOUTH KOREA

Headquarters of the North Sea Naval Fleet. *Probable location of China's Xia class ballistic missile nuclear submarine.*

Shangai Institute of Nuclear Research. *Engaged in ballistic missile and nuclear weapons development.*

Chinese Academy of Engineering Physics. *This is a duplicate of the nuclear weapons research and design facility at Haiyan.*

Nuclear Fuel Component Plant. *Used for producing and processing plutonium for nuclear weapons.*

East China Sea

HEILONGJIANG

JILIN

LIAONING

Harbin

Tonghua

Dengshahe

Tianjin

Qingdao

Shanghai

NEI MONGOLIA

Beijing

HEBEI

SHAN-DONG

Yidu

Jinan

JIANGSU

ANHUI

Lianyuang

ZHEJIANG

TAIWAN

Xuephua

Wuzhai

SHANXI

HENAN

Luoning

Sundian

HUBEI

JIANGXI

FUJIAN

HONG KONG

China Nuclear Energy Industry Corporation. *Commercial arm of the government-owned China National Nuclear Corp. Sold ring magnets manufactured at the Yibin plant to Pakistan in 1994-95.*

Jiuquan Atomic Energy Complex. *Location of plutonium production, processing and fabrication facilities, processing plant for uranium hexafluoride, the Nuclear Fuel Processing Plant (converting weapons-grade uranium hexafluoride to uranium metal), and the Nuclear Component Manufacturing Plant and workshop for final weapons assembly.*

CHINA

Baotou

Xi'an

SHAANXI

Guangyuan

Mianyang

SICHUAN

Chengdu

Yibin

Heping

Tongdao

GUIZHOU

HUNAN

GUANGDONG

GUANGXI

HAINAN

Helan Shan

Lanzhou

NINGXIA

Jiuquan

GANSU

Subei

Da Qaidam

Xiao Qaidam

Delingha

Haiyan

Datong

QINGHAI

Kunming

YUNNAN

Jianshui

VIETNAM

LAOS

Lop Nur Nuclear Weapons Test Site. *Also possible site of nuclear weapons stockpile.*

RUSSIA

MONGOLIA

Malan

Lop Nur

XINJIANG

Guangyuan. *Site of China's largest plutonium production reactor and plutonium separation (reprocessing) plant, believed to be the main hub of nuclear weapons production in China.*

Large-scale uranium enrichment plant; under construction.

Heping. *Site of China's second gaseous diffusion uranium enrichment plant; can produce between 750 and 2,950 kg of weapons-grade uranium per year.*

KAZAKHSTAN

0 **500**

Miles

KYRGYZSTAN

TAJIKISTAN

Northwest Nuclear Weapons Research and Design Academy (Qinghai Academy).

Lanzhou Gaseous Diffusion Plant. *China's main facility for producing weapons grade uranium; possible pilot-scale commercial reprocessing plant under construction.*

BHUTAN

BANGLA-DESH

TIBET

NEPAL

PAKISTAN

INDIA

MYANMAR (BURMA)

■ Nuclear weapons research or production

▲ Missile deployment or air base

(See associated charts for site-specific details)

Carnegie Endowment for International Peace, *Tracking Nuclear Proliferation*, 1998

SOURCES: Robert S. Norris et al., Nuclear Weapons Databook, Natural Resources Defense Council, March 1994; and "Datafile: China," *Nuclear Engineering International*, October 1993, pp. 16-22.

CHINA Chart 1: Nuclear Weapons Systems[a]

TYPE	OPERATING PARAMETERS (km/kg)	NUMBER OF WEAPONS/ LOCATIONS	COMMENTS
LAND-BASED MISSILES			
Dong Feng-3 (3A)/CSS-2	DF-3: 2,650/2,150 DF-3A: 2,800/2,150 Warhead: 3.3 MT	Total: 38 + Yidu, Jianshui, around Kunming, Tonghua, Dengshahe, Datong, Lianxiwang.[b]	First indigenously produced missile. Extended range DF-3A produced in late 1980s. In 1988, 30 conventionally armed DF-3s sold to Saudi Arabia.
Dong Feng-4/CSS-3	4,750/2,200 Warhead: 3.3 MT	Total: 10 + Xiao Qaidam, Da Qaidam, Delingha (cave-based); Tongdao, Sundian (silo-based).	China's first missile capable of striking Moscow.
Dong Feng 5 (5A)/CSS-4	DF-5: 12,000/3,200 DF-5A: 13,000/3,200 Warhead: 4-5 MT	Total: 7-18[c] Luoning Province (2 silos), Xuanhua. Others possibly deployed as war reserves at Jiuquan and Wuzhai Centers.	China's first and only deployed intercontinental ballistic missile (ICBM); identical airframe to CSS-2 space launch vehicles.
Dong Feng-21 (21A)/CSS-5	DF-21: 1,700/600 DF-21A: 1,800/600 Warhead: 200-300 Kt	Total: 30 + Tonghua, Jianshui, and Lianxiwang.	China's first road-mobile, solid-fuel missile; will replace the DF-3 (CSS-2), perhaps by 2002.
Dong Feng-25	1,700/2,000	Under development.[d]	Solid-fuel, road-mobile.
Dong Feng-31	8,000/700 Warhead: 100-200 Kt	Under development.	Solid-fuel, road-mobile ICBM. Tested May 1995, deployment planned around 2000.
Dong Feng-41	12,000/800	Under development.	May have multiple warheads.
SUBMARINE-LAUNCHED BALLISTIC MISSILES (SLBMs)			
Julang-1/CSS-N-3	1,700/600 Warhead: 200-300 Kt	Total: 12 Deployed on one Daqingyu (Xia) class nuclear submarine likely based at North Sea Naval Fleet in Qingdao.	China's first SLBM; solid-fuel; sea-based version of DF-21.
Julang-2	8,000/700 Warhead: 100-200 Kt	Under development. The new Type 094 nuclear submarine is expected to be in service by 2005 and carry 16 JL-2 missiles.	A sea-based version of the DF-31; would allow China's submarines to target the United States for the first time from locations near Chinese coast.[e]
TACTICAL MISSILES			
Dong Feng-15/CSS-6	600/500 nuclear-capable	Total: ? Jiangxi and Fujian Provinces.	Solid-fuel, road-mobile; M-9 export.
Dong Feng-11/CSS-7	280/800 nuclear-capable	Total: ?	Solid-fuel, road-mobile; M-11 export; supplied to Pakistan.
CSS-X[f]	300 + /?	Under development.	Improved CSS-7.

Explanation of Terms:

Dong Feng	=	"East Wind"
Julang	=	"Giant Wave"
CSS	=	U.S. designation for "Chinese Surface-to-Surface"
CSS-N	=	U.S. designation for "Chinese Surface-to-Surface Naval"
?	=	Uncertain
MT	=	megaton
Kt	=	kiloton

NOTES (China Chart 1)

[a]Principal sources: International Institute for Strategic Studies, *The Military Balance 1997/98* (London: Oxford University Press for IISS, 1997) p. 176; Robert Norris, Andrew Burrows, and Richard Fieldhouse, *Nuclear Weapons Databook Volume V: British, French and Chinese Nuclear Weapons* (Washington, DC: Natural Resources Defense Council, 1994); Robert Norris and Willam Arkin, "Nuclear Notebook," *Bulletin of the Atomic Scientists*, November/December 1996, p. 67; John Wilson Lewis and Hua Di, "China's Ballistic Missile Program: Technologies, Strategies and Goals," *International Security*, Fall 1992; Bill Gertz, "New Chinese Missile Target All of East Asia," *Washington Times*, July 10, 1997; and David Shambaugh, "China's Military: Real or Paper Tiger," *Washington Quarterly*, Spring 1996, pp. 19-36.

[b]These facilities were listed in a secret report by the National Air Intelligence Center, which detailed Chinese IRBM deployments, as reported by Gertz, "New Chinese Missile," op. cit.

[c]Recent press reports refer variously to 13 and 17-18 as the number of ICBMs known to be deployed by China. The most specific such report claims to be based on a new CIA report that is said to give 13 as the number of DF-5 (CSS-4) ICBMs aimed at the United States, and another 5 aimed elsewhere. See Bill Gertz, "China Targets Nukes at U.S.: CIA Missile Report Contradicts Clinton," *Washington Times*, May 1, 1998, p. A1. Since this report has not been confirmed publicly by U.S. officials, the chart information here, which is based on public sources, provides the estimate of 7-18, acknowledging uncertainty about the number of deployed Chinese ICBMs. The lower bound of the range used in strategic arms negotiations to decide whether a ballistic missile is an ICBM is 5,500 km. China currently deploys only one type, the DF-5, with a demonstrated range above that limit.

[d]According to one missile expert, China has abandoned the DF-25 program, although this has not been confirmed by other sources. Eric Arnett, "Chinese Blow Cold on East Wind Missile Plan," *Jane's Defence Weekly*, December 4, 1996, p. 3. Interestingly, a recent Pentagon report on China's military does not mention the DF-25 in its examination of current and projected Chinese ballistic missile capabilities. Department of Defense, *Selected Military Capabilities of the People's Republic of China,* Report to Congress Pursuant to Section 1305 of the FY97 National Defense Authorization Act, April 2, 1997, pp. 3-4.

[e]*World Submarine Challenges 1997*, Office of Naval Intelligence, February 1997, p. 22.

[f]Department of Defense, *Selected Military Capabilities of the PRC,* op. cit., p. 3.

CHINA Chart 2: Nuclear Weapons–Related Sites of Proliferation Concern[a]

NAME/LOCATION OF FACILITY	TYPE/STATUS
N U C L E A R W E A P O N S C O M P L E X [b]	
Northwest Nuclear Technology Institute, in the Scientific Research District outside Malan, Xinjiang	Archive on nuclear explosions, warfare, and weapons research and design; associated with testing at Lop Nur.
Jiuquan Atomic Energy Complex (Plant 404), Subei, Gansu	Fabrication of fissile materials into bomb cores, and final weapons assembly.
Northwest Institute of Nuclear Technology, Xi'an, Shaanxi	Diagnostic support for nuclear test program.
Lop Nur Nuclear Weapons Test Base, Xinjiang	Nuclear weapons test site and possible nuclear weapons stockpile.
Chinese Academy of Engineering Physics (CAEP), Mianyang, Sichuan	Nuclear weapons research, design, and technology complex; called the "Los Alamos of China," 11 institutes, 8 located in Mianyang.[c]
Institute 905 of CAEP, outside Mianyang	Ordnance engineering lab for non-nuclear components of nuclear weapons; "the Chinese Sandia."[d]
Institute of Applied Physics and Computational Mathematics, Beijing	Conducts research on nuclear warhead design computations for CAEP.
Shanghai Institute of Nuclear Research, Shanghai, Zhejiang	Engaged in tomography, tests solid missile propellants, explosives, and detonation packages for nuclear weapons.
Fudan University, Shanghai, Zhejiang	Engaged in tomography, tests solid missile propellants, explosives, and detonation packages for nuclear weapons.
Harbin, Heilongjiang	Possible warhead assembly and production site.
Plant 821, Guangyuan, Sichuan	Nuclear weapon assembly facility.
P L U T O N I U M P R O D U C T I O N R E A C T O R S	
Plant 821 Guangyuan, Sichuan	LWGR, nat. U, 1,000 MW; operational. Largest plutonium producing reactor in China.
Jiuquan Atomic Energy Complex (Plant 404), Subei, Gansu	LWGR, nat. U, 400-500 MW; operational.
R E S E A R C H R E A C T O R S	
HFETR Nuclear Power Institute of China, Chengdu, Sichuan	Tank, LW; HEU (90%), 125 MWt; operational.
HFETR critical Nuclear Power Institute of China, Chengdu, Sichuan	Critical assembly, LW; HEU (90%), 0 MWt; operational.
MJTR Nuclear Power Institute of China, Chengdu, Sichuan	Pool, LW; HEU (90%), 5 MWt; operational.
MNSR IAE China Institute for Atomic Energy, Tuoli, near Beijing	Tank in pool, LW; HEU (90%), .027 MWt; operational.
MNSR-SD Shandong Geology Bureau, Jinan, Shandong	Tank in pool, LW; HEU (90%), .027 MWt; operational.
MNSR SZ Shenzhen University, Guangdong	Tank in pool, LW; HEU (90%), .027 MWt; operational.
Zero Power Fast Critical Reactor Southwest Research Institute, Chengdu, Sichuan	Critical fast; HEU (90%), 0 MWt; operational.

NAME/LOCATION OF FACILITY	TYPE/STATUS
HWRR-II China Institute for Atomic Energy, Tuoli, near Beijing	Heavy water; LEU (3%), 15 MWt; operational. Under IAEA safeguards.
SPR IAE China Institute for Atomic Energy, Tuoli, near Beijing	Pool, LW; LEU (10%), 3.5 MWt; operational.
SPRR-300 Southwest Research Institute, Chengdu, Sichuan	Pool, LW; LEU (10%), 3.7 MWt; operational.
Tsinghua Pool Institute of Nuclear Energy Technology, Tsinghua University, Beijing	Pool, two cores, LW; LEU (10%), 2.8 MWt; operational.
PPR Pulsing Reactor Nuclear Power Institute of China, Chengdu, Sichuan	Pool, HEU (20%), 1 MWt; operational.

URANIUM ENRICHMENT

Heping Uranium Enrichment Plant, Heping, Sichuan	Gaseous diffusion plant: estimated to produce 750-2950 kg HEU/year[e]; operational.
Lanzhou Nuclear Fuel Complex, Lanzhou, Gansu	Gaseous diffusion plant: estimated to produce at least 150-330 kg HEU/year[f]; operational.[g]
Lanzhou Nuclear Fuel Complex, Lanzhou, Gansu	Gaseous diffusion plant: new cascade under construction, for LEU export.[h]
China Institute of Atomic Energy, Tuoli, near Beijing	Laboratory-scale gaseous diffusion: developed enrichment process later installed at Lanzhou.
Russian-supplied centrifuge enrichment plant, Chengdu, Sichuan[i]	Large-scale centrifuge enrichment facility; under construction;[j] capacity: 200,000 SWU/yr.

PLUTONIUM REPROCESSING[k]

Jiuquan Atomic Energy Complex (Plant 404), Subei, Gansu	Large-scale reprocessing plant, capacity: 300-400kg Pu/yr, and pilot reprocessing plant (both use PUREX method); and Nuclear Fuel Processing Plant for refining plutonium into weapons-usable metals.
Plant 821, Guangyuan, Sichuan	China's largest plutonium separation facility, capacity: 300-400 kg Pu/yr.
Nuclear Fuel Component Plant (Plant 812), Yibin, Sichuan	Plutonium fuel rod fabrication, and plutonium production and processing for nuclear weapons; operating.
Lanzhou Nuclear Fuel Complex, Lanzhou, Gansu	Pilot spent fuel reprocessing plant, nominal capacity of 100 kg/heavy metal per day; under construction, completion in 2000.[l]

URANIUM PROCESSING

Nuclear Fuel Component Plant (202), Baotou, Nei Mongolia province	Fuel rod fabrication; operating.
Nuclear Fuel Component Plant (Plant 812), Yibin, Sichuan	Fuel rod fabrication; operating.
Jiuquan Atomic Energy Complex, (Plant 404), Subei, Gansu	Nuclear Fuel Processing Plant: Converts enriched UF_6 to UF_4 for shaping into metal; operational.

CHINA Chart 2 (cont'd.)

NAME/LOCATION OF FACILITY	TYPE/STATUS
TRITIUM, LITHIUM DEUTERIDE, AND BERYLLIUM	
Ningxia Non-Ferrous Metal Research Institute (Plant 905), Helan Shan, Ningxia	China's main research and production site for beryllium.
Nuclear Fuel Component Plant (Plant 202), Baotou, Nei Mongolia	Tritium, Li-6 deuterium production; operational.
Nuclear Fuel Element Plant (Plant 812), Yibin, Sichuan	Probable production of tritium and Li-6 deuterium.

Abbreviations:

HEU	=	highly enriched uranium
LEU	=	low-enriched uranium
nat. U	=	natural uranium
MWe	=	millions of watts of electrical output
MWt	=	millions of watts of thermal output
KWt	=	thousands of watts of thermal output

NOTES (China Chart)

[a]Principle sources for this chart: Robert S. Norris, Andrew S. Burrows, and Richard W. Fieldhouse, *Nuclear Weapons Databook V* (Boulder: Westview Press, 1994); *Nuclear Engineering International: World Nuclear Industry Handbook 1997*; "Datafile: China," *Nuclear Engineering International*, October 1993, pp. 16-22; John Wilson Lewis and Xue Litai, *China Builds the Bomb* (Stanford: Stanford University Press, 1988); David Albright, Frans Berkhout and William Walker, *Plutonium and Highly Enriched Uranium 1996: World Inventories, Capabilities and Policies* (New York: Oxford University Press for Stockholm Peace Research Institute International, 1997); International Atomic Energy Agency, *Nuclear Research Reactors in the World*, December 1995; Wisconsin Project, "Nuclear Profile: China," *Risk Report*, November 1995, pp. 3-9.

[b]In addition to the sites listed under Nuclear Weapons Complex, the following sites are engaged in nuclear research, though perhaps not explicitly weapons related: Atomic Research Center, Xinjiang; Institute of Nuclear Energy Technology (INET), Tsinghua University, Beijing; Institute of Nuclear Science and Technology, Sichuan University, Chengdu, Sichuan; Institute of Materials and Elements at the Sichuan Institute of Nuclear Power, Chengdu, Sichuan province; China Institute for Radiation Protection (CIRP), Yaiyuan, Shanxi; Beijing Nuclear Engineering R&D Academy, Beijing; and Nuclear R&D Institute, Tianjin, SE of Beijing.

[c]CAEP is an identical copy of the Northwest Nuclear Weapons Research and Design Academy in Haiyan, the original Chinese weapons design facility that has since been phased out, and the work transferred to CAEP. See Norris et al., *Nuclear Weapons Databook V*, op. cit., p. 338ff.

[d]Ibid. p. 348; and *Risk Report*, op. cit., p. 6.

[e]U.S. Defense Intelligence Agency, *Soviet and Peoples' Republic of China Nuclear Weapons Employment Policy and Strategy*, TCS-65475-72, March 1972; see discussion in Albright, Berkhout, and Walker, *1996 World Inventories*, op. cit., p. 126ff.

[f]This estimate was based on the 1972 DIA report, op. cit.; Albright et al., op. cit., speculate that Lanzhou had a capacity of approximately 24,000-53,000 SWU/yr at that time, but subsequent increases in separative membrane technology are thought to have boosted the capacity to 300,000 SWU/yr and therefore higher levels of HEU production.

[g]Chinese officials have stated that once the centrifuge enrichment plant provided by Russia is fully operational, China will close the Lanzhou gaseous diffusion plant because it is uneconomical to operate. Mark Hibbs, "With More Russian Centrifuges, China Will Close Lanzhou Plant," *Nuclear Fuel*, October 6, 1997, p. 3.

[h]In the 1992 edition of Albright, Berkhout, and Walker, *1996 World Inventories*, op. cit., the authors note that "China is building a new cascade at Lanzhou to produce low-enriched uranium that will be more suitable for export, but this facility is not expected to be completed until the mid-1990s." No further information on the status of this project has surfaced, although it is possible that with the construction of the Russian centrifuge enrichment plant coupled with Chinese statements that the Lanzhou plant will close, this project has been discontinued.

[i]There has been conflicting information as to the exact location of this facility. The most recent reports suggest that the facility is in Chengdu; see Mark Hibbs, "China Will Close Lanzhou," op. cit., and "China's Centrifuge SWU Plant Up and Running, MINATOM Says," *Nuclear Fuel*, January 27, 1997, p. 3. Earlier reports suggested that the facility might be located in Shaanxi province, perhaps Xi'an or Hanzhong; see Mark Hibbs, "Russian Centrifuge Plant in China to be Finished, Operating Next Year," *Nuclear Fuel*, September 25, 1995, p. 1. The World Nuclear Industry Handbook 1997 further suggests that the plant is at Lanzhou, alongside the original gaseous diffusion plant.

[j]The first module of the plant began operating in 1996, and the second in late September 1997. No finish date for the third and last module has been given. Hibbs, "China Will Close Lanzhou," op. cit.

[k]Additional military reprocessing facilities are thought to be located at Urumqi, Xinjiang province, and Yumen, Gansu province. "Datafile: China," *Nuclear Engineering International*, October 1993, p. 22.

[l]Mark Hibbs, "Chinese Separation Plant to Reprocess Spent HEU Fuel," *Nuclear Fuel*, January 13, 1997, p. 3, and Ann MacLachlan, "Chinese Official Outlines Plans for Complete Nuclear Fuel Cycle," *Nuclear Fuel*, April 24, 1995, p. 15.

4

DE-NUCLEARIZED POST-SOVIET STATES

Belarus

Upon the collapse of the Soviet Union in 1991, Belarus was one of the three Soviet-successor states with strategic nuclear weapons on their territories that committed themselves—in the May 1992 Lisbon Protocol to START I—to de-nuclearization and accession to the Nuclear Non-Proliferation Treaty (NPT) as "non-nuclear-weapon states." Although there was never real doubt that Belarus would abide by these commitments, it was the last of the three to have all former Soviet strategic delivery systems and nuclear warheads removed to Russia. In late November 1996, the remaining 16 SS-25 road-mobile intercontinental ballistic missiles (ICBMs) deployed in Belarus, each equipped with a single warhead, and the remaining 18 road-mobile launchers were withdrawn by Russia's Strategic Rocket Forces to Russian territory.[1] All tactical nuclear weapons in former Soviet republics, including Belarus, had been removed to Russia by April 1992.[2] First scheduled for completion in 1995, the withdrawal of the remaining strategic systems from Belarus was delayed, however, by domestic political battles between President Aleksandr Lukashenko and leaders of the Belarusian parliament,[3] who were influenced by reactions to NATO's planned enlargement[4] as well as by Russian-Belarusian disagreements over which state should be financially responsible for the dismantlement and environmental clean-up of the ICBM support facilities located in Belarus.

BACKGROUND

When the Soviet Union was dissolved in December 1991, Belarus emerged as an independent state that had former Soviet strategic nuclear delivery systems—specifically, 81 single-warhead road-mobile SS-25 ICBMs—deployed on its territory. In addition, 725 tactical nuclear weapons were deployed in Belarus.[5] Russia retained the command and control over these nuclear systems, including the arming and launch codes needed to use them. Nonetheless, outsiders were apprehensive initially that Belarus might attempt to assert ownership and control over the nuclear arms and declare itself a new nuclear-weapon state, which would have dealt a serious blow to international efforts to curb the spread of nuclear arms.

De-Nuclearization Commitments. With close ties to and dependency upon Russia, Belarus not only cooperated in the removal of nuclear arms to Russia but accepted firm nuclear non-proliferation commitments at an early stage. Belarus took the first steps toward becoming nuclear-weapon-free when—along with Kazakhstan, Russia, and Ukraine—it signed the December 21, 1991, Alma-Ata Declaration on Nuclear Arms. Under this Declaration, Belarus pledged to join the NPT as a non-nuclear-weapon state and to remove to Russia all tactical nuclear weapons located in Belarus by July 1, 1992. In addition, it agreed not to transfer nuclear weapons on its territory to others, except Russia, in anticipation of the ultimate return of all nuclear weapons from Belarus to Russia.[6]

In the Minsk accord of December 30, 1991, Belarus agreed, together with the ten other members of the Commonwealth of Independent States (CIS), that a "decision on the need [to use nuclear weapons would be] made by the President of the Russian Federation in agreement with the heads of the Republic of Belarus, the Republic of Kazakhstan, and Ukraine, and in consultation with the heads of the other member states of the Commonwealth."[7] (Arrangements for sharing authority in this area under the CIS military umbrella ended in June 1993, when Russia formally took full command and control over all nuclear arms in the Soviet successor states.)

START Framework of De-Nuclearization. In the May 23, 1992, Lisbon Protocol to START I, Belarus agreed to participate in START jointly with Kazakhstan, Russia, and Ukraine, as successors to the former Soviet Union—and to "implement the Treaty's limits and restrictions" (Article II of the Protocol). Belarus also agreed to accede to the NPT as a non-nuclear-weapon state party "in the shortest possible time" (Article V of the Protocol); in a side letter to President George Bush, Belarus's president pledged to eliminate all strategic nuclear arms in Belarus within the seven-year START I implementation period.[8] A month earlier, all tactical nuclear weapons had been removed to Russia, several months ahead of the schedule established under the agreement signed in Alma-Ata.[9]

The Belarusian parliament ratified START I on February 4, 1993, and Belarus formally acceded to the NPT on July 22, 1993—well before Ukraine did so. Steps were also taken in 1993 to begin the withdrawal of SS-25 ICBMs deployed on the territory of Belarus to Russia, but the process was later interrupted before all the systems were removed.

Arms Dismantlement Assistance. To assist Belarus, Kazakhstan, and Ukraine in the removal of nuclear weapons and delivery systems from their territories, and to help Russia reduce nuclear arms under the START treaty and other arms control arrangements, the United States in 1992 began the Cooperative Threat Reduction (CTR) program, also known as the Nunn-Lugar program, after Senators Sam Nunn and Richard Lugar, who sponsored the legislation providing funding for the effort. The CTR program was designed to provide technical and financial assistance in the safe handling, transport, and storage of nuclear weapons, as well as in the dismantlement or elimination of the reduced weapons and their delivery systems and bases.

As of December 1993, the United States and Belarus had proposed $66 million in CTR-related contracts for environmental restoration, the purchase of emergency response equipment, and defense conversion, including $6 million for the elimination of ICBMs and their launchers. On January 15, 1994, during a visit to Belarus, President Bill Clinton promised an additional $25 million in CTR funds for Belarus. Japan also pledged $8.37 million for CTR-related purposes.[10]

DEVELOPMENTS

De-Nuclearization Completed. Belarus had committed itself in 1993 to allow the removal of the former Soviet SS-25 ICBMs deployed on its territory to Russia. But in mid-1995, with some 18 strategic launchers and associated missiles and warheads remaining, Belarus suspended the removal process. In December 1995, Russia and Belarus reached a new agreement to extricate the remaining missiles by September 1, 1996.[11] Hinting at an economic reason for the Belarusian holdup, on February 27, 1996, the two nations agreed on an arrangement to compensate Belarus financially for the value of the fissile materials in the strategic weapons that were leaving its territory. Under the deal, Russia forgave approximately $500 million of Belarus's natural gas debt.[12] Despite these arrangements, President Lukashenko disrupted the schedule a second time,[13] forcing another round of talks in July 1996. As a result of these talks, Belarus agreed to allow Russia to remove the remaining SS-25s by the end of 1996.[14] Notwithstanding the delays, all SS-25s located in Belarus remained under Russian control until withdrawal to Russia was completed in late November 1996.[15]

Dismantlement Assistance. After the inception of the CTR program in 1992, considerable time elapsed as legal agreements providing for implementation and transfer of assistance were painstakingly worked out. As of August 5, 1996, however, the Pentagon had notified Congress that it planned to allocate a total of nearly $119 million in CTR-related contracts in Belarus for environmental restoration, the purchase of emergency response equipment, and defense conversion, as well as almost $34 million for the elimination of ICBMs and their launchers.[16] Japan and Germany also signed framework agreements with Belarus to provide assistance for ICBM dismantlement, infrastructure dismantlement, and environmental clean-up.[17]

Civil Nuclear Program and Safeguards. Belarus had begun negotiating a "full-scope" safeguards agreement with the International Atomic Energy Agency (IAEA) in 1993. After signature in April 1995, this agreement authorized the IAEA to apply safeguards on all Belarusian civil nuclear activities as of August 1995.[18] (Nuclear weapons were not involved, as they were under Russian control—the jurisdiction of a nuclear-weapon state—during the time they remained in Belarus.) Even before the IAEA safeguards took effect, the danger of diversion of nuclear materials in Belarus was relatively low, inasmuch as Belarus had little civil nuclear infrastructure; it had no nuclear power plants, uranium-enrichment facilities, or spent-fuel reprocessing facilities.

The greatest proliferation concern in Belarus was the possibility, until late November 1996, that a complete nuclear weapon en route to Russia could be attacked, stolen, or diverted. A residual concern was the presence at the Institute of Power Engineering Problems, in Sosny, Minsk, of enough weapons-grade uranium to make one or two nuclear bombs. Furthermore, the site contained about 330 kg of non-weapons-grade highly enriched uranium.[19] These materials represented a potential for diversion or theft. Under the auspices of the U.S. Department of Energy's program on Material Protection, Control, and Accounting (MPC&A), the United States has helped design and fund physical security improvements at the Institute, including training programs, alarm upgrades, and the installation of tamper-indication devices. These MPC&A programs have also received support from Japan and Sweden.[20]

Continuing political problems in Belarus, particularly the curtailment of human rights and freedom of speech, led President Clinton to revoke CTR certification for Belarus in March 1997 and again in 1998. CTR projects for which funds had been obligated before the decertification will be completed, but funding in excess of $25 million for agreed projects has been frozen. This funding would have contributed to the continued dismantling of the strategic offensive weapons infrastructure and other projects in Belarus.

Nuclear Export Controls. Belarus has passed several export control laws but, with strained resources and no experience in export control prior to independence, its system remains inchoate. Because of its contiguity with Russia and its proximity to Western Europe, Belarus's territory could be a transit point for nuclear materials being smuggled out of Russia. In November 1993, Belarusian officials announced that they had prevented an attempt to smuggle uranium into Poland,[21] but overall reports of incidents of smuggled radioactive materials from the former Soviet Union declined dramatically after 1994.

About $16 million of U.S. CTR funding was committed to improving the Belarusian export control system, for procurement of radiation detection equipment to install at border posts, and computer hardware and software to establish and maintain export control records. A customs union formed by Belarus, Kazakhstan, and Russia under an agreement signed on January 28, 1996, has resulted in the elimination of checkpoints along the Belarusian-Russian border, leaving well-guarded only the Belarusian-Polish border, which is manned partly by Russian forces. Belarus has yet to join the Nuclear Suppliers Group (NSG), but it did sign a commitment to adhere to the NSG export control standards.[22]

The Union with Russia. On April 2, 1996, Belarus and Russia signed the "Treaty on the Formation of the Community of Belarus and Russia" to establish a closer relationship—a form of "union" that has created some doubt about whether Belarus will be able to maintain genuine independence. In the treaty's ambiguous language, the two nations aim "to form a profoundly politically and economically integrated Community of Belarus and Russia with a view to pooling the material and intellectual potential of their states . . ."[23] The new union calls for a common economic market with free movement of capital and labor, and for shared defense responsibilities. It gives Russia a larger role in guarding Belarusian borders and air space. The two partners have initiated joint air-defense activities.[24] However, plans for a currency union and other steps toward economic integration have been deferred.

Nuclear-Weapon-Free Zone Proposal. Belarusian officials have repeatedly called for establishing a Central European nuclear-weapon-free zone. This proposal, originally suggested in October 1990,[25] has paralleled Ukrainian proposals for such a zone and received more prominence in 1996, as Belarus and Russia sought strategies to counter NATO enlargement.[26]

PROSPECTS

Belarus made a major contribution to the nuclear non-proliferation regime when it voluntarily affirmed non-nuclear-weapon commitments in the wake of Soviet disintegration, agreed to the START I Lisbon Protocol provisions for the elimination of all nuclear arms on its territory, and followed through with its commitments to accede to the NPT as a non-nuclear-weapon state. Despite some hesitation in the final withdrawal of nuclear weapons and strategic delivery systems from its territory to Russia during 1996, that Belarusian commitment was fulfilled too, before the end of 1996, completing the Belarusian process of de-nuclearization. To ensure physical protection of the limited quantities of special nuclear materials in its nuclear research facilities, Belarus has accepted full-scope IAEA safeguards, adopted nuclear export control laws, and accepted U.S. cooperation in establishing MPC&A systems. By 1997, therefore, Belarus was a virtually complete non-proliferation success story.

Belarus has had a troubled domestic political evolution since independence, however, and its deep economic problems have led it to request closer economic ties with—indeed a form of dependence on—Russia; it is not clear that it will progress as a fully independent state. While President Lukashenko is personally popular, his government is authoritarian, retarding both economic and political reform and potentially storing up problems of future instability. It seems unlikely, however, that future political evolution in Belarus would undermine the country's non-proliferation commitments.

NOTES

[1] "Adherence to and Compliance with Arms Control Agreement," U.S. Arms Control and Disarmament Agency, August 15, 1997.

[2] Testimony of Assistant Secretary of Defense Ashton Carter before the Senate Armed Services Committee, April 28, 1994.

[3] Lukashenko scheduled and won a November 24, 1996, national referendum on modifying the Belarusian constitution to consolidate his presidential powers. Under the changes, the president's term of office was extended from five to seven years, a second legislative chamber was created with its members appointed by the president, and a new Constitutional Court was established with the president naming half the judges. Members of the Belarusian Parliament opposed Lukashenko's efforts to weaken the legislature, and, in mid-November 1996, one group initiated impeachment proceedings, although these were not completed. The referendum controversy resulted in the resignation or firing of several senior government officials, including Prime Minister Mikhail Chigir, Labor Minister Alexander Sosnov, and the chairman of the Central Electoral Commission. "Belarus Opposition Denounces President," *Washington Post,* July 30, 1996; "Belarus Deputies Seek to Impeach President," *Reuters,* November 18, 1996. The United States took the view that Lukashenko was acting outside his authority and urged him to work within the context of the existing constitution. The United States also offered asylum to two Belarusian opposition leaders who fled Minsk in April 1996, saying their lives were in danger. U.S. State Department briefing, November 18, 1996.

[4] In a speech to the Russian State Duma on November 13, 1996, Lukashenko hinted that he might link the transfer of the remaining SS-25s to Russia to receiving a pledge from NATO that it would not deploy nuclear weapons near Belarus: "I hate to think that it may happen that the removal of nuclear weapons from Belarusian territory will coincide in time with the deployment of nuclear missiles and warheads on the territories of new NATO members. . . And withdrawing the nuclear weapons from Belarus—a little more than ten missiles remain—we might request from the Western states a pledge not to deploy such weapons close to our borders." *Federal News Service,* November 13, 1996.

[5] The basic source for the strategic system figures, as well as for those in the chart that follows, is the START I Memorandum of Understanding (MOU) on Data. Updated every six months after entry into force in December 1994, the last available update being January 1998, the MOU is an annex to the START I treaty that specifies the numbers and locations of the strategic forces located in Belarus, Kazakhstan, Russia, Ukraine, and the United States as of the last updated date. See "START-Related Facilities by Republic as Declared in MOU Data Exchange, Sept. 1, 1990," *Hearings on the START Treaty,* Committee on Foreign Relations, U.S. Senate, 102nd Cong., 2nd Sess., February 6, 1992, p. 496. See also Gen. Roland LaJoie, special briefing on the Cooperative Threat Reduction Program for the Senate Foreign Relations Committee, February 23, 1995; Dunbar Lockwood, "New Data From the Clinton Administration on the Status of Strategic Nuclear Weapons Deactivations," Memorandum, Arms Control Association, Washington, D.C., December 7, 1994; unclassified CIA report, September 1994, as cited in "'Nuclear Weapons Deactivation Continue in FSU," *Arms Control Today,* November 1994. p. 27; Robert S. Norris, "The Nuclear Archipelago," *Arms Control Today,* January/February 1992, p. 25.

A total of 54 SS-25 ICBMs were declared to be on Belarusian territory in the first (December 1990) START I MOU, but 27 additional SS-25s were subsequently deployed. See *Radio Free Europe/Radio Liberty Daily* Report, December 23, 1993, quoting a spokesman from the Belarusian defense ministry. See also "FSU Strategic Nuclear Weapons Outside Russia," Arms Control Association Fact

Sheet, January 1994. The START I treaty did not come into force until December 1994.

[6]See "Texts of Accords by Former Soviet Republics Forming Commonwealth of Independent States," *Facts on File,* 1991, p. 972.

[7]See "Minsk Agreement on Strategic Forces. December 30, 1991," *Arms Control Today,* January/February 1992, p. 39.

[8]See "Documents: Protocol to the Treaty Between the United States of America and the Union of Soviet Socialist Republics on the Reduction and Limitation of Strategic Offensive Arms," *Arms Control Today,* June 1992, p. 33; "START I: Lisbon Protocol and the Nuclear Non-Proliferation Treaty," ACDA Fact Sheet, March 17, 1994.

[9]See Dunbar Lockwood, "Nuclear Weapon Developments," *SIPRI Yearbook* (London: Oxford University Press, 1994); "Chronology of Commonwealth Security Issues," *Arms Control Today,* May 1992, p. 27.

[10]"CTR Programs by Country" and "CTR Obligations by Country/Project," Department of Defense, Office of Cooperative Threat Reduction, February 1995; "Four Ex-Soviet States Share Japanese Aid," *Defense News,* April 11-17, 1994. See Naoaki Usui, "Japan's Denuclearization Programs Take Off in Ex-USSR," *Nucleonics Week,* November 11, 1993, p. 12; Douglas Jehl, "Clinton Promises Help for Belarus Before Changing Focus to Mideast," *New York Times,* January 16, 1994; *Radio Free Europe/Radio Liberty Daily Report,* January 17, 1994.

[11]*Interfax,* December 9, 1995, in *FBIS-SOV-95-237,* December 11, 1995.

[12]Brian Killen, "Russia, Belarus strengthen links, write off debts," *Reuters,* February 27, 1996; *Post-Soviet Nuclear and Defense Monitor,* March 4, 1996, p. 22. The Belarusian demands echoed those made in 1993-94 by Ukraine. Minsk may have perceived that Ukraine received a more favorable settlement from Moscow than Belarus originally obtained. See Ukraine chapter in this volume.

[13]Earlier, on January 18, 1996, Lukashenko cautioned "I am afraid we will have to redeploy in Belarus the nuclear weapons that were withdrawn from it" if NATO expands. In addition to concerns over NATO expansion, Lukashenko was reportedly concerned about the pending Russian presidential elections in June and July. (While President Boris Yeltsin, with whom Lukashenko had worked out a special relationship, was reelected in July 1996, the election could have gone another way—the most likely alternative being the election of Communist Party leader Gennady Zyuganov, probably forcing Belarus to reevaluate its relationship with Russia.) *Financial Times,* January 19, 1996; *OMRI Daily Digest,* June 14, 1996.

[14]Radio Rossii, July 6, 1996, cited by *OMRI Daily Digest* July 8, 1996; *UPI,* September 13, 1996; *OMRI Daily Digest,* October 17, 1996.

[15]Other terms of the START agreement, particularly the destruction of SS-25 launch pads, had not progressed smoothly. According to Belarusian Minister of Environmental Protection and Natural Resources Charnyawski, Belarus suspended pad destruction after one operation to destroy a pad resulted in massive damage exceeding treaty requirements: "Namely, the forest was leveled within a radius of 100 meters around the site of the explosion and the installation was turned into mountains of gravel and concrete debris." Charnyawski said Belarus would resume pad destruction when the United States developed a better method. As of July 1, 1996, 36 launch pads remained to be destroyed. *Zvyazda* (Minsk), October 28, 1996, in *FBIS-SOV-96-198,* October 28, 1996; START Memorandum of Understanding, July 1, 1996.

[16]Of the total funds intended for Belarus, just over $41 million had actually been disbursed by August 5, 1996. Other CTR program elements included emergency response and training equipment ($5 million notified), export control development ($16.26 million notified), and site restoration ($25 million notified). *Weapons of Mass Destruction: Status of the Cooperative Threat Reduction Program,* U.S. General Accounting Office, GAO/NSIAD-96-222, September 1996.

[17]For Japan, see note 10, above. For Germany, see "Belarus: Details on German Aid in 'Liquidating Nuclear Weapons,'" *Belapan* (Minsk), July 4, 1996, in *FBIS-TAC-96-008,* July 16, 1996.

[18]Belarus acceded to the NPT on July 22, 1993, and signed a full-scope safeguards agreement on April 14, 1995. That agreement entered into force on August 2, 1995. Carnegie Endowment for International Peace and Monterey Institute of International Studies, *Nuclear Successor States of the Soviet Union: Nuclear Weapon and Sensitive Export Status Report,* No. 4, May 1996, pp. 5, 61; International Atomic Energy Agency, *The Annual Report for 1995,* p. 64.

[19]See *Nuclear Successor States,* No. 4, op. cit., p. 31; William Potter, *Nuclear Profiles of the Soviet Successor States* (Monterey, CA: Monterey Institute of International Studies, May 1993), p. 7; Mark Hibbs, "U.S.-Ukraine Safeguards Proposal Protested as Dangerous Precedent," *Nucleonics Week,* October 28, 1993, p. 6.

[20]*Nuclear Successor States,* No. 4, op. cit., p. 31.

[21]William Scally, "Key U.S. Senator Says Belarus Stopped Uranium-Smuggling Effort," *Reuters,* November 25, 1993.

[22]*Nuclear Successor States,* No. 4, op. cit., p. 63.

[23]See full text in *The Vector,* Vol. I, No. 1, 1996, p. 26.

[24]"Ten Military Agreements Signed With Belarus," *Interfax,* May 14, 1996, in *FBIS-SOV-96-094,* May 14, 1996, p. 18; "Belarusian President Exaggerates Success in Russia," *OMRI Daily Digest,* September 10, 1996.

[25]*Arms Control Reporter,* 1990, p. 408.B.116.

[26]The Czech Republic, Hungary, and Poland have been invited to become the first three nations of Eastern Europe that NATO will take in as new members in the year 2000. Mirroring Lukashenko's threats to keep the SS-25s in Belarus if NATO enlarges, some Russian officials have suggested that Russia would respond by redeploying tactical nuclear weapons in Belarus. "Parliament Proposes Nuclear-Free Zone," *Itar-Tass,* July 16, 1996, in *FBIS-SOV-96-138,* July 16, 1996; "Official Views Possible NATO Nuclear Threat," *BTK Television Network* (Minsk), May 10, 1996, in *FBIS-SOV-96-095,* May 10, 1996.

Belarus:
Map and Chart

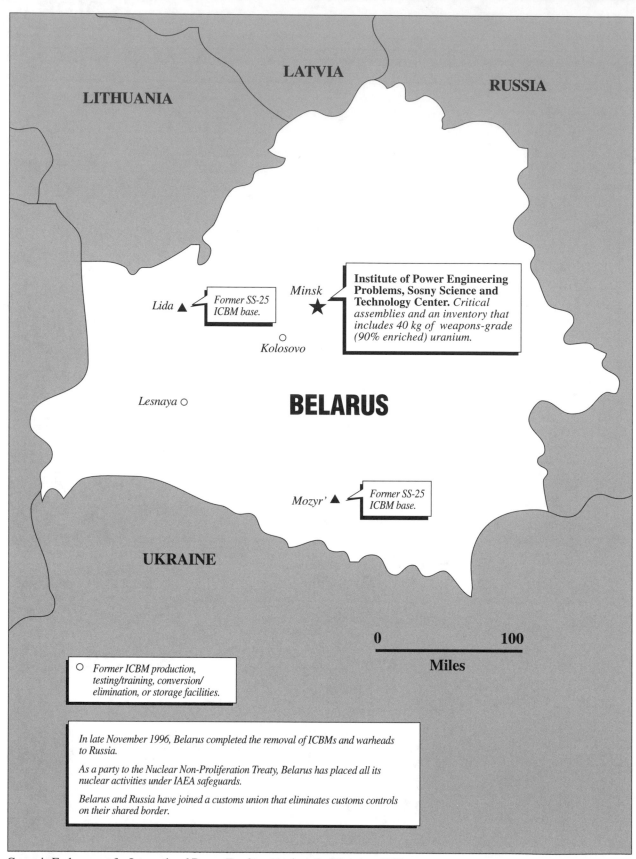

LITHUANIA

LATVIA

RUSSIA

Lida ▲ — Former SS-25 ICBM base.

Minsk ★ — **Institute of Power Engineering Problems, Sosny Science and Technology Center.** *Critical assemblies and an inventory that includes 40 kg of weapons-grade (90% enriched) uranium.*

○ Kolosovo

Lesnaya ○

BELARUS

Mozyr' ▲ — Former SS-25 ICBM base.

UKRAINE

0   100
Miles

○ *Former ICBM production, testing/training, conversion/ elimination, or storage facilities.*

In late November 1996, Belarus completed the removal of ICBMs and warheads to Russia.

As a party to the Nuclear Non-Proliferation Treaty, Belarus has placed all its nuclear activities under IAEA safeguards.

Belarus and Russia have joined a customs union that eliminates customs controls on their shared border.

Carnegie Endowment for International Peace, *Tracking Nuclear Proliferation*, 1998

SOURCES: NIS Nuclear Profiles Database, Center for Nonproliferation Studies, Monterey Institute of International Studies; START Treaty Memoranda of Understanding on Data (MOU), September 1990 - January 1998.

BELARUS: Nuclear Infrastructure and Other Sites of Proliferation Concern[a]

NAME/LOCATION OF FACILITY	TYPE/STATUS	IAEA SAFEGUARDS[b]
NUCLEAR RESEARCH FACILITIES		
Institute for Power Engineering Problems, Sosny, Minsk	Fresh and spent fuel storage; approximately 14 g plutonium and 40 kg weapons-grade HEU present.[c]	Yes
Scientific Research Institute of Nuclear Problems, Belarus State University, Minsk	Research-training facility; no fissile material present.	Yes
RESEARCH REACTORS[d]		
IRT-M (Institute for Power Engineering Problems), Sosny, Minsk	Pool, HEU, 4-8 MWt; decommissioned.	Yes
Critical Assembly No. 1, Sosny, Minsk	Fast critical assembly, LEU; not operating.	Yes
Critical Assembly No. 2, Sosny, Minsk	Fast critical assembly, 90% enriched U; not operating.	Yes
Experimental Reactor, Sosny, Minsk	Neutron generator; operating.[e]	Yes

Abbreviations:

HEU	=	highly enriched uranium
LEU	=	low-enriched uranium
nat. U	=	natural uranium
MWe	=	millions of watts of electrical output
MWt	=	millions of watts of thermal output
KWt	=	thousands of watts of thermal output

NOTES (Belarus Chart)

[a]Belarus cooperated in the removal to Russia of the last nuclear weapons located on its soil in late November 1996. All nuclear warheads had been deployed on Russian SS-25 missiles at Lida and Mozyr'. Angela Charlton, "Belarus Marks Nuke Withdrawal," *Associated Press*, November 27, 1996.

[b]Belarus acceded to the NPT as a non-nuclear-weapon state in July 1993, and the IAEA safeguards agreement entered into force in July 1995.

[c]In addition to the weapons-usable fissile material noted above, 330 kg of non-weapon-grade HEU and approximately 94 kg of LEU are present. See Carnegie Endowment for International Peace and Monterey Institute of International Studies, *Nuclear Successor States of the Soviet Union: Status Report on Nuclear Weapons, Fissile Materials, and Export Controls*, No. 5, March 1998.

[d]Belarus currently has no operational reactors. The two critical assemblies at the Institute for Power Engineering Problems have not been operating due to a lack of funding, although they have not been formally decommissioned. The fuel from these critical assemblies has been moved into the fresh fuel storage facility. K. Murakami et al., "IAEA Safeguards and Verification of the Initial Inventory Declarations in the NIS," paper distributed at a workshop on protection of fissile materials, Stanford University, July 28-30, 1997, p. 3.

In October 1993, Belarusian officials announced preliminary plans to build one or two VVER-type power reactors to help alleviate Belarus's chronic energy shortages. A year later, officials announced that they had discussed alternative reactor projects with Canada, the United States, Germany, and France. No subsequent decision on when and where a reactor might be built has been announced. Mark Hibbs, "Belarus Widens Sphere of Contacts in Bid to Get Nuclear Reactors," *Nucleonics Week*, October 13, 1994, p. 1; and Mark Hibbs, "Energy Strapped Belarus Leans Toward VVER Project," *Nucleonics Week*, October 28, 1993, p. 1.

[e]In July 1997, Belarus announced it had installed a neutron generator, with help from the St. Petersburg Nuclear Physics Institute, for nuclear physics and waste research at Sosny. Lidia Peresypkina, "Neutron generator put into commission near Minsk," *TASS*, July 18, 1997.

Kazakhstan

When the Soviet Union dissolved in December 1991, Kazakhstan was one of four Soviet-successor states with both strategic and tactical nuclear weapons deployed on their territories at independence. Kazakhstan has since been a model state both for cooperating in the removal of nuclear arms from its territory and for fully embracing international nuclear non-proliferation norms. In fulfilling de-nuclearization commitments, Kazakhstan preceded Belarus and Ukraine in removing all nuclear warheads on its soil to Russia and was the first of these three successor states to the Soviet Union's START treaty obligations to join the Nuclear Non-Proliferation Treaty (NPT) as a non-nuclear-weapon state. It has also signed a full-scope safeguards agreement with the International Atomic Energy Agency (IAEA), allowing international inspectors to visit all of its nuclear facilities, and it has accepted U.S. assistance in improving security and materials accounting practices at its nuclear facilities. Kazakhstan has cooperated in securing and shipping to the United States weapons-useable nuclear materials left in storage on its territory, complied with START I requirements to destroy the SS-18 silos on its territory, and cooperated with Russia to remove SS-18 missile airframes, heavy bombers, and associated air-launched cruise missiles (ALCMs). It closed the former Soviet nuclear weapon test site at Semipalatinsk and has signed the Comprehensive Test Ban Treaty (CTBT).

BACKGROUND

Kazakhstan emerged as an independent state in December 1991, with approximately 1,410 strategic nuclear warheads deployed on its territory as well as a still undisclosed number of tactical nuclear arms. The strategic warheads were deployed on 104 ten-warhead SS-18 intercontinental ballistic missiles (ICBMs) and on 370 single-warhead ALCMs, the latter deliverable by Bear-H bombers.[1] Russia, however, retained the military command and control over the strategic missiles and warheads and heavy bomber armament in Kazakhstan, including the arming and launch codes required to use these systems.[2]

Early De-Nuclearization Commitments. With close ties to, and some measure of continued dependency upon Russia, Kazakhstan cooperated from the beginning with Russia's removal of nuclear arms from its territory. Kazakhstan took its first non-proliferation steps when—in cooperation with Belarus, Russia, and Ukraine—it signed the December 21, 1991, Alma-Ata

Declaration on Nuclear Arms. This Declaration provided for Kazakhstan to return to Russia all tactical nuclear weapons on its territory by July 1, 1992. Kazakhstan also undertook not to transfer nuclear weapons on its territory to other post-Soviet states, reflecting an understanding that all strategic nuclear weapons would be removed from Kazakhstan to Russia.[3] (Unlike Belarus and Ukraine, however, Kazakhstan did not then pledge in the Alma-Ata Declaration to join the NPT as a non-nuclear-weapon state.)

In the Minsk accord of December 30, 1991, Kazakhstan agreed, together with the ten other members of the Commonwealth of Independent States (CIS), that a "decision on the need [to use nuclear weapons would be] made by the President of the Russian Federation in agreement with the heads of the Republic of Belarus, the Republic of Kazakhstan, and Ukraine, and in consultation with the heads of the other member states of the Commonwealth."[4] (Arrangements for sharing authority in this area ended in June 1993, when Russia formally took full control over the use of all nuclear arms still present in the other successor states.)

Lisbon Protocol. Under the May 23, 1992, Lisbon Protocol to START I, Kazakhstan agreed to be bound jointly with Belarus, Russia, and Ukraine as successors to START obligations of the former Soviet Union, and to "implement the Treaty's limits and restrictions" (Article II of the Protocol). Kazakhstan also agreed to adhere to the NPT as a non-nuclear-weapon state party "in the shortest possible time" (Article V of the Protocol).[5] In a "side letter" from President Nursultan Nazarbayev to President George Bush, Kazakhstan further pledged to eliminate all nuclear and strategic arms on its territory within the seven-year START I implementation period.

NPT Adherence. Kazakhstan's parliament ratified START I on July 2, 1992, and approved Kazakhstan's accession to the NPT on December 13, 1993. Its NPT instrument of ratification was deposited on February 14, 1994.[6]

De-Nuclearization Steps. By late January 1992—some four months ahead of the schedule established under the Alma-Ata Declaration on Nuclear Arms—all tactical nuclear weapons on Kazakhstan's territory had been withdrawn to Russia.[7]

An agreement on the disposition of strategic nuclear weapons on Kazakhstan's territory was reached at a March 28, 1994, summit between presidents Yeltsin and Nazarbayev. According to press reports, the agreement provided for the withdrawal to Russia of all strategic warheads within 14 months and for the dismantlement of all missile silos in Kazakhstan within three years. This schedule was far more rapid than required under the Lisbon Protocol to START I.

Operation Sapphire. In late 1994, the disclosure that Soviet fissile materials had been stored in Kazakhstan at a facility with only primitive security arrangements graphically illustrated how easily nuclear weapons-usable materials could have been stolen during the aftermath of the Soviet breakup and then diverted to proliferant states or terrorist organizations. The U.S. government announced on November 23, 1994, that approximately 600 kg of highly enriched uranium (HEU)—previously stored behind only a padlocked door at a uranium conversion (UO₂) and fuel pellet production facility at Ust-Kamenogorsk, Kazakhstan— had been air-lifted secretly to the United States in Operation Sapphire.[8] Although the material had been stockpiled for use as fuel in Soviet naval propulsion reactors rather than for nuclear weapons, the bulk of the HEU was in a form that could be used directly for weapons construction, or for weapons fabrication after some additional processing.[9] Kazakhstani officials had become concerned about the material after learning that Iranian government representatives had visited Ust-Kamenogorsk seeking undisclosed nuclear support or materials, according to Bolat Nurgaliyev, then chief of national security and arms control.[10]

U.S. spokesmen noted that the HEU had been transported to the United States in cooperation with the government of Kazakhstan, and in consultation with Russia, to remove the risks of diversion, theft, or smuggling. The United States planned to blend the HEU with natural uranium or LEU to produce fuel for nuclear power plants. Kazakhstan reportedly received $20-30 million in U.S. economic assistance in return for relinquishing the material.[11] The question that many asked in light of this episode was how many other such locations might exist in the former Soviet Union, with fissile materials that could easily be removed and sold in a black market.

IAEA Safeguards. On July 26, 1994, Kazakhstan signed a safeguards agreement with the International Atomic Energy Agency (IAEA), which provides for inspection of all Kazakhstani nuclear activities (excluding Russian-controlled nuclear weapons still then on Kazakh territory). Following signature of the agreement, representatives of the IAEA began "'visiting" a number of facilities on an informal basis until the agreement formally entered into force on August 11, 1995.[12]

Nuclear Infrastructure. Kazakhstan inherited a small number of nuclear facilities, including a commercial-scale nuclear reactor (a fast-breeder reactor) at Aktau; research reactors at the Institute of Nuclear Physics in Almaty and at the Baikal Test Facility in Semipalatinsk; a fuel fabrication facility at Ust-Kamenogorsk; and uranium mines.[13] However, no Soviet ura-

nium-enrichment or plutonium-reprocessing facilities had been built in Kazakhstan. Although Kazakhstan's reactors generally are fueled with low-enriched uranium (LEU), a significant amount of weapons-usable HEU (over 30 kg of HEU, enriched to 90 percent) is located at the Baikal complex.[14] In addition, Kazakhstan has notified the IAEA that more than 200 kg of weapons-grade HEU—left over from the Soviet nuclear rocket engine research program—is stored in rocket fuel at Semipalatinsk.[15] All nuclear materials at Kazakhstani facilities are safeguarded by the IAEA with the exception of the rocket fuel, which Russia claims as its property.[16] In 1993, Russia proposed the construction of an integrated fast-reactor complex at Aktau that would include two or three additional reactors and a spent-fuel reprocessing facility.[17] If this complex were built, Kazakhstan would acquire a plutonium-production capability.

Nuclear Export Controls. Kazakhstan's export control regulations have been under development since 1995. At the outset, Kazakhstani controls were based on decrees rather than national legislation, but laws are being considered that will establish a system of export controls, limit export destinations, and designate responsible government agencies.[18] While a body to coordinate export control administration among different agencies has been absent, plans exist to create a Commission on Export Control. In January 1995, Kazakhstan joined Belarus and Russia in establishing a customs union, which was used to eliminate border checks between the parties.[19] In addition, Kazakhstan entered into negotiations anticipating its eventual joining of the Nuclear Suppliers Group (NSG).

Dismantlement Assistance. U.S. arms dismantlement assistance to Kazakhstan has been channeled through the Cooperative Threat Reduction (CTR) program, also known as the Nunn-Lugar program after its sponsors, Senators Sam Nunn and Richard Lugar. As of March 1993, the United States had proposed $99.9 million in CTR-related contracts, the bulk of which were for the elimination of ICBMs and their silos. Disbursement of these funds began after Kazakhstan's accession to the NPT in February 1994, when President Clinton also promised an additional $311 million in economic assistance to Kazakhstan. Japan signed framework agreements with Kazakhstan and pledged at least $11.43 million to provide assistance for de-nuclearization, improved control over nuclear materials, and environmental clean-up.[20]

DEVELOPMENTS

De-Nuclearization. Kazakhstan preceded Belarus and Ukraine in becoming nuclear-weapon-free and joining the NPT as a non-nuclear-weapon state. According to a Russian Strategic Rocket Forces official, all strategic nuclear warheads remaining in Kazakhstan had been withdrawn to Russia by April 24, 1995.[21] There were no references at the time to Kazakhstan's earlier demand that Russia provide compensation for the fissile material contained either in these strategic weapons or in previously withdrawn tactical nuclear weapons,[22] but the two nations continued to discuss the compensation issue and had negotiated a draft agreement on the subject by November 25, 1995. Under that deal, Kazakhstan would get about 9 percent of all proceeds Russia received as part of its agreement to sell the United States LEU blended down from 500 metric tons of weapons-grade HEU.[23]

Semipalatinsk Nuclear Test Facility. The former Soviet Semipalatinsk Nuclear Test Site, located in northeastern Kazakhstan, was permanently closed to nuclear explosive tests in August 1991, but there were residual problems. Before environmental clean-up of radioactive contamination, something had to be done about the undetonated nuclear explosive device (with an expected yield of approximately 0.4 kt) that had been left in a tunnel 130 meters below the surface of the test site. A Russian-Kazakhstani commission considered removing the device for dismantlement, but safety considerations prevented unearthing it. Instead, the device was destroyed with conventional explosives on May 31, 1995.[24]

In October 1995, Kazakhstan announced a plan to seal the tunnels used for testing at the Degelen mountain and Balapan areas of the Semipalatinsk test site. Using $16 million in assistance from the U.S. CTR program, Kazakhstan is scheduled to close and seal 186 test tunnels in the Degelen mountain range with conventional explosives by fiscal year 1999.[25]

Dismantlement Assistance. By August 1997, the Pentagon had notified Congress that it had allocated a total of $172 million toward CTR-related contracts in Kazakhstan, including $104 million for the destruction of ICBMs and the elimination of missile silos.[26]

In addition to the CTR programs, Kazakhstan is receiving assistance from the U.S. Department of Energy to improve security over materials at its nuclear facilities. Begun in 1994, the Materials Protection, Control, and Accounting (MPC&A) program has been installing improved physical security and inventory controls at Kazakhstan's nuclear facilities at Semipalatinsk, Aktau, and Ust-Kamenogorsk.[27]

Implementing a September 1994 agreement, Japan supplied equipment and instituted an exchange of experts in order to establish a better control and monitoring system for nuclear materials in Kazakhstan. Japan spent $9.36 million to assist Kazakhstan in dismantling functions and in meeting IAEA safeguards obligations.[28] In 1996-97, Japan agreed to provide the BN-350 fast-breeder reactor at Aktau with communication systems equipment and a physical protection system. Japan also plans to conduct medical surveys at the Semipalatinsk nuclear test site to assess the effects of nuclear exposure on local residents. Other countries providing MPC&A assistance to Kazakhstan are Japan, Sweden, and the United Kingdom.[29]

START I Implementation. All nuclear warheads—a total of approximately 1,410 strategic warheads—were withdrawn from Kazakhstan to Russia by April 1995.[30] As of December 1996, all 104 SS-18 heavy ICBM silos deployed in Kazakhstan had been destroyed,[31] all the SS-18 missile airframes in Kazakhstan had been moved to Russia, and 40 heavy bombers and approximately 370 associated ALCMs based in Kazakhstan had been moved to Russia (a few unflyable heavy bombers were still present in early 1997 at the Semipalatinsk air base in Kazakhstan, subject to an agreement to destroy them on site).[32] In addition, as of September 5, 1996, all Russian strategic rocket forces were withdrawn from Kazakhstan.[33] Thus, by the end of 1996, Kazakhstan was free of both nuclear warheads and strategic delivery systems—in early compliance with its START I and Lisbon Protocol obligations.

By allowing the removal of all SS-18 ICBM airframes and launch canisters to Russia for dismantlement, Kazakhstan had eased Russia's ability to comply later with its START II obligation to eliminate all SS-18 heavy ICBMs, including those located outside its territory in Kazakhstan.

The original START I (1990) Memorandum of Understanding on Data indicated that 27 Bear-H6 and 13 Bear-H16 bombers, capable of carrying a total of 370 ALCMs, were deployed in Kazakhstan at the time of the Soviet breakup, but these operable strategic bombers and all ALCMs associated with strategic bombers in Kazakhstan subsequently have been moved to Russia.[34]

Civil Nuclear Infrastructure. Kazakhstan has four civil nuclear sites with both industrial and research facilities. Weapons-usable nuclear material is stored at three of these sites. To improve the security of this material, the United States and Kazakhstan signed an agreement on December 13, 1993, providing for U.S. MPC&A assistance.[35] Kazakhstani nuclear facility staff have been working together with U.S. Department of Energy technical teams to identify ways to improve MPC&A and bring the Kazakhstani facilities up to international standards. As agreed, U.S. assistance focused first on the Ulba Metallurgy Plant, then on the fast-breeder reactor, and finally on the two National Nuclear Center research facilities near Semipalatinsk and Almaty. The Department of Energy continues to provide assistance to all four sites in Kazakhstan to enhance MPC&A systems, techniques, hardware, and software, as well as to provide training.[36]

In 1995, Kazakhstani authorities notified the IAEA that approximately 205 kg of weapons-grade HEU, left over from Soviet-era experiments, was still located at Baikal-1.[37] As the material was claimed by the Russian Federation, it was not subject to IAEA safeguards. After a series of trilateral discussions between Kazakhstan, Russia, and the IAEA, a protocol was signed in which Russia agreed to finance and organize the return of the material to Russian territory.[38]

Although Russia's financial constraints delayed the project, on October 25, 1996, the non-irradiated portion of the material was returned to Russia. There have been subsequent shipments of irradiated material as well, but a portion of the irradiated material remains in storage on-site.[39] The National Nuclear Center has filed a project proposal with the International Science and Technology Center to remove the remaining material to Russia,[40] but as of late 1997, the matter was still unresolved.

The BN-350 sodium-cooled (liquid metal) fast-breeder reactor at Aktau (one unit), which generates power and desalinates water for the Mangyshlyak Peninsula, was designed to use uranium fuel enriched to 17-26 percent, as well as uranium-plutonium mixed-oxide (MOX) fuel (23.19 percent Pu).[41] The BN-350 is capable of generating more than 110 kg of plutonium annually.[42] As Kazakhstan does not return its spent fuel to Russia, at least 3 metric tons of high-grade plutonium in the form of low-irradiated spent fuel from the reactor blanket remain on-site at Aktau in cooling ponds.[43] An IAEA inventory verification is still in progress at this site.[44] In 1990, experiments were conducted in which weapons-grade plutonium-based MOX fuel assemblies were loaded into the reactor. This research and development program, which appears to have been halted in 1991 after Kazakhstan gained independence, foreshadowed proposals by the Russian Ministry of Atomic Energy (Minatom) to introduce plutonium from dismantled warheads into the civilian nuclear fuel cycle.[45]

IAEA Safeguards. Kazakhstan signed a safeguards agreement with the IAEA on July 26, 1994, providing for IAEA inspection of all Kazakhstani nuclear activities. This agreement entered into force on August 11, 1995.[46] On September 4, 1995, the IAEA received from Kazakhstan an initial inventory report on nuclear materials subject to safeguards at the four major sites; as of the end of 1997, the IAEA was still in the process of conducting inventory verifications.[47]

Nuclear Export Controls.[48] Kazakhstan has not joined the multi-national Nuclear Suppliers Group (NSG), but it has agreed to adhere to NSG guidelines[49] and has also expressed interest in joining the group.[50] Given its extensive nuclear industry, it is crucial that Kazakhstan establish nuclear export controls. Kazakhstan has begun this work, but the system is still evolving. The legal basis for Kazakhstani nuclear export controls consists of a series of executive branch decrees and regulations, as well as two national laws. In fact, Kazakhstan was the first newly independent country of the former Soviet Union to pass comprehensive legislation on non-proliferation export controls.

On February 9, 1993, Kazakhstan reached an agreement with five other members of the CIS to cooperate in controlling exports on items that could be used to manufacture weapons of mass destruction.[51] As with most CIS agreements, however, little has been done to implement coordinated export control policies. Coordination was discussed most recently on October 29,

1997, in efforts to harmonize national laws and to institutionalize an export control mechanism under the aegis of the CIS's Council of Foreign Ministers.[52]

A complication in efforts to control the export of sensitive technologies from former Soviet states is the reduction or elimination of border controls along internal FSU borders. On January 6, 1995, Kazakhstan, Belarus, and Russia agreed to establish a Customs Union, which will abolish tariffs and customs controls along their common borders. Kyrgyzstan joined this Customs Union on March 29, 1996. Kazakhstani Resolutions No. 367 and No. 381, passed on September 6 and September 19, 1995, respectively, established the legal basis in Kazakhstan for the Customs Union. Russia and Kazakhstan have eliminated tariffs and trade volume restrictions and no longer operate most major customs checkpoints along their common border.[53] However, as of early 1998, the Customs Union had not yet been fully implemented on the Russia-Kazakhstan border.[54]

Other Nuclear Arms Control. Kazakhstan has closed down the Semipalatinsk nuclear weapon test site (see above), and it signed the Comprehensive Test Ban Treaty on September 30, 1996.

Chemical and Biological Arms Control. Kazakhstan is not believed to possess chemical or biological weapons, but a former Soviet biological weapons production facility is located at Stepnogorsk. Kazakhstani officials have indicated that they plan to convert the plant, with U.S. CTR program assistance appropriated in 1997, into a vitamin-production facility.[55]

PROSPECTS

After Russia, Kazakhstan is the largest of the new states to emerge from the breakup of the Soviet Union. With vast natural resources, especially oil and gas, and a population of only 16 million, it has favorable economic development prospects—provided it manages political and social reform successfully. These prospects have been enhanced in considerable measure by Kazakhstan freeing itself voluntarily of the former Soviet nuclear weapons deployed on its territory and by its accession to the NPT as a non-nuclear-weapon state. Its early compliance with these commitments was a major source of reassurance for the future stability of the non-proliferation regime.

Kazakhstan's path to a more prosperous future may be troubled by regional and even domestic political instability, however. It is important that the U.S. Cooperative Threat Reduction and Department of Energy assistance programs for weapons dismantlement, MPC&A, and nuclear clean-up be well funded and energetically implemented to enable Kazakhstan to secure and manage the residual nuclear infrastructure—including the substantial array of research facilities built there by the former Soviet Union. Kazakhstan's cooperation with Russia in developing export control and customs measures to prevent nuclear theft and smuggling through its borders needs to be monitored, but also should be commended and encouraged as a necessary beginning. Apart from Russia, no former Soviet state is more pivotal than Kazakhstan in combating the dangers of loose nukes and black-market nuclear materials. Fortunately, Kazakhstan has embarked on a consistent path since 1993, first complying steadily with de-nuclearization, and then committing itself to full participation in the nuclear non-proliferation regime. This good record greatly reduces the danger that nuclear proliferation will take root in Central Asia.

NOTES

[1]The basic source for these figures, as well as for those in the chart that follows, is the START I Treaty Memorandum of Understanding on Data (MOU). Initially declared as of September 1, 1990, and current as of January 1998, the MOU is an annex to START I that specifies the numbers and locations of the strategic forces of the United States and the Soviet Union as of the initial date and as of each six-month update after treaty entry into force. See also "START-Related Facilities by Republic as Declared in MOU Data Exchange—Sept. 1, 1990," *Hearings on the START Treaty*, Committee on Foreign Relations, U.S. Senate, 102nd Cong., 2nd Sess., February 6, 1992, p. 496. See also Gen. Roland LaJoie, Deputy for Cooperative Threat Reduction to the Assistant to the Secretary of Defense for Atomic Energy, special briefing on the Cooperative Threat Reduction Program for the Senate Foreign Relations Committee, February 23, 1995; Dunbar Lockwood, "New Data From the Clinton Administration on the Status of Strategic Nuclear Weapons Deactivations," Memorandum, Arms Control Association, Washington, D.C., December 7, 1994; Unclassified CIA report, September 1994, as cited in "Nuclear Weapons Deactivation Continues in FSU," *Arms Control Today*, November 1994, p. 27.

[2]Russia also had "administrative control" over the ICBMs, i.e., Russia was responsible for the security of the missiles and the administration of the missile facilities. See Carnegie Endowment for International Peace and Monterey Institute of International Studies, *Nuclear Successor States of the Soviet Union: Nuclear Weapon and Sensitive Export Status Report*, No. 4, May 1996, p.10.

[3]See "Texts of Accords by Former Soviet Republics Forming Commonwealth of Independent States," *Facts on File*, 1991, p. 972.

[4]See "Minsk Agreement on Strategic Forces, December 30, 1991," *Arms Control Today*, January/February 1992, p. 39.

[5]"Documents: Protocol to the Treaty Between the United States of America and the Union of Soviet Socialist Republics on the Reduction and Limitation of Strategic Offensive Arms," *Arms Control Today*, June 1992, p. 33; "START I: Lisbon Protocol and the Nuclear Non-Proliferation Treaty," ACDA Fact Sheet, March 17, 1994.

[6]Inasmuch as Kazakhstan had never asserted control of any kind over the nuclear weapons on its territory, the strategic nuclear arms remaining there after Kazakhstan joined the NPT were deemed to be Russian arms for the purposes of the treaty and their presence did not impair Kazakhstan's status as a non-nuclear-weapons state under the accord. All nuclear weapons had been withdrawn from Kazakhstan by April 1995.

[7]See "Chronology of Commonwealth Security Issues," *Arms Control Today*, May 1992, p. 27.

[8]R. Jeffrey Smith, "U.S. Takes Nuclear Fuel," *Washington Post*, November 23, 1994; Steven Erlanger, "Kazakhstan Thanks U.S. on Uranium," *New York Times*, November 25, 1994.

[9]Interviews with U.S. officials, December 1994.

[10]Rowan Scarborough, "Tale Told of How Iran Nearly Got Nuke Gear," *Washington Times*, November 2, 1996.

[11]Ibid.; Smith, "U.S. Takes Nuclear Fuel," op. cit.; Erlanger, "Kazakhstan Thanks U.S. on Uranium," op. cit. A later concern that the shipment was not complete was satisfactorily resolved. See Rowan Scarborough, "Kazakh Uranium Shipment is Shy Enough for Two Bombs," *Washington Times*, October 24, 1996.

[12]International Atomic Energy Agency, *The Annual Report for 1995*, p. 65; See "Kazakhstani-IAEA Safeguards Agreement: Hans Blix in Almaty," *Sovety Kazakhstana*, August 19, 1994, in *JPRS-TND-94-016*, August 19, 1994, p. 54; "Nuclear Safeguards Pact Signed with IAEA," *Nuclear News*, September 1994, p. 92.

[13]Kazakhstan's uranium reserves comprise 25 percent of the world's prospected uranium reserves, according to specialists cited by a Kazakhstani journal. Prospected reserves in the country total 926,000 metric tons and there are an estimated 700,000 metric tons not yet prospected, but low world uranium prices currently make the extraction of Kazakhstani uranium uneconomical. "Foreign Cooperation in Uranium Industry Development Viewed," *Delovaya Nedelya* (Almaty), September 20, 1996, in *FBIS-SOV-96-190*, September 20, 1996.

[14]William Potter, *Nuclear Profiles of the Soviet Successor States* (Monterey, CA: Monterey Institute of International Studies, 1993), p. 19.

[15]William Potter, "Nuclear Leakage from the Post-Soviet States," testimony before the Permanent Subcommittee on Investigations, U.S. Senate Committee on Governmental Affairs, March 13, 1996.

[16]Jessica Eve Stern, "Nunn-Lugar Activities to Improve Fissile Material Protection, Control, and Accountability in the Former Soviet Union," in John Shields and William Potter, eds., *The Nunn-Lugar Cooperative Threat Reduction Program: Donor and Recipient Country Perspectives* (Cambridge, MA: MIT Press, 1998).

[17]See Mark Hibbs, "Russian Industry Seeks Pact for Kazakhstan FBR Complex," *Nucleonics Week*, December 16, 1993, p. 14.

[18]For early assessment of Kazakhstan's nuclear export controls, see Potter, *Nuclear Profiles of the Soviet Successor States*, op. cit., pp. 16-32; and B. Ayaganov, "Nuclear Export Controls in Kazakhstan," a paper prepared for the CIS Non-Proliferation Project, Monterey Institute of International Studies, April 1993.

[19]"Yeltsin Lifts Customs Controls at Kazakhstan Border," *ITAR-TASS*, January 3, 1996 in *FBIS-SOV-96-002*, January 3, 1996.

[20]"CTR Programs by Country" and "CTR Obligations by Country/Project," Department of Defense, Office of Cooperative Threat Reduction, February 1995; *Nuclear Successor States of the Soviet Union*, No. 4, op. cit., p. 23; "Four Ex-Soviet States Share Japanese Aid," *Defense News*, April 11-17, 1994. See also Naoaki Usui, "Japan's Denuclearization Programs Take Off in Ex-USSR," *Nucleonics Week*, November 11, 1993, p. 12; "Japan to Provide Nuclear System to Kazakhstan," *Reuters*, September 6, 1996.

[21]This was confirmed by the Kazakhstani Foreign Ministry on May 24, 1995. See Doug Clarke, "Kazakstan Free of Nuclear Weapons," *OMRI Daily Digest*, April 26, 1995; Doug Clarke, "Kazakstan Confirms It Is Nuclear Free," *OMRI Daily Digest*, May 25, 1995, p. 3; Prepared Remarks of U.S. Undersecretary of Defense for Policy Walter B. Slocombe before the Senate Armed Services Committee, May 17, 1995.

The evacuation of the remaining nuclear weapons appears to have followed the agreement signed at the March 28, 1994, summit between Russian President Yeltsin and Kazakhstani President Nazarbayev, under which all nuclear weapons in Kazakhstan were to be removed to Russia within 14 months, and all SS-18 ICBM silos and missiles in Kazakhstan were to be dismantled by a three-year deadline. Kazakhstan adhered to the transfer schedule, completing the transfer of all warheads, containing more than 44 metric tons of weapons-grade HEU, by the spring of 1995.

Although Kazakhstan was not a party to START II, Russia undertook in that treaty to physically destroy all the former Soviet SS-18 ICBMs (the missile airframes and launch canisters), including those located in Kazakhstan, for which it had to obtain Kazakhstan's separate cooperation.

[22]See *Radio Free Europe/Radio Liberty Daily Report*, May 4, 1994.

[23]Kazakhstan also received fighter aircraft, including 21 MiG-29s and 32 MiG-31s by the end of 1995, as part of the compensation package. Kazakhstan agreed to use the aircraft to participate in joint air-defense efforts with Russia. "Russia-Kazakhstan Protocol on Nuclear Munitions Recycling," *Rossiskaya Gazeta*, November 25, 1995, in *FBIS-TAC-95-007*, December 27, 1995, pp. 55-57; "Kazakhstan to Receive Military Jets From Russia," *OMRI Daily Digest*, November 13, 1995; International Institute for Strategic Studies, *The Military Balance 1995/96* (London: Oxford University Press for IISS, 1996), p. 152.

[24]The Russian-Kazakhstani commission had considered removing the device and shipping it to the Chelyabinsk-70 nuclear center for further disassembly. Concern over a possible accident, however, led the commission to recommend that the device be destroyed by conventional explosives. The device, which was to be used in a 1991 physical irradiation experiment, had been buried in a tunnel 592 meters long and approximately 130 meters from the surface. When the test range was closed in August 1991, the test was never conducted, and the undetonated bomb was left buried in Degelen Mountain until its subsequent destruction. Bruce Pannier, "Kazakhstan Nuclear-Free," *OMRI Daily Digest*, June 1, 1995, p. 3; Douglas Busvine, "Kazakhstan to Blow Up Four-Year-Old Nuclear Device," *Reuters*, May 25, 1995; Bruce Pannier, "Kazakhstan to Explode Nuclear Device," *OMRI Daily Digest*, May 24, 1995, p. 2; "Nuclear Bomb to be Removed from Kazakhstan Test Site," *Komsomolskaya Pravda*, May 13, 1994, in *FBIS-SOV-94-093*, May 13, 1994, pp. 13-14.

[25]See "U.S.–Kazakstan Agreement to Seal Up World's Largest Nuclear Test Tunnel Complex," U.S. Department of Defense News Release, October 3, 1995; "Deal Signed to Seal Former Soviet Nuclear Test Site," *Reuters*, October 3, 1995; "U.S. and Kazakhstan Agree Details on Closing Semipalatinsk Test Site," *Nuclear Proliferation News*, October 12, 1995, p.14; "Kazakhstan Defends Nuclear Arms Control Record," *Reuters*, October 4, 1996; "U.S. Officials to Witness Destruction of Nuclear Site," Kazakh Television, March 26, 1996, in *FBIS-SOV-96-061*, March 26, 1996; Joseph Harahan, "The Kazakhstan Center for Monitoring Arms Reductions and Supporting Inspection Activities," *On-Site Insights*, June 1996, pp. 6-7; Emily Ewell, "Trip Report: "International Conference on Non-Proliferation Problems," Kazakhstan, September 1997.

[26]"Cooperative Threat Reduction," U.S. Department of Defense, August 1997, pp. 12f.

[27]*Nuclear Successor States of the Soviet Union,* No. 4, op. cit., pp. 32-33.

[28]"Disarmament Assistance to Kazakhstan," *Kyodo*, September 6, 1994, translated in *JPRS-TAC-94-012-2*, September 6, 1994.

[29]Interview with Kazakhstani nuclear official by Center for Non-Proliferation Studies' staff, May 1997.

[30]See section on de-nuclearization and its citations in this chapter. A Russian Strategic Missile Forces official stated in February 1995 that 632 [strategic] warheads had been withdrawn from Kazakhstan and 266 remained. This total of 898 strategic warheads, far less than the 1,410 warheads attributable to strategic delivery systems under START I counting rules, suggests that a portion of the 104 SS-18s deployed in Kazakhstan were actually single-warhead Mod. 1/3/6 versions. "Strategic Missile Forces Chief Interviewed," *Krasnaya Zvezda*, February 8, 1995, in *FBIS-SOV-95-027*, February 9, 1995, p. 15; Dunbar Lockwood, "New Data on the Strategic Arsenal of the Former Soviet Union," *Jane's Intelligence Review*, June 1995, pp. 246-49.

[31]"Last Russian Nuclear Missile Silos Destroyed," *ITAR-TASS*, September 6, 1996, in *FBIS-SOV-96-174*, September 6, 1996; "Russia Completes Withdrawal of Nuclear Military Facilities," Kazakh Television, September 5, 1996, in *FBIS-SOV-96-174*, September 5, 1996.

[32]See Table 1-C for Kazakhstan (Nuclear Weapons Systems and Associated Warheads), and citations, Carnegie Endowment for International Peace and Monterey Institute of International Studies, *Nuclear Successor States of the Soviet Union: Status Report on Nuclear Weapons, Fissile Material, and Export Controls,* No. 5, March 1998.

[33]"Russia Completes Withdrawal of Nuclear Military Facilities," Kazakh Television, September 5, 1996, in *FBIS-SOV-96-174*, September 5, 1996.

[34]*Radio Free Europe/Radio Liberty Daily Report,* February 23, 1994. According to the December 1995 START MOU, seven unrepaired Bear-G heavy bombers, which cannot be relocated due to their condition, are located at Semipalatinsk air base. The July 1997 START MOU indicated that elimination of the bombers will be carried out on-site according to the schedule agreed to by Kazakhstan and the United States. See General LaJoie, special briefing on the CTR Program, op. cit.; Dunbar Lockwood, "New Data From the Clinton Administration," op. cit.; International Institute for Strategic Studies, *The Military Balance 1994/95* (London: Oxford University Press for IISS, 1994), p. 149.

[35]U.S. Department of Energy Public Information, Office of Non-Proliferation and National Security, January 27, 1995.

[36]G. Tittemore et al. , "United States Assistance to Kazakhstan in the Area of Nuclear Material Security," *United States/Former Soviet Union: Program of Cooperation on Nuclear Materials Protection, Control and Accounting*, Department of Energy Nuclear Material Security Task Force, December 1996, p. NIS 5.

[37]Interviews with U.S. administration official, December 18, 1995, and Kazakhstani nuclear official, May 1997, by Center for Non-Proliferation Studies' staff. See also "More HEU Said To Be in Kazakhstan," *Nuclear Fuel*, December 4, 1995, p. 2.

[38]Interview with Kazakhstani nuclear official, op. cit.

[39]Presentation by William C. Potter at the American Nuclear Society, November 11, 1996; and Center for Non-Proliferation Studies staff discussions with Baikal-1 reactor site engineers, September 1997.

[40]Correspondence with Kazakhstani nuclear official by Center for Non-Proliferation Studies' staff, March 1997.

[41]*Nuclear Engineering International: World Industry Handbook 1992*, p. 58.

[42]V. Shmelev, "Estimation of the Quantities of Nuclear Materials at the Facilities in the New Independent States," unpublished manuscript, Monterey Institute of International Studies, December 1992.

[43]Interview with U.S. government official by Center for Non-Proliferation Studies, April 1996. Kazakhstani officials have preliminary plans either to store the material at Aktau indefinitely, or to move it to a site at the former Semipalatinsk nuclear test range, currently under the auspices of the National Nuclear Center. See Mark Hibbs, "Lack of Home for Vitrified Waste Stalls Aktau Spent Fuel Transport," *Nuclear Fuel*, October 20, 1997, p. 6.

[44]K. Murakami et al., "IAEA Safeguards and Verification of the Initial Inventory Declarations in the NIS," paper distributed at the workshop on "A Comparative Analysis of Approaches to the Protection of Fissile Materials," Stanford University, July 28-30, 1997.

[45]Oleg Bukharin and William Potter, "Kazakhstan: A Nuclear Profile," *Jane's Intelligence Review*, April 1994, p. 184.

[46]"Situation on 31 December 1996 with respect to the Conclusion of Safeguards Agreements between the Agency and Non-Nuclear-Weapons States in Connection with NPT," International Atomic Energy Agency homepage (http://www.iaea.org).

[47]Murakami et al., "IAEA Safeguards and Verification," op. cit.

[48]See section on "Kazakhstan" in 2-A of Carnegie Endowment and Monterey Institute, *Nuclear Successor States* No. 5, op. cit.

[49]*Nuclear Successor States of the Soviet Union,* No. 4, op. cit.

[50]Discussion with Kazakhstani nuclear official, Center for Non-Proliferation Studies' staff, summer 1997.

[51]"Six CIS States Join Forces to Enforce Export Control," *ITAR-TASS* (Moscow), February 9, 1993, in *FBIS-SOV-93-026*, February 10, 1993.

[52]Sergei Ryabikin, "Representatives of CIS States Discuss Export Control Over Products Used for the Creation of Mass Destruction Weapons," *RIA Novosti Hotline*, October 29, 1997.

[53]"Derbisov on Customs Affairs, Security," *Kazakhstanskaya Pravda,* August 30, 1995, in *FBIS-SOV-95-173*, August 30, 1995.

[54]Correspondence with Alexander Pikayev, Carnegie Moscow Center, January 1998.

[55]"U.S. to Increase Aid for Conversion of Nuclear Weapons," Kazakh Television, June 10, 1996, in *FBIS-SOV-96-113*, June 10, 1996; Office of the Secretary of Defense, *Proliferation: Threat and Response,* November 1997, p. 56.

Kazakhstan:
Map and Chart

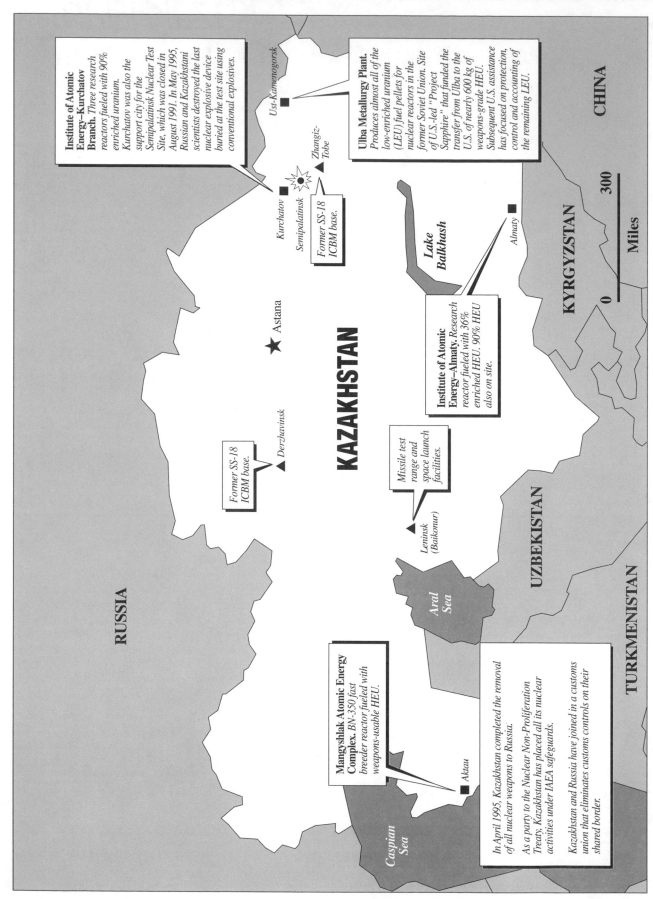

Institute of Atomic Energy–Kurchatov Branch. *Three research reactors fueled with 90% enriched uranium. Kurchatov was also the support city for the Semipalatinsk Nuclear Test Site, which was closed in August 1991. In May 1995, Russian and Kazakhstani scientists destroyed the last nuclear explosive device buried at the test site using conventional explosives.*

Ulba Metallurgy Plant. *Produces almost all of the low-enriched uranium (LEU) fuel pellets for nuclear reactors in the former Soviet Union. Site of U.S.-led "Project Sapphire" that funded the transfer from Ulba to the U.S. of nearly 600 kg of weapons-grade HEU. Subsequent U.S. assistance has focused on protection, control and accounting of the remaining LEU.*

Institute of Atomic Energy–Almaty. *Research reactor fueled with 36% enriched HEU. 90% HEU also on site.*

Former SS-18 ICBM base.

Former SS-18 ICBM base.

Missile test range and space launch facilities.

Mangyshlak Atomic Energy Complex. *BN-350 fast breeder reactor fueled with weapons-usable HEU.*

In April 1995, Kazakhstan completed the removal of all nuclear weapons to Russia.

As a party to the Nuclear Non-Proliferation Treaty, Kazakhstan has placed all its nuclear activities under IAEA safeguards.

Kazakhstan and Russia have joined in a customs union that eliminates customs controls on their shared border.

RUSSIA

Ust-Kamenogorsk

Kurchatov

Semipalatinsk

Zhangiz-Tobe

Astana

Derzhavinsk

KAZAKHSTAN

Lake Balkhash

Almaty

KYRGYZSTAN

CHINA

Leninsk (Baikonur)

Aral Sea

UZBEKISTAN

TURKMENISTAN

Caspian Sea

Aktau

0   300

Miles

Carnegie Endowment for International Peace, *Tracking Nuclear Proliferation*, 1998

SOURCES: NIS Nuclear Profiles Database, Center for Nonproliferation Studies, Monterey Institute of International Studies; START Treaty Memoranda of Understanding on data (MOU), September 1990 - January 1998.

KAZAKHSTAN: Nuclear Infrastructure and Other Sites of Proliferation Concern

NAME/LOCATION OF FACILITY	TYPE/STATUS	IAEA SAFEGUARDS[a]
N U C L E A R W E A P O N S F A C I L I T I E S		
Derzhavinsk	Former ICBM base; the last SS-18 silos were destroyed in 1996. All nuclear weapons and heavy bombers were removed to Russia earlier.	No
Zhangiz Tobe	Former ICBM base.	No
Semipalatinsk	Former Soviet nuclear test range (closed August 1991). Former Soviet strategic bomber base; all bombers and associated ALCMs transferred to Russia.	
Leninsk (Baikonur)	Missile test range and space launch facilities.	
Kurchatov (Semipalatinsk-21)	Possible former nuclear weapon assembly facility.	
N U C L E A R R E S E A R C H C E N T E R S		
Institute of Atomic Energy, Almaty (also Institute of Nuclear Physics)	Hot cell facilities and nuclear material storage; seven laboratories including cyclotron, HEU present; see below for research reactor.	Yes
P O W E R R E A C T O R S		
Aktau	BN-350 (sodium-cooled, fast-breeder), medium-enriched uranium, 335 MWe.[b]	Yes
R E S E A R C H R E A C T O R S		
Institute of Nuclear Physics, Almaty	WWR-K, 36% HEU, 10 MWe; resumed operation in December 1997.	Yes
Almaty	Critical assembly; operating.	Yes
IGR (Baikal Test Facility) Semipalatinsk	Graphite-moderated, water-cooled, fueled with 90% HEU; operating. HEU reactor fuel in storage; some Russian-owned HEU (not safeguarded).	Yes
IVG-1M, Semipalatinsk	60 MWt reactor; 90% HEU; operating.	Yes
RA, Semipalatinsk	0.4 MWt experimental reactor, 90% HEU; operating.	Yes
U R A N I U M P R O C E S S I N G		
Stepnogorsk	Uranium mining; operating.	Yes
Ulba Metallurgy Plant, Ust-Kamenogorsk	Uranium conversion facility (UO_2) and fuel pellet production for VVER and RBMK reactors; operating.	

Abbreviations:

HEU	=	highly enriched uranium
LEU	=	low-enriched uranium
nat. U	=	natural uranium
MWe	=	millions of watts of electrical output
MWt	=	millions of watts of thermal output
KWt	=	thousands of watts of thermal output

NOTES (Kazakhstan Chart)

[a]As required by its adherence to the NPT, Kazakhstan signed a full-scope safeguards agreement with the IAEA, which entered into force on August 11, 1995, that subjects all nuclear materials and activities in Kazakhstan to IAEA monitoring.

[b]By agreement between the Kazakhstan Atomic Energy Agency, Russia's Gosatomnadzor, and the U.S. Nuclear Regulatory Commission, Russia reprocesses the spent fuel from this reactor and will eventually return the final nuclear waste to Kazakhstan. See Carnegie Endowment for International Peace and Monterey Institute for International Studies, *Nuclear Successor States of the Soviet Union: Nuclear Weapons and Sensitive Export Status Report*, No. 4, May 1996, p. 32.

Ukraine

As Ukraine pressed for independence in 1990-91—with the Chernobyl tragedy embedded in the public's mind—the Ukrainian government pledged to become nuclear-weapons free. But after independence, when Ukraine's tensions with Russia mounted on the issue of dividing post-Soviet assets and its economy started downhill, Ukrainian leaders had second thoughts about independent control over the nuclear weapons on Ukrainian soil. Following an intensive trilateral diplomatic process with both Russian and Western involvement, however, Ukraine on December 5, 1994, acceded to the Nuclear Non-Proliferation Treaty (NPT) as a non-nuclear-weapon state. Ukraine also agreed then on a final schedule for the withdrawal of the nuclear weapons remaining on its territory. The removal of nuclear weapons was completed in June 1996, when the last of more than 4,400 nuclear weapons originally located in Ukraine arrived in Russia.[1] Security assurances by the nuclear-weapon states, Western economic and technical assistance, energy concessions by Russia, and the benefits of broader integration in Europe and the world economy all played a part in this de-nuclearization outcome.

Since its accession to the NPT as a non-nuclear-weapon state, Ukraine has taken many other steps consistent with international non-proliferation norms. It signed a comprehensive safeguards agreement with the International Atomic Energy Agency (IAEA) on September 21, 1995, and its parliament ratified this agreement on December 17 the same year. Ukraine was admitted to the Nuclear Suppliers Group (NSG) in April 1996 and has instituted a nuclear export control regime that meets international standards. It has readily accepted U.S. and other Western assistance in improving the security and materials accounting practices at its nuclear facilities. Moreover, Ukraine has sought to work out with the United States an agreement for peaceful nuclear cooperation, although on this matter Ukraine's nuclear export ambitions, which could involve nuclear equipment supply to Iran, have surfaced as a "serious irritant in an otherwise close relationship" with Washington.[2] In addition, Ukraine has expressed its intent to become a member of the Missile Technology Control Regime (MTCR) and has agreed to adhere to the MTCR guidelines for missile technology transfers, but reaching common understandings on permissible missile-related trade has proved difficult (see Missile Proliferation chapter in this volume).

BACKGROUND

Soviet Nuclear Legacy. Following the breakup of the Soviet Union in December 1991, Ukraine—with a population of 50 million (large by European standards) and a substantial industrial sector—emerged as an independent state of some weight. The former Soviet nuclear weapons and delivery systems located on Ukraine's territory would have constituted the world's third largest nuclear arsenal, had Ukraine seized sovereign control over them. The strategic nuclear weapons were deployed on 46 ten-warhead SS-24 ICBMs (total of 460 warheads), 130 six-warhead SS-19 ICBMs (780 warheads), 25 Bear-H16 strategic bombers, each capable of carrying up to 16 warheads on air-launched cruise missiles (ALCMs), and 19 Blackjack strategic bombers, each carrying up to twelve warheads on ALCMs.[3] In addition, between 2,650 and 4,200 former Soviet tactical nuclear weapons were estimated to have been deployed or stored in Ukraine, although all had been removed to Russia by May 1992.[4]

Unlike Belarus and Kazakhstan, which stayed on comparatively close terms with Russia and cooperated on the removal of nuclear arms to Russia, Ukraine was concerned about the division of former Soviet financial assets, and Russia's potential claim to the Black Sea port of Sevastopol and the Crimea, a Russian-majority province. Ukraine was therefore tempted to try to become an independent nuclear-weapon state and threatened, until early 1994, to retain the nuclear weapons on its territory. As a result, Ukraine's progress toward de-nuclearization appeared halting and erratic. Ukraine's ambivalence was reflected in an executive-legislative battle that resulted in the postponement of the de-nuclearization and non-proliferation commitments Ukraine had announced unilaterally in 1990 and 1991, and those negotiated in the Lisbon Protocol to START I.

Early De-Nuclearization Commitments. In declaring independence on December 1, 1991, Ukraine's government had unequivocally renounced the possession of nuclear weapons and affirmed the intent to become a nuclear-weapon-free state. On December 21, 1991, Ukraine pledged in the Alma-Ata Declaration on Nuclear Arms, along with Belarus and Kazakhstan, to join the NPT as a non-nuclear-weapon state, and to return to Russia by July 1, 1992, all tactical nuclear weapons present on its territory. Ukraine also agreed not to transfer nuclear weapons on its territory to any other states, except Russia, reflecting the understanding that it would remove all strategic nuclear weapons to Russia.[5] However, Ukraine's parliament, the Verkhovna Rada, neglected to ratify this executive accord, and later claimed that it was not binding on Ukraine.

In the Minsk Agreement on Strategic Forces of December 30, 1991, Ukraine again made a series of nuclear pledges, promising that all nuclear weapons on its territory would be dismantled by the end of 1994 (with the dismantling of tactical nuclear weapons to be completed by July 1, 1992). The Minsk Agreement also stipulated that a "decision on the need [to use nuclear weapons would be] made by the president of the Russian Federation in agreement with the heads of the Republic of Belarus, the Republic of Kazakhstan, and Ukraine, and in consultation with the heads of the other member states of the Commonwealth."[6] (Arrangements for sharing authority in this area ended in June 1993, when Russia formally took full control over the use of all nuclear arms in the post-Soviet states.) Once again, however, the Rada did not ratify the agreement, undercutting its credibility.

Ukraine's Second Thoughts. Ukraine's military commanders never acquired independent control over the launch mechanisms for use of the strategic missiles deployed in Ukraine. Russian military officers and units never relinquished the arming and targeting codes necessary to fire the missiles or detonate the warheads. Nevertheless, shortly after independence had been secured in December 1991, Kiev insisted on the right to block Russia's unilateral use of the weapons that were deployed in Ukraine. In March 1992, Ukraine began to consider retaining some of the weapons and temporarily halted the transfer of tactical nuclear weapons to Russia.[7] In June 1992, in the first of several steps to establish a political claim and some form of control over the nuclear arms on its soil, Ukraine asserted what it called "administrative control" over the strategic bombers, air-launched cruise missiles, and silo-based ICBMs by replacing the Russian soldiers who were guarding them with Ukrainian forces.[8] In late 1992 and early 1993, Ukraine also publicly claimed ownership of warhead components as a means of establishing its right to get financial compensation for the energy value of the plutonium and highly enriched uranium (HEU) they contained. Ukraine also asserted ownership of the strategic delivery vehicles (i.e., bombers and missiles).[9] These challenges to Russian control over nuclear weapons in Ukraine coincided with a highly publicized debate in the Rada on whether the country should keep nuclear weapons to ensure its security against what many Ukrainians perceived to be the Russian threat to their still fragile independence.

Lisbon Protocol to START I. On May 23, 1992, Ukraine's President Leonid Kravchuk signed the Lisbon Protocol to START I, under which Ukraine agreed to be bound by START I—jointly with Belarus, Kazakhstan, and Russia, as successors to the obligations of the former Soviet Union—and to "implement the Treaty's limits and restrictions" (Article II of the Protocol). Ukraine also agreed to adhere to the NPT as a non-nuclear-weapon state party "in the shortest possible time" (Article V of the Protocol). In a side letter to President George Bush, President Kravchuk also pledged to eliminate all nuclear and strategic arms on Ukrainian territory within the seven-year START I implementation period.[10]

In deliberating on the Lisbon Protocol, the Rada passed a resolution on November 18, 1993, purportedly to "ratify" START I; but it also attached a number of qualifications and conditions, some of which attempted to undercut the Lisbon Protocol and Kravchuk's de-nuclearization commitment, and therefore were unacceptable to Russia and the United States. The resolution declared that only 36 percent of the former Soviet Union's strategic delivery vehicles and 42 percent of its strategic warheads deployed on Ukrainian territory would be subject to elimination under the START treaty, allowing Ukraine to retain the remainder on its territory indefinitely. This not only contradicted the commitment in President Kravchuk's Lisbon letter but also could have been construed as a bid by Ukraine for nuclear-weapon-state status.

Furthermore, the Rada made the elimination of the remaining strategic nuclear warheads and delivery vehicles conditional on Ukraine's receiving aid to cover dismantlement costs, compensation for nuclear materials to be extracted from the warheads, and complex security guarantees. At the same time, the Rada resolved that Ukraine was not bound by Article V of the Lisbon Protocol, the provision that called for Ukraine's quick accession to the NPT as a non-nuclear-weapon state, and, by implication, established Ukraine's obligation to relinquish all nuclear weapons.[11] Coming in the wake of Ukraine's growing assertion of administrative control over the strategic nuclear arms still on its territory, this new challenge by the Rada triggered a period of intensive negotiations among Ukraine, Russia, and the United States.

Turning the Corner: The Trilateral Statement. The result of stepped-up negotiations with Ukraine was a deal that satisfied a number of Ukraine's practical concerns and that was reflected in the January 14, 1994, Trilateral Statement. Signed by Presidents Kravchuk, Clinton, and Yeltsin, the statement was a key turning point that would lead, eventually, to Ukraine's fulfillment of its de-nuclearization and non-proliferation pledges. Under its terms, Ukraine would cooperate in the withdrawal to Russia of all remaining nuclear weapons—approximately 1,800 were still on Ukrainian soil—over a period that could not exceed seven years.[12] In Russia, the warheads would be dismantled, and the highly enriched uranium (HEU) extracted from the warheads would be blended down to low-enriched uranium (LEU). Some of the LEU, in turn, would be put in the form of fuel pellets in fuel rods and transferred to Ukraine for use in its nuclear power reactors, in compensation for relinquishing the energy value of the uranium in the strategic warheads. In addition to power reactor fuel, Ukraine would also receive U.S. economic aid and U.S. technical assistance for the safe, secure dismantlement of its strategic nuclear arms. Russia and the United States promised to provide security assurances to Ukraine upon Ukraine's accession to the NPT.

Acting on the deals made in the Trilateral Statement, the Rada on February 3 approved a resolution instructing Kravchuk to exchange the instruments of ratification of START I. The resolution acknowledged that Article V of the Lisbon Protocol, which called for three successor states' rapid adherence to the NPT as non-nuclear-weapon states, applied to Ukraine after all. The Rada also implicitly endorsed the Trilateral Statement. It did not at that juncture, however, specifically approve accession to the NPT.[13]

Although the Trilateral Statement alluded to a seven-year dismantlement schedule, Ukraine and Russia privately agreed in one of several confidential "side letters" that Ukraine would cooperate in the removal of all nuclear warheads on its territory to Russia within three years.[14] Russia promised to forgive large portions of Ukraine's debt for energy supplies as compensation for Ukraine's prior transfer of tactical nuclear weapons to Russia.[15]

On November 16, 1994, the Rada took the next step to confirm its de-nuclearization commitments, approving Ukraine's accession to the NPT. Once again, however, it imposed a condition, making Ukraine's accession contingent upon its first receiving security guarantees by the nuclear-weapon states. The nuclear-weapon states had already prepared documents in consultation with Ukraine's executive leadership to satisfy this condition. Security assurances were finally conveyed in the form of a multilateral memorandum, to be signed by the United Kingdom, the United States, and Russia. The draft text was made available to Ukraine's authorities just before the Rada's vote on November 16, 1994.

NPT Accession and START I's Entry into Force. The Summit of the Conference on Security and Cooperation in Europe (CSCE) that was held in Budapest on December 5, 1994, was chosen as the occasion for the United Kingdom, the United States, and Russia to convey their identical security assurances to Ukraine, as well as similar assurances to Kazakhstan and Belarus.[16] France also provided a security assurance to Ukraine at the CSCE summit in a separate document. On the same occasion, Ukraine presented its instruments of accession to the NPT. This action, together with the earlier accessions by Belarus and Kazakhstan, satisfied Russia's conditions for exchanging the instruments of ratification for START I. Consequently, at the same meeting, the United States, Russia, Belarus, Kazakhstan, and Ukraine exchanged their START I instruments of ratification, finally bringing the treaty into force.[17]

Dismantlement Assistance. U.S. assistance for the safe, secure dismantlement of Ukrainian nuclear weapons is provided for under the Cooperative Threat Reduction (CTR) program, also known as the "Nunn-Lugar" program, after its sponsors, Senators Sam Nunn and Richard Lugar. On March 4, 1994, during the visit of President Kravchuk to Washington, President Clin-

ton announced that the United States would nearly double its aid to Ukraine over the next year to $700 million. This amount included an increase in dismantlement-related funds to $350 million and an increase in conventional economic assistance from the $155 million announced in January 1994 to $350 million. However, the slow pace of disbursal of dismantlement-related funds—only $6 million by August 1994—became an issue in U.S.–Ukrainian relations in the summer of 1994. Japan signed framework agreements with Ukraine to provide assistance for de-nuclearization and environmental clean-up and pledged $17.08 million for those purposes.[18]

De-Nuclearization. Ukraine's de-nuclearization process was guided by the Trilateral Statement noted earlier, which called for a phased process of missile de-activation and removal of nuclear weapons to Russia. In the first phase, which was to be completed by mid-November 1994, all SS-24 ICBMs on Ukrainian territory were to be de-activated. In fact, by early December 1994, Ukraine had not only de-activated all its SS-24s, but it had also de-activated 40 out of its 130 SS-19s. Second, the Trilateral Statement called for Ukraine to remove at least 200 warheads from its SS-19s and SS-24s to Russia by mid-November.[19] By February 1995, it had withdrawn a total of 420 SS-24, SS-19, and heavy bomber warheads back to Russia.[20] (For later steps, see Developments section below.)

Nuclear Infrastructure. Ukraine's nuclear power program comprises five stations, each with a number of reactors either operating or under construction. These stations are located at Pripyat/Chernobyl, Neteshin, Kuznetsovsk, Kostantinovsk, and Energodar.[21] The country's nuclear research base includes the Institute for Nuclear Research in Kiev, housing a 10-MWe research reactor, and the Defense Ministry's High Marines School at Sevastopol, which also has a research reactor.[22]

There are no reprocessing or uranium-enrichment plants in Ukraine that would give it the capability to produce weapons-usable plutonium or highly enriched uranium (HEU). However, the Kharkiv Physical-Technical Institute had in its possession up to 75 kg of weapons-grade HEU in bulk form enriched up to 90 percent, a matter of proliferation concern before IAEA safeguards came into place in 1995.[23] Ukraine also has several heavy-water production plants located in Dnepropetrovsk with the capacity to produce about 250 metric tons of such material per year.[24]

IAEA Safeguards. A full-scope IAEA safeguards agreement that Ukraine had signed on September 28, 1994, came into force on January 13, 1995, opening the door for routine inspections of all Ukrainian nuclear facilities (the nuclear weapons on Ukrainian territory were not subject to IAEA inspections). An NPT-type safeguards agreement had not been placed into effect at that time, although negotiations were under way.

Nuclear Export Controls. Ukraine's domestic export control system for nuclear and nuclear-related technology and materials remained in the process of development in early 1995. Although several presidential decrees had established a government body to administer export controls, these decrees were yet to be replaced by more permanent national legislation. Some progress on this front was achieved in February 1995 when the Rada approved the Law on Nuclear Energy Utilization and Radiation Safety.[25]

Missile Program. Ukraine inherited important components of the Soviet missile production industrial base, which it planned to utilize for the manufacture of space launch systems for export. This infrastructure, however, also gives Ukraine the capability to produce or export strategic and theater ballistic missiles. Certain space equipment is already being produced at the Yuzhmash Plant, formerly the SS-18 (heavy) ICBM production facility at Dnepropetrovsk. Moreover, the former SS-24 production plant at Pavlograd, which is also believed to be operating, may be engaged in solid-fuel space launch vehicle research and development activities.[26] In a memorandum of understanding signed in Washington on May 13, 1994, Ukraine agreed to conduct its missile- and space-related exports according to the criteria and standards of the Missile Technology Control Regime (MTCR),[27] but Ukraine did not find it easy to meet all the requirements of this regime and still is not a member.

DEVELOPMENTS

De-Nuclearization. The final steps in the de-nuclearization of the three successor states—the removal of all strategic warheads from Belarus, Kazakhstan, and Ukraine to Russia—took place in 1995 and 1996. Kazakhstan's de-nuclearization was the first to be accomplished, and Ukraine's took just over a year longer. Guided by a schedule connected with the Trilateral Statement, Ukraine shipped batches of 60 strategic warheads to Russia about every two months during 1994-96. Approximately 3,068 nuclear weapons located on Ukraine's soil in 1990 had all been withdrawn to Russia by June 1996.[28] About 1,800 of these nuclear weapons were associated with strategic delivery systems.[29] Removal of mobile ICBMs and strategic warheads from Belarus was accomplished five months later.

START I Implementation in Ukraine. Implementation of the reductions prescribed for the Soviet successor states by START I proceeded rapidly after the treaty's entry into force on December 5, 1994, and, as of the fall of 1997, was more than a year ahead of schedule in meeting the first phase of START I reductions.[30] While all strategic nuclear warheads were removed from Belarus, Kazakhstan, and Ukraine by November 1996, some strategic delivery systems in those states had yet to be eliminated. According to the treaty, this elimination could take up to seven years after entry into force (i.e., until December 2001), but both the United States and Russia have encouraged a more rapid reduction process in Belarus, Kazakhstan, and Ukraine. Russia salvaged heavy bombers and air-launched cruise missiles from their previous basing locations in Kazakhstan, for instance, and seriously considered purchasing the 44 heavy bombers located in Ukraine.[31]

As for reductions of the strategic delivery systems in Ukraine, of the 130 SS-19 ICBM silos present in 1991, 107 had been destroyed by December 1997, with the remainder to be destroyed in 1998; the 46 SS-24 ICBM silos and all 55 SS-24 solid-fuel ICBMs in Ukraine were scheduled to be destroyed in 1998 with U.S. Cooperative Threat Reduction (CTR) assistance; and 44 heavy bombers remain in Ukraine, subject to elimination.[32] Ukraine has plans to eliminate all of its formerly deployed 130 SS-19 missiles (airframes) with U.S. CTR assistance, and it has signed an agreement to sell 43 non-deployed SS-19 missiles (the "spares" inventory) to Russia, since Russia may continue to deploy SS-19 missiles under START II.[33]

Dismantlement Assistance. While the disbursement of CTR funds was slow to begin (with only $6 million disbursed by August 1994), the pace accelerated thereafter. By August 1996, more than $158 million had been disbursed for Ukraine, and the U.S. Department of Defense had planned CTR assistance projects for Ukraine totaling about $396 million, including $243 million for eliminating strategic nuclear weapons.[34] In addition, the United States had pledged $350 million in conventional economic assistance, much of which was provided immediately after Ukraine's January 1994 reaffirmation of its commitment to remove all nuclear weapons to Russia. As of late 1997, $446 million in CTR assistance had been notified to Congress. The largest category of CTR assistance to Ukraine was for "strategic nuclear arms elimination," for which $318 million had been notified.[35] Significant assistance had also been committed to Ukraine for industrial partnerships (defense conversion), material control and accounting, the science and technology center (funding for scientists for non-military research), and development of nuclear export controls; and some additional U.S. Department of Energy funds had been disbursed for Materials Protection, Control, and Accounting systems (MPC&A).[36]

A number of other countries and entities have provided dismantlement assistance, or related economic assistance, to Ukraine. Since 1995, Germany, for example, has assisted Ukraine in developing techniques for missile silo elimination. In 1996, Japan funded two projects: one for an MPC&A system at the Kharkiv Institute, and another that provided medical equipment and pharmaceutical supplies for military personnel engaged in dismantling strategic systems.[37]

Nuclear Infrastructure. The research reactor at the Kiev Institute of Nuclear Research (INR), shut down since 1993 to address safety problems, was being considered for restart in November 1997 but had not received a license from the State Nuclear Inspectorate. The research reactor is a 10-MW pool-type reactor built in 1960. A Western-type physical protection system is expected to be in place soon under a $3.6 million joint U.S.–Ukraine program.[38]

Nuclear Safeguards. Ukraine had signed a full-scope safeguards (*sui generis*) agreement on September 28, 1994, allowing IAEA inspection of all Ukrainian nuclear activities; this agreement had been in force since January 13, 1995.[39] However, because Ukraine had not yet acceded to the NPT when it signed the September 1994 safeguards agreement, it was required to sign a second safeguards agreement in accordance with its obligations as a non-nuclear-weapon state party to the NPT. This second, NPT-type safeguards agreement—which was signed on September 21, 1995, and ratified by the Rada on December 17, 1997—superseded the 1994 agreement.[40]

Nuclear Export Controls. Ukraine has received assistance for, and has been responsive in improving, its internal legal and personnel arrangements for nuclear export controls. Ukraine was formally admitted into the Nuclear Suppliers Group (NSG) on April 20, 1996, at the NSG plenary meeting in Buenos Aires, after having attended earlier NSG meetings as an observer.[41] However, a major issue has arisen between the United States and Ukraine on a specific nuclear export case, and this in turn has held up the finalization of a U.S.–Ukraine agreement for peaceful nuclear cooperation. Turboatom, a heavy equipment vendor in the Ukrainian city of Kharkiv, has developed lucrative arrangements with Russia to build special turbines for the 1,000-MWe nuclear power reactor at Bushehr in Iran. Russia would install these turbines as part of its construction contract with Iran. The United States opposes Russia's nuclear deal with Iran and is attempting to persuade Ukraine to forego its turbine sale. Ukraine's prospects for importing nuclear power technology from the United States and for certain other forms of U.S. assistance are at stake. The accord was eventually signed in May 1998 after Ukraine pledged to end its nuclear cooperation with Iran.[42]

Missile Technology Control Regime. Ukraine has declared its readiness to adhere to the MTCR guidelines and has applied for membership, but it has not been accepted yet as a formal member of the MTCR. Ukraine has not been willing to meet the U.S. conditions of membership,[43] which call for Ukraine to demonstrate the effective implementation of export controls, to end production of MTCR-limited missiles, and to renounce possession of its MTCR-class ballistic missiles (including Scud missiles).[44] Ukraine has so far rejected these conditions because it seeks a place in the global space launch and conventional arms markets.[45] In addition, there have been reports of Russian and Ukrainian technical exchanges with China on ballistic missile guidance—possibly related to SS-18 multiple-warhead dispensing (MIRV) capabilities. Russia

still depends on Ukraine for the manufacture of some of the guidance and control components that it needs for its ICBMs and SLBMs, and the production plants may seek overseas customers for such technology.[46]

Other Arms Control. Ukraine signed the Comprehensive Test Ban Treaty (CTBT) on September 27, 1996, and has also signed the Chemical Weapons Convention (CWC) but not yet ratified it. Ukraine has no chemical weapons program, although there may be remnants there of the former Soviet chemical warfare infrastructure. Ukraine also has no biological weapons program.[47]

PROSPECTS

Ukraine's fulfillment of its de-nuclearization commitments and adherence to the nuclear non-proliferation regime requirements was indispensable to avoiding tension across a wide range of political and economic relationships with European and other Western countries and critical also to security and stability in Central Europe. Despite Ukraine's solid nuclear non-proliferation commitments since 1994, however, Ukraine's export activities remain a source of concern, as illustrated by the dispute with the United States over Ukraine's interest in supplying nuclear equipment to Iran, and in Ukraine's efforts to market ballistic and cruise missiles.

The tragic accident at the Chernobyl nuclear power plant remains a matter of serious regional concern, since the containment of the structure that experienced a meltdown and gas explosions is breaking down and contamination could leak out. The danger of another leak is a matter of intense attention by the European Union (which would like to see the other reactors of that type in Ukraine shut down), as well as by the IAEA and others among its member states. The Chernobyl experience may cement Ukraine's dedication to nuclear safeguards and controls, including those needed for careful nuclear export policies.

Tensions between Russia and Ukraine have been managed, on the whole, relatively well. Yet there have been worrisome episodes, and they could recur—especially if Ukraine's economy does not progress more efficiently. Ukraine has lagged in applying the needed reforms to convert the economy to market incentives, and it is therefore likely to pay a higher price later; it may find it harder to reduce its almost total dependence on both Russian oil and natural gas supplies, and its continued export dependence on the vast interior Russian market. In March 1997, a breakthrough occurred between Russia and Ukraine—one that arguably is critical for their ability to cooperate in the future—with the conclusion of a Friendship and Cooperation Treaty and an agreement on the division of the Black Sea Fleet (clarifying Russian access to the naval port of Sevastopol).

NOTES

[1] "Kuchma Issues Statement on Removal of Nuclear Weapons," *UT-1 Television*, June 1, 1996, in *FBIS-SOV-96-107*, June 5, 1996.

[2] See "Nuclear Exports" in the Developments section of this chapter.

[3] The basic source for these figures, as well as for those in the chart that follows, is the START I Memorandum of Understanding (MOU) on Data. Current as of January 1998, the MOU is an annex to START I, which specifies the numbers and locations of the strategic forces of the United States and former Soviet Union declared as of September 1, 1990, with regular six-month data updates that have been declared since the treaty entered into force in December 1994. See *The Treaty Between the United States of America and the Union of Soviet Socialist Republics on the Reduction and Limitation of Strategic Offensive Arms, signed in Moscow on July 31, 1991* (Washington, DC: U.S. Arms Control and Disarmament Agency, 1991). Also see "START-Related Facilities by Republic as Declared in MOU Data Exchange–Sept. 1, 1990," Hearings on the START Treaty, the Committee on Foreign Relations, U.S. Senate, 102nd Cong., 2nd Sess., February 6, 1992, p. 495.

The START MOU under-counts the number of gravity bombs and air-to-surface ballistic missiles, and even of ALCMs, that heavy bombers can carry, attributing 8 to each Soviet ALCM-equipped heavy bomber. The actual equipage of the Blackjack and the Bear-H are 12 and 16 ALCMs respectively, and these are the numbers to be used for START II. See Dunbar Lockwood, "FSU Strategic Nuclear Weapons Outside Russia," Arms Control Association Fact Sheet, January 1994. See also Gen. Roland LaJoie, Deputy for Cooperative Threat Reduction to the Assistant Secretary of Defense for Atomic Energy, special briefing on the Cooperative Threat Reduction Program for the Senate Foreign Relations Committee, February 23, 1995; Dunbar Lockwood, "New Data from the Clinton Administration on the Status of Strategic Nuclear Weapons Deactivations," Memorandum, Arms Control Association, December 7, 1994; Unclassified CIA report, September 1994, as cited in "Nuclear Weapons Deactivation Continue in FSU," *Arms Control Today*, November 1994, p. 27.

[4] See "U.S. Confident on Soviet A-Weapons," *New York Times*, December 16, 1991; "57 Percent of Arms Removed," *Komsomolskaya Pravda*, March 26, 1992, in *FBIS-SOV*, March 26, 1992, pp. 3-4; "Chronology of Commonwealth Security Issues," *Arms Control Today*, May 1992, p. 27.

[5] See "Texts of Accords by Former Soviet Republics Forming Commonwealth of Independent States," *Facts on File*, 1991, p. 972.

[6] See "Minsk Agreement on Strategic Forces, December 30, 1991," *Arms Control Today*, January/February 1992, p. 39.

[7] "Ukraine Says Arms Transfer Delay Temporary," *Reuters*, March 25, 1992.

[8] In June 1992, the Ukrainian Defense Ministry established the Center for the Administrative Command and Control of the Troops of the Strategic Nuclear Forces, setting up a dual administrative structure with Russia for controlling the strategic nuclear forces. See "Ukraine Said Seeking Command of Nuclear Forces," *Izvestiya*, June 11, 1992, in *FBIS-SOV*, June 11, 1992, p. 2. Ukrainian scientists also reportedly initiated work during 1992 on developing the capability to bypass the codes for using the nuclear weapons in Ukraine, but there are no indications that any such efforts were successful. Naturally, Ukraine exercised administrative and flight control over the strategic bombers based on its territory.

[9] Under the START treaty's Lisbon Protocol, Ukraine undertook to eliminate "all nuclear and strategic arms" located on its territory. The treaty's procedures for elimination do not preclude transfer of strategic arms to Russia, and do not necessarily require the physical elimination of strategic *missiles* (airframes, fuel), even though the *launchers* in Ukraine are to be eliminated and must be physically destroyed during the seven-year period of reductions of strategic offensive arms. Even where missiles themselves must be eliminated, as in the case of mobile ICBMs that exceed treaty limits, strategic missiles may be used as space launch vehicles (this means their elimination by launch) but, for Ukraine, this is permissible using strategic missiles only for as long as the reductions period lasts.

[10] "Documents: Protocol to the Treaty Between the United States of America and the Union of Soviet Socialist Republics on the Reduction and Limitation of Strategic Offensive Arms," *Arms Control Today*, June 1992, p. 33; "START I: Lisbon Protocol and the Nuclear Non-Proliferation Treaty," ACDA Fact Sheet, March 17, 1994.

[11] *Arms Control Today*, June 1992, p. 34; "Parliament Ratifies START I Treaty, Lisbon Protocol," *Interfax* (Moscow), November 18, 1993, in *FBIS-SOV-93-222*, November 19, 1993, p. 45; "Supreme Council START I Ratification Resolution," *UNIAR* (Kiev), November 18, 1993, in *FBIS-SOV-93-222*, November 19, 1993, p. 45.

[12] General LaJoie, special briefing on the CTR Program, op. cit. In congressional testimony in October 1994, Assistant Secretary of Defense Ashton Carter reported that there were 1,734 warheads in Ukraine prior to the initiation of the dismantlement process in January 1994, as opposed to 1,564 warheads as cited in the START I Memorandum of Understanding (MOU). See Testimony of Assistant Secretary of Defense Ashton Carter, before the Senate Foreign Relations Committee, October 4, 1994.

[13] John W. R. Lepingwell, "Ukrainian Parliament Removes START-I Conditions," *Radio Free Europe/Radio Liberty Research Report*, February 25, 1994, p. 37.

[14] The confidential side agreement to the Trilateral Statement that stipulated the three-year schedule for warhead withdrawal from Ukraine was formalized by Ukraine's acting Prime Minister Yefim Zvyagilsky and Russian Prime Minister Viktor Chernomyrdin on May 16, 1994. See "Ukraine Pledges to Double Speed of Disarmament," *Reuters*, May 19, 1994.

[15] Dunbar Lockwood, "U.S. Reaches Understanding with Ukraine, Russia on Denuclearization," *Arms Control Today*, January-February 1994, pp. 19-20.

[16] The security assurance text (identically worded in each country's assurance) was as follows:

1. The United States of America, the Russian Federation, Ukraine, and the United Kingdom of Great Britain and Northern Ireland reaffirm their commitment to Ukraine, in accordance with the principles of the CSCE Final Act, to respect the independence and sovereignty and the existing borders of Ukraine.

2. The United States of America, the Russian Federation, Ukraine, and the United Kingdom of Great Britain and Northern Ireland reaffirm their obligation to refrain from the threat or use of force against the territorial integrity or political independence of Ukraine, and that none of their weapons will ever be used against Ukraine except in self-defense or otherwise in accordance with the charter of the United Nations.

3. The United States of America, the Russian Federation, Ukraine, and the United Kingdom of Great Britain and Northern Ireland reaffirm their commitment to Ukraine, in accordance with the principles of the CSCE Final Act, to refrain from economic coercion designed to subordinate to their own interest the exercise by Ukraine of rights inherent in its sovereignty and thus to secure advantages of any kind.

4. The United States of America, the Russian Federation, Ukraine, and the United Kingdom of Great Britain and Northern Ireland reaffirm their commitment to seek immediate United Nations Security Council action to provide assistance to Ukraine, as a non-nuclear-weapon State Party to the Treaty on the Non-Proliferation of Nuclear Weapons, if Ukraine should become victim of an act of aggression or an object of a threat of aggression in which nuclear weapons are used.

5. The United States of America, the Russian Federation, Ukraine, and the United Kingdom of Great Britain and Northern Ireland reaffirm their commitment not to use nuclear weapons against any non-nuclear-weapon State Party to the Treaty on the Non-Proliferation of Nuclear Weapons, except in the case of an attack on themselves, their territories or dependent territories, their armed forces, or their allies, by such a state in association or alliance with a nuclear weapon state.

6. The United States of America, the Russian Federation, Ukraine, and the United Kingdom of Great Britain and Northern Ireland will consult in the event a situation arises which raises a question concerning these commitments.

[17] See "Text of Resolution Detailing NPT Reservations," *Kiev Radio Ukraine World Service in the Ukraine*, in *FM FBIS London UK*, November 16, 1994; "Ukraine Joins Treaty Curbing Nuclear Arms," *Washington Post*, November 17, 1994; "Ukraine Accedes to NPT Treaty," *United Press International*, December 5, 1994; "Remarks by President Clinton at Signing of Denuclearization Agreement," *Federal News Service*, December 5, 1994; "France Signs NPT Security Guarantee Document," *Interfax* (Moscow), December 5, 1994, in *FBIS-SOV-94-234*, December 6, 1994, p. 44.

[18]"CTR Programs by Country" and "CTR Obligations by Country/ Project," Department of Defense, Office of Cooperative Threat Reduction, February 1995; Carnegie Endowment for International Peace and Monterey Institute of International Studies, *Nuclear Successor States of the Soviet Union: Nuclear Weapon and Sensitive Export Status Report,* No. 2, December 1994, p. 24; "Four Ex-Soviet States Share Japanese Aid," *Defense News,* April 11-17, 1994. See also Naoaki Usui, "Japan's Denuclearization Programs Take Off in Ex-USSR," *Nucleonics Week,* November 11, 1993, p. 12; William Potter, *Nuclear Profiles of the Soviet Successor States* (Monterey, CA: Monterey Institute of International Studies, 1993), p. 81.

[19]Although START I would have allowed up to seven years, after entry into force, as the timetable for the withdrawal (or elimination) of all the strategic systems, a protocol signed by Ukraine's acting Prime Minister Yefim Zvyagilsky and Russian Prime Minister Victor Chernomyrdin on May 16, 1994, obligated Ukraine to withdraw all nuclear warheads to Russia within three years of the signing of the Trilateral Statement. See "Ukraine Pledges to Double Speed of Disarmament," *Reuters,* May 19, 1994.

[20]See General LaJoie, special briefing on the CTR Program, op. cit. In congressional testimony in October 1994, Assistant Secretary of Defense Carter reported that there were 1,731 warheads in Ukraine prior to the initiation of the dismantlement process in January 1994, as opposed to 1,564 warheads as cited in the START I Memorandum of Understanding (MOU). See Testimony of Assistant Secretary Carter, op. cit.

[21]Potter, *Nuclear Profiles,* op. cit., p. 83; Monterey Institute of International Studies, *CIS Nonproliferation Database,* January 1995; and International Atomic Energy Agency, *The Annual Report for 1995,* July 1996, p. 81.

[22]See Potter, *Nuclear Profiles,* op. cit., p. 87.

[23]*Nuclear Successor States of the Soviet Union,* op. cit., No. 4, May 1996, p. 41.

[24]Mark Hibbs, "Nonproliferation Policy on Hold, Kiev's Heavy Water at Issue," *Nuclear Fuel,* August 17, 1992, p. 8.

[25]*Nuclear Successor States of the Soviet Union,* op. cit., No. 4, May 1996, p. 71.

[26]U.S. Congress, Office of Technology Assessment, *Technologies Underlying Weapons of Mass Destruction,* OTA-BPISC-I 15, December 1993, p. 12; "Perry Visits Strategic Missile Unit," Moscow, *ITAR-TASS,* March 22, 1994, in *FBIS-SOV-94-056,* March 23, 1994, p. 27; "Implementation of Lisbon Protocol," *Hearings on the START Treaty,* Committee on Foreign Relations, U.S. Senate, 102nd Cong., 2nd Sess., June 23, 1992, p. 199.

As a result of the breakup of the Soviet Union's armed forces, Ukraine has also inherited a number of advanced tactical strike aircraft that could be used to carry nuclear weapons. They include the MiG-29 Fulcrum, Su-24 Fencer, Tu-22/26 Blinder, and MiG-27 Flogger D. See International Institute for Strategic Studies, *The Military Balance 1993/94* (London: Oxford University Press for IISS, October 1993), p. 91; OTA, *Technologies Underlying WMD,* op. cit., pp. 235, 243.

[27]The MTCR restricts exports of missiles and related technology with respect to systems able to deliver weapons of mass destruction to a distance of more than 300 km. Space launch vehicles are, by definition, ballistic missiles—even though they are not equipped to deliver weapons.

[28]"Kuchma Issues Statement on Removal of Nuclear Weapons," *UT-1 Television,* June 1, 1996, in *FBIS-SOV-96-107,* June 5, 1996.

[29]Office of the Secretary of Defense, *Proliferation: Threat and Response,* November 1997, p. 43.

[30]Ibid., p. 41.

[31]On February 2, 1995, Ukraine agreed to sell to Russia all of its strategic bombers. Russian experts estimated the value of the total bomber force at $75 million, a tiny fraction of their original cost. It proved difficult, however, to reach agreement on a price. Russian officials noted that Ukraine plans to use this money to reduce its enormous energy debt to Russia. See Anton Zhigulsky, "Future of Disputed Black Sea Fleet Remains Uncertain," *Defense News,* March 13-19, 1995, p. 8; "Russia Says Ukraine to Hand Over Strategic Bombers," *Reuters,* February 24, 1995. As of late 1997, the Russian government appeared to have lost interest in the bombers in Ukraine, having learned that they were not in good operating condition and would be very expensive to put back into operation. Given the Russian sentiment, Ukraine requested U.S. assistance for the destruction of the bombers. See Barbara Starr, "Stalemate on 'Scuds' As Latest US-Kiev Talks Fail," *Jane's Defence Weekly,* July 23, 1997.

[32]At first reluctant, Ukraine finally agreed to physically eliminate the SS-19 missiles (airframes) that had been deployed in Ukraine, and later agreed to eliminate the SS-24 missiles. This was not strictly required by the terms of the START I treaty (which generally focuses on the elimination of the launchers), but physical elimination has been encouraged by the U.S. dismantlement assistance (Nunn-Lugar) program. For details on both launchers and missiles destroyed, and on the status of strategic bombers in Ukraine, see Table 1-C for Ukraine, "Nuclear Weapons Systems and Associated Warheads," *Nuclear Successor States of the Soviet Union,* op. cit., No. 5, March 1998.

[33]*Proliferation: Threat and Response 1997,* op. cit., p. 47.

[34]U.S. General Accounting Office, "Weapons of Mass Destruction: Status of Cooperative Threat Reduction," GAO-NSIAD-96-222, September 1996, pp. 30-31.

[35]See *Nuclear Successor States of the Soviet Union,* No. 5, op. cit., Table I-F, "Cooperative Threat Reduction."

[36]See "Cooperative Threat Reduction Program: Summary of Obligations and Disbursements by Country/Project," Department of Defense, Assistant to the Secretary of Defense (Atomic Energy), Office of Cooperative Threat Reduction, May 15, 1995; "U.S. Assistance and Related Programs for the New Independent States of the Former Soviet Union: 1994 Annual Report," Department of Defense, Office of Cooperative Threat Reduction, January 1995; "Semi-Annual Report on Program Activities to Facilitate Weapons Destruction and Nonproliferation in the Former Soviet Union," Department of Defense, Office of Cooperative Threat Reduction, October 30, 1994; "Weapons of Mass Destruction: Status of Cooperative Threat Reduction Program," U.S. General Accounting Office, Report to Congress, September 1996; "Cooperative Threat Reduction: Status of Defense Conversion Efforts in the Former Soviet Union," U.S. General Accounting Office, Report to the House Committee on National Security, April 1997; Office of Nonproliferation and National Security, U.S. Department of Energy, "MPC&A Program Strategic Plan," January 1998.

[37]See *Nuclear Successor States of the Soviet Union,* No. 5, op. cit., Table I-F, "Other Disarmament Assistance Programs."

[38]Alexei Breus, "Ukraine Research Reactor Nears Restart After Four-Year Overhaul," *Nucleonics Week,* November 6, 1997.

[39]"Ukraine: International Organizations and Treaties," *NIS Nuclear Profiles Database,* Center for Nonproliferation Studies, Monterey Institute of International Studies.

[40]Correspondence with Ukrainian official from Ministry of Environmental Protection and Nuclear Safety, by Center for Nonproliferation Studies' staff, January 1998. See IAEA, *The Annual Report for 1995,* p. 68; *Nuclear Successor States of the Soviet Union,* No. 5, op. cit., p. 6.

[41]Emily Ewell, John Parachini, and William Potter, "Ukrainian Nuclear Export Controls: A Status Report," Center for Nonproliferation Studies, Monterey Institute of International Studies, prepared for the Office of Nonproliferation and Arms Control at the U.S. Department of Energy, December 1996.

[42]"U.S., Ukraine Sign Nuclear Cooperation Accord," *Agence France Presse,* May 6, 1998.

[43]The United States has three primary conditions that nations must meet to join the MTCR: (1) they must be party to the NPT (or equivalent), the CWC, and the BWC; (2) they must have "substantially effective" export control mechanisms in place and have a successful track record of implementation; and (3) they must forgo possession of Category I offensive military systems (with the exception of China and Russia, which may retain ICBMs because of their status as established nuclear-weapon states). Discussion with U.S. official, December 6, 1996.

Ukraine, however, was not ready to accept these conditions and was instead seeking a special status of MTCR membership due to its extensive past experience with missile production and related industrial infrastructure. At a workshop in Kiev in May 1996, two Ukrainian officials explained that Ukraine wanted to retain the right to produce MTCR-class ballistic missiles. The preservation of Ukraine's established technological capabilities was considered key to its survival, and some observers believed the United States was mistaken to place Ukraine in the same category as other new MTCR members (including Hungary, Switzerland, and Luxembourg) that had no missile production industries. See John C. Baker, *Non-Prolifer-*

ation Incentives Project: Aerospace Industries Workshop and Ukraine Trip Report, International Institute for Strategic Studies, August 1996.

[44]Ukraine's short-range ballistic missile arsenal includes 132 Scud-Bs (considered to be MTCR-class missiles) and 140 SS-21s (not MTCR-class because of their 120-km range). See International Institute for Strategic Studies, *The Military Balance, 1995/96* (London: Oxford University Press for IISS, 1996), p. 100.

[45]In April 1995, for example, Ukraine entered into an agreement with firms in the United States, Russia, and Norway to create a consortium, Sea Launch Co. Ltd., to produce a sea-based satellite launching system. Sea Launch Co. received its first order in December 1995 to launch at least ten Hughes satellites beginning in 1998. Under the plan, Boeing (United States) will provide overall management and will provide port facilities in Long Beach, California; Kvaerner A.S. (Norway) will build a modified self-propelled oil-drilling platform to serve as the launch vehicle transporter and launch pad; NPO-Yuzhnoye (Ukraine) will provide most components of the launcher, based on a Zenit space launch vehicle; and RSC-Energia (Russia) will provide the upper stage of the launcher. See *Space Launch Today—The Online Edition* (http://www.tui.edu/STO/Rockets/BoeingSeaLaunch.html).

[46]*Proliferation: Threat and Response 1997,* op. cit., pp. 47-48.

[47]Ibid., p. 46.

Ukraine:
Map and Chart

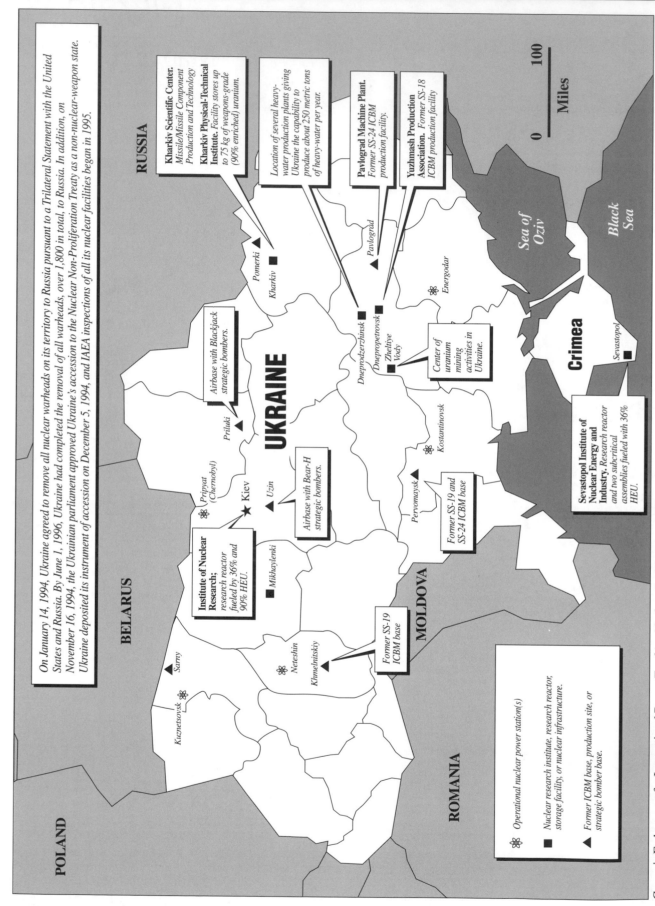

On January 14, 1994, Ukraine agreed to remove all nuclear warheads on its territory to Russia pursuant to a Trilateral Statement with the United States and Russia. By June 1, 1996, Ukraine had completed the removal of all warheads, over 1,800 in total, to Russia. In addition, on November 16, 1994, the Ukrainian parliament approved Ukraine's accession to the Nuclear Non-Proliferation Treaty as a non-nuclear-weapon state. Ukraine deposited its instrument of accession on December 5, 1994, and IAEA inspections of all its nuclear facilities began in 1995.

POLAND

BELARUS

RUSSIA

UKRAINE

MOLDOVA

ROMANIA

Crimea

Sea of Oziv

Black Sea

Kharkiv Scientific Center: *Missile/Missile Component Production and Technology*

Kharkiv Physical-Technical Institute. *Facility stores up to 75 kg of weapons-grade (90% enriched) uranium.*

Location of several heavy-water production plants giving Ukraine the capability to produce about 250 metric tons of heavy-water per year.

Pavlograd Machine Plant. *Former SS-24 ICBM production facility.*

Yuzhmash Production Association. *Former SS-18 ICBM production facility.*

Airbase with Blackjack strategic bombers.

Airbase with Bear-H strategic bombers.

Institute of Nuclear Research; *research reactor fueled by 36% and 90% HEU.*

Center of uranium mining activities in Ukraine.

Former SS-19 and SS-24 ICBM base

Former SS-19 ICBM base

Sevastopol Institute of Nuclear Energy and Industry. *Research reactor and two subcritical assemblies fueled with 36% HEU.*

Pomerki

Kharkiv

Dneprodzerzhinsk

Dnepropetrovsk

Zheltiye Vody

Energodar

Pavlograd

Kostantinovsk

Pervomaysk

Priluki

Pripyat (Chernobyl)

Kiev

Uzin

Mikhaylenki

Neteshin

Khmelnitskiy

Samy

Kuznetsovsk

Sevastopol

Operational nuclear power station(s)

Nuclear research institute, research reactor, storage facility, or nuclear infrastructure.

Former ICBM base, production site, or strategic bomber base.

0   100

Miles

Carnegie Endowment for International Peace, *Tracking Nuclear Proliferation*, 1998

SOURCES: NIS Nuclear Profiles Database, Center for Nonproliferation Studies, Monterey Institute of International Studies; START Treaty Memoranda of Understanding on Data (MOU), September 1990-January 1998; and Department of Energy, "MPC&A Program: Strategic Plan," January 1998.

UKRAINE: Nuclear Infrastructure and Other Sites of Proliferation Concern

NAME/LOCATION OF FACILITY	TYPE/STATUS	IAEA SAFEGUARDS[a]
NUCLEAR-WEAPON BASES AND SUPPORT FACILITIES[b]		
Pervomaysk	Former ICBM base for SS-19 and SS-24 missiles. As of July 1997, 19 SS-19s and 46 SS-24s at Pervomaysk were still accountable under START; in 1998, with U.S. CTR assistance, Ukraine will destroy the remaining SS-19s and begin SS-24 destruction.[c]	
Khmelnitskiy	Former ICBM base. As of July 1997, 45 SS-19s at Khmelnitskiy were still accountable under START, but will be destroyed by the end of 1998.	
Uzin	Former strategic bomber base and bomber conversion and elimination facility. As of July 1997, 25 Bear-H bombers at Uzin were still accountable under START, even though the bombers are not in operable condition and all warheads for air-launched cruise missiles (ALCMs) have been removed to Russia.[d]	
Priluki	Former strategic bomber base. As of July 1997, 19 Blackjack bombers still remained at Priluki, all accountable under START, although none are currently operable.	
Mikhaylenki	ICBM storage facility with 4 SS-11, 3 SS-17, and 80 SS-19 non-deployed ICBMs as of July 1997.	
Pavlograd Machine Plant	Former SS-24 production facility with 1 non-deployed, rail-mobile SS-24 (5 silo-based SS-24s and 3 rail-mobile SS-24s are at the conversion and elimination facility) as of July 1997.	
Yuzhmash Plant, Dnepropetrovsk	Former SS-18 production facility with 2 SS-17 and 7 SS-19 non-deployed ICBMs as of July 1997.	
Pomerki	Former SS-18 training facility with 1 SS-18 training missile as of July 1997.	
Sarny	ICBM conversion and elimination facility; no ICBMs present as of July 1997.	
NUCLEAR RESEARCH FACILITIES		
Institute of Nuclear Research, Kiev	Research center and nuclear material storage with HEU in fuel assemblies (see below for research reactors) and small amounts of Pu.	Yes
Kharkiv Physics and Technology Institute, Kharkiv	Nuclear physics research and nuclear material storage. Up to 75 kg of 90% enriched HEU in bulk and item form.[e]	Yes
Sevastopol Institute of Nuclear Energy and Industry, Sevastopol	Reactor training facility and subcritical assemblies; HEU present (see research reactors below).	Yes
POWER REACTORS		
Chernobyl, Unit 3[f], Pripyat	RBMK, LEU, 925 MWe; operating.	Yes
Khmelnitskiy Unit 1, Neteshin	VVER-1000, LEU, 950 MWe; operating.	Yes
Khmelnitskiy Unit 2, Neteshin	VVER-1000, LEU, 950 MWe; under construction.	Yes
Rovno Units 1 and 2, Kuznetsovsk	VVER-440, LEU, 361 and 384 MWe, respectively; operating.	Yes

NAME/LOCATION OF FACILITY	TYPE/STATUS	IAEA SAFEGUARDS[a]
Rovno Unit 3, Kuznetsovsk	VVER-1000, LEU, 950 MWe; operating.	Yes
Rovno Unit 4, Kuznetsovsk	VVER-1000, LEU, 950 MWe; operating.	Yes
South Ukraine Units 1-3, Kostantinovsk	VVER-1000, LEU, 950 MWe; operating.	Yes
Zaporozhe Units 1-6, Energodar	VVER-1000, LEU, 950 MWe; operating.	Yes
RESEARCH REACTORS		
WWR-M (Institute of Nuclear Research), Kiev	Tank WWR, 36% and 90% enriched HEU, 10 MWt; awaiting operating license.	Yes
IR-100 (Sevastopol Institute of Nuclear Energy and Industry), Sevastopol	Pool, up to 36% enriched HEU, 200 KWt; unlicensed.	Yes
Subcritical Assemblies, Sevastopol	2 subcritical assemblies fueled with up to 36% enriched HEU; operating.	Yes
URANIUM PROCESSING		
Zheltiye Vody	Uranium mining and milling; operating.	
HEAVY-WATER PRODUCTION		
Dnepropetrovsk	Pridneprovsky Chemical Plant; can produce up to 250 metric tons of heavy water/year.	Yes

Abbreviations:

HEU	=	highly enriched uranium
LEU	=	low-enriched uranium
nat. U	=	natural uranium
MWe	=	millions of watts of electrical output
MWt	=	millions of watts of thermal output
KWt	=	thousands of watts of thermal output

NOTES (Ukraine Chart)

[a]Ukraine acceded to the NPT as a non-nuclear-weapon state on December 5, 1994, and on September 21, 1995, it signed a comprehensive safeguards agreement with the IAEA pursuant to its obligations under Article III of the NPT. This agreement was ratified by the Ukrainian Parliament on December 17, 1997. Prior to its NPT accession, however, Ukraine had signed a temporary safeguards agreement with the IAEA on September 28, 1994, that covered all nuclear material and peaceful nuclear activities in Ukraine; this agreement was superseded by the new safeguards agreement when it entered into force in December 1997.

[b]All nuclear warheads have been removed from Ukraine to Russia. The last of more than 1,800 warheads were shipped to Russia on May 31, 1996. However, under the terms of the Strategic Arms Reduction Treaty (START) Ukraine must destroy its remaining strategic launch capabilities, including SS-19 and SS-24 ICBMs. See "Kuchma Issues Statement on Removal of Nuclear Weapons," UT-1 Television, June 1, 1996, in FBIS-SOV-96-107, June 5, 1996.

Much of the data on facilities has been derived from the July 1997 START Memorandum of Understanding that lists numbers of weapons and locations for the five START parties.

[c]See "Ukraine is fulfilling nuclear-free pledge," *St. Louis Post-Dispatch*, December 27, 1997; and "Ukraine will destroy remaining SS-19 missiles in 1998," *Agence France Presse*, December 17, 1997.

[d]Russia had originally agreed to purchase the remaining bombers from Ukraine, but the deal was canceled due to deterioration of the bombers. Ukraine has since requested U.S. CTR assistance to help with the destruction. See Barbara Starr, "Stalemate on 'Scuds' as latest US-Kiev talks fail," *Jane's Defence Weekly*, July 23, 1997, p. 3.

[e]See Table I-E in Carnegie Endowment for International Peace and Monterey Institute of International Studies, *Nuclear Successor States of the Soviet Union: Status Report on Nuclear Weapons, Fissile Materials, and Export Controls,* No. 5, March 1998.

[f]The Chernobyl Unit-3 was temporarily closed in September 1997 to repair cracks in the primary pipe welds. The discovery of new cracks in January 1998 will extend the outage for several months. "Chernobyl restart postponed as new primary cracks discovered," *Nucleonics Week*, January 8, 1998, p. 5.

The other Chernobyl units have not been in operation since late November 1996. Unit 1 was permanently shut down on November 30, 1996, based on an agreement signed between Ukraine and the G-7. Unit 2 has been off-line since a turbine hall fire in October 1991. Unit 4 was closed in April 1986 after the meltdown in the reactor core.

Due to energy needs, Ukraine has considered a plan to repair and restart Unit 2, but as of December 1997, no commitment to this plan had been made. The decommissioning of Unit 1 is imminent once the financial arrangements have been finalized. See Alexei Breus, "Ukraine decrees formal end to operation of Chernobyl-1," *Nucleonics Week*, July 3, 1997, p. 7; Peter Coryn, "Chernobyl-1 is shut but Ukraine keeps units 1, 2 restart option," *Nucleonics Week*, January 2, 1997, p. 14.

5

EASTERN EUROPE

Romania

Romania ratified the Nuclear Non-Proliferation Treaty (NPT) on February 4, 1970, pledging not to manufacture nuclear weapons and agreeing to place all of its nuclear materials and facilities under International Atomic Energy Agency (IAEA) safeguards. However, just as the winds of political change began to affect Eastern Europe in April and May 1989, the Communist leader of Romania, Nicolae Ceausescu, stated that, from the standpoint of technical competence, his country had the "ability to manufacture nuclear weapons."[1] Two months later, Romanian officials reiterated that the country possessed this capability, adding that it would soon be able to manufacture medium-range missiles as well.[2]

These statements were reason enough to give close scrutiny to Romania in the early 1990s. Evidence has accumulated that Ceausescu had been in the process of attempting to build an ambitious nuclear weapons production and nuclear technology export capability, and might have done so except for his overthrow, the collapse of the Warsaw Pact, and the seeds of political and economic reform taking root in Eastern Europe.

It appears, however, that Romania's leadership since Ceausescu's overthrow has adhered to a path that is consistent with NPT obligations and non-proliferation norms. Romania is bidding for entry to the North Atlantic Treaty Organization (NATO) and the European Union (EU), and while its chances for success depend on its progress with democratic and economic reform, doubts about its non-proliferation commitments certainly would give pause, jeopardizing its integration into broader European institutions and activities.

BACKGROUND

Discovery of Safeguards Violation. In early 1989, shortly before the overthrow of his regime, Nicolae Ceausescu and several of his officials hinted at the possibility that Romania had the capability to manufacture nuclear weapons and to produce medium-range missiles. Following the overthrow of the Ceausescu regime in December 1989, the newly elected government of Ion Iliescu initially dissociated itself from those nuclear-weapons-related statements. However, in April 1992, a vessel containing 470 ml of a mysterious nuclear substance was discovered at the Nuclear Research Institute (ICN) in Pitesti. Analysis showed the material to be nuclear waste from plutonium separation.

Then-Prime Minister Theodor Stolojan reported the discovery to the IAEA and invited the Agency to conduct a "visit" or special inspection of Romania's nuclear program. As a result, in June 1992, IAEA Director General Hans Blix told the Agency's Board of Governors that, in December 1985, Romania's (Communist) government had violated the country's safeguards agreement with the IAEA by separating about 100 mg of plutonium from irradiated uranium in a laboratory-scale experiment. According to one report, the experiment was intended to serve as the basis for setting up a production capacity of 1 kg of plutonium a year. The same report noted that, during or after the 1992 special IAEA visit, IAEA officials told the Stolojan government that they had been aware of Ceausescu's clandestine nuclear weapons program all along.[3]

Secret Weapons Program. A 1993 report in a Romanian newspaper quoted the former head of Romania's Department of Foreign Intelligence and sources close to the Romanian Intelligence Service as saying that, during the Ceausescu era, secret planning took place for developing a medium-range missile with nuclear warheads. This report added that, in 1968-70, "Ceausescu had ordered the establishment of a large espionage network intended to obtain the documentation necessary for production of the nuclear weapon." The purpose of manufacturing such weapons was to "intimidate both the NATO adversaries and those that were members of the Warsaw Pact" and to sell the weapons to countries in the Middle East.[4]

U.S. officials familiar with the Romanian case have confirmed the existence of a nuclear weapons program under Ceausescu but have declined to provide additional details.[5]

DEVELOPMENTS

Since early 1995, some additional information has come to light about the scale of the nuclear industrial and export program Ceausescu had envisaged. Romania has also been in the news as a result of illicit nuclear trafficking from Russia through its territory. While there does not appear to be any continuation of a secret nuclear weapons program, the fact that there was such a program and no specific public disavowal—together with Romania's past heavy investment in nuclear industrial infrastructure, existing plans for nuclear power based on heavy-water reactor designs, and the nuclear smuggling reports—suggests that it may be reasonable to keep Romania on the nuclear proliferation watch list.

Massive Nuclear Industrial Program. In 1996, Romanian officials and technicians reportedly were trying to salvage what remained from a $10-billion, 20-year investment by Ceausescu to turn Romania into the leading nuclear vendor of the Third World.[6] Seven years after Ceausescu's overthrow, leaders of Romania's nuclear establishment were regretting the migration out of the country of highly-skilled personnel and the fact that over 80 percent of the firms and organizations that had been part of the ambitious nuclear program (there had been over 150 in 1990) were being forced to go out of the nuclear business. Those in charge of the remaining 20 or so nuclear laboratories, machine works, and engineering offices were making an effort to stem the "brain drain" and to keep the Romanian nuclear industry afloat by developing business with utilities and governments in Eastern Europe and Asia.

One official who had been involved in reactor negotiations during the 1970s with Canada, the United States, and the Soviet Union said that the experts wanted to build a solid foundation, slowly and methodically, by constructing a small number of reactors in steps, but that Ceausescu "schemed to play off the West and the USSR against each other" and insisted on efforts to build both Soviet VVER pressurized light-water reactors (PWRs) and Canadian CANDU pressurized heavy-water reactors (PHWRs) in large numbers. "After we imported the first VVERs and CANDUs, the plan was to build 15-20 units—all by ourselves. In the meantime, we would begin to export Romanian reactors to the Third World."

Under Ceausescu, Romania invested large sums in developing facilities to make heavy water and uranium fuel, with huge service capacities, long before the power reactors themselves could be completed. Some of the engineering and manufacturing know-how is still intact, atomic energy officials claim, for the basic components of nuclear power reactors—e.g., calandria, steam generators, turbogenerator equipment, fuel channels, heat exchangers, and valves—that could be used to substitute for imports for future reactors. But others believe that too much of the nuclear industry has been idle for too long, or has dispersed, for Romania to compete with contemporary nuclear suppliers.

Romania's own nuclear plans have been stalled for lack of funds, so that nearly 25 years after beginning its nuclear program, only Cernavoda-1, a single CANDU-6 PHWR, is actually on-line generating electricity.[7] Cernavoda-2 is only 40 percent complete, and three shells, built at huge cost for the next three reactors, sit empty on the Black Sea Canal. Plans to buy three VVERs from the USSR were scrapped altogether after the accident at Chernobyl.

Heavy-Water Production. Romania's large investment in heavy-water production plants also created capacities that could be troublesome for non-proliferation purposes if its international trade were not subject to rigorous controls. In this regard, there have been unexplained gaps between production and inventories,

according to Mark Hibbs.[8] Romanian records at the end of 1995 indicate, for instance, that 325 metric tons of heavy water had been produced, although officials claim none was exported. However, Romanian industry could supply only 150 metric tons of the 500 metric tons of heavy water needed by the new Cernavoda PHWR for it to operate, forcing Romania to borrow 355 metric tons of heavy water from Canada. Romania expects to pay Canada back from future Romanian production of heavy water. This leaves the question of what happened to 175 metric tons of Romanian heavy water.[9]

PROSPECTS

The unsettling nuclear program that was the legacy of the Ceausescu regime in the late 1980s has been brought under more effective political control. While the Romanian nuclear industry might have had strong compulsions to sell its expertise and technology to proliferant countries in the Middle East and elsewhere in the Third World, these have been offset, on one hand, by some measure of progress at home with the completion of Cernavoda-1 and plans to continue constructing the partially completed Cernavoda-2, and, on the other hand, by the growing importance to Romania of its trade with, and investment from, the European Union countries. Instead of selling dangerous technology to the Third World, Romania has actually been a participant in a large number of U.N. peacekeeping operations in the Balkans, the Middle East, and Africa.

Moreover, political change within Romania has swung more clearly in the direction of democratic and market-economy reform. While the elected regime of President Ion Iliescu was a major improvement over the long dictatorial regime of Ceausescu and did produce a significant level of positive economic growth from 1992 to 1996, Iliescu's attachments to the old communist and state-run configuration of the economy inhibited a full-fledged democratic opening and slowed the needed economic restructuring. Fresh elections in November 1996 produced the surprise victory of an authentically democratic coalition, leading to the first alternation in the presidency by genuine popular elections with the ascendancy of President Emil Constantinescu and Prime Minister Victor Ciorbea. Although Romania has a long way to go in overhauling and reforming its state-centric economy, the pluralism that has emerged in the political system together with the overwhelming domestic popular leaning toward integration with Western Europe increase the chances that Romania will exercise appropriate controls over its nuclear industrial sector, that routine IAEA inspections there will engender transparency, and that Romania's incentives for legitimate trade and industrial expansion will outweigh the temptations to engage in questionable nuclear commerce with other parts of the world.

NOTES

[1] Alison Smale, "President Says Romania Has Nuclear Weapons Potential," *Associated Press*, April 15, 1989, which cites Romania's *Agerpress*.

[2] See "SPIEGEL Reports Missile Aid to Romania," Hamburg, *Der Spiegel*, May 8, 1998, in *FBIS-WEU-89*, May 8, 1989, p. 8; Henry Kamm, "Hungarian Accuses Rumania of Military Threats," *New York Times*, July 11, 1989; "Past Attempt to Produce Plutonium Disclosed," *Rompres* (Bucharest), May 25, 1993, in *FBIS-EEU-93-100*, May 26, 1993, p. 25; "Romania Planned Atom Bomb," *Reuters*, May 26, 1993.

[3] See "Past Attempt to Produce Plutonium Disclosed," Bucharest, op. cit.; "Romania Planned Atom Bomb," op. cit.; Ann MacLachlan, "Romania Produced Unsafeguarded Pu, Blix Tells IAEA Board of Governors," *Nuclear Fuel*, June 22, 1992, p. 16.

[4] See "Ceausescu Effort to Build Nuclear Bomb Reported," *Evenimentul Zilei* (Bucharest), May 10, 1993, in *FBIS-EEU-93-092*, May 14, 1993, p. 14.

[5] Interviews, December 1994.

[6] For this and other information in this section, see Mark Hibbs, "Romania Hopes to Save Remains of a $10-Billion Know-How Investment," *Nucleonics Week*, July 18, 1996, pp. 6ff.

[7] Cernavoda-1, a 650-MWe power reactor, was finally started up, nearly a decade late, by the state-owned electric utility, RENEL (Regia Atonoma De Electricitate), in April 1997. "Romania: Joint Venture Construction Plans for Proposed $750,000,000," *ESP-Report on Engineering Construct and Operations in the Developing World*, No. 2, Vol. 7, February 1, 1998. In this relatively small country of 23 million, Cernavoda-1 alone could provide, if operated effectively at full capacity, about 10 percent of Romania's electrical energy needs and correspondingly reduce the current imports of oil and gas, or coal, for electricity. See claims made after the first full year of Cernavoda-1 operation, producing 5.4 billion kilowatt-hours of electricity. "Canadian-built nuclear plant generates 10 percent of power," *Rompres* (the Romanian news agency), in *BBC Summary of World Broadcasts*, (London: British Broadcasting Corporation, February 19, 1998).

[8] See "Romania Aims to Double Current Heavy Water Inventory by 1999," *Nuclear Fuel*, July 15, 1996, p. 13; Mark Hibbs, "Tritium Decontamination Plant Planned for Cernavoda Reactors," *Nuclear Fuel*, July 15, 1996, p. 14.

[9] It is at least possible that some was shipped to India, much as shipments via Romania of Russian and Norwegian heavy water to India were reported in earlier years. See Leonard Spector, *Nuclear Ambitions: The Spread of Nuclear Weapons, 1989-1990* (Boulder, CO: Westview Press, 1990), pp. 36, 73. See also Wisconsin Project, *Risk Report*, March 1995, p. 8.

POLAND

0   100
Miles

SLOVAKIA

UKRAINE

HUNGARY

Uranium mining

■ Botusana

Crucea

Uranium mining

Avram Iancu

● Cluj

MOLDOVA

ROMANIA

Location of heavy-water production plant intended to support the operation of the Cernavoda power station.

Brasov ■

Uranium milling; also location of UO₂ powder fabrication plant, subject to IAEA inspection.

Uranium mining

Dobrei South

Drobeta Turnu Severin

■ *Pitesti*

Bucharest
★

Cernavoda ■

SERBIA

Black Sea

Nuclear Research Institute (ICN).
Location of "hot cells" that presumably could be used to extract small amounts of plutonium from spent nuclear fuel. In 1985, the then-communist government separated about 100 milligrams of plutonium, presumably at this site, as part of a nuclear-weapons research and development effort. Also site of fuel fabrication plant, subject to IAEA inspection.

■ *Magurele*

BULGARIA

Cernavoda nuclear power station–one 700 MWe heavy-water reactor began operating in 1996, second unit 40% complete. All facilities subject to IAEA inspection once completed.

GREECE

TURKEY

Carnegie Endowment for International Peace, *Tracking Nuclear Proliferation*, 1998

ROMANIA: Nuclear Infrastructure

NAME/LOCATION OF FACILITY	TYPE/STATUS	IAEA SAFEGUARDS
POWER REACTORS		
Cernavoda I	Heavy-water, natural U, 706 MWe; began operating in April 1996.	IAEA
Cernavoda II[a]	Heavy-water, natural U, 700 MWe; under construction.	IAEA (planned)
RESEARCH REACTORS		
Triga II Nuclear Research Institute (ICN), Pitesti	LEU, 14 MWt materials testing reactor; operating.[b]	IAEA
VVR-S (Units I and II) Magurele	LEU/HEU, tank, 3 MWt; operating.	IAEA
REPROCESSING (PLUTONIUM EXTRACTION)		
ICN, Pitesti	Laboratory-scale hot cells.	No[c]
URANIUM PROCESSING		
Avram Iancu and Bihor, Apuseni mountains; Dobrei South, Banat mountains; Botusana and Crucea, Eastern Carpathians	Uranium mining; operating.	N/A (Not applicable)
Feldioara, Brasov	Uranium milling; operating.	N/A
Feldioara, Brasov	UO$_2$ powder fabrication plant; operating.	IAEA
Romfuel, Pitesti	Fuel fabrication plant; operating.	IAEA
HEAVY-WATER PRODUCTION		
ROMAG, Drobeta Turnu Severin	Operating.[d]	No

Abbreviations:

HEU	=	highly enriched uranium
LEU	=	low-enriched uranium
nat. U	=	natural uranium
MWe	=	millions of watts of electrical output
MWt	=	millions of watts of thermal output
KWt	=	thousands of watts of thermal output

NOTES (Romania Chart)

[a]Five CANDU-type reactors were originally planned for the Cernavoda site as part of the Ceausescu-era nuclear plan. However, Cernavoda II is only 40 percent complete and the approximately $1.4 billion necessary to complete the reactor has not been budgeted. If funding is found, the reactor could be completed by 2005. The prospects for the completion of the other Cernavoda units are uncertain, especially as lack of funds continue to be a problem. See "No Moldova help for Romania plant-president," *Reuters*, February 21, 1998.

[b]Originally rated at 40 MWt, the TRIGA reactor at Pitesti was the largest of its type in the world. Supplied by the United States, it was fueled with U.S.-origin weapons-usable HEU throughout the Ceausescu era. Although the facility was under IAEA monitoring from the time it began operating, Romania would have been able to use the unit's HEU fuel to fabricate a nuclear weapon had it been prepared to violate the IAEA safeguards covering the facility. During

the mid-1980s, Romania did, in fact, violate IAEA rules on a smaller scale by separating a small quantity of plutonium without notifying the agency (see Discovery of Safeguards Violation in this chapter) and, reportedly, by clandestinely shipping a quantity of heavy water to India, again without notifying the IAEA.

Between 1989 and 1991, the reactor was shut down because the United States was no longer prepared to supply HEU fuel for the facility. After Romania agreed to convert the reactor to LEU fuel (not usable for nuclear arms), Washington approved the transfer of five LEU fuel elements for the plant. As part of an overall agreement on the final disposition of Romania's HEU fuel for the reactor, the U.S. Department of Energy has agreed to convert fourteen highly enriched fuel elements owned by the Romanian government to low-enriched elements. See "U.S. and Romania Agree on Use of Low Enriched Uranium for Research Reactor," *DOE News*, November 8, 1991.

^cThe IAEA inspected this facility under the auspices of a "special" invitation by the Romanian government in May 1992. The agency discovered that about 100 milligrams of pure plutonium had been separated in an experiment in 1985. See Ann MacLachlan, "Romania produced unsafeguarded Pu, Blix tells IAEA Board of Governors," *Nuclear Fuel*, June 22, 1992, p. 16.

^dAs of the end of 1995 Romania had produced about 325 metric tons of heavy water since the facility began operating in 1988. In order to meet the needs of the Cernavoda I PHWR and to repay Canada, the plant operators plan to double output by 1999, also with a view toward producing the necessary material to operate the Cernavoda II reactor, should it be completed. See Mark Hibbs, "Romania aims to double current heavy water inventory by 1999," *Nuclear Fuel*, July 15, 1996.

Three of the four production units of the plant were shut down in 1994 for safety checks. To meet the projected deficit in heavy water production, in September 1994, Romanian authorities in charge of the nuclear power program signed a contract with India's department of atomic energy for the import of 350 tons of heavy water. There is considerable irony in this purchase, inasmuch as during the mid-1980s, Romania is believed to have transferred heavy water to India clandestinely, in violation of Romania's safeguards commitments. At the time, India lacked sufficient heavy water to operate three unsafeguarded reactors that it was about to bring on line. At least one of these, the Dhruva reactor at the Bhabha Atomic Research Center, was intended to produce plutonium for India's nuclear weapons program. See "Romania to Import 350 Tonnes of India Heavy Water," *Reuters*, September 23, 1994.

6
SOUTH ASIA AND EAST ASIA

India

India breached the international taboo on "going nuclear" in 1998, by testing a series of nuclear explosive devices on May 11 and 13 and officially declaring itself a new "nuclear-weapons power."[1] These events triggered Pakistan's nuclear explosive testing response two weeks later,[2] suddenly springing on the world stage two self-declared, non-NPT nuclear-weapon states and radically challenging the efficacy of the nuclear non-proliferation regime. The damage done to the nuclear non-proliferation regime was limited only slightly by the fact that both states had long been viewed as *de facto* nuclear-weapon states and neither had joined the Nuclear Non-Proliferation Treaty (NPT) or such other legally binding nuclear non-proliferation instruments as full-scope International Atomic Energy Agency (IAEA) safeguards.

The profound international outrage over India's action was all the stronger because of the absence of credible nuclear security threats to India as a justification for its nuclear testing[3]—and because of India's own early aversion to nuclear weapons and its once prominent leadership in seeking non-proliferation and disarmament measures. In reacting to India, other nations objected that India's nuclear tests and self-declaration ran counter to the prevailing world tide of nuclear arms reductions, the negotiated 1996 ban on nuclear weapons testing, and accumulated non-proliferation successes in other regions.

India had demonstrated a nuclear weapons capability in May 1974, nearly a quarter century earlier, by detonating a nuclear device in what it called a "peaceful nuclear experiment." Officially, India thereafter claimed, until 1998, that it did not possess and had no plans for nuclear weapons. Nevertheless, India maintained a nuclear weapons research program and a nuclear posture of ambiguity from the early 1970s, and actively pursued the development of space launchers and nuclear-capable ballistic missiles for over two decades. Consequently, in the years between 1974 and 1997, India was regarded as a threshold nuclear-weapon state that could "go nuclear" on short notice.[4]

An original sponsor of Nuclear Non-Proliferation Treaty (NPT) principles, India nonetheless refused to sign the document that emerged from NPT negotiations in 1968—arguing that it did not fulfill the original mandate. Thereafter, India consistently opposed regional nuclear-weapon-free-zone (NWFZ) and other non-proliferation proposals for South Asia, calling instead for global nuclear disarmament. Similarly, India had long championed the development of a global nuclear test ban treaty and contributed positively to early drafts of the Comprehensive Test Ban Treaty (CTBT) of 1996, but finally rejected the CTBT as well.

A recent technical analysis estimated that, as of the end of 1995, India's safeguards-free nuclear weapons potential involved enough *separated* weapons-grade plutonium for at least 65 early-generation nuclear weapons; it also projected that this stockpile will rise to the equivalent of 85 to 90 weapons by the year 2000.[5] Unseparated plutonium residing in unsafeguarded spent fuel in India could, if reprocessed, at least double this inventory. India has also been developing uranium-enrichment facilities that could enable construction of hydrogen bombs.[6]

India began to make investments in a space program as early as 1970. It has since developed both space launch vehicles and satellites and is beginning to launch its own heavy-satellite payloads. The design and engineering of space rockets has provided India with many of the essentials for developing nuclear-capable ballistic missiles. India has been testing two such missile types—the Prithvi short-range missile (150-250 km) and the Agni medium-range missile (1,500-2,500 km)—for several years. It is now testing space launch vehicles of sufficient range and capacity for converted versions to become prototypes of long-range ballistic missiles. India is not an adherent to the Missile Technology Control Regime (MTCR) guidelines. Indeed, the Indian Space Research Organization (ISRO) actually was a target of related U.S. sanctions in 1992-94.[7]

Those in India's own small circle of strategic analysts who believe that China poses a nuclear military threat to India have regarded India's long-range missile development program as a basis for the nuclear deterrence of China. Insofar as perceived security threats have mattered to the Indian public at large, however, it is India's preoccupation with threats posed by weaker Pakistan that has served as the main driving factor—politically and psychologically—in the day-to-day, public orchestration of India's nuclear and missile development programs.[8] For the senior elected officials and a larger domestic constituency, the motives for India's nuclear, space, and missile development have arisen more from status than security needs. Developing India's scientific and technological capacity—civilian and military—is seen as the means of demonstrating India's world-class leadership potential and of satisfying India's pressing need to have advanced technology to modernize the nation's still underdeveloped infrastructure and economy.

BACKGROUND

Nuclear Weapons Program. India was an early beneficiary of the U.S.–sponsored "Atoms for Peace" program launched in 1953. This program was intended to stem the proliferation of nuclear weapons by offering access to civil uses of nuclear technology in exchange for pledges not to apply the technology to weapons purposes. Based on the prevailing atmosphere of trust in the early Atoms for Peace years, Canada in 1955 supplied the Cirus 40-MWt heavy-water-moderated research reactor from which India later derived the plutonium for the 1974 nuclear explosive device. In lieu of IAEA safeguards, which did not exist until after the Agency was founded in 1957, Canada required only written "peaceful assurances" that the reactor would be used exclusively for peaceful purposes. The United States sold India some of the heavy water needed for Cirus operations under the same assurances. Before the mid-1950s, there was only slight evidence that India had any interest in nuclear weapons.

India's first atomic energy chief, Homi Bhahba, however, already understood the dual uses of many nuclear technologies—especially that of plutonium separation. In 1958, India began to acquire the equipment for its Trombay plutonium-reprocessing facility—even then justifying it as a scheme to pave the way in the civilian power program for breeder reactors.[9] The plant was commissioned in late 1964, shortly before China detonated its first nuclear explosive device in October of the same year.[10] When fully operational, the plant had the capacity to separate up to 10 kg of plutonium annually (enough for at least two bombs a year). Ten years later, India's nuclear explosion—using plutonium generated in Cirus and separated in the Trombay reprocessing facility—demonstrated India's nuclear weapons option.[11]

India single-mindedly pursued self-sufficiency in atomic energy and, with few exceptions, rejected the imposition of IAEA safeguards, even on its indigenous electric power plants.[12] As a result, IAEA safeguards are missing from every component of the Indian nuclear research program and from all but two pressurized heavy-water reactors (PHWRs) in the civil power program.[13] Virtually all fuel-cycle facilities have been kept outside safeguards.[14] India thus faces few constraints in using fissile materials for military as well as civilian purposes, and India's civil PHWRs and fast-breeder reactors could be (and some believe intermittently were) diverted to produce weapons-grade materials.[15]

The estimate that India's plutonium stockpile at the end of 1995 probably was sufficient for about 65 weapons, and would rise to 85 or 90 weapons by the year 2000, is derived from cautious analysis by David Albright, Frans Berkhout, and William Walker.[16] Their estimate of 330 kg in India's safeguards-free separated plutonium inventory at the end of 1995 could be low by as much as 30 percent; India's actual plutonium stockpile then might have been sufficient for 80 to 90 weapons. Their estimates of high-quality plutonium are based primarily on India's decades-long operation of

two unsafeguarded, heavy-water-moderated research reactors (the 40-MWt Cirus and 100-MWt Dhruva,[17] both located at the Bhabha Atomic Research Center, or BARC), but they also take into account the more recent start-up operations of five unsafeguarded 220-MWe PHWRs (Madras I and II, Narora I and II, and Kakrapar I) constructed indigenously by India for its civil program. They omit, however, the most recent Kakrapar II power plant start-up in 1995.[18]

India's stockpile of separated plutonium has been constrained by the capacity of its three existing reprocessing facilities. Hence the estimates are based on what is known about the operational history of India's current reprocessing facilities at Trombay, Tarapur (Prefre), and Kalpakkam. With additional reprocessing capacity, the plutonium stockpile could be increased at a much more rapid rate from existing as well as future spent fuel. India reportedly has a second and larger (commercial scale) reprocessing facility under construction at Kalpakkam with a planned capacity to handle about 1,000 tons of spent fuel a year, or nearly four times the amount (275 tons of spent fuel) that India's three smaller facilities together can currently handle each year.[19]

The generation of weapons-quality plutonium in spent fuel could also be expanded significantly by fast-breeder reactors, which can "produce" more plutonium than they "consume." The Indian Atomic Energy Commission (IAEC) began its breeder program with the pilot-scale (15-MWe) Fast-Breeder Test Reactor (FBTR), based on French cooperation and the Phénix design during the 1970s. The FBTR was kept free of safeguards and commissioned at Kalpakkam in south India in 1987.[20] The IAEC recently announced that India soon would break ground for a long-envisaged 500-MWe Prototype Fast-Breeder Reactor (PFBR) with a hoped-for completion date of 2007.[21]

India also has a centrifuge-based, uranium-enrichment program that could eventually augment the fissile material stockpile for weapons by producing highly enriched uranium (HEU). HEU is believed to be useful for thermonuclear weapon (H-bomb) development.[22] India has had no need to enrich uranium for its indigenous civilian reactors, which operate on natural uranium fuel.[23] The capacity of India's two enrichment facilities—one at the Trombay (BARC) complex and the other at Rattehalli, near Mysore, in Karnataka state—has not been disclosed. However, these plants are presumed to be pilot rather than commercial in scale.[24]

Setbacks to Civil Nuclear Program. India's autarkic approach to its civil nuclear program, resistance to IAEA safeguards, and rejection of the NPT all played some part in distancing the advanced nuclear supplier countries from expanding peaceful nuclear cooperation with India, but the biggest blow came from the Indian nuclear explosion in 1974. The test seemed to defy the Atoms for Peace premises at the heart of early U.S. and Canadian peaceful nuclear cooperation with India. To develop, demonstrate, and protect its nuclear weapons option, India paid an unexpectedly high diplomatic and economic price. Part of that price was severe, cumulative setbacks to India's civil nuclear power program. The lost electric power supply opportunities that were a consequence slowed natural growth in India's industrial base and economy as a whole and have reached crippling levels today.[25]

India's nuclear explosion of 1974 shocked the institutionalized system of peaceful nuclear cooperation and was the primary catalyst for decisions by the advanced nuclear supplier states to upgrade their export control policies—by forming the Nuclear Suppliers Group (NSG) and adopting more stringent export criteria. Canada tried for two years to persuade India to accept additional non-proliferation constraints, and, having failed, terminated peaceful nuclear cooperation with India altogether in 1976. Although the United States did not sever its Tarapur contractual relationship with India for the supply of low-enriched uranium (LEU) fuel to the Tarapur nuclear power plant,[26] it sought to persuade India to adopt new non-proliferation measures—at least IAEA safeguards on civilian facilities. When this approach failed, U.S. interest in new nuclear cooperation projects with India dropped off sharply and eventually ceased.[27]

For India, the unexpected loss of Canadian cooperation was particularly costly. India found it impossible to complete on schedule the second power plant that Canada had contracted to supply. It also experienced serious technical and operational setbacks with both of the Rajasthan power reactors that Canada was no longer willing to help remedy. Moreover, India had in the late 1960s decided to standardize its planned construction of a large number of indigenous power plants on the CANDU (Canadian deuterium-uranium) PHWR design,[28] but it found that implementing this plan after 1974, without continued Canadian technical support, was both more expensive and technically difficult than expected. By 1995, nearly a quarter century after the start of domestic procurement of indigenous PHWR plants in 1967 and 1971, the Indian power program had installed only six additional CANDU-type, 235-MWe (220-MWe net) power reactors—two at each of three sites.[29] Although the first indigenously built reactors at the Madras site got off to a reasonably good start, their performance in later years was disappointing. The performance of the twin reactors at the other sites, Narora and Kakrapar, has been troubled, partly due to turbine defects, leading in one case to a serious fire.[30]

While nuclear power installation and operational delays are not uncommon in the advanced states, the Indian setbacks have been exceptionally severe. By the late 1980s, together with increasing disclosure of safety problems, the setbacks had begun to throw official cost-effectiveness calculations into doubt and threatened to discredit the role of nuclear power in India.[31] One measure of the severity of the setbacks is how far India fell behind its planned targets for the installation of nuclear electric capacity. In the early 1970s, the IAEC target for installed nuclear power capacity by 1981 had

been 8,000 MWe; the actual nuclear capacity achieved by that year, with four installed power reactors, was only 600-800 MWe, or less than one-tenth the goal.[32] By 1985, capacity had been boosted slightly, to 1,095 MWe, and in that year the target was reset to 10,000 MWe of operating nuclear capacity installed by the year 2000—requiring a tenfold increase from the 1985 base.[33]

By 1995, however, after completing the six new power reactors first planned in 1980, India's rated nuclear-electric capacity had risen to only 2,200 MWe and its actual (operating) output to no more than 1,500 MWe—slightly more than doubling, but still well under one-fourth of the 1981 target.[34] This installed nuclear capacity represented only about 2.7 percent on the high side (less on the low side—1.9 percent—when the actual operating nuclear electric-output figure is used) of India's total of 80,000 MW electricity generating capacity instead of the 10 to 15 percent nuclear-electric proportion once hoped for.[35]

Nuclear Exports. India has played a very limited role in the nuclear export arena, partly as a matter of policy and partly because its domestic nuclear equipment and materials production capacity has been fully absorbed by domestic requirements. Having rejected the NPT, India is not legally bound by the Treaty's prohibition against assisting non-nuclear-weapon states to acquire or develop nuclear weapons or nuclear explosive capabilities.[36] India has not joined the International Nuclear Export (Zangger) Committee, and it has been a target rather than a member of the Nuclear Suppliers Group. However, India has never—as a policy—encouraged nuclear proliferation elsewhere. It has been generally cautious in its approach to nuclear exports.[37]

India has not published a formal and transparent nuclear export control system that clearly allocates licensing authority, or itemizes regulations or criteria that would explain what it regards as permissible exports and how it deals, if it does, with recipient end-use certifications. India has, however, made diplomatic representations to the United States and to other parties that it will not engage in sensitive nuclear transactions in troubled regions, particularly in the Middle East.[38]

Missile Program. As with nuclear technology, India has striven to achieve self-sufficiency in military armaments production and in allied areas, especially modern electronics and the exploration of the upper atmosphere and outer space. In 1970, at the initiative of then Department of Atomic Energy chief Vikram Sarabhai, India's electronics and space programs were given separate organizational and budgetary footings—enhancing their ability to take advantage of foreign cooperation and technology transfer. India's surface-to-surface ballistic missile program was organized under defense department auspices but has benefited from the technology transfer opportunities, personnel expertise, and development of rockets and launch vehicles within the space program.[39]

In developing its space and missile programs, India profited as early as the 1960s from extensive cooperation with the U.S. National Aeronautics and Space Administration (NASA), and subsequently with Britain, France, West Germany, and the former Soviet Union.[40] India's initial exposure to space-launch propulsion came from access to U.S. Scout sounding rockets, which utilized solid-rocket motor technology and could be reconfigured for use as short-range missiles, although not readily for typical nuclear payloads.[41] India was able to purchase off-the-shelf rocket engines and their technology from France,[42] and it has obtained Russian assistance with cryogenic rockets for heavy space-lift vehicles.[43]

India's indigenous missile development began in the 1970s and was accelerated by an integrated development program beginning in 1983.[44] By the late 1980s, India had work under way on prototypes for nuclear-capable, short-range ballistic missiles (for service against Pakistan) as well as nuclear-capable, medium-range ballistic missiles (presumably to deter potential threats from China).[45] The shorter-range missile, Prithvi, which began initial testing in 1989, is a liquid-fueled, single-stage missile designed to be fired from a mobile launcher and comes in two versions.[46] Prithvi I, the Army version, is said to have a range of 150 km with a 1,000-kg warhead. The other version for the Air Force is designed to carry a 500-kg warhead to a range of 250 km,[47] which could strike most of urban Pakistan, especially in the north. The Prithvi is a derivative of the Soviet-supplied SA-2 surface-to-air missile (SAM) designed for high-altitude air defense.[48]

While the Prithvi is theoretically nuclear-capable, the official line is that both versions will be fielded with conventional warheads. The mission of the Army version of the Prithvi is suppression of concentrated armored vehicles and personnel by bombardment with warheads that contain clusters of submunitions. The Air Force version is to be used for air base attack, to destroy aircraft in the open, and to hamper runway repairs.[49] It is clear from the lack of enthusiasm of India's military services for these missile systems that their military effectiveness as conventionally armed systems is dubious.[50] Armed with nuclear warheads, however, they unarguably would pose a mass-destruction threat to Pakistan's urban areas and population. In any case, production of the Prithvi and its storage near Pakistan conveyed just such a political signal.[51]

Agni, the medium-range ballistic missile, has been described as a "technology demonstrator."[52] In fact, it is an experiment in rocket hybridization. It combines a solid-fuel first stage (based on the American Scout's first-stage, solid-rocket motor) with the Prithvi liquid-fuel booster (derived from the Soviet SA-2 SAM) as the second stage.[53] Agni was tested in 1994 to a range of approximately 1,500 km. After further development, it is to be capable of traveling 2,500 km with a payload of at least 1,000 kg.[54] Based in eastern India, it could therefore reach some targets beyond Tibet, in southwestern China. Presumably, the same missile with a smaller but still nuclear-capable payload of 500 kg could reach farther east into more urbanized parts of China.

In the early 1990s, the Indian Space Research Organization (ISRO) sought to obtain assistance and technology transfer from the Soviet Union's space agency, Glavkosmos, to enable India to enter the field of cryogenic (cooled liquid-fueled) engines. While this was for heavy-lift, space launch vehicles, cryogenic engine technology happens to be what the United States, the Soviet Union, and China each adopted for their first ICBMs. Since the Soviet-Indian deal involved transfer of technology proscribed by the MTCR, the United States objected strenuously and, on May 11, 1992, imposed sanctions on Glavkosmos and ISRO for two years.[55] Russia then modified the $250-million deal to provide no more than seven off-the-shelf cryogenic engines and dropped the commitment to transfer production technology. This permitted removal of U.S. sanctions on Russia's Glavkosmos; those on ISRO ran their full two-year course.[56]

Nuclear-Capable Aircraft. India has had nuclear-capable aircraft delivery systems for more than two decades. Its advanced nuclear-capable aircraft from the 1980s includes the British-French Jaguar, French Mirage 2000, and Soviet-supplied MiG-27 and MiG-29 strike aircraft.[57]

Regional Tensions and U.S. Policy. Over the past decade, Indo-Pakistani relations have been marked by cycles of military tension as New Delhi has accused Islamabad of supporting militant separatist movements in Punjab and in Kashmir. In the winter of 1986-87, and again in the spring of 1990, and once again in 1993, it was widely feared that India and Pakistan might go to war. By the time of the 1990 crisis, both countries presumably possessed the ability to assemble and deploy nuclear weapons quickly, triggering concerns that if war erupted, it might lead to a nuclear confrontation or exchange.[58]

India and Pakistan have adopted a number of limited, bilateral confidence building measures—e.g., pledges not to attack each other's nuclear facilities, hot-line communications links, and military exercise notifications—that are intended to reduce the risk of inadvertent military conflict. These are described more fully in the Pakistan chapter of this book. India and China also have eased tensions along their border, with small steps dating back to Rajiv Gandhi's visit to Beijing in December 1988[59] and, more recently, through their agreement to a partial troop pullback by the end of 1995.[60]

In recent years, the United States had shifted the focus of its non-proliferation policy toward India. From the time of India's 1974 test until the mid-1980s, it gave priority to persuading India to reconsider joining the NPT and, short of that, to accept IAEA inspection on all of its nuclear facilities (full-scope safeguards). As the goal of convincing India to join the NPT faded under Presidents Bush and Clinton, however, U.S. policy efforts placed higher priority on fostering greater stability in the relationship between India and Pakistan—by means of Indo-Pakistani confidence-building measures, political accommodation, and normalization of relations.[61] Washington also sought to persuade both states to cap their nuclear and missile capabilities as an initial step toward their ultimate elimination. It was assumed that India and Pakistan would recognize the end of the Cold War, deep reductions in U.S. and former Soviet strategic arsenals, and the commitment to a comprehensive nuclear test ban treaty as strong incentives for curtailing their nuclear competition with one another.

Despite the shock to the non-proliferation regime of India's 1974 test, Washington had never backed up its non-proliferation diplomacy toward India with the same kind of far-reaching sanctions on arms transfer and security assistance that it imposed on Pakistan in unsuccessful attempts to head off its development of nuclear arms in the 1970s and 1980s (see Pakistan chapter).[62] In late 1992, however, the U.S. Congress added new provisions to the Foreign Assistance Act (Section 620F) calling on the U.S. president to pursue regional nuclear non-proliferation initiatives in South Asia and requiring the president to submit twice-yearly reports, beginning in April 1993, on the nuclear weapon and ballistic missile programs of China, India, and Pakistan. The law expected the president to determine whether either of the two South Asian states of concern possessed a nuclear explosive device. While not imposing specific sanctions, this U.S. legislation for the first time specifically treated India on a par with Pakistan as a proliferation concern.

In a significant overhaul of U.S. non-proliferation legislation in 1994, Congress passed the Nuclear Proliferation Prevention Act (NPPA). This legislation for the first time contained financial sanctions that would be triggered by Indian acts of proliferation, such as a nuclear test, an official declaration of a nuclear weapons program, and certain other stipulated possibilities. Clinton Administration diplomacy toward India assumed that the Indian economic policy liberalization measures of 1991 could open up new ways of dealing with proliferation and security problems in the Subcontinent. Priority was given to dissuading India from developing and deploying nuclear-capable ballistic missiles.

DEVELOPMENTS

India is one of the handful of countries in which proliferation activities steadily worsened between early 1995 and 1998—a trend few acknowledged until India resumed nuclear testing in May 1998. Although not a party to it, India lobbied behind the scenes against indefinite extension of the NPT. India also showed signs in 1995 of readiness to resume nuclear testing; pressed forward with the fast-breeder reactor program; turned against the Comprehensive Test Ban Treaty and the Fissile Material Cutoff initiative; reopened a former Soviet (now Russian) deal to supply nuclear reactors; provocatively moved Prithvi missiles to locations near its border with Pakistan; and began a major new buildup in acquisition of strike aircraft, smart bombs, and defensive missiles—with destabilizing implications for its relations with the presumably nuclear-armed Pakistan.

Nuclear Weapons Program: 1995 Test Scare. In the mid-1990s, India moved into a condition of governing-party instability at the national level and came close to reversing its official policy of disclaiming nuclear weapons in 1995 and 1996 before breaking out openly with fresh nuclear testing in 1998. Maintaining denial of a nuclear weapons posture, External Affairs Minister Pranab Mukherjee of the outgoing Congress Party government stated in late 1995: "We have the capability but we have deliberately opted not to manufacture nuclear weapons."[63] This official line was maintained by the two successor United Front coalition governments of Deve Gowda and I. K. Gujral. But pressure from domestic pro-nuclear interest groups and electoral competition with the pro-nuclear Bharatiya Janata Party (BJP) in 1995-96 brought India to the verge of new nuclear explosive testing. U.S. detection and disclosure of that effort temporarily checked it at that time.

In December 1995, the *New York Times* reported that U.S. spy satellites had detected increased activity at Pokaran, the site of India's 1974 nuclear test, and intelligence experts inferred that the activity signified preparation for another nuclear test.[64] India's Foreign Ministry described the report as "highly speculative" and later denied that India was intending to stage a nuclear test.[65] The NPPA contained automatic, no-waiver sanctions for any "non-nuclear-weapon state" that might detonate a nuclear device.[66] In January 1996, after warning India about the consequences of a nuclear test, the United States accepted Indian assurances that no test was planned.[67] However, India did not remove the monitoring equipment it installed at the test site before international pressure forced it to suspend work at the site,[68] and the same equipment probably was used for the May 1998 tests.

The testing controversy preceded India's April-May 1996 parliamentary elections, which pitted the ruling Congress Party against the ultra-nationalist BJP. The BJP had stated it would deploy nuclear weapons and both the Prithvi and Agni missiles, and that it would refuse to sign any international non-proliferation agreements.[69] In the elections, the BJP won the largest bloc of parliamentary seats and attempted to form a government under Atal Bihari Vajpayee, but he could not assemble a majority coalition to support his government and relinquished power within two weeks. It has since been reported that Vajpayee tried to initiate the nuclear tests then, but could not get his orders carried through because the BJP could not win a vote of confidence. The United Front, which then took over the national government, was a fragile center-left coalition of numerous parties. It vowed to retain the "nuclear option" until there is global nuclear disarmament but showed no enthusiasm for any major nuclear policy shift.[70]

In the meantime, India's nuclear energy establishment renewed its commitment to the fast-breeder and plutonium-reprocessing programs. In early 1997, Rajagopal Chidambaram, chairman of India's Atomic Energy Commission (IAEC), announced that the 500-MWt Prototype Fast Breeder Reactor (PFBR), then still at the proposal stage, "could be built in seven years" once given the go-ahead. The PFBR, he said, "will be used to breed, not burn up, plutonium." The PFBR will use plutonium separated from the unsafeguarded spent fuel from India's "indigenous" pressurized, heavy-water reactors (PHWRs), although it may take many years for the Kalpakkam facility to separate enough plutonium from unsafeguarded PHWR spent fuel for the core of the PFBR.[71] The Department of Atomic Energy has requested funding to begin construction of the PFBR in 1999, aiming to have the reactor ready for operation in 2007.[72]

In 1996, India significantly increased its ability to reprocess plutonium free from safeguards by commissioning a large-scale separation facility at Kalpakkam. A year before, IAEC Chairman Chidambaram had announced that the semi-commercial-scale reprocessing plant at Kalpakkam, India's third plutonium-separation facility, was "nearly completed" and would undergo trial operations "in less than one year's time."[73] The new reprocessing plant at Kalpakkam was then officially inaugurated in March 1996 and began "cold" commissioning the following quarter.[74] Rated with a capacity of 125 metric tons heavy metal (MTHM) per year, the Kalpakkam plant is to separate plutonium for India's PFBR as well as for the future commercial-scale, fast-breeder reactor.[75] The most recent reports indicate that the Kalpakkam plant will begin operation in 1998.[76]

At the end of 1997, India's DAE reported new efforts to upgrade the centrifuge uranium-enrichment program—ostensibly for submarine reactors.[77] U.S. government awareness of these efforts prompted the U.S. Department of Commerce to place the DAE subsidiary, Indian Rare Earths, Ltd. (IRE), which operates the Rattehalli (Mysore) enrichment facility, "on a short list of Indian organizations, which, because of their role in procuring [importing] unsafeguarded nuclear equipment and ballistic missile equipment, were to be denied any transfer of technology or U.S.–origin exports without express permission of the U.S. government after an interagency review."[78]

Civil Nuclear Power Program. India's Department of Atomic Energy has endeavored to build indigenous nuclear electric capacity to meet its planned goals, but setbacks have forced improvisation in its "go it alone" approach. India's import options have been constrained since the late 1970s by the reluctance of advanced supplier countries to sell it nuclear equipment. In 1992, all NSG members finally subscribed to the policy of denying nuclear exports to states like India that refuse full-scope IAEA safeguards.

In the early 1990s, however, Indian discussions with Russia resumed on a tentative agreement dating back to 1987 in which the Soviet Union had been prepared to sell India two light-water reactors.[79] The original Indian deal with the Soviet Union was to purchase two 440-MWe VVERs, but the revised deal calls for

Russia to provide two 1,000-MWe VVERs on a turnkey basis.[80] Russia intends that these reactors will be under IAEA safeguards but does not insist that India accept full-scope safeguards (on all its nuclear facilities) to complete this deal.

The United States has questioned the legality of this Russian-Indian nuclear supply plan on the grounds that Russia agreed in 1992 to require the NSG full-scope safeguards condition on future nuclear exports. Russia, the nuclear successor of the Soviet Union, has taken the view that this particular agreement is "grandfathered" as a Soviet commitment predating 1992. If Russia fulfills this plan to construct two power reactors in south India, the added capacity of 2,000 MWe will move India a significant step forward toward the goal it set in 1996 of installing 20,000 MWe by the year 2020. This will, however, represent a major break with India's past policy of attempting to rely exclusively on internal resources for its expansion of nuclear power.

Ballistic and Cruise Missile Programs. India stepped up its ballistic missile activities in the 1995-97 period. The Prithvi was further tested on January 27, 1996, and February 23, 1997,[81] and the Army version was put into low-rate production.[82] Despite international calls for restraint, reports indicated that India might have "deployed" about a dozen Prithvi missiles—said to be equipped only with conventional warheads—in the spring of 1997, at Jullundur, Punjab, near the border with Pakistan.[83] Indian officials later clarified that the missiles were not operationally deployed—presumably, that is, *not* mounted on mobile launchers or on concrete launch pads, fueled with their liquid propellant, mated with warheads, or ready for immediate launch, but instead stored in military facilities. Whatever the immediate launch status is of these Prithvi missiles, their transfer to deployment areas in the border region implies that they could be put into operation within days, if not hours, and certainly compresses the period of time for diplomatic intervention in a military crisis.

This semi-deployment of Prithvi in early 1997 was a serious setback to years of U.S. policy efforts to avert nuclear-capable missile deployment in South Asia—and was bound to provoke some form of reciprocal military action by Pakistan. One result was soon evident in Pakistan's announced testing in July 1997 of the Hatf-3 ballistic missile, with a claimed range of 600 km, easily sufficient to strike New Delhi.[84]

Other setbacks to U.S. urging of Indian restraint in missile development appear likely. Domestic pressures mounted in 1997 to revive the Agni program, which had been tentatively shelved in March 1994.[85] Prime Minister Deve Gowda's government initially seemed to resist pressure in December 1996 when it deferred a decision to revive development of the missile on the grounds that it was not needed and would be very expensive to deploy.[86] In April 1997, however, a BJP-influenced parliamentary panel fought back, demanding that the government revive the Agni program as essential to Indian national security. In late

July 1997, Defense Minister Mulayam Singh Yadav bowed to pressure and announced in Parliament that India would revive the Agni medium-range-missile development program.[87]

India claims to be developing a submarine-launched ballistic missile (SLBM) known as Sagarika, apparently based on the Prithvi.[88] There have been reports that India began development in 1994 of an intercontinental-range ballistic missile (ICBM) called Surya; an ICBM capability could be derived from the solid fuel stages of its Polar Satellite Launch Vehicle (PLSV).[89] A. P. J. Abdul Kalam, head of India's missile development program, told the Indian press in the fall of 1997 that India is also developing cruise missiles, i.e., unmanned air vehicles (UAVs) that can carry warheads.[90] One type of Indian UAV, known as Lakshya, is used as a target drone. Another, the Nishant, is designed with sensors as a cross-border surveillance and target-acquisition platform.[91]

Nuclear-Capable Aircraft. India also has been enhancing its nuclear air-delivery capability by purchasing and mass producing under license from Russia the Su-30MK fighter-bomber (supposedly equivalent to the American F-15E). The order was placed in November 1996, and deliveries of the first 8 of 40 aircraft began in 1997.[92] India also has just concluded a $300-million deal with Russia to acquire 6 Ilyushin-78 air-refueling tankers to extend the range of its Su-30MK and other strike aircraft.[93]

Missile Defense Plans. A new phase of missile competition was launched in South Asia by India's steps to acquire integrated air defense and anti-tactical ballistic missile (ATBM) systems through the restoration of military sales channels with Russia and growing ties with Israeli suppliers.[94] India has reviewed both the Arrow system, being developed by Israel in cooperation with the United States, and Russia's SA-10 and SA-12 systems. India reportedly will concentrate on a combination of the Russian S-300V (SA-12, Giant) ATBM system (touted as similar to the U.S. Patriot system).[95]

India's acquisition of a sophisticated air defense system with anti-missile capabilities theoretically could offset Pakistan's planned reliance on the M-11 ballistic missiles supplied by China and on Pakistan's high-performance tactical strike aircraft (e.g., F-16 and reconditioned Mirage III) as its primary nuclear-capable delivery systems. Indian anti-missile systems could therefore impair Pakistan's confidence in the deterrent value of its current nuclear capabilities. If this change occurred suddenly, Pakistan might, in order to restore that deterrent value, feel compelled to adopt a nuclear launch-on-warning (hair-trigger) posture, creating an inherently unstable military relationship.[96] If India's introduction of defenses took a long time, however, Pakistan—notwithstanding its smaller defense budget and indigenous resource base—probably would respond to this offense-defense challenge from India by building up its nuclear offensive deterrent incrementally. This could entail increasing the number of nuclear weapons available for delivery by both missiles and aircraft, acquiring cruise missiles, and developing decoys and penetration aids to saturate India's active defenses.

Reaction to the Comprehensive Test Ban Treaty. India's 1996 decision to oppose the Comprehensive Test Ban Treaty (CTBT)—an arms control and disarmament measure India had championed for the past forty years—probably was motivated by fear that compliance with the treaty would deprive it of a militarily meaningful nuclear option. On June 20, eight days before the U.N.–sponsored Conference on Disarmament (CD) was to complete a draft of the CTBT, India announced it would not sign the treaty. The official reason it gave was that the declared nuclear-weapon states refused to agree to the new Indian demand that the treaty must contain a provision for a "timebound framework for nuclear disarmament," obligating the nuclear-weapon states to negotiate the elimination of their nuclear weapons within a fixed period of ten or so years.[97]

Shortly after, India withdrew from the treaty's verification system in an effort to keep itself off of the list of states that must ratify the treaty for it to enter into force. The entry-into-force provision was then changed to require that the 44 countries that are members of the CD and that operate nuclear reactors must ratify the treaty for it to enter into force. India opposed this provision as an infringement on its sovereignty. Accordingly, on August 20, 1996, India formally vetoed the proposed text of the treaty, which had been negotiated by the CD for over two and a half years.[98] Despite India's opposition to the CTBT, the text of the treaty was presented to the U.N. General Assembly by Australia and approved overwhelmingly by a vote of 158-3, with only India, Libya, and Bhutan voting against. The treaty was opened for signature at the United Nations on September 24, 1996, and over 130 states, including all 5 declared nuclear-weapon states, had signed it as of late 1997.

India subsequently opposed the proposed Fissile Material Cut-off Treaty to end the production of weapons-usable fissile material; indeed, India's Ministry of Defense opposed the treaty concept in its annual report for 1995-96.[99]

Kashmir. In October 1996, the pro-India/pro-autonomy National Conference Party led by Farooq Abdullah won handily in the first State Assembly elections held in Jammu and Kashmir since 1990, when New Delhi assumed emergency control over the province and sent in large army and paramilitary forces to help quell uprisings by Muslim insurgents.[100]

In mid-1996, after the United Front assumed power at the center, Prime Minister Gowda offered Kashmir "autonomy" in return for an end to the violence—a sign of potential flexibility not apparent in previous Congress governments. However, the United Front coalition government in Delhi was inherently weak, and Prime Minister Gowda was pushed aside on April 13, 1997, by pressure from the Congress Party, whose support he needed to avoid a parliamentary vote of no-confidence. I. K. Gujral, who succeeded Gowda on April 19, was even more dependent on the Congress Party and was forced to resign on November 28, 1997.[101] Meanwhile, waiting in the wings, the BJP—a rising power in national politics—opposed "autonomy" for Jammu and Kashmir and blocked further flexibility in Delhi. In May 1998, shortly after the BJP formed the new government, L. K. Advani, the BJP minister for Home Affairs (internal security) greatly escalated tension with Pakistan by bellicose statements that India should prepare to forcibly recover the areas of Kashmir under Pakistani control. This and stepped up Indian military pressure along the line of control in Kashmir were said to have been pivotal factors in forcing Pakistan, instead of taking the high road, to react immediately to India's nuclear tests of May 11 and 13 with tests of its own.[102]

India's Relations with Pakistan and China.

Following Gujral's installation as India's Prime Minister and the February 1997 election of Nawaz Sharif as Pakistan's Prime Minister, the two had exchanged overtures aiming for a resumption of genuine bilateral dialogue. India and Pakistan began a new series of high-level meetings in March 1997—the first at the foreign ministerial level in four years, and the first at the head-of-government level in eight years.[103] When Gujral and Sharif met at a summit of South Asian leaders on May 12, 1997, they agreed to establish a hot line between the prime ministers' offices.[104] In a compromise, India agreed to include discussion of Kashmir in a broader agenda of dialogue with Pakistan, while Pakistan agreed to drop its insistence that progress on Kashmir be a prior condition for solving issues in other areas.

Nevertheless, talks in the summer and fall of 1997 made little progress. By November, moreover, crisis had overtaken both governments: Nawaz Sharif was caught in a tri-cornered battle with the president and chief justice of Pakistan,[105] and Gujral's United Front coalition government was ousted by Congress Party pressure, setting the stage in India for mid-term parliamentary elections. Roughly as foreseen at the end of 1997, the BJP, which has a very hard line on Kashmir, won enough parliamentary seats in April 1998 to be able to form a government with the help of several small, allied parties.

With respect to China, India's relations had been improving slowly but markedly for over a decade. Prime Minister Rajiv Gandhi had initiated a rapprochement with China by visiting Beijing in December 1988—in the first visit by an Indian head of government since his grandfather, Jawaharlal Nehru.[106] Limited improvements in official exchange and local cross-border trade had begun in the late 1980s, and working-level discussions of the boundary disputes followed. Sino-Indian relations continued to improve after early 1995 with the December 1996 visit of Chinese President Jiang Zemin to India, where the two sides signed an agreement to reduce border tensions.[107] India's May 1998 nuclear tests appear to have taken China just as much by surprise as they did other members of the international community. Early Indian cabinet-level statements justifying the tests on the basis of a nuclear threat from China threatened to undo years of confidence-building between Beijing and Delhi.

Chemical and Biological Weapons. India, an early signatory of the Chemical Weapons Convention (CWC), hurriedly ratified the convention on September 3, 1996, taking a place as chair on the CWC's executive council.[108] On June 26, 1997, the last day allowed by the CWC provisions for such declarations, India announced that it had a hitherto secret chemical weapons stockpile as well as production facilities and declared that it would eliminate them.[109] Although previously not known to be producing chemical weapons, India's well-developed chemical industry was known to have produced and exported certain precursors necessary for chemical weapons agents to countries of concern.[110] An Indian firm has been accused of assisting Iran's chemical weapons program.[111] India is also a party to the Biological Weapons Convention (BWC) and is assessed by the Pentagon to have the technical capability to develop offensive biological warfare agents—although, in the case of biological weapons, India is believed to have worked on defensive measures only.[112]

PROSPECTS

Even before conducting its May 1998 nuclear tests and declaring itself a nuclear-weapon power, India had been pressing ahead with sensitive nuclear activities in enrichment, plutonium reprocessing, and breeder reactor installation, as well as with ballistic missile development. India apparently was barely restrained by diplomatic intervention from new nuclear testing in 1995 and again, during the uncertainty of the BJP's 13-day tenure, in early 1996. India was poised to quickly resume nuclear and medium-range missile testing and to step up production and deployment of short-range missiles before the BJP came to power in April 1998. Pakistan was responding in 1996-97, trying to match each nuclear and missile development in India. Most hesitated then to label the South Asia action-reaction cycle as a full-fledged nuclear arms race, but that conclusion was unavoidable after May 1998. The immediate issue now is whether this nuclear and missile arms race can be slowed and eventually capped, short of actual war.

Since the Kashmir issue is still unresolved, the India-Pakistan nuclear arms competition brings the Subcontinent closer to the edge of a nuclear catastrophe. The nuclear tests triggered U.S. 1994 Nuclear Proliferation Prevention Act (NPPA) sanctions on India, and then on Pakistan.[113] Since the tests, the primary efforts of the U.S. Administration and of other leading states in the United Nations and in the Group of Eight (G-8) have been designed to contain the effects of India's and Pakistan's proliferation, to begin looking for the means to defuse the root problems between India and Pakistan (including the Kashmir dispute), and to stabilize the arms race pressures between both countries.

Undoubtedly, efforts will be made to commit both India and Pakistan, notwithstanding the changed situation, to engage in serious bilateral dialogue and to return to arms control and non-proliferation measures that are in their interests. India hinted right after its May 1998 detonations that it may, under certain conditions, be prepared to commit itself to certain provisions of the CTBT. This contorted posture should be explored warily, if at all; bait and switch has often been the rule in India's positioning on international non-proliferation treaties. No one should now be surprised to find that India's conditions for joining just some parts of the CTBT will detour and bog down, rather than smoothe, that treaty's entry into force.

The most far-reaching danger in need of policy attention is that India's defiance of the non-proliferation regime, unless stemmed, will start a chain reaction of nuclear proliferation, prompting weak NPT adherents and problem states not only to step up their own efforts to acquire nuclear weapons but to leave the NPT, or threaten to, arguing that the Treaty and regime enforcement mechanisms are no longer viable. Repairing this damage is going to be a difficult job, but a necessary one. Unless this is done, the non-proliferation regime may actually begin to wither. Repair and reconstruction of the regime will require a sustained review of non-proliferation policies and tools and the development of more effective approaches. Otherwise, as *The Economist* of London depicted on a recent cover, the 1998 detonations on the Subcontinent may lead to "a bomb in every backyard."[114]

NOTES

[1]India claimed to have carried out three simultaneous explosive device tests on May 11, one of a Hiroshima-size atomic device, another of a higher-yield "thermonuclear" device, and the third a low-yield "tactical" device, and claimed to have detonated two additional, low-yield devices on May 13. See R. Jeffrey Smith, "India Sets Off Nuclear Devices," *Washington Post*, May 12, 1998; "Ground Zero," a special report in *Newsweek*, May 25, 1998, pp. 28-37; Michael Elliott, "Out of Pandora's Box," *Newsweek*, June 8, 1998, pp. 20-27.

Analysis of the seismic shocks set off by the Indian and Pakistani tests left little doubt that each had detonated nuclear explosive devices of militarily significant yield, but raised questions about whether the numbers and size of the tested devices were as claimed. The seismic signal of Pakistan's claimed five detonations on May 28, according to preliminary analysis, showed a single event (possibly the cumulative effect of simultaneous detonations) that registered a magnitude of between 4.8 and 4.9 on the Richter scale, indicating an explosive force of between 8 and 17 kilotons (the Hiroshima bomb had a yield of about 15 kilotons). Analysis of the three Indian detonations on May 11 also showed what might have been a single event (or simultaneous detonations), but registered at 5.3 on the Richter scale, suggesting a total yield of 25 to 30 kilotons. This result would seem to exclude a true thermonuclear (H-bomb) device, but could be consistent with a so-called "boosted" device. See William J. Broad, "Explosion is Detected by U.S. Scientists," *New York Times*, May 29, 1998, and Michael Hirsh and John Barry, "Nuclear Jitters," *Newsweek*, June 8, 1998, p. 24.

[2]Pakistan claimed to have carried out five nuclear explosive tests on May 28 and a sixth on May 30. See Tim Weiner, "Pakistan, Answering India, Carries Out Nuclear Tests," and John F. Burns, "Arms Race Feared," *New York Times*, May 29, 1998; John Ward Anderson and Kamran Khan, "Pakistan Sets Off Nuclear Blasts," and Steve Coll, "The Race May be On—And May Be Hard to Stop," *Washington Post*, May 29, 1998; *The Economist*, May 30, 1998, pp. 16, 41-42.

[3]A Washington editorial distilled this assessment: "India's tests [were] strategically gratuitous: They did not emanate from any threat that reasonable people could perceive, certainly not one from Pakistan." *Washington Post*, May 29, 1998.

[4]A 1997 Pentagon report on proliferation stated: "India is believed to have a stockpile of fissile material sufficient for fabricating several nuclear weapons and could probably assemble at least some of these weapons within a short time of deciding to do so." Office of the Secretary of Defense, *Proliferation: Threat and Response*, November 1997, p. 17.

[5]See subsection on Nuclear Weapons Program, in this chapter.

[6]*Proliferation: Threat and Response*, 1997, op. cit.

[7]Sanctions were imposed on May 11, 1992, on both the Russian Glavkosmos organization, as the supplier of cryogenic engines, and on ISRO, as the recipient, for two years. These U.S. MTCR-related sanctions invoked the Arms Export Control Act and the Export Administration Act. For a detailed account based on both U.S. and Russian sources, see Alexander A. Pikayev, Elina V. Kiritchenko, Leonard S. Spector, and Ryan Gibson, *The Soviet-Russia Sale of Cryogenic Booster Technology to India and Its Implications for Russia's Adherence to Missile Technologies Control Regime*, Adelphi Paper, International Institute of Strategic Studies, 1998.

[8]Security analysts have long understood that the Indian defense establishment needs external threats to justify popular support for its desired defense expenditures. Potential threats from Pakistan are more palpable to the ordinary public than from other neighbors, such as China. Despite the enormous disparity between India and Pakistan, therefore, Pakistan looms large in India's public security perceptions. It is interesting in this context that whereas Indian diplomats and publicists regularly underscore the dangers of Pakistan's possession of nuclear weapons to both domestic and international audiences, many of India's "defense insiders"—civilian and military—either have been skeptical or disbelieved that Pakistan had usable nuclear weapons, or could quickly create them. Eric Arnett, for instance, wrote: "There are strong indications that Indian military planners do not take the Pakistani nuclear capability seriously and continue to plan for conventional war. The top priority of the Indian Air Force (IAF) ... [is] destroying Pakistani air bases." "Nuclear Stability and Arms Sales to India: Implications for U.S. Policy," *Arms Control Today*, Vol. 27, No. 5, August 1997, p. 8.

[9]After President Eisenhower's Atoms for Peace proposal, a large amount of nuclear process information was declassified in the United Nations Conference on the Peaceful Uses of Atomic Energy held in Geneva in August 1955. France, not then a nuclear-weapon state, disconcertingly published its method of plutonium extraction (chemical reprocessing), lifting the veil of secrecy from this weapons-related process. See Bertrand Goldschmidt, *The Atomic Complex: A Worldwide Political History of Nuclear Energy* (La Grange Park, IL: The American Nuclear Society, 1982), p. 259. By putting this information in the public domain, France expedited India's entry into plutonium reprocessing.

[10]China's May 1958 announcement that it intended to develop nuclear weapons did not evoke wide public discussion in India, but China's brief military invasion of eastern India in 1962 drastically changed Indian perceptions of China as a threat and of India's conventional defense requirements. With the 1962 Chinese invasion as the backdrop, China's first nuclear test two years later triggered a major debate in India about the value of nuclear weapons options.

[11]After the Chinese nuclear test of October 1964, Homi Bhabha lobbied for the start of a "subterranean nuclear explosive project" (SNEP), ostensibly for peaceful nuclear excavation activities. This program was approved by Prime Minister Lal Bahadur Shastri in November 1964, nominally shelved in 1966 by Vikram Sarabhai, Bhabha's successor, but reinvigorated in 1970 or 1971. The nuclear explosive test followed several years later, in May 1974.

[12]Only the original U.S. and Canadian power reactors built at Tarapur in Maharashtra and Kohta in Rajasthan, respectively, were placed under IAEA safeguards, as a condition of supply.

[13]All uranium-fueled reactors produce plutonium that could be used in nuclear weapons. However, the natural uranium-fueled, pressurized heavy-water reactor (PHWR) type—which India originally imported from Canada and chose as the design basis for its indigenous reactor construction program—is somewhat better suited to, and can be more easily operated for, the purpose of producing "high-quality" weapons-grade plutonium than the low-enriched uranium (LEU) fueled, light-water reactor (LWR) type. PHWR designs typically permit on-line refueling, which can be used to replace irradiated fuel rods after low burn-up, maximizing plutonium isotopes desirable for weapons or materials-handling.

[14]India's second reprocessing plant, the Prefre facility at Tarapur, is subject to IAEA inspection if and when U.S.-origin spent fuel irradiated in the Tarapur reactors is being reprocessed there, as a condition of the U.S.-India (Tarapur) agreement for cooperation. Any facility that reprocesses spent fuel from the two Canadian-supplied reactors in Rajasthan, if India ever lets this occur, would also be subject to IAEA inspection in perpetuity, as a result of the "full pursuit" safeguards provisions in the Indo-Soviet cooperation agreement negotiated to cover Soviet supplies of heavy water used in the Rajasthan reactors in the 1980s. With these, still hypothetical, exceptions, India's fuel-cycle facilities—reprocessing, enrichment, fuel fabrication and heavy-water production facilities—are all outside safeguards.

[15]India's oldest atomic research facility, the Tata Institute of Fundamental Research (TIFR), founded in Bombay (Mumbai) in 1944, helped to advance physics research and to train the Indian scientific community. It is not known to have played a direct role in the nuclear weapons program. The Center for Advanced Technology (CAT) in Indore, in Madhya Pradesh, and the Indira Gandhi Atomic Research Center (IGARC) in Kalpakkam, south of Madras in Tamil Nadu, may play support roles in weapons program research or technology development.

[16]David Albright, Frans Berkhout, and William Walker, *Plutonium and Highly Enriched Uranium 1996: World Inventories, Capabilities and Policies* (New York: Oxford University Press for Stockholm International Peace Research Institute, 1997), pp. 269ff.

[17]India built the Dhruva plutonium production reactor on the Cirus model, but by indigenous means, and placed it in full operation in January 1988, following two and a half years of start-up difficulties. Ibid., p. 266. Work on Dhruva (then designated R-5) began in 1972-73, with a target completion date, originally, of about 1980. See Rodney W. Jones, *Nuclear Proliferation: Islam, the Bomb, and South Asia*, The Washington Papers No. 82 (Washington, DC: Center for Strategic and International Studies, 1981), p. 26.

[18]The start-up and testing operations of PHWRs are ideal for production of high-quality plutonium in spent fuel, since they involve a short uranium burn-up period, which ensures that the resulting Pu-239, the isotope desired for weapons, is only minimally intermixed with other plutonium isotopes, such as Pu-240, 241 and 242, which complicate weapons production. These estimates also exclude the possibility that India may have chosen to operate some or all of these six power reactors *after* start-up in a mode that would maximize the production of high-quality plutonium, a step India could have taken by refueling the units more frequently than would normally be the case for the efficient production of electricity. It should be noted that even if India refueled these power reactors at normal rates, the lower quality plutonium produced in the reactors could still be used in nuclear explosives, if India chose to use it for that purpose.

[19]*Nuclear Engineering International: World Nuclear Industry Handbook 1997*, p. 122.

[20]Albright, et al., *1996 World Inventories*, op. cit., p. 206. The authors note that no operating information has been published about the FBTR, making it difficult to calculate both the amount of plutonium used to fuel this reactor, and the amount produced by its operation. The authors' estimates of weapons-grade plutonium in India take into account the amount of plutonium removed from the stockpile for fuel-loadings of research reactors, and assume for the FBTR a 50 percent (typical) operating capacity. If its performance has been significantly poorer, less plutonium would have been utilized in fabricating this reactor's fuel loadings. Albright, et al., ibid., p. 207.

[21]"Commissioning of Kalpakkam Nuclear Power Reactor in 2007," *Deccan Herald*, January 23, 1997, in *FBIS-NES-97-015*, January 24, 1997.

[22]The German foreign intelligence agency Bundesnachrichtendienst (BND) claimed in 1985, when the BARC cascade began operating, that then-BARC director P.K. Iyengar, who was involved in India's 1974 nuclear explosion effort, "aimed to develop an advanced fusion or boosted fission warhead 'in about two years'." Recent reports from the Indian DAE suggest that India has not successfully accumulated HEU for this purpose. See Mark Hibbs, "India to equip centrifuge plant with improved rotor assemblies," *Nuclear Fuel*, December 1, 1997, p. 8.

[23]If Russia builds two turnkey 1,000-MWe VVER light-water power reactors in South India, at Koodankulam, India presumably could also obtain appropriate LEU fuel from Russia, which has abundant supplies. Since Russia is (and the Soviet Union was) a member of the Nuclear Suppliers Group, these imported reactors, fuel, and the spent fuel would be subject to IAEA safeguards. By purchasing such LEU-fueled reactors, however, India technically could create a civil nuclear power rationale (although not a cost-effective one) for developing domestic enrichment technology. Separate from the civilian power program and another proliferation concern, India has claimed since the 1980s to have a program to develop a nuclear-propulsion reactor for submarines. R. Roy, "India-nuclear submarine," *Associated Press*, December 8, 1994, cited in Albright, et al., *1996 World Inventories*, p. 271, note 44. This may also be connected with the DAE's report that it is developing a small research reactor that would use enriched-uranium fuel. Government of India, Department of Atomic Energy, *Annual Report 1990-91*, cited in Albright, et al., note 43. Most naval nuclear-propulsion systems—to date, these exist operationally only among the established nuclear-weapon states—have been based on reactors that use HEU fuel.

[24]The previously available information on India's two small enrichment facilities at Trombay and Rattehalli (Mysore) has been collected in Albright, et al., *1996 World Inventories*, op. cit., pp. 269-271. See Developments section of this chapter, for additional detail on the enrichment program.

[25]As a contemporary note, Indian economists believe that electric power shortages in India today annually cost the economy the local equivalent of $2.7 billion, which represents about 1.5 percent of India's GDP. Dilip Ganguly, "India-Nuclear Quest," *Associated Press*, February 12, 1997. Methodical installation of nuclear power plants could have overcome the current electric power shortfalls in India. If, for instance, India had realized its Department of Atomic Energy plan targets for the installation of 8,000 MWe nuclear electric capacity in 1980-81, this alone would have made up the currently measured (mid-1990s) 9 percent baseload deficit in Indian electric power supply nationwide. Today's peak period electricity supply deficits run as high as 18 percent. This too could have been offset if India had methodically met its 1970s nuclear power installation targets for the 1990s, for installed capacity between 15,000 and 20,000 MWe.

[26]The two American-supplied Tarapur LWRs were commissioned and began operating in 1969.

[27]U.S. supply of LEU fuel to India was terminated after a final shipment in 1980, following several years of unsatisfactory negotiations. By prior agreement with the United States, France supplied LEU fuel for Tarapur in the 1980s, and recently China has been supplying LEU to India for Tarapur. India evidently plans to keep Tarapur operating at reduced operating capacity long past its design service life, which ended in 1993, until 2007. See Hibbs, "India to Equip Centrifuge Plant with Improved Rotor Assemblies," op. cit.

[28]The CANDU (Canada deuterium-uranium) design is a natural uranium-fueled, pressurized heavy-water-moderated reactor. The two Canadian-supplied power plants in Rajasthan, RAPS 1 and RAPS 2, were ordered in 1964 and 1967, respectively. RAPS 1 was finished in 1972 and went into commercial operation at the end of 1973. RAPS 2 began construction in 1968 but did not become operational until 1980-81, due in part to shortages in India's supplies of heavy water, which neither Canada nor the United States were then willing to supply. See *Nuclear Engineering International 1997*, op. cit., pp. 20-21. With the termination of Canadian assistance, the retrofits Canada developed to solve operational problems with its own reactors in Canada were not available to India, so that declining performance in the RAPS plants was difficult for India to rectify.

[29]The additional six reactors ordered after 1967 and actually installed as of 1997 are:

	Construction Began	Start-Up, Criticality	Commercial Operation
Madras, MAPS 1	Jan 1971	July 1983	Jan 1984
Madras, MAPS 2	Oct 1972	Aug 1985	Mar 1986
Narora 1	Dec 1976	Mar 1989	Jan 1991
Narora 2	Oct 1977	Oct 1991	Jun 1992
Kakrapar 1	Dec 1984	Sept 1992	May 1993
Kakrapar 2	Apr 1985	Jan 1995	Sept 1995

Nuclear Engineering International 1997, op. cit., pp. 20-21. See also chart on India's Nuclear Infrastructure, in this chapter.

[30]By 1995, although India's installed design capacity for ten nuclear power reactors amounted to about 2,200 MW electrical, the actual output, due to the requirement to run several reactors at much lower than their rated capacity, typically has not exceeded 1,500 MWe. See Neel Patri, "India and Russia Revive Talks for Two VVER-1000s in South India," *Nucleonics Week*, Vol. 37, No. 43, October 24, 1996, p. 8. Poor reactor performance was chronicled for fiscal 1994 in a report to Parliament, and is summarized in Neel Patri, "Rajasthan-2 down for 3 Years to Replace all Pressure Tubes," *Nucleonics Week*, Vol. 36, No. 21, May 25, 1995, pp. 3ff. For 1996-97, *Nuclear Engineering International*, op. cit., gives 1,790 MWe as India's net nuclear operating capacity.

[31]Dr. A. Gopalakrishnan, chairman of India's Atomic Energy Regulatory Board (AERB), who played an active role in identifying and pressing the Department of Atomic Energy to correct nuclear safety problems during his 1993-96 term, was victimized for his apparently unflinching watchdog role by non-renewal of his appointment in June 1996. See R. Ramachandran, "DAE drags its feet over extension of regulatory board chief's term," *Economic Times* (Bombay), June 13, 1996; "Act on AERB," *Economic Times*, editorial, June 20, 1996; "Timely Warning," *Times of India* editorial, June 20, 1996. For coverage of the nature of the safety problems, see also S.R. Valluri, "Nuclear safety options," *Economic Times*, May 10, 1996.

[32]Jones, *Nuclear Proliferation*, op. cit., p. 24.

[33]Under Prime Minister Rajiv Gandhi, a new push for nuclear power expansion was made in the mid-1980s, with the creation of a Nuclear Power Board, as part of a reorganization under the Department of Atomic Energy, to coordinate quality control for equipment and component manufacture by private industrial firms, and domestic acquisition of equipment for standardized PHWRs, to support the year 2000 (15-year) plan. See Pearl Marshall, "Indian Nuclear Industry: Preparing for the Great Leap Forward," *Nucleonics Week*, Vol. 26, No. 21, May 23, 1985, pp. 14ff.

[34]See note 25 above.

[35]According to India's then-Minister of Science and Technology, Y. K. Alagh, in India's total "commercial energy supply" picture today, 60 percent comes from coal, 27 percent petroleum, 7 percent natural gas, 3 percent hydro, and only 0.3 percent nuclear. "N-Power Will Get High Priority," *Times of India*, January 23, 1997.

India's optimistic new target for nuclear power generation for the year 2020 is 20,000 MWe, a tenfold increase on current capacity, but this time allowing two and a half decades for achievement.

[36]India, by striving for self-sufficiency in nuclear technology, escaped most U.S. nuclear non-proliferation sanctions laws, which are either based on NPT obligations or presuppose that the target country is an importer of sanctionable items (e.g., reprocessing or enrichment technology). India's potential role as a nuclear exporter could, nonetheless, trigger sanctions in the 1994 Nuclear Proliferation Prevention Act (NPPA), which do not depend on whether a state that commits a defined act of proliferation is a member of the NPT or not, and seeks to hold states (and entities) accountable irrespective of whether they are exporters or importers. Sanctions under the NPPA have now been triggered against India not by its exports, but by its May 1998 nuclear weapons testing.

[37]For a study of Indian potential as a third-tier (emerging) nuclear supplier and its decision-making structure and practices, circa 1989, covering Indian nuclear exports and other foreign nuclear cooperation, see Rodney W. Jones, "India," in William C. Potter, ed., *International Nuclear Trade and Nonproliferation: The Challenge of the Emerging Suppliers*, (Lexington, MA: Lexington Books/D. C. Heath, 1990), pp. 153-179.

India discussed supplying to Iran a 5-MWt research reactor but later dropped the offer when suspicions about Iraq's intentions became more widespread. India has explored the sale of small research reactors to NPT member countries in the Persian Gulf, South Asia, and Southeast Asia, and it has supplied heavy water to South Korea, where IAEA safeguards are regularly applied to nuclear facilities and materials in any case. India briefly contemplated nuclear cooperation with Libya in the late 1970s, a venture then promoted by the current BJP government's defense minister, George Fernandes, but dropped after external and internal criticism materialized.

[38]Jones, "India," ibid.

[39]Separate organizations were created for the civil space and military missile programs, and they are separately budgeted, but the same rocket technology has been accessible to both organizations, key personnel (notably, the head of the space and later of the military rocket programs, Dr. A. P. J. Abdul Kalam) have shuttled between them, and shifting priorities in favor of one tends to be at the expense of the other. The civil space program has been centered in the Indian Space Research Organization (ISRO) founded in 1969, under the ministries concerned with civilian space or science and technology, while the missile program has been the offspring of the Defense Research and Development Organization (DRDO), which is under the Defense Department but also has ties to the Department of Atomic Energy.

[40]In November 1963, the United States began launching sounding rockets from Indian soil in a cooperative program, and between 1963 and 1975, more than 350 U.S., French, British, and Soviet sounding rockets were launched from India's Thumba Test Range. Gary Milhollin, "India's Missiles—With a Little Help from Our Friends," *Bulletin of the Atomic Scientists*, November 1989, pp. 31-35. Milhollin traces back the basis of most of India's space launch vehicles and military ballistic missiles to foreign training, technical assistance, and space launch hardware or technology.

[41]Dr. A. P. J. Abdul Kalam (see note 39) spent four months at NASA's Wallops Island center, the home of the Scout space launch vehicle. India thereafter copied the Scout to produce its first space launch vehicle (SLV), and the first stage of this SLV was adapted to become the first stage of the Agni MRBM. Milhollin, "India's Missiles," ibid.; and K. S. Ramamurthy, "Commentary Lists Accomplishments of Indian 'Missile Man,'" *All India Radio*, November 30, 1997, in *FBIS-TAC-97-334*, November 30, 1997.

[42]France licensed to India both the Centaure sounding rockets and the Viking high-thrust liquid rocket motor, used on the European Space Agency's Ariane satellite launcher. Milhollin, "India's Missiles," op. cit., p. 32.

[43]See subsection on Ballistic Missile Program under Developments section of this chapter.

[44]According to W.P.S. Sidhu, "India's original missile programme began in the 1970s." *Enhancing Indo-U.S. Strategic Cooperation*, Adelphi Paper 313, International Institute of Strategic Studies, 1997, p. 19. Also according to Sidhu, five missile types—the Trishul and Akash surface-to-air missiles (SAMs), the Nag anti-tank missile (ATM), and the Prithvi and Agni surface-to-surface missiles (SSMs)—were all started under the DRDO's Integrated Missile Development Programme in 1983, partly anticipating restrictions on technology transfer that would attend the creation of the MTCR, pp. 23-27.

[45]*Nuclear-capable* is a term of art that makes allowance for the typical mass (500 kg or more) of an early-generation atomic warhead configured for use on a missile. Surface-to-surface missiles that are designed to carry payloads of at least 500 kg are considered nuclear-capable. Considerable refinement of early-generation nuclear devices typically is needed to produce a version that can be mounted in the front end of a missile and withstand the stresses of aerodynamic flight and atmospheric reentry. India's May 1998 nuclear test series almost certainly had as one of its objectives testing a warhead design that could be mounted on ballistic missiles. Pakistan's tests right after may also have had this objective.

[46]Pravin Sawhney, "Prithvi's Position: India Defends Its Missile," *Jane's International Defence Review*, Vol. 30, July 1997, pp. 43-45.

[47]For an evaluation of the destabilizing consequences of short-range ballistic missiles (SRBMs) in the Indo-Pakistani context, see Neil Joeck, *Maintaining Nuclear Stability in South Asia*, Adelphi Paper 312, International Institute of Strategic Studies, 1997, p. 69.

[48]Apparently yet another Indian-planned adaptation of this former Soviet air defense missile is the Sagarika, a short-range submarine-launched ballistic missile (SLBM). Rahul Bedi, "Political Pressure May Change India's Course on Disarmament," *Jane's Defence Weekly*, January 31, 1996, p. 27; Ranjit Kumar, "Plan to Develop Submarine-

Launched Missile," *Navbharat Times*, August 2, 1994 in *JPRS-TND-94-016*, August 19, 1994, p. 23. According to the "President's Summary" of a November 1995 National Intelligence Estimate on missile proliferation, India is planning to deploy the Sagarika by 2010. Bill Gertz, "Intelligence Report Warns of Missile Launches Against U.S.," *Washington Times*, May 14, 1996.

[49]See Eric Arnett, "Nuclear Stability and Arms Sales to India: Implications for U.S. Policy," *Arms Control Today*, Vol. 27, No. 5, August 1997, p. 8; and his citation of J.P. Joshi, "Employment of Prithvi Missiles," *Journal of the United Services Institution of India*, October/December 1996.

[50]Joeck, *Maintaining Nuclear Stability*, op. cit., p. 68, and his note 7. Joeck reflects the expert consensus that the Prithvi is "cumbersome to manage in the field and will be a tempting target . . . [and is of] high cost, limited range and questionable accuracy." Even the Pakistanis, he notes, regard the Prithvi as an implausible military system as long as it is only conventionally armed, ibid., note 8.

[51]See Raj Chengappa, "Boosting the Arsenal," *India Today*, February 29, 1996, pp. 98-99.

[52]The most important technology demonstrations associated with Agni missile testing were autonomous (on-board computer-controlled) missile guidance and nose cone heat shields (a warhead atmospheric reentry requirement), using training and technology from West German sources, obtained before the MTCR went into effect. Milhollin, "India's Missiles," op. cit., pp. 32-35.

[53]Milhollin, "India's Missiles," op. cit., pp. 34-35.

[54]International Institute of Strategic Studies, *The Military Balance, 1995/96*, (London: Oxford University Press for IISS, October 1995), p. 283.

[55]The deal originated in 1991 while the Soviet Union still existed; the Soviet Union ceased to exist at the end of 1991, and Russia, the nuclear successor state, also inherited Glavkosmos in 1992.

[56]Pikayev et al., *Soviet-Russia Sale of Cryogenic Technology to India*, op. cit.

[57]International Institute for Strategic Studies, *The Military Balance 1996/97* (London: Oxford University Press for IISS, 1996), p. 161; *Aviation Week & Space Technology*, August 5, 1996, p. 15.

For an assessment of the pattern of arms imports and the impact on the India-Pakistan military balance in the 1980s and early 1990s, see Rodney W. Jones, "Principal Purchasers and Recipient Regions: South Asia," in Andrew J. Pierre, ed., *Cascade of Arms: Managing Conventional Weapons Proliferation* (Cambridge, MA: The World Peace Foundation, and Washington, DC: The Brookings Institution Press, 1997), pp. 305-39.

[58]If India and Pakistan had gone to war over Kashmir in 1990, it would have been the first major military conflict in history between two states that each had ready access to nuclear arms. If significant hostilities had appeared imminent, moreover, there is good reason to believe that both sides would have readied their nuclear arms— Pakistan to protect against a preemptive attack by superior Indian nuclear and/or conventional forces, and India to protect against being placed at a disadvantage by nuclear-ready Pakistan. One report asserted that during the crisis the two states in fact came to the nuclear brink as Pakistan loaded nuclear weapons on U.S.-made F-16 strike aircraft. See Seymour M. Hersh, "On the Nuclear Edge," *New Yorker*, March 29, 1993, p. 86. Another report was skeptical, however; see Douglas Jehl, "Assertion India Pakistan Faced Nuclear War Is Doubted," *New York Times*, March 23, 1993.

[59]On CBM activity in South Asia in the 1980s, and on the China visit, see Rodney W. Jones and Harald Mueller, "Preventing a Nuclear Sarajevo: Proliferation in the Middle East and South Asia," *Arms Control Today*, Vol. 19, No. 1, January/February 1989, pp. 20-22. That visit was an important bilateral watershed; Rajiv Gandhi made known to the press, based on his talks in Beijing, that he believed China was not targeting India with nuclear missiles. Ibid., p. 22.

[60]*Arms Control Reporter 1995*, 454.B.213.

[61]Although diplomatic relations were restored between India and Pakistan after the Simla Agreement of 1972, and certain air travel and communications links exist, trade relations and ordinary travel between the two countries remain highly constrained.

[62]After 1974, the United States declined to expand peaceful nuclear cooperation with India. The Indian test also inspired a U.S.-led, comprehensive upgrading of international nuclear export controls, along with the formation of the Nuclear Suppliers Group. But the United States did not seek to legislate special sanctions in non-nuclear areas of international exchange that would be triggered by Indian acts of proliferation, until 1994 (see note 36 above).

[63]"Mukherjee Calls Nuclear Program 'Peaceful'," *The Hindustan Times,* December 18, 1995, in *FBIS-NES-95-245*, December 21, 1995, p. 44.

[64]Tim Weiner, "U.S. Suspects India Prepares to Conduct Nuclear Test," *New York Times,* December 15, 1995. See also Joeck, *Maintaining Nuclear Stability,* op. cit., p. 42 (and his notes) for a thorough account of the first appearance of Indian test preparation reports, of India's first response (denial), India's secondary response (grudging admission that preparations had been made, but the test would not be carried out), and Pakistan's response.

[65]Krishnan Guruswamy, "India-Nuclear Test," *Associated Press*, December 15, 1995; "India Says Does Not Plan Nuclear Test," *Reuters*, December 19, 1995.

[66]U.S. law and the NPT recognize only the original five nuclear powers as "nuclear-weapon states," since they declared their programs before the NPT was negotiated, and U.S. law therefore would apply sanctions to any non-nuclear-weapon state, including India, that breaches the nuclear explosive threshold. The sanctions in the 1994 NPPA include a cut-off of all economic and military aid, credits, bank loans, and export licenses, and would require that the United States veto loans by international financial institutions, such as the World Bank, to offending states. The sanctions may be delayed by the president once for 30 days and waived only if both houses of Congress pass a joint resolution authorizing the waiver. India receives only $170 million a year from the United States in direct assistance, but receives about $2 billion per year from the World Bank, and benefits from billions of dollars of other foreign investment activity that is guaranteed by U.S. OPIC and Export-Import Bank programs that would be disrupted by triggering this law. Jim Mann, "U.S. Warns India an A-Test Would Imperil Aid, Ties," *Los Angeles Times*, January 16, 1996.

[67]Sid Balman, Jr., "India Assures U.S. on Nuke Test," *United Press International,* January 19, 1996.

[68]"India Delivers Blow to Nuclear Test Ban," *Jane's Defence Weekly*, July 3, 1996, p. 29.

[69]"BJP Declares Readiness To Deploy Nuclear Weapons," *Business Standard* (India), April 8, 1996, in *FBIS-NES-96-070*, April 11, 1996.

[70]Jawed Naqvi, "Indian Government Sets Nuclear, Kashmir Policies," *Reuters*, June 5, 1996.

[71]Mark Hibbs, "Tarapur-2 to Join Twin BWR in Burning PHWR Plutonium," *Nuclear Fuel*, September 25, 1995, p. 19. NOTE: Albright says initial core for FBTR has been fabricated using 50 kg of plutonium, but it had only half of the design number of fuel elements. Albright et al., *1996 World Inventories*, op. cit., p. 268.

[72]"Commissioning of Kalpakkam Nuclear Power Reactor in 2007," *Deccan Herald*, January 23, 1997, in *FBIS-NES-97-015*, January 24, 1997.

[73]India's first reprocessing facility was the unsafeguarded pilot-scale plant at BARC in Trombay, rated with a capacity of 50 metric tons heavy metal (MTHM) per year, and used to separate plutonium for India's 1974 nuclear explosive test program as well as for small research reactors. The Trombay facility had been shut down for refurbishment for some years, before reopening around 1990. India's second reprocessing facility, Prefre (at Tarapur), was originally intended to reprocess fuel from the two U.S.-origin Tarapur LWRs and the two Canadian-supplied Rajasthan PHWRs. It was assumed IAEA safeguards would be applied at Prefre when fuel from those reactors was being processed. However, the United States declined to give India permission to reprocess U.S.-origin spent fuel from the Tarapur reactors. Moreover, India may have decided not to reprocess spent fuel from the Canadian reactors there because a condition of the Soviet heavy-water agreement with India required that safeguards not only apply *in perpetuity* to the plants and fuel in which the heavy water was first used (this heavy water was procured for and used in the Rajasthan reactors), but also in perpetuity to any plant in which the heavy water or the affected spent fuel (or derivative material) was later used. This could explain why, as Indian experts have reported, Prefre, which had a nominal design capacity of 100 MTHM/year, operated for more than a decade at under 25 MTHM/year. This would correspond to the spent fuel output at that time of the then small number of operating reactors of indigenous origin, whose spent fuel is not subject to safeguards. Hibbs, "Tarapur-2 to Join Twin

BWR," op. cit., p. 19. See also "Third Reprocessing Plant Opened at Kalpakkam," *Nuclear News*, May 1996.

[74]PPNN Newsbrief, Second Quarter 1996, p. 7, citing *NucNet News*, March 27.

[75]"Third Reprocessing Plant Opened at Kalpakkam," *Nuclear News*, May 1996.

[76]According to reports in December 1997, the existing Kalpakkam Reprocessing Facility (KARP) was delayed by subcontractor failures, and has been cold tested, but will have begun hot operations only from 1998. It will have a nominal throughput capacity of 100 metric tons heavy metal (MTHM) in spent fuel per year, with some expansion potential. The Indian DAE now says that KARP will be used exclusively to reprocess MAPS (Madras) PHWR spent fuel. A second line that would also nominally reprocess 100 MTHM is under construction in the same plant, but is planned to come on line only after the first line is shut down around 2008. The DAE plan is to use the plutonium recovered from KARP for fuel loading of the FTBR. See Mark Hibbs, "First separation line at Kalpakkam slated to begin operations next year," *Nuclear Fuel,* December 1, 1997, p. 8.

[77]In these latest reports on India's uranium centrifuge activities, there are a number of new points and nuances: (1) technicians at BARC, where the pilot enrichment facility was said to have about 100 centrifuges in its array, have done experimental work on sophisticated ("supercritical") centrifuges; (2) the Rattehalli pilot plant, which is operated by a DAE subsidiary known as Indian Rare Earths, Ltd., had a cascade of several hundred relatively simple ("subcritical") centrifuges intended to enrich to between 30 and 45 percent U-235, for fueling nuclear submarine reactors, but did not produce 90 percent enrichment levels; (3) the Rattehalli equipment encountered "operational difficulties"; (4) the DAE now intends to install "improved (centrifuge) rotor assemblies" at the Rattehalli plant; (5) there is no planned use for the Rattehalli enriched uranium output, DAE claims, in power reactors (nor for the Tarapur power plant, which has sufficient LEU stockpiled from Chinese supply); and "very little real progress has been made in India's long-standing goal to develop a nuclear-powered submarine." See Hibbs, "India to Equip Centrifuge Plant with Improved Rotor Assemblies," *Nuclear Fuel,* December 1, 1997, pp. 7-8.

[78]Ibid., p. 7.

[79]Michael Gordon, "Russia Selling Atomic Plants to India; U.S. Protests Deal," *New York Times*, February 6, 1997.

[80]The Indo-Soviet deal was formalized under Indian Prime Minister Rajiv Gandhi in 1988, and languished after Rajiv Gandhi was assassinated the following year. Neel Patri, "India and Russia Revive Talks for Two VVER-1000s in South India," *Nucleonics Week*, Vol. 37, No. 43, October 24, 1996, p. 8.

[81]Narayanan Madhavan, "India Launches Advanced Medium-Range Missile," *Reuters*, January 27, 1996. "India Test-Fires Missile," *Washington Post*, February 24, 1997.

[82]"Army 'Very Close' to Inducting 'Prithvi' Missile," *The Pioneer* (India), January 27, 1997, in *FBIS-NES-97-020*, January 31, 1997.

[83]Rahul Bedi, "India Ignores West and Test Fires Prithvi II," *Jane's Defence Weekly*, February 7, 1996, p. 12; R. Jeffrey Smith, "India Moves Missiles Near Pakistani Border," *Washington Post*, June 3, 1997.

[84]This reportedly 600-km range solid-fuel Hatf-3 missile was described in an Indian source as a "clone" of the Chinese-origin M-9 MRBM. Unlike the M-11, whose 280-km range from Pakistan's territory falls short of India's capital at New Delhi, the 600-km range M-9 could reach not only New Delhi but deep into India's interior, including Bombay (Mumbai), India's premier industrial and financial city. Manoj Joshi, "In the Shadow of Fear," *India Today International*, Vol. XXII, No. 17, July 15-21, 1997, pp. 50ff. No other evidence has appeared, however, of Pakistani acquisition of M-9 missiles.

[85]Rahul Bedi, "Countdown Starts for India's Ballistic Missile," *Jane's Defence Weekly*, September 11, 1996, p. 21; Nelson Graves, "India Shelves Agni Ballistic Missile," *Reuters*, December 5, 1996.

[86]Bedi, "Countdown Starts for India's Ballistic Missile," ibid., p. 21; Graves, "India Shelves Agni," ibid.

[87]See *Reuters* report from New Delhi, July 30, 1997; Manoj Joshi, "In the Shadow of Fear," op. cit.

[88]See note 48.

[89]According to Office of Secretary of Defense, *Proliferation: Threat and Response 1997*, op. cit., pp. 19-20, India has the capability to convert space launch vehicles into either IRBMs (3,000-5,500 km range) or ICBMs (5,500-km or greater range), but it has not done so. Reports suggest, however, that a missile with a range between 8,000 and 12,000 km, based on the components of the existing, four-stage PSLV, possibly is under development: "India, Ballistic Missile Threats: National Briefings," Internet: http://www.cdiss.org/countrya.htm#INDIA (September 27, 1996); Ali Abbas Rizvi, "Indian Missile Programme," *Asian Defence Journal,* May 1995, p. 22; "India's Intercontinental Missile Program Criticized," *Jang,* in *FBIS-TAC-95-004,* July 28, 1995; and "Missile and Space Launch Capabilities of Selected Countries," *Nonproliferation Review,* Spring/Summer 1996, p. 193. India's Ariane-based three-stage Geostationary Satellite Launch Vehicle (GSLV), partly based on cryogenic engines, hypothetically could be converted to an ICBM with a range of about 14,000 km with a payload of over two tons.

[90]"Reusable Missiles Under Development," *The Pioneer*, November 28, 1997, p. 1, in *FBIS-TAC-97-334*, November 30, 1997.

[91]N. K. Pant: "Ruling Over the Skies," *The Pioneer*, February 8, 1997, p. 11, in *FBIS-NES-97-027*.

[92]International Institute of Strategic Studies, *The Military Balance, 1997/98* (London: Oxford University Press for IISS, October, 1997), pp. 150, 153; *Aviation Week & Space Technology*, August 5, 1996, p. 15. The reported value of the Russian sale to India of 40 Su-30MK is $2 billion. See Anatoliy Yurkin, "India to Buy Six Russian Tanker Aircraft," *ITAR-TASS*, December 2, 1997, in *FBIS-UMA-97-336*.

[93]Yurkin, "India to Buy," ibid.; Nikolay Novichkov, "Russia's Sukhoy Finalizing Second Su-30MKI Pilot," *ITAR-TASS*, December 12, 1997, in *FBIS-UMA-97-346*.

[94]For a more detailed assessment, see Gregory Koblentz, "Theater Missile Defense and South Asia: A Volatile Mix," *Nonproliferation Review*, Vol. 4, No. 3, Spring/Summer 1997, pp. 54-62.

[95]One report claims the Russian ATBM system will be a new S-300 variant, the S-300-PMU. See Ranjit Kumar: "Preparations for Defense Against Possible Pakistani Missile Attack," *Navbharat Times*, February 18, 1996, p. 1. Kumar reports that the system would be deployed around both Delhi and Bombay (Mumbai), against Pakistani M-11 missiles, and would be integrated with the indigenous Rajendra phased-array radar system (claimed to be capable of tracking multiple objects from 60 km out) together with the indigenous Akash high-altitude surface-to-air missile (SAM) system (claimed to be capable of defending local areas as large as 300 square km—a defense footprint suitable not only for most military facilities but also for smaller cities). These figures should be taken with a grain of salt, since promoters of future systems are prone to exaggerate the prospective performance. The announcements are significant less for their performance claims than for their political messages and destabilizing, arms race implications. India's interest in such defenses puts new pressure on Pakistan, whose far more limited resources preclude its adopting comparable defensive measures and therefore increase its incentives to augment its offensive capabilities.

[96]Certain capabilities, such as space-based photography and sensors, provided they are available to both sides, can be stabilizing to a military balance, even an asymmetrical one. However, India alone has satellite-based information about its adversary. Since launched in December 1995, India's locally built IRS-1C satellite has been used exclusively by the Indian military to monitor developments in Pakistan and China. The satellite's panchromatic camera reportedly has a resolution of 5.8 meters. Vivek Raghuvanshi, "India Exerts Military Control of Satellite," *Defense News*, June 17-23, 1996, p. 10. Pakistan has no independent access to satellite intelligence. The effects of this and other military asymmetries in the relationship with India are likely to increase Pakistan's reliance on weapons (and methods) of last resort.

[97]Barbara Crossette, "India Warns It Won't Sign Test Ban Pact As It Stands," *New York Times*, June 21, 1996.

[98]Barbara Crossette, "India Vetoes Pact to Forbid Testing of Nuclear Arms," *New York Times*, August 21, 1996.

[99]Vivek Raghuvanshi, "India Blasts Nuclear Regimes," *Defense News*, August 26-September 1, 1996, p. 24.

[100]John F. Burns, "India Counts on Vote to Blunt Kashmir Insurgency," *New York Times*, September 7, 1996; "Pro-India Party in Kashmir Wins a Landslide Victory in Elections," *New York Times*, October 3, 1996.

[101]Kenneth J. Cooper, "Government Falls, India Premier Quits," *Washington Post*, November 29, 1997; Cooper, "Indian Parliament Ordered Dissolved, Mid-Term Vote Set," *Washington Post,* December 5, 1997.

[102]Barbara Crossette, "South Asian Arms Race: Reviving Dormant Fears of Nuclear War," *New York Times*, May 29, 1998.

[103]See John F. Burns, "New Report from India-Pakistan Meeting, *New York Times*, May 13, 1997.

[104]Kenneth Cooper, "Leaders of India, Pakistan Agree on Gestures of Goodwill," *Washington Post*, May 13, 1997.

[105]Nawaz Sharif apparently prevailed on December 2, 1997, when the Army declined to back the president, who then resigned; this seemed to enhance the prospect that an elected, majority government would finally enjoy the normal five-year tenure between parliamentary elections and have a more realistic opportunity to undertake long-term commitments. See Kenneth J. Cooper, "Pakistani Prime Minister Bests Rivals in Feud," *Washington Post,* December 3, 1997.

[106]See Jones and Mueller, op. cit., note 59.

[107]Clarence Fernandez, "India Concern on Pakistan Persists After Jiang Trip," *Reuters*, December 1, 1996.

[108]"India's Ratification of Chemical Weapons Convention," *Deccan Herald*, June 30, 1997.

[109]"India Sets an Example," *International Herald Tribune*, August 7, 1997; "India declares chemical weapons," *The Hindu*, June 27, 1997; *Proliferation: Threat and Response,* November 1997, op. cit., p. 17.

[110]Office of the Secretary of Defense, *Proliferation: Threat and Response,* April 1996, op. cit., p. 38.

[111]Con Coughlin, "Iran Secures Aid to Make Poison Gas in Deal with India," *London Sunday Telegraph*, June 23, 1996.

[112]*Proliferation: Threat and Response,* April 1996, op. cit., p. 38.

[113]These sanctions require the cutoff of all but humanitarian U.S. government-to-government assistance and government-backed credit facilities to India and Pakistan, with effects that are likely to be much more damaging to Pakistan's more externally indebted economy than to India's. The sanctions also put into question roughly $2 billion of proposed World Bank loans to India annually. They block further U.S. Overseas Private Investment Corporation (OPIC) and Export-Import backed credit for U.S. private investment activity in India, which could derail projects valued at another $2 or $3 billion a year. They will also stand in the way of private U.S. bank loans to the Indian government and to its public industrial sector. Technically, they do not affect private American investment in the strictly private sector of India's (or Pakistan's) economy, except in sensitive technology areas (e.g., defense, atomic energy, arms production, and supercomputers), but since much of India's economy is subject to government funding, credit, or control, the ripple effects of these sanctions on private trade and investment could be very substantial. For rationale of NPPA sanctions, see also notes 36 and 66.)

[114]*The Economist*, June 6-12, 1998.

Additional References

Francine R. Frankel, *Bridging the Non-Proliferation Divide: The United States and India* (Lanham, MD: University Press of America, 1995); P.R. Chari, *Indo-Pak Nuclear Standoff* (New Delhi: Manohar and Columbia MO: South Asia Books, 1995); David Cortright and Amitabh Mattoo, eds., *India and the Bomb: Public Opinion and Nuclear Options* (Notre Dame: University of Notre Dame Press, 1996); Shekhar Gupta, *India Redefines its Role,* Adelphi Paper 293 (Oxford: Oxford University Press for the International Institute of Strategic Studies, London, 1995); T.T. Poulouse, *The CTBT and the Rise of Nuclear Nationalism in India* (New Delhi: Lancers Books, 1996); General K. Sundarji, *Blind Men of Hondoostan: Indo-Pak Nuclear War* (New Delhi: UBS Publishers, 1993); Jasjit Singh, *Abolishing Nuclear Weapons: Why and How?* (New Delhi: Institute for Defence Studies and Analysis, 1997); Sundeep Waslekar, *Abolishing Nuclear Weapons: Rajiv Gandhi Plan Revisited* (Urbana: Program in Arms Control, Disarmament, and International Security, University of Illinois, July 1994); Neil Joeck, *Maintaining Nuclear Stability in South Asia,* Adelphi Paper 312 (Oxford: Oxford University Press for the International Institute for Strategic Studies, 1997); *Preventing Nuclear Proliferation in South Asia,* Report of a Study Group sponsored by The Asia Society (New York: The Asia Society, 1995); George Perkovich, "A Nuclear Third Way in South Asia," *Foreign Policy,* No. 91, Summer 1993, pp. 85-104; Kanti Bajpai et. al., *Brasstacks and Beyond: Perception and Management of Crisis in South Asia* (New Delhi: Manohar and Columbia MO: South Asia Books, 1995); Devin T. Hagerty, "Nuclear Deterrence in South Asia: The 1990 Indo-Pakistani Crisis," *International Security,* Vol. 20, No. 3 (Winter 1995/96), pp. 79-114; Sumit Ganguly and Ted Greenwood, *Mending Fences: Confidence-and Security Building Measures in South Asia* (Boulder: Westview Press, 1996); Stephen P. Cohen, ed, *Nuclear Proliferation in South Asia: The Prospects for Arms Control* (Boulder: Westview Press, 1991).

India:
Map and Chart

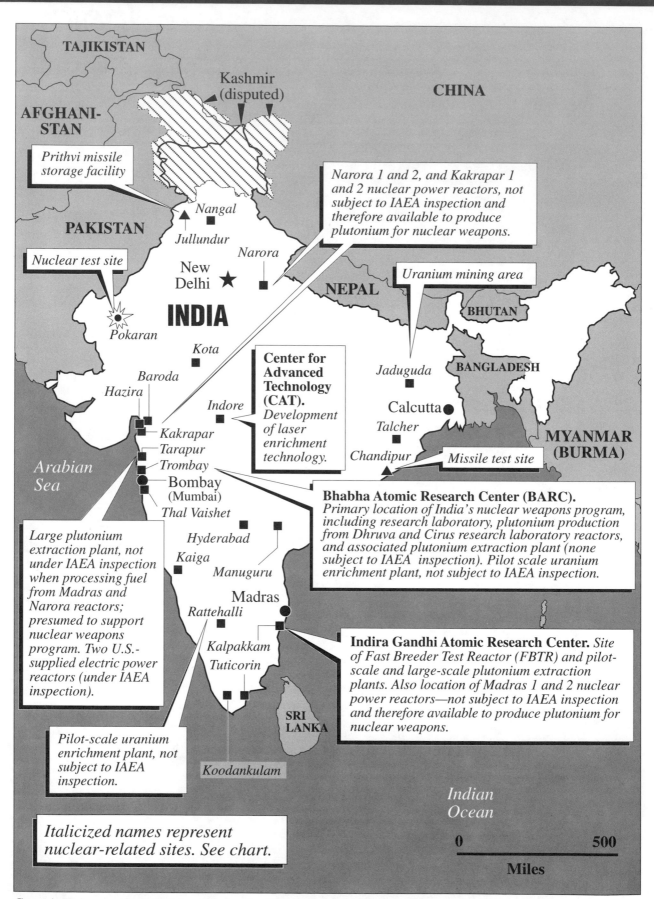

TAJIKISTAN

AFGHANI-
STAN

Kashmir
(disputed)

CHINA

**Prithvi missile
storage facility**

Nangal

PAKISTAN

Jullundur

*Narora 1 and 2, and Kakrapar 1
and 2 nuclear power reactors, not
subject to IAEA inspection and
therefore available to produce
plutonium for nuclear weapons.*

Narora

New
Delhi

INDIA

NEPAL

Nuclear test site

Pokaran

Kota

Uranium mining area

BHUTAN

Jaduguda

BANGLADESH

Baroda

Hazira

Indore

Calcutta

**Center for
Advanced
Technology
(CAT).**
*Development
of laser
enrichment
technology.*

Talcher

Chandipur

**MYANMAR
(BURMA)**

Kakrapar
Tarapur
Trombay

*Arabian
Sea*

Bombay
(Mumbai)

Thal Vaishet

Missile test site

Bhabha Atomic Research Center (BARC).
*Primary location of India's nuclear weapons program,
including research laboratory, plutonium production
from Dhruva and Cirus research laboratory reactors,
and associated plutonium extraction plant (none
subject to IAEA inspection). Pilot scale uranium
enrichment plant, not subject to IAEA inspection.*

*Large plutonium
extraction plant, not
under IAEA inspection
when processing fuel
from Madras and
Narora reactors;
presumed to support
nuclear weapons
program. Two U.S.-
supplied electric power
reactors (under IAEA
inspection).*

Hyderabad

Kaiga

Manuguru

Madras

Rattehalli

Kalpakkam

Tuticorin

Indira Gandhi Atomic Research Center. *Site
of Fast Breeder Test Reactor (FBTR) and pilot-
scale and large-scale plutonium extraction
plants. Also location of Madras 1 and 2 nuclear
power reactors—not subject to IAEA inspection
and therefore available to produce plutonium for
nuclear weapons.*

SRI
LANKA

*Pilot-scale uranium
enrichment plant, not
subject to IAEA
inspection.*

Koodankulam

*Indian
Ocean*

**Italicized names represent
nuclear-related sites. See chart.**

0   500

Miles

Carnegie Endowment for International Peace, *Tracking Nuclear Proliferation*, 1998

INDIA: Nuclear Infrastructure

NAME/ LOCATION OF FACILITY	TYPE AND CAPACITY: GROSS DESIGN (NET) OUTPUT[a]	COMPLETION OR TARGET DATE	IAEA SAFEGUARDS
POWER REACTORS: OPERATING			
Tarapur 1	Light-water, LEU and MOX 210 (150) MWe.	1969	Yes
Tarapur 2	Light-water, LEU[b] 210 (160) MWe.	1969	Yes
Rajasthan, RAPS-1, Kota	Heavy-water, natural U 220 (90) MWe.	1972	Yes
Rajasthan, RAPS-2, Kota	Heavy-water, natural U 220 (187) MWe.[c]	1980	Yes
Madras, MAPS-1, Kalpakkam	Heavy-water, natural U 235 (170) MWe.	1983	No
Madras, MAPS-2, Kalpakkam	Heavy-water, natural U 235 (170) MWe.	1985	No
Narora 1	Heavy-water, natural U 235 (202) MWe.	1989	No
Narora 2	Heavy-water, natural U 235 (202) MWe.	1991	No
Kakrapar 1	Heavy-water, natural U 235 (170) MWe.	1992	No
Kakrapar 2	Heavy-water, natural U 235 (202) MWe.	1995	No
POWER REACTORS: UNDER CONSTRUCTION			
Kaiga 1	Heavy-water, natural U 235 (202) MWe.	1998	No
Kaiga 2	Heavy-water, natural U 235 (202) MWe.	1998	No
Rajasthan, RAPP-3, Kota	Heavy-water, natural U 235 (202) MWe.	1999	No
Rajasthan, RAPP-4, Kota	Heavy-water, natural U 235 (202) MWe.	1999	No
POWER REACTORS: PLANNED AND PROPOSED			
Tarapur 3	Heavy-water, natural U 500 (450) MWe.	2004	No
Tarapur 4	Heavy-water, natural U 500 (450) MWe.	-	No
Kaiga 3	Heavy-water, natural U 235 (202) MWe.	-	No
Kaiga 4	Heavy-water, natural U 235 (202) MWe.	-	No
Kaiga 5	Heavy-water, natural U 235 (202) MWe.	-	No
Kaiga 6	Heavy-water, natural U 235 (202) MWe.	-	No

NAME/ LOCATION OF FACILITY	TYPE AND CAPACITY: GROSS DESIGN (NET) OUTPUT[a]	COMPLETION OR TARGET DATE	IAEA SAFEGUARDS
Rajasthan, RAPP-5, Kota	Heavy-water, natural U 500 (450) MWe.	-	No
Rajasthan, RAPP-6, Kota	Heavy-water, natural U 500 (450) MWe.	-	No
Rajasthan, RAPP-7, Kota	Heavy-water, natural U 500 (450) MWe.	-	No
Rajasthan, RAPP-8, Kota	Heavy-water, natural U 500 (450) MWe.	-	No
Koodankulam 1	Russian VVER Light-water, LEU 1000 (953) MWe.[d]	-	Yes
Koodankulam 2	Russian VVER Light-water, LEU 1000 (953) MWe.	-	Yes
RESEARCH REACTORS			
Apsara BARC, Trombay	Light-water, medium-enriched Uranium, pool type, 1 MWt.	1956	No
Cirus BARC, Trombay	Heavy-water, natural U 40 MWt.	1960	No
Dhruva BARC, Trombay	Heavy-water, natural U 100 MWt.	1985	No
Kamini IGCAR, Kalpakkam	Uranium-233 30 KWt.	1996	No
Zerlina BARC, Trombay	Heavy-water, variable fuel, 100 Wt, decommissioned.	1961	No
Purnima 1 BARC, Trombay	Fast neutron, critical assembly, zero power, decommissioned.	1972	No
Purnima 2 BARC, Trombay	Uranium-233 .005 KWt, dismantled.	1984	No
Purnima 3 BARC, Trombay	Uranium-233.[e]	-	No
BREEDER REACTORS			
Fast Breeder Test Reactor (FBTR) IGCAR, Kalpakkam	Plutonium and natural U 40 MWt.	1985	No
Prototype Fast Breeder Reactor (PFBR) IGCAR, Kalpakkam	Mixed-oxide fuel, 500 MWe, planned.	2008[f]	No
URANIUM ENRICHMENT			
Trombay	Pilot-scale ultracentrifuge plant; operating.	1985	No
Trombay	Laser enrichment research site.	early 1980s	No
Rattehalli (Mysore)	Pilot-scale ultracentrifuge plant; operating.[g]	1990	No
Center for Advanced Technology, Indore	Laser enrichment research site.	1993[h]	No

INDIA (cont'd.)

NAME/ LOCATION OF FACILITY	TYPE AND CAPACITY: GROSS DESIGN (NET) OUTPUT[a]	COMPLETION OR TARGET DATE	IAEA SAFEGUARDS
REPROCESSING (PLUTONIUM EXTRACTION)			
Trombay	Medium-scale, 50 tHM/y; operating.	1964/1985	No
Tarapur (Prefre)	Large-scale, 100 (25) tHM/y; operating.[l]	1977	Only when safeguarded fuel is present.
Kalpakkam	Laboratory-scale, operating.[j]	1985	No
Kalpakkam	Large-scale, two lines, 100 tHM/y each; under construction.[k]	1998/2008[l]	No
URANIUM PROCESSING			
Rakh, Surda, Mosaboni[m]	Uranium recovery plant at copper concentrator; operating.		N/A (Not Applicable)
Jaduguda, Narwpahar, Bhatin[n]	Uranium mining and milling; operating.		N/A
Hyderabad	Uranium purification (UO_2); operating.		No
Hyderabad	Fuel fabrication; operating.		Partial
Trombay	Uranium conversion (UF_6); operating. Fuel fabrication.[o]		No
Tarapur	Mixed uranium-plutonium oxide (MOX) fuel fabrication; operating.		Only when safeguarded fuel is present.
HEAVY-WATER PRODUCTION			
Trombay	Pilot-scale; operational?[p]		-[q]
Nangal	14 t/y; operating.	1962	-
Baroda	67 t/y; intermittent operation.	1980	-
Tuticorin	71 t/y; operating.	1978	-
Talcher phase 1	62 t/y; operating.	1980	-
Talcher phase 2	62 t/y; operating.	1980	-
Kota	100 t/y; operating.	1981	-
Thal-Vaishet	110 t/y; operating.	1991	-
Manuguru	185 t/y; operating, under expansion.	1991	-
Hazira	110 t/y; operating.	1991	-

Abbreviations:

HEU	=	highly enriched uranium
LEU	=	low-enriched uranium
nat. U	=	natural uranium
MWe	=	millions of watts of electrical output
MWt	=	millions of watts of thermal output
KWt	=	thousands of watts of thermal output
tHM/y	=	tons of heavy metal per year
MOX	=	mixed natural U and plutonium oxide fuel

NOTES (India chart)

[a]The gross design capacity of the reactor is its original power rating, while the net operating capacity refers to *current* output as reported for the latest operational use. See *Nuclear Engineering International: 1997 World Nuclear Industry Handbook.*

[b]Up to 30 percent mixed oxide (MOX) fuel was planned for loading in late 1995, but no subsequent reporting has confirmed this. See Marks Hibbs, "Tarapur-2 to Join Twin BWR in Burning PHWR Plutonium," *Nuclear Fuel*, September 25, 1995, p. 18f. Under contract, China supplied enough LEU to India to operate both units at Tarapur at 125 MWe until 2007. Mark Hibbs, "India to Equip Centrifuge Plant With Improved Rotor Assemblies," *Nuclear Fuel*, December 1, 1997, p. 7f.

[c]RAPS-2 was shut down in 1994 for at least three years, and as of late 1997 had not been restarted. "Rajasthan-2 Down for 3 Years to Replace All Pressure Tubes," *Nucleonics Week*, May 25, 1995, p. 3.

[d]Based on a general agreement reached in October 1995, Russia plans to supply the two VVER reactors to India. The original provisions were for turnkey reactors, but India wants to change the sales terms so that it can build the reactors itself. This would amount to a technology-transfer, which Russia has not yet agreed to. Russia is reportedly under strong U.S. pressure to change the agreement to include a safeguards requirement, which would also cover spent fuel. See Mark Hibbs, "India Seeks China-style Deal for Two VVERs, MINATOM Says," *Nucleonics Week*, January 11, 1996, p. 4; and Jyoti Malhotra, "U.S. Pressure Cited for Faltering Russian Nuclear Deal," *Business Standard* [India], April 23, 1996, in *FBIS-NES-96-080*, April 24, 1996, p. 67.

[e]India listed Purnima 3 as an operating research reactor when it exchanged lists of nuclear facilities with Pakistan; no power rating was given. See "India and Pakistan exchange lists of nuclear facilities," *Nucleonics Week*, January 9, 1992.

[f]According to Indian Department of Atomic Energy Secretary Rajagopol Chidambaram, the design engineering for PFBR is complete, construction is expected to begin in 2000, and completion is expected in 2008. Mark Hibbs, "Despite Chronic Delays, DAE Maintains Prototype Breeder to Be Built Soon," *Nuclear Fuel*, December 1, 1997, p. 9.

[g]The Mysore plant, operated by India Rare Earths Ltd. (IRE), is intended to produce a small amount of HEU, enriched to 30-45 percent U-235, for use in a nuclear submarine reactor, which has thus far not been designed or built. Although the nuclear-powered submarine program has been under development since the 1980s, little progress has been made. India may also have requested centrifuge technology from Brazil based on a nuclear cooperation agreement signed between the two in 1996. In 1997 the U.S. Department of Commerce placed IRE on a list of companies that may not receive any U.S.-origin technology due to its procurement of unsafeguarded nuclear and ballistic missile equipment. Mark Hibbs, "India to Equip Centrifuge Plant with Improved Rotor Assemblies," *Nuclear Fuel*, December 1, 1997, p. 7; and Mark Hibbs and Mike Knapik, "U.S. Aims to Kill Our Program, India Says After Brazil Trade Cutoff," *Nuclear Fuel*, November 3, 1997, p. 4f.

[h]Construction on the Indore research center continued in 1993, but some of the facilities, perhaps including the laser enrichment site, were operational. See "India Funds Nuclear Construction, Operations, and Research in FY-92," *Nucleonics Week*, March 19, 1992.

[i]The Power Reactor Reprocessing Plant (Prefre) has a nominal output capacity of 100 tHM/y, but has operated for more than a decade at about 25 tHM/y. Hibbs, "Tarapur-2," op. cit., p. 19.

[j]Reportedly built to reprocess spent fuel from the FTBR. Mark Hibbs, "First Separation Line at Kalpakkam Slated to Begin Operations Next Year," *Nuclear Fuel*, December 1, 1997, p. 8.

[k]According to a recent report, the first line is scheduled to begin hot operations in 1998, reprocessing spent fuel from the Madras heavy water power reactors. The second line, reportedly identical to the first but still under construction, is scheduled to begin operations when the first closes, in approximately 2008. While not fully clear on this point, this report may imply that a separate large-scale (1000 tHM/y) facility devoted to reprocessing fuel from India's fast-breeder reactors, also planned for Kalpakkam according to the *1997 World Nuclear Industry Handbook*, p. 122, has been shelved due to financial constraints. Given this possibility, the second line could be adapted to separate this type of fuel. Mark Hibbs, "First Separation Line," op. cit., p. 8f.

[l]The initial target date for completion of the first line was 1990, but it was delayed by subcontractors' failure to supply key equipment. See *1997 World Nuclear Industry Handbook*, op. cit., p. 122; Mark Hibbs, "First Separation Line," op. cit., p. 8f.; and Hibbs, "Tarapur-2," op. cit., p. 18f.

[m]Sites listed in OECD Nuclear Energy Agency and International Atomic Energy Agency, *Uranium: 1991 Resources, Production, and Demand*, p. 197.

[n]These uranium milling sites are located in a 10-km area near Jaduguda. Listed in the Wisconsin Project *Risk Report*, March 1995, p. 9.

[o]This is a small plutonium fuel fabrication facility for Purnima II (5 KWe) that was expanded to produce fuel for the FBTR. David Albright, Frans Berkhout and William Walker, *Plutonium and Highly Enriched Uranium 1996: World Inventories, Capabilities and Policies* (New York: Oxford University Press for Stockholm International Peace Research Institute, 1997), p. 206.

[p]See Andrew Koch, "Nuclear Testing in South Asia and the CTBT," *Nonproliferation Review,* Spring-Summer 1996, p. 99.

[q]The non-proliferation regime does not include the application of safeguards to heavy-water production facilities, but safeguards are required on the export of heavy water.

Pakistan

Pakistan is not a party to the Nuclear Non-Proliferation Treaty (NPT) and was long regarded as a *de facto* nuclear power that "could assemble a limited number of nuclear weapons in a relatively short timeframe."[1] India's May 11 and 13, 1998, nuclear tests and nuclear-weapons declaration produced a matching reaction from Pakistan, which, after briefly hesitating, tested a series of nuclear devices of its own on May 28 and 30 and also declared itself a nuclear-weapon power.[2]

Pakistan has been locked in a conflict relationship with India that has led to three wars since both became independent in 1947. As a result of Pakistan's defeat by India in the last war of 1971, Pakistan was dismembered; its former eastern wing became the independent state of Bangladesh. Pakistan secretly commenced its nuclear weapons program shortly thereafter.

Since the late 1980s, the top military and civilian leadership of Pakistan has sought to project an ambiguous form of nuclear deterrence—non-weaponized deterrence—to check any major attack and related political and military pressure from its much larger and also nuclear-capable neighbor. Although Pakistan had not declared or demonstrated nuclear weapons before May 1998, it was believed to have a secret nuclear arsenal consisting of a small number of complete but unassembled nuclear weapons that could be quickly readied for use.[3] By conservative estimates, Pakistan by 1995 would have been able to deploy about 10 nuclear weapons; by other estimates, the number could have been as high as 15-25.[4]

Pakistan reportedly possesses about 30 nuclear-capable M-11 surface-to-surface missiles with a 280-300-km range, supplied by China, and is reported to be constructing a factory to build similar missiles.[5] In July 1997, as a riposte to India's semi-deployment of the Prithvi missile in Punjab, where it could strike Lahore, Pakistan reportedly tested the Hatf-3, a 600-km ballistic missile, and then in the spring of 1998 tested the Ghauri missile, which is claimed to have a range upwards of 1,500 km that could reach much more deeply into Indian territory. Pakistan halted further production of weapons-grade uranium in 1991, temporarily placing a ceiling on the size of its stockpile of highly enriched uranium (HEU). It has made efforts to expand other elements of its nuclear weapons program, however, including work on weapons design, on unsafeguarded facilities to produce plutonium and, possibly, on facilities to increase the production capacity for weapons-grade uranium.[6]

BACKGROUND

Nuclear Weapons Program. Pakistan secretly launched its nuclear weapons program in 1972, in the aftermath of the 1971 war. The program, which gained new impetus after India' s nuclear test in May 1974, had made substantial progress in acquiring sensitive uranium-enrichment know-how and technology by the early 1980s. This was expedited by the return to Pakistan in 1975 of Dr. Abdul Qadeer Khan, a German-trained metallurgist, who was employed at the classified Urenco uranium-enrichment plant at Anselmo in the Netherlands in the early 1970s. Dr. Khan brought to Pakistan personal knowledge of gas-centrifuge equipment and industrial suppliers, especially in Europe, and was put in charge of building, equipping, and operating Pakistan's Kahuta enrichment facility.[7] In 1977 and again in 1979, the United States terminated economic and military aid to Pakistan in a sanctions-based effort to dissuade it from continuing the nuclear weapons program.[8]

Glenn-Symington Amendment. The 1979 economic and military aid cutoff was made pursuant to the 1977 "Glenn-Symington Amendment." This amendment requires the termination of assistance to any state that imported uranium-enrichment equipment or technology after 1977 and refused to place it under IAEA inspection.[9] Pakistan transgressed this law in 1979 because of its importation of equipment for its secret uranium-enrichment plant at Kahuta.[10]

In 1981, in the wake of the Soviet occupation of Afghanistan, the United States for six years suspended the application of the uranium-enrichment sanctions provisions of the Glenn-Symington Amendment to Pakistan and provided greatly increased military and economic assistance to Pakistan.[11] Washington's fundamental goal was to create a bulwark against further Soviet expansionism and to establish Pakistan as a strategic partner supporting anti-Soviet forces in Afghanistan. Reagan Administration officials also argued that the restoration of aid would advance U.S. non-proliferation objectives by enhancing Pakistan's overall security, thereby reducing Islamabad's motivation to acquire nuclear arms.

Pakistan continued its nuclear weapons program, however. A 1983 U.S. State Department analysis of the effort declared that there was "unambiguous evidence that Pakistan is actively pursuing a nuclear weapons development program." The report highlighted Pakistan's progress in key areas of weapons manufacture, its critical dependence on clandestine efforts to procure nuclear equipment from private Western firms, and its receipt of nuclear assistance from China, including assistance "in the area of fissile material production and possibly also nuclear device design."[12]

The program reached a key milestone in 1985, when, despite numerous pledges to the United States that it would not produce weapons-grade uranium, Pakistan crossed this threshold.[13] By 1986, Pakistan had apparently produced enough material for its first nuclear device, thereby acquiring a *de facto* nuclear weapons capability, although it is believed to have refrained at this juncture from fabricating the key nuclear components for nuclear arms.[14] Although the United States sought to discourage Pakistan from pursuing its nuclear program throughout this period, Washington restrained its pressure on Islamabad because of the need for continued Pakistani cooperation in the campaign to oust Soviet forces from Afghanistan.[15]

The Pressler Amendment. The Afghanistan-related duality in U.S. policy toward Pakistan was reflected in the enactment of a 1985 law known as the Pressler Amendment, which specified that U.S. aid and government-to-government military sales to Pakistan would be cut off unless the president certified at the beginning of each U.S. fiscal year that Pakistan did "not possess a nuclear explosive device and that the proposed U.S. assistance program will significantly reduce the risk that Pakistan will possess a nuclear explosive device."[16] This formulation underscored U.S. concerns about the Pakistani nuclear program but did not trigger an immediate termination of U.S. aid, inasmuch as Pakistan was believed not to have an assembled device at the time.[17] Despite further Pakistani advances toward nuclear weapons, through October 1989, Presidents Reagan and Bush made the certifications necessary to permit U.S. aid and arms sales. The 1989 certification that Pakistan did not possess a nuclear device reportedly was made only after Pakistan's Prime Minister Benazir Bhutto agreed to suspend the further production of weapons-grade uranium.[18]

In late 1989 and early 1990, perhaps because of the threat of war with India, Pakistan apparently ended this freeze and fabricated cores for several nuclear weapons from pre-existing stocks of weapons-grade uranium.[19] As a result, in October 1990, the Bush Administration declined to make the certification required by the Pressler Amendment and terminated all aid and government-to-government military sales to Pakistan.[20] At the time, Pakistan had 28 additional F-16 aircraft and certain other military hardware on order, to be acquired on a government-to-government (rather than on a commercial) basis, and therefore unquestionably subject to the Pressler Amendment embargo.[21] Islamabad continued making payments on these purchases after October 1990 so that it could receive the armaments at issue in the event that the prohibition against such U.S. military sales was rescinded.[22]

In late 1991, Prime Minister Nawaz Sharif, who succeeded Benazir Bhutto in November 1990, reinstated the freeze on the production of weapons-grade uranium. This freeze appears to have remained in effect.[23] Pakistan continued to produce low-enriched uranium (LEU), however, thereby enlarging its overall nuclear weapons potential.[24] Other aspects of the Pakistani nuclear program also continued to advance. These included work on nuclear weapon designs; construction of a 40-MWt nuclear reactor at Khushab that is not subject to IAEA inspection and is apparently intended for the production of plutonium; work on safeguards-free facilities for separating plutonium from the Khushab reactor's spent fuel; and the enlargement of Pakistan's capacity to enrich uranium, reportedly through the construction of a second enrichment plant at Golra.[25]

Pakistan's Ambiguous Nuclear Posture. Although evidence of Pakistan's ability to deploy nuclear weapons had been clear at least since President Bush failed to certify in October 1990 that Pakistan did not possess a nuclear device, rather than declare itself a nuclear-weapon state, Pakistan preferred merely to hint at this capacity in official statements. In August 1994, however, eleven months after he lost the prime ministership to Benazir Bhutto in the October 1993 elections, Nawaz Sharif openly stated: "I confirm that Pakistan possesses the atomic bomb."[26] This did not, however, comprise an official statement of the Pakistani government. Prime Minister Bhutto thereafter invoked the more traditional, ambiguous official line, stating in April 1995, for example: "We have enough knowledge and capability to make and assemble a nuclear weapon. But we have voluntarily chosen not to either assemble a nuclear weapon, to detonate a nuclear weapon, or to export technology."[27] In another pronouncement in a similar vein, she stated in April 1996 that Pakistan's nuclear program would "remain peaceful so long as our national survival and territorial integrity is not threatened."[28] After his return to power in the elections of February 1997, Prime Minister Nawaz Sharif stayed within the official policy line, until his hand was forced by India's May 1998 tests (see Developments section of this chapter).

Pakistan's quest for a nuclear deterrent has been motivated principally by fears of domination by India, whose population, economy, and military resources dwarf those of its western neighbor. A desire for leadership in the Islamic world, popular nationalist sentiment, and bureaucratic pressure also contribute to Pakistan's bid for nuclear arms. Since the 1971 India-Pakistan War, relations between Islamabad and New Delhi have alternated between periods of relative peace and periods of considerable tension, punctuated with crises that nearly erupted into war during the winter of 1986-87 and the spring of 1990. In the latter crisis, heated by Indian accusations that the insurgency by Muslim extremists in the Indian-held portion of Kashmir had been instigated and was fueled by Pakistan, there were fears that Pakistan might take steps to deploy its nascent nuclear arsenal. These concerns spurred intensive, and ultimately successful, U.S. diplomatic efforts to defuse the situation.[29]

Arms Control and Confidence-Building Measures. Over the years, Pakistan has proposed numerous bilateral nuclear arms control initiatives with India, declaring, for example, that it would be prepared to join the NPT or accept other non-proliferation measures if India did so.[30] India has rejected these proposals, arguing that they do not address the nuclear threat India faces from China and that nuclear disarmament questions should be addressed as global rather than regional issues. Pakistan and India have, however, adopted a number of bilateral confidence-building measures, including a military-to-military hot line and an agreement, which entered into force in January 1991, prohibiting the two states from attacking each other's nuclear installations. Lists of facilities covered by this agreement are now exchanged periodically.[31]

In August 1992, the two states brought into force agreements on mutual advance notification of military exercises and on the avoidance of overflights of military aircraft. They also signed a bilateral accord banning the possession, manufacture, and use of chemical weapons. This accord, however, did not contain any verification measures. Both states also became original signatories to the Chemical Weapons Convention (CWC) in mid-January 1993. India ratified the CWC in September 1996, and Pakistan ratified it in October 1997. Both India and Pakistan have also ratified the Biological Weapons Convention (BWC).

Ballistic Missile Program. Pakistan's efforts to acquire ballistic missiles intensified in the mid-1980s, when, with Chinese assistance, it launched a program to develop two short-range ballistic missile (SRBM) systems: the 80-km-range Hatf-1 and the 300-km-range Hatf-2.[32] A 1994 study indicated that the Hatf-2 was not expected to be available as a militarily deployable system for a number of years, but a 1997 Pentagon report observed that it may have been discontinued.[33] In parallel with these programs, Pakistan also sought to acquire the 280-300-km-range, nuclear-capable M-11 ballistic missile system and associated equipment from China.

The precise nature of China's support for Pakistan's ballistic missile program is not known. The 1997 Pentagon proliferation report says, "Pakistan received SRBMs and associated equipment from China during the early 1990s."[34] This latest official report makes clear publicly that the U.S. government believes actual short-range ballistic missiles (SRBMs) were transferred to Pakistan in the early 1990s but does not clarify whether these missiles were captured by the 300-km-range/500-kg-payload parameters of the Missile Technology Control Regime (MTCR).[35] On June 25, 1991, pursuant to the missile-transfer sanctions provisions of the 1990 Defense Authorization Act, the United States imposed Category II sanctions for two years on governmental or government-owned entities in China and Pakistan because of M-11 missile-related equipment transfers by China to Pakistan.[36] Category II sanctions are those specified in the law for transfers of dual-use missile technology or equipment. Some U.S. government sources believed at the time that the transfer actually involved complete M-11 missiles,[37] which would justify tougher, Category I sanctions.

The sanctions against China were waived in March 1992, after China had sent a written message to the Bush Administration in which Beijing agreed to abide by the "guidelines and parameters" of the MTCR.[38] In August 1993, Washington imposed Category II sanctions against Chinese and Pakistani entities for a second time, however, because of China's renewed transfers of M-11-related items to Pakistan; again, the sanctions were those the U.S. law specified for transfers of dual-use missile technology or equipment, although transfers of actual missiles may have been involved. The sanctions against China were lifted in October 1994, after it had reaffirmed its previous commitments to abide by the MTCR "guidelines and parameters" and agreed to ban the sale of "ground-to-ground" missiles inherently capable of carrying a 500-kg payload to a distance of at least 300 km (the primary threshold for missiles of concern under the MTCR)—a ban that China agreed prohibited further exports of the M-11 missiles.[39]

DEVELOPMENTS

The major strands of Pakistan's nuclear development described above have continued to unfold since early 1995. During 1995-96, in one effort to regain influence over proliferation trends after the imposition of Pressler sanctions on Pakistan in 1990, the United States sought to promote a package of incentives to encourage proliferation restraint in Islamabad. New disclosures of Chinese and Pakistani transactions, however, prevented the full implementation of the initiative. Meanwhile—despite its apparent preparations for a nuclear test in anticipation of a new Indian test, and its matching of India's refusal to join the Comprehensive Test Ban Treaty—Pakistan maintained the voluntary freeze on weapons-grade uranium enrichment even as it attempted to advance other aspects of its nuclear and missile programs.

Partial Release of Frozen Arms Package. By early 1995, the failure of the United States to deliver the 28 F-16s and other military equipment embargoed by the Pressler Amendment—or to return the nearly $1.3 billion that Pakistan had already paid for these arms—had become a source of increasing strain between Washington and Islamabad. Indeed, elements in the Pakistan military reportedly had threatened to end the freeze on the production of weapons-grade uranium if the matter were not satisfactorily resolved. In March, the Clinton Administration announced that it would address the issue by seeking a modification of the Pressler Amendment. The principal objective of a modification was to create incentives for Pakistan to continue the restraints that it had voluntarily imposed on its nuclear program.[40] These included not only the weapons-grade uranium production freeze but also decisions not to conduct nuclear tests, not to deploy nuclear weapons or nuclear-capable missiles, and not to export sensitive nuclear items.

When Prime Minister Benazir Bhutto visited Washington in April 1995, President Bill Clinton confirmed that he would address the issue, and by the summer, the Clinton Administration had introduced legislation to modify the Pressler Amendment to permit the release of $368 million in arms contracted for prior to 1990 and to provide an initial cash refund of $120 million. None of the F-16s Pakistan had purchased would be released to Pakistan, however, in part because of their potential as nuclear delivery systems. Rather, the United States would seek the resale of the F-16s elsewhere, with the proceeds being used to reimburse Pakistan. The change in the Pressler Amendment would also end its prohibition on U.S. economic assistance to Pakistan and on certain military assistance (for anti-narcotics, anti-terrorism, peacekeeping, and military-to-military contacts).[41] In return, Pakistan would continue to implement the existing restraints on its nuclear weapons program, or, as phrased in a State Department letter to Senator Sam Nunn, "Pakistan knows that the decision to resolve the equipment problem is based on the assumption that there will be no significant change on nuclear and missile non-proliferation issues of concern to the United States."[42]

The Brown Amendment. In November 1995, in a provision known as the Brown Amendment—named after its sponsor, Senator Hank Brown—Congress approved the Clinton Administration's proposed modification of the Pressler Amendment.[43] Because of an unrelated conflict with Congress over the federal budget, President Clinton did not sign the Brown Amendment into law until February 1996. As the Administration and Congress worked to enact the measure, Pakistan continued its freeze on the production of weapons-grade uranium, and it refrained from conducting nuclear tests, exporting nuclear materials or technology, and deploying M-11 missiles. At the same time, however, Pakistan sought to advance its nuclear weapons capabilities along the plutonium track, as well as to upgrade its equipment on the uranium track.

Plutonium Track. According to U.S. officials, Pakistan continued work on its 40-MWt, heavy-water research reactor at Khushab, with Chinese assistance, although Washington was apparently unable to discern the precise nature of this assistance.[44] Prime Minister Bhutto claimed that the project is "a small reactor for experimental purposes" and that the country has "no plans to produce plutonium."[45] The Khushab reactor—which Pakistan claims is of indigenous origin, and therefore probably would not be placed under IAEA inspection—has the potential to contribute importantly to Pakistan's nuclear weapons program. Once operational, it could provide Pakistan with the country's first source of plutonium-bearing spent fuel free from IAEA controls.

Weapons-grade plutonium from the Khushab reactor's spent fuel could be extracted at the nearby Chasma reprocessing plant, if that facility becomes operational, or at the pilot-scale New Labs reprocessing facility at the Pakistani Institute of Nuclear Science and Technology (PINSTECH) in Rawalpindi—both facilities being outside IAEA purview. The Khushab reactor is estimated to be capable of generating enough plutonium for between one and two nuclear weapons annually. Not only would this increase Pakistan's overall weapons production capabilities by perhaps 20-30 percent (assuming that the Kahuta enrichment plant can produce enough weapons-grade uranium for three to four weapons per year), but the availability of plutonium would permit Pakistan to develop smaller and lighter nuclear warheads.[46] This in turn might facilitate Pakistan's development of warheads for ballistic missiles. In addition, Pakistan might employ the Khushab reactor to irradiate lithium-6 to produce tritium, a material used to "boost" nuclear weapons so as to improve their yield-to-weight efficiency.

The Khushab reactor was reported to have been completed in 1996, although it had not been fueled, according to U.S. officials.[47] As of late 1997, the Khushab reactor still was not operational, apparently because of Pakistan's inability to procure (or produce) a sufficient supply of unsafeguarded heavy water.[48]

China was also reported to be assisting Pakistan with completing a facility linked to the Khushab reactor and thought to be either a fuel fabrication plant or a plutonium separation (reprocessing) plant.[49] Pakistan previously was not thought to have a fuel fabrication facility to manufacture fuel for the new reactor. There was, however, construction at an "auxiliary location" just south of the Khushab reactor. Whereas in mid-1996 officials worried this might represent work on a reprocessing plant to handle spent fuel discharged from the Khushab reactor, more recently they have said categorically that the auxiliary location is "not a reprocessing plant."[50]

The status of Pakistan's reprocessing capabilities at New Labs in Rawalpindi and at the Chasma site, however, has not been altogether clear from published sources. A classified U.S. State Department analysis prepared in 1983 said that the New Labs facility was "nearing completion" at that time; thus the facility could well be available for use today.[51] Reports on the Chasma reprocessing facility in the early 1990s suggested that it was progressing, but probably still several years from completion.[52] According to an analysis by the CIA quoted in the press, as of April 1996, China was providing technicians and equipment to help finish the facility.[53] According to reports of August 1997, however, U.S. officials believe that, while some Chinese assistance and equipment may have trickled into the Chasma reprocessing project, the reprocessing complex at Chasma "is an empty shell."[54] If this description is correct, Pakistan may have only the laboratory-scale reprocessing capability at New Labs and may be further from major plutonium reprocessing activities than once thought.

Uranium-Enrichment Track. In the mid-1990s, Pakistani specialists also pursued efforts to improve the Kahuta enrichment plant and, possibly, to expand the country's capacity to enrich uranium.[55] The best-publicized episode was Pakistan's purchase from China of 5,000 custom-made ring magnets, a key component of the bearings that support high-speed rotation of centrifuges. Shipments of the magnets, which were sized to fit the specific type of centrifuge used at the Kahuta plant, were apparently made between December 1994 and mid-1995 and became known to the Clinton Administration by August 1995.[56] It was not clear whether the ring magnets were intended for Kahuta as a "future reserve supply," or whether they were intended to permit Pakistan to increase the number of uranium-enrichment centrifuges, either at Kahuta or at another location.[57]

As discussed in the chapter on China, the ring magnet transaction, valued at $70,000, raised the possibility that China had violated a provision of the Export-Import Bank Act, added in 1994, requiring a cutoff of all U.S. Export-Import Bank financing to any country that "has willfully aided or abetted any non-nuclear-weapon state" in acquiring enriched uranium or plutonium not subject to IAEA monitoring.[58] In this instance, however, the principal impact of sanctions would have been on U.S. firms doing business in China, as the sanctions would have jeopardized as much as $1 billion annually in unrelated U.S. exports to China.

After the ring magnet story became public, the Clinton Administration entered into active negotiations with China over the sale, temporarily suspending new Export-Import Bank credits, without formally declaring that China had violated the statutory sanctions provision. It also postponed the release of military hardware to Pakistan, notwithstanding the intent of the Brown Amendment. In mid-April, however, the Administration eased both restrictions, apparently in anticipation of the resolution of the controversy that would be announced on May 10, 1996.[59]

On that date, the Clinton Administration announced that it would not impose sanctions against China under the Export-Import Bank Act. The Administration accepted the Chinese government's statement that it had not been aware of the ring magnet sale, and, because it was not made "willfully," the transaction did not transgress the statutory standards requiring the termination of Export-Import Bank financing.[60] As part of the resolution, the Administration stated that China would a) make a public commitment not to provide assistance to any nuclear facility not subject to IAEA monitoring—a commitment U.S. officials stated would prevent future ring magnet sales, and b) engage in a dialogue with the United States on strengthening export controls. The following day, China issued a statement declaring, "China will not provide assistance to unsafeguarded nuclear facilities."[61]

If this undertaking is strictly implemented, it would appear to rule out Chinese assistance to activities at unsafeguarded Pakistani facilities that could support the manufacture of nuclear weapons. Still, the phraseol-ogy of the May 1996 pledge is quite vague, leaving unclear, for example, whether China's pledge will ban transfers of dual-use items, technology (such as blueprints), and expert advice. Many specialists consider it likely that China will, as in the past, interpret its obligations narrowly. On the basis of the history of China's assistance to Pakistan's nuclear weapons and ballistic missile programs, some observers, especially in India, have come to believe that China perceives Pakistan to be a strategic ally and partner with which it is working to keep India in check. If China does have such an objective, it is doubtful that it will stop all assistance to Pakistan's nuclear and missile programs—notwithstanding any pledges Beijing may have given the United States.[62] However, this may overestimate the closeness of the China-Pakistan tie, and other observers—even a few in India—have not jumped to this conclusion.[63] Moreover, the recent upgrading of Chinese nuclear export control policies (see China chapter in this volume) is likely to constrain Chinese assistance to unsafeguarded nuclear activities in Pakistan.

While the May 1996 understanding averted the imposition of sanctions against China, the ring magnet episode undercut the Clinton Administration's efforts to restore a measure of non-proliferation influence in the relationship with Pakistan and curtailed the intended benefits of the Brown Amendment. After the Brown Admendment's enactment in February 1996—which was followed by the brief suspension of arms transfers noted above—Pakistan received $124 million in cash as a first *tranche* of the reimbursement of funds it had paid to the United States and, through September 1996, received some $150 million in military equipment contracted and paid for prior to 1990. However, the ring magnet case prevented Pakistan from receiving any economic or targeted military *aid*—benefits that the Clinton Administration and many legislators earlier had anticipated would be extended to Pakistan after passage of the Brown Amendment.

At that time it was recognized that, even if the Pressler Amendment were modified as the Brown Amendment contemplated, all economic and military aid to Pakistan would still be barred because Pakistan's importation of uranium-enrichment equipment in the 1970s and 1980s violated provisions of the 1977 Glenn-Symington Amendment. As noted above, however, under special legislation, U.S. presidents had been given the authority to waive these sanctions upon a finding that this was in the national interest. Most recently, the 1994 Nuclear Proliferation Prevention Act (NPPA) had given the president authority to waive Glenn-Symington uranium-enrichment sanctions on this national interest ground with respect to *all Pakistani violations prior to June 29, 1994.*[64] Thus, in the fall of 1995, before the ring magnet case emerged, it was assumed that the prohibitions against economic aid and certain military aid in the Pressler Amendment would be rescinded by means of the Brown Amendment, and that the prohibitions on such aid in the Glenn-Symington Amendment would be neutralized by waiver—ending all legal hurdles to U.S. assistance to Pakistan in these specified categories.

But Pakistan's importation of the ring magnets for the Kahuta enrichment plant took place *after* June 29, 1994. For such actions, the NPPA offered no relief from the uranium-enrichment sanctions of the Glenn-Symington Amendment. This meant that while the Brown Amendment would eliminate the barriers to economic and certain military aid in the Pressler Amendment, the only way for the president to waive the prohibitions in the Glenn-Symington Amendment was to employ the original waiver provision in that statute. This necessitated a certification that he had "received reliable assurances" that Pakistan "will not acquire or develop nuclear weapons"—a certification no president has been able to make since the law was adopted in 1977.[65]

Thus the ring magnets case, though it involved only subcomponents for a nuclear installation, had major consequences. It led China to accept important new undertakings regarding assistance to unsafeguarded nuclear facilities, and it deprived Pakistan of the opportunity to obtain U.S. economic assistance and certain military aid.[66]

The Harkin Amendment. As a result of the cumulative statutory impediments to the Executive Branch having even limited opportunities to provide assistance to Pakistan, and thereby to maintain influence with the government of Pakistan, efforts have continued (beyond the Brown Amendment) to acquire some diplomatic flexibility through legislative modifications and interpretation.[67] One of these was the Harkin Amendment of July 1997: a series of proposed modifications of the Foreign Assistance Act of 1961, supported by the Clinton Administration and sponsored by the Senate, to provide avenues for modest initiatives to improve communication and retain influence with Pakistan. The proposed modifications were a) to restore the option of U.S. education and training of Pakistani officers under the International Military Education and Training (IMET) Program, b) to provide authority for the Overseas Private Investment Corporation (OPIC) to support commercial ventures in Pakistan, c) to permit the Trade and Development Agency (TDA) to facilitate exports to Pakistan, and d) to offer financial support for democracy-building activities.[68]

The original Harkin Amendment would not have authorized resumption of direct military aid to Pakistan, nor would it have specifically countered the Glenn-Symington sanctions. Some believed, however, that its IMET provision would be inconsistent with the spirit of Glen-Symington. In the course of Senate conference with the House of Representatives, the IMET and democracy-building provisions were struck from the Harkin Amendment. The version sent to the president for signature in late 1997 retained only the OPIC and TDA provisions.

Civilian Nuclear Power Program. In a somewhat less politically charged area, China is also assisting Pakistan in the construction of a civilian nuclear facility that will be placed under IAEA safeguards, a 300-MWe nuclear power plant at Chasma. This unit is not expected to contribute directly to Pakistan's nuclear weapons program. However, China's sale of the facility is inconsistent with the practices of the other major nuclear supplier states, which have banned such sales to countries that refuse full-scope safeguards (i.e., that refuse to place all of their nuclear installations under IAEA inspection). Although civil work at the facility was completed in early 1996 with the placement of the reactor's containment dome, there is some question as to whether China will be able to supply the machinery and equipment to complete this facility.[69]

Missile Program. In parallel with the consideration of the Brown Amendment and the controversy over the ring magnets, U.S. concern continued about China's transfers of M-11 surface-to-surface missiles to Pakistan. In spring 1995, for example, press reports indicated that Washington believed that China had recently transferred components that could be used with the M-11, and, by the summer of 1995, the U.S. intelligence community had apparently concluded that Pakistan had more than 30 complete M-11 missiles on hand. The weapons, which some believed were received as early as November 1992, were said to be sitting in storage crates at the Sargodha Air Force Base, west of Lahore.[70] The Clinton Administration declined to impose sanctions on the two countries, however, arguing that it lacked sufficiently firm evidence to support such action.[71]

The M-11 issue resurfaced in the summer of 1996, when press reports disclosed the conclusion of a U.S. National Intelligence Estimate (NIE) that, as previously estimated, Pakistan had roughly three dozen M-11 missiles. The NIE reportedly stated that these were stored in canisters at the Sargodha Air Force Base, along with maintenance facilities and missile launchers; that the missiles could be launched in as little as 48 hours, even though the missiles had not been used in actual training exercises; and that two teams of Chinese technicians had been sent to Pakistan to provide training and to help unpack and assemble the missiles.[72]

In addition, the document reportedly surmised that Pakistan probably had designed a nuclear warhead for the system, based on evidence that Pakistan had been working on such an effort for a number of years.[73] As noted earlier, however, Pakistan had not conducted a full-scale test of any nuclear explosive device, nor had it flight-tested a prototype nuclear warhead with the M-11. These factors led some in the U.S. intelligence community to doubt that any warhead Pakistan may have developed could be deemed ready for use.[74]

In late August, another U.S. intelligence finding was leaked to the press: Using blueprints and equipment supplied by China, Pakistan reportedly had in late 1995 begun construction of a factory to produce short-range missiles based on the Chinese-designed M-11.[75] The factory, located near Rawalpindi, was expected to be operational in one or two years. It was not clear whether the facility would be able to build complete missiles, or whether it would manufacture some components and use imported parts to produce complete systems.[76]

None of these China-Pakistan missile-transfer events in 1996 triggered the imposition of U.S. missile-transfer sanctions on China or Pakistan, however. Indeed, throughout this period, modest shipments of U.S. military hardware continued under the Brown Amendment.[77]

India-Pakistan Nuclear and Missile Arms Race. Although in March 1994 India had, after a relatively successful launch test, shelved the Agni medium-range ballistic missile program (the decision was reaffirmed by the United Front government in December 1996), India's missile activities intensified in 1996 and 1997, producing the earmarks of a regional nuclear-missile arms race.[78] Rejecting foreign overtures and advice, India began test-firing the Prithvi II, the Air Force version capable of targeting nearly all of Pakistan, in early 1996. Then, in June 1997, India took the provocative step of moving Prithvi I mobile missile systems from factories in the south into Punjab, bringing Pakistan's most heavily inhabited region and cities within direct range of the missiles.[79] In July 1997, moreover, India's defense ministry announced revival of the Agni medium-range missile program.[80] The Prithvi relocation in Punjab created direct pressure on Pakistan to deploy the Chinese-origin M-11 missiles reportedly stored at Sargodha, which would have triggered U.S. MTCR-related sanctions, probably on both Pakistan and China as well as on entities in China.

Pakistan chose instead to respond rhetorically, pointing out the threatening and destabilizing features of Indian missile actions, and also announced the first test of a new ballistic missile, called Hatf 3.[81] The announced 600-km-range/500-kg-payload capability of Hatf-3 implies that it would be both nuclear-capable and capable of reaching New Delhi and other targets deeper in India's interior. Subsequently, Pakistani sources claimed that development of an even more powerful and versatile missile, the Ghauri, was under way, with sufficient range to reach south India—indeed, any city in India—and then announced on April 6, 1997 that the Ghauri had been tested.[82] Indian publicists highlighted these presumed capabilities in what appeared to be a media campaign in India to win defense budgetary support for a major procurement program for both offensive and defensive missile systems.[83]

Equally disturbing is the recent worsening of the air-combat military imbalance between India and Pakistan, which could exacerbate nuclear and missile arms race instability by increasing the propensity toward "hair-trigger" nuclear weapon deployments on the Subcontinent. This is particularly the case for Pakistan, which has no depth of defense and therefore no airfields out of range of Indian air attack. The low-key U.S. transfer to India of smart-bomb technology, which is ideally suited for disabling aircraft at air bases, sharply increases Pakistan's incentive to put its nuclear deterrent on high alert (adopting a launch-on-warning or launch-under-attack posture), because it must now fear the possibility of successful Indian preemptive air attacks.[84]

Nuclear Test Scare in 1995. Islamabad also faced an intensification of the nuclear challenge from India in late 1995, when U.S. agencies detected indications that India was preparing to conduct a nuclear explosive test at the Pokaran site in Rajasthan. India's only previous nuclear detonation, described as a "peaceful nuclear experiment," had been in 1974. Indian nuclear program custodians may have pushed for a new test (or test series) due to their concern that the expected opening for signature of the Comprehensive Test Ban Treaty (CTBT) during 1996 would soon make it politically difficult for any state, whether or not a party to the treaty, to conduct nuclear tests for fear of incurring severe international condemnation.[85]

The disclosure of the test preparations triggered a major diplomatic effort by the United States and a number of other industrialized countries to dissuade Indian Prime Minister Narasimha Rao from proceeding, and, by early 1996, the threat of a test appeared to have subsided. Nonetheless, testifying before the U.S. Senate in late February, Director of the Central Intelligence Agency John Deutch stated, "We are concerned India is considering the possibility of a nuclear test. We have judged that if India should test, Pakistan would follow."[86]

Barely two weeks after Deutch's statement, preparations for a Pakistani nuclear test were disclosed. Reportedly, U.S. satellite photos revealed evidence of Pakistani nuclear test preparations at a site in the Chagai Hills—seemingly a direct response to India's earlier preparations.[87] Pakistan's Foreign Ministry described the story as "speculation" based on "deliberate leaks of faulty intelligence reports," but Foreign Minister Asif Ahmad Ali lent substance to the allegation when he said soon afterward: "If India wants to prove its manhood by conducting a nuclear test, then we have the capability to prove our manhood."[88]

International Arms Control. On September 24, 1996, the Comprehensive Test Ban Treaty (CTBT) was opened for signature at the United Nations in New York. Earlier that summer, India had denounced the treaty and declared that it would not sign it. Given the intense domestic opposition in Pakistan to accepting any nuclear restraints that India is not bound by, Pakistan indicated that it would become a party to the CTBT only if India joined too.

In the fall of 1997, Pakistan ratified the Chemical Weapons Convention (CWC). Like India, it was already a party to the Biological Weapons Convention (BWC).[89]

Political Leadership Changes. On November 5, 1996, Pakistan's President Farooq Leghari dismissed Prime Minister Benazir Bhutto on charges of corruption and economic mismanagement. Leghari also dismissed the National Assembly (Pakistan's directly elected lower house of Parliament) and set new National Assembly elections for February 1997. Former Prime

Minister Nawaz Sharif was returned to power by a landslide. His Pakistan Muslim League (PML) won a clear majority of National Assembly seats, enabling it to form a strong elected government in Islamabad.

The most important implication of this election result for Pakistan's relations with India and for Pakistan's nuclear policy was that Pakistan now had a civilian government with sufficient voting strength to conduct serious negotiations with India, and if India acted in a reciprocal spirit, to make and defend the politically sensitive agreements that would be necessary to begin resolving long-standing disputes, to initiate steps that could genuinely reduce military tension in the Subcontinent, and to join in confidence-building measures that could cap, if not reverse, the nuclear proliferation in the region.

Regrettably, elected Indian governments in the mid-1990s were becoming progressively weaker and were unable to get traction for substantive negotiations with Pakistan. The BJP, campaigning on a pro-nuclear weapons platform, was the rising power. Since it was able to form a government majority after the 1998 elections only after winning the support of several small parties, many assumed that it could not precipitously change India's policy of nuclear ambiguity. But it did so within weeks of assuming office, conducting nuclear weapon tests on May 11 and 13, 1998, declaring India a nuclear weapons power, and plunging the Subcontinent into an open nuclear arms race. Despite the looming U.S. sanctions which would hit Pakistan far harder than India, Nawaz Sharif reluctantly gave the go-ahead for Pakistan to respond in kind less than two weeks later.

PROSPECTS

India's and Pakistan's May 1998 nuclear tests and open declarations on the possession of nuclear weapons have almost uncertainly unleashed a continuing nuclear arms and missile arms race on the Subcontinent. The constraints so tenuously maintained on Pakistan's nuclear and missile acquisitions for the last decade may now give way to a determined effort in Pakistan to build a formidable nuclear arsenal, with assembled bombs for aircraft delivery, warheads for its ballistic missiles, and the fielding and training of deployed nuclear forces.

With U.S. NPPA sanctions applied automatically under law, and almost certain to have a profoundly debilitating effect on Pakistan's externally indebted economy (unless superseded by new measures), Nawaz Sharif's declaration of a national emergency (invoking martial law regulations) represents both a desperate effort to shelter Pakistan from the coming economic shock and the first step in a domestic regimentation that may be seen as needed to extract resources to compete effectively with India on the military plane. The tension over Kashmir has already risen since the first tests and could easily ignite an escalating war.

The immediate reaction of the United States, members of the Group of Eight, and the U.N. Security Council has been to deplore the nuclear breakout in South Asia and to begin a process of cooperation that would aim, in the short run, to tamp down tension, stabilize the India-Pakistan relationship, and urge a slowdown in the steps that India and Pakistan are both already taking to reallocate resources to their military programs. The search for a strategy to head off nuclear confrontation and the risks of war in South Asia will be given a much higher priority, with new attention to the Kashmir stalemate and the other root issues of conflict between India and Pakistan. This strategy will not be able to ignore the deeper security problems of both countries. It will have an important immediate focus on developing crisis-management measures, and firebreaks, such as easily monitored commitments not to actually deploy weapons of mass destruction and the ballistic missiles that could compress nuclear-use decision time to minutes and seconds.

Finally, the response will also involve measures to repair and bolster the nuclear non-proliferation regime—hopefully *with*, but if necessary *without*, the direct participation of the two self-declared nuclear powers on the Subcontinent. In the new situation that has arisen, and given the failure of automatic U.S. sanctions to deter this outcome, a new, more robust combination of incentives and disincentives will have to be designed—and developed through negotiations—to explore ways in which India and Pakistan may yet be able to join non-proliferation undertakings and step back from the nuclear and missile arms race that their actions have greatly accelerated.

NOTES

[1]U.S. State Department, "Report to Congress: Update on Progress Toward Regional Non-proliferation in South Asia," April 1994.

[2]Pakistan claimed to have carried out five nuclear explosive tests on May 28 and a sixth on May 30. See Tim Weiner, "Pakistan, Answering India, Carries Out Nuclear Tests," and John F. Burns, "Arms Race Feared," *New York Times*, May 29, 1998; John Ward Anderson and Kamran Khan, "Pakistan Sets Off Nuclear Blasts," and Steve Coll, "The Race May Be On—and May Be Hard to Stop," *Washington Post*, May 29, 1998; *The Economist*, May 30, 1998, pp. 16, 41-42.

Analysis of the seismic shocks set off by the Indian and Pakistani tests left little doubt that each had detonated nuclear explosive devices of militarily significant yield, but raised questions about whether the numbers and size of the tested devices were as claimed. The seismic signal of Pakistan's claimed five detonations on May

28, according to preliminary analysis, showed a single event (possibly the cumulative effect of simultaneous detonations) and registered a magnitude of between 4.8 and 4.9 on the Richter scale, indicating an explosive force of between 8 and 17 kilotons (the Hiroshima bomb had a yield of 15 kilotons). See William J. Broad, "Explosion Is Detected by U.S. Scientists," *New York Times*, May 29, 1998, p. A8, and Michael Hirsh and John Barry, "Nuclear Jitters," *Newsweek*, June 8, 1998, p. 24.

[3]A 1996 Pentagon report stated, "Pakistan possesses all the components necessary for producing a nuclear device, and it probably has sufficient fissile material now to assemble a few nuclear weapons." Office of the Secretary of Defense, *Proliferation: Threat and Response*, April 1996, p. 38. The 1997 version adds, "Like India, Pakistan probably could assemble the weapons fairly quickly and it has aircraft and possibly ballistic missiles that are believed capable of delivery." *Proliferation: Threat and Response,* November 1997, p. 17.

[4]Barbara Opall, "U.S. Seeks to Bypass Pakistani Fighter Ban," *Defense News,* April 3-9, 1995 ("According to Senator Larry Pressler, who was briefed March 28 by the CIA, Pakistan has nine or ten assembled nuclear weapons"); R. Jeffrey Smith and Thomas W. Lippman, "Pakistan Is Building Reactor That May Yield Large Quantities of Plutonium," *Washington Post,* April 8, 1995 ("U.S. intelligence officials say that Pakistan has an arsenal of around 10 nuclear weapons"); "Pakistan Has Seven Nuclear Weapons," *Reuters,* December 1, 1992 (reporting on an NBC News story stating that Pakistan possessed "at least seven" nuclear devices); Hedrick Smith, "A Bomb Ticks in Pakistan," *New York Times Magazine,* March 6, 1988; David Albright and Mark Hibbs, "Pakistan's Bomb: Out of the Closet," *Bulletin of the Atomic Scientists,* July/August 1992, p. 38; U.S. Department of State, "Memorandum for Dr. Kissinger, Subject: Official Visit of Pakistan Prime Minister Mohammad Khan Junejo: Background and Talking Points," July 18, 1986, SECRET/SENSITIVE, released under the Freedom of Information Act to the National Security Archive (When fully operational, the Kahuta enrichment plant "could probably produce enough highly enriched uranium for several [nuclear] devices per year.") The National Security Archive is a private research organization based in Washington, D.C.

Pakistan's bombs in the basement were presumed credible because of reports that they were based on a design supplied by sources in China in the early 1980s. Leslie H. Gelb, "Pakistan Links Peril U.S.-China Nuclear Pact," *New York Times,* June 22, 1984; Leslie H. Gelb, "Peking Said to Balk at Nuclear Pledges," *New York Times,* June 23, 1984; R. Jeffrey Smith, "U.S. Aides See Troubling Trend in China Pakistan Nuclear Ties," *Washington Post,* April 1, 1996; "Pakistan's Atomic Bomb," *Foreign Report,* January 12, 1989, p. 1. Pakistan was reported to have conducted a "cold test" of a nuclear device based on the Chinese design—i.e., a fully-instrumented test of a dummy weapon, using a core of natural (unenriched) uranium. The event is said to have taken place in September 1986, near Chagai. Howard Hough, "Pakistan's Nuclear Stand: Confusion or Strategy?" *Jane's Intelligence Review,* June 1995, p. 270.

[5]Bill Gertz, "Pakistan Deploys Chinese Missiles," *Washington Times,* June 12, 1996; R. Jeffrey Smith, "Report Cites China-Pakistan Missile Links," *Washington Post,* June 13, 1996. (See also China chapter in this volume.)

[6]In addition, Pakistan is continuing to produce low-enriched uranium (LEU), i.e., uranium enriched to less than 20 percent. Although weapons-grade uranium is enriched to more than 90 percent, much of the effort to reach this level is expended in producing LEU. As a result, Pakistan's LEU stocks could be rapidly enriched to a weapons-grade level. Its growing stocks of LEU thus provide an expanding reserve for its nuclear weapons program.

[7]For the A.Q. Khan story, see Leonard S. Spector, *The Undeclared Bomb* (Cambridge, MA: Ballinger Publishing Co., 1988), pp. 122ff, and notes; and Steven R. Weisman and Herbert Krosney, *The Islamic Bomb* (New York: Times Books, 1981). For an early study devoted to understanding Pakistan's entire nuclear program, civilian and military, see Ashok Kapur, *Pakistan's Nuclear Development* (London: Croon Helm, 1987).

[8]The 1977 cutoff of aid to Pakistan, aimed at discouraging Pakistan's completion of a French-origin plutonium separation facility at Chasma, was implemented as a matter of U.S. policy, rather than pursuant to statute.

[9]The Amendment was to the Foreign Assistance Act of 1961, Sec. 669, 22 U.S. Code Sec. 2429 (1977), now Arms Export Control Act, Chapter 10, Sec. 101; 22 U.S. Code Sec. 2799a (1994). The provision was originally adopted in a somewhat different form in 1976, Foreign Assistance Act of 1961, Sec. 669, 22 U.S. Code Sec. 2429 (1976). *(Editorial Note: To assist the reader in finding the full text of the statutory provisions discussed herein, citations are normally given to [1] the statute containing the provision, using the popular name of that statute, and [2] the official compilation of U.S. laws known as the United States Code, which organizes and codifies portions of various statutes according to their subject. Because statutes are amended from time to time, provisions are further identified by the year of their enactment. Omnibus laws, such as annual authorization and appropriations laws, which contain amendments to existing statutes as well as new provisions, are usually referred to herein by the "Public Law" [P.L] number they are assigned upon enactment.)*

The 1994 recodification of the Glenn-Symington Amendment within the Arms Export Control Act and the enactment of a number of additional provisions dealing with nuclear proliferation was accomplished in Title VIII of the Foreign Relations Authorization Act, Fiscal Years 1994 and 1995, P.L. 103-236 (1994). Title VIII of that act is also known as the Nuclear Proliferation Prevention Act (NPPA) of 1994.

[10]The Pakistani nuclear weapons effort relied on a massive smuggling program, which began with the clandestine acquisitions of key technology for the Kahuta plant from the Netherlands and included the illicit importation of an entire facility from West Germany for producing uranium hexafluoride, as well as many other episodes, some involving smuggling from the United States. For an overview, see Leonard S. Spector and Jacqueline R. Smith, *Nuclear Ambitions* (Boulder, CO.: Westview Press, 1990), Chapters 4 and 7.

[11]The uranium-enrichment provisions of the Glenn-Symington Amendment specify that the sanction (termination of U.S. economic and military assistance) may be waived if the president (1) determines that the termination of U.S. assistance would have a "serious adverse effect on vital U.S. interests" and (2) the president has "received reliable assurances that the country in question will not acquire or develop nuclear weapons or assist other nations in doing so." Arms Export Control Act, Sec.101(b); 22 U.S. Code Sec. 2799aa (1994), formerly Foreign Assistance Act of 1961, Sec. 669(b), 22 U.S. Code Sec. 2429(b) (1977). Given the status of the Pakistani nuclear weapons program in 1981, President Ronald Reagan was unable to make these determinations. Instead, special legislation was enacted permitting the president to waive the application of these Glenn-Symington sanctions with respect to Pakistan, for six years, if he certified that this was "in the national interest of the United States." Foreign Assistance Act of 1961, Sec. 620E(d), 22 U.S. Code Sec. 2375 (1981). The flexible waiver law was subsequently extended through September 30, 1994, but beginning in October 1990, U.S. economic and military aid to Pakistan, as well as all non-commercial U.S. military sales to that country were terminated because of the Pressler Amendment, discussed later in this chapter. Since the Pressler Amendment independently prohibited U.S. economic and military aid to Pakistan, along with military sales, neither President Reagan nor President Bush exercised the special waiver authority enacted for Glenn-Symington in 1981.

By 1982, Pakistan was also subject to sanctions under the reprocessing sanctions provisions of the 1977 Glenn-Symington Amendment. Arms Export Control Act, op. cit.. These provisions specified that U.S. economic and military aid were to be terminated to any state that imported reprocessing technology (i.e., technology for separating plutonium from spent reactor fuel) after 1977 when the law was enacted. Presumably, this sanctions law was triggered by Pakistan's acquisition of equipment to complete a pilot-scale reprocessing plant, known as the "New Labs" at the Pakistan Institute of Nuclear Technology (PINSTECH), and by its continued work on a larger reprocessing plant at Chasma, which France had originally agreed to design and build in the early 1970s. At U.S. request, France ceased work on the facility in 1976, and terminated its contract in 1978.

Unlike the Glenn-Symington uranium-enrichment provisions, however, that law's reprocessing provisions originally included a more flexible waiver provision, requiring only that the president certify to Congress that the termination of U.S. assistance "would be seriously prejudicial to the achievement of United States nonproliferation objectives or otherwise jeopardize the common defense and security." President Ronald Reagan did exercise this waiver, which had an indefinite duration, in February 1982.

As explained in the text in connection with the Khushab reactor, Pakistan did not have the technical option to produce plutonium during the 1980s, but actively pursued this option in the early 1990s. The 1994 Nuclear Proliferation Prevention Act (NPPA) specified that the 1982 presidential waiver of sanctions under Glenn-Symington reprocessing provisions would not apply to any Pakistani reprocessing technology import activities after June 29, 1994. Thus should the reprocessing sanctions provisions of the Glenn-Symington Amendment be triggered after that date, a new presidential waiver would be required to lift the ban on U.S. economic and military assistance to Pakistan that would be triggered by this provision.

[12]U.S. Department of State, "The Pakistani Nuclear Program." June 23, 1983, SECRET/NOFORN/ORCON released under the Freedom of Information Act to the National Security Archive, January 17, 1991.

[13]Hedrick Smith, "A Bomb Ticks in Pakistan," op. cit.

[14]Bob Woodward and Don Oberdorfer, "Pakistan A-Project Upsets Superpowers," *Washington Post,* July 15, 1986; Gerald M. Boyd, "Pakistan Denies Developing Bomb," *New York Times,* July 17, 1986; Don Oberdorfer, "Nuclear Issue Clouds Junejo Visit," *Washington Post,* July 17, 1986. See also "Pakistan Persists," *Foreign Report,*

March 27, 1986; Smith, "A Bomb Ticks in Pakistan," op. cit.; Bob Woodward, "Pakistan Reported Near Atom Arms Production," *Washington Post,* November 4, 1986. By this time, Pakistan was also believed to have tested the non-nuclear "triggering package" of a nuclear device. See John Scali, "Good Morning America," *American Broadcasting Company,* July 11, 1985.

[15]For a discussion of this period in U.S.–Pakistan nuclear relations, see Spector and Smith, *Nuclear Ambitions,* op. cit. Regarding the intimacy of U.S.–Pakistani relations during the 1980s, see Steve Coll, "Anatomy of a Victory: CIA's Covert Afghan War $2 Billion Program Reversed Tide for Rebels," *Washington Post,* June 19, 1992. U.S. officials, including Presidents Reagan and Bush, also continued to argue as late as 1989 that the provision of assistance to Pakistan contributed to U.S. non-proliferation goals by providing Pakistan an alternative to nuclear arms for enhancing its security.

[16]Foreign Assistance Act of 1961, Sec. 620E(e); 22 U.S. Code Sec. 2375 (1985). The U.S. Department of State has interpreted this provision as not prohibiting commercial sales of military hardware by U.S. vendors, a position strongly opposed by some in Congress. See *Interpreting the Pressler Amendment,* Hearings before the Committee on Foreign Relations, U.S. Senate, July 30, 1992, (scrutinizing the decision of the Bush Administration to permit commercial sales to Pakistan of spare parts for F-16 combat aircraft). Whatever the merits of the State Department view, U.S. practice precludes commercial sales of major military systems, such as tanks and aircraft, except on a government-to-government basis. Both the Executive and Congress interpret the Pressler Amendment as prohibiting government-to-government arms sales to Pakistan.

[17]The Pressler Amendment applied only to Pakistan. This reflected the fact that Pakistan (and only Pakistan) had been the recipient of a waiver from the uranium-enrichment provisions of the Glenn-Symington Amendment in 1981. This waiver allowed aid to flow. The Pressler law sought to restore the threat of sanctions if Pakistan continued to pursue its nuclear weapons program, but it sought to impose this threat in a manner that would not require the immediate cessation of assistance and military sales during the height of the Afghan crisis.

Pakistan points out that during the 1980s (when India was expanding its nuclear weapons capability), India was not subject to similar threats of sanctions. This is because the Glenn-Symington Amendment imposed sanctions only for the importation, after 1977, of enrichment and reprocessing technology, while India used indigenous resources to develop these elements of its nuclear capabilities after that date.

[18]David B. Ottaway, "U.S. Relieves Pakistan of Pledge Against Enriching Uranium," *Washington Post,* June 15, 1989; William Beecher, "Pakistan Will Halt Nuclear Arms Work to Keep U.S. Aid," *Minneapolis Star-Tribune,* June 14, 1989; Stephen Engelberg, "U.S. Sees Pakistan Seeking an A-Bomb," *New York Times,* June 11, 1989.

[19]The year when Pakistan, for practical purposes, first "possessed" a nuclear explosive device has been an issue of some dispute. Some observers believe that this threshold was crossed by 1987 and that the Reagan and Bush Administrations in 1987, 1988, and 1989 improperly certified that Pakistan did not possess this capability, in order to avoid the imposition of sanctions under the Pressler Amendment. Seymour M. Hersh, "On the Nuclear Edge," *The New Yorker,* March 29, 1993; "Pakistani Quoted as Citing Nuclear Test in '87," *Reuters,* July 25, 1993 (quoting former Army Chief of Staff Mirza Aslam Beg to this effect). At a minimum, by 1987 it appears that Pakistan possessed the necessary weapons-grade uranium for a nuclear device, along with most, if not all, of the necessary non-nuclear components. This would have given the ability to manufacture a nuclear device rapidly. Reportedly, it was not until 1990, however, that Pakistan first took the step of machining the uranium metal components for a nuclear device, the event that apparently left the Bush Administration no choice but to withhold certifying that Pakistan did not possess such a device.

[20]Soviet forces, it may be noted, had been withdrawn from Afghanistan in February 1989.

[21]Barbara Crossette, "Pakistan May Consider Suing U.S. Over Aircraft," *The New York Times,* May 24, 1997.

[22]In all, Pakistan paid $658 million toward the F-16s and $368 million for the other military equipment, a total of nearly $1.3 billion. Seventeen of the F-16s were to be paid for in cash, with the remainder to be paid for through U.S. Foreign Military Financing grants and loans. As of 1990, the Glenn-Symington uranium-enrichment provisions did not ban these credits and loans because sanctions under

the law were waived (pursuant to an extension of the 1981 legislation easing the law's waiver standards). This waiver expired on April 1, 1991. Although Presidents Bush and Clinton had the authority for several years thereafter to waive the Glenn-Symington uranium-enrichment sanctions, upon a finding that this was in the national interest, they did not exercise this authority. Thus, the Glenn-Symington uranium-enrichment sanctions were applied to Pakistan after April 1, 1991—along with the partially overlapping Pressler Amendment sanctions. The 1994 Nuclear Proliferation Prevention Act (NPPA) continued the liberal waiver authority, but only with respect to Glenn-Symington Amendment uranium-enrichment sanctions stemming from Pakistani actions prior to June 29, 1994, the effective date of that Act. It should also be noted that the Glenn-Symington Amendment uranium-enrichment sanctions do not prohibit U.S. arms transfers for cash, whether government-to-government or commercial, but only economic and military assistance.

[23]Interviews with U.S. officials, summer 1996; U.S. State Department, "Report to Congress," op. cit.; R. Jeffrey Smith, "Pakistan Can Build One Nuclear Device, Foreign Official Says," *Washington Post,* February 7, 1992; "Khan Notes Freeze on Program," *AMN* (Karachi), February 9, 1992, in *JPRS-TND,* April 3, 1992, p. 6; Gene Kramer, "U.S.–Pakistan," *Associated Press,* February 10, 1992; Rauf Siddiqi, Ann MacLachlan, "No 'Direct Progress' in Talks, But Pakistan, U.S. Continue Effort," *Nucleonics Week,* February 20, 1992, p. 15; Ali Sarwar Naqvi, "Don't Blame Pakistan," *Washington Post,* July 16, 1992.

[24]See footnote 7.

[25]Mark Hibbs, "Bhutto May Finish [Khushab] Plutonium Reactor Without Agreement on Fissile Stocks," *Nucleonics Week,* October 6, 1994, p. 10; Simon Henderson, "Pakistan Builds Second Plant to Enrich Uranium," *Financial Times,* December 11, 1987; Neil A. Lewis, "Reports of Second Pakistani Uranium Plant Weighed," *New York Times,* January 10, 1988.

Pakistan may also have been continuing its efforts of the late 1980s to develop the capability to produce tritium, used in advanced nuclear weapons. According to various press accounts describing the conclusions of a number of official investigations, during the mid-1980s, two related West German firms provided Pakistan with test quantities of tritium gas, a tritium purification and storage plant, tritium precursor materials, the design for a reactor that could be used for tritium production, and material and equipment for fabricating fuel for that reactor, including special American-made welding lasers. See Mark Hibbs, "Illegal Export Charges May Spur Tighter German Export Controls," *Nucleonics Week,* January 5, 1989; Mark Hibbs, "German Firms Exported Tritium Purification Plant to Pakistan," *Nuclear Fuel,* February 6, 1989; "Germans Sell Nuke Equipment to Pakistan," *News India,* March 3, 1989; Mark Hibbs, "U.S. Repeatedly Warned Germany on Nuclear Exports to Pakistan," *Nuclear Fuel,* March 6, 1989; Mark Hibbs, "German Firm's Exports Raise Concern About Pakistan's Nuclear Capabilities," *Nuclear Fuel,* March 6, 1989; John J. Fialka and Thomas F. O'Boyle, "West German Firms Admit Supplying Nuclear-Weapons Material to Pakistan," *Wall Street Journal,* April 21, 1989; Mark Hibbs, "Prosecutors Link Tritium Plant to Pakistan Weapons Program," *Nuclear Fuel,* May 1, 1989; "NTG Nuclear Proliferation Case," *Der Spiegel,* November 6, 1989, translated in *JPRS-TND,* November 29, 1989, p. 35.

[26]B. Barber, "Ex-Premier Declares Pakistan Has A-Bomb," *Washington Times,* August 24, 1994; Alistair Lyon, "Pakistani Leaders Deny Nuclear Bomb Claim," *Reuters,* August 24, 1994; Steve Pagani, "IAEA Says Unable to Verify Pakistan Atom Bomb Report," *Reuters,* August 24, 1994; Alistair Lyon, "Pakistani Ex-Premier Stands By Nuclear Revelation," *Reuters,* August 25, 1994.

[27]"Clinton Pledges to Settle Dispute with Pakistan," *Xinhua,* April 12, 1995, in *FBIS-CHI,* September 27, 1996.

[28]Raja Asghar, "Pakistan Vows Tit-for-Tat Nuclear Reply to India," *Reuters,* March 12, 1996. When addressing U.S. audiences, Bhutto emphatically denied that Pakistan was pursuing nuclear arms.

[29]Seymour M. Hersh, "On the Nuclear Edge," op. cit. Some U.S. officials intimately familiar with events at this time dispute a key point in Hersh's account, namely that the U.S.-led diplomatic effort that eased the crisis was triggered by Washington's detection of Pakistani actions to deploy its nuclear weapons. These observers state that no reports of such activities circulated at senior levels of the U.S. government and that the U.S. diplomatic initiative predated the Pakistani actions that Hersh alleges took place. Interviews, September 1996.

[30]Various Pakistani nuclear arms control and non-proliferation proposals are listed in "Statement of Ambassador Munir Akram," at the Carnegie Endowment Conference: *Nuclear Non-Proliferation and the Millennium*, Washington, D.C., February 12-13, 1996; see also "'Text' of Sharif Speech on Nuclear Issue," *Nation*, June 7, 1991, in *FBIS-NES*, June 10, 1991, p. 68.

[31]The first such data exchange, in January 1992, was marred by accusations that both sides had failed to list at least one important nuclear plant. Pakistan protested the absence of a gas centrifuge uranium-enrichment facility in Karnataka state (presumably the Rattehalli plant) from the Indian list, while India objected to Pakistan's failure to list the Golra enrichment facility near Islamabad. Mark Hibbs, "Second Indian Enrichment Facility Using Centrifuges Is Operational," *Nucleonics Week*, March 26, 1992; "India and Pakistan Fail to Include New SWU Plants on Exchanged Lists," *Nuclear Fuel*, March 30, 1992.

[32]Pakistan has 18 deployed launchers of Hatf-1, an indigenous missile, according to the International Institute of Strategic Studies, *The Military Balance, 1997/98* (London: Oxford University Press for IISS, October 1997), p. 159. According to a detailed study by an Indian analyst, the Hatf-2 was based on French sounding-rocket engines obtained by Pakistan. See S. Chandrashekar, "An Assessment of Pakistan's Missile Capability," *Jane's Strategic Weapon Systems*, March 1990, p. 4.

[33]See William C. Potter and Harlan W. Jencks, *The International Missile Bazaar* (Boulder, CO: Westview Press, 1994), p. 81. According to the 1997 Pentagon report, "the Hatf-2 was based on two Hatf-1 stages, but appears to have been discontinued." *Proliferation: Threat and Response*, 1997, op. cit., p. 20.

[34]*Proliferation: Threat and Response*, 1997, op. cit.

[35]For a detailed discussion of the MTCR and the related U.S. sanctions law, see Missile Proliferation chapter in this volume. A concise assessment of missile proliferation, suppliers, and missile type characteristics as of mid-1995 is available in International Institute of Strategic Studies, *The Military Balance, 1995/96* (London: Oxford University Press for IISS, October 1995), pp. 281-84.

[36]See "Imposition of Missile Proliferation Sanctions Against Chinese and Pakistani Entities," Public Notice 1423, U.S. Department of State, Bureau of Politico-Military Affairs, July 17, 1991.

[37]Communications with U.S. officials, 1993.

[38]*Federal Register*, July 17, 1991; *Federal Register*, April 7, 1992; see also Elaine Sciolino, "U.S. Lifts Its Sanctions on China Over High-Technology Transfers," *New York Times*, February 22, 1992.

[39]*Federal Register*, August 27, 1993; *Federal Register* November 7, 1994; Elaine Sciolino, "U.S. and Chinese Reach Agreement on Missile Export," *New York Times*, October 5, 1994; Daniel Williams, "U.S. Deal With China Allows High-Tech Sales in Exchange for Pledge," *Washington Post*, October 5, 1994.

[40]Based on discussions with U.S. officials, 1995-96 and letter from Acting Secretary of State Peter Tarnoff to Senator Sam Nunn, August 3, 1995. Washington also hoped to build stronger ties with Pakistan in order to foster its evolution as a moderate Islamic democracy and ease the growing sense of isolation that could intensify the country's pursuit of nuclear arms.

[41]Elaine Sciolino, "Despite Nuclear Fears, Senate Acts to Lift Pakistan Curbs," *New York Times*, September 22, 1995. The released military equipment included artillery, P-3C Orion anti-submarine-warfare aircraft, Harpoon anti-shipping missiles, and AIM-9L air-to-air missiles, spares and explosives. Although the new F-16s were themselves excluded from the release package, spare parts and engine upgrades for Pakistan's existing force of F-16s were included.

[42]Letter from Acting Secretary Tarnoff to Senator Nunn, op. cit.

[43]Foreign Assistance Act of 1961, Sec. 620E(e), (f), (g), and (h), 22 U.S. Code, Secs. 2375 (e), (f), (g), and (h) (1996). As discussed below, although the Brown Amendment ended the prohibition in the Pressler Amendment on U.S. economic aid to Pakistan, such assistance remains prohibited by the uranium-enrichment sanctions provisions of the Glenn-Symington Amendment, op. cit.

[44]See Hibbs, "Bhutto May Finish Plutonium Reactor," op. cit.; interview with U.S. official, July 1994; Mark Hibbs, "China Said Aiding Kahuta Project; U.S. Credits, NPT Status On Line," *Nucleonics Week*, February 8, 1996, p. 1; Mark Hibbs, "China Challenges U.S. Data Pointing to Pakistani Aid," *Nucleonics Week*, February 22, 1996, p. 3 ("[U.S. officials] said this week that China continues to assist Pakistan at both Kahuta and Khushab").

[45]R. Jeffrey Smith and Thomas W. Lippman, "Pakistan Is Building Reactor That May Yield Large Quantities of Plutonium," *Washington Post*, April 8, 1995.

[46]For a fission device of a given yield, much less plutonium (by mass) is needed for the charge than highly enriched uranium.

[47]Interviews with U.S. officials, summer 1996; "Pakistan: First Indigenously Developed Nuclear Reactor Completed," *Dawn*, March 7, 1996, in *FBIS-NES*, March 11, 1996, p. 105 (describes reactor's power as 50 MWs); C. Raja Mohan, "Plutonium Reactor May Give Pak A-Leverage," *Hindu*, March 11, 1996, in *FBIS-TAC-95-005*, March 11, 1996.

[48]See Mark Hibbs, "China Accord Would Turn Up U.S. Heat on Pakistani Reactor," *Nucleonics Week*, August 14, 1997, p. 8.

[49]Hibbs, "China Challenges U.S. Data Pointing to Pakistan Aid," op. cit.

[50]Hibbs, "China Accord Would Turn Up U.S. Heat," op. cit., p. 9.

[51]U.S. Department of State, "Memorandum for Dr. Kissinger," op. cit.

[52]Smith and Lippman, "Pakistan Building Reactor that May Yield Large Quantities of Plutonium," op. cit.

[53]Bill Gertz, "China Aids Pakistani Plutonium Plant," *Washington Times*, April 3, 1996.

[54]Hibbs, "China Accord Would Turn Up U.S. Heat," op. cit., p. 8.

[55]Pakistan's enrichment program manager, Dr. A. Q. Khan, announced that a team of specialists had developed machinery to control vibrations in ultracentrifuges, extolling efforts that had clearly taken many months, if not years of work. "KRL [Khan Research Laboratories] Achieves Breakthrough in Ultracentrifugal Technic," *Nawa-I-Waqt* (Pakistan), September 8, 1996, in *FBIS-NES*, September 13, 1996. The Kahuta enrichment plant, formally known as the Khan Research Laboratories (KRL) was named after Dr. A. Q. Khan.

[56]Bill Gertz, "China Nuclear Transfer Exposed," *Washington Times*, February 5, 1996; R. Jeffrey Smith, "China Sent Nuclear Aid to Pakistan," *Washington Post*, February 7, 1996; Hibbs, "China Said Aiding Kahuta Project," op. cit.; R. Jeffrey Smith, "U.S. Decides to Transfer Weapons That Pakistan Paid for in 1980s," *Washington Post*, March 20, 1996.

Kahuta plant centrifuges installed between 1985 and 1990 may require renovation or replacement for effective operation. See the analysis in David Albright, Frans Berkhout, and William Walker, *Plutonium and Highly Enriched Uranium 1996: World Inventories, Capabilities, and Policies* (New York: Oxford University Press for Stockholm International Peace Research Institute, 1997), pp. 274-78.

[57]Background Briefing by Senior U.S. Official, Department of State, May 10, 1996; Hibbs, "China Said Aiding Kahuta Project," op. cit. ("future reserve supply," according to U.S. government sources). In the late 1980s, Pakistan was reported to be building a second enrichment plant at Golra, but there has been little published since regarding this facility. A recent report stated that the second enrichment plant was located at Wah and that the Pakistani government had confirmed the existence of a second enrichment facility. Mark Hibbs, "Pakistan Said Ready to Counter Indian Nuclear Test with Its Own," *Nucleonics Week*, February 29, 1996, p. 14.

[58]Export-Import Bank Act of 1945, Sec. 2(b)(4); 12 U.S. Code Sec. 635(b)(4) (1994). The new sanctions were added to the Export-Import Bank Act in 1994 by Sec. 825 of the Nuclear Proliferation Prevention Act of 1994, Title VIII, Foreign Relations Authorization Act, Fiscal Years 1994 and 1995, P.L. 103-236 (1994).

[59]Smith, "U.S. Decides to Transfer Weapons," *Washington Post*, March 20, 1996; Thomas W. Lippman and Paul Blustein, "U.S. Clears, Pakistan, China Deals," *Washington Post*, April 17, 1996.

The fact that the imposition of the Export-Import Bank sanctions would have significantly harmed U.S. exporters involved in unrelated areas of commerce created pressure on the Clinton Administration to find a solution that would avoid the harm. Recognizing that the "boomerang" effect impeded the utility of such sanctions, Congress amended the Export-Import Bank Act in the summer of 1996 to target the termination of loan guarantees on the specific entities involved in aiding and abetting in the acquisition of a nuclear explosive device or of unsafeguarded special nuclear material, rather than on all loans to the country in which the sanctioned activity originated. Export-Import Bank Act of 1945, Sec. 2(b)(4); 12 U.S. Code Sec. 635(b)(4) (1996).

[60]U.S. Department of State, "Special Briefing on U.S.-China Discussions on Non-Proliferation and Nuclear-Related Exports," Washington, D.C., May 10, 1996.

[61]"Foreign Ministry Spokesman on U.S. Decision Not to Impose Sanctions," *Xinhua,* May 11, 1996.

[62]Questions also remain as to whether the Chinese government will establish mechanisms to ensure that entities, such as the China Nuclear Energy Industry Corporation, which transferred the magnets to Pakistan, fully comply with national export control pledges.

[63]For a dispassionate Indian analysis of how the Pakistan-China relationship has been misrepresented in the Indian press, for example, see Achin Vainik, "Nuclear Notebook: Three Misrepresentations," *Economic and Political Weekly,* (Mumbai), September 6, 1997.

[64]Nuclear Proliferation Prevention Act Sec. 822(b)(2), amending Foreign Assistance Act, Sec. 620E9(d), 22 U.S. Code Sec. 2375(d) (1994).

[65]As discussed earlier (see note 11), the aid ban in the uranium-enrichment provisions of the Glenn-Symington Amendment can be waived only if the president had (1) determined that the termination of U.S. assistance would have a "serious adverse effect on vital U.S. interests" and (2) the president has "received reliable assurances that the country in question will not acquire or develop nuclear weapons or assist other nations in doing so." Arms Export Control Act Sec. 101(b); 22 U.S. Code Sec. 2799aa(b) (1994).

Under the 1994 NPPA, the president was authorized to waive the ban on aid (for Pakistani actions prior to June 29, 1994), "if he determines that to do so is in the national interest of the United States," a relatively easy standard to satisfy. Foreign Assistance Act Sec. 620E9(d), 22 U.S. Code Sec. 2375(d) (1994), amended in Nuclear Proliferation Prevention Act Sec. 822(b)(2).

At the time this change was made in 1994, however, it had no immediate impact on U.S. aid flows to Pakistan, and President Clinton never exercised his new waiver authority, because economic and military assistance (and U.S. military sales) to that country were then prohibited, in any event, by the Pressler Amendment.

With this background in mind, after the ring magnet episode, rather than make a formal determination that Pakistan once again violated the uranium-enrichment provisions of the Glenn-Symington Amendment, the Clinton Administration chose simply not to exercise the waiver provision for pre-1994 Glenn-Symington Amendment enrichment-related violations. The result is that the pre-existing ban on economic and military aid to Pakistan remains in force.

As a separate matter, the 1994 NPPA also addressed the reprocessing (plutonium separation) provisions of the Glenn-Symington Amendment (see note 6), which ban U.S. economic and military aid to states importing or exporting reprocessing technology. The provision had apparently been invoked against Pakistan sometime between the imposition of sanctions under the uranium-enrichment provisions of the Glenn-Symington Amendment in May 1979 and February 1982, when both provisions were formally waived by President Reagan. The uranium-enrichment provisions of the Glenn-Symington Amendment were waived, initially for six years, by means of the 1981 legislation, and the reprocessing provisions, by means of the waiver mechanism included within the reprocessing provisions of the Glenn-Symington law. The latter waiver (of reprocessing sanctions) was treated as having indefinite duration. The 1994 NPPA specified that this waiver would not apply with respect to Pakistani reprocessing importation activities after June 29, 1994. Despite allegations that China has assisted Pakistan in completing the Chasma reprocessing plant, the Clinton Administration has not made a determination that Pakistan or China has violated the reprocessing provisions of the Glenn-Symington Amendment.

[66]The ring magnets case was shortly followed by another controversy over the sale by the China Nuclear Energy Industry Corporation of specialized furnaces and high-technology diagnostic equipment to Pakistan, potentially useful in Pakistan's nuclear weapons program. Initial press stories indicated that the sale took place after China's May 11, 1996, pledge not to provide assistance to unsafeguarded nuclear installations, and that U.S. officials raised this matter with the Chinese government in August 1996. U.S. officials shortly declared, however, that, on the basis of Chinese assurances that the transaction had taken place in late 1995 and early 1996, the Clinton Administration had determined that the sales predated China's new commitment. The items were apparently destined for the Khushab nuclear reactor. Bill Gertz, "Beijing Flouts Nuke-Sale Ban," *Washington Times,* October 9, 1996; Bill Gertz, "State Department Mum on Chinese Nuke Sale to Pakistan," *Washington Times,* October 10, 1996; R. Jeffrey Smith, "China Sold Nuclear Items Before Vow," *Washington Post,* October 10, 1996.

[67]Some support has emerged in Congress for the State Department's interpretation that current sanctions do not stand in the way of commercial military sales to Pakistan, i.e., cash sales of other than major military equipment, and not provided under terms of assistance.

[68]Harkin Amendment 899 to S.955 in the Senate was put forward on July 16, 1997, by Senators Tom Harkin, John Warner, Robert Torricelli, and Tim Johnson, to modify Foreign Assistance Act of 1961 Sections 239(f) [22 U.S. Code 2199(f)]; 638(b) [22 U.S. Code 2398(b)]; and 661 [22 U.S. Code 2421].

[69]The unit is based on a nuclear power plant in China for which China imported key equipment from French, German, and Japanese vendors. Because these three states are members of the Nuclear Suppliers Group, whose rules prohibit sales of nuclear facility components to states like Pakistan that have refused to place all of their nuclear installations under IAEA safeguards, the three have apparently refused to supply China with equipment to be used in the Chasma nuclear power plant. There is considerable doubt as to whether China can manufacture such items itself. See, "Chasma Milestone," *Nuclear Engineering International,* February 1996; Mark Hibbs, "South Korea Could Provide Vessel for Pakistan's PWR," *Nucleonics Week,* November 30, 1995; Vessel Supply Problem for Chasma PWR Project," *Nuclear News,* November 1995, p. 38; Shahid-Ur-Rehman Khan, "Chasma Vessel Manufacture Said to Be Under Way in China," *Nucleonics Week,* November 30, 1995. The project has also come under financial pressure. Shahid-Ur-Rehman Khan, "Finance Preview Urges Pakistan to Drop Costly Chasma Project, "*Nucleonics Week,* August 3, 1995.

[70]"Missile Issue Further Clouds U.S.–Chinese Ties," *Reuters,* June 22, 1995; R. Jeffrey Smith, "Spy Photos Suggest China Missile Trade," *Washington Post,* July 3, 1995; R. Jeffrey Smith, "An M-11 Missile Violation By Any Other Name," *Washington Post,* August 3, 1995.

[71]A serious deterioration in U.S.–Chinese relations caused by the Clinton Administration's decision to grant Taiwanese President Lee Teng-hui a visa to visit the United States in June 1995 contributed, some believe, to Washington's reluctance to invoke new sanctions against Beijing.

[72]Bill Gertz, "Pakistan Deploys Chinese Missiles," *Washington Times,* June 12, 1996; R. Jeffrey Smith, "Report Cites China-Pakistan Missile Links," *Washington Post,* June 13, 1996.

[73]One piece of evidence of Pakistan's efforts to refine its nuclear weapons was Great Britain's expulsion in early 1996 of an employee of the Pakistan Embassy in London for attempting to export illegally specialized laser instruments used in the manufacture of nuclear weapons. "Pakistan Nuclear Program at a 'Screwdriver Level,'" *Washington Times,* February 20, 1996.

[74]Smith, "Report Cites China-Pakistan Missile Links," op. cit.

[75]R. Jeffrey Smith, "China Linked to Pakistani Missile Plant," *Washington Post,* August 25, 1996; *Time,* Vol. 149, No. 26, June 30, 1997.

[76]Smith, "China Linked to Pakistani Missile Plant," ibid.

[77]Various factors apparently contributed to this stance. First, the existence of M-11 missiles in Pakistan was thought to date back to 1992-1993. The possibility that complete Chinese missiles had been transferred to Pakistan was apparently taken into account when sanctions were imposed against organizations in both countries in August 1993. Those sanctions had been rescinded for China and had expired for Pakistan, and it was not clear that a "new" violation of U.S. sanctions law had occurred (even though the Category II sanctions imposed in 1993 were for the transfer of missile-related components, not the more severe Category I sanctions that applied to transfers of complete missiles). With respect to the missile factory, to be a violation of U.S. sanctions laws, any assistance that China might have provided for such a plant would have to contribute to the production of missiles inherently capable of carrying a 500-kg payload to a distance of at least 300 km (see Appendix G on MTCR in this volume). According to U.S. officials, however, the United States did not have sufficient intelligence data on the facility to make a firm judgment on this question. (Interviews, fall 1996.) Another factor that likely contributed to U.S. restraint was that overall U.S.-Chinese relations were once again embittered because of China's intimidating military maneuvers (including missile tests) near Taiwan during that country's first-ever presidential elections, and because of a major dispute over China's failure to enforce U.S. intellectual property rights—a dispute in which Washington was threatening to impose $2 billion in trade penalties. To have imposed missile-transfer sanctions in this setting would have driven relations to a new low point,

from which they might not have recovered for many years. With respect to Pakistan, finally, imposing Category I missile-transfer sanctions against it would have meant the end of arms shipments under the Brown Amendment, a step that would have undermined the last surviving component of this U.S. initiative.

[78]For other details and citations on India's missile program activities, see chapter on India.

[79]The Prithvi I Army version missile is rated as having a 150-km range with a 1,000-kg (one ton) payload, which is not only nuclear-capable but capable of delivering a rather large conventional warhead, a canister of anti-personnel or anti-runway mines, or even a fuel-air explosive or chemical payload. The Prithvi II Air Force version is attributed with a 250-km range with a 500-kg payload—probably much the same missile, technically, but with greater range achieved by cutting back the payload. For reported range and payload, see *The Military Balance 1995/96*, op. cit., p. 283.

[80]*Reuters* report from New Delhi, July 30, 1997; Manoj Joshi, "In the Shadow of Fear," *India Today International*, Vol. XXII, No. 17, July 15-21, 1997, pp. 50ff.

[81]Indications of a Hatf-3 600-km missile program in Pakistan were reported as early as 1995 in IISS, *The Military Balance, 1995/96*, op. cit., p. 283.

[82]Reportedly, the Ghauri missile, unveiled in March 1998, is indigenously designed and manufactured, has a strike range of 1,500 to 2,000 km, can be used in either a surface-to-surface or air-to-surface mode, and will be produced at a missile factory in Attock, apparently the same factory disclosed in 1996 in U.S. media sources. See report in *Jang*, January 3, 1998, in *FBIS*, January 5, 1998; for the U.S. reports on a missile factory, see Smith, "Report Cites China-Pakistan Missile Links," op. cit., and the chapter on China in this volume. Pakistan claimed to have successfully tested the Ghauri on April 6, 1998. See "Pakistan Tests Medium-Range Missile," *Washington Post*, April 7, 1998; and "Nuclear Arms Race in South Asia," *Washington Post*, May 29, 1998.

[83]One author characterized Pakistan's just-tested Hatf-3 as a "clone" of the Chinese export type of medium-range, mobile missile designated M-9. See Manoj Joshi, "In the Shadow of Fear," op. cit.

The M-9 is reported to have a 600-km range with a 500-kg payload, more than twice the Chinese-claimed 280-km range of the M-11. See *The Military Balance 1995/96*, op. cit., p. 281. While a Pakistani M-11 with 280-km-range capability probably would not be able to reach India's capital at Delhi, the M-9 not only could target Delhi but possibly reach Mumbai (Bombay), India's largest industrial city, from Pakistani territory. For India's new defensive missile procurement objectives, see chapter on India.

[84]This unstable condition is known as the "use them or lose them" dilemma; Pakistani planners would fear that their nuclear-equipped aircraft or missiles, if preemptively attacked, might be destroyed, disarming Pakistan's retaliatory capability, and thus undermining the crediblity of its nuclear deterrent. See Eric Arnett, "Nuclear Stability and Arms Sales to India: Implications for U.S. Policy," *Arms Control Today*, Vol. 27, No. 5, August 1997, pp. 7-11.

[85]It is not clear that a decision to conduct the test had been sanctioned at the highest political levels, and the foreign disclosure may have forced high-level attention. However, with general elections to be held in the spring of 1996, it is also possible that Indian Prime Minister and Congress Party leader Narasimha Rao had been persuaded to allow preparations to go forward to deflect pressure from the increasingly powerful Hindu nationalist Bharatiya Janata Party (BJP), whose platform had long advocated India's becoming an overt nuclear power.

[86]"Testimony of John Deutch, Director, Central Intelligence," *Current and Projected National Security Threats to the United States and Its Interests Abroad*, Select Committee on Intelligence, U.S. Senate (Washington, DC: GPO, February 22, 1996), p. 12.

[87]R. Jeffrey Smith, "Pakistan Plans Tit-for-Tat Test of Nuclear Blast, Officials Say," *Washington Post*, March 6. The site was the location of one or more "cold tests," i.e., heavily instrumented detonations of dummy nuclear devices, that Pakistan had conducted in the 1980s.

[88]"Pakistan Dismisses Nuclear Test Report," *Reuters*, March 6, 1996; Raja Asghar, "Pakistan Vows Tit-for-Tat Nuclear Reply to India," op. cit.

[89]*Proliferation: Threat and Response,* 1997, op. cit., p. 17.

Additional References

Zia Mian, *Pakistan's Atomic Bomb and the Search for Security,* (Islamabad: Sustainable Development Policy Institute, 1995). Stephen P. Cohen, *The Pakistan Army* (Berkeley: University of California Press, 1984, and Karachi: Oxford University Press, 1993). Neil Joeck, *Maintaining Nuclear Stability in South Asia,* Adelphi Paper 312, International Institute for Strategic Studies, 1997. *Preventing Nuclear Proliferation in South Asia,* Report of a Study Group sponsored by The Asia Society (New York: The Asia Society, 1995). George Perkovich, "A Nuclear Third Way in South Asia," *Foreign Policy,* No. 91, Summer 1993, pp. 85-104. Kanti Bajpai et al., *Brasstacks and Beyond: Perception and Management of Crisis in South Asia* (New Delhi: Manohar, and Columbia, MO: South Asia Books, 1995). Devin T. Hagerty, "Nuclear Deterrence in South Asia: The 1990 Indo-Pakistani Crisis," *International Security,* Vol. 20, No. 3, Winter 1995/96, pp. 79-114, with correspondence in subsequent issues. Sumit Ganguly and Ted Greenwood, *Mending Fences: Confidence and Security Building Measures in South Asia* (Boulder: Westview Press, 1996). Stephen P. Cohen, ed., *Nuclear Proliferation in South Asia: The Prospects for Arms Control* (Boulder: Westview Press, 1991).

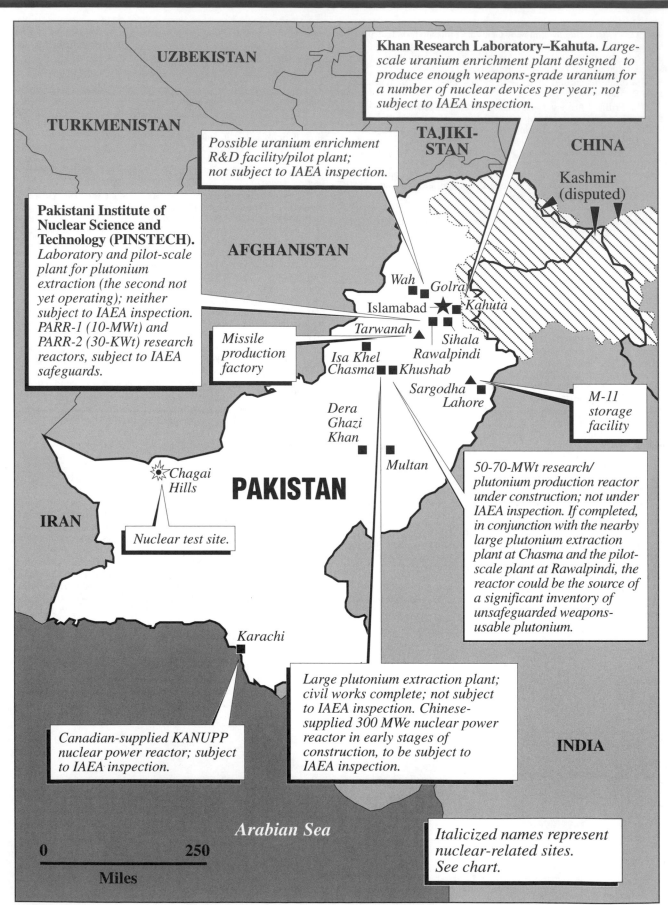

Khan Research Laboratory–Kahuta. *Large-scale uranium enrichment plant designed to produce enough weapons-grade uranium for a number of nuclear devices per year; not subject to IAEA inspection.*

Possible uranium enrichment R&D facility/pilot plant; not subject to IAEA inspection.

Pakistani Institute of Nuclear Science and Technology (PINSTECH). *Laboratory and pilot-scale plant for plutonium extraction (the second not yet operating); neither subject to IAEA inspection. PARR-1 (10-MWt) and PARR-2 (30-KWt) research reactors, subject to IAEA safeguards.*

Missile production factory

M-11 storage facility

50-70-MWt research/plutonium production reactor under construction; not under IAEA inspection. If completed, in conjunction with the nearby large plutonium extraction plant at Chasma and the pilot-scale plant at Rawalpindi, the reactor could be the source of a significant inventory of unsafeguarded weapons-usable plutonium.

Nuclear test site.

Large plutonium extraction plant; civil works complete; not subject to IAEA inspection. Chinese-supplied 300 MWe nuclear power reactor in early stages of construction, to be subject to IAEA inspection.

Canadian-supplied KANUPP nuclear power reactor; subject to IAEA inspection.

Italicized names represent nuclear-related sites. See chart.

UZBEKISTAN

TURKMENISTAN

TAJIKI-STAN

CHINA

Kashmir (disputed)

AFGHANISTAN

Wah Golra Kahuta
Islamabad
Tarwanah Sihala
Rawalpindi
Isa Khel
Chasma Khushab
Sargodha
Lahore

Dera Ghazi Khan

Multan

Chagai Hills

PAKISTAN

IRAN

INDIA

Karachi

Arabian Sea

0   250
Miles

Carnegie Endowment for International Peace, *Tracking Nuclear Proliferation*, 1998

PAKISTAN: Nuclear Infrastructure

NAME/LOCATION OF FACILILTY	TYPE/STATUS	IAEA SAFEGUARDS
NUCLEAR WEAPONS R&D COMPLEX		
Khan Research Laboratories (KRL), Kahuta	Fabrication of HEU into nuclear weapon.	No
Chagai Hills	Nuclear test site.	No
Pakistan Ordnance Factory, Wah	Possible nuclear weapons assembly site.[a]	No
POWER REACTORS		
KANUPP, Karachi	Heavy-water, natural U, 137 MWe; operating.	Yes
Chasma-1	Light-water, LEU, 310 MWe; under construction.[b]	Planned
Chasma-2	Light-water, LEU, 310 MWe; planned.[c]	Planned
RESEARCH REACTORS		
Pakistan Atomic Research Reactor 1 (PARR 1), Rawalpindi	Light-water, originally HEU, modified to use LEU, 9 MWt; operating.	Yes
PARR 2, Rawalpindi	Pool-type, light-water, HEU, 30 KWt; operating.	Yes
Research/Plutonium Production Reactor, Khushab	Heavy-water, natural U, 50 MWt; under construction, expected completion 1998.[d]	No
URANIUM ENRICHMENT		
Khan Research Laboratories (KRL), Kahuta	Large-scale ultracentrifuge facility; operating.	No
Sihala	Experimental-scale ultracentrifuge facility; operating.	No
Golra	Ultracentrifuge plant reportedly to be used as testing facility; operational status unknown.[e]	No
Wah	Enrichment plant possibly under construction.[f]	
REPROCESSING (PLUTONIUM EXTRACTION)[g]		
Chasma	Terminated by France (1978); indigenous construction of the building shell may be nearly complete; reportedly not equipped.[h]	No[i]
New Labs, PINSTECH, Rawalpindi	Pilot-scale, "hot cell" facility; design capacity up to 20 kg/y.[j]	No
PINSTECH, Rawalpindi	Experimental-scale lab for research on solvent extraction.[k]	No
URANIUM PROCESSING		
Baghalchar	Uranium mining; operating.	N/A (Not Applicable)
Dera Ghazi Khan	Uranium mining and milling; operating.	N/A
Isa Khel	Uranium ore processing; planned.	N/A
Qabul Khel, near Isa Khel	Uranium mining and milling; operating.	N/A
Lahore	Uranium milling; operating.	N/A

PAKISTAN (cont'd.)

NAME/LOCATION OF FACILILTY	TYPE/STATUS	IAEA SAFEGUARDS
Dera Ghazi Khan	Uranium conversion (UF$_6$); operating.	No
Chasma/Kundian	Fuel fabrication; operating.[l]	No
HEAVY-WATER PRODUCTION		
Multan	Operating.	No
Karachi	Operating.	No

Abbreviations:

HEU	=	highly enriched uranium
LEU	=	low-enriched uranium
nat. U	=	natural uranium
MWe	=	millions of watts of electrical output
MWt	=	millions of watts of thermal output
KWt	=	thousands of watts of thermal output

NOTES (Pakistan Chart)

[a]See "India Denies Atom-Test Plan but Then Turns Ambiguous," *New York Times*, December 16, 1996.

[b]The civil works for the Chasma-1 power plant were completed by November 21, 1995, and the plant is expected to begin commercial operation by October 1998. See "Chasma Milestone," *Nuclear Engineering International,* February 1996, p. 9.

[c]Plans to build the second Chasma-2 reactor may have been shelved due to financial problems and pressure from the United States, although Pakistani officials have denied these reports. "PAEC head denies report that U.S., money ills derail Chasma-2," *Nucleonics Week,* July 6, 1995, p. 5.

[d]Some reporting suggests that the Khushab research reactor is already complete, but is awaiting unsafeguarded heavy water from China. Pakistani officials claimed in July 1997 that the plant was operational, but U.S. officials rejected this claim, noting that "all the data at hand indicates that the reactor is still cold." See "U.S. believes Khushab still cold, no heavy water by China," *Nucleonics Week*, July 3, 1997, p. 16; and Mark Hibbs, "China accord would turn up U.S. heat on Pakistani reactor," *Nucleonics Week*, August 14, 1997, p. 8.

[e]See David Albright, Frans Berkhout, and William Walker, *Plutionium and Highly Enriched Uarnium 1996: World Inventories, Capabilities and Policies* (New York: Oxford University Press for Stockholm International Peace Research Institute, 1997), p. 269ff.

[f]A January 4, 1996, article in *The Muslim* reported that during a visit to Islamabad, U.S. official Robert Oakley accused Pakistan of constructing another enrichment facility at Wah with Chinese assistance. Pakistani officials confirmed the existence of the project. As reported in "Pakistan said ready to counter Indian nuclear test with its own," *Nucleonics Week*, February 29, 1996, p. 14.

[g]It was suspected that Pakistan was also constructing a secondary facility to extract plutonium from spent reactor fuel at Khushab. In early August 1997, however, U.S. intelligence officials categorically declared that the secondary facility at Khushab is "not a reprocessing plant." See Albright et al., *1996 World Inventories*, op. cit., p. 281; Hibbs, "China Accord Would Turn Up U.S. Heat," op. cit., p. 8.

[h]A 1996 report suggested that China was aiding Pakistan in the construction of the Chasma facility. See Bill Gertz, "China aids Pakistan's plutonium plants," *Washington Times*, April 3, 1996. Further reports from early August 1997, however, indicate that Chinese and French assistance has stopped, and that U.S. officials believe the Chasma complex is "an empty shell." See Hibbs, "China Accord Would Turn Up U.S. Heat," op. cit., p. 8.

[i]Safeguards may be required because of the use of French technology supplied in the 1970's under the Franco-Pakistani bilateral supply agreement for the plant, which requires such monitoring. Because France refused to complete the facility, however, Pakistan has never acknowledged its obligation to place the facility under IAEA inspection, despite its incorporation of the French technology. If past reports of Chinese assistance to Pakistan to complete the reprocessing facility were true, China would be in violation of Article 3, Paragraph 2 of the NPT for failing to secure IAEA safeguards on the transfer of reprocessing technology to Pakistan.

[j]Contradictory reports have surfaced over the real plutonium output capacity of New Labs. Reports from the early 1980's before New Labs was operational suggested that it had a design output capacity of 10-20 kg/y. See Milton Benjamin, "Pakistan Building Secret Nuclear Plant," *Washington Post*, September 23, 1980; a secret U.S. Department of State report dated June 23, 1983, and titled "The Pakistani Nuclear Program"—subsequently released in 1992 under the Freedom of Information Act—supports this claim. A 1997 report, however, suggests that New Labs can produce only about 1 kg/y. See Hibbs, "China Accord Would Turn Up U.S. Heat," op. cit., p. 8.

[k]The secret 1983 Department of State report, op. cit., notes that in the basement of the main PINSTECH building exists a small laboratory for research on solvent extraction. Solvent extraction in Pakistan should be subject to IAEA inspection pursuant to a trilateral safeguards agreement (France, Pakistan, IAEA—see INFCIRC/239).

[l]"In parallel with efforts to manufacture fuel for its Canadian-supplied KANUPP-1 PHWR, Pakistan already has developed the capability to manufacture the NATU [natural Uranium] fuel for the production reactor [Khushab] on a pilot basis." See "Bhutto may finish Plutonium reactor without agreement on fissile stocks," *Nucleonics Week,* October 6, 1994, p. 10. Under contract, China will supply fuel for the first three cores of the Chasma power reactor, and help Pakistan set up a fuel fabrication plant. See "Chasma vessel manufacture said to be underway in China," *Nucleonics Week,* November 30, 1995, p. 6.

North Korea

North Korea, a party to the Nuclear Non-Proliferation Treaty (NPT) since 1985, is believed to have pursued an active nuclear weapons program, in violation of the Treaty, centered around a number of facilities at the Yongbyon Nuclear Research Center. North Korea blocked International Atomic Energy Agency (IAEA) inspections and threatened to withdraw from the NPT in 1993, forcing an unprecedented regime crisis. In October 1994, as part of a special agreement with the United States, North Korea pledged to freeze operations at most of these facilities, halting the production of new weapons-usable nuclear materials, and promised to eventually dismantle its gas-graphite moderated reactors and reprocessing facility. Under the agreement, the United States, South Korea, and Japan formed a multilateral consortium to build two light-water reactors in the North and to deliver 500,000 tons of heavy fuel oil annually until the first nuclear reactor is completed. Some observers suspect, however, that—in the absence of effective IAEA inspections—North Korea is continuing secret work on nuclear weapons, such as designing a nuclear device or fabricating components from materials it already possesses.

BACKGROUND

The key facilities at Yongbyon include an operational 5-MWe experimental nuclear power reactor, a partially completed large-scale reprocessing plant for plutonium extraction, a number of radiochemistry laboratories (or "hot cells") that can be used for plutonium extraction, a high-explosive testing facility, a fuel fabrication plant, and a partially completed 50-MWe power reactor. North Korea was also building a 200-MWe reactor at Taechon until it agreed to freeze construction of the facility under its October 1994 understanding with the United States.[1]

Although North Korea signed the NPT in 1985, it did not permit the IAEA to conduct inspections, as required by the Treaty, until May 1992. In the early 1990s, U.S. intelligence agencies judged that North Korea had extracted plutonium at the Yongbyon reprocessing plant—and possibly at a number of hot cells— using irradiated fuel rods from the 5-MWe reactor, which is thought to have been partially or fully refueled in 1989. Technically, North Korea could have obtained as much as 12 kg of plutonium—enough to have manufactured one or two nuclear weapons. Most U.S. intelligence agencies at the time assessed that the amount of plutonium recovered by North Korea was more than

that declared to the IAEA, and that the excess would have been enough for one or possibly two nuclear weapons.[3]

The 5-MWe reactor's inventory of spent fuel was again unloaded in May 1994. If reprocessed, this material could provide enough plutonium for four or five nuclear weapons. In addition, if completed, the 50-MWe reactor would have the potential to produce enough material for ten to twelve nuclear bombs a year.[4]

Under the terms of the U.S.–North Korean "Agreed Framework" concluded on October 21, 1994, however, North Korea has pledged to:

(1) Freeze operations at, or cease construction of, all of these reactors and cease operating the Yongbyon reprocessing plant, with the freeze to be verified by the IAEA;

(2) Not separate plutonium from the spent fuel removed from the 5-MWe reactor in May 1994 (the status of the fuel to be monitored by the IAEA);

(3) Ship the spent fuel out of North Korea; and

(4) Thereafter dismantle all facilities of nuclear proliferation concern. In exchange, North Korea will be provided with two less proliferation-prone light-water reactors (LWRs) and a number of other energy-related inducements as well as security assurances.[5]

The Inspection Controversy. North Korea's acceptance of the Agreed Framework culminated a decade of ups and downs in the relationship between North Korea and the international non-proliferation regime. As noted above, although North Korea became a party to the NPT in 1985, it did not finalize a safeguards agreement with the IAEA, as required by the Treaty, until April 9, 1992. Under the NPT, North Korea is required to declare all of its nuclear materials and related facilities for IAEA inspection. In May 1992, the IAEA initiated a series of inspections and "visits" to verify North Korea's initial inventory of nuclear facilities and materials.[6] During this process, in the summer and fall of 1992, the IAEA found discrepancies in North Korea's declaration of levels of past plutonium production.

Specifically, the IAEA's chemical analysis of samples of plutonium provided by Pyongyang contradicted the latter's claim that it had previously separated only grams of plutonium in a one-time "experiment." Instead, the IAEA results indicated that the North had separated plutonium in four campaigns over three years, starting in 1989.[7]

The findings raised further concern because they also appeared to contradict North Korea's claim that it had not replaced the fuel core of the 5-MWe reactor since the unit began operating in 1986 but had separated plutonium only from a handful of defective fuel rods that it had removed from the facility. U.S. intelligence analysts believed, however, that the reactor's core had been replaced during a 100-day period when the unit was shut down in 1989, providing the North with a stockpile of plutonium-bearing spent fuel from which it had subsequently extracted a significant amount of plutonium at the Yongbyon reprocessing plant—possibly enough for one or two nuclear devices.[8] The IAEA finding that the North had engaged in multiple plutonium separation campaigns thus lent credence to the U.S. view that North Korea might have a significant quantity of weapons-usable plutonium.

In an effort to resolve the discrepancies that the IAEA found in North Korea's declaration regarding plutonium production, the IAEA called in early 1993 for a "special inspection" of two undeclared sites near the Yongbyon nuclear complex that were thought to contain wastes from the plutonium separation process. North Korea refused to allow the inspection and announced it was withdrawing from the NPT, which permits such action on a 90-day notice if a party's "supreme national interests" are jeopardized. After a round of negotiations with the United States in June 1993, North Korea agreed to suspend its withdrawal. North Korea asserted, however, that it was no longer a full party to the NPT and that the IAEA no longer had the right to conduct even normal routine and ad hoc inspections. Over the ensuing nine months, Pyongyang severely constrained IAEA inspection activities needed to preserve the "continuity of safeguards," leading IAEA Director General Hans Blix to declare in December 1993 that Agency safeguards in North Korea could no longer provide "any meaningful assurances" that nuclear materials were not being diverted to weapons uses.[9]

In March 1994, as part of a complicated package deal with the United States, North Korea initially agreed to an IAEA inspection of its declared facilities, but then blocked the Agency from taking key radioactive samples at the plutonium extraction plant at Yongbyon when it believed that key elements of the deal had not been fulfilled.[10] The crisis escalated further in mid-May 1994, when North Korea started to defuel the 5-MWe reactor while refusing to implement procedures demanded by the IAEA to segregate 300 carefully selected fuel rods from the 8,000-rod core.[11] Analysis of the radioactive signature of the segregated rods would have indicated how long they had been in the reactor, permitting the IAEA to determine whether it had been refueled in 1989—and, thus, whether North Korea might have been able to obtain plutonium for one or two nuclear devices.

As Pyongyang accelerated and completed the defueling, Hans Blix declared in a letter to the U.N. Security Council, on June 2, 1994, that the "agency's ability to ascertain, with sufficient confidence, whether nuclear material from the reactor has been diverted in the past, has been . . . lost."[12] A special inspection of the two undeclared waste sites thus apparently remained the IAEA's principal option for determining past levels of plutonium production. However, North Korea continued to insist that it would never allow inspections at the two sites, which it claimed were military facilities and therefore off limits to the Agency. To penalize North Korea for refusing to comply with IAEA inspection requirements during the defueling of the Yongbyon reactor, the Agency in early June suspended all technical assistance to the North. This led Pyongyang to announce on June 13 that it was withdrawing from the IAEA (a step that did not, however, amount to a renunciation of its safeguards obligations under the NPT).[13]

These developments prompted the United States to circulate, on June 15, a proposal to the U.N. Security Council calling for two phases of sanctions against North Korea. The first phase of the sanctions, which were to be activated after a grace period, consisted of a worldwide ban on arms imports from, and arms exports to, North Korea, along with a downgrading of diplomatic ties. In the second phase, to be triggered if the North continued to reject the IAEA's demands, a worldwide ban on financial dealings with Pyongyang would be implemented.[14]

The crisis eased after former President Jimmy Carter met with North Korean President Kim Il Sung on June 16-17. The North Korean leader agreed to freeze his country's nuclear program if the United States resumed high-level talks. These negotiations—which took place in July but were then suspended until early August because of the sudden death of Kim Il Sung on July 9—proved successful in hammering out an "Agreed Statement" on August 12, 1994, under which, in broad terms, North Korea agreed to dismantle the elements of its nuclear program that appeared to be linked to the production of nuclear arms.[15]

The "Agreed Framework." The two sides proceeded with a series of expert-level discussions and another round of high-level talks to work out the modalities of an agreement. After a period of stalemate, they managed to conclude the "Agreed Framework," signed on October 21, 1994.[16] The accord provides, among other things, for the establishment of a multinational consortium that will finance and supply North Korea with two LWRs by the target date of 2003. In return, North Korea agreed to freeze its nuclear program immediately; pledged not to refuel the 5-MWe Yongbyon reactor; undertook to halt construction of the 50-MWe reactor at that site and of the 200-MWe reactor at Taechon; and agreed to seal the Yongbyon plutonium separation plant and the fabrication plant at the site, and to leave the spent fuel discharged from the 5-MWe reactor in June 1994 in storage, without plutonium separation. Pyongyang also agreed that the spent fuel would be removed from North Korea as nuclear components for the first LWR are supplied, and that all of the facilities where activities were frozen would be dismantled by the time that the second LWR was completed.

To offset the energy deficit that North Korea claimed it would face by the freezing of its graphite-moderated reactors and related facilities, the United States was to arrange for the delivery to North Korea (within three months) of heavy oil for heating and electricity production "that will reach a rate of 500,000 tons annually." This grant of heavy fuel oil would stop with the completion of the first LWR.

Under the Agreement Framework, North Korea would remain party to the NPT. However, it would not be required to come into full compliance with its IAEA safeguards agreement until a "significant portion of the LWR project is completed, but before delivery of key nuclear components." This delay, estimated to last from four to six years, will result in postponement of IAEA verification of the accuracy and completeness of North Korea's initial report on the nuclear materials in its possession. More specifically, it will postpone IAEA special inspections of the two waste sites noted above and thus a determination of whether the North possesses sufficient plutonium for one or more nuclear weapons.

The Agreed Framework also provided for steps toward the normalization of relations between North Korea and the United States, U.S. assurances against the threat or use of nuclear weapons against the North, and a North Korean commitment to implement the 1992 North-South Joint Declaration on the De-Nuclearization of the Korean Peninsula.[17]

Proponents of the Agreed Framework have pointed to its inherent security benefits. They stress that it freezes, and then dismantles, nuclear facilities that would have given North Korea the capability to produce dozens of nuclear weapons per year, some of which might have been exported. Another advantage cited is that North Korea has effectively agreed, for the first time, to IAEA inspection of the two undeclared waste sites, which will help reveal the history of past plutonium production. Proponents of the agreement note, moreover, that it places restrictions on North Korea beyond those imposed by the NPT by banning reprocessing of existing spent fuel and requiring the dismantling of North Korea's most sensitive nuclear facilities. As a by-product of the agreement, the construction of the LWRs would require thousands of South Korean engineers, technicians, and laborers to work, live, and socialize in the North for a decade, thereby improving the chances for more normal relations between Pyongyang and Seoul and lifting, at least partially, the veil of secrecy surrounding the North.[18]

On the other hand, the Agreed Framework is controversial. Its critics contend that the agreement guarantees nothing and gives away too much. First, by postponing IAEA inspection of the two undeclared sites for an extended period (four to six years), the accord delays attaining full compliance with IAEA safeguards and creates an unprecedented "special" safeguards status for North Korea (i.e., it introduces a double standard and a troubling precedent). Postponing inspections, it is argued, compromises the integrity of IAEA safeguards, especially as they relate to the conduct of the Agency's "special inspections."[19] The accord also will not attempt to rule out, for four to six years, the possibility that North Korea possesses a pre-existing stock of plutonium or possibly one or two nuclear weapons. Moreover, the critics stress, the agreement preserves for a somewhat longer period North Korea's ability to acquire additional nuclear weapons rapidly— since, if implementation of the pact breaks down, Pyongyang would have immediate access to the stored spent fuel from the 5-MWe reactor as well as to the Yongbyon reprocessing plant. A final criticism is that the agreement sets a precedent for others to "toy" with the NPT. Iran, for example, has already hinted it might withdraw from the Treaty because it is the object of a U.S.–led nuclear embargo.[20]

On balance, it seems clear that the Agreement Framework, although an unorthodox adaptation to North Korea's singular defiance, still provides a credible means of keeping North Korea in the regime and of blocking nuclear weapons manufacture while time is used to construct other incentives and build constructive working relationships with North Korean authorities.

DEVELOPMENTS

Implementation of the Agreed Framework has proceeded slowly due to time-consuming negotiations with North Korea and periodic crises on the Korean peninsula. North Korea's continuing freeze on its graphite-moderated reactors and reprocessing facility has been verified by the IAEA. John Holum, Director of the U.S. Arms Control and Disarmament Agency, has stated, "In fact, I understand that the reactors are gathering rust and wouldn't be useful without an enormous investment again."[21] Progress on implementing the political, economic, and reactor-related aspects of the Agreed Framework has been slow, but overall the project to construct the reactors has made the most headway. North Korea has been receiving regular oil shipments since January 1995.[22]

Korean Peninsula Energy Development Organization. On March 9, 1995, the United States, Japan, and South Korea formed a multinational consortium, called the Korean Peninsula Energy Development Organization (KEDO), to supply North Korea with the two promised light-water reactors.[23] Besides being the agency responsible for implementing the reactor deal, KEDO has also taken over responsibility for raising the funds to pay for the oil deliveries that the United States sponsored initially. One of the initial stumbling blocks in carrying out the reactor-related portion of the Agreed Framework was North Korea's refusal to accept South Korean reactors.[24] On June 13, North Korea and the United States issued a joint statement, which resolved some of the more contentious issues that had been stalling implementation of the Agreed Framework. Both sides agreed that KEDO would select a reactor model based on a U.S.–origin design and would also select the prime contractor for the project. The program coordinator would be an American firm chosen by KEDO. On the same day, KEDO announced that the 1,000-MWe Korean Standard Nuclear Power Plant (KSNP), based on the System 80 reactor design of the U.S. firm Asea Brown Boveri-Combustion Engineering, (ABB-CE), would be the model for the reactors to be supplied to North Korea.[25]

After months of further negotiation, North Korea and KEDO concluded a Supply Agreement on December 15, 1995, for the actual financing and supply of the reactors.[26] The Supply Agreement has three main components: setting out the scope of supply for the two light-water reactors; outlining the terms of repayment by North Korea for the cost of the reactors; and outlining the general terms and conditions under which KEDO will operate at the project site. In addition, according to a senior White House official, the Supply Agreement is important because "it codifies in a legally binding instrument, those same non-proliferation commitments which were the core of the Agreed Framework of 1994."[27] This means that delivery of fuel oil and construction work on the LWRs will stop immediately if North Korea violates its contractual commitments.

The terms and conditions of the Supply Agreement are detailed in subsequent protocols negotiated between KEDO and North Korea. On July 11, 1996, KEDO and North Korea signed three protocols on privileges and immunities, transportation, and communication.[28] In March 1996, KEDO selected Korea Electric Power Corporation (KEPCO), South Korea's electrical utility with nuclear power reactor experience, as the prime contractor for the reactor project.[29] In July, KEDO selected the U.S. firm Duke Engineering & Services, Inc., as its program coordinator (later renamed as its technical support consultant).[30] The same month, KEPCO submitted a rough cost estimate for the LWR project—reportedly, $5.5-$6 billion.[31] (In November 1997, KEDO officially declared that the cost of the LWR construction project would be $5.1785 billion.) South Korea is prepared to assume a "central role" and pay up to 70 percent of the cost of the project, while Japan will play a "meaningful role," paying up to 20-25 percent. North Korea will repay the cost of the project over a 20-year, interest-free period, with a three-year grace period, following the completion of the LWRs.

In early September 1996, Stephen W. Bosworth, then head of KEDO, stated, "We have put in place nearly all of the basic political agreements with the North Koreans that will be required for us to launch work in North Korea at the designated site for the reactors."[32] At the time, negotiations were under way on two additional protocols, but the implementation of the Agreed Framework was halted by the September 18 discovery of a North Korean reconnaissance submarine grounded on South Korea's coast. South Korea allowed KEDO to complete the negotiations, but refused to allow it to initial the protocols on "site use" and "use of

DPRK manpower, materials, and services" until North Korea apologized for the submarine incident.[33]

On December 29, 1996, after a series of meetings with the United States, North Korea expressed "deep regret" for the submarine incident.[34] On January 8, 1997, KEDO and North Korea signed the protocols on site use and use of manpower, materials, and services.[35] In April, a KEDO delegation traveled to the LWR project site via a sea transportation route for the first time.[36] On May 4, KEDO and North Korea initialed a protocol on "actions in the event of nonpayment."[37] In July, KEDO and North Korea concluded negotiations on the final steps needed before physical work could begin at the LWR project site at Sinpo. In August 1997, KEDO formally broke ground on the LWR project.

Three months earlier, on May 15, KEDO and the European Union had initialed an agreement for EURATOM to become an executive board member, with contributions to KEDO to total $86 million over five years.[38] As of mid-1997, KEDO had 11 members and had received international contributions from 23 countries.[39]

Oil Deliveries. As part of the Agreed Framework, the United States committed itself to compensate North Korea with fuel oil for the energy it lost by shutting down its 5-MWe reactor and abandoning plans to finish the two larger power reactors. In January 1995, the United States delivered 50,000 tons of heavy fuel oil to North Korea. KEDO then assumed responsibility for the delivery of the remaining 100,000 tons due by November 1995, and the 500,000 additional tons due every twelve months thereafter. These oil shipments will continue until the first LWR is completed. Reports emerged in mid-1995 that North Korea was diverting fuel oil to the military.[40] In response, KEDO installed oil flow meters at the thermal power plants that were receiving the fuel oil.[41] KEDO met its fuel oil commitments to North Korea in 1995, 1996, and 1997.[42]

Spent Fuel Canning. The Agreed Framework also specifies that North Korea would store, without reprocessing, the spent fuel discharged in June 1994 from its 5-MWe reactor, and complete the removal of the spent fuel from its territory when the major nuclear components had been completely shipped to the North for the first reactor. Since North Korea has claimed in the past that it has engaged in reprocessing because it is unable to store spent fuel safely for long periods of time, the United States began a project to place the spent fuel in corrosion-resistant canisters that would allow for long-term storage. The U.S. Department of Energy awarded a contract to NAC International to stabilize and can the approximately 8,000 spent fuel rods.[43] The first stage of canning the spent fuel rods was to install a water-purification device in the holding pool; this was accomplished by the end of September 1995.[44] North Korea began removing the spent fuel rods from the pool and placing them in dry storage in January 1996.[45] The actual canning, conducted by North Korea, began April 27, 1996, and was expected to be completed by April 1, 1998.[46] The cost of canning, which will be borne by the United States, is estimated at $26.5 million.[47] Although IAEA inspectors supervised the canning, they were not allowed to sample the fuel rods for radiation measurements.[48] The ultimate fate of the spent fuel has not yet been determined.

IAEA. The IAEA has continuously monitored the freeze on North Korea's indigenous nuclear activities since November 1994.[49] The Agency has been allowed to conduct routine and ad hoc inspections of "unfrozen" nuclear facilities but not of the reprocessing plant, and it has been allowed to measure but not analyze the spent fuel.[50] A North Korean representative to the IAEA has stated that North Korea will not provide any additional information on its inventory of nuclear material until the LWRs are operational.[51] This stance would be inconsistent with the Agreed Framework, which states that North Korea must be in full compliance with IAEA safeguards before it can receive key nuclear components of the LWRs. During 1997, the IAEA and North Korea continued to hold talks about uncovering the North's nuclear history, but no progress was reported.

Steps Toward Normalized Relations. Normalized diplomatic, political, and economic relations between the United States and North Korea have not yet been realized. In early January 1995, President Clinton signed an executive order reducing some sanctions on North Korea.[52] However, the Trading with the Enemy Act, which has applied to North Korea since the Korean War and prevents virtually any trade with North Korea, remains in effect, although some exceptions have been made. On December 30, 1996, the United States approved a license sought by Cargill, Inc., a U.S. firm, to negotiate a commercial deal to sell North Korea up to 500,000 tons of grain.[53] Cargill and North Korea reportedly reached an agreement on a shipment of an unknown size.[54] In April 1997, the United States approved a joint venture signed in September 1996 between another U.S. firm, the Stanton Group, and North Korea's Sungri petrochemical company to refurbish an oil refinery in the Rajin-Sonbong free trade zone.[55]

In addition to this limited reduction of economic barriers, over the past two years, the United States has provided $33 million for medical supplies and food, including $10 million pledged in February 1997 and $15 million pledged in April 1997, in response to emergency appeals by the U.N. World Food Programme.[56] The humanitarian aid offered to North Korea was both a sign of good will and an attempt to forestall disaster in the famine-stricken country. According to one report, U.S. government sources predicted in April 1997 that as many as 100,000 North Koreans could die from starvation and disease over the next four months.[57] However, U.S., South Korean, and Japanese officials refused to assist with large-scale humanitarian aid until North Korea agreed to the proposed four-party peace talks (see below).

The Agreed Framework calls for the United States and North Korea to establish liaison offices in each other's capitals as a prelude to full diplomatic recognition and the opening of embassies. In early 1997, a State Department official with responsibility for Korea declared that "conditions appear to be improving for the realization of the establishment of liaison offices" in Washington and Pyongyang.[58] It is likely that the pace of opening liaison offices will be tied to the pace of the four-party talks.

The United States and North Korea will need to sign a bilateral nuclear cooperation accord to allow U.S. firms to supply nuclear equipment to the LWR project.[59] A U.S. firm, Combustion Engineering, Inc., supplies some of the key nuclear components for South Korea's reactors and is expected to receive an order for these same components for the LWRs that KEDO will provide to the North. If Congress finds the cooperation agreement meets U.S. law, it will become effective 90 days after being submitted by the president. For Congress to kill the accord, it would have to pass a joint resolution of disapproval. If the agreement does not meet all of the statutory requirements, Congress would have to pass a joint resolution of approval for the agreement to enter into force.[60]

Korean Peace Talks. Following a series of incursions into the Demilitarized Zone (DMZ) separating North and South Korea, North Korea announced on April 4, 1996, that it was renouncing the armistice that ended the 1950-53 Korean War.[61] Later that month, Presidents Bill Clinton and Kim Young-Sam offered peace talks, also involving China, to North Korea.[62] In July, China's Foreign Minister Qian Qichen said that China would play a constructive role in the four-party talks.[63] On December 30, after expressing "deep regret" for the submarine intrusion in September, North Korea agreed to receive a joint briefing from the United States and South Korea on the four-party talks.[64] In January 1997, South Korea and the United States decided not to stage their joint military exercise 'Team Spirit,' which had been held for the previous three years.[65]

The defection of Hwang Jang Yop, founder of North Korea's *juche* philosophy,[66] to the South Korean embassy in China in early February 1997 heightened tension on the peninsula; unease was exacerbated by the shooting shortly thereafter of a North Korean defector living in South Korea (North Korean agents were suspected in the incident).[67] After North Korea dropped its threats of retaliation for the defection of Hwang, the crisis eased, and the United States and South Korea announced that they were resuming food aid to North Korea.[68] Following a March 5 joint briefing by the United States and South Korea on the proposed four-party talks, and a March 7 bilateral meeting with the United States, North Korea announced it was seeking U.S. diplomatic recognition, increased food aid, an end to U.S. economic sanctions, and trilateral talks with the United States and South Korea before it would attend the four-party talks.[69] With the refusal of the United States and South Korea to accept North Korea's preconditions, movement toward a replacement of the 1953 armistice agreement with a peace treaty stalled. Nonetheless, after a number of preliminary meetings throughout the year, the four parties were finally able to meet in Geneva on December 9-10, 1997. At this meeting, the parties agreed to reconvene in Geneva in March 1998.

Taiwan's Nuclear Waste. In January 1997, Taiwan Power Co. announced that it would ship 200,000 barrels of low-level waste (LLW) to North Korea for burial at Pyongsan, the same site where North Korea has disposed of its own LLW and the same site that KEDO plans to use for disposal of LLW from the LWR project. North Korea would receive $270 million.[70] The IAEA would not supervise the waste shipment or inspect the storage site.[71] After strenuous objections from the international community, especially from South Korea and the United States, Taiwan announced in September 1997 that it had agreed with North Korea to postpone the shipments.[72]

Missile Programs. North Korea has an expanding ballistic missile program, based on the reverse engineering of Soviet Scud-B missiles reportedly supplied by Egypt. With substantial Iranian financing, North Korea has developed and deployed the Scud Mod. B (320- to 340-km range and 1,000-kg payload) and Scud Mod. C (500-km range and 700-kg payload). The Department of Defense estimates that North Korea's arsenal includes "several hundred" of these missiles.[73] A South Korean press report indicates that North Korea can produce 150 surface-to-surface missiles a year.[74] A Defense Intelligence Agency (DIA) report estimates that North Korea can produce about 50 to 100 Scud missiles a year.[75]

In return for its financial assistance, Iran has received from North Korea 100 Scud Mod. B and 100 Scud Mod. C missiles as well as the infrastructure to assemble, and in the future to produce, the missiles.[76] In addition, Syria has received Scud Mod. C missiles and assembly facilities, and Egypt has reportedly received Scud missiles and production equipment from North Korea.[77] Official government statements disagree as to whether or not Libya has obtained Scud missiles from North Korea.[78]

North Korea is also in the "late stages" of developing the Nodong, a short-range ballistic missile with a range of 1,000 kilometers.[79] When deployed, this missile will give North Korea the capability to hit targets throughout South Korea; Niigata and Osaka in Japan; Khabarovsk in Russia; and Beijing and Shanghai in China. The Nodong's first and only flight test was in May 1993.[80] Particularly worrisome is North Korea's interest in selling the Nodong to a number of countries, including Iran, Libya, and Syria. If deployed in Iran or Syria, the missile could reach Israel; if deployed in Libya, it could reach U.S. bases and allied capitals in the Mediterranean region.

According to some sources, North Korea is also developing more advanced, two-stage missiles, including the Taepo Dong 1 (more than 1,500-km range) and the Taepo Dong 2 (more than 4,000-km range). Currently, both systems are in the design stage. In February 1996, John Deutch, then head of the CIA,

stated that the Taepo Dong 1 missile "could be operational after the turn of the century."[81] The intelligence community believes that the Taepo Dong 2 "could conceivably have sufficient range to strike portions of Alaska or the far western Hawaiian islands."[82]

In April 1996, the United States and North Korea held two days of talks on North Korea's ballistic missile program. The United States wants North Korea to abandon its development of longer-range missiles and stop its missile exports.[83] In return, the United States would be willing to lift some of the trade restrictions currently in place.[84] The United States and North Korea agreed to a second round of talks that was tentatively scheduled for August.[85] However, the United States imposed sanctions on North Korea in May for the supply of missile-related technology to Iran, and when the sanctions became public in July, North Korea refused to attend the second round of talks.[86] In November 1996, North Korea, under pressure from the United States, canceled a planned launch of the Nodong.[87] New reports of North Korea readying the Nodong for testing or deployment emerged in mid-April 1997, around the same time that the United States and North Korea were discussing having a second round of missile talks.[88] These talks were initially scheduled to be held on May 12-13 but were postponed at North Korea's request to June 11-13, 1997.[89]

North Korea also has an indigenous cruise missile program based on Soviet and Chinese technology. North Korea has been manufacturing the Chinese-designed Silkworm anti-shipping missile for many years and has produced two variants with ranges of about 100 km. It is also developing an anti-shipping missile with a range of 160 km that was tested in July 1994.[90] North Korea has also acquired European-built unmanned aerial vehicles (UAVs) and has a program to develop its own UAVs that could be used for reconnaissance or delivering chemical or biological agents.[91]

Chemical and Biological Weapons. North Korea is believed to have an active chemical weapons program and the ability to produce biological weapons. According to the U.S. Department of Defense, North Korea can produce "large quantities" of nerve, blister, and blood agents and "limited quantities" of biological warfare agents. Possible delivery systems include ballistic missiles, combat aircraft, artillery, multiple rocket launchers, mortars, and agricultural sprayers.[92] South Korea's Foreign Ministry has stated that North Korea maintains a chemical weapons stockpile estimated at 5,000 tons, consisting mainly of mustard, phosgene, and nerve agents.[93] According to a Pentagon official, large amounts of chemical weapons have been stockpiled close to the DMZ.[94] North Korea is a party to the Biological Weapons Convention (BWC), but not the Chemical Weapons Convention (CWC).

PROSPECTS

As of early 1998, the basic bargain of the Agreed Framework has held together. The nuclear freeze on the North's nuclear program remains in place. KEDO is scheduled to start construction work on the two LWRs by the fall of 1998, and it is anticipated that hundreds, and eventually thousands, of Koreans from both sides of the DMZ will work together to build the two plants. This direct interaction between North and South Koreans at the project site, as well as in KEDO–North Korea negotiations to agree on the detailed implementation of the Supply Agreement, although little-advertised, has been a significant accomplishment.

It is all the more worrisome, then, that financial difficulties may imperil KEDO's continued success. KEDO faces an annual bill of approximately $60-$65 million to finance the supply of heavy fuel oil (HFO) to the North, and it has had to borrow funds through long-term suppliers' credits to meet this commitment. In addition, although the KEDO member countries have pegged the cost of the LWR construction project at $5.1785 billion, none of this money has yet been appropriated by South Korea's National Assembly or the Japanese Diet. However, KEDO has weathered a number of political storms in the past few years and now appears to be widely recognized as a functioning part of security agreements in Northeast Asia.

Other aspects of the North's behavior remain troublesome. High on this list are its ballistic missile program and its continued chemical and biological weapons activities. It is expected that these issues will be addressed, if not resolved, in the four-party talks.

Finally, the uncertain political situation on the Korean Peninsula complicates charting the future for all of the actors involved. In the South, it could be expected that the financial crisis that swept the country in late 1997 will cause Seoul to turn inward and pay less attention to the North. On the other hand, the personality of long-time opposition leader Kim Dae-jung, who was elected president in December 1997 and assumed office in February 1998, may dictate otherwise. Kim has spoken often in the past of placing North-

South relations on a better footing. He may understand that dealing with Pyongyang in a more positive fashion than his predecessor may build mutual confidence, lower the military threat from the North, and provide the South with a much-needed "peace dividend."

By comparison, the situation in the North is much more grave; the economy has all but collapsed. The North will again need to rely on foreign benefactors to feed its people in 1998, and despite some modest attempts at agricultural reform (although never labeled as such), the food situation is likely to remain a chronic problem. Questions over who, if anyone, was really running North Korea have largely receded as it has become clearer over time that Kim Il Sung's son, Kim Jong Il, has solidified his grip on power. Yet, given the oblique nature of the regime, the most accurate characterization may be that there is no sign that Kim Jong Il is not in control in the North.

Since mid-1996, senior U.S. officials have increasingly questioned North Korea's ability to survive in its current form.[95] The three options usually discussed are implosion (collapse of the state), explosion (war with South Korea), or absorption (reform and reunification). In May 1997, the acting head of the CIA, George Tenet, referring to the possible outcomes of North Korea's increasing difficulties, stated, "One of the things that worries us most is an implosion internally."[96] The consequences of regime collapse could mean millions of North Korean refugees flooding into South Korea or westward to northern China. Signs of imminent collapse may cause Seoul to take the agonizing decision to bar refugees, perhaps forcibly, from entering the South. It is not far-fetched to think that China may take preemptive measures in its border area with North Korea that would result in its forces occupying North Korean territory. For these and other reasons, none of the major actors in the region are likely to favor reunification of the peninsula anytime soon.

NOTES

[1]See "IAEA Director General Completes Official Visit to the Democratic People's Republic of Korea," IAEA Press Release (PR 92/25), May 15, 1992; "Democratic People's Republic of Korea (DPRK) Submits Initial Report to IAEA Under Comprehensive Safeguards Agreement in Connection With the Non-Proliferation Treaty," IAEA Press Release (PR 92/24), May 5, 1992; Mark Hibbs, "North Korea Said to Have Converted Separated Plutonium into Metal," *Nucleonics Week,* July 8, 1993, p. 2; Lally Weymouth, "Peninsula of Fear: Will North Korea Start an Asian Nuke Race?" *Washington Post,* October 24, 1993; Mark Hibbs, "No U.S. Agency Consensus on DPRK Nuclear Progress," *Nucleonics Week,* January 6, 1994, p. 9; Mark Hibbs, "North Korea Obtained Reprocessing Technology Aired by Eurochemic," *Nuclear Fuel,* February 28, 1994, p. 6; Remarks by Secretary of Defense William Perry: "U.S. Security Policy in Korea," National Press Club, Washington, D.C., May 3, 1994.

[2]See Stephen Engelberg, "Intelligence Study Says North Korea Has Nuclear Bomb," *New York Times,* December 26, 1993; Hibbs, "No U.S. Agency Consensus," ibid.

[3]Responses to questions for the record, dated May 10, 1996, from John H. Moseman, Director, Congressional Affairs, Central Intelligence Agency, *Current and Projected National Security Threats to the United States and Its Interests Abroad,* Senate Select Committee on Intelligence, February 22, 1996, p. 78. But some U.S. government analyses reportedly estimated that the North may have separated significantly less plutonium, perhaps less than a bomb's worth. See

Leon V. Sigal, *Disarming Strangers: Nuclear Diplomacy with North Korea* (Princeton, NJ: Princeton University Press, 1998), p. 94.

[4]Remarks by Secretary Perry: "U.S. Security Policy in Korea," op. cit.

[5]"Agreed Framework Between the United States of America and the Democratic People's Republic of Korea," October 21, 1994; Testimony of Leonard S. Spector, Director of the Nuclear Non-Proliferation Project, Carnegie Endowment for International Peace, before the Senate Foreign Relations Committee, January 25, 1995.

[6]See IAEA Director General Hans Blix, "Travel Report: Visit to the Democratic People's Republic of Korea," May 11-16, 1992, (Vienna: IAEA, June 11, 1992); "IAEA Director General Completes Official Visit," op. cit.; "DPRK Submits Initial Report to IAEA Under Comprehensive Safeguards Agreement," op. cit.; Ann MacLachlan, "North Korea Files Initial Report With IAEA, Declares Reprocessing Facility," *Nucleonics Week,* May 5, 1992.

[7]Mark Hibbs, "IAEA Special Inspection Effort Meeting Diplomatic Resistance," *Nucleonics Week,* February 18, 1993, p. 16; R. Jeffrey Smith, "N. Korea and the Bomb: High-Tech Hide-and-Seek," *Washington Post,* April 27, 1993; Mark Hibbs, "U.S. Might Help North Korea Refuel Reactor," *Nuclear Fuel,* November 8, 1993, p. 1; R. Jeffrey Smith, "West Watching Reactor for Sign of North Korea's Nuclear Intentions," *Washington Post,* December 12, 1993.

[8]Smith, "West Watching Reactors," ibid.

[9]See David Sanger, "U.N. Agency Finds No Assurance North Korea Bans Nuclear Arms," *New York Times,* December 3, 1993. For a detailed examination of the IAEA's relationship with the DPRK, see Sigal, *Disarming Strangers,* op. cit. Note that discontinuities in or disruptions of inspections scheduled at times chosen by the IAEA make it easier for the operators of the nuclear facilities to conceal irregular nuclear activities and materials.

[10] R. Jeffrey Smith, "N. Korean Conduct in Inspection Draws Criticism of U.S. Officials," *Washington Post,* March 10, 1994; R. Jeffrey Smith, "Inspection of North Korea's Nuclear Facilities Is Halted," *Washington Post,* March 16, 1994; David E. Sanger, "North Korea Said to Block Taking of Radioactive Samples from Site," *New York Times,* March 16, 1994; Michael R. Gordon, "U.S. Goes to U.N. to Increase the Pressure on North Korea," *New York Times,* March 22, 1994. For a comprehensive assessment of the March 1994 inspection, see Sigal, *Disarming Strangers,* op. cit., pp. 95-108.

[11]Mark Hibbs, "Fuel Readiness Means North Korea Can Start Reactors Up on Schedule," *Nucleonics Week,* April 7, 1994, p. 14; R. Jeffrey Smith, "N. Korea Refuses Demand to Inspect Reactor Fuel," *Washington Post,* April 28, 1994; Remarks by Secretary Perry: "U.S. Security Policy in Korea," op. cit.; Mark Hibbs, "U.S. Warns North Koreans to Accept IAEA Presence at Reactor Refueling," *Nuclear Fuel,* May 9, 1994, p. 10; David E. Sanger, "Nuclear Agency to Send a New Inspection Team to North Korea," *New York Times,* May 13, 1994; R. Jeffrey Smith, "Inspectors Returning to North Korea," *Washington Post,* May 14, 1994; "IAEA Safeguards in the DPRK," IAEA Press Release, May 19, 1994; Mark Hibbs, "North Korea Needs 6-9 Months to Reprocess Discharged Core," *Nucleonics Week,* May 26, 1994, p. 17; Mark Hibbs, "North Korea Has Machines to Refuel Faster Than West's Experts Thought," *Nucleonics Week,* June 2, 1994, p. 1; Mark Hibbs and Kathleen Hart, "IAEA, U.S. Agencies Underestimated North Korea's Refueling Capability," *Nuclear Fuel,* June 6, 1994, p. 5.

[12]See "Letter From the Director General of the IAEA Addressed to the Secretary General [of the United Nations] Relating to North Korea," June 2, 1994.

[13]R. Jeffrey Smith and T. R. Reid, "North Korea Quits U.N. Nuclear Body," *Washington Post,* June 14, 1994.

[14]Ann Devroy, "U.S. to Seek Sanctions on N. Korea," *Washington Post,* June 3, 1994; Michael Gordon, "White House Asks Global Sanctions on North Koreans," *New York Times,* June 3, 1994; David B. Ottaway, "N. Korea Forbids Inspections," *Washington Post,* June 8, 1994; Julia Preston, "U.S. Unveils Proposal for Sanctions," *Washington Post,* June 16, 1994.

[15]T. R. Reid, "Leaders of 2 Koreas Seek First Summit," *Washington Post,* June 19, 1994; Michael R. Gordon. "Back from Korea, Carter Declares the Crisis Is Over," *New York Times,* June 20, 1994; T. R. Reid, "North Korean President Kim Il Sung Dies at 82," *Washington Post,* July 9, 1994; "Agreed Statement Between the United States of America and the Democratic People's Republic of Korea, Geneva, August 12, 1994," IAEA Media Talking Points, August 16, 1994; "Seoul Says North Must Accept South's Model Reactor," *Reuters,* August 18, 1994. For a detailed account of the Carter-Kim meeting, see Sigal, *Disarming Strangers,* op. cit., pp. 150-162.

[16]See Mark Hibbs, "U.S., DPRK to Meet in Berlin on LWR Transfer, Spent Fuel Details," *Nucleonics Week,* September 8, 1994. p. 17; "North Korea Rejects Special Nuclear Inspections," *Reuters,* September 16, 1994; Jan Krcmar, "IAEA Wants Action on N. Korea, Nuclear Smuggling," *Reuters,* September 23, 1994; "N. Korea to Allow Inspections Once Pact Agreed," *Reuters,* September 24, 1994; "Pyongyang Rejects Call to Open Atomic Plants," *Reuters,* September 25, 1994; R. Jeffrey Smith, "Stalemate in North Korea Talks May Strain Relations, Officials Say," *Washington Post,* October 2, 1994; "Agreed Framework Between the United States of America and the Democratic People's Republic of Korea," October 21, 1994.

[17]Under this de-nuclearization accord, signed on December 31, 1991, and effective on February 19, 1993, both Koreas pledged not to "test, manufacture, produce, receive, store, deploy, or use nuclear weapons." Two provisions of the agreement were particularly noteworthy—one mandating bilateral nuclear inspections (separate from the IAEA inspections required in both states under the NPT) and a second prohibiting both states from building or operating plutonium reprocessing or enrichment plants, which could provide access to weapons-usable nuclear materials. (See Joint [North/South Korea] Declaration on the De-Nuclearization of the Korean Peninsula. February 19, 1992, Articles III and IV.) Bilateral talks on implementing the agreement foundered over the issue of mutual inspections,

and it has not been implemented. In addition, North Korea has claimed that the Yongbyon reprocessing plant is merely a radiochemistry laboratory and therefore is not covered by the accord. Thus, it was not until the signing of the October 21, 1994, Agreed Framework with the United States that the North implemented a freeze on all activities at the facility.

[18]Spector Testimony, Senate Foreign Relations Committee, op. cit.; Douglas Hamilton, "IAEA Concerned by Terms of U.S.-N. Korea Pact," *Reuters,* October 20, 1994; R. Jeffrey Smith, "N. Korea Accord: A Troubling Precedent?" *Washington Post,* October 20, 1994; "IAEA Comments on Agreed Framework Between United States and Democratic People's Republic of Korea," IAEA Press Release, October 20, 1994; Mitchell Reiss, *Bridled Ambition: Why Countries Constrain Their Nuclear Capabilities* (Washington, DC: Woodrow Wilson Center Press, 1995), pp. 276-80.

[19]The IAEA had previously conducted special inspections in Sweden and Romania, but these were of a fundamentally different nature than the ones proposed for North Korea. See Sigal, *Disarming Strangers,* op. cit., p. 49.

[20]See also Iran chapter in this volume, p. 173.

[21]House International Relations Committee, Subcommittee on International Operations and Human Rights, FY98 Authorization for the U.S. Arms Control & Disarmament Agency, March 5, 1997.

[22]R. Jeffrey Smith, "U.S. Prepares Oil Shipment for N. Korea," *Washington Post,* January 6, 1995.

[23]Julia Preston and R. Jeffrey Smith, "Consortium Established for N. Korean A-Plants," *Washington Post,* March 10, 1995.

[24]R. Jeffrey Smith, "North Korea Rejects Reactor Deal," *Washington Post,* February 7, 1995.

[25]Resolution No. 1995-2, Executive Board of the Korean Peninsula Energy Development Organization, June 13, 1995.

[26]Kathleen Hart, "KEDO Signs Contract to Supply Two LWRs to North Korea," *Nucleonics Week,* December 21, 1995, p. 1.

[27]Press Briefing by Dan Poneman, Senior Director for Non-Proliferation and Export Controls, National Security Council, December 15, 1995.

[28]Korean Peninsula Energy Development Organization, *Annual Report 1995,* July 31, 1996, p. 8.

[29]"KEDO To Commission KEPCO as LWR Project's Main Contractor," *Yonhap,* March 19, 1996, in *FBIS-EAS-96-054,* March 19, 1996, p. 53.

[30]General Accounting Office, *Nuclear Nonproliferation: Implications of the U.S./North Korean Agreement on Nuclear Issues,* GAO/RCED/NSIAD-97-8, October 1996, p. 15.

[31]Kim Kyon-ho, "ROK, US, Japan Face 'Tough Job' Splitting LWR Costs," *The Korea Herald,* July 22, 1996, in *FBIS-EAS-96-142,* July 23, 1996, p. 36.

[32]Testimony of Stephen Bosworth, Hearing before the Senate Foreign Relations Committee, East Asian and Pacific Affairs Subcommittee, *U.S. Policy Toward North Korea,* September 12, 1996.

[33]Yi Pyong-son, "U.S. 'Afraid' DPRK to Suspend Sealing of Nuclear Fuel Rods," *Munhwa Ilbo,* November 19, 1996, in *FBIS-EAS-96-224,* November 20, 1996; Willis Witter, "S. Korea Unforgiving After Submarine Flap," *Washington Times,* December 13, 1996.

[34]Kevin Sullivan, "North Korea Apologizes for Sub Incident," *Washington Post,* December 30, 1996. "North Korea's Apology to South May Smooth Way for LWR Plan to Resume," *Nucleonics Week,* January 2, 1997.

[35]"N. Korea and KEDO to Sign Nuclear Protocols," *Reuters,* January 7, 1997.

[36]"54-Member KEDO Team to Visit North Via Sea Route," *Korea Times,* April 5, 1997; "KEDO to Construct Infrastructure for NK Reactors in July," *Korea Times,* May 15, 1997.

[37]"KEDO and North Korea Reach Agreement on Protocol," KEDO Press Release, May 4, 1997.

[38]"European Union and KEDO Reach Agreement," *Reuters,* May 22, 1997. Also in May, the European Union contributed food aid worth more than $40 million to the U.N. World Food Program. "Europe to Send Food to North Korea," *United Press International,* May 24, 1997.

[39]KEDO's Executive Board consists of the United States, Japan, Republic of Korea, and EURATOM. Other official members are Argentina, Australia, Canada, Chile, Finland, Indonesia, and New Zealand. Non-member contributing states are: Great Britain, Singa-

pore, Malaysia, Netherlands, Thailand, Brunei, Germany, Philippines, Greece, Norway, Switzerland, and Oman.

[40]"Reports of diversion were confirmed by Assistant Secretary of State Winston Lord, who noted: "The oil that's being provided to them compensates for the energy they lose from their reactor they've shut down. It is not feasible for military use. It is a heavy fuel oil that is not usable in tanks or airplanes, and so on. There was a diversion, which we took very seriously, but it was an industrial diversion, not a military diversion." See *U.S. Security Interests in Asia*, Hearing of the Asia and the Pacific Subcommittee of the House International Relations Committee, June 27, 1995.

[41]Korean Peninsula Energy Development Organization, *Annual Report 1995*, July 31, 1996, p. 19.

[42]Korean Peninsula Energy Development Organization, *Annual Report, 1996/97*, July 31, 1997, pp. 9-11.

[43]"NAC to Help N. Korea Stabilize Waste," *Nuclear Fuel*, June 5, 1995, p. 11.

[44]Cha Man-sun, "U.S. Ends 1st Stage of Fuel Rod Storage Work," *KBS-1*, September 20, 1995, in *FBIS-EAS-95-183*, September 21, 1995, p. 31.

[45]Song Ui-tal, "DPRK Reportedly Starts Dry Storage of Spent Fuel," *Choson Ilbo*, January 10, 1996, in *FBIS-TAC-96-001*, January 26, 1996, p. 15.

[46]As of December 17, 1997, the canning was "virtually complete," according to a conversation with a U.S. official, December 17, 1997. And, according to Presidential Determination No. 98-14, issued on February 9, 1998, "North Korea is cooperating fully in the canning and safe storage of all spent fuel from its graphite-moderated nuclear reactors and that such canning and safe storage is scheduled to be completed by April 1, 1998." "Memorandum on the Korean Peninsula Energy Development Organization," Presidential Determination No. 98-14, *Public Papers of the Presidents*, February 9, 1998.

[47]This is an estimate of total cost, including the removal of the fuel, the canning, sealing, establishing of safeguards, and clean-up. U.S. Department of Energy Official, March 12, 1998.

[48]"DPRK Hindering Measurement of Spent Nuclear Fuel Rods," *KBS-1*, May 2, 1996, in *FBIS-EAS-96-087*, May 3, 1996, p. 26.

[49]Testimony of Charles Kartman, Acting Assistant Secretary of State for East Asian and Pacific Affairs, Hearing before the House International Relations Committee, Asian and Pacific Affairs Subcommittee, *U.S. Policy Toward North Korea*, February 26, 1997.

[50]*Nuclear News*, March 1996, p. 48.

[51]Mark Hibbs, "DPRK Won't Comply With Safeguards Until New Reactors Are Finished," *Nuclear Fuel*, September 23, 1996, p. 1.

[52]R. Jeffrey Smith, "Clinton Slightly Lowers Some Bars To U.S. Trade With North Korea," *Washington Post*, January 21, 1995.

[53]Charles Abbott, "U.S. Issues Rare License for Food Sales to N. Korea," *Reuters*, January 6, 1997.

[54]Shim Jae Hoon, "Death Awaits," *Far Eastern Economic Review*, April 17, 1997, p. 22.

[55]"N. Korea Seeks Diplomatic Ties With US as Prerequisite to Starting Peace Treaty," *Korea Times*, April 19, 1997.

[56]Prepared Testimony of Charles Kartman before the Senate Appropriations Committee, Foreign Operations Subcommittee, April 17, 1997.

[57]Jim Hoagland, "Rush Toward Reunification," *Washington Post*, April 10, 1997.

[58]Kartman Testimony, House Asian and Pacific Affairs Subcommittee, op. cit.

[59]See Zachary S. Davis, et al., "Korea: Procedural and Jurisdictional Questions Regarding Possible Normalization of Relations with North Korea," CRS Report, 94-933S, November 29, 1994; General Accounting Office, *Nuclear Nonproliferation: Implications of the U.S./ North Korean Agreement on Nuclear Issues*, GAO/RCED/NSIAD-97-8, October 1996, pp. 13, 57.

[60]See Davis, et al., *Procedural and Jurisdictional Questions*, ibid.; GAO, *Nuclear Nonproliferation*, ibid., p. 58.

[61]"N. Korea Gives Up DMZ Duties," *Korea Times*, April 5, 1996.

[62]John F. Harris and R. Jeffrey Smith, "U.S. Backs Talks on Korean Peace," *Washington Post*, April 16, 1996.

[63]"Qian Qichen: PRC To Play 'Constructive' Role in 4-Way Talks," *The Digital Choson Ilbo* (South Korea), July 25, 1996, in *FBIS-EAS-96-145*, July 26, 1996, p. 39.

[64]Thomas Lippman, "North Korea Steps Toward Peace Talks," *Washington Post*, December 31, 1996.

[65]"'Team Spirit' Cancelled to Make Way for Peace Talks," *Jane's Defence Weekly*, March 12, 1997, p. 5.

[66]"Often translated as 'self-reliance,' especially in economic matters, *juche* is concerned at heart with political independence and Korean nationalism." Charles K. Armstrong, "The Politics of Transition in North and South Korea," in David R. McCann, ed., *Korea Briefing: Toward Reunification* (Armonk, NY: M.E. Sharpe, 1997), p. 21.

[67]Andrew Pollack, "Korean Shooting Is Casting Cloud on Signs of Thaw," *New York Times*, February 17, 1997.

[68]Kevin Sullivan, "N. Korea Eases Stance on High-Level Defector," *Washington Post*, February 18, 1997.

[69]Andrew Browne, "N. Korea Details Conditions for Four-Party Talks," *Washington Post*, April 25, 1997; Zeno Park, "Pyongyang Calls For Three-Way Talks, Seoul Says Demand Unacceptable," *Agence France Presse*, April 24, 1997.

[70]Margaret Ryan and Mark Hibbs, "Seoul Accepted Pyongsan Site for KEDO Waste, Taipower Says," *Nucleonics Week*, May 1, 1997, p. 2.

[71]"IAEA Won't Monitor N. Korean Nuke Storage," *Agence France Presse*, May 27, 1997.

[72]Son Key-young, "NK, Taiwan Agree to Postpone N-Waste Shipment," *Korea Times*, September 11, 1997.

[73]Office of the Secretary of Defense, *Proliferation: Threat and Response*, April 1996, p. 8.

[74]James Bruce, "S. Korea Tables North's Ballistic Missile Sales," *Jane's Defence Weekly*, July 17, 1996, p. 3.

[75]Defense Intelligence Agency, *North Korea: The Foundations for Military Strength Update 1995*, December 1995, p. 5.

[76]Bruce, "S. Korea Tables North's Ballistic Missile Sales," op. cit., p. 3; *Proliferation: Threat and Response 1996*, op. cit., p. 16.

[77]Central Intelligence Agency, *The Weapons Proliferation Threat*, March 1995, p. 10. According to Admiral Studeman, "Pyongyang has provided Scud missiles and production equipment to Egypt." See Senate Committee on Armed Services, *Worldwide Threat to the United States*, January 17, 1995, p. 39. For the most recent incident, see Bill Gertz, "Cairo's Missile Buy Violates U.S. Laws," *Washington Times*, June 21, 1996.

[78]According to the Pentagon, Libya's only operational missiles are Scud-Bs acquired from the USSR. *Proliferation: Threat and Response 1996*, op. cit., p. 27. According to a March 1995 CIA report, *The Weapons Proliferation Threat*, Libya has only Scud-Bs but the supplier is not identified. However, John Deutch, head of the CIA, lists Libya as one of the recipients of North Korean Scud missiles. See Senate Select Committee on Intelligence, *Current and Projected National Security Threats to the United States and Its Interests Abroad*, February 22, 1996, p. 9. The DIA also lists Libya as a recipient of missile-related technology from North Korea. Defense Intelligence Agency, "Global Missile Proliferation Threat," Presented to the Missile Technology Control Regime Transshipment Seminar, July 15, 1996.

[79]*Proliferation: Threat and Response 1996*, op. cit., p. 8. Ten mobile launchers for the Nodong have been observed in North Korea, but the missile is not considered operational. Paul Beaver, "Ten Nodongs Fielded but Accuracy is Low, says USA," *Jane's Defence Weekly*, May 28, 1997, p. 4.

[80]Joseph Bermudez, Jr., and Greg Gerardi, "An Analysis of North Korean Ballistic Missile Testing," *Jane's Intelligence Review*, Vol. 7, No. 4, April 1995, p. 186.

[81]See Senate Select Committee on Intelligence, *Current and Projected National Security Threats*, op. cit.

[82]Lt. Gen. Patrick Hughes, Director, Defense Intelligence Agency, before the Senate Select Committee on Intelligence, *Current and Projected National Security Threats to the United States and Its Interests Abroad*, February 22, 1996, p. 250.

[83]"DPRK Delegate at Missile Talks With U.S. Notes 'Good Start,'" *KBS-1*, April 21, 1996, in *FBIS-EAS-96-078*.

[84]Bill Gertz, "U.S. Will Pull Sanctions If Pyongyang Halts Missile Program," *Washington Times*, June 5, 1996.

[85]"U.S., N.K. Agree to Hold 2nd Missile Talks," *Korea Times*, June 20, 1996.

[86]"Imposition of Missile Proliferation Sanctions Against Entities in Iran and North Korea," *Federal Register,* June 12, 1996, p. 29785; "N. Korea-Missiles," *Associated Press,* July 9, 1996.

[87]"North Koreans Decide Against Testing Missile," *Washington Post,* November 9, 1996.

[88]"DPRK Deploys Nodong-1 Missile on Northeast Coast," *Sankei Shimbun,* April 10, 1997, in *FBIS-EAS-97-100,* April 14, 1997; Barbara Opall, "Japan Nears Commitment to BMD Buy," *Defense News,* April 21-27, 1997, p. 1.

[89]Korea Balks at Missile Talks," *United Press International,* May 6, 1997; Patrick Worsnip, "U.S.–N. Korea Missile Talks Rescheduled for June," *Reuters,* May 27, 1997.

[90]*Proliferation: Threat and Response 1996,* op. cit., p. 9. Duncan Lennox, "Cruise Missiles," *Jane's Defence Weekly,* May 1, 1996, p. 20.

[91]"Serial Provocation," *Aviation Week & Space Technology,* October 14, 1996, p. 25; Defense Intelligence Agency, *North Korea: The Foundations for Military Strength Update 1995,* December 1995, p. 5.

[92]*Proliferation: Threat and Response 1996,* op. cit., p. 9.

[93]"ROK, US to Block DPRK Chemical Weapons Development," *Choson Ilbo,* May 8, 1997, in *FBIS-TAC-97-128,* May 9, 1997; Kim Yon-kwang, "Foreign Ministry Estimates North Chemical Weapons," *Choson Ilbo,* September 24, 1995, in *FBIS-EAS-95-185,* September 23, 1995, p. 48; Joseph S. Bermudez, Jr., "Inside North Korea's CW Infrastructure," *Jane's Intelligence Review,* August 1996, p. 382.

[94]Barbara Starr, "USA to Ponder N. Korean Defector's Nuclear Riddle," *Jane's Defence Weekly,* April 20, 1997, p. 13.

[95]"USFK Commander Gen. Luck Predicts NK Disintegration," *Korea Times,* March 30, 1996; R. Jeffrey Smith, "Dim Prospects Seen for N. Korean Regime," *Washington Post,* August 10, 1996.

[96]Senate Select Committee on Intelligence, Hearing on the Nomination of George Tenet for CIA Director, May 6, 1997.

Additional References

The single best source of information on North Korea's nuclear program and nuclear diplomacy toward North Korea is Leon V. Sigal, *Disarming Strangers: Nuclear Diplomacy with North Korea* (Princeton, NJ: Princeton University Press, 1998). Sigal's book is likely to be the authoritative text on the US-DPRK nuclear negotiations for some time to come. Additional behind-the scenes information is provided in Don Oberdorfer, *The Two Koreas: A Contemporary History* (Reading, MA: Addison-Wesley, 1997), pp. 249-368. Two earlier studies also worth reading are Mitchell Reiss, *Bridled Ambition: Why Countries Constrain Their Nuclear Capabilities* (Washington, DC: Woodrow Wilson Center Press, 1995), pp. 231-319; and Michael J. Mazarr, *North Korea and the Bomb: A Case Study in Nonproliferation* (New York: St. Martin's Press, 1995). KEDO's annual reports are available from the organization, which is located at 600 Third Ave., 12th Floor, New York, NY 10016.

North Korea:
Map and Chart

Yongbyon Nuclear Research Center. *Site of a 5-MWe experimental nuclear power reactor;* a partially completed plutonium extraction facility;* a fuel fabrication plant;* fuel storage facilities;* and a Soviet-supplied IRT research reactor** and critical assembly.** 50 MWe power reactor also under construction.*

Under the Oct. 21, 1994, U.S.-North Korean "Agreed Framework," activities at the 5-MWe gas-graphite reactor, the fuel fabrication facility, and the reprocessing plant have been frozen; construction also has been halted on the 50-MWe gas-graphite reactor.

U.S. intelligence agencies believe that North Korea has used the 5-MWe reactor and extraction plant to produce plutonium (possibly enough for 1 or 2 nuclear weapons). Wastes from the extraction process are believed to be stored at two undeclared sites near the Center.

CHINA

NORTH KOREA

Hwaedae-Gun missile testing range and production facilities.

200-MWe nuclear power reactor; construction halted under U.S.-N.K. "Agreed Framework."

Taechon

Yongbyon

Shinpo

Site of two 1,000-MWe, light-water reactors financed by KEDO according to the terms of the "Agreed Framework;" construction began in August 1997.

Pakchon

★Pyongyang

■ Pyongsan

Uranium mining, and uranium concentrate production plant.

Uranium concentrate production plant, using ore from Sunchon-Wolbingson mine (50 km to the south).

Seoul
★

Sub-critical assembly.

Soviet-supplied laboratory-scale "hot cells" that may have been used to extract small quantities of plutonium. (Similar cells may exist at other locations.)

Yellow Sea

SOUTH KOREA

Sea of Japan

* Subject to IAEA safeguards as of May 1992 pursuant to North Korea's obligations under the Non-Proliferation Treaty (NPT); future application of safeguards uncertain.

** Under IAEA safeguards pursuant to NPT obligations and a trilateral U.S.S.R.-North Korea-IAEA agreement.

JAPAN

0   50

Miles

Carnegie Endowment for International Peace, *Tracking Nuclear Proliferation*, 1998

NORTH KOREA: Nuclear Infrastructure

NAME/LOCATION OF FACILITY	TYPE/STATUS	IAEA SAFEGUARDS
POWER REACTORS		
Sinpo (Kumho)	Light-water, 1000 MWe; ground broken in August 1997.	Yes
Yongbyon	Gas-graphite, natural U, 5 MWe; operations frozen.	IAEA verifying freeze in operations.
Yongbyon	Gas-graphite, natural U, 50 MWe; construction halted.	IAEA verifying construction freeze.
Taechon	Gas-graphite, natural U, 200 MWe; construction halted.	IAEA verifying construction freeze.
RESEARCH REACTORS		
IRT, Yongbyon	Pool-type, HEU, 4 MWt; operating.	Yes[a]
Yongbyon	Critical assembly.	Yes[b]
Pyongyang	Sub-critical assembly.	Yes
REPROCESSING (PLUTONIUM EXTRACTION)[c]		
Yongbyon	Partially completed; operations frozen.	Yes[d]
Pyongyang	Soviet-supplied laboratory-scale "hot cells."	No
URANIUM PROCESSING[e]		
Pyongsan	Uranium mining; status unknown.	N/A (Not Applicable)
Pakchon (Sunchon-Wolbingson mine)	Uranium mining; status unknown.	N/A
Pyongsan	Uranium milling; status unknown.	N/A
Pakchon	Uranium milling; status unknown.	N/A
Yongbyon	Uranium purification (UO_2) facility; operating.	Yes[f]
Yongbyon	Fuel fabrication facility; operations frozen.	Yes[g]
Yongbyon	Pilot-scale fuel fabrication facility; dismantled, according to North Korean officials.[h]	No

Abbreviations:

HEU	=	highly enriched uranium
LEU	=	low-enriched uranium
nat. U	=	natural uranium
MWe	=	millions of watts of electrical output
MWt	=	millions of watts of thermal output
KWt	=	thousands of watts of thermal output

NOTES (North Korea Chart)

[a]This facility is covered by the 1992 IAEA safeguards agreement and an earlier trilateral U.S.S.R.-North Korea-IAEA agreement.

[b]This facility is covered by the 1992 IAEA safeguards agreement and an earlier trilateral U.S.S.R.-North Korea-IAEA agreement.

[c]There have been allegations that North Korea is constructing a uranium enrichment facility, but U.S. officials discount these reports.

[d]North Korea has consistently maintained that the 600-foot-long plutonium separation facility at Yongbyon should be characterized as a "radiochemical laboratory" because it had not been fully tested and because, when first observed by the IAEA in mid-1992, only 80 percent of its civil engineering had been completed and only 40 percent of its equipment installed. U.S. officials believe, however, that the facility was designed to handle all the spent fuel from both the 5 MWe reactor and the 50 MWe reactor at Yongbyon. They theorize that, even in its incomplete state, the plant had the capacity to process all the spent fuel produced by the smaller reactor and thus could have separated one to two bombs' worth of plutonium prior to 1992 from the spent fuel thought to have been discharged from the 5 MWe unit in 1989. During their March 1994 inspection of this facility, IAEA inspectors made certain observations that led them to believe that, since their previous inspection a year earlier,

North Korea had built and possibly operated a second, unsafeguarded plutonium separation line. (See Mark Hibbs and Naoaki Usui, "Second, Hidden Reprocessing Line Feared Opened at Yongbyon Plant," *Nucleonics Week,* March 24 1994, p. 1; Mark Hibbs, "North Korea Needs 6-9 Months to Reprocess Discharged Core," *Nucleonics Week,* May 2 1994, p. 17.) All operations at the facility are currently frozen, pursuant to the U.S.-North Korean Agreed Framework, and the IAEA has verified this status.

[e]The mining and milling operatings at Pakchon and Pyongsan are not subject to the "freeze" agreement between the IAEA and North Korea, and inspectors have no authority to see these facilities. According to one IAEA official interviewed in February 1998, inspectors have not visited these facilities for a considerable amount of time and have no information on their operational status.

[f]According to an IAEA official interviewed in February 1998, the uranium processing facility at Yongbyon is permitted to operate under the terms of the "freeze" agreement between the IAEA and North Korea. However, the facility is only permitted to produce yellowcake, and IAEA inspectors are monitoring the facility to ensure this.

[g]Associated with this plant are fuel storage facilities that are covered by North Korea's 1992 safeguards agreement with the IAEA.

[h]In the August 1996 IAEA Director General's report, mention was made of this pilot-scale facility. An IAEA official noted in a February 1998 interview that North Korean nuclear officials have claimed that the facility, part of the Yongbyon complex, was destroyed in a fire prior to the initial IAEA inspections in 1991. Apparently, in this fire, all records of the facility were destroyed, including record of the manufacture of the first reactor core for the 5 MW reactor, making it impossible for inspectors to determine this piece of North Korea's proliferation story. Implementation of the Agreement Between the Agency and the Democratic People's Republic of Korea for the Application of Safeguards in Connection with the Treaty on the Non-Proliferation of Nuclear Weapons, Report by the Director General to the General Conference, GC (40)/16, August 20, 1996, p. 4.

7

NORTH AFRICA
AND THE
MIDDLE EAST

Algeria

In 1991, the international community feared that Algeria might be seeking to develop nuclear weapons through the use of a large, unsafeguarded research reactor. These fears abated after Algeria agreed to place the facility under International Atomic Energy Agency (IAEA) inspection in 1991, pledged to join the Nuclear Non-Proliferation Treaty (NPT) in 1993, and formally honored that pledge in early 1995. The threat that on-going political strife might bring a radical government to power, however, makes Algeria's nuclear future a continuing source of concern.

BACKGROUND

Algeria was initially linked with nuclear weapons in February 1960, when France detonated its first nuclear device at Reganne, in the Algerian portion of the Sahara Desert. Even after Algeria gained independence from France in 1962, Reganne continued to serve as the location for French nuclear tests through 1966, when France shifted its nuclear testing to the South Pacific.[1] Indigenous nuclear activities in Algeria remained extremely limited through the late 1980s, with the country acquiring only one nuclear installation, the 1-MWt Nur research reactor. The facility has been subject to IAEA monitoring since it began operating in 1989. Algeria refused at that time to join the NPT; as a leader of the Non-Aligned Movement, it objected to the Treaty as an instrument through which the nuclear powers sought to keep non-nuclear nations in a permanent state of inferiority.

In early 1991, U.S. intelligence agencies discovered that Algeria was secretly building a sizable research reactor at the Ain Oussera nuclear complex. Because the facility was unusually large in view of Algeria's rudimentary nuclear research program, was being built in secret, and was not subject to IAEA inspection, Washington suspected the facility might be used to produce plutonium for a nuclear weapons program.[2] Not then a party to the NPT, Algeria could have developed nuclear weapons using unsafeguarded installations.

After the foreign disclosure and inquiries, Algeria acknowledged it was building the Ain Oussera reactor and that China was the supplier. Algeria disclosed that the unit's power rating was 15 MWt (indicating that it could not produce large amounts of plutonium) and that it would use highly enriched uranium as fuel and heavy water as its moderator. Noting the facility's unusually large cooling towers, however, U.S. and other foreign analysts worried that the reactor might have a capacity as high as 60 MWt. Other factors, especially the presence of SA-5 surface-to-air missile defense batteries near the facility, also suggested a possible military use of the reactor. In addition, several unconfirmed reports indicated that Algeria had also begun to construct a reprocessing facility next to the reactor—an installation that presumably could have been used to separate weapons-usable plutonium from the reactor's spent fuel or from uranium targets irradiated in the reactor. These developments aroused suspicions that Algeria was embarking on a nuclear weapons program.[3]

In May 1991, following the exposure of the nuclear reactor construction program, Algiers agreed to place the reactor at Ain Oussera (denominated the Es Salam reactor) under IAEA safeguards.[4] This step significantly reduced the immediate threat of nuclear weapons development in Algeria. In addition, during the December 21, 1993, inauguration of the Es Salam reactor, Algerian Foreign Minister Salah Dembri pledged that Algeria "resolved to adhere to the Non-Proliferation Treaty." He added that Algeria was "absolutely dedicated to the peaceful use of the atom" and "confidently and unequivocally affirms its commitment to the non-proliferation regime."[5] Algeria completed the constitutional process needed for adherence to the NPT in late 1994, and, on January 12, 1995, formally acceded to the Treaty.[6]

By this time, Algeria was plunged into political turmoil bordering on civil war. In January 1992, after the socialist National Liberation Front, which had governed Algeria since independence, was threatened with loss of its parliamentary majority to the radical Islamic Salvation Front (FIS), the Algerian army seized power, ousted President Chadli Benjadid, cancelled the country's impending elections, and banned the FIS. With the FIS forced underground, the organization's military arm and an Islamic extremist faction known as the Armed Islamic Group (GIA) launched a campaign combining guerrilla warfare and widespread anti-government/anti-secular terrorism, which cost tens of thousands of lives. The GIA, if not the FIS itself, was said to receive clandestine support from Iran.[7] These events formed a violent backdrop to Algeria's nuclear decision making. One possible factor that motivated the Algerian government to join the NPT was the desire to garner favor with France and other Western powers whose political and economic support Algiers desperately needed as it confronted such grave challenges at home.

DEVELOPMENTS

Like the then-recent NPT adherence of Argentina, China, France, and South Africa, Algeria's decision to join the NPT after decades of refusing to do so further strengthened the Treaty as a central pillar of international law. Algeria's demonstration of support for the Treaty had additional significance because of the imminence of the April-May 1995 NPT Review and Extension Conference, at which the state parties were to decide whether to extend the Treaty for a fixed term or terms, or indefinitely. By joining the NPT, Algeria became eligible to participate in the Review Conference, at which the industrialized nations, led by the United States, were pressing strongly for the Treaty's indefinite extension. Precedent called for the extension decision to be made by consensus. This practice gave individual states a veto over the outcome of the Conference.

At the Review Conference, Algeria joined a group of Arab states led by Egypt that attempted to use the review process to put pressure on Israel to abandon its nuclear weapons program. At the fourth Preparatory Committee session of the Conference in January 1995, the members of the group, which also included Libya and Syria, declared that they would consent to an indefinite extension of the Treaty only if Israel agreed to accede to it—a step that would require Israel to renounce nuclear arms and to place all of its nuclear installations and all of the plutonium it had produced over the years under IAEA inspection.[8] Egypt and Algeria underscored these demands in a joint declaration in late March after a meeting between Egyptian Foreign Minister Amr Moussa and Algerian Foreign Minister Mohamed Salah Dembri.[9]

As detailed in Appendix B on the NPT Review Conference in this book, under considerable U.S. pressure, Egypt and its allies ultimately softened their position and, during the Conference's last stages, consented to the NPT's indefinite extension. They did so in exchange for passage of a resolution calling for a Middle East nuclear-weapon-free-zone, sponsored by the United States, the Russian Federation, and the United Kingdom. Although the resolution did not mention Israel by name, it called on states that had not joined the NPT to do so.[10]

On March 30, 1996, Algeria signed a comprehensive IAEA safeguards agreement providing for IAEA inspections of all of Algeria's nuclear facilities and for IAEA technical assistance to Algeria. On that occasion, the Director General of the IAEA, Hans Blix, visited the Es Salam research reactor at Ain Oussera and praised the commitment of the Algerian authorities to the peaceful use of nuclear energy.[11] After the agreement entered into force on January 7, 1997, Algeria made a declaration of its initial nuclear inventory to the Agency, which IAEA inspectors could verify. If any discrepancies were to be found, the Agency would then move to resolve these with Algerian authorities.

Algeria's nuclear ties to China were renewed on June 1, 1996, when the two countries signed a draft agreement for "the second stage" of cooperation in nuclear technology.[12] In October 1996, the two states began to implement the accord by signing a "letter of intent" under which China was to assist Algeria with the construction of facilities for the research and production of radio isotopes to be used in the medical, industrial, and agricultural fields.[13]

During 1996, Western governments learned that China intended to move to "phase three" of its nuclear cooperation with Algeria. Under this program, China will provide know-how to enable Algeria to operate hot cells in a facility under construction since 1992 at a site adjacent to the Es Salam reactor. These hot cells would give Algeria the capability to separate plutonium from irradiated fuel. But in declaring the facility to the IAEA, Algeria stated that the intended purpose of the hot cells is to make Algeria a leading supplier of medical isotopes.[14] In the context of U.S.–Chinese discussions over U.S. certification of China's non-proliferation credentials, the United States raised concerns about the possible use of the hot cells for plutonium separation. However, after IAEA consultations with Algeria over the matter, the United States is reportedly "satisfied" that the hot cells will be operated under IAEA safeguards, and will be subject to environmental sampling.[15]

PROSPECTS

Over the past two years, political turmoil in Algeria appeared to ease as the military-backed government in Algiers made gains vis-a-vis Islamic fundamentalist rebels operating under the banner of the Islamic Salvation Front (FIS). On November 16, 1995, retired General Liamine Zeroual was elected president, winning 61 percent of the vote. A year later, in a referendum, 70 percent of the Algerian electorate approved an authoritarian constitution, banning religion-based political parties (e.g., the FIS) while declaring Islam to be the state religion. In parliamentary and municipal elections, held in June 1997 and October 1997 respectively, the government appeared to be making some progress in its efforts to gain legitimacy and promote a pluralistic system.[16]

The erosion of support for the FIS has reduced fears of a militant Islamic government emerging in Algeria that might opt for the development of nuclear weapons as a way to gain legitimacy, prestige, or military power in a hostile international environment.[17] However, an increase in violence ostensibly perpetrated by both Islamic radicals and government forces during the latter part of 1996 and throughout 1997 is a sobering reminder that Algeria's political future remains far from certain.[18]

Algeria's original motivation for the acquisition of the Es Salam reactor remains obscure. Possibly its goal was not to develop nuclear weapons in the near term but to create the capability to launch such an effort at a later date, if nuclear developments in neighboring Libya or elsewhere in the Middle East warranted such action. Today, the Zeroual government is cautiously expanding Algeria's civilian nuclear research program, in compliance with the requirements of the NPT. Nonetheless, Algeria's nuclear activities are likely to remain a continuing focus of international attention in coming years because of uncertainties about the country's long-term vision for its nuclear program and about its political future.

NOTES

[1] In a highly unusual episode in April 1961, as France was preparing its fourth nuclear test at the Algerian test site, a group of French generals in Algeria, who were opposed to the decision of President Charles de Gaulle to grant the country independence, revolted against the French government and seized power in Algiers. As the attempted coup unraveled, the test device was apparently detonated ahead of schedule to ensure that it did not fall into the hands of the rebel generals. See "Le Putch des Généraux d'Algier," *Le Monde,* April 4, 1986; D.G. Brennan, "The Risks of Spreading Weapons: A Historical Case," *Arms Control and Disarmament,* Vol. 1 (1968); Leonard S. Spector, *Going Nuclear* (Cambridge, MA: Ballinger Publishing Company, 1987), pp. 25–31.

[2] Elaine Sciolino and Eric Schmitt, "Algerian Reactor: A Chinese Export," *New York Times,* November 15, 1991; "China Helps Algeria Build First Arab Atom Bomb," *Sunday Times,* April 28, 1991; Bill Gertz, "China Helps Algeria Develop Nuclear Weapons," *Washington Times,* April 11, 1991.

[3] See Ann MacLachlan and Mark Hibbs, "Algeria Confirms Secret Reactor; Questions About Purpose Remain," *Nucleonics Week,* May 2, 1991, p. 3; Barbara Gregory, *Algeria: Contemplating A Nuclear Weapons Option?* (McLean, VA: Science Applications International Corporation, March 25, 1995); interviews with former U.S. officials.

[4] "Algeria: IAEA, Algeria Sign Safeguards Agreement," *Nuclear Fuel,* March 16, 1992, p. 15; "Atomic Energy Inspectors Tour Nuclear Reactor," *Algiers Radio,* January 19, 1992, in *FBIS-NES-92-014,* January 22, 1992, p. 15; Gamini Senevirante, "IAEA Governors Defer Decision on Expanding Safeguards Powers," *Nucleonics Week,* December 12, 1991, p. 10.

[5] "Algeria Pledges Peaceful Use of PRC-Built Nuclear Reactor," *Xinhua Domestic Service* (Beijing), December 24, 1993, in *JPRS-TND-93-003,* January 31, 1994, p. 45; "Decision to Join Nuclear Non-Proliferation Treaty Announced," *Radio Algiers Network,* December 21, 1993, in *JPRS-TND-94-002,* January 18, 1994, p. 12; "Reactions to Dedication of Nuclear Reactor," *El Moudjahid* (Algiers), December 22, 1993, in *JPRS-TND-94-005,* February 25, 1994, p. 10.

[6] "Algeria Accedes to the Treaty on the Non-Proliferation of Nuclear Weapons," IAEA Press Release PR 95/2, January 13, 1995. Algeria deposited its instruments of accession to the NPT in Washington, Moscow, and London.

[7] James Philips, "The Rising Threat of Revolutionary Islam in Algeria," Heritage Foundation Backgrounder No. 1060, November 9, 1995.

[8] Mark Hibbs, "Last NPT PREPCOM Moves Toward Limited Extension," *Nucleonics Week,* February 2, 1995, p. 6. Also see Kathleen Hart, "Clinton Administration Accelerates Push For NPT Indefinite Extension," *Nuclear Fuel,* April 10, 1995, p. 5; "To Sign or Not to Sign: Israel Embattled Over NPT Refusal," *Jane's Defence Weekly,* March 25, 1995.

[9] "Algeria Against NPT Extension Without Israel," *Reuters,* March 21, 1996.

[10] Mark Hibbs, "Weapon States Face Pressure on NPT Pledge, Chairman Says," *Nucleonics Week,* May 18, 1995, p. 8; "Russian Federation, the United Kingdom and Northern Ireland, and the United States: Resolution," *Arms Control Reporter* (Section 453.D), 1995, p. 21.

[11] "IAEA Chief Visits Algerian Nuclear Reactor," *Reuters,* March 31, 1996.

[12] "Algeria Signs Nuclear Draft Agreement With China," *Reuters,* June 2, 1996; "Algerian Official Discusses Nuclear Energy Cooperation," *Xinhua Domestic Service* (Beijing), June 3, 1996, *FBIS-CHI-96-107,* June 3, 1996.

[13] See "Talks Held With Algerian Ministers on Medicare, Nuclear Industry," *Xinhua* (Beijing), October 18, 1996, in *FBIS-CHI-96-204,* October 18, 1996.

[14] Mark Hibbs, "China Attends Zangger Meeting, Might Join Committee After Talks," *Nuclear Fuel,* June 2, 1997, p. 8; David Albright, Frans Berkhout and William Walker, *Plutonium and Highly Enriched Uranium 1996: World Inventories, Capabilities and Policies* (London: Oxford University Press for Stockholm Peace Research Institute, 1997), p. 363.

China announced the commencement of "phase three" of nuclear cooperation with Algeria on May 21, 1997. According to China, "phase three" will provide "blueprints and plans of the third stage of construction" of the Algerian Center for Nuclear Energy Research involved in "control of isotopes" and waste management. Hibbs, "China Attends Zangger Meeting," op. cit., p. 8.

According to one report Western officials have stated that there is "another large facility nearby that was not observed by intelligence agencies until its roof was in place, preventing an identification of its purpose via overhead surveillance. Algeria has not declared this facility to the IAEA as a nuclear facility. Nevertheless, some officials believe this facility may have been intended as a large-scale plutonium separation or reprocessing facility." Albright, Berkhout and Walker, *1996 World Inventories,* op. cit., p. 364.

[15] Mark Hibbs, "Move to Block China Certification Doesn't Concern Administration," *Nucleonics Week,* August 7, 1997, p. 1.

[16] Charles Trueheart, "Referendum Results Strengthen Algeria's Army-Backed Regime," *Washington Post,* November 29, 1996; Roger Cohen, "Algerians, Backing Constitution, Seem Poised to Accept Authority," *New York Times,* November 29, 1996; Roger Cohen, "Algeria Says Charter Passes, But Critics Charge Vote Fraud," *New York Times,* November 30, 1996. Also see Roddy Scott, "Algeria: Peace Remains Uncertain," *Middle East,* January 1996, p. 6; John Lancaster, "Pro-Government Parties Win In Disputed Algerian Election," *Washington Post,* June 7, 1997; John Lancaster, "Government Seeks Greater Legitimacy in Algerian Vote," *Washington Post,* October 24, 1997; John Lancaster, "Algerian Ruling Party Wins Local Vote," *Washington Post,* October 25, 1997.

[17] In such circumstances, the risk of proliferation could be significantly increased if such a government chose to work with Iran in a common effort to acquire nuclear arms.

[18] "Massacre and Bomb Kill Dozens in Wave of Violence in Algeria," *New York Times,* January 20, 1997; Charles Trueheart, "U.N., Vatican Condemn Massacres in Algeria," *Washington Post,* September 9, 1997; Charles Trueheart, "Attackers Massacre Up to 200 Civilians In Suburb of Algiers," *Washington Post,* September 24, 1997; John Lancaster, "As Algeria's Savagery Grows, So Does Mystery Shrouding It," *Washington Post,* October 18, 1997; John Lancaster, "Algerian Minister Rejects Foreign Role in Ending Violence," *Washington Post,* October 19, 1997; "Opposition Vows Protests In Algeria," *Washington Post,* October 26, 1997.

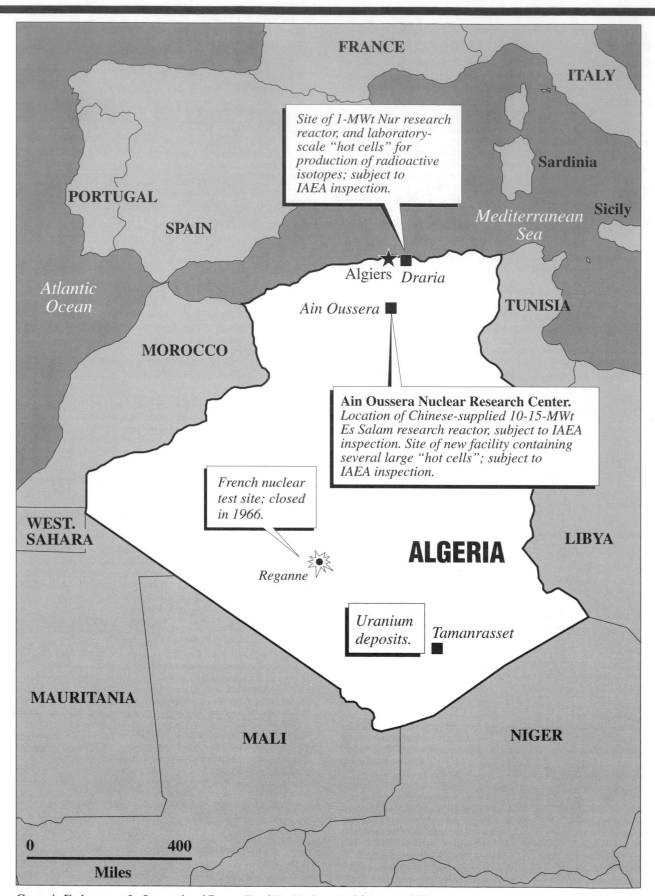

Site of 1-MWt Nur research reactor, and laboratory-scale "hot cells" for production of radioactive isotopes; subject to IAEA inspection.

FRANCE

ITALY

Sardinia

Sicily

PORTUGAL

SPAIN

Mediterranean Sea

Atlantic Ocean

Algiers *Draria*

Ain Oussera TUNISIA

MOROCCO

Ain Oussera Nuclear Research Center. *Location of Chinese-supplied 10-15-MWt Es Salam research reactor, subject to IAEA inspection. Site of new facility containing several large "hot cells"; subject to IAEA inspection.*

French nuclear test site; closed in 1966.

WEST. SAHARA

LIBYA

ALGERIA

Reganne

Uranium deposits. *Tamanrasset*

MAURITANIA

MALI

NIGER

0   400

Miles

Carnegie Endowment for International Peace, *Tracking Nuclear Proliferation*, 1998

ALGERIA: Nuclear Infrastructure

NAME/LOCATION	TYPE/STATUS	IAEA SAFEGUARDS
RESEARCH REACTORS		
Nur, Draria, Algiers	Small pool-type, LEU, 1 MWt; operating.	Yes
Es Salam, Ain Oussera	Heavy-water, LEU 15 MWt; operating.	Yes[a]
REPROCESSING (PLUTONIUM EXTRACTION)		
Ain Oussera	New facility containing hot cells for use in the production of radioactive isotopes.	Yes
Draria	Hot cells for use in the production of radioactive isotopes.	Yes
URANIUM PROCESSING		
West of Tamanrasset, southern Algeria	Uranium deposits; status unknown.	N/A (not applicable)

Abbreviations:

HEU	=	highly enriched uranium
LEU	=	low-enriched uranium
nat. U	=	natural uranium
MWe	=	millions of watts of electrical output
MWt	=	millions of watts of thermal output
KWt	=	thousands of watts of thermal output

NOTES (Algeria Chart)

[a]On February 27, 1992, Algeria and the IAEA signed a facility-specific safeguards agreement. The agreement provided for the inspection of the reactor, its nuclear fuel, and its heavy water, but apparently did not guarantee access to other facilities in the Ain Oussera nuclear research complex. However, on March 30, 1996, pursuant to its obligations under the NPT, Algeria signed a comprehensive inspection agreement with the IAEA that placed all nuclear activities in the country under IAEA safeguards. The agreement entered into force on January 7, 1997.

Iran

Although Iran had been a party to the Nuclear Non-Proliferation Treaty (NPT) since 1970, it is believed to have pursued a secret nuclear weapons program since the mid-1980s.[1] Iran's motives for seeking nuclear weapons stem from its rivalry with Iraq, from its quest for preeminence in the Persian Gulf, and, possibly, from the desire for a deterrent against major power intervention.

In 1996 congressional testimony, CIA Director John M. Deutch said: "We judge that Iran is actively pursuing an indigenous nuclear weapons capability. . . . Specifically, Iran is attempting to develop the capability to produce both plutonium and highly enriched uranium. In an attempt to shorten the timeline to a weapon, Iran has launched a parallel effort to purchase fissile material, mainly from sources in the former Soviet Union."[2] Iran's indigenous uranium-enrichment program appears to be focused on the development of gas centrifuges.[3] U.S. intelligence testimony in 1996 indicated that Iran's nuclear weapons program was still at a relatively rudimentary stage, at least eight to ten years away from producing nuclear arms—or less with foreign assistance.[4]

Iran's efforts to acquire nuclear arms has gone hand in hand with Iran's promotion of Islamic fundamentalism through violence and subversion. The Clinton Administration has branded Iran a "backlash state" because of its sponsorship of terrorism and assassination, subversion of the Middle East peace process, campaign to intimidate smaller countries in the Gulf region, and its human rights abuses.[5] Washington has sought to contain Iran through an energetic campaign of diplomatic isolation and wide-ranging economic sanctions—some targeted on its weapons-of-mass-destruction and missile programs.

China and Russia have been Iran's main suppliers of nuclear technology. In the U.S.–China summit of October 1997, however, China made a commitment to cancel almost all of its existing nuclear assistance to Iran and to provide Iran no new nuclear assistance. China at that time declined to give explicit assurances that it would stop assisting Iran's acquisition of missiles.[6] Russia has sought to expand civilian nuclear cooperation with Tehran and is building a nuclear power plant for Iran at Bushehr.[7] In the course of consultation with the United States, however, Russia has dropped its previously contemplated uranium-enrichment assistance to Iran.

Iran is believed to have one of the world's largest chemical weapon (CW) stockpiles and reportedly acquired stocks of biological weapons (BW) for the first time in 1996. Iran might soon be able to mate these weapons with ballistic missiles. Iran possesses the 300-km range Scud-B and the 500-km range Scud-C missiles and is able to strike targets in Iraq, Saudi Arabia, and elsewhere in the Persian Gulf region. Iran is also seeking to acquire the 1,000-km range Nodong missile from North Korea, which would enable it to target Israel for the first time. In addition, Iran is working on a missile with a 1,300-1,500 km range with assistance from Russian firms,[8] and seeking to develop the Shahab-3 and Shahab-4 ballistic missiles with ranges up to 2,000 km.[9]

Thus, although Iran probably is at least eight to ten years away from acquiring nuclear weapons, it may be able to threaten its adversaries' population centers with other mass destruction weapons far sooner. Iran appears to be following the model adopted by Iraq in the 1980s: obtaining "strategic" capabilities based, initially, on more easily developed chemical and biological weapons while working toward the acquisition of nuclear arms.

BACKGROUND

The revolutionary Islamic regime of Ayatollah Khomeini that came to power in Iran in 1979 inherited two partially completed, German-supplied nuclear power reactors at Bushehr. Under construction in the late 1970s, the structures were severely damaged by Iraqi bombing during the 1980-88 Iran-Iraq War. Germany later refused to repair and finish the plants because of Iran's apparent interest in nuclear weapons.[10] The Khomeini regime also inherited a nuclear research base and continued the nuclear research activities.[11] The Tehran Research Center, for example, trained specialists and operated a small U.S.–supplied research reactor, which remained under International Atomic Energy Agency (IAEA) safeguards.[12] Specialists at the center presumably had access to the research done during the Shah's reign, possibly including undeclared nuclear-weapons research. The Khomeini regime's commitment to continued nuclear research was so strong that in 1984—in the midst of the Iran-Iraq War—it opened a new nuclear research center in Esfahan.[13]

Iran's great losses from the war with Iraq played a key part in Iran's decisions to invest in modern conventional arms and in weapons of mass destruction (WMD). During the war, Iraq had used chemical weapons against poorly protected Iranian forces with devastating effect, and Iraq's bombardment of Tehran with conventionally armed, extended-range Scud missiles during the spring 1988 "War of the Cities" was an important factor leading Iran to accept a cease-fire in October of that year. Shortly after the cease-fire, Akbar Hashemi-Rafsanjani, then the speaker of the Iranian parliament and commander-in-chief of Iran's armed forces and later Iran's president, declared:

> With regard to chemical, bacteriological, and radiological weapons training, it was made very clear during the war that these weapons are very decisive. It was also made clear that the moral teachings of the world are not very effective when war reaches a serious stage and the world does not respect its own resolutions and closes its eyes to the violations and all the aggressions which are committed in the battle field.
>
> *We should fully equip ourselves both in the offensive and defensive use of chemical, bacteriological, and radiological weapons.* From now on you should make use of the opportunity and perform this task [emphasis added].[14]

To produce nuclear weapons material, Iran sought the needed expertise by enlarging its nuclear research and energy program with assistance from China and Russia. Iran also conducted covert research on fissile material production, supported by smuggling activities, particularly in Western Europe. Because development of an indigenous capability to produce fissile material might take from eight to ten years, however, Iran added a second track to its nuclear weapons program, seeking to purchase nuclear weapons material illicitly in the former Soviet Union.

Civil Nuclear Assistance: First Track. China provided significant assistance to Iran's civil nuclear program from the mid-1980s.[15] China reportedly trained Iranian nuclear technicians and engineers in China under a ten-year agreement for cooperation signed in 1990. China supplied Iran with two "mini" research reactors installed at Esfahan. China also supplied Iran with a calutron—the type of equipment used in Iraq's EMIS enrichment program for separation of weapons-grade uranium. The calutron is a smaller model which, according to the Iranians, is used only for stable isotope production.[16] Both countries claim the aid has been exclusively for peaceful purposes, in line with Iran's NPT obligations. The United States has objected to such assistance on the grounds that it could bolster Iran's nuclear technology base and indirectly support its efforts to acquire nuclear weapons.

In 1992, Washington persuaded China to indefinitely postpone the sale to Iran of a plutonium-producing research reactor and convinced Argentina not to export supporting fuel-cycle and heavy-water production facilities.[17] On the other hand, China in March 1992 agreed to supply two 300-MWe nuclear power reactors to Iran based on its Qinshan-1 design. The reactors were to be located at Esteghlal, a site adjacent to Bushehr.[18]

On January 8, 1995, Russia signed an $800-million agreement with Iran under which Russia is to complete one of the two partially constructed nuclear power reactors at Bushehr.[19] Under the contract, Russia is also to provide low-enriched uranium (LEU) fuel for a period of ten years starting in 2001 at an annual cost of $30 million, as well as technical training. If the project goes well, the deal may be extended to include Russia's completion of the other partially constructed unit at the same site.[20] During the discussions over the Bushehr agreement, Tehran expressed strong interest in purchasing two more power reactors, 440 MWe in this case, and a research reactor from Russia.

The Chinese and Russian agreements to supply Iran with nuclear power reactors aroused strong concern in Washington. While it acknowledged that the contracts are legal under international non-proliferation guidelines, the Clinton Administration strongly protested them as providing expertise and training that would contribute indirectly, but substantially, to Iran's nuclear weapons program.[21]

By 1992, press reports of Western intelligence findings helped explain the basis for Washington's concerns. They indicated that Iran had established experimental programs in fissile material production at Sharif University in Tehran, and possibly at other locations. These programs reportedly included research and development in both centrifuge uranium enrichment and plutonium reprocessing. Iran was said to be supporting these efforts by means of a clandestine procurement network; it was secretly approaching Western European companies to acquire nuclear-related, dual-use technologies and purchasing a number of small companies—particularly in Germany—to serve as export platforms for sensitive equipment to Iran.[22]

Although there had been a number of allegations during the late 1980s that Pakistan might be contributing to the Iranian nuclear weapons effort, such reports were not substantiated and eventually died away in the early 1990s.[23] Indeed, in March 1996, then-CIA Director John Deutch advised Congress, "We have no concrete evidence of WMD cooperation between Iran and Pakistan."[24]

Part of Iran's nuclear weapons program was believed to be under the authority of the civilian-run Atomic Energy Organization of Iran (AEOI), while the procurement activities abroad were reportedly controlled by the Iranian Defense Ministry. According to American and German intelligence officials, the Defense Ministry uses front organizations like Sharif University to help buy nuclear-related equipment.[25] The defense unit concerned has also been implicated in possible nuclear weapons research and development activities at military sites.[26]

Direct Purchase: Second Track. Iran is also thought to be trying to accelerate nuclear weapons development by direct "purchase [of] fissile material, mainly from sources in the former Soviet Union," according to former CIA Director Deutch. In this context, Iranian agents are said to have contacted officials at nuclear facilities in Kazakhstan on several occasions.[27] For example, in 1992, Iranians approached the

Ulba Metallurgical Plant at the production complex at Ust-Kamenogorsk to buy enriched uranium and beryllium metal, although they were unsuccessful. There are conflicting reports on whether the Iranians wanted to buy LEU as reactor fuel for future use or, instead, wanted to buy or smuggle some of the more than 500 kg of weapons-usable highly enriched uranium (HEU) stored at the complex at the time.[28]

Special IAEA "Visits." In 1991, in an effort to dispel recurring suspicions about its nuclear program, Iran agreed that, in addition to permitting routine IAEA inspections on all nuclear activities as required by the NPT, it would also allow the IAEA to visit any location within the country to check for undeclared nuclear activities. The Agency has made two such special "visits." A February 1992 visit observed several locations not on Iran's list of declared nuclear sites but found no violations of the NPT. In a follow-on visit in November 1993, IAEA officials viewed facilities in Esfahan, Karaj, and Tehran, but again found no violations of the pact.[29] Nevertheless, the outcomes of the visits have not allayed U.S. concerns.

Ballistic Missile Program. During the early 1990s, Iran sought to acquire ballistic missile capabilities that could be used for delivering nuclear weapons—turning to Libya, North Korea, and China for missile systems and related technologies. Iran possesses two versions of the nuclear-capable and North Korea–supplied Scud ballistic missile, the Mod. B (300-km range) and the Mod. C (500-km range). It also has in its inventory the Chinese-supplied CSS-8 missile with an estimated range of 150 km.[30]

North Korea agreed in 1992 to sell Iran the Scud, Mod. D (Nodong 1) ballistic missile, then under development, with a range of 1,000 km (capable of reaching Israel).[31] Some sources have reported that North Korea has postponed the Nodong 1 sale indefinitely, possibly at the request of Israel, or as a result of ongoing negotiations with the United States. Iran apparently has acquired much of its current ballistic missile capability in exchange for providing long-term financing for North Korea's missile program.[32] China reportedly had agreed in 1988 to provide Iran with "M-class" missile technology that would enable it to produce nuclear-capable ballistic missiles with ranges of 300 to 1,000 km, but later reports said that this offer had been withdrawn.[33]

Western Nuclear Embargo. China and Russia have been the only major nuclear supplier states willing to make nuclear transfers to Iran openly. The Western nuclear suppliers, in contrast, have adopted, from the regime's earliest days, a U.S.–led embargo on nuclear sales to the Iranian Revolutionary Government. The United States has relied on the Nuclear Suppliers Group (NSG) to coordinate the Western embargo and persuaded other like-minded states to withhold goods that were regulated under the NSG's core export control guidelines. Controlled items include complete nuclear power plants, major components for them, and sensitive "nuclear-unique" items or equipment (relat-

ing to uranium enrichment, spent fuel reprocessing, and heavy-water production). NSG rules permit the sale of such items, provided they are subject to IAEA inspection in the recipient state, but Washington has convinced its Western trading partners to adopt the stricter policy in the case of Iran. China is not an NSG member, and Russia, though a member, explicitly rejects the U.S.–initiated ban on major nuclear exports to Iran. Moscow argues that the United States has not presented persuasive evidence that Iran is pursuing nuclear weapons and that the light-water type of reactor that Russia is supplying, which will be under IAEA inspection, is not a proliferation risk.[34] As noted below, Iran has vehemently protested U.S. efforts to block its access to nuclear technology on the grounds that the U.S. action violates Article IV of the NPT.

U.S. efforts to curtail foreign nuclear sales to Iran intensified during the Bush Administration when, in the aftermath of the 1991 Gulf War, it was learned that Iraq, despite its status as an NPT party, had pursued a massive nuclear weapons program that relied heavily on the procurement of goods from abroad. This experience led the NSG in April 1992 to extend its controls to nuclear "dual-use" items—i.e., items with both nuclear and non-nuclear end uses—prohibiting exports of items on the list "when there is unacceptable risk of diversion [to the production of nuclear explosives] or when the transfers are contrary to the objective of averting the proliferation of nuclear weapons." Once the new NSG rules were adopted, Washington sought agreement from the leading Western members of the group to prohibit all transfers of nuclear dual-use goods to Iran but only Great Britain and Germany complied.[35] An initially unsuccessful, parallel U.S. proposal, launched in 1992, was to curtail Western sales of (non-nuclear) strategic dual-use items to Iran; the initiative took four years to materialize in the form of the Wassenaar Agreement in 1996.[36] Washington in early 1993 sought to persuade other Western industrialized states not to reschedule any credits they had issued to Iran, not to issue any new credits, and to oppose new loans for Iran from multilateral banks. Again, Washington achieved only partial success.[37]

U.S. Sanctions. After the U.S.–Iran agreement for nuclear cooperation expired in April 1979, the essential preconditions for U.S. exports of nuclear equipment and materials to Iran were absent. Passage of the 1992 Iran-Iraq Arms Non-Proliferation Act expressly prohibited such transfers as well as exports to Iran of *all* dual-use commodities and U.S. government and commercial arms sales.[38] In addition, during the 1980s, the United States imposed a wide range of sanctions on Iran because of its support for international terrorism, its attacks in 1987 on U.S.–flagged Kuwaiti tankers, and other actions hostile to U.S. interests. These sanctions blocked economic and military assistance to Iran, prohibited the importation of Iranian-origin goods, and restricted U.S. contributions to multilateral organizations that assist Iran and U.S. Export-Import Bank credits for Iran.[39]

On March 6, 1992, the United States imposed sanctions, under missile non-proliferation provisions of the Arms Export Control and Export Administration Acts, against the Iranian Ministry of Defense and Armed Forces Logistics and against two North Korean entities for engaging in "missile proliferation activities."[40] The sanctioned activities involved North Korea's transfer to Iran of Scud missiles and production technology for such missiles.[41] Because the transferred items fell within Category I of the MTCR Annex (see the description of the MTCR in Appendix G on the Missile Technology Control Regime in this volume), the sanctions imposed on the three entities consisted of a two-year ban on U.S. export licenses for all dual-use and military goods and a ban on all U.S. government contracts. In addition, because the transfers were considered to make a "substantial" contribution to the Iranian missile program, the Bush Administration also invoked a provision of the law permitting the imposition of an additional sanction: a ban on all imports to the United States from the sanctioned entities.[42] Since U.S. trade with North Korea was already prohibited under a U.S. embargo dating from the Korean War, and since Iran was prohibited by other statutes from receiving all but the least sensitive exports (and the Iranian Defense Ministry was unlikely to receive U.S. export licenses of any kind), the new sanctions did not impose significant new penalties on the targeted entities in either state. The imposition of sanctions did, however, serve to highlight and publicize the fact that important missile-related transfers were taking place between the two states involved and to underscore U.S. concerns about such transactions.

DEVELOPMENTS

Since early 1995, Iranian efforts to advance its nuclear capabilities—and U.S.-led efforts to block such progress and to isolate Iran more generally—have continued. In recent years, the United States expanded non-proliferation and more generalized sanctions against Iran and succeeded in persuading Russia and China to curtail the most troubling of the planned nuclear transfers to Iran. This Russian and Chinese retrenchment, it appears, did slow the progress of the overall Iranian nuclear weapons effort. In October 1997, China agreed that it would terminate most previous nuclear assistance projects with Iran and provide no new nuclear assistance. Over the last three years, however, Iran has expanded its missile and chemical weapon capabilities and for the first time has acquired stocks of biological weapons.

Disclosure of Iran's Secret Enrichment Program. In the spring of 1995, details emerged on Iran's nuclear procurement activities, publicly substantiating its suspected efforts to establish a secret gas centrifuge uranium-enrichment program. Specifically, Western intelligence sources were quoted as stating that, since 1990, Iran had approached German and Swiss firms to purchase balancing machines, as well as diagnostic and monitoring equipment—all dual-use items potentially valuable for laboratory-scale centrifuge development. In addition, Iranian agents were said to have contacted a British company to obtain samarium-cobalt magnetic equipment, potentially useful in the development of centrifuge top bearings.[43]

Also during early 1995, Russia proceeded with its contract to help Iran build a nuclear reactor at Bushehr. Tensions rose with Russia when the Clinton Administration learned in March-April 1995 that, as part of a secret protocol to the reactor sale contract, Russia had agreed to provide Iran with a gas centrifuge uranium-enrichment facility. Such a facility, though itself under IAEA inspection and dedicated to the production of low-enriched (non-weapons grade) uranium, could enable Iran to build and operate a similar plant clandestinely to produce weapons-grade uranium. Other disturbing elements of the protocol were an agreement in principle for Russia to supply a 30-50-MWt light-water research reactor, 2,000 metric tons of natural uranium, and training of Iranian graduates in the nuclear field in Russia.[44]

Just as these facts emerged, the Clinton Administration was completing the review of U.S. policy toward Iran that led it to impose additional trade sanctions on Iran on April 30, 1995. Concerned that continued purchases of Iranian oil by U.S. companies overseas gave the impression that Washington was not serious about isolating Iran, and under congressional pressure to impose tougher measures, the Clinton Administration extended a number of trade prohibitions to cover the overseas subsidiaries of U.S. companies.[45] The new sanctions included a ban on all imports of Iranian origin-goods (including those transshipped largely unchanged through third countries), a ban on U.S. exports to Iran of all dual-use goods regulated under the Export Administration Act (including those transshipped largely unchanged through third countries), a ban on investment in Iran by U.S. persons and their subsidiaries, and a ban on trading by U.S. persons and their subsidiaries in Iranian oil.[46] In explaining these new measures, President Clinton made clear that one purpose of the broadened U.S. trade sanctions was to curtail Iran's ability to pursue the development of nuclear arms:

> I am formally announcing my intention to cut off all trade and investment with Iran and to suspend nearly all other economic activity between our nations. This is not a step I take lightly, but I am convinced that instituting a trade embargo with Iran is the most effective way our nation can help to curb that nation's drive to acquire devastating weapons and its continued support for terrorism.[47]

This demonstration of U.S. resolve may have influenced Russian President Boris Yeltsin's decision to cancel the transfer of an enrichment facility to Iran, the most dangerous element of the Russian nuclear deal. At their May 10 summit in Moscow, Yeltsin advised Clinton that Russia would not supply militarily useful nuclear technology to Iran and that, as part of this undertaking, would remove the centrifuge plant provisions from the protocol with Tehran, acknowledging that certain elements of the protocol had "the potential for creating weapons-grade fuel."[48] Yeltsin refused to abandon other aspects of the protocol, however.

Iran has regularly objected to U.S. efforts to impose the nuclear embargo. Indeed, at the third Preparatory Committee (PrepCom) session of the NPT Review and Extension Conference in September 1994, Iran threatened to withdraw from the NPT on the grounds that the Western embargo violated Article IV of the Treaty. This article guarantees "the inalienable right of all Parties to the Treaty to develop research, production and use of nuclear energy for peaceful purposes," as well as full access to "equipment, materials and scientific and technological information" for such uses. Iranian officials later toned down their threat of withdrawal and did not renew it at the fourth PrepCom in January 1995. But at the NPT Review and Extension Conference, which concluded on May 11, 1995, Iran revisited the "peaceful uses" issue by threatening until the last minute to block consensus on indefinite extension of the treaty. Ultimately, Iran backed down, reportedly after Russia warned that blocking consensus might jeopardize Moscow's sale of nuclear reactors to Tehran.[49]

Chinese Reactor Cooperation Suspended. In the fall of 1995 China's reactor sale to Iran was suspended, ostensibly because of difficulties over site selection, although the underlying cause may have been Iran's difficulties in raising financing. Other factors may also have been involved. Some reports indicated that China suspended or even terminated the deal because of strong U.S. pressure.[50] Also, France, Germany, and Japan apparently had declined to supply China with essential components that it might have needed for the reactors it had offered Iran. It is also possible that Iran lost interest in the arrangement once it was confident that Russia would complete the Bushehr project.

New U.S. Sanctions Laws. In February 1996, President Clinton signed two additional pieces of legislation aimed at constraining Iranian WMD programs. The first amended the 1992 Iran-Iraq Arms Non-Proliferation Act to impose sanctions on any person or foreign government that "transfers or retransfers goods or technology so as to contribute knowingly and materially to the efforts by Iran or Iraq to acquire chemical, biological, or nuclear weapons."[51] The sanctions to be imposed against persons—including corporate entities—were a two-year ban on U.S. government procurement contracts and a two-year ban on the issuance of export licenses to the person. The sanctions to be imposed against governments—all for one year—were a ban on U.S. assistance, opposition to multilateral loans, suspension of co-development or co-production agreements, and suspension of military and dual-use technical exchange agreements. In addition, the president was given the discretion to halt all dual-use exports to the country in question. Previously the law had imposed sanctions only when aid to Iran or Iraq was intended to assist either to acquire destabilizing numbers and types of advanced conventional weapons. The original Iran-Iraq Arms Non-Proliferation Act had allowed the president to waive these sanctions upon a finding that doing so was "essential to the national interests of the United States."[52] In many respects, the triggers for sanctions and the sanctions to be imposed under the 1996 amendment to the Iran-Iraq Arms Non-Proliferation Act overlap with other anti-proliferation sanctions laws, such as the 1994 Nuclear Proliferation Prevention Act. However, the new provision, with its specific targeting of assistance provided to Iran and Iraq, served to underscore U.S. concerns about the WMD programs of these states.

Congress directed the second new sanctions law against Russia's sale of nuclear equipment and technology to Iran. Adopted in February 1996, the legislation conditioned U.S. economic assistance to Russia on a presidential determination, to be made every six months, that Russia had terminated "arrangements to provide Iran with technical expertise, training, technology, or equipment necessary to develop a nuclear reactor or related nuclear research facilities or programs."[53] The legislation permitted the president to waive this restriction at six month intervals, however, upon a determination that making U.S. funds available to Russia "is important to the national security interests of the United States."[54] Such waivers were exercised in May 1996, November 1996, May 1997, and November 1997 (see below).[55]

Having obtained President Yeltsin's commitment in May 1995 to drop uranium enrichment from Russian nuclear cooperation with Iran, U.S. officials believed that Iran's program to develop and bench-test gas centrifuges for uranium enrichment would still be at the experimental stage in early 1996. Strictly speaking, Iran would be obligated to declare a uranium-enrichment program to the IAEA under the country's NPT safeguards agreement, but only at the stage that it was acquiring and installing the equipment. There had been some fear that Pakistan would help Iran acquire enrichment technology.[56] In early 1995, for example, reports indicated that some U.S. officials suspected that Iran had obtained gas centrifuge uranium-enrichment technology, including European-origin design information, from Pakistan. CIA Director John Deutch testified in March 1996, however, that the United States had no "concrete evidence of WMD cooperation between Iran and Pakistan."[57] Thus, U.S. efforts to dissuade nuclear suppliers from openly assisting Iran with sensitive uranium-enrichment technology seemed to have had success.

The March 1996 parliamentary elections in Iran held open the possibility that moderates might make significant gains within the Majlis (Iranian parliament), possibly leading to a gradual opening to the West. These hopes were disappointed, however. While the centrist bloc, the so called Servants of Iranian Reconstruction, achieved some gains, and the conservative bloc, the Society of the Combatant Clergy, lost its majority, the results did not lead to a decisive realignment, and Iranian activities of concern to the United States continued unabated.[58] In subsequent months, therefore, Washington intensified its efforts to constrain nuclear transfers to Iran.

U.S. Pressure on China and Russia. Although China had halted its planned reactor sales to Iran, in April 1996 the U.S. Department of Defense still regarded China to be Iran's "main" source of nuclear assistance.[59] China apparently was still assisting Iran with the construction of a proliferation-sensitive uranium conversion plant near Esfahan.[60] The facility was to produce uranium hexafluoride (UF_6), the feedstock in the gas centrifuge uranium-enrichment process.[61] If built, the facility could enable Iran to produce the fissile materials for nuclear weapons under the guise of mastering a link in the nuclear fuel cycle. Although the plant would be subject to IAEA inspection, Iran would be able to use the engineering knowledge to construct a similar, undeclared conversion plant.

In May, however, after the U.S.–China negotiations over China's sale of ring magnets to Pakistan's uranium-enrichment facility, Beijing restated its non-proliferation commitments and pledged to cease all assistance to foreign nuclear facilities not subject to IAEA inspection. Although no alleged Chinese assistance to Iran fell into this category because all known Iranian nuclear facilities are under IAEA monitoring, the commitment suggested that China was becoming more responsive to U.S. nuclear non-proliferation concerns. Indeed, in November 1996, the Chinese government reportedly indicated to the Clinton Administration that it might be willing to cancel the uranium conversion plant deal with Iran to help gain U.S. certification that China was in compliance with U.S. non-proliferation laws (see China chapter in this volume). Although this understanding nearly unraveled, a Chinese official confirmed in March 1997 that the Iranian uranium conversion plant sale had, indeed, been suspended.[62]

Meanwhile, Washington stepped up pressure on Russia to halt its work on the Bushehr nuclear reactor, but without success. Among other initiatives, President Clinton pressed the issue with President Yeltsin at their April 1996 summit and in May invoked the sanctions provisions of the FY 1996 Foreign Appropriations Act, calling for the termination of U.S. foreign assistance for Russia. Because of the overriding U.S. commitment to support economic and political reforms in Russia, however, the President simultaneously exercised the waiver provision in the law, permitting continued U.S. aid to Russia.[63]

As Washington sought to constrain Chinese and Russian nuclear exports to Iran, Iran's clandestine effort to develop a uranium-enrichment capability apparently continued. In August 1996, British customs officials intercepted a shipment of 110 pounds of "maraging steel" at the London port of Barking. The material, which had been ordered by the Iranian military, can be used in the manufacture of uranium-enrichment centrifuges. It had been shipped by a U.S. manufacturer to a British defense company but was actually destined for Iran.[64]

Also in August, Washington further intensified economic pressure on Iran by imposing "secondary" sanctions on it and Libya, through the Iran and Libya Sanctions Act of 1996. Signed by President Clinton on August 5 at a time when Iran was seeking international bids on eleven major energy projects, the law imposes sanctions on foreign enterprises that invest $40 million or more in the energy sector of Iran or Libya.[65] Section 3 of the law, entitled "Policy with Respect to Iran," states: "it is the policy of the United States to deny Iran the ability to support acts of international terrorism and to fund the development and acquisition of weapons of mass destruction and the means to deliver them by limiting the development of Iran's ability to explore for, extract, refine, or transport by pipeline petroleum resources of Iran."[66] By the fall of 1997, this legislation was facing a serious challenge from Russian, French, and Malaysian oil companies that signed a deal with Iran to help recover and market oil and natural gas.[67] The Clinton Administration backed away from imposing these sanctions because of the economic crisis in East Asia and in Russia in the fall of 1997 and spring of 1998, which placed larger U.S. foreign policy interests at stake.

Comprehensive Test Ban Treaty. On September 24, 1996, Iran signed the Comprehensive Test Ban Treaty (CTBT). Iran had supported India's objections to the treaty until immediately before the treaty was approved by the U.N. General Assembly on September 10. Iran had also objected to the inclusion of Israel in representing the Middle East and South Asian region in the treaty's Executive Council. Iran also criticized the use of "national technical means" of intelligence for monitoring the treaty because they could be used as a cover for big-power intelligence gathering.[68] As of May 1998, Iran had taken no visible steps to ratify the CTBT.

Iranian Nuclear Program Setbacks. In November 1996, U.S. aid to Russia was again called into question under the Foreign Operations Appropriations Act because of Moscow's continuing participation in the Bushehr reactor project. Once again, President Clinton waived the aid cutoff as permitted by the legislation. A memorandum explaining this decision highlighted the nature of U.S. concerns about the deal and the efforts that had been made to persuade Russia to terminate it:

> The Administration shares the deep concern of the Congress over Russian nuclear cooperation with Iran. Such cooperation, which could contribute over time to a nuclear-armed Iran, continues to be a threat not only to U.S. security interests, the Middle East Peace Process, and global stability, but also to Russian security interests as well. In dealing with this pressing issue, the Administration has repeatedly and strenuously objected to any form of nuclear cooperation with Iran.[69]

The President then explained that the urgent need to sustain the process of reform in Russia necessitated the exercise of the waiver so that U.S. aid to Moscow might continue.

Ironically, for reasons completely apart from U.S. pressure, it is possible that Russia may have second thoughts about finishing the Bushehr project. Initially, Russian officials had estimated that, once construction commenced by early 1996, it would take about 55 to 60 months to build the reactor and load it with fuel.[70] However, by the fall of 1996, the project clearly faced complex engineering problems. Specifically, Russian experts were grappling with the incompatibility of metallurgical specifications of equipment supplied by Siemens during the 1970s with those of components to be fitted in the reactor under the Russia-Iran deal.[71] In addition, Russia's promised sale to Iran of a sizable research reactor, encompassed in the original Bushehr deal, also faltered. At U.S. urging, Russia refused to provide a heavy-water system—an efficient plutonium producer—as requested by the Iranians. The original agreement had called for a light-water research reactor.[72]

By the fall of 1996, China had suspended its assistance to Iran on the uranium conversion facility. Coupled with the seizure of the maraging steel in Great Britain in August and Russian retrenchment on sensitive assistance, Iran's plan to expand its nuclear program was running into growing obstacles. Continued IAEA monitoring in Iran—and pressure from the Agency to expand its inspection activities there—provided another major constraint on the country's clandestine nuclear activities for the remainder of 1996 and 1997.[73]

In connection with Russia's reactor sale agreement, the United States was particularly troubled by the arrangements for the disposition of the plutonium-bearing spent fuel from Bushehr. Take-back of spent fuel had been a standard feature of Soviet nuclear export agreements. In practice, this meant that plutonium in spent fuel was returned to the fuel supplier. In Iran's case, spent-fuel return to Russia could prevent Iranian diversion of plutonium for weapons. Throughout the protracted U.S.–Russian dialogue over Russia's contracts with Iran, the United States had urged Russia to agree to take back and keep the spent fuel from the Bushehr reactors. Washington feared that, even though spent fuel stored in Iran would be under IAEA inspection, if Iran chose to violate its obligations to the IAEA, it could, with adequate pre-planning, rapidly recover the plutonium and transform it into nuclear weapons.[74] The Russian Ministry of Atomic Energy (Minatom), however, fearful of jeopardizing the commercial terms already agreed to with Iran, was reluctant to insist upon the permanent return of the spent fuel to Russia. Minatom's position was that imposing such a condition on Iran would go "far beyond" the safeguards requirements of the NPT.[75]

Ultimately, the United States convinced Russia to stipulate to Iran that spent fuel from the reactor would be returned to Russia.[76] This did not resolve the related issue, however, as to whether there would be sufficient safeguards in place for the ongoing monitoring of significant quantities of irradiated fuel in cooling ponds at the reactor site, awaiting transport to Russia (see below).

Iran's Presidential Elections of May 1997. In a stunning upset, moderate Islamic cleric Mohammed Khatami was elected president of Iran on May 24, 1997, winning approximately 70 percent of the vote.[77] This raised expectations of an easing of tension between Iran and the United States, possibly beginning a bilateral dialogue. The elections came against the backdrop of a debate in Western circles on whether the U.S. policy of "dual containment" had run its course.[78]

President Clinton called the election of Khatami "interesting" and "hopeful" but made clear that "a reconciliation" with Iran would have to overcome "three big hurdles." Iran's new leadership would have to demonstrate that Iran (1) has ceased to believe that terrorism is a legitimate extension of political policies, (2) will not use violence to wreck a peace process in the Middle East, and (3) will not develop weapons of mass destruction.[79] Since the Khatami election, Iranians have hinted they would favor a dialogue with the United States, provided that the United States demonstrates its sincerity and good faith (e.g., lifting sanctions and dropping terrorism charges).[80] Some saw the Clinton Administration's late 1997 decision to defer sanctions against foreign companies involved in huge energy deals with Iran as a sign of flexibility toward the new Iranian leadership.[81]

In a surprise move in August 1997, President Khatami appointed Gholam Reza Aghazadeh both as his vice president and as president of the Atomic Energy Organization of Iran (AEOI). Replacing Reza Amrollahi with Aghazadeh as head of AEOI stirred new speculation about the future course of the Iranian nuclear program. Some argue that the change of the AEOI leadership reflects growing opposition within the Iranian parliament to the Bushehr project. According to one report, parliamentary opponents to the deal have questioned the $800-million figure cited by the AEOI and Minatom as the cost for completing the reactor and have charged that "Russian documentation for the project is inadequate," and that "there are no commercial contracts under Iranian law for completing" the reactor. Some parliamentarians have raised safety issues and urged the new Iranian leadership "to shore up relations with Western countries so as to be able to import Western reactor equipment or simply to scuttle the effort to complete the 20-year old Bushehr reactors and build a new nuclear power station instead."[82] On the other hand, some observers believe that Amrollahi was replaced by Aghazadeh because of management ineffectiveness that allegedly had caused delays in the Iranian nuclear weapons program.[83]

Bushehr Stalled and Chinese Nuclear Assistance Ends. The issue of safeguards for the interim storage of spent fuel at the Bushehr site resurfaced in September 1997 during talks between Vice President

Albert Gore and Russian Premier Viktor Chernomyrdin. Reports indicated that, during the meeting, Russia had accepted the U.S. assessment of the proliferation risks posed by the Bushehr project and had agreed to a program of "mutual inspections."[84] However, within days, a senior Russian official dismissed Gore's renewed allegations of an Iranian nuclear weapons program and stated that there "[would] be no mutual inspections." He asserted: "Iran is sovereign. The reactors (for Bushehr) will be provided under full-scope IAEA safeguards. Iran is a member in good standing of the [NPT]. So there will be no additional [inspection] arrangements."[85]

On the other hand, another Russian official described Bushehr as "on hold for right now" because of lack of finance and inconclusive commercial arrangements with the AEOI.[86] Reportedly, as of early October 1997, some 200 to 300 Russian experts were still in Iran completing an engineering evaluation at the Bushehr installation, but no components for the reactor's nuclear steam system had been delivered yet. Because of the delays, the projected date for completing Bushehr 1 had been moved further ahead to 2003.[87]

In addition to the delays of the Bushehr project, the Iranian nuclear program has had to grapple in 1997 with the official termination of Chinese nuclear assistance. To achieve U.S. certification that it was in compliance with U.S. non-proliferation laws and gain access to advanced U.S. nuclear technology under the 1985 U.S.–China agreement for nuclear cooperation, President Jiang Zemin agreed at the October 29, 1997, summit with President Clinton that China would provide no further nuclear assistance to Iran (i.e., no fuel-cycle equipment or materials, and no power reactors).[88] Jiang's assurances that China would end the sale of cruise missiles and missile-related technology to Iran and avoid transfer of chemical weapons capabilities to Iran were less clear cut.[89]

Missile Program. According to a November 1997 U.S. Defense Department report, Iran is making significant progress on becoming self-sufficient in the production of both liquid-fueled and solid-propellant ballistic missiles. Iran is already assembling missiles utilizing foreign-made parts and may be able at some point in the future to produce such components domestically. Iran was known to be in the market for missile-related technology and know-how for the production of a medium-range ballistic missile (MRBM).[90]

In June 1995, the press cited U.S. intelligence reports as evidence that "strongly implicates" China in the transfer to Iran of equipment, materials, and scientific know-how that could be used in the manufacture of short-range ballistic missiles such as the Chinese M-9 or M-11.[91] China was believed to have transferred "dozens, perhaps hundreds, of missile guidance systems and computerized machine tools" to Iran, as well as rocket propellant ingredients that could be used on its current stockpile of short-range Scud Mod. Bs and Cs, as well as on Scud variants that Iran might produce in the future.[92] In the final analysis, however, the United States did not find that China's missile transactions with Iran violated China's MTCR-related pledges and declined to impose MTCR-related sanctions against China or Iran.[93]

In 1996, it became clear that North Korea was exporting missile capabilities to Iran. As a result, the United States did impose sanctions on May 26, 1996, on the Iranian Ministry of Defense Armed Forces Logistics, the Iranian State Purchasing Office, and the Korea Mining Development Trading Bureau.[94] The precise nature of the offending transactions remains classified, but U.S. officials indicated that North Korea had sold missile components, equipment, and materials to Iran, although not complete missiles, production technology, or major subsystems. The sanctions amounted to a political statement because U.S. dealings with the entities concerned were already banned by other legislation.

During 1997, U.S. press reports quoted U.S. and Israeli intelligence findings that Russian enterprises, including cash-strapped Russian technical institutes, research facilities, and defense-production companies were transferring to Iran Russian SS-4 MRBM technologies. According to these assessments, Iran hoped to employ these SS-4 MRBM technologies to develop two Iranian derivatives of the 1,000-km range North Korean Nodong missile. The first indigenous missile, the Shahab-3, is projected to have a range between 1,300 and 1,500 km. The second, the Shahab-4, which would have an improved guidance system, is expected to have a range up to 2,000 km. The Shahab-4 could hit targets as far as Germany and western China.[95]

At first, Russia repeatedly denied that it was supplying missile technology to Iran.[96] Vice President Gore raised the issue in Moscow with Prime Minister Chernomyrdin in September 1997. While the Russian government continued to deny official involvement in missile technology transfers to Iran, an official of the Russian Federal Security Service acknowledged on October 2 that his organization had "thwarted" an attempt by Iran, earlier this year, to custom order "joints and parts for a liquid-fuel missile engine" manufactured by a Russian factory. He also said that there were "separate occasions of cooperation with Iran as result of which Russian deliveries may have contradicted requirements of the Missile Technology Control Regime," but they all had been detected and stopped at an early stage.[97] The Russian official also said that Iranian missile technicians were being trained at two Russian universities, but claimed that the information they have access to is disseminated widely.

In spite of these Russian assurances, during the fall of 1997, Israel put increasing pressure on a reluctant Clinton Administration to impose economic sanctions on Russian entities reported to be supplying ballistic missile technology to Iran.[98] At the same time, the House Foreign Relations Committee marked up legislation to that effect. On November 4, 1997, the committee referred the Iran Missile Proliferation Sanctions Act of 1997 to the full House. According to the committee report:

The bill requires the President to submit a report to Congress 30 days after the date of enactment, and periodically thereafter, identifying those entities where there is credible evidence they have transferred key missile components or technology to Iran. Thirty days after this report is required to be submitted, three sanctions (denying munitions licenses, dual use licenses and U.S. foreign assistance to these entities) would be imposed for a period of at least two years on these entities identified in the report.[99]

Clinton Administration officials have complained that this law unfairly targets Russia, and, if implemented, would not only interfere with U.S. attempts to secure Russian cooperation on many important nonproliferation goals but could also sour U.S.–Russia relations, jeopardizing reform efforts in Russia. The bill (HR 2709) passed both houses of Congress by wide margins, though, and Clinton officials indicated in June 1998 that a veto was likely, but with such broad support in Congress a veto probably would be overturned.[100] In fact, in late June 1998, the Clinton Administration announced a veto of this legislation

Chemical and Biological Weapons. The U.S. CIA stated in February 1996 that Iran was continuing to expand and diversify its chemical weapons program, already among the largest in the Third World. The agency estimated that Tehran currently controls a CW stockpile of several thousand tons of sulfur, mustard, phosgene, and cyanide agents, and has the potential of producing 1,000 tons of these agents each year. The delivery means for these agents include "artillery, mortars, rockets, aerial bombs, and, possibly, even Scud warheads."[101] Importantly, the chemical agents that Iran possesses are World War I era weapons; it has yet to produce more advanced nerve agents, such as Soman, Tabun, Sarin, or VX.[102]

In addition, the CIA stated in a May 1996 document that: "Iran has had a biological warfare program since the early 1980s. Currently, the program is mostly in the research and development stages, but we believe Iran holds some stocks of BW agents and weapons."[103] The agency estimated that Iran's stockpile of biological weapons then was limited, but that it could deploy biological weapons using the delivery systems it already had. The CIA is concerned that Iran has the potential to develop a biological warhead for its ballistic missiles, but does not expect this to occur before the end of the century.[104] China has been implicated in supporting aspects of Iran's CW and BW activities.[105]

PROSPECTS

John Holum, the director of the Arms Control and Disarmament Agency, testified before Congress in March 1997 that Iran remained eight to ten years away from acquiring nuclear weapons—virtually the same assessment that U.S. officials had given two years earlier. Queried whether this meant that Iran's nuclear program was making little progress, Holum replied: "I think they have slipped rather than gained on the timetable. That is my current recollection. I may also want to give you a classified response."[106] During the course of 1997, press accounts and congressional testimony by U.S. officials also indicated that U.S. economic sanctions against Iran were beginning to affect its energy sector, possibly contributing to these setbacks.[107]

At the same time, there have been no reports that Iran succeeded in acquiring whole weapons or nuclear materials on the black market from Russian or other sources. Indeed, there have been no new reported cases involving the smuggling of weapons-usable materials from the former Soviet Union by any party since 1994.[108] On the other hand, hundreds of tons of weapons-usable nuclear materials remain poorly secured in Russia and are likely to remain so for many years, despite important U.S.–Russian collaborative efforts to enhance controls over such materials. Thus the potential danger that Iran may be able to obtain such materials will continue.

The May 1997 election of President Khatami raises the possibility of moderation in Iran's behavior. This could eventually alter the overall orientation of Iranian foreign policy or lead Iran to suspend its WMD and missile programs. However, until the Khatami regime takes steps to meet U.S. conditions for U.S.–Iranian "reconciliation," the United States is likely to continue its policy of containing Iran through diplomatic isolation and sanctions.

This may enable the United States and its allies to retard Iran's bid for nuclear arms, but the overall threat posed by Iran's other weapons of mass destruction and missile capabilities appears destined to grow stronger in coming years.[109]

NOTES

[1]State Department Briefing, "Statement by Secretary of State Warren Christopher Regarding U.S. Sanctions Against Iran," May 1, 1995.

[2]Testimony of John M. Deutch, Director of Central Intelligence, before the Permanent Subcommittee on Investigations of the Committee on Governmental Affairs, U.S. Senate, March 20, 1996. See Irwin Arieff, "U.S. Says Iran Wants to Steal Nuke Arms Capability," *Reuters*, February 29, 1996.

[3]Supplementary materials submitted by John H. Moseman, CIA Director of Congressional Affairs, *Hearings on Current and Projected National Security Threats to the United States and Its Interests Abroad*, Select Committee on Intelligence, U.S. Senate, February 22, 1996 (supplementary materials supplied May 10, 1996), p. 81.

[4]Supplementary materials submitted by Lt. Gen. Patrick M. Hughes, Director of the Defense Intelligence Agency, *Hearings on Current and Projected National Security Threats to the United States and Its Interests Abroad*, Select Committee on Intelligence, U.S. Senate, February 22, 1996 (supplementary materials supplied May 6, 1996), p. 205.

[5]See Anthony Lake, "Confronting Backlash States," *Foreign Affairs*, March/April 1994, p. 52.

[6]R. Jeffrey Smith, "China's Pledge to End Iran Nuclear Aid Yields U.S. Help," *Washington Post*, October 30, 1997; Bill Gertz "Albright Concedes 'Concern' Over China-Iran Transfers," *Washington Post*, January 24, 1997.

[7]See, e.g., Ann MacLachlan and Sergie Ryback, "Iran Rejects Russian Banks for Bushehr Over Jewish Officers," *Nucleonics Week*, February 13, 1997.

[8]See sections on Ballistic Missile Programs in this chapter.

[9]See chapter on Missile Proliferation in this volume.

[10]See Mark Hibbs, "Bonn Will Decline Teheran Bid to Resuscitate Bushehr Project," *Nucleonics Week*, May 2, 1991, p. 17.

[11]Leonard S. Spector, "Threats in the Middle East," *Orbis*, Spring 1992, p. 186.

[12]Akbar Etemad, "Iran," in Harald Mueller, *European Non-Proliferation Policy* (Oxford: Oxford University Press, 1987). Etemad was the chairman of the Atomic Energy Organization of Iran under the Shah. The research reactor was able to operate intermittently, despite the termination of U.S. fuel supplies for the reactor, which employed weapons-usable 93 percent enriched uranium. In 1987, Iran signed a $5.5 million contract with Argentina under which the latter agreed to reconfigure the Tehran research reactor to use 20 percent enriched uranium fuel (not usable for weapons) and to supply new fuel for the facility. The deal undercut U.S. efforts to establish a total embargo on nuclear sales to Tehran. See "Iran to Receive Nuclear Technology, Know-How," *Noticias Argentinas*, May 18, 1987, in *Foreign Broadcast Information Service (FBIS)/Latin America*, May 19, 1987.

[13]Richard Kessler, "Argentina to Enforce Curbs on Nuclear Trade with Iran," *Nucleonics Week*, March 14, 1987, p. 12; "Iranian Reactor to Go Critical," *Nuclear Engineering International*, December 1984.

[14]See "Hashemi-Rafsanjani Speaks on the Future of the IRGC [Iranian Revolutionary Guards Corps]," *Tehran Domestic Service*, October 6, 1988, in *FBIS-NES*, October 7, 1988, p. 52.

[15]"Iran Confirms Nuclear Cooperation with China," *United Press International*, November 6, 1991; R. Jeffrey Smith, "China-Iran Nuclear Tie Long Known," *Washington Post*, October 31, 1991.

[16]"Iran's Weapons of Mass Destruction," *Jane's Intelligence Review*, Special Report No. 6, 1995, pp. 12-13; Smith, "China-Iran Nuclear Tie," ibid.; Roland Evans and Robert Novak, "Beijing's Tehran Connection," *Washington Post*, June 26, 1991; R. Jeffrey Smith, "Officials Say Iran Is Seeking a Nuclear Arms Capability," *Washington Post*, October 30, 1991; Testimony of Gary Milhollin, Director, Wisconsin Project on Arms Control, Hearings on U.S.–China Relations, U.S. Senate Foreign Relations Committee, June 13, 1991. The mini research reactors are the Miniature Neutron Source Reactor (MNSR) and the Heavy-Water Zero-Power Reactor (HWZPR). In addition, there are two Chinese-supplied sub-critical assemblies located at Esfahan, the Light Water Sub-Critical "Reactor" (LWSCR) and the Graphite Sub-Critical "Reactor" (GSCR). See International Atomic Energy Agency, *The Annual Report for 1995*, GC (40)-8, July 1996, pp. 83, 90; Mark Hibbs, "U.S. Warned Not to Try Using IAEA to Isolate or Destabilize Iran," *Nucleonics Week*, October 8, 1992, p. 10.

[17]See Mark Hibbs, "Iran Sought Sensitive Nuclear Supplies from Argentina, China," *Nucleonics Week*, September 24, 1992, p. 2; Steve Coll, "U.S. Halted Nuclear Bid by Iran," *Washington Post*, November 17, 1992.

[18]See "World Survey: Iran," *Nuclear Engineering International*, June 1993, p. 21; "China in Pact to Help Iran Build A-Plant," *New York Times*, July 7, 1993; "Nuclear Energy Chief on Iran's Program, Israel," *Tehran Times*, August 18, 1993, in *FBIS-NES-93-166*, August 30, 1993, p. 75; Mark Hibbs, "Russian, Chinese Reactors Might Be Sited at Bushehr," *Nucleonics Week*, October 14, 1993, p. 9; "Beijing Exports Nuclear Power Plants to Pakistan, Iran," *Xinhua Domestic Service* (Beijing), in *JPRS-TND-93-038*, December 29, 1993, p. 1; R. Jeffrey Smith, "China Nuclear Deal With Iran Is Feared," *Washington Post*, April 17, 1995.

[19]Siemens of Germany began construction of the reactors in 1976, but completion was halted after the 1979 Iranian Revolution. At that point, about 85 percent of the civil work on Bushehr I was complete: The inner steel containment vessel had been completed and tested; the outer concrete dome was incomplete. Work on Bushehr II was also partially finished when construction stopped in 1979. In the intervening years, both reactors were damaged during bombing raids in the Iran-Iraq War. Iran failed to convince Siemens to resume construction, largely due to pressure from the United States. The Russian-Iranian nuclear agreement envisions the installation of a VVER-1000 (1,000-MWe) power reactor at Bushehr I. Although the original facility was designed for a Siemens-designed 1,300-MWe pressurized water reactor, the Russians plan to retrofit into the original structure as much of their VVER-1000 technology as possible. One source noted that the primary circuit for the VVER-1000 reactor, which utilizes horizontal steam generators, occupies a much larger space than the original German construction, requiring the enlargement of the current structure. See "Russian German Hybrid for Bushehr?" *Nuclear Engineering International*, November 1994, p. 10.

[20]For general background on the deal see "Russia to Help Set Up Nuclear Plant in Bushehr," *Mena* (Cairo), April 13, 1994, in *FBIS-NES-94-072*, April 14, 1994; "Russia Helps Build Bushehr Nuclear Power Plant," *Jomhuri-Yeeslami* (Tehran), April 13, 1994, in *FBIS-NES-94-079*, April 25, 1994, p. 82; Mark Hibbs, "Minatom Says It Can Complete One Siemens PWR in Iran in Five Years," *Nucleonics Week*, September 29, 1994; "Agreement Signed for Bushehr," *Nuclear Engineering International*, November 1994, p. 4; Elaine Sciolino, "Iran's Nuclear Goals Lie in Half-Built Plant," *New York Times*, May 19, 1995; Boris Konovalov, "Russia on Track to Start Work on Iran's Bushehr-1 in October," *Nucleonics Week*, September 7, 1995, p. 7; David Albright, "An Iranian Bomb?" *Bulletin of the Atomic Scientists*, July/August 1995, p. 22.

[21]In early 1995, several Republican members of Congress suggested that the United States substantially curtail its aid to Russia unless it canceled the reactor deal. See Thomas W. Lippman, "Russia-Iran Atomic Deal Irks U.S.," *Washington Post*, February 12, 1995; Elaine Sciolino, "Congress Presses Russia, and Clinton, Over Iran Deal," *New York Times*, February 23, 1995. Congress subsequently adopted legislation to this effect (see New U.S. Sanctions Laws subsection of this chapter).

[22]See Mark Hibbs, "U.S. Officials Say Iran Is Pursuing Fissile Material Production Research," *Nuclear Fuel*, December 7, 1992, p. 5; "Iran and the Bomb," *Frontline*, PBS Network, April 13, 1993; Mark Hibbs, "German-U.S. Nerves Frayed Over Nuclear Ties to Iran," *Nuclear Fuel*, March 14, 1994, p. 9; Mark Hibbs, "Sharif University Activity Continues Despite IAEA Visit, Bonn Agency Says," *Nuclear Fuel*, March 28, 1994, p. 10; Elaine Sciolino, "Iran Says It Plans 10 Nuclear Plants But No Atom Arms," *New York Times*, May 16, 1995.

[23]Leonard S. Spector and Jacqueline R. Smith, *Nuclear Ambitions* (Boulder, CO: Westview Press, 1990), p. 212.

[24]Supplemental questions for the record submitted by John M. Deutch, Director of Central Intelligence, *Hearings on Global Proliferation of Weapons of Mass Destruction*, Permanent Subcommittee on Investigations, Governmental Affairs Committee, U.S. Senate, March 20, 1996, p. 867.

[25]Sciolino, "Iran Says It Plans 10 Nuclear Plants," op. cit. In 1994, based on reports from its foreign intelligence agency that Iran's Sharif University was involved in procurement activities to acquire nuclear-weapons-related technology and materials, the German government began to block nuclear-related exports to Iran. (See discussion of international embargo later in this chapter.) Steve Vogel, "Allies Oppose Bonn's Iran Links," *Washington Post*, November 6, 1993; Elaine Sciolino, "U.S. and Germany at Odds on Isolating Iran," *New York Times*, December 2, 1993; David A. Schwarzbach, *Iran's Nuclear Program: Energy or Weapons?* (Washington, DC: Natural Resources Defense Council, 1995), p. 5.

[26]Albright, "An Iranian Bomb?" op. cit., p. 21.

[27]Testimony of CIA Director Deutch, Senate Comm. on Governmental Affairs, March 20, 1996, op. cit. Deutch highlighted a 1993 incident in which three Iranians apparently associated with Iran's intelligence service were captured in Turkey while seeking to acquire nuclear material from smugglers from the former Soviet Union.

[28]The threat of diversion raised by the incident, as well as U.S. concerns over inadequate security arrangements at the storage site, led to "Operation Sapphire." Following arrangements with Kazakhstan, and in consultation with Russia, a U.S. technical team transported the HEU to Oak Ridge National Laboratory. See R. Jeffrey Smith, "U.S. Takes Nuclear Fuel," *Washington Post*, November 23, 1994; Steven Erlanger, "Kazakhstan Thanks U.S. on Uranium," *New York Times*, November 25, 1994; Elaine Sciolino, "Calling Iran 'Outlaw State,' Christopher Defends U.S. Trade Ban," *New York Times*, May 2, 1995; Mark Hibbs, "Kazakhs Say Iran Sought LEU For VVER Fuel, Not 'Sapphire' Fuel," *Nuclear Fuel*, July 17, 1995.

[29]Mark Hibbs, "IAEA Explores Iran's Intentions, Minus Evidence of Weapons Drive," *Nucleonics Week*, February 13, 1992, p. 12; "Atomic Team Reports on Iran Probe," *Washington Post*, February 14, 1992; "Iran: IAEA Inspection Team Finds Nothing Suspicious," *Nuclear Engineering International*, April 1992, p. 67; Steve Coll, "Nuclear Inspectors Check Sites in Iran," *Washington Post*, November 20, 1993; Mark Hibbs, "IAEA Says It Found No Non-Peaceful Activity

During Recent Iran Visit," *Nucleonics Week*, December 16, 1993, p. 11. Israeli officials believe that, during the February 1992 inspection, the IAEA inspectors were taken to the wrong sites. At the time, the Israeli government warned that it would take military action to halt Iran from developing nuclear weapons if political measures prove ineffective. See "Israeli Warns of Iran," *Washington Post*, June 15, 1992; "Efforts to Halt Iranian Program," *Ha'aretz*, translated by *FBIS-NES*, June 12, 1992, p. 29. On October 3, 1994, IAEA Director General Hans Blix had said that his agency would continue to provide technical assistance to Iran until conclusive evidence was presented that Iran is violating its NPT obligations. See Mark Hibbs, "IAEA Sees No Current Grounds to Deny Iran Technical Assistance," *Nucleonics Week*, October 6, 1994, p. 11.

[30]See Statement by Joseph S. Bermudez Jr. before the Subcommittee on International Security, International Organizations and Human Rights, House Committee on Foreign Affairs, September 14, 1993; William C. Potter and Harlan W. Jencks, eds., *The International Missile Bazaar* (Boulder, CO: Westview Press, 1994), p. 65; Office of the Secretary of Defense, *Proliferation: Threat and Response*, April 1996, p. 16. Also see Barbara Starr, "Iran Gets 'Scud' TELs From North Korea," *Jane's Defence Weekly*, May 13, 1995, p. 5; International Institute of Strategic Studies, *The Military Balance 1993/94* (London: Oxford University Press for IISS, 1993), p. 116.

[31]*Los Angeles Times*, April 11, 1992; "Iran Buying North Korean Nodong-1?" *Arms Control Reporter*, 1992, p. 706.B.84.

[32]See Testimony of Director of Central Intelligence R. James Woolsey before the Subcommittee on International Security, International Organizations, and Human Rights, House Committee on Foreign Affairs, July 28, 1993; "Allegations of 'Secret' Contacts With DPRK on Missiles to Iran," IDF Radio (Tel Aviv), March 22, 1994, in *JPRS-TND-94-008*, April 1, 1994, p. 34.

[33]Statement by Joseph S. Bermudez Jr., House Committee on Foreign Affairs, op. cit.; "Iran's Weapons of Mass Destruction," *Jane's*, op. cit., p. 21.

[34]In arguing this case, Russia noted that the United States itself had promoted the sale of a light-water reactor to North Korea—a state widely viewed as in violation of the NPT—under the October 1994 Agreed Framework. In that context, Russian officials noted, Washington argued that the IAEA inspections would be able to ensure that the facility was not misused for weapons purposes. In arguing the United States had not presented evidence about the existence of an Iranian nuclear weapons program, Russia was contradicting its own 1993 intelligence assessment. It stated that Iran had "a program of military applied research in the nuclear realm" and that "the Iranian leadership had created a system of purchasing 'dual use' technology overseas." "Proliferation Issues: Russian Federation Foreign Intelligence Service Report," *JPRS-TND-93-007*, March 5, 1993, p. 28. Also, see Albright, "An Iranian Bomb?" op. cit., p. 25.

[35]In March 1993, Great Britain announced that, in the context of its support of a "harmonized approach" among G-7 and European Community countries for controlling exports to Iran, it had decided not to approve licenses for (1) items on international lists of regulated military and atomic energy equipment or (2) for goods "where there was knowledge or reason to suspect" that such goods would be used for military purposes. "U.K. Support for U.S. Embargo on Iran is Linked to Rushdie Affair," *Islamic Republic News Agency* (Tehran), March 3, 1993, reported by *British Broadcasting Corporation*, March 4, 1994. In 1994, the German government also began to block nuclear-related exports to Iran.

[36]See Appendix H on Wassenaar Arrangement.

[37]Kenneth Katzman, *Iran: U.S. Policy and Options*, Congressional Research Service, Report 97-231f, February 11, 1997, p. 8.

[38]Iran-Iraq Arms Non-proliferation Act of 1992, Division A, Title XVI, Sec. 1603, P.L. 102-484, (Oct. 23, 1992) 106 Stat. 2571, (50 U.S. Code Section 1701, note). The restriction applies both to *nuclear* dual-use commodities, i.e., those having nuclear and non-nuclear uses and which are regulated internationally by the NSG, and *strategic* dual-use commodities, i.e., those having military and non-military uses, which were formerly regulated under the Coordinating Committee on Multilateral Export Controls (COCOM) and are currently regulated under the Wassenaar Arrangement. (See Appendices on NSG and Wassenaar Arrangement; the latter also elaborates on COCOM.) Within the United States, exports of both categories of dual-use items are licensed by the Commerce Department, pursuant to the Export Administration Act.

[39]For an excellent review of U.S. sanctions against Iran, see Kenneth Katzman, *Iran: U.S. Policy and Options*, op. cit. See Export

Administration Act of 1979, as amended, Sec. 40 (22 U.S. Code 2780) and Sec. 6(j) (50 U.S. Code App 2405 [j]).

[40]"Imposition of Missile Proliferation Sanctions Against North Korean and Iranian Entities," *Federal Register*, April 7, 1992, p. 11767. The North Korean entities were Lyongakasan Machineries and Equipment Export Corporation (North Korea) and the Changgwang Credit Corporation (North Korea). The sanctions expired 24 months later.

[41]Interview with U.S. officials, March 6, 1997, Washington, D.C.

[42]See "Imposition of Missile Proliferation Sanctions," *Federal Register*, op. cit. Under a provision of the missile non-proliferation law applicable to states with non-market economies that are not former members of the Warsaw Pact, the sanctions extended not only to the two entities cited above, but to all activities of the North Korean government affecting the development or production of electronics, space systems or equipment, and military aircraft. Also, interview with U.S. officials, March 6, 1997, Washington, D.C.

[43]In light of these activities, the German export control authorities have begun denying licenses for any equipment destined for Sharif University. See Mark Hibbs, "No German Nuclear Equipment Getting to Iran, Bonn Vows," *Nuclear Fuel*, April 10, 1995, p. 5; Thomas W. Lippman, "Stepped-Up Nuclear Effort Renews Alarm About Iran," *Washington Post*, April 17, 1995; Mark Hibbs, "Investigators Deny Iran Smuggled Weapons Material From Germany," *Nucleonics Week*, February 1, 1996, p. 14.

[44]"Clinton's Iran Embargo Initiative Impedes U.S. NPT Diplomatic Effort," *Nuclear Fuel*, May 8, 1995, p. 6; Mark Hibbs, "Countering U.S. Claims, Moscow Says Iran Nuclear Program Is Peaceful," *Nucleonics Week*, February 9, 1995, p. 4; Mark Hibbs, "Iran's Arab Neighbors Don't Believe U.S. Has Proof of Weapons Ambitions," *Nucleonics Week*, April 20, 1995, p. 10.

[45]The Congress, as a result of the November 1994 elections, was now dominated by Republicans.

[46]Executive Order 12959, April 30, 1995; "Statement by Secretary of State Warren Christopher Regarding U.S. Sanctions Against Iran," *Federal News Service*, May 1, 1995; U.S. Department of State, "Press Briefing by Secretary of State Warren Christopher on the President's Executive Order on Iran," May 1, 1995.

[47]Office of the White House Press Secretary, "Remarks by the President at World Jewish Congress Dinner, New York, April 30, 1995."

[48]Albright, "An Iranian Bomb?" op. cit., p. 22. Also see Mark Hibbs, "Russia, Others Pressed Iran Prior to NPT Extension Vote," *Nuclear Fuel*, May 22, 1995, p. 9.

[49]See Mark Hibbs, "Iran May Withdraw From NPT Over Western Trade Barriers," *Nucleonics Week*, September 22, 1994, p. 1; Mark Hibbs, "Western Group Battles Iran at Third Prep Com Session," *Nucleonics Week*, September 22, 1994, p. 9; Mark Hibbs, "It's 'Too Early' for Tehran to Leave NPT, Delegates Say," *Nuclear Fuel*, September 26, 1994, p. 9; Hibbs, "Russia, Others Pressed Iran Prior to NPT Extension Vote," op. cit., p. 9.

[50]See "'Source': Nuclear Plans With China Near Collapse," *Al-Sharq Al-Awsat* (London), May 21, 1995, in *FBIS-NES-95-099*, May 23, 1995, p. 54; "Moscow to Proceed With Nuclear Deal With Iran," *ITAR-TASS* (Moscow), October 2, 1995, in *FBIS-SOV-95-191*, October 3, 1995, p. 22; Mark Hibbs, "Iran, China Said to Disagree Only on Site Selection for New PWRs," *Nucleonics Week*, October 5, 1995, p. 1; "China/Iran: Reactor Plans Shelved—Again?" *Nucleonics Week*, January 11, 1996, p. 9; Supplementary materials submitted by Barbara Larkin, Acting Assistant Secretary for Legislative Affairs, U.S. State Department, *Hearings on Current and Projected National Security Threats to the United States and Its Interests Abroad*, Select Committee on Intelligence, U.S. Senate, February 22, 1996 (supplementary materials supplied May 23, 1996), p. 135.

[51]Iran-Iraq Arms Non-Proliferation Act, P.L. 102-484, Division A, Title XVI, Secs. 1604 and 1605, (October 23, 1992), 106 Stat. 2571, (50 U.S. Code 1701, note), as amended by the Defense Authorization Act for Fiscal Year 1996, P.L. 104-107, Sec. 1408, (Feb. 10, 1996).

[52]Iran-Iraq Arms Non-Proliferation Act, ibid., Sec. 1606.

[53]Foreign Operations, Export Financing and Related Programs Appropriations Act, for Fiscal Year 1996, P.L. 104-107, Title II, subsection (o) under the heading "Assistance for the New Independent States of the Former Soviet Union"; Department of Defense Appropriations, 1997, P. L. 104-208, Title IX, subsection (o) under the heading "Assistance for the New Independent States of the Former Soviet

Union." See also "Russia Firm on Iran Reactor Sale; Could Mean Loss of U.S. Aid," *Post-Soviet Nuclear & Defense Monitor*, November 17, 1995, p. 4.

[54]See references to Appropriations Act, P.L. 104-107 and 104-208 in preceding note.

[55]Presidential Determination No. 96-24 of May 9, 1996, *Federal Register*, May 23, 1996; Presidential Determination No. 97-01 of November 8, 1996, p. 26031; *Federal Register* November 20, 1996, pp. 59169-59172; Presidential Determination No 97-23 of May 5, 1997, *Federal Register*, May 22, 1997; Presidential Determination No. 98-4 of November 14, 1997, *Federal Register*, December 2, 1997; "President Clinton Says Aid to Russia Critical to National Security," *Post-Soviet Nuclear & Defense Monitor*, May 31, 1996, p. 1.

[56]Mark Hibbs, "IAEA Will Explore New Charges Iran Has Enrichment Program," *Nucleonics Week*, February 22, 1996, p. 4.

[57]See Hibbs, "No German Nuclear Equipment Getting to Iran," op. cit.; "Pakistan: Iran Links Denied," *Nucleonics Week*, June 15, 1995, p. 15. Supplemental questions for the record, submitted by CIA Director Deutch, *Hearings on Global Proliferation*, op. cit. One report indicated that Karl-Heinz Schaab, a former expert with Urenco (a European uranium-enrichment consortium) suspected of passing design information to Iraq's clandestine nuclear program, may have sought refuge from German authorities in Iran. See Mark Hibbs, "Hunted German Expert May Be Hiding in Iran," *Nucleonics Week*, February 8, 1996, p. 12.

[58]"Iran Cleric Says Enemies of Islam Barred From Vote," *Reuters*, February 23, 1996; Bizhan Torabi, "Four Factions Fight for Control of the Iranian Majlis," *Deutsche Presse-Agentur*, February 28, 1996; Kathy Evans, "Iranian Clerics Reject a Third of Candidates," *Guardian*, February 29, 1996; "Strong Turnout in Iran Parliamentary Elections," *Reuters*, March 8, 1996; "Run-Offs to Decide Half of Iran Parliament Seats," *Reuters*, March 14, 1996; William Maclean, "Iran Conservatives Appear Largest Bloc in Polls," *Reuters*, April 20, 1996; Robin Allen, "Iran's Reformers Face Uphill Battle: Despite Electoral Success, Tehran Moderates are Opposed by a Range of Entrenched Interests," *Financial Times*, April 26, 1996.

[59]Office of the Secretary of Defense, *Proliferation: Threat and Response 1996*, op. cit., p. 14.

[60]Bill Gertz, "Iran Gets China's Help on Nuclear Arms," *Washington Times*, April 17, 1996.

[61]The facility was legal under the NPT and had been declared to the IAEA, but Iran's interest in acquiring a nuclear weapons capability inevitably made this a suspect facility in the eyes of the non-proliferation community. (Interview with senior U.S. administration official, October 1996.)

[62]Interview with Chinese official, Washington, D.C., March 1997. But see R. Jeffrey Smith, "China May Cancel Proposed Sale of Nuclear Facility to Iran," *Washington Post*, November 6, 1996; Mark Hibbs, "China Has Far to Go Before U.S. Will Certify, Agencies Now Say," *Nucleonics Week*, December 12, 1996, p. 1; Mark Hibbs, "Iran Told IAEA It Will Build Chinese UF6 Plan at Isfahan," *Nuclear Fuel*, December 16, 1996, p. 1.

[63]*Federal Register,* May 23, 1996, p. 26031.

[64]Con Coughlin, "Britain Seizes Bomb-Grade Steel Cargo," *Washington Times*, August 12, 1996.

[65]Iran and Libya Sanctions Act of 1996, P.L. 104-172, Sec. 5(A),50 U.S. Code 1701; see David E. Sanger, "Congress Curbs Iran Investment From Overseas," *New York Times*, June 20, 1996; Clay Chandler, "U.S. Expects Furor Over Trade Sanctions at Summit," *Washington Post*, June 27, 1996; Rick Atkinson, "Divergent Policies Toward Iran Strain U.S.–German Relations," *Washington Post*, June 27, 1996; Eric Pianin, "Clinton Approves Sanctions for Investors in Iran, Libya," *Washington Post*, August 6, 1996. The act provides the lowering of the threshold for imposing sanctions to $20 million a year after enactment.

[66]Iran and Libya Sanctions Act of 1996 in preceding note, P.L. 104-172, Sec. 3.

[67]For the controversy over sanctions, see "U.S. Ponders Sanctions for Oil Deal in Iran," *Washington Post*, May 14, 1997; Dan Morgan and David B. Ottaway, "U.S. Won't Bar Pipeline Across Iran," *Washington Post*, July 27, 1997; Anne Swardson, "France, U.S. At Odds on Iran Oil Deal," *Washington Post*, September 30, 1997; Thomas W. Lippman, "U.S. Defers Sanctions on Iran Gas Deal," *Washington Post*, October 4, 1997; David B. Ottaway and Dan Morgan, "Deal Tests U.S. Policy on Tehran," *Washington Post*, October 12, 1997; David E. Sanger,

"U.S. Sanctions May Backfire on Russian-Iran Oil Deal," *Washington Post*, October 16, 1997.

[68]"Iran Threat to Block N-Test Treaty," *Financial Times*, August 13, 1996; "India: Iranian Support Over CTBT Seen as Possible 'Liability,'" *Telegraph* (Calcutta), August 14, 1996, in *FBIS-NES-96-160*, August 14, 1996; "India Blocks Consensus on CTB, Treaty May Still Go to UN," *Arms Control Today*, August 1996, p. 31.

[69]Presidential Determination 97-01, op. cit.

[70]In early October 1995, upon the completion of preliminary studies at the Bushehr reactor site, Reza Amrollahi, the head of the Iranian Atomic Energy Organization (AEOI) optimistically declared that the unit would be finished within three years. Konovalov, "Russia on Track to Restart Work," op. cit.; "Preliminary Studies Completed at Bushehr," *OMRI Daily Digest*, November 8, 1995, p. 2; Mark Hibbs, "Russian Industry Now Tapping Iran Bushehr Credit, AEOI Says," *Nucleonics Week*, January 25, 1996, p. 4.

[71]Mark Hibbs, "Russia-Iran Bushehr PWR Project Shows Little Concrete Progress," *Nucleonics Week*, September 26, 1996, p. 3.

[72]Michael Eisenstadt, "Halting Russian Aid to Iran's Nuclear and Ballistic Programs," *PolicyWatch*, September 25, 1997; Mark Hibbs, "Iran, Russia Still Settling Countertrade Terms for PWR's," *Nucleonics Week*, October 5, 1995, p. 9.

[73]In early 1996 it was reported that the IAEA would discuss with Iran renewed charges that the latter had embarked on a clandestine uranium enrichment program. This discussion apparently was going to take place as part of the Agency's campaign to convince Iran to accept the IAEA's "93+2" enhanced safeguards program, which provides for more intrusive inspections and environmental surveillance than would be carried out under Iran's existing NPT safeguards agreement. Hibbs, "IAEA Will Explore New Charges," op. cit.

In September 1996, however, Iran refused to permit the IAEA to begin taking environmental monitoring samples at declared sites as called for in the then still voluntary Part 1 of the "93+2" program. The Agency was able to conduct a "routine" inspection at the Esfahan Nuclear Technology Center. Mark Hibbs, "Iran Balking at Approval of IAEA Environmental Monitoring," *Nuclear Fuel*, September 23, 1996, p. 2; Mark Hibbs, "IAEA Plans Safeguards Inspection at Key Iranian Technology Center," *Nuclear Fuel*, October 7, 1996, p. 9; Hibbs, "Iran Told IAEA It Will Build Chinese UF6 Plan at Isfahan," op. cit.

In July 1997, IAEA Director General Hans Blix visited two new Iranian nuclear research centers, the first located at Bonab in West Ajarbaijan, and the second at Ramsar, in Mazandaran Province. At Bonab, Blix was shown research in the use of nuclear isotopes for food preservation. During his visit to Ramsar, Blix was briefed on research activities focusing on above-average levels of natural radioactivity. Subsequently, IAEA officials stated that there was no sign of any undeclared or clandestine nuclear activity at the two sites. Mark Hibbs, "No Sign of Undeclared Activity at New Iranian Sites, IAEA Says," *Nucleonics Week*, August 7, 1997, p. 9.

On September 29, 1997, at the opening session of the IAEA General Conference, the new president of the Atomic Energy Organization of Iran (AEOI), Gholam Reza Aghazadeh, stated that "our facilities have proven transparent through the [IAEA's] various inspections." In response, Director General Blix, in a private meeting with Aghazadeh, expressed dissatisfaction with the statement as well as with numerous similar Iranian statements claiming that the IAEA's Department of Safeguards "has exonerated [Iran] from unsubstantiated reports it has a nuclear weapons development program." (Mark Hibbs, "Blix Told Iran Not to Distort Result of Safeguards Inspections," *Nucleonics Week*, October 16, 1997, p. 15.) Blix proceeded to explain that under Part II of the IAEA Program 93+2, the IAEA's authority to pursue unofficial reports of unauthorized nuclear activities will be enhanced (see Appendix D on IAEA safeguards).

[74]Iraq's crash program to develop a nuclear device on the eve of the 1991 Gulf War, it may be noted, was based on the seizure of highly enriched uranium that was under IAEA inspection at the time. See Iraq chapter.

[75]Mark Hibbs, "Iran May Keep Russian Spent Fuel Or Take Plutonium, REPU, Waste," *Nuclear Fuel*, December 18, 1995, p. 1; Hibbs, "Iran, Russia Still Settling Countertrade Terms," op. cit.

Interviewed in late 1995, a Russian Minatom official stated that Moscow had offered Iran several alternatives for disposing of the spent fuel produced in the Russian-supplied reactors: Iran could chose to store the spent fuel in that country, return it to Russia for interim storage for a period of 25 to 30 years (after which the spent fuel would be returned to Iran for storage), or have the fuel reprocessed in Russia, an activity that would chemically separate the spent fuel into plutonium, reprocessed uranium (REPU), and radioactive high-level waste (HLW). If the last option were chosen, Russia would return all three, including the weapons-usable plutonium, to Iran. The returned REPU and plutonium would be placed under IAEA safeguards.

[76]Eisenstadt, "Halting Russian Aid," op. cit.

[77]John Lancaster, "The Large Turnout in Iranian Election," *Washington Post*, May 24, 1997; John Lancaster, "Moderate Iranian Wins," *Washington Post*, May 25, 1997; John Lancaster, "Iranians Voted for New Ideas, Not a New System," *Washington Post*, May 26, 1997; Ed Blanche, "Iran Under Khatami; Pariah or Potential Peace Partner," *Jane's Intelligence Review*," November 1997, p. 505. John Lancaster, "New Iranian Regime, Arab Neighbors Show Signs of Easing Tense Relations," *Washington Post*, September 20, 1997.

[78]In an article in *Foreign Affairs* in April 1997, Zbigniew Brzezinski and Brent Scowcroft, former national security advisors during the Carter, Ford and Bush administrations, argued for a relaxation of economic sanctions against Iran and Iraq. They wrote: "In trying to isolate both of the Gulf's regional powers, the policy lacks strategic viability and carries high financial and economic cost." They called for a "more nuanced approach" to Iran, using both a carrot and a stick to control the "single most worrisome aspect of Iranian behavior," which is its alleged pursuit of nuclear weapons. In their view, the policy was driving Iran towards Russia. As cited in Blanche, "Iran Under Khatami," op. cit., p. 506.

[79]John F. Harris, "Clinton 'Hopeful' But Skeptical on New Iranian Leader," *Washington Post*, May 30, 1997.

[80]"Iranian Minister: U.S. Can't Divide and Rule," *Washington Post*, October 5, 1997. Also see Anwar Faruqui, "Iran—President," *Associated Press*, May 27, 1997; "U.S. Should Start Rapprochement With Iran," *Reuters*, July 29, 1997; "Iran Says U.S. Should Drop Charges of Terrorism," *Reuters*, August 21, 1997; "Iran Paper Repeats Conditions for Talks With U.S.," *Reuters*, August 25, 1997.

[81]Thomas W. Lippman, "U.S. Defers Sanctions on Iran Gas Deal," *Washington Post*, October 4, 1997; David B. Ottaway and Dan Moran, "Deal Tests U.S. Policy On Tehran," *Washington Post*, October 12, 1997.

[82]Mark Hibbs, "Amrollahi Ouster Challenges Stalled Bushehr PWR Project," *Nucleonics Week*, October 9, 1997, p. 12.

[83]Eisenstadt, "Halting Russian Aid," op. cit.

[84]Mark Hibbs, "IAEA, Russia to U.S.: Go Public in U.N. Bodies or Drop Claim," *Nucleonics Week,* October 9, 1997, p. 1. Also see R. Jeffrey Smith, "Administration Concerned About Russia's Nuclear Cooperation With Iran," *Washington Post,* July 3, 1997; David Hoffman, "Yeltsin Denies Selling Arms to Iran," *Washington Post*, September 27, 1997.

[85]Hibbs, "IAEA, Russia to U.S.," ibid.

[86]Hibbs, "Amrollahi Ouster Challenges Stalled Bushehr," op. cit., p. 13.

[87]Ibid. But also see "Russia: Iran Pays the First Installment on Bushehr Nuclear Plant," *Interfax* (Moscow), March 19, 1997, in *FBIS-SOV-97-078*, March 19, 1997.

[88]Smith, "China's Pledge to End Iran Nuclear Aid," op. cit.; R. Jeffrey Smith, "China to Purchase U.S. Reactors After Curbing Ties to Iran," *Washington Post*, October 25, 1997; Mark Hibbs and Michael Knapik, "China Agrees to End Nuclear Trade With Iran When Two Projects Completed," *Nuclear Fuel,* November 3, 1997, p. 3. Also see Mark Hibbs and Michael Knapik, "U.S. Aims for China Certification Timed with Fall Visit by Jiang," *Nuclear Fuel,* July 28, 1997, p. 1; John Pomfret, "U.S. May Certify China on Curbing Nuclear Exports," *Washington Post*, September 18, 1997; Bill Gertz, "U.S. Offers Deal to Stop China's Iran Nuke Sales," *Washington Times*, October 14, 1997. Under the agreement China would be allowed to complete two ongoing projects. The first was the heavy-water zero-power reactor under construction at the Esfahan Nuclear Technology Center. According to a senior U.S. official, the unit, which uses natural uranium, cannot produce "any significant amount" of plutonium. The second project, a zirconium tube factory, does not pose a proliferation risk because Iran "lacks the ability to fabricate the reactor fuel rods that need such cladding." (Smith, "China's Pledge to End Iran Nuclear Aid," op. cit.)

[89]Smith, "China's Pledge to End Iran Nuclear Aid," ibid.

[90]Office of the Secretary of Defense, *Proliferation: Threat and Response,* November 1997, p. 27. See also *Proliferation: Threat and Response,* 1996, op. cit.; Alan George, "Iran Puts Together Scud-B Missiles," *Washington Times*, December 3, 1994.

[91]R. Jeffrey Smith, "Iran's Missile Technology Linked to China, Report Says," *Washington Post*, June 17, 1995; Barbara Opall, "U.S. Queries China on Iran," *Defense News*, June 19-25, 1995, p. 1; "China Denies Violating Missile Treaty," *United Press International*, June 20, 1995; Jim Mann, "U.S. Says China May Have Aided Iran Missile Program," *Los Angeles Times*, June 23, 1995; Eisenstadt testimony, op. cit.

[92]Elaine Sciolino, "CIA Report Says Chinese Sent Iran Arms Components," *New York Times*, June 21, 1995; "Chinese Shipments Violate Controls," *Jane's Defence Weekly*, July 1, 1995, p. 3.

[93]Even though these transactions apparently did not violate U.S. missile-export sanctions laws, Congress and the Clinton Administration in late May 1997 debated whether sanctions against China should be triggered under the Gore-McCain Act (aimed at preventing sales that destabilize countries or regions). See Thomas W. Lippman, "U.S. Confirms China Missile Sale to Iran," *Washington Post*, May 31, 1997. China is the primary supplier of Iran's inventory of land-based and shipborne anti-ship cruise missiles and is believed to be assisting Iran in the development of anti-ship missiles based on Chinese prototypes. Leonard S. Spector, "U.S. Efforts to Halt Weapons of Mass Destruction and Missile Programs in Iran," testimony before the Subcommittee on Near Eastern and South Asian Affairs of the Committee on Foreign Relations, U.S. Senate, April 17, 1997.

[94]*Federal Register*, June 28, 1996, p. 29785; "Daily on U.S. Government Notice of Sanctions Against DPRK," *Chosun Ilbo* (Seoul), June 30, 1996, in *FBIS-EAS-96-127*, July 3, 1996.

[95]Bill Gertz, "Iran Nuclear Missile Program," *Washington Times*, September 10, 1997; Bill Gertz, "Missiles in Iran of Concern to State," *Washington Times*, September 11, 1997. Also see Director of Central Intelligence, *The Acquisition of Technology Relating to Weapons of Mass Destruction and Advanced Conventional Munitions*, June 1997, p. 4.

[96]"White House Raises Missile Concerns," *United Press International,* February 2, 1997; Adam Tanner, "Russia Says It Is Not Helping Iran With Missiles," *Reuters*, March 5, 1997; "Report: Russian Missile Deal With Iran," *United Press International*, March 31, 1997; Steven Erlanger, "U.S. Telling Russia to Bar Aid to Iran by Arms Experts," *New York Times*, August 22, 1997; "Russia Denies Helping Iran Make Nuclear Missiles," *Reuters*, September 10, 1997; David Hoffman, "Russia Says It Thwarted Attempt by Iran to Get Missile Technology," *Washington Post*, October 3, 1997; Bill Gertz, "Russians Admit to Training Iranian Missile Technicians," *Washington Times*, October 3, 1997; Ed Blanche, "Russia Is Assisting Iran's Missile Drive, Says USA," *Jane's Defence Weekly*, October 1, 1997, p. 3.

[97]Gertz, "Russians Admit to Training," ibid.; Hoffman, "Russia Says It Thwarted Attempt," ibid.

[98]Thomas W. Lippman, "Israel Presses U.S. to Sanction Russia Missile Firm Aiding Iran," *Washington Post*, September 25, 1997; Bill Gertz, "U.S. May Punish Russia for Iran Sales," *Washington Post*, October 16, 1997.

[99]Iran Missile Proliferation Sanctions Act of 1997, Report 105-375, Committee on International Relations, U.S. House of Representatives, 105th Cong, 1st Sess., November 4, 1997, p. 6. Also see Bill Gertz, "House Seeks Sanctions on Russia for Iran Arms," *Washington Times*, October 10, 1997.

[100]See Miles A. Pomper, "Sanctions on Missile Aid to Iran Are Cleared by a Veto-Proof Margin," *Congressional Quarterly Weekly*, June 13, 1998, p. 1629.

[101]Supplementary materials submitted by Director Moseman, *Hearings on National Security Threats*, op. cit., p. 82; Supplementary materials submitted by Lt. Gen. Hughes, *Hearings on National Security Threats*, op. cit., p. 206.

[102]W. Seth Carus, "Iran's Weapons of Mass Destruction," paper presented at the Nixon Center for Peace and Freedom, February 20, 1997. On November 3, 1997, Iran officially ratified the Chemical Weapons convention by depositing the instruments of ratification at the United Nations. ("Iran: IRNA Correction—Iran Ratifies Chemical Weapons Treaty," *Irna* (Tehran), November 4, 1997, in *FBIS-TAC-97-308*, November 4, 1997.) Skeptics speculate that Iran became a party as a cover for its chemical weapons program; that is, by joining it is guaranteed access to the latest technology for developing pharmaceuticals and industrial chemicals. See Leonard S. Spector, "Chinese Assistance to Iran's Weapons of Mass Destruction and Missile

Programs," prepared testimony for the House International Relations Committee, September 12, 1996; Thomas W. Lippman, "Iran Ratifies Chemical Weapons Pact, Allowing International Inspections," *Washington Post,* November 10, 1997.

[103]Supplementary materials submitted by Director Moseman, *Hearings on National Security Threats,* op. cit., p. 82.

[104]The CIA has stated that while Iran's BW program is mostly in the research and development stages—likely investigating both toxins and live organisms as BW agents—Iran has "the technical infrastructure to support a significant BW program and needs little foreign assistance." Supplementary materials submitted by Director Moseman, *Hearings on National Security Threats,* op. cit., p. 82.

[105]Chinese firms have apparently played a role in supplying CW precursors to Iran, leading to the imposition of sanctions against several firms and persons in 1994, 1995, and May 1997. See Thomas W. Lippman, "U.S. Imposes Sanctions on China Firms," *Washington Post,* May 23, 1997; Steven Mufson, "China Demands U.S. Lift New Embargo," *Washington Post,* May 24, 1997. Also see Gary Milhollin and Meg Dennison, "China's Cynical Calculation," *New York Times,* April 24, 1995. A June 1997 CIA report stated that, during the period July-December 1996, "Iran [had] obtained considerable CW-related assistance from China in the form of production equipment and technology," See Director of Central Intelligence, *The Acquisition of Technology,* op. cit., p. 5.

[106]Testimony of John Holum, Director, Arms Control and Disarmament Agency, before the Subcommittee on International Operations and Human Rights, House International Relations Committee, on the FY 1998 Authorization for ACDA, March 5, 1997.

[107]Thomas W. Lippman, "U.S. Economic Offensive Against Iran's Energy Industry is Bearing Fruit," *Washington Post,* March 3, 1997.

[108]Mark Hibbs, "No Plutonium Smuggling Cases Confirmed by IAEA Since Munich," *Nucleonics Week,* March 6, 1997, p. 13.

[109]Undoubtedly a key Iranian security concern is that Iraq, in a future, post–UN sanctions environment, can be expected to try to reconstitute its own nuclear weapons program. Indeed, Iraq has been able to preserve a significant edge in conventional armaments vis-à-vis Iran and maintains residual chemical and biological warfare capabilities. Michael Eisenstadt, *Iranian Military Power: Capabilities and Intentions* (Washington, DC: The Washington Institute for Near East Policy, 1996), p. 10; Spector, "Threats in the Middle East," op. cit., p. 188.

Iran:
Map and Chart

University of Tehran. *U.S.-supplied, Argentine-fueled 5-MWt research reactor, subject to IAEA inspection.*
Sharif University of Technology. *Alleged experimental centrifuge uranium enrichment program, and possible research on plutonium separation.*

Esfahan Nuclear Research Center. *Chinese-supplied mini research reactors and sub-critical assemblies, subject to IAEA inspection. Possible location of nuclear-weapons design research.*

Civilian nuclear research facilities; first inspected by IAEA in July 1997.

Yazd Province. Location of uranium deposits.

Partially completed Bushehr 1 and 2 power reactors (1,300 MWe each). Damaged during the Iran-Iraq War; construction of Bushehr 1 restarted with Russian assistance.

Carnegie Endowment for International Peace, *Tracking Nuclear Proliferation*, 1998

IRAN: Nuclear Infrastructure

NAME/LOCATION OF FACILITY	TYPE/STATUS	IAEA SAFEGUARDS
P O W E R R E A C T O R S		
Bushehr I	Light-water, LEU, 1,000 MWe; under construction; damaged by Iraqi air strikes (1987, 1988).	Planned[a]
Bushehr II	Light-water, LEU, 1300 MWe; construction suspended; damaged by Iraqi air strikes (1987, 1988).	Planned[a]
R E S E A R C H R E A C T O R S		
Tehran	Light-water, HEU, 5 MWt; operating.[b]	Yes
Esfahan	Miniature Neutron Source Reactor (MNSR), 900 grams of HEU, 27 kw; operating.[c]	Yes
U R A N I U M E N R I C H M E N T		
Tehran	Alleged uranium centrifuge research program, Sharif University of Technology.[d]	
R E P R O C E S S I N G (P L U T O N I U M E X T R A C T I O N)		
Tehran	Laboratory-scale hot cells; may not be operational.[e]	
U R A N I U M P R O C E S S I N G		
Yazd Province	Discovery of uranium deposits announced in 1990.[f]	N/A (Not Applicable)
Tehran	Uranium-ore concentration facility; incapacitated.[g]	N/A
Esfahan	Planned uranium conversion plant that could produce UF_4, UF_6 and UO_2.[h] China cancelled its assistance in this area in 1997.	Yes

Abbreviations:

HEU	=	highly enriched uranium
LEU	=	low-enriched uranium
nat. U	=	natural uranium
MWe	=	millions of watts of electrical output
MWt	=	millions of watts of thermal output
KWt	=	thousands of watts of thermal output

NOTES (Iran Chart)

[a]This facility will be subject to IAEA safeguards, but since the reactors have not been installed and as there has been no nuclear material present at the site, standard IAEA inspections there have not yet begun. The Bushehr complex reportedly was among the locations "visited" by the IAEA in February 1992. U.S. government sources have indicated that, during the Iran-Iraq War, Iran was planning to move 22.4 kg of uranium hexafluoride (UF_6) to the Bushehr site to trigger limited IAEA monitoring, which Iran apparently believed might deter recurrent Iraqi air strikes on the Bushehr plants. However, the plan apparently was not implemented. Interviews with U.S. officials, December 1993.

[b]The reactor is located at the Amirabad Technical College, also called Tehran Nuclear Research Center. See "Iran's Weapons of Mass Destruction," *Jane's Intelligence Review,* Special Report No. 6, 1995, p. 10.

[c]Another Chinese-supplied miniature research reactor at the Esfahan Nuclear Technology Center is the heavy-water zero-power reactor (HWZPR). In addition, there are two Chinese-supplied sub-critical assemblies, the light-water sub-critical "reactor" (LWSCR), and the graphite sub-critical "reactor" (GSCR). These units, in themselves, do not pose a proliferation threat since their operation does not yield significant amounts of sensitive nuclear materials. (Interview with U.S. State Department official, December 1993.) Nevertheless, they provide for the development of nuclear technical expertise.

According to one report, a significant portion of the staff and equipment of the Amirabad Nuclear Research Center may have been moved to the Esfahan facility when the latter opened in the mid-1980s. See David A. Schwarzbach, *Iran's Nuclear Program: Energy or Weapons?* (Washington, DC: Natural Resources Defense Council, 1995), p. 6.

[d]Sharif University was one of the sites "visited" by the IAEA in November 1993, but reportedly no suspicious activity was discovered there. During their February 1992 "visit," IAEA officials reportedly observed a small Chinese-supplied calutron at Karaj and concurred with Iran's assertion that it was being used only for stable isotope production and not for uranium enrichment purposes. After the IAEA discovery in 1991 that Iraq was using large-size calutrons in the electromagnetic isotope separation (EMIS) process to enrich uranium, concerns increased that Iran might be pursuing a similar path. Despite its small size, some experts believe that the calutron could play a role in the development of an Iranian EMIS capability if it

were to be reverse engineered. See David Albright, "An Iranian Bomb?" *Bulletin of the Atomic Scientists,* July/August 1995, p. 25. In the last years of the Shah's regime, Iran began a laser isotope-separation (LIS) research program on uranium enrichment, and in October 1978 the Amirabad Nuclear Research Center in Tehran reportedly received four suitable lasers. See "Iran's Weapons of Mass Destruction," *Jane's,* op. cit., p. 11. According to one report, research is currently being performed at the Center employing those lasers. See Schwarzbach, *Iran's Nuclear Program,* op. cit., p. 6.

[e]This "hot cell" facility at the Amirabad Nuclear Research Center, which is small and only capable of separating grams of plutonium, was supplied (along with training) by the United States in the same timeframe as the 5-MWt thermal research reactor. If operational, the facility could serve as a tool for training Iranian scientists in separation techniques. See David Albright, "An Iranian Bomb?," op. cit., p. 25; "Iran's Weapons of Mass Destruction," *Jane's,* op. cit., p. 11.

[f]During its February 1992 "visit," the IAEA went to the desert town of Saghand in Yazd Province to check on reports that Iran was constructing a uranium-ore processing plant there, but only uranium-ore drilling rigs were found.

[g]Located at the University of Tehran, the facility was viewed by IAEA officials during their February 1992 "visit."

[h]This facility, reportedly, was to be built with Chinese assistance. See Bill Gertz, "Iran Gets China's Help on Nuclear Arms," *Washington Times,* April 17, 1996; Interview with senior U.S. administration official, October 1996. China withdrew from supporting uranium conversion and all its other nuclear assistance to Iran in late 1997—with two exceptions, neither of which was regarded as critical for nonproliferation objectives. (See also China chapter in this volume.)

Iraq

Iraq's near-term potential to develop nuclear weapons has been curtailed by the implementation of U.N. Security Council Resolution 687, adopted in April 1991 following Iraq's defeat in the 1991 Persian Gulf War. Resolution 687 established procedures for the destruction of Iraq's unconventional weapons and ballistic missile capabilities and for a subsequent monitoring program to prevent their reconstruction. Operation Desert Storm and the inspection and dismantling efforts of the International Atomic Energy Agency (IAEA), assisted by the U.N. Special Commission on Iraq (UNSCOM), are believed to have left no fissile materials and no nuclear-weapons-related production facilities in Iraq.

The U.S. intelligence community believes, however, that Iraq "has not abandoned its nuclear program and is taking steps designed to thwart the inspection process . . . [and] would seize any opportunity to buy nuclear weapons materials or a complete weapon," if these should become available (through, for example, leakage from the former Soviet Union).[1] The U.S. Department of Defense warned that if the U.N. sanctions were lifted and IAEA inspections were eased or terminated, Iraq "could probably rebuild its nuclear weapons program and manufacture a device in about five to seven years."[2] This timeline would be shortened if Iraq obtained fissile materials through illicit sources.

To preserve its weapons of mass destruction (WMD) capabilities, Iraq has resorted to a strategy of frustrating and hindering the U.N. inspection process. Iraq has forgone approximately $120 billion in oil revenues over the past six years—an indication of the price it has been prepared to pay in order to keep as much of its weapons infrastructure as possible.[3] Iraq's recalcitrance has been particularly apparent, lately, in the areas of ballistic missiles and biological weapons (BW).[4] By early 1996, UNSCOM had come to the conclusion that Iraq had resumed its foreign acquisition efforts to support development of long-range missiles. In late 1997, UNSCOM believed that Iraq may have been hiding a residual missile force of 18 to 25 indigenously produced Al Hussein missiles, which could be armed with biological or chemical warheads.

At the time of the defection of Lt. Gen. Hussein Kamel (Saddam Hussein's son-in-law and the official in charge of Iraq's WMD programs) Iraq disclosed to UNSCOM in August 1995 that, following the August 1990 invasion of Kuwait, it had embarked on a "crash program"—in parallel with its longer-term effort—to develop nuclear weapons and to develop a nuclear device by extracting weapons-grade material from safeguarded research-reactor fuel. Iraq also confirmed that, as UNSCOM had long suspected, it had developed an extensive array of biological weapons. This BW capability included 25 600-km-range Al Hussein missiles equipped with BW warheads. UNSCOM remained concerned in 1997 that Iraq may have retained stocks of BW and related manufacturing capabilities. Iraq also revealed more details about its extensive chemical weapon (CW) program, including the fact that it had deployed 50 Al Hussein missiles equipped with potent CW warheads as part of its active forces. In 1996, Iraqi officials indicated to UNSCOM that they considered their missile-based BW and CW weapons to be "strategic" capabilities, for potential use against cities in nearby countries. Although Iraq did not succeed in acquiring nuclear arms prior to the Gulf War, its other WMD posed an extremely grave threat to the populations of neighboring states, including Israel.

BACKGROUND

Nuclear Weapons Program. After Iraq's defeat in the 1991 Gulf War, the IAEA discovered that Iraq had violated its NPT obligations[5] by secretly pursuing a multi-billion-dollar nuclear weapons program, code-named "Petrochemical 3," with thousands of workers in numerous facilities.[6] In the course of its sixth inspection, the IAEA located thousands of pages of documents that revealed the extent of the Iraqi nuclear weapons program, forcing the Iraqi authorities to finally acknowledge its existence. The IAEA investigation revealed details of Baghdad's efforts to design an implosion-type nuclear explosive device and to test its non-nuclear components, including Iraq's plans to produce large quantities of lithium-6, a material used usually for the production of "boosted" atomic bombs and hydrogen bombs. In addition, the inspectors found that Iraq was pursuing a parallel program to develop a missile-delivery system for its nuclear arms. IAEA officials estimated that Iraq might have been able to, had the war not intervened, manufacture its first atomic weapons, using indigenously produced weapons-grade uranium, as early as the fall of 1993.[7]

Uranium-Enrichment Program. Iraq's efforts to produce weapons-grade uranium used virtually every viable uranium-enrichment process, including electromagnetic isotope separation (EMIS), the use of gas centrifuges, chemical enrichment, gaseous diffusion, and laser isotope separation. IAEA inspectors discovered that Iraq's EMIS infrastructure for enriching uranium was being built on an industrial scale.[8] The program had been initiated in 1982, when the Iraqi authorities decided to abandon Iraq's reactor program after Israel's 1981 bombing of the Osiraq research reactor.[9] The inspectors concluded, however, that by the time the 1991 Gulf War began, Iraq had succeeded in building and operating only a small number of EMIS units, near the Tuwaitha Nuclear Research Center and at a partially completed industrial-scale facility in Al Tarmiyah. The Iraqi Atomic Energy Commission (IAEC) had planned to install a total of 90 separators at the Al Tarmiyah plant and to build a replica facility at Ash Sharqat.[10] At the time of the Coalition bombings, 8 separators were operational and 17 were in the process of installation at Tarmiyah. The Ash Sharqat facility was about 85 percent completed, with no separators installed. The Coalition attacks, along with the Iraqis' subsequent dismantlement and deception activities, extensively damaged both installations.[11]

Estimates vary as to when Iraq could have achieved full production at Al Tarmiyah if the construction activities there had not been interrupted by the war. In the early stages of the inspection process, the IAEA team projected that, had construction not been halted, full production was 18 to 36 months away.[12] A more recent analysis of the Iraqi EMIS program—with the advantage of more information—concluded that the earliest the first goal quantity of HEU (15 kg) could have been achieved was mid-1994, with a more realistic date being somewhere around mid-1995.[13] By either estimate, Iraq had come much closer to a nuclear weapons breakthrough than Western authorities were aware before the Gulf War.

Iraq's EMIS program went undetected because it did not rely on state-of-the-art, imported equipment whose acquisition might have given the effort away. The Iraqis developed a number of prototype EMIS devices by: (1) using unclassified data that had entered the public domain simply because the enrichment process of the Manhattan Project era had become obsolete by Western standards; and (2) incorporating "modern microprocessor, fiber optic and computer-assisted manufacturing controls into the system to achieve gains in reliability, precision, and availability."[14] Iran also built impressive indigenous production facilities to fabricate the magnets, vacuum chambers, ion sources, and collector components of the EMIS separators.[15] Indeed, the EMIS program might have remained hidden from the IAEA inspection teams but for the fact that it was revealed by an Iraqi nuclear engineer who had defected to U.S. forces after the war.[16]

Iraq's gas centrifuge program for uranium enrichment was started later than the EMIS program, but given its scope, the Iraqis must have attached high importance to it.[17] The program relied heavily on foreign contractors who were willing to circumvent export controls and to sell classified design information of early Western-type centrifuges and high-tensile "maraging" steel used for the manufacture of centrifuges.[18] Three German experts, Bruno Stemmler, Walter Busse, and Karl-Heinz Schaab, provided crucial technical assistance to the Iraqi centrifuge program. All three had worked on centrifuge programs at MAN Technologie AG, a German firm that was a partner in Urenco, the European commercial enrichment consortium. In separate channels, these individuals advised Iraq on centrifuge design, sold machine tools and maraging steel, and supplied high-speed centrifuge components.[19]

Early in the inspection process Iraqi scientists insisted that development and testing work on centrifuges was carried out only at the Al Tuwaitha Nuclear Research Center. However, during the 15th IAEA inspection, they admitted that they had also done computer simulation research on centrifuges at Rashdiya, north of Baghdad.[20] The program intensified in mid-1987 and, within a year, work centered on two prototype centrifuges, one using a carbon fiber rotor tube, the other using a maraging steel cylinder. The Iraqis proved unsuccessful in their efforts to shape maraging steel into rotor tubes, or cylinders, on flow-forming machines, but they succeeded in building and testing two carbon fiber rotor machines obtained illegally from abroad.[21]

Based on high levels of foreign procurement, the Iraqis began construction of an industrial-scale plant to manufacture and test centrifuges. Under the codename Al Furat Project, the plant was designed to make all the components for the centrifuges, and was slated for completion by mid-1991. By IAEA estimates, it could have achieved a production capacity of more than 2,000 centrifuges per year.[22] The project called for the construction of a 100-machine cascade of centrifuges at Al Furat by the end of 1992 and commencement of cascade operations by mid-1993. In addition, a 500-machine cascade was to be built and operated by early 1996, but at an unknown location.[23]

Iraqi scientists apparently did not progress very far with their work on chemical enrichment—a third, laborious uranium-enrichment route. Similarly, while they admitted they had carried out a detailed feasibility study on gaseous diffusion, they maintained that they abandoned work in this area in mid-1987 because they lacked the necessary industrial infrastructure.[24] Iraqi officials initially denied the existence of any activities in the field of laser isotope separation (LIS). In the course of an IAEA investigation during the Agency's 26th inspection in August-September 1994, however, the Iraqi side admitted that a research LIS program did in fact exist but stated that it had made little progress since it never achieved separation of uranium either in the metallic or the molecular form.[25]

Plutonium Separation. Iraqi scientists also organized secret attempts to produce and separate small quantities of plutonium in IAEA-safeguarded facilities at Tuwaitha. One of four campaigns undertaken involved extracting plutonium from one fuel element removed from the Russian-supplied IRT-5000 reactor. In three other campaigns, the Iraqis fabricated fuel elements from undeclared uranium dioxide (UO_2) in their Experimental Reactor Fuel Fabrication Laboratory, irradiated this fuel secretly in the IRT-5000 reactor, and then chemically processed the fuel in Al Tuwaitha Building No. 9, a radiochemical laboratory that had not been accessible to IAEA safeguard inspectors prior to the 1991 war. As a result of the four campaigns, the Iraqis produced approximately six grams of plutonium and acquired a rudimentary mastery of the plutonium separation process. Without any changes to the configuration of the radiochemical laboratory, the Iraqis would have been unable to separate more than 60 grams of plutonium per year, quantities insufficient to produce the five to eight kilograms needed for a first nuclear device.[26]

Weaponization. The program to design Iraq's first nuclear weapon device and to fabricate its components was centered at the Al Atheer complex, which served as the prime development and testing site; the Al Qa Qaa site and the Al Hateen High Explosive site also played important supporting roles in the program.[27] IAEA inspectors concluded that the Iraqis were focusing their efforts on developing an implosion-type of weapon.[28] The basic design is to surround a subcritical mass or core of fissile material—in this case, highly enriched uranium—with conventional high-explosive charges. These charges are uniformly detonated to compress the nuclear material into a supercritical configuration. The weaponization program was in its early stages at the time of the Gulf War. Iraqi scientists were still struggling to master the high-explosive charges that have to be precisely fabricated in order to produce homogeneous shock waves against the core after ignition.[29]

Violations of NPT Safeguards. On July 18 and August 9, 1991, the IAEA formally declared Iraq to be non-compliant with its safeguards agreement with the Agency (INFCIRC/172) for undeclared possession of fissile materials and operations on those fissile materials.[30] Iraq had also engaged in nuclear weapons research and development activities in violation of Article II of the Nuclear Non-Proliferation Treaty (NPT) prohibiting the "manufacture" of such weapons.[31] While the research activities did not constitute a violation specifically of Iraq's IAEA safeguards agreement, the comprehensive inspections mandated by Security Council Resolution 687 that uncovered the nuclear weapons activities enabled the United States to determine in its 1995 annual report on compliance with arms control treaties that Iraq's nuclear activities were indeed in violation of its obligations under NPT Article II.[32]

Dismantlement of Weapons Program. The 1991 Gulf War and its aftermath set back Iraq's nuclear weapons program many years. Many of the installations involved in the effort were destroyed or damaged by U.S. bombing raids during the conflict, although, in some cases, key equipment had been previously removed from them. Other facilities, many of which had been unknown to the United States and its Coalition partners, were leveled by Iraq itself after the war in an effort to deceive the IAEA inspectors about the nature of the installations. French- and Soviet-origin weapons-usable uranium that Iraq had obtained for running research reactors supplied by these countries was placed in IAEA custody and was eventually removed from Iraq.[33]

During the seventh IAEA inspection, in October 1991, the inspectors started to destroy enrichment-related equipment, as well as equipment for the separation of plutonium, which they had discovered in earlier inspections. In April 1992, during the eleventh inspection, inspectors destroyed buildings and equipment at the Al Atheer/Al Hateen site, Iraq's key complex for designing, fabricating, assembling, and cold-testing nuclear weapons. On September 19, 1994, after an additional 15 inspections, IAEA Director General Hans Blix stated that his agency had completed the destruction, removal, or rendering harmless of all known nuclear weapons-usable material, facilities, and equipment in Iraq that might have the potential to contribute to the development of nuclear weapons.[34]

Long-Term IAEA Monitoring Plan. On November 26, 1993, Iraq formally agreed to accept long-term IAEA monitoring of its industries as assurance that it was not reviving programs to manufacture weapons of mass destruction. The IAEA had already instituted, in September 1992, a periodic survey at selected locations of the principal bodies of water and waterways in Iraq, to help detect any sizable nuclear activity. This was later supplemented by the use of helicopters and vehicles equipped with radiation sensors. The plan also prescribed the ongoing monitoring of selected "dual-use" facilities and equipment that could be utilized in reconstructing the Iraqi nuclear weapons program, and involved the continued use of short-notice inspections.[35] In August 1994, the IAEA established a continuous presence in Iraq that would enable it to conduct no-notice inspections at all suspected sites.[36] On September 29, 1994, Ambassador Rolf Ekeus, then head of UNSCOM, reported to the Security Council that the "commission's ongoing monitoring and verification system [in Iraq] is provisionally operational," and that a period of testing of the system had begun.[37]

While Ekeus had earlier indicated that a six-month period of testing would have been sufficient for determining the effectiveness of the system, his report did not set a time limit. The United States campaigned at the United Nations to delay, for an unspecified period, the lifting of U.N. economic sanctions against Iraq imposed at the end of the 1991 Gulf War because of the indications that Iraq was still concealing portions of its WMD programs.[38]

At meetings in Baghdad between Ekeus and Iraqi officials on October 4 and 5, Iraq demanded, in language amounting to an ultimatum, that the commission should: (1) declare that all actions required by Iraq under the Security Council were complete; (2) delete the word "provisionally" from the UNSCOM report so that the verification system would be considered complete; and (3) declare immediately the start of a six-month period for testing the system. Iraqi officials warned that, without these three steps, Iraq would resort to a new policy toward UNSCOM and, possibly, against Kuwait.[39]

Ekeus rejected this ultimatum for three reasons. First, Iraq had not completed the actions required and, indeed, was concealing large quantities of prohibited weapons capabilities. Second, the monitoring system was nothing else but provisional insofar as only missile and nuclear monitoring had begun (i.e., the system of biological and chemical monitoring was far from implementation). Third, because of the incompleteness of the overall system for monitoring prohibited WMD and missile capabilities, no assurance of time limit could be given (i.e., only when the whole system with its four components was in place, would a six-month time limit be appropriate).[40]

For the Iraqis, the lack of a specific testing period for the monitoring system implied an indefinite extension of the sanctions. The impending release of the Ekeus report coincided with the eruption of a week-long crisis triggered by the massing of Iraqi troops on the Kuwait border and the redeployment of U.S. forces to the region.[41]

DEVELOPMENTS

The disclosures made by Lt. Gen. Hussein Kamel (former Iraqi Minister of Industry and Military Industrialization) after his defection to Jordan on August 8, 1995, prompted the Iraqi government to invite UNSCOM Chairman Ekeus and an IAEA delegation to Baghdad, so that it could make new information available about past nonconventional-weapons activities that allegedly had been withheld by General Kamel. These discussions and subsequent inspections revealed that following the invasion of Kuwait in August 1990 Iraq had embarked on a "crash program" to develop a nuclear device by extracting weapons-grade material from safeguarded research reactor fuel.[42] The Iraqis now admitted that they had also pursued an extensive biological warfare program and had produced and weaponized a large number of biological agents, including ten tons of anthrax, botulinum toxin, and an agent called aflatoxin.[43] Moreover, they acknowledged that Iraq's chemical weapons program had continued until December 1990 (not September 1988 as previously claimed), producing sufficient quantities of precursor materials for almost 500 tons of the nerve agent VX.[44] In addition, Iraqi officials disclosed that Iraqi engineers had made advances in the development and production of ballistic missiles exceeding those that Iraq had reported earlier to UNSCOM inspectors.

The scope and magnitude of Iraq's WMD capabilities just prior to the 1991 Gulf War was one element of these disclosures. The other was the role that these capabilities played in the strategic calculus of Saddam Hussein. In the nuclear realm, Saddam Hussein ordered an accelerated effort to fabricate a single nuclear device as soon as possible. This would have provided him with the ultimate symbol of military power and, possibly, a deterrent against the Coalition forces as the confrontation over Kuwait evolved. In parallel, Saddam Hussein

readied an alternative "strategic" capability. Iraqi forces filled about 25 missile warheads and 150 to 200 bombs with biological agents and dispersed them in forward storage positions for rapid employment.[45] Similar arrangements were made for 50 missile warheads that were filled with chemical agents.[46] Reportedly, Saddam Hussein fully intended to use chemical weapons and gave local commanders authority to use them at their discretion, perhaps as a last resort if the Iraqi border was breached or in the event Baghdad was attacked with weapons of mass destruction.[47]

Iraq's interest in preserving as many of its WMD-related capabilities as possible in spite of U.N. resolutions was reflected in its strategy of frustrating and hindering the U.N. inspection process in March 1996, and again in June and July 1996, when the Iraqis delayed U.N. inspectors' access to legitimate inspection sites. This was particularly apparent in inspections focusing on the ballistic missile program but also, to some extent, on the chemical and biological weapons programs. In this context, on April 11, UNSCOM reported to the Security Council that "the Commission has serious concerns that a full accounting and disposal of Iraq's holdings of prohibited items has not been made."[48] During 1997 Iraq blocked or hindered a number of UNSCOM inspections relating to its chemical and biological programs, culminating in a standoff with the United Nations in late October 1997 (see Prospects section of this chapter). During this period, Iraq was much more cooperative in answering IAEA inquiries about the "crash program," and also in providing new details about the uranium-enrichment component of the longer-term program.

"Crash Nuclear Weapon Program." Launched in September 1990, this "crash" project called for (1) the diversion of approximately 36 kg of IAEA-safeguarded unirradiated and slightly irradiated highly enriched uranium (HEU) from the Soviet-supplied IRT-5000 research reactor and the French-supplied Tammuz II research reactor (13.7 kg of unirradiated Soviet-supplied 80-percent uranium; 11.9 kg of lightly irradiated French-supplied 93-percent fuel; 400 grams of unirradiated French-supplied 93-percent material; and about 11 kg of irradiated Soviet-supplied 80-percent material);[49] (2) the chemical processing of both unirradiated and irradiated fuel to extract the HEU; (3) the re-enrichment of the 80-percent-enriched material of Soviet-origin in a 50-machine gas centrifuge cascade specifically constructed for that purpose; and (4) the conversion of the HEU chemical compounds to metal. The program also provided for such measures as the accelerated design and fabrication of the implosion package, the selection and construction of a test site, and development of a delivery vehicle. The deadline for producing a weapon under the "crash program" apparently was April 1991.[50]

If uninterrupted, the "crash program" might have enabled the Iraqis to extract about 25 kg of HEU from the unirradiated and lightly irradiated fuel by the end of April 1991 (with an average enrichment of 86 percent).

However, recovery of the HEU from fuel with higher irradiation levels would have proven more difficult, probably delaying availability of that material until the end of October 1991. Under the assumption that Iraqi scientists would have been able to construct the 50-machine gas centrifuge cascade by early spring 1991 to re-enrich the 80-percent-enriched material and resolve questions relating to the fabrication, testing, and delivery of the device, they might have succeeded in commissioning a deliverable weapon by the end of 1992.[51]

In any case, the "crash program" was short-lived. By January 1991, Iraq had managed only to commission a small-scale reprocessing facility at Al Tuwaitha (the LAMA hot cells) for recovery of the HEU—the first stage of the program. The facility was ready to start operating but all activities ceased there after the Coalition bombing of January 17. (It was dismantled shortly after the beginning of the Gulf War, but not all of its equipment has been accounted for.)

Centrifuge Program. The new revelations of August 1995 confirmed IAEA suspicions that the Rashdiya Engineering Design Center (EDC) had been the central site of Iraq's centrifuge research and development efforts. Iraqi officials also revealed that in addition to the Al Furat site, which already had been disclosed during the 1991 inspections as the manufacturing site for centrifuges (as well as the site for a planned prototype 100-centrifuge cascade), Iraq was planning to build a 1,000-machine cascade at Taji.[52] By the middle of 1990, the EDC scientists had managed to build five prototype centrifuges incorporating carbon fiber rotors (presumably fabricated abroad) and magnetic bearings. A cascade of 1,000 such machines could have yielded up to 10 to 15 kg of HEU per year, potentially enough for a single nuclear weapon.[53]

By that time the Iraqis had also decided that carbon fiber technology was the preferred option for manufacturing centrifuges, as compared with making them from maraging steel. They attempted to procure a filament-winding machine and enough carbon fiber and epoxy resin to produce 1,000 rotor cylinders, but the U.N. embargo imposed after Iraq's invasion of Kuwait apparently blocked that effort. In September 1996, it was revealed that the IAEA had seized a filament-winding machine in Jordan sometime in the previous year. Karl-Heinz Schaab, who was convicted in 1993 by a German court for supplying Iraq in 1990 with more than 20 carbon fiber centrifuge rotor tubes, had reportedly built the machine and had organized its export to Iraq via Switzerland, Singapore, and Jordan.[54]

In addition, the earlier IAEA findings had indicated that Iraq had based its centrifuge program on 1960s-era technology developed by the British-German-Dutch uranium-enrichment consortium, Urenco. Following the August 1995 revelations, evidence emerged that the Iraqi program was also seeking to develop an advanced 3-meter supercritical centrifuge, and was apparently receiving technical assistance to that end from Karl-Heinz Schaab.[55] In addition to selling Iraq design blueprints of the advanced "TC-11" centrifuge, Schaab apparently provided Iraqi scientists with three samples of bellows and other components and also assisted with the assembly of Iraq's single-cylinder subcritical test machine.[56] In this context, during the 29th IAEA inspection, Iraqi officials admitted that the cascade hall at the EDC was being constructed to accommodate supercritical centrifuges.

Notwithstanding this assistance, the IAEA came to the conclusion that, by the time the 1991 Gulf War broke out, no practical progress had been made toward the completion of the 50-machine cascade that would have been used to re-enrich HEU in the "crash program." EDC scientists asserted that they were awaiting production of a number of components at the Al Nida (Al Rabiya) Establishment before assembling the centrifuges. However, the IAEA estimated that, at best, the EDC would have been able to build only about 20 machines, assuming the availability of a sufficient number of foreign-origin parts. For the EDC to have any realistic chance for completing the cascade it would have required "arrangements to procure all the necessary components and expert assistance, through their extensive clandestine foreign supply network."[57]

Weaponization. Prior to August 1995, a missing link in the IAEA's knowledge of Iraq's longer-term program to develop nuclear arms concerned weaponization activities for the period June 1990 to June 1991. As part of their new disclosures, the Iraqis provided the IAEA with a detailed document indicating that work on designing and fabricating a nuclear weapon continued at Al Atheer and Al Tuwaitha until the commencement of the Coalition bombing campaign, and that, following the cessation of hostilities, activities centered on efforts to salvage equipment. They acknowledged, for the first time, that activities at those two sites were for the sole purpose of manufacturing nuclear weapons and not just for defining the requirements of producing them.[58]

Among the advances not revealed earlier was the fact that the Iraqi weaponization group at the beginning of 1991 was close to deciding on a final design for an implosion device based on a version that had been under consideration since early summer 1990. Another revelation was that further progress had been made in the high-explosives testing program, with work being conducted on generating spherical implosions.[59]

IAEA Re-Assessment. Based on the new revelations, the IAEA concluded that the original plan of the Iraqi nuclear weapons program, as set out in 1988, was to "produce a small arsenal of weapons" with the first one readied in 1991. While the weaponization team made significant progress in designing a viable device, the original deadline could not have been met because progress in the production of HEU—utilizing the EMIS and gas centrifuge processes—had lagged far behind. The fact that domestically produced HEU would not have been available for some time led Iraq to modify the objective of the original plan and to undertake the "crash program" to develop a nuclear device by extracting weapons-grade material from safeguarded research reactor fuel.

In its October 1996 assessment, the IAEA stated that the "industrial infrastructure which Iraq had set up to produce and weaponize special nuclear material has been destroyed." However, the Agency was aware "that the know-how and expertise acquired by Iraqi scientists and engineers could provide an adequate base for reconstituting a nuclear-weapons-oriented program."[60] The IAEA environmental monitoring regime in Iraq is more intrusive than that under Part I of the IAEA's "93 + 2" enhanced safeguards program (see Appendix D on IAEA Safeguards in this volume),[61] enabling the Agency to detect clandestine small-scale activities related to uranium enrichment, "such as cold testing of centrifuges using gaseous feedstocks."[62] However, the monitoring regime apparently does not have the capability to trace certain activities in the field of uranium metallurgy, such as casting uranium metal into a configuration for use in a nuclear device.

This raises the question of whether Iraq has made enough progress in the weaponization process (design of a device and development of the non-nuclear components) to clandestinely produce a weapon if it were to acquire nuclear materials through illicit sources. According to Konrad Porzner, head of Germany's BND secret service, Iraq has been seeking to purchase nuclear materials in the black market through third parties.[63]

The IAEA believes that Iraq has a workable design but has never conducted a "full-up" test of an implosion device with a dummy core. Although it may make sense to assume, as a worst-case planning scenario, that Iraq would need only the fissile material to build a device, in reality Iraq has not mastered all of the non-nuclear parts of the bomb. It had not conducted the necessary implosion tests prior to the Gulf War and there is "no evidence" that it has conducted them since.[64] For this, a special facility with appropriate diagnostic equipment would be needed, and procurement would likely be detected.

On September 7, 1996, Iraq submitted to the IAEA what Baghdad considered to be the final version of the "Full, Final, and Complete Declaration" called for in Security Council Resolution 707 (1991). The IAEA evaluated the report over the next several months, focusing on those areas where Iraq's WMD missile activities may have been understated.[65] By mid-1997, the IAEA reportedly believed that it had, as a physical matter, shut down the Iraqi nuclear weapons program.[66] Iraqi ambitions and accumulated nuclear technical expertise remains, however, and with it the capability to restart the program covertly.

Post-Sanctions Monitoring. In light of Iraq's continuing strategy of deception and concealment regarding past and current WMD-related programs and activities—especially biological and chemical weapons, and ballistic missiles—U.N. sanctions were not eased during the period 1995-96. Nevertheless, on July 18, 1996, Secretary-General Boutros Boutros-Ghali approved a plan to allow Iraq to sell up to $2 billion in oil for relief supplies over a six-month period. This exemption to U.N. sanctions was to be renewable.[67] Implementation of the "oil for food" deal was postponed by the United Nations until December 1996, however, because of the August 1996 incursion of the Iraqi army into northern Iraq in support of a Kurdish faction.[68]

Earlier, on March 27, 1996, the U.N. Security Council unanimously adopted Resolution 1051 (1996) establishing the export/import monitoring system for Iraq. This system, which was developed by UNSCOM (in conjunction with the IAEA and the U.N. Sanctions Committee) provides for notifications, both by Iraq and supplier countries, of planned supplies of dual-use items to Iraq that could have applications in U.N.–proscribed WMD and missile programs. Under the system, these items will be subject to inspection upon their arrival in Iraq and will be monitored at the end-user site. This mechanism, adopted as one component of ongoing monitoring and verification in Iraq, was expected to assume added importance once overall U.N. sanctions were lifted because of the need to check the increased flow of imported items into Iraq. The benefit, in the near term, would be that the mechanism might assist supplier states in identifying and closing cracks in their current regulations for carrying out sanctions against Iraq.[69]

Continuing problems with the U.N. inspection regime arose in February 1998 when Iraq began further limiting inspectors and declaring off-limits many facilities, including several large presidential palaces thought to be hiding prohibited equipment. After a large U.S. military build-up in the region, U.N. Secretary-General Kofi Annan brokered a deal with Iraq to allow the inspections to continue, but with some changes in format to include the presence of international diplomats as observers at some inspections. Since the agreement, UNSCOM inspections have continued without any known disruptions, but UNSCOM Chairman Richard Butler still reports that not all the information he has requested of the Iraqis has been delivered, suggesting that the inspection regime will continue to be enforced for some time.

Ballistic and Cruise Missile Program. Prior to the 1991 Gulf War, Iraq had extensive short-range ballistic missile capabilities, including a stockpile of Soviet-supplied, single-stage liquid-fueled Scud-Bs (300-km range and 1,000-kg payload) and three indigenously produced variants of the Scud-B, the Al Hussein, the Al Hussein Short, and the Al Hijarah, all three with an approximate range of 600-650 km. Iraq was developing a domestic manufacturing capability for these modified Scuds, which included a sophisticated missile technology base to reverse-engineer these systems. According to then UNSCOM Chairman Ekeus, Iraq had the capability to produce Scud-type engines, airframes, and warheads.[70] Iraq had also undertaken a joint venture with Argentina and Egypt to develop a two-stage solid-fueled missile with an intended range of 750 to 1,000 km, the Badr 2000.[71] (The Argentine version was called Condor.)

Under the cease-fire agreement and the terms of Security Council Resolution 687, Iraq was obliged to eliminate ballistic missiles with ranges exceeding 150 km, but allowed to keep missiles with ranges up to 150 km. In early July 1991, UNSCOM destroyed Iraq's known 48 ballistic missiles that had a range capability greater than 150 km, and dismantled a large part of the related infrastructure. However, in March 1992, Iraq admitted that it had withheld 85 missiles from UNSCOM's controlled destruction. Iraq had destroyed these missiles in mid-July and October 1991 (after the official destruction of the 48) in a secret operation. While the UNSCOM inspectors confirmed in April 1992 that most of Iraq's remaining Scud-based missile force had been eliminated, the clandestine character of Iraq's destruction of the 85 missiles showed that Iraq was desperately trying to preserve missiles and missile components.[72]

As part of its long-term monitoring and verification plan, UNSCOM started regular inspections of facilities involved in research and production of missiles with a range of less than 150 km. There are, however, no U.N. restrictions on Iraq's development of cruise missiles.

Iraq was able to preserve a residual ballistic-missile-production technology base for four reasons. First, UNSCOM allowed Iraq to keep certain missile-production-related, dual-use items for use in its civilian industry. Second, a number of liquid-propellant missile production technologies utilized in permitted missile programs—particularly in the Ababil-100 surface-to-surface missile (with an estimated maximum range of 150 km)—are "compatible with Scud production."[73] Third, range/payload tradeoffs allow missiles with lighter warheads to travel to greater ranges, as Iraq demonstrated in its doubling of the range of the Soviet-supplied Scud missile type. Fourth, Iraq's SA-2 air defense missiles have been adapted as surface-to-surface missiles with ranges in excess of 150 km.[74]

By early 1995, UNSCOM believed that it had a fairly complete overview of facilities, equipment, and materials used in Iraq's past missile program. However, because Iraq repeatedly withheld and falsified information, UNSCOM had unresolved issues, partly on past research and development activities, and partly on numerical accounting of missiles, warheads and supporting/auxiliary equipment.[75] UNSCOM also found itself in disagreement with the United States over whether all of Iraq's illegal missiles had been accounted for. The U.S. intelligence community believed that Iraq may have successfully hidden up to a hundred such missiles.[76]

Iraq disclosed new information on its past missile activities during Ambassador Ekeus's Baghdad visit in August 1995, after the defection of Lt. Gen. Hussein Kamel. Iraqi officials now admitted that Iraq, prior to the 1991 Gulf War, had carried out research and development work on advanced rocket engines and that it had manufactured rocket engines "made of indige-nously produced or imported parts and without the cannibalization of the imported Soviet-made Scud engines."[77] Iraq was more specific in a new "full, final and complete disclosure" on November 16, when it revealed that Iraq itself had produced about 80 major subsystems of Scud-type engines. Iraq explained that out of the total, 53 had been rejected as unfit, 17 had been disposed of during testing, and 10 had been unilaterally destroyed.[78]

The 28th and 29th IAEA inspections revealed that, until the Gulf War, Iraq had focused on ballistic missiles as the only really viable delivery system for its nuclear weapons. Iraq was apparently pursuing three options. The first option was tailored to the longer-term plan, initiated in 1988, of producing the first of a number of nuclear weapons in 1991. The delivery vehicle would have been based on a modification of the Al Abid satellite launcher, and would have had the capability to deliver a one-ton warhead to a distance of almost 1,200 km.[79] However, since work on the engines for this system did not begin until April 1989, it would not have been ready until 1993. The second option, a fall-back position, would have been to put the nuclear warhead on an unmodified Al Hussein missile, which would have limited the range to 300 km. The third option, initiated in August/September 1990 under the "crash" program, was to produce "a derivative of the Al Hussein/Al Abbas short-range missile designed to deliver a warhead of one ton to 650 km and to accommodate a nuclear package (80 centimeters in diameter)."[80] The estimated timeframe for completing the third option was six months.

In December 1995, UNSCOM reported that some elements in Iraq's final missile declaration were still unaccounted for, including ten missile engine systems that Iraq claimed it had destroyed.[81] UNSCOM also was not satisfied that it had accounted for the number of indigenously produced warheads and of "such major components for operational missiles as guidance and control systems, liquid propellant fuels and ground support equipment." A third gap was incomplete Iraqi declarations on the relationship of the missile program to past activities in the chemical, biological, and nuclear weapons areas.[82]

UNSCOM was also concerned that Iraq had resumed foreign procurement of banned missile technologies and components.[83] Iraq defended these procurement activities as intended for the legal Ababil-100 missile program. However, Iraq was ordering the import of equipment and materials without making the required notifications to UNSCOM and the imports would violate the U.N. sanctions in place.[84] Evidence also emerged that after the 1991 Gulf War, Iraq had set up a covert network of purchasing agents and dummy companies to stockpile key missile components for future use and conceal them from UNSCOM inspectors.[85]

In November 1995, Jordanian authorities intercepted 115 missile guidance system components (including gyroscopes), which had been shipped from sources in Russia to Iraq.[86] On December 21, Ambassador Ekeus revealed that divers had retrieved from the Tigris Canal in Baghdad missile guidance gyroscopes like those intercepted in Jordan—apparently another, earlier shipment to Iraq from Russian sources.[87] UNSCOM missile experts inferred that Iraq was trying to develop an advanced variant of the Al Hussein with a range of up to 3,000 km.[88] An MRBM with that range fired from Iraq could easily reach a number of European capitals.

Iraqi missile program controversies persisted through 1996; UNSCOM reported in October that "in the missile area, Iraq still has not fully accounted for all proscribed weapons, items, and capabilities."[89] UNSCOM Chairman Ekeus told the U.S. Senate in March 1996 that Iraq seemed to be hiding at least 6, and maybe as many as 16, indigenously produced Al Hussein missiles.[90] A month later, a Pentagon report rekindled the dispute with UNSCOM over the accounting of Iraq's missiles, stating: "The United States believes Iraq has hidden a small number of mobile launchers and *several dozen* Scud-type missiles produced before Operation Desert Storm (emphasis added)."[91] In December 1996, UNSCOM officials indicated that they believed that 18 to 25 missiles, along with support equipment, were still being hidden—enough, in the words of Ambassador Ekeus, "to constitute a complete missile force."[92]

In October 1997, UNSCOM finally reported that it had made significant progress in the missile area, being now able to account for 817 of the 819 missiles Iraq had imported from the Soviet Union before the end of 1988. UNSCOM had analyzed the remnants of those missiles that Iraq unilaterally destroyed in July and October 1991 and was able to verify that 83 engines out of the 85 declared missiles were, in fact, destroyed."[93] But, UNSCOM had not yet completed its accounting of proscribed missile warheads, of particular concern because the warhead accounting could be connected with chemical/biological weapons activities.[94]

Iraq also had an active interest in cruise missiles, importing Chinese Silkworm cruise missiles before the Gulf War. Although Silkworms are normally ground- or ship-launched, Iraq explored launching them from aircraft. Iraq has tested remotely piloted vehicles (RPVs) for chemical and biological weapon delivery and has adapted Polish cropdusters as RPVs that could easily be used for CW or BW delivery.[95]

PROSPECTS

Iraq's Saddam Hussein regime has long pursued WMD as a means of achieving Iraqi political and military preeminence in the Middle East and Persian Gulf. The regime has already used chemical weapons not only against Iran but against its own people. It has used ballistic missiles for tactical, strategic, and psychological purposes.[96] If and when U.N. sanctions are lifted, Iraq certainly will attempt to reconstitute its WMD programs and ballistic missile capabilities (indeed, it has already started to do so).[97]

An October 1996 assessment indicated that Saddam Hussein had already restored the effectiveness of Iraq's army, with "a qualitative superiority" over Iran's armed forces and all others in the Persian Gulf region.[98] Iraq strengthened its stature in the region on August 31, 1996, when 30,000 to 40,000 Iraqi troops and 350 tanks were dispatched into northern Iraq to prop up an ally, the Kurdistan Democratic Party.[99] The fact that UNSCOM believes it has yet to unearth all of Iraq's prohibited ballistic missiles and all of its CW and BW stocks and manufacturing base makes this resurgent Iraqi threat all the more serious.[100]

Saddam Hussein's advances in Northern Iraq also revealed cracks in the Coalition. France and Russia, among others, refused to support the U.S. call for a strong response to the Iraqi aggression. Disunity within the Coalition was evident again in November 1997 in a U.N. standoff with Iraq over its demand that American inspectors be expelled from UNSCOM inspection teams. Iraq accused the United States of manipulating American inspectors in order to prolong U.N. sanctions in Iraq. In the early phases of the crisis, Russia, France, and a number of moderate Arab states, including Egypt, argued against threatened U.S. military action to force a solution. Russia then brokered a preliminary agreement with Iraq that would allow the return of the U.S. inspectors and the resumption of UNSCOM inspections. However, this accord was based on the understanding that Russia would push for an easing of U.N. sanctions against Iraq, a quid pro quo unacceptable to the United States as long as the accounting and elimination of Iraq's WMD programs remained incomplete. The crisis persisted into late February 1998, with Iraq threatening to block UNSCOM inspections of "sovereign" presidential sites suspected of hiding elements of Iraq's proscribed biological and chemical weapons programs,[101] until U.N. Secretary-General Kofi Annan negotiated a deal that allowed the inspections to continue.

Russia's and others' more lenient attitude in this crisis vis-à-vis Iraq, including a greater readiness to declare Iraq's WMD programs dismantled and relax the comprehensive sanctions regime, suggests that, in a post-sanctions environment, it may be more difficult for the United States to organize a united front in the U.N. Security Council against Iraq to respond to new challenges. This problem was particularly evident among the United States' European and Middle East allies, who publicly refused to support any U.S. military action against Iraq during the February 1998 inspections crisis. With waning support of Security Council powers such as Russia and France, as well as Iraq's neighbors, the continuity of the IAEA and UNSCOM inspection regimes will come into question. This, in turn, is likely to complicate U.S. and international actions to stem Iraq's efforts to reconstitute its programs for weapons of mass destruction.

NOTES

[1]Testimony of the Director of Central Intelligence John M. Deutch, before the Permanent Subcommittee on Investigations of the Senate Committee on Governmental Affairs, March 20, 1996.

[2]Office of the Secretary of Defense, *Proliferation: Threat and Response*, April 1996, p. 18. An earlier CIA estimate stated that if U.N. monitoring ceased "it would probably take (Iraq) about five to seven years to develop the infrastructure necessary to provide fissile material for nuclear weapons." See William O. Studeman, Acting Director of Central Intelligence, supplementary materials submitted to *Hearings on Worldwide Intelligence Review*, before the Senate Select Committee on Intelligence, U.S. Senate, 104th Cong., 1st Sess., January 10, 1995 (supplementary materials supplied April 3, 1995), p. 110.

[3]Rick Marshall, "Ekeus: Weapons of Mass Destruction of Higher Value to Iraq Than Oil," *USIS Washington File*, June 10, 1997. For earlier estimate see Briefing by Ambassador Rolf Ekeus, Executive Chairman, United Nations Special Commission, *Hearings on Global Proliferation of Weapons of Mass Destruction*, Committee on Governmental Affairs, U.S. Senate, March 13, 20, and 22, 1996, p. 91.

[4]Iraq was more cooperative in answering IAEA questions about its nuclear weapons program after the August 1995 defection of Hussein Kamel, the official responsible for the country's pre–Gulf War WMD and missile programs. Mark Hibbs, "Future of IAEA in Iraq at Stake After Middle East Tension Rises," *Nuclear Fuel*, September 23, 1996, p. 3. The IAEA was confident that it had destroyed Iraq's nuclear-weapons-related industrial infrastructure, but questions remained about Iraqi claims to have destroyed certain nuclear equipment after the Gulf War. See *IAEA*, "Report on the Twenty-Eighth IAEA On-Site Inspection in Iraq Under Security Council Resolution 687 (1991)," S/1995/1003, December 1, 1995, p. 8.

[5]Iraq ratified the Non-Proliferation Treaty on October 29, 1969, pledging not to manufacture nuclear weapons and agreeing to place all its nuclear materials and facilities under IAEA safeguards. Iraq's fissile-material-related research activities date back to the early 1980s.

[6]Saudi Arabia is reported by one source to have provided financial and technological support to the Iraqi nuclear weapons program during the 1980s in exchange for access to nuclear weapons technology. This allegation was made by Mohammed Khilewi, a Saudi diplomat assigned to the Saudi mission to the United Nations in New York, who defected in May 1994. Khilewi also asserted that Saudi Arabia's nuclear-weapons-related effort included attempts in 1989 to buy nuclear research reactors from China and an American company. (See "Britain's Gulf War Ally Helped Saddam Build a Nuclear Bomb," *Sunday Times* (London), July 24, 1994; Steve Coll and John Mintz, "Saudi Aid to Iraqi A-Bomb Alleged; Asylum-Seeking Diplomat," *Washington Post*, July 25, 1994; *New York Times*, August 7, 1994.)

[7]This review of the Iraqi nuclear weapons program and related IAEA activities is based on the following sources: International Atomic Energy Agency, "Reports on On-Site Inspections in Iraq Under Security Council Resolution 687 (1-30)," 1991-1996; David Albright and Mark Hibbs, "Iraq's Bomb: Blueprints and Artifacts," *Bulletin of the Atomic Scientists*, January/February 1992, pp. 30-40; Gary Milhollin, "Building Saddam Hussein's Bomb," *New York Times Magazine*, March 8, 1992, pp. 30-36; International Atomic Energy Agency, "IAEA Inspections and Iraq's Nuclear Capabilities," IAEA/PI/A35E, April 1992; David Albright and Mark Hibbs, "Iraq's Shop-Till-You Drop Nuclear Program," *Bulletin of the Atomic Scientists*, April 1992, pp. 27-37; Jay C. Davis and David A. Kay, "Iraq's Secret Nuclear Weapons Program," *Physics Today*, July 1992, p. 21; Paul Lewis, "U.N. Experts Now Say Baghdad Was Far From Making an A-Bomb Before Gulf War," *New York Times*, May 20, 1992; Maurizio Zifferero, "The IAEA: Neutralizing Iraq's Nuclear Weapons Potential," *Arms Control Today*, April 1993, p. 7.

[8]In the electromagnetic process, uranium in the form of uranium tetrachloride (UCl_4) is ionized and the beam of charged uranium atoms is put through a series of powerful electromagnets, separating the desired uranium-235 atoms from the more common uranium-238 atoms. The process played an important role in the early stages of the Manhattan Project, helping to enrich uranium for the Hiroshima bomb, but was abandoned in favor of more efficient enrichment technologies. No other emerging nuclear state is known to have pursued this enrichment method, which is very difficult to operate on an industrial scale and is extremely energy intensive.

[9]IAEA, "Report on the Fourth IAEA On-Site Inspection in Iraq Under Security Council Resolution 687 (1991)," S/22986, August 28, 1991, p. 5.
Until the Israeli attack on Osiraq on June 7, 1981, Iraq had chosen plutonium (versus highly enriched uranium [HEU]) as the preferred fissile material for its nuclear weapons program. The Osiraq research reactor, purchased from France in 1976, was unusually large and was therefore capable of irradiating uranium specimens to produce significant quantities of plutonium. See Jed C. Snyder, "The Non-Proliferation Regime, Managing the Impending Crisis," *Journal of Strategic Studies*, December 1985, p. 11. Also see Shyam Bhatia, *Nuclear Rivals in the Middle East*, (London: Routledge, 1988), p. 85; Leonard S. Spector, *Nuclear Proliferation Today* (New York: Vintage Books, 1984), p. 170.

[10]See IAEA, "Report on the Third IAEA On-Site Inspection in Iraq Under Security Council Resolution 687 (1991)," S/22837, July 25, 1991, pp. 2-3, 5-6; "Report on the Fourth On-Site Inspection," op. cit., pp. 5-9.

[11]For additional details on the Iraqi EMIS program, see IAEA, "Report on the Seventh IAEA On-Site Inspection in Iraq under Security Council Resolution 687 (1991)," S/23215, November 14, 1991, pp. 17-19, Annex 4 (pp. 1-4); Albright and Hibbs, "Iraq's Bomb: Blueprints and Artifacts," op. cit., pp. 37-39.

[12]IAEA, "Report on the Fourth On-Site Inspection," op. cit., p. 8.

[13]David Albright, Frans Berkhout, and William Walker, *Plutonium and Highly Enriched Uranium 1996: World Inventories, Capabilities and Policies* (New York: Oxford University Press for Stockholm International Peace Research Institute, 1997), pp. 318-26.

[14]Ibid., p. 23.

[15]See IAEA, "Report on the Fourth On-Site Inspection," op. cit., p. 6, and "Report on the Seventh On-Site Inspection," op. cit., Annex 4 (p. 4).

[16]See Bill Gertz, "Saddam Close to Nuclear Weapon," *Washington Post*, June 11, 1991; "Iraqi Defector," *Associated Press*, June 14, 1991; R. Jeffrey Smith, "Iraqi Nuclear Program Due Further Inspections," *Washington Post*, June 14, 1991.

[17]For an explanation of the centrifuge enrichment process, see Appendix J in this volume.

[18]For descriptions of the Iraqi gas centrifuge program, see IAEA, "Report on the Fourth On-Site Inspection," op. cit., pp. 3, 9-13; "Report on the Seventh On-Site Inspection," op. cit., pp. 17, 19, 21, Annex 4 (pp. 5-10); Albright and Hibbs, "Iraq's Bomb: Blueprints and Artifacts," op. cit, pp. 39-40; Albright and Hibbs, "Iraq's Shop-Till-You Drop Nuclear Program," op. cit., pp. 27-37; David Albright and Mark Hibbs, "Iraq: Supplier-Spotting," *Bulletin of the Atomic Scientists*, January/February 1993, pp. 8-9; David Albright, "Engineer for Hire," *Bulletin of the Atomic Scientists*, December 1993, pp. 29-36.

[19]It was originally thought that Pakistan was the likely provider of G-1 design drawings to Iraq. However, in February 1996, the IAEA revealed that Bruno Stemmler is believed to have sold to Iraq "between four and six" centrifuge design blueprints for Urenco's G-1 and G-2 machines in 1988-1989. See Mark Hibbs, "Stemmler, Too, Sold Baghdad Urenco Centrifuge Blueprints," *Nuclear Fuel*, February 12, 1996, p. 1. Also see Caroline Drees, "Second German Sold Nuclear Data to Iraq—IAEA," *Reuters*, February 12, 1996. Urenco's G-1 and G-2 machines utilize maraging steel rotor tubes, the former consisting of one tube and the latter of two tubes connected by a bellows. See IAEA, "Report on the Eighth IAEA On-Site Inspection in Iraq Under Security Council Resolution 687 (1991)," S/23283, December 12, 1991, p. 13; IAEA, "Report on the Ninth IAEA On-Site Inspection in Iraq Under Security Council Resolution 687 (1991)," S/23505, January 30, 1992, p. 11; Mark Hibbs, "German Couple Convicted for Centrifuge Exports to Iraq," *Nucleonics Week*, November 11, 1993, p. 8.

[20]IAEA, "Report on the Fifteenth IAEA On-Site Inspection in Iraq Under Security Council Resolution 687 (1991)," S/24981, December 17, 1992, p. 11.

[21]See IAEA, "Report on the Fourth On-Site Inspection," op. cit., pp. 10-12; "Report on the Seventh On-Site Inspection," op. cit., p. 17. Albright and Hibbs, "Iraq's Shop-Till-You Drop Nuclear Program," op. cit., pp. 32-34.

[22]See "Report on the Fourth On-Site Inspection," ibid., p. 14.

[23]Ibid., pp. 10, 12.

[24]See IAEA "Report on the Seventh On-Site Inspection," op. cit., p. 17.

[25]Ibid., p. 54; IAEA, "Sixth Report of the Director General of the International Atomic Energy Agency on the Implementation of the IAEA's Plan for Future Ongoing Monitoring and Verification of Iraq's Compliance With Paragraph 12 of Resolution 687 (1991)," S/1994/1151, October 10, 1994, p. 8; IAEA, "Report on the Twenty-Sixth IAEA On-Site Inspection in Iraq Under Security Council Resolution 687 (1991)," S/1994/1206, October 22, 1994, p. 5.

[26]See IAEA "Report on the Fourth On-Site Inspection," op. cit., pp. 17-19; also see "Report on the Seventh On-Site Inspection," op. cit., pp. 23, 27; "IAEA Inspections and Iraq's Nuclear Capabilities," op. cit.

[27]See Davis and Kay, "Iraq's Secret Nuclear Weapons Program," op. cit., p. 26; "IAEA Inspections and Iraq's Nuclear Capabilities," op. cit., p. 9.

[28]See IAEA "Report on the Eighth On-Site Inspection," op. cit., p. 15; "Report on the Eleventh IAEA On-Site Inspection in Iraq Under Security Council Resolution 687 (1991)," S/23947, May 22, 1992, p. 20.

[29]See "First Report on the Sixth IAEA On-Site Inspection in Iraq Under Security Council Resolution 687 (1991)," S/23122, October 8, 1991, p. 4; "Report on the Seventh On-Site Inspection," op. cit., pp. 8, 9, 13; Paul Lewis, "U.N. Experts Now Say Baghdad Was Far From Making an A-Bomb," op. cit. In the fall of 1995 the IAEA discovered, however, that Iraq had conducted experimental work on the explosive assembly, including single-unit tests of spherical wave lenses. See Developments section in the chapter.

[30]See IAEA, "Iraq's Non-Compliance With Its Safeguards Obligations," IAEA Document GC(XXXV)/978, Attachments 1 and 3, September 16, 1991.

[31]U.S. Arms Control and Disarmament Agency, "Adherence to and Compliance with Arms Control Agreements," August 1996, p. 13.

[32]In 1992, the United States imposed sanctions against Iraq under the Iran-Iraq Arms Non-Proliferation Act expressly prohibiting the transfer of U.S. nuclear equipment and materials, as well as exports to Iraq of all dual-use commodities, and U.S. government commercial arms sales. The restriction applies both to nuclear dual-use commodities, i.e., those having nuclear and non-nuclear uses and which are regulated internationally by the NSG (see this volume's Appendix F on Nuclear Supplier Organizations), and strategic dual-use commodities, i.e. those having military and non-military uses, which were formerly under the Coordinating Committee on Multilateral Export Controls (COCOM) and are currently regulated under the Wassenaar Arrangement (see Appendix H in this volume). Within the United States, exports of both categories of dual-use items are licensed by the Commerce Department, pursuant to the Export Administration Act. Iran-Iraq Arms Non-proliferation Act of 1992, Division A, Title XVI, Sec. 1603, P.L. 102-484, 106 Stat. 2571, 50 U.S.C. Sec. 1701, note (October 23, 1992).

Earlier, in 1990, the United States had enacted the Iraq Sanctions Act providing the continuation of "the trade embargo and other economic sanctions with respect to Iraq and Kuwait that the United States [had imposed] in response to Iraq's invasion of Kuwait, pursuant to Executive Orders Numbered 12724 and 12725 . . . (August 9, 1990) and, to the extent they [were] still in effect, Executive Orders Numbered 12722 and 12723 . . . (August 2, 1992)." Iraq Sanctions Act of 1990, P.L. 101-513, Title V. Sec. 586-586J, Nov. 5, 1990. 104 Stat. 2047-2054.

[33]See IAEA, "Consolidated Report on the First Two IAEA Inspections Under Security Council Resolution 687 (1991) of Iraqi Nuclear Capabilities," S/22788, July 15, 1991, p. 22; IAEA, "First Semi-Annual Report (Covering the Period 17 June–17 December 1991) on the Implementation by the IAEA of the Plan for the Destruction, Removal or Rendering Harmless of Items Listed in Paragraph 12 of U.N. Security Council Resolution 687 (1991)," S/23295, December 17, 1991, p. 4; IAEA, "Report On the Twelfth IAEA On-Site Inspection in Iraq Under Security Council Resolution 687 (1991)," S/24223, July 2, 1992, p. 41; "IAEA to Transfer Batch of Enriched Uranium to Russia," *Agence France Presse*, January 9, 1994, reported in *JPRS-TND-93-003*, January 31, 1994; "Last of HEU in Iraq Shipped to Russia," *Arms Control Today*, March 1994, p. 40.

[34]IAEA, "Highlights of IAEA Director General's Statement to the 38th Regular Session of the IAEA General Conference," 94 PR/33, September 19, 1994; IAEA, "Sixth Report of the Director General on Monitoring and Verification," op. cit., p. 9.

[35]See IAEA, "Report on the Fourteenth IAEA On-Site Inspection in Iraq Under Security Council Resolution 687 (1991)," S/24593, September 28, 1992; Zifferero, "The IAEA: Neutralizing Iraq's Nuclear Weapons Potential," op. cit., p. 9; Paul Lewis, "U.N. Sends Atom-Detecting Copters to Iraq," *New York Times*, September 19, 1993; Evelyn Leopold, "IAEA Says Iraqi Nuclear Capacity 'Neutralized,'" *Reuters*, November 1, 1993; Paul Lewis, "Bowing to U.N., Iraq Will Permit Arms Monitors," *New York Times*, November 27, 1993.

Another element of the plan was the development by the IAEA, in conjunction with UNSCOM and the U.N. Sanctions Committee, of a mechanism for monitoring future sales and supplies by other countries to Iraq. This so called "export-import" mechanism was not approved by the Security Council until March 1996. See IAEA, "Sixth Report of the Director General of the International Atomic Energy Agency on the Implementation of the IAEA's Plan for Future Ongoing Monitoring and Verification of Iraq's Compliance With Paragraph 12 of Resolution 687 (1991)," op. cit., p. 16; UNSCOM, "First Consolidated Report of the Secretary-General on the Activities of the Special Commission Established by the Secretary-General Pursuant to Paragraph 9 (b) (i) of Resolution 687 (1991)," S/1996/258, April 11, 1996, p. 22.

[36]See UNSCOM, "Report of the Secretary-General on the Status of the Implementation of the Special Commission's Plan for the Ongoing Monitoring and Verification of Iraq's Compliance With Relevant Parts of Section C of Security Council Resolution 687 (1991)," S/1994/1138, October 7, 1994; Mark Hibbs, "Permanent IAEA Monitors Now on the Job in Iraq," *Nucleonics Week*, September 1, 1994, p. 16.

[37]See UNSCOM, "Report of the Secretary-General on the Status," ibid.; Barbara Crossette, "Head of U.N. Inspection Team Says Baghdad Threatens Weapons-Monitoring Effort," *New York Times*, October 12, 1994.

[38]See Sid Balman, Jr., "CIA: Saddam Building and Hiding Weapons," *United Press International*, September 26, 1994; Patric Worsnip, "CIA Chief Attacks Iran, Iraq Weapons Programs," *Reuters*, September 26, 1994; Al Kamen, "Tunnel Vision," *Washington Post*, November 4, 1994.

[39]Interview with Rolf Ekeus, spring 1997.

[40]Ibid.

[41]See "U.S. Sends Force as Iraqi Soldiers Threaten Kuwait: Iraq Denounces Sanctions," *New York Times*, October 8, 1994; "October 2-8: Threat to Kuwait; Iraq Moves It's Troops Toward the Brink Again; Clinton Responds Quickly," *New York Times*, October 9, 1994; "Threats in the Gulf: The Military Buildup; At Least 36,000 U.S. Troops Going in Response to Continued Iraqi Buildup," *New York Times*, October 10, 1994; "Iraq Pledges Pullback; Clinton Orders 350 Aircraft to Gulf," *Los Angeles Times*, October 11, 1994; "U.S. Says Iraqis Start Pullback But Crisis Is Not Over," *Los Angeles Times*, October 12, 1994; "U.S. Puts Limit on Its Military Buildup in Gulf," *New York Times*, October 21, 1994.

[42]IAEA, "Eighth Report of the Director General of the International Atomic Energy Agency on the Implementation of the Agency's Plan for Future Ongoing Monitoring and Verification of Iraq's Compliance With Paragraph 12 of Resolution 687 (1991)," S/1995/844, October 6, 1995; IAEA, "Report on the Twenty-Eighth IAEA On-Site Inspection in Iraq, op. cit.; "Report on the Twenty-Ninth IAEA On-Site Inspection in Iraq Under Security Council Resolution 687 (1991)," S/1996/14, January 10, 1996.

[43]Interview with Rolf Ekeus, spring 1997. By November 1997, UNSCOM had discovered documents indicating that Iraq had produced and weaponized 8,500 liters of anthrax, 20,000 liters of botulinum toxin, 2,200 liters of aflatoxin, and the biological agent Ricin. See White House, "Iraq's Program of Mass Destruction: Threatening the Security of the International Community," Factsheet, November 14, 1997.

[44]The Al Hussein ballistic missile was flight tested in April 1990 carrying a chemical warhead (see subsection on ballistic missile capabilities). See Testimony of Gordon C. Oehler on the Continuing Threat From Weapons of Mass Destruction, before the Permanent Subcommittee on Investigations of the Senate Committee on Governmental Affairs, March 27, 1996; Briefing by Ambassador Ekeus, *Hearings on Global Proliferation*, op cit., p. 91.

[45]Briefing by Ambassador Ekeus, ibid.; UNSCOM, "Report of the Secretary-General on the Status of the Implementation of the Special Commission's Plan for the Ongoing Monitoring and Verification of Iraq's Compliance With Relevant Parts of Section C of Security Council Resolution 687 (1991)," S/1995/864, October 11, 1995, p. 26.

46"Briefing by Ambassador Ekeus," *Hearings on Global Proliferation*, op. cit., p. 91; UNSCOM, "Second Consolidated Report of the Secretary-General on the Activities of the Special Commission Established by the Secretary-General Pursuant to Paragraph 9 (b)(i) of Resolution 687 (1991)," S/1996/848, October 11, 1996, p. 21.

47Various explanations have been offered as to why Iraq did not launch chemical or biological weapons during the war. One is that, just prior to the outbreak of the war, the United States implicitly threatened it would use nuclear weapons against Iraq if chemical or biological weapons were used against the Coalition forces. Another is that the Coalition's advance into Iraq during the ground war occurred too rapidly for the Iraqi leadership to react. It has also been suggested that the U.S. decision to halt the ground war after only four days was influenced by concerns that Iraq might use chemical or biological weapons if Coalition forces closed in on Baghdad. See Arthur Spiegelman, "Iraq Ordered Chemical Warfare in Gulf War—Expert," *Reuters*, op. cit., January 17, 1996; Briefing by Ambassador Ekeus, *Hearings on Global Proliferation*, op. cit., p. 92.

48See UNSCOM, "First Consolidated Report of the Secretary-General Pursuant to Paragraph 9," April 11, 1996, op. cit., pp. 6-8, 27. Also see John M. Goshko, "UN Official Asserts Iraq Still Hiding Banned Arms," *Washington Post*, June 15, 1996; Barbara Crossette, "Years After War, Iraq Is Probably Still Hiding Arms, UN Says," *New York Times*, June 13, 1996; Barbara Crossette, "Iraq Isn't Doing So Well at Hide and Seek," *New York Times*, June 16, 1996; Adnan Malik, "Iraq Gives UN Inspector Banned-Weapons Records," *Washington Post*, June 23, 1996.

Iraq's apparent intent to reconstitute its programs of weapons of mass destruction was demonstrated in November 1995 when Jordanian authorities intercepted 115 missile guidance systems destined for Iraq in violation of U.N. resolutions. See "Jordan Intercepts Missile Parts for Iraq—Officials," *Reuters*, December 7, 1995; "U.S. Praises Jordan for Seizure," *Reuters*, December 8, 1995; "Jordan Says Shipment 'Ominous' Sign of Iraq Intent," *Reuters*, December 12, 1995; "Jordanians Intercept Chemicals Bound for Iraq," *Associated Press*, December 27, 1995, printed in *New York Times*, December 28, 1995.

49See Mark Hibbs, "Experts Say Iraq Could Not Meet Bomb Deadline Even With Diversion," *Nucleonics Week*, August 31, 1995, p. 1; David Albright and Robert Kelley, "Has Iraq Come Clean at Last?," *Bulletin of the Atomic Scientists*, November/December 1995, p. 53. For a description of the "crash program," see IAEA "Eighth Report of the Director General Monitoring and Verification," op. cit., p. 6; IAEA, "Report on the Twenty-Eighth On-Site Inspection," op. cit. p. 3; "Report on the Twenty-Ninth On-Site Inspection," op. cit., p. 3.

50According to UNSCOM Chairman Ekeus, the deadline of April 1991 was based on instructions from the Iraqi leadership, including Gen. Hussein Kamel. However, in a number of meetings with IAEA inspectors, some Iraqi officials remained steadfast in their assertion that the April 1991 deadline was for the recovery of the HEU from the reactor fuel, and that no other deadlines had been set. See Hibbs, "Experts Say Iraq Could Not Meet Bomb Deadline Even With Diversion," op. cit.; IAEA, "Report on the Twenty-Eighth On-Site Inspection," op. cit., p. 14; Briefing by Ambassador Ekeus, *Hearings on Global Proliferation,* op. cit., p. 99.

51In discussions with IAEA inspectors, Iraqi scientists indicated that they might have been able to fabricate a nuclear device before the end of 1992 if they were successful in their tests of single full-size lenses. In that case, "the first full-scale non-nuclear implosion with a natural uranium pit and an internal neutron initiator could have taken place sometime in 1991." See IAEA, "Report on the Twenty-Ninth On-Site Inspection," op. cit., pp 7-8. Also see "Report on the Twenty-Eighth On-Site Inspection," op. cit., p. 14.

52IAEA, "Report on the Twenty-Ninth On-Site Inspection," op. cit., pp. 5, 10.

53IAEA, "Report on the Twenty-Eighth On-Site Inspection," op. cit., p. 11. Iraq reportedly stated that it planned to commission a 1000-machine cascade in 1994. See Albright, Berkhout, and Walker, *1996: World Inventories,* op. cit., p. 331.

54Mark Hibbs, "IAEA Recovers Gear in Jordan Sold to Iraq by German Fugitive," *Nucleonics Week*, September 19, 1996, p. 1; Mark Hibbs, "Future of IAEA in Iraq at Stake After Middle East Tension Rises," *Nuclear Fuel*, September 23, 1996, p. 3. As noted earlier, Karl-Heinz Schaab was an ex-employee of the firm MAN Technologie AG, which manufactures centrifuge parts for the German Division of Urenco.

55Mark Hibbs, "EXTRA: Iraq Bought—And Still Has—Design for Advanced Urenco Gas Centrifuge," *Nucleonics Week*, January 22, 1996, p. 1; Mark Hibbs, "Internal Security Probe Underway Following Urenco Design Diversion," *Nuclear Fuel*, January 29, 1996, p. 1.

56IAEA, "Report on the Twenty-Ninth On-Site Inspection," op. cit., p. 7. Urenco's G-1 and G-2 machines utilize maraging steel rotor tubes, the former consisting of one tube and the latter of two tubes connected by a bellows. The supercritical TC-11 centrifuge machine consists of seven composite carbon fiber rotor tube segments, linked together by bellows (thin rings three millimeters or less in thickness). Hibbs, "EXTRA: Iraq Bought—And Still Has—Design," op. cit.

In February 1996, the IAEA revealed that Bruno Stemmler, another former employee of MAN Technologie AG who was known to have provided expert advice to Iraq's centrifuge program, had also sold Urenco gas centrifuge blueprints during the period 1988-1989. See Drees, "Second German Sold Nuclear Data," op. cit.; Hibbs, "Stemmler, Too, Sold Baghdad Urenco Centrifuge Blueprints," op. cit., p. 1.

57IAEA, "Report on the Twenty-Eighth On-Site Inspection," op. cit., p. 12. Also see "Report on the Twenty-Ninth On-Site Inspection," op. cit., p. 6; Mark Hibbs, "Iraqi Design Engineers May Have Tapped German Cascade Know-How," *Nuclear Fuel*, February 12, 1996, p. 12; Mark Hibbs, "Siemens, IAEA Don't Agree About Firm's Role in Iraq," *Nuclear Fuel*, February 26, 1996, p. 4.

58IAEA, "Report on the Twenty-Eighth On-Site Inspection," op. cit., "Report on the Twenty-Ninth On-Site Inspection," op. cit.

59IAEA, "Report on the Twenty-Ninth On-Site Inspection," op. cit., p. 9; Hibbs, "Experts Say Iraq Could Not Meet Bomb Deadline," op. cit., p. 11. Following the seventh IAEA inspection in the fall of 1991, IAEA inspectors had tentatively concluded that the group had conducted experiments limited to generating planar shock waves (i.e., they had only developed and tested plane-wave lenses). They assumed, however, that the Iraqi scientists had "a basic knowledge of the initiation of a spherical implosion." (See "Report on the Seventh IAEA On-Site Inspection in Iraq," op. cit., p. 11.) But during the 28th and 29th inspections, the IAEA team found out that a large number of shock-wave and high-explosive experiments had been made, mainly at Al Atheer, but also at Al Qa Qaa. They also discovered that work on spherical lenses had started as early as 1988 and that an experimental unit of the weaponization group had made several, single unit tests of spherical wave lenses. See IAEA, "Report on the Twenty-Ninth On-Site Inspection," op. cit., p. 9; IAEA, "Report on the Twenty-Eighth On-Site Inspection," op. cit., p. 16.

60IAEA, "Second Consolidated Report of the Director General of the International Atomic Energy Agency Under Paragraph 16 of Resolution 1051 (1996)," S/1996/833, p. 11.

61Part I of the IAEA's "93-2" enhanced safeguards program provides for stronger environmental monitoring procedures than those carried out under INFCIRC-153, the Agency's model safeguards agreement for the parties to the NPT.

62Hibbs, "Future of IAEA in Iraq at Stake After Middle East Tension Rises," op. cit. A former senior IAEA inspector has questioned the adequacy of the IAEA monitoring system in Iraq to detect clandestine small-scale reprocessing of spent fuel. Interview on February 1997.

63Irwin Arieff, "U.S. Says Iran Wants to Steal Nuke Arms Capability," *Reuters*, February 29, 1996.

64Interview with senior U.S. Administration official, October 1996; also see Briefing by Ambassador Rolf Ekeus, *Hearings on Global Proliferation*, op. cit., p. 99.

65"Second Consolidated Report of the Director General of the International Atomic Energy Agency Under Paragraph 16 of Resolution 1051 (1996)," op. cit., p. 11.

66Barbara Crossette, "Iraqis Still Defying Arms Ban, Departing U.N. Official Says," *New York Times*, June 25, 1997. Also see Evelyn Leopold, "France Says IAEA Should Close Nuclear File on Iraq," *Reuters*, October 17, 1997. UNSCOM, "Report of the Secretary-General on the Activities of the Special Commission Established by the Secretary-General Pursuant 9 (b)(i) of Resolution 687 (1991)," S/1997/301, April 11, 1997, p. 23.

67See Barbara Crossette, "UN Chief Approves a New Plan to Allow Iraq to Start Selling Oil," *New York Times*, July 19, 1996. Also see Nicholas Burns, "State Department Regular Briefing," January 31, 1996; "Israeli Says Iraq Could Use Oil Money for Arms," *Reuters*, February 13, 1996; Nicholas Doughty, "Iraq Sanctions Expected to Stay Despite Oil Deal," *Reuters*, May 21, 1996; Barbara Crossette,

"Accord Reached by Iraq and UN For Oil Exports," *New York Times*, May 21, 1996.

[68]Barbara Crossette, "Iraq Gets U.N. Approval to Sell Oil to Meet Civilian Needs," *New York Times*, December 10, 1996; John M. Goshko and Martha M. Hamilton, "U.N. Backs Oil-for-Food Deal for Iraq," *Washington Post*, December 10, 1996; Douglas Jehl, "Iraq Resumes Pumping Oil Through Pipeline to Turkey," *New York Times*, December 11, 1996.

[69]See UNSCOM, "First Consolidated Report of the Secretary-General Pursuant to Paragraph 9," April 11, 1996, p. 22. Also see IAEA, "Sixth Report of the Director General on Monitoring and Verification," op. cit., p. 16. In February 1996, President Clinton signed legislation that amended the 1992 Iran-Iraq Arms Non-Proliferation Act to impose sanctions on any person or foreign government that "transfers or retransfers goods or technology so as to contribute knowingly and materially to the efforts by Iran or Iraq to acquire chemical, biological, or nuclear weapons." Iran-Iraq Arms Non-Proliferation Act, P.L. 102-484, Division A. Title XVI, Secs. 1604 and 1605, (October 23, 1992), 106 Stat. 2571, (50 USC 1701, note), as amended by the Defense Authorization Act for Fiscal Year 1996, P.L. 104-107, Sec. 1408, (February 10, 1996). (For details, see Iran chapter in this volume.)

[70]Note that short-range ballistic missiles (SRBMs) with ranges up to 1,000 km are valued as "strategic" weapons in the relatively compact geography of the Near East and Gulf States. As classified by the United States, ground-based medium-range ballistic missiles (MRBMs) have ranges between 1,000 and 3,000 km and intermediate-range ballistic missiles (IRBMs) have ranges between 3,000 and 5,500 km. Ground-based ballistic missiles that exceed 5,500 km range are considered intercontinental ballistic missiles (ICBMs).

Ekeus testified that "Iraq [had] not been able to produce guidance and control systems . . . [It had to use] spare kits from the Soviet deliveries to put into those homemade type of missiles." See Briefing by Ambassador Ekeus, *Hearings on Global Proliferation*, op. cit., p. 93.

[71]Office of the Secretary of Defense, *Proliferation: Threat and Response*, 1996, op. cit., p. 21; UNSCOM, "Report of the Secretary-General on the Status of the Implementation of the Special Commission's Plan for the Ongoing Monitoring and Verification of Iraq's Compliance With Relevant Parts of Section C of Security Council Resolution 687 (1991)," S/1995/284, April 10, 1995, p. 6. UNSCOM's assessment is that no complete Badr 2000 missiles were ever produced in Iraq. According to the DOD report noted above, "Baghdad also had plans for a 2,000-kilometer range missile, called the Tammouz I." The Tammouz I was to have a Scud-derivative first stage and an SA-2 sustainer as the second stage.

[72]Interview with Rolf Ekeus, spring 1997; UNSCOM, "Report of the Secretary-General on the Activities of the Special Commission Established by the Secretary-General Pursuant to Paragraph 9 (b) (i) of Resolution 687 (1991)," S/1997/774, October 6, 1997, p. 6.

[73]Office of the Secretary of Defense, *Proliferation: Threat and Response*, 1996, op. cit., p. 21. The development program for the Ababil-100 is considering both solid- and liquid-propellant versions. The missile's overall configuration will have great potential for range extension.

[74]R. Jeffrey Smith, "U.N. Finds New Evidence of Iraqi Long-Range Missile Research," *Washington Post*, February 5, 1997.

[75]UNSCOM, "Report of the Secretary-General on Compliance," April 10, 1995, p. 6; UNSCOM, "Report of the Secretary-General on Iraq's Compliance," October 11, 1995, op. cit., p. 14.

[76]In 1994, Rolf Ekeus, head of UNSCOM, stated his belief that, subject to verification, his commission had accounted for all missiles delivered from the Soviet Union. However, the subsequent verification of activities showed that all Scud missiles had not been identified. (Interview with Rolf Ekeus, spring 1997.) In his September 1994 speech (see note 38), then CIA Director Woolsey said that Iraq was still hiding Scud missiles. See David C. Isby, "Iraq's Residual Scud Force," *Jane's Intelligence Review*, March 1995; Balman, "CIA: Saddam Building and Hiding Weapons," op. cit.; Worsnip, "CIA Chief Attacks Iran, Iraq Weapons Programs," op. cit.

[77]UNSCOM, "Report of the Secretary-General on Iraq's Compliance," October 11, 1995, op. cit., p. 14.

[78]UNSCOM, "Tenth Report of the Executive Chairman of the Special Commission Established by the Secretary-General Pursuant to Paragraph 9 (b) (i) of Resolution 687 (1991), and Paragraph 3 of Resolution 699 (1991)," S/1995/1038, December 17, 1995.

[79]The Al Abid's first stage consisted of five lengthened Scuds in parallel. Office of the Secretary of Defense, *Proliferation: Threat and Response*, 1996, op cit.

[80]IAEA, "First Consolidated Report of the Director General of the International Atomic Energy Agency Under Paragraph 16 of Resolution 1051 (1996)," S/1996/261, April 11, 1996, p. 7. Also see "Report on the Twenty-Eighth On-Site Inspection in Iraq," op. cit., p 15; "Report on the Twenty-Ninth On-Site Inspection," op. cit., p. 10.

[81]Evelyn Leopold, "UN Official Unsatisfied With Iraqi Missile Data," *Reuters*, December 5, 1995.

[82]UNSCOM, "Tenth Report of the Executive Chairman," op. cit.

[83]UNSCOM, "Report of the Secretary-General on Iraq's Compliance," October 11, 1995, op. cit., p. 13. Also see UNSCOM, "Tenth Report of the Executive Chairman," op. cit.; Barbara Crossette, "UN Panel Says Iraq May Still Be Trying to Produce Missiles," *New York Times*, December 22, 1996.

[84]UNSCOM, "Report of the Secretary-General on Iraq's Compliance," October 11, 1995, op. cit., p. 12.

[85]This equipment included "key pieces of advanced missile systems, such as accelerometers and gyroscopes, a variety of specialty metals, a set of special machine tools, and a high-tech furnace that can be used to fabricate missile engine parts." See R. Jeffrey Smith, "Iraq Buying Missile Parts Covertly; Officials Say Effort Violates Trade Ban," *Washington Post*, October 14, 1995. In this report, a senior U.S. official was quoted as saying that the suppliers of this equipment were European countries, including Germany, France and Ukraine, but that of particular concern were recent, missile-related sales to Iraq from Russia.

[86]See "Jordan Intercepts Missile Parts," op. cit.; "U.S. Praises Jordan for Seizure," op. cit.; "Jordan Says Shipment 'Ominous' Sign of Iraq Intent," op. cit.; "Jordanians Intercept Chemicals," op. cit.; R. Jeffrey Smith, "U.N. Is Said to Find Russian Markings on Iraq-Bound Military Equipment," *Washington Post*, December 15, 1997.

[87]Crossette, "Iraq May Still Be Trying to Produce Missiles," op. cit.; Briefing by Ambassador Rolf Ekeus, *Hearings on Global Proliferation*, op. cit., p. 95; R. Jeffrey Smith, "Iraq Accused of Hiding Prohibited Weapons," *Washington Post*, October 12, 1996. In September 1997, it was reported the gyroscopes that were fished out of the Tigris river had originated from the Scientific Testing Institute of Chemical Machine Building at the Russian city of Sergiyev Posad. The facility has disassembled SS-N-8 missiles removed from Russian submarines under START I reductions. The gyroscopes reportedly were transferred to Iraq through a Moscow-based company and a Lebanese middleman. See David Hoffman, "Russian Missile Gyroscopes Were Sold to Iraq," *Washington Post*, September 12, 1997.

[88]Stewart Stogel, "Missile Plans by Iraq May Aim at Europe," *Washington Times*, February 16, 1996.

[89]UNSCOM, "Report of the Secretary-General on the Activities," p. 9; Smith, "Iraq Accused of Hiding Prohibited Weapons," op. cit.

[90]Briefing by Ambassador Ekeus, *Hearings on Global Proliferation*, op. cit., p. 93. Also see Peter F. Sisler, "Ekeus: Iraq Still Hiding Missiles," *United Press International*, March 20, 1996; "Weapons Inspector: Iraq May Be Hiding Biological-Warhead Missiles," *Associated Press*, March 21, 1996; "Iraq May Have 16 Banned Missiles," *Washington Times*, July 2, 1996.

[91]Office of the Secretary of Defense, *Proliferation: Threat and Response*, 1996, op. cit., p. 24.

[92]"Iraq Likely Has Hidden Missiles, Inspector Says," *Washington Times*, December 19, 1996; Barbara Crossette, "UN Says Iraq May Be Hiding More Missiles Than Suspected," *New York Times*, December 19, 1996.

[93]UNSCOM, "Report of the Secretary-General on the Activities of the Special Commission Established by the Secretary-General Pursuant to Paragraph 9 (b) (i) of Resolution 687 (1991)," S/1997/774, October 6, 1997, pp. 6-8; White House, "Iraq's Program of Mass Destruction," op. cit.

[94]UNSCOM, "Report of the Secretary-General on the Activities," October 6, 1997, op. cit., pp. 6-8; see also R. Jeffrey Smith, "Iraq's Drive for a Biological Arsenal," *Washington Post*, November 21, 1997.

[95]Briefing by Ambassador Ekeus, *Hearings on Global Proliferation*, op. cit.; Office of the Secretary of Defense, *Proliferation: Threat and Response,* 1996, op cit.; Marie Colvin and Uzi Mahnaimi Amman, "Saddam Invents Germ Warfare Crop-duster to Spray Cities," *Sunday Times* (London), November 9, 1997.

[96]Office of the Secretary of Defense, *Proliferation: Threat and Response*, 1996, op. cit., p. 19.

[97]Ibid., p. 21; Testimony of Lt. Gen. James R. Clapper, Jr., USAF, Director of the Defense Intelligence Agency, *Hearings on Worldwide Threat to the United States*, before the Armed Services Committee, U.S. Senate, 104th Cong., 1st Sess., January 17, 1995, p. 50; Testimony of Joseph S. Nye, Jr., Assistant Secretary of Defense for International Security Affairs, *Hearings on U.S. Policy toward Iran and Iraq*, before the Foreign Relations Committee, U.S. Senate, 104th Cong., 1st Sess., March 2 and August 3, 1995, pp. 171, 173.

[98]"Iraq Reportedly Restores Army," *Associated Press*, printed in *Washington Post*, October 6, 1996; Sean Boyne, "How Saddam Rebuilt," *Jane's Intelligence Review*, November 1996, p. 506.

[99]See R. Jeffrey Smith, "Iraq Stronger Since August, Deutch Says," *Washington Post*, September 20, 1996. Also see R. Jeffrey Smith and David B. Ottaway, "Anti-Saddam Operation Cost CIA $100 Million," *Washington Post*, September 15, 1996.

[100]UNSCOM, "Report of the Secretary-General on the Activities," op. cit., pp. 3, 16, 17; UNSCOM, "Report of the Secretary-General on the Activities," October 6, 1997, op. cit., pp. 3, 10, 16, 27, 37; White House, "Iraq's Program of Mass Destruction," op. cit.; Smith, "Iraq's Drive for a Biological Arsenal," op. cit. Also see Rolf Ekeus, Executive Chairman, U.N. Special Commission, "Iraq," remarks before the Washington Institute for Near East Policy, January 29, 1997.

[101]John M. Goshko, "U.N. Inspectors Told to Ignore Iraqi Warning," *Washington Post*, October 31, 1997; John M. Goshko, "Iraq Persists In Blocking Inspectors," *Washington Post*, November 4, 1997; John Lancaster, "Iraq Defends Expulsion Order," *Washington Post*, November 8, 1997; John F. Harris, "U.S. Urging U.N. to Pressure Iraq to Yield on Arms," *Washington Post*, November 10, 1997; John M. Goshko, "Council May Condemn Iraqi Moves," *Washington Post*, November 12, 1997; Charles Trueheart and David Hoffman, "France, Russia Differ From U.S. in Agendas on Iraq," *Washington Post*, November 13, 1997; John M. Goshko, "Iraq Expels 6 American Inspectors," *Washington Post*, November 14, 1997; John Lancaster, "Egypt Urges Diplomacy, Not Force, in U.S.-Iraq Dispute," *Washington Post*, November 14, 1997; Steven Erlanger, "Iraq Sends Signal It Does Not Want to Fight with U.S.," *New York Times*, November 17, 1997; John F. Harris, "Cohen Cites Iraqi Ability on Weapons," *Washington Post*, November 17, 1997; John M. Goshko, "U.N. Arms Inspectors Returning to Iraq in Reversal by Baghdad," *Washington Post*, November 21, 1997; John M. Goshko, "U.N. Panel on Iraq Supports Sanctions," *Washington Post*, November 23, 1997; R. Jeffrey Smith, "Iraq Calls Some Areas Off-Limits," *Washington Post*, November 27, 1997; Waiel Faleh, "Iraq Drops Insistence on End to Embargo," *Associated Press*, November 29, 1997, published in *Washington Post*, November 30, 1997.

For a review of Iraq's obstructionist behavior vis-à-vis UNSCOM inspections during 1997, see UNSCOM, "Report of the Secretary-General on the Activities," October 6, 1997, op. cit., p. 31; R. Jeffrey Smith, "Iraqis' Resistance Grew for Months," *Washington Post*, November 9, 1997.

Additional References

1990: Leonard S. Spector with Jacqueline R. Smith, *Nuclear Ambitions* (Boulder, CO: Westview Press, 1990). **1992:** Gary Milhollin, "Building Saddam Hussein's Bomb," *New York Times Magazine*, March 8, 1992, pp. 30-36; IAEA, "IAEA Inspections and Iraq's Nuclear Capabilities," IAEA/PI/A35E, April 1992; Jay C. Davis and David A. Kay, "Iraq's Secret Nuclear Weapons Program," *Physics Today*, July 1992, p. 21; Paul Lewis, "U.N. Experts Now Say Baghdad Was Far From Making an A-Bomb Before Gulf War," New York Times, May 20, 1992. **1993:** Maurizio Zifferero, "The IAEA: Neutralizing Iraq's Nuclear Weapons Potential," *Arms Control Today*, April 1993, p. 7. **1996:** Robert Kelley, "The Iraqi and South African Nuclear Weapon Programs," *Security Dialogue* Vol. 27, No. 1, pp. 24-38, 1996. **1997:** "Ambassador Rolf Ekeus; Leaving Behind the UNSCOM Legacy in Iraq," *Arms Control Today*, June/July 1997, p. 3; Judy Aita, "U.N. Dissatisfied With Two Iraqi Weapons Inspections," *USIS Washington File*, September 17, 1997; Robert H. Reid, "UN-Iraq," *Associated Press*, October 2, 1997; Anthony Goodman, "U.S. to Have 'Strong Response' to Iraq Arms Report," *Reuters*, October 10, 1997; Evelyn Leopold, "France, Russia Oppose US, Britain on Iraq Sanctions," *Reuters*, October 17, 1997; John M. Goshko, "U.S. May Delay Pressing New Iraq Sanctions," *Washington Post*, October 21, 1997; John Lancaster, "Iraq to Oust American Inspectors," *Washington Post*, October 31, 1997.

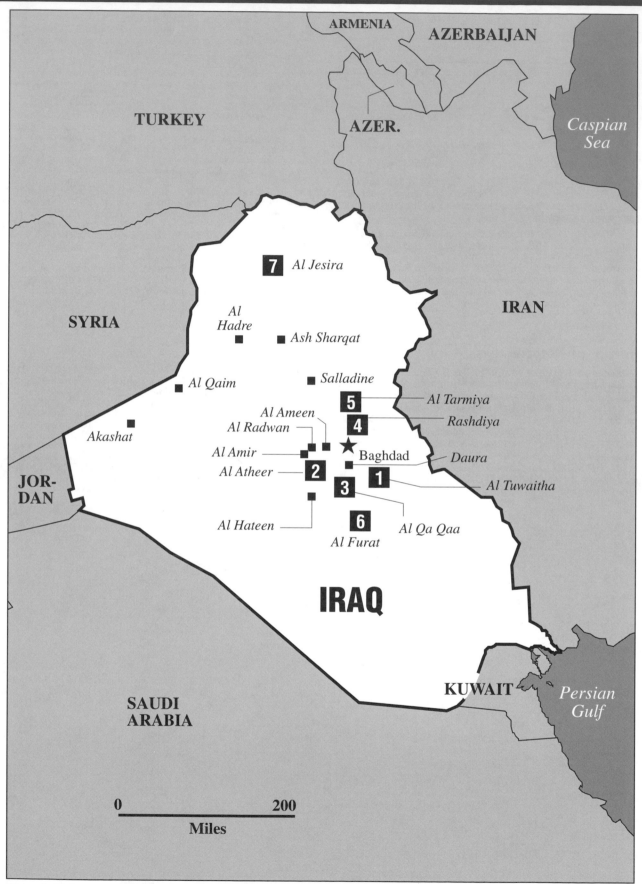

Carnegie Endowment for International Peace, *Tracking Nuclear Proliferation*, 1998

Italicized names on map represent nuclear-related sites either declared by Iraq or discovered by IAEA inspectors during implementation of Security Council Resolution 687 adopted at the end of the 1991 Gulf War. The facilities and equipment at these sites that escaped damage during the war were subsequently dismantled or destroyed by the IAEA or came under IAEA monitoring; sensitive nuclear materials have been removed. See chart.

1 **Al Tuwaitha Nuclear Research Center.** *Tammuz I (Osiraq), Tammuz II (Isis), and IRT-5000 research reactors (the first destroyed by Israel in 1981); subject to IAEA inspection prior to Gulf War.*

Site of research and development (R&D) programs in uranium enrichment, including gas centrifuges, Electromagnetic Isotope Separation (EMIS), chemical separation, and gaseous diffusion.*

Location of "hot cells" used for separation of grams of plutonium.* Experimental program for the production of lithium-6 which, if irradiated in a reactor, yields tritium for use in advanced nuclear weapons.

Weapons-related R&D activities in nuclear physics, uranium metallurgy, and triggering system capacitors.**

2 **Al Atheer.** *Prime development and testing site for nuclear weaponization program, including facilities and equipment for large-scale uranium metallurgy and production of weapons components; computer simulations of nuclear weapon detonations; and experiments for the development of an implosion-type explosive structure in nearby "bunker" at Al-Hateen. Possible testing of explosive structures at Al Hadre.***

3 **Al Qa Qaa High Explosives and Propellant Facility.** *Military and nuclear weapons R&D facility: development of exploding bridge wire detonators (EBW) used in the firing system of nuclear weapons; high-explosive experiments; storage of large quantities of HMX high explosive used in nuclear weapons.***

4 **Rashdiya.** *Central site of Iraq's centrifuge research and development efforts.*

5 **Al Tarmiya.** *Industrial-scale complex for EMIS designed for the installation of 70 1,200-millimeter separators plus twenty 600-millimeter separators. Eight units were operational prior to Desert Storm bombings; if all separators had been installed, plant could have yielded 15 kg of HEU annually, possibly enough for one nuclear weapon. Replica facilities were under construction at Ash Sharqat.**

6 **Al Furat Project.** *Large-scale manufacturing and testing facility, designed for the production of centrifuges for uranium enrichment. Site of a planned 100-centrifuge experimental cascade, with an initial operational capability by mid-1993. A 1000-centrifuge cascade was to be built at Taji.**

7 **Al Jesira.** *Large-scale facility for the production of uranium dioxide (UO_2) and uranium tetrachloride (UC_4), feed materials for EMIS. Intended site for the production of uranium hexafluoride (UF_6) to feed the centrifuge enrichment program.**

* Activities found by IAEA to be in violation of Iraq's safeguards agreement with the IAEA.

** Activities found by the United States to be in violation of Iraq's obligations under Article II of the Nuclear Non-Proliferation Treaty (NPT) prohibiting the "manufacture" of nuclear weapons.

IRAQ: Nuclear Infrastructure

NAME/LOCATION OF FACILITY	TYPE/STATUS	IAEA SAFEGUARDS[a]
NUCLEAR WEAPONS COMPLEX		
Al Atheer	Prime development and testing complex for nuclear weaponization program; large-scale uranium metallurgy that could produce reflectors, tampers, and other weapons components; location of two isostatic presses (hot and cold) suitable for making shaped charges, plus other remote-controlled machining equipment suitable for production of explosive structures. Operational until damaged by Coalition air attacks (1991); subsequently destroyed by IAEA inspectors.	NPT Violation
Al Tuwaitha	Nuclear physics and uranium metallurgy laboratories; research and development (R&D) in triggering system capacitors; possible site for experimental work on neutronic initiators. Operational until damaged by Coalition air attacks (1991); under IAEA monitoring.	NPT Violation
Al Qa Qaa	Military R&D facility; development and fabrication of exploding bridge wire detonators and high-explosive lenses (plane and spherical); site of shock-wave and high-explosive experiments; storage of large quantities of HMX high explosive; under IAEA monitoring.	NPT Violation
Al Musaiyib (Al Hateen Establishment)	High-explosive testing site; facility for hydrodynamic studies; facilities and equipment destroyed by the IAEA.	NPT Violation
Al Hadre	Open firing range for fuel-air bombs and fragmentation testing, suitable for experimentation with entire non-nuclear explosive structure of an implosion-type nuclear device; damaged by Coalition air attacks; under IAEA monitoring.	NPT Violation
RESEARCH REACTORS[b]		
Osiraq/Tammuz I	Light-water, HEU, 40 MWt; destroyed by Israeli air attack (1981).	Yes
Isis/Tammuz II	Light-water, HEU, 800 KWt; operational until destroyed by Coalition air attack (1991).	Yes
IRT-5000	Light-water, HEU, 5 MWt; operational until destroyed by Coalition air attack (1991).	Yes
URANIUM ENRICHMENT		
Al Tuwaitha	Prototype-scale, electromagnetic isotope separation (EMIS) method; operational until damaged by Coalition air attack (1991).	IAEA Violation
Al Tuwaitha	Prototype-scale, gas centrifuge method; operations relocated to Rashdiya in 1987.	IAEA Violation
Rashdiya	Prototype-scale, gas centrifuge method; operations terminated at the outbreak of the 1991 Gulf War; under IAEA monitoring.[c,d]	IAEA Violation
Al Tuwaitha	Laboratory-scale, chemical exchange isotope separation method; operational until damaged by Coalition air attack (1991).	IAEA Violation
Al Tarmiya	Industrial-scale, EMIS method[e]; partially operational until damaged by Coalition air attack (1991); EMIS-related installations and equipment subsequently destroyed by IAEA.[f]	IAEA Violation
Ash Sharqat	Industrial-scale, EMIS method; under construction until damaged by Coalition air attack (1991); EMIS-related installations and equipment subsequently destroyed by IAEA.	IAEA Violation?

NAME/LOCATION OF FACILITY	TYPE/STATUS	IAEA SAFEGUARDS[a]
Al Furat	Large manufacturing and testing facility for centrifuge production[g]; under construction until it came under IAEA monitoring.	IAEA Violation?
REPROCESSING (PLUTONIUM EXTRACTION)		
Al Tuwaitha	Laboratory-scale; three hot cells used for separating plutonium from irradiated uranium; operations terminated as a result of Gulf War (1991); equipment largely escaped damage; destroyed or rendered inoperable subsequently by IAEA inspectors.	IAEA Violation[h]
URANIUM PROCESSING		
Akashat	Uranium mine; operational until damaged by Coalition air attack (1991).	N/A (Not Applicable)
Al Qaim	Phosphate plant that produced uranium concentrate (U_3O_8); operational until damaged by Coalition air attack (1991); recovered material under IAEA monitoring.	N/A
Al Tuwaitha	Laboratory-scale uranium purification facility (UO_2); operational until heavily damaged by Coalition air attack (1991); recovered equipment under IAEA monitoring.	IAEA Violation
Al Tuwaitha	Laboratory-scale, uranium tetrachloride facility (UCL_4); operational until heavily damaged by Coalition air attack (1991); recovered equipment under IAEA monitoring.	IAEA Violation
Al Tuwaitha	Laboratory-scale production of uranium hexafluoride (UF_6); operational until damaged by Coalition air attack (1991).	IAEA Violation
Al Tuwaitha	Fuel fabrication laboratory; operational until destroyed by Coalition air attack (1991); recovered nuclear material under IAEA monitoring.	IAEA Violation
Mosul (Al Jesira)	Industrial-scale, uranium tetrachloride facility (UCL_4); operational until damaged by Coalition air attack (1991).	IAEA Violation
Mosul (Al Jesira)	Production-scale uranium purification facility (UO_2); operational until heavily damaged by Coalition air attack (1991); production area sustained greatest damage by subsequent Iraqi deception activities.	IAEA Violation

Abbreviations:

HEU	=	highly enriched uranium
LEU	=	low-enriched uranium
nat. U	=	natural uranium
MWe	=	millions of watts of electrical output
MWt	=	millions of watts of thermal output
KWt	=	thousands of watts of thermal output
?	=	uncertain

NOTES (Iraq Chart)

[a]For the purposes of this chart, the designations "Yes" and "N/A" (not applicable) are used to describe the safeguards in place prior to the 1991 Gulf War at facilities processing or using nuclear materials that were declared by Iraq to the IAEA under Iraq's safeguards agreement with the IAEA (INFCIRC/172). "IAEA Violation" denotes clandestine facilities involved in processing or using nuclear *materials* that were discovered in the course of the post-war IAEA inspections and found by the IAEA to be violations of the IAEA-Iraq safe-guards agreement. "NPT Violation" denotes clandestine facilities that were discovered in the course of the post-war IAEA inspections and were involved in nuclear weapons-related *activities* inconsistent with Iraq's NPT pledge not to manufacture nuclear arms.

[b]In late 1992–early 1993, rumors surfaced about the possible existence of an underground, plutonium-bearing, heavy-water reactor. During the tenth and eighteenth IAEA inspections, a number of sites were visited but no such facility was found. In early 1996,

Iraqi officals admitted that feasibility studies had been carried out in 1984-1988 to replace the capability that would have been provided by the Osiraq research reactor. However, the project was allowed to lapse in mid-1988 because of the "lack of available resources resulting from the higher priority needs of the EMIS enrichment and weapon development programs." See First Consolidated Report of the Director General of the International Atomic Energy Agency Under Paragraph 16 of Resolution 1051 (1996), p. 4. Also see "Report on the Tenth IAEA On-Site Inspection in Iraq Under Security Council Resolution 687 (1991)," S/23644, February 26, 1992, p. 17; "Report on the Eighteenth IAEA On-Site Inspection in Iraq Under Security Council Resolution 687 (1991)," S/25666, April 26, 1993, p. 20; Gary Milholin, "The New Arms Race: The Iraqi Bomb," *New Yorker*, February 1, 1993, p. 47; Diana Edensword and Gary Milholin, "Iraq's Bomb—an Update," *New York Times*, April 26, 1993; Maurizio Zifferero, "The IAEA: Neutralizing Iraq's Nuclear Weapons Potential," *Arms Control Today,* April 1993, p. 7.

[c]A cascade hall was being constructed to accommodate super-critical centrifuges. It might have ended up housing the 100-machine cascade envisioned for the Al Furat plant, if the latter had continued to experience construction delays (see endnote g). It was also the planned site for the 50-machine cascade that would have been used to reenrich HEU in the "Crash Program."

[d]All known centrifuge components and manufacturing equipment have been destroyed or rendered inoperable by IAEA inspection teams.

[e]Component manufacturing facilities for the Iraqi EMIS program were located at: Al Ameen (prototype components); Al Radwan and Al Amir (magnet cores, return irons, ion sources, collector parts); Sehee at Daura (vacuum chamber parts); Salladine (electrical control panel assembly); and Tuwaitha (coil manufacturing). In January 1993, a U.S. cruise missile attack destroyed Al Rabee, an EMIS-related industrial complex near Zaafarniyah (about 20 km from Baghdad) in retaliation to Iraqi violations of Security Council resolutions establishing no-fly zones in Iraq. Al Rabee and Al Dijjla, another site at Zaafarniyah that was not hit in the attack, were manufacturing plants whose activities were useful in producing EMIS components. Their capabilities included coil winding, chassis assembly, computer-aided design, printed circuit-board fabrication, and control system design and assembly. Reportedly the two plants had manufactured some EMIS equipment installed at the Al Tarmiya facility. See Mark Hibbs, "IAEA in 'Difficult Position' After U.S. Attack on Iraq Site," *Nucleonics Week*, January 21, 1993.

[f]All equipment at the Al Tuwaitha and Al Tarmiya sites that might have revealed the existence of the EMIS program was removed and transported by the Iraqi Army to six locations where Iraqi personnel attempted to destroy the tell-tale signs of the EMIS effort. After IAEA inspection teams obtained access to those locations, the inspectors concentrated their efforts on identifying key EMIS components that were still recognizable to verify Iraqi statements regarding their program. This equipment was then destroyed under the supervision of the IAEA inspectors.

[g]These facilities, which escaped damage during the Gulf War, were far from completion when work stopped in August 1990.

[h]One of the fuel elements processed was from the IRT-5000 reactor and was exempt from safeguards under Article 37 of INFC-IRC/172, Iraq's safeguards agreement with the IAEA. The other three were fabricated indigenously from undeclared nuclear material, in violation of the safeguards agreement. A total of 6 grams of plutonium was recovered.

Israel

Israel is not a party to the Nuclear Non-Proliferation Treaty (NPT) and has not acknowledged that it has nuclear weapons, but generally is regarded as a *de facto* nuclear-weapon state. In recent years, unclassified estimates of Israel's nuclear capabilities have been based in large part on former Israeli nuclear technician Mordechai Vanunu's revelations to the *Sunday Times* of London in October 1986.[1] Based on Vanunu's information about Israeli plutonium production, the *Sunday Times* projected that Israel might have as many as 200 nuclear devices.[2] U.S. officials who attempted at the time to harmonize Vanunu's testimony with other relevant information concluded, however, that, given the relatively small size of Israel's only plutonium-producing reactor, located at the Dimona research complex, Israel's nuclear inventory probably contained fewer than 100 weapons, and perhaps as few as 50 or 60. Extrapolating from these lower figures to the present, the Israeli nuclear arsenal could have grown to between 70 and 80 weapons today.[3] Vanunu also indicated that Israel had produced tritium and lithium deuteride, suggesting that Israel may have developed "boosted" nuclear weapons, i.e., weapons that use a nuclear fusion reaction to increase their efficiency. Since Israel is not known to have conducted any nuclear tests (see below), it is assumed that it could not have advanced to the point of producing thermonuclear weapons ("hydrogen bombs").

A 1991 book by American investigative journalist Seymour Hersh argued that Israel's arsenal was considerably larger and more advanced than even Vanunu's information suggested. Relying largely on interviews with U.S. intelligence analysts and Israelis knowledgeable about the country's nuclear program, Hersh concluded that Israel possessed "hundreds" of low-yield enhanced-radiation type warheads, many in the form of artillery shells and land mines, as well as full-fledged thermonuclear weapons.[4]

A 1994 report alleged plausible new details about Israel's nuclear weapons infrastructure, identifying Nahal Soreq as the installation where Israel conducts research on nuclear weapons design. It claimed that Israel's nuclear weapons are assembled at a facility in Yodefat, that Israel's nuclear missile base and bunker for storing nuclear gravity bombs is in Kfar Zekharya, and that tactical nuclear weapons are stored at Eilabun.[5]

BACKGROUND

Nuclear Weapons Program. The Israeli nuclear weapons program was launched in the fall of 1956, in the wake of the Suez crisis. At the time, France's Socialist government, led by Guy Mollet, was deeply committed to Israel's survival, and the two states confronted dangers stemming from Arab nationalism—Israel because of its isolated position in the Middle East and France because of growing unrest in French Algeria. France secretly pledged to assist Israel in developing nuclear arms and agreed to supply a sizable plutonium-producing reactor to be built at Dimona, in the Negev, some 40 miles from Beersheba.[6]

In mid-1957, with French Atomic Energy Commission approval, Israel signed an agreement with the French firm of St. Gobain Techniques Nouvelles for the construction of several additional facilities at the Dimona site, including the key installation—where Vanunu would subsequently work—for extracting plutonium from the Dimona reactor's spent fuel. Soon thereafter, France also gave Israel important information on the design and manufacture of nuclear weapons themselves. Francis Perrin, the scientific head of the French Atomic Energy Commission from 1951 to 1970, was intimately involved with the French Israeli nuclear program. In an on-the-record 1986 interview with the London *Sunday Times*, Perrin acknowledged that France supplied the Dimona reactor and the plutonium extraction plant and that, for at least two years during the late 1950s, France and Israel collaborated on the design and development of nuclear weapons.[7]

There has been no conclusive proof that Israel has ever conducted a full-scale nuclear test. Its nuclear arsenal is thought to have been developed in part through the testing of non-nuclear components and computer simulations, and through the acquisition of weapons design and test information from abroad. Israel is thought, for example, to have obtained data from France's first nuclear test, in 1960.[8] It may also have obtained data from U.S. nuclear tests at approximately that time. According to a May 1989 U.S. television documentary, Israel was able to gain access to information concerning U.S. tests from the 1950s and early 1960s. The test data could have included the results of tests of U.S. boosted and thermonuclear weapons that were being developed at the time.[9]

There has been speculation, however, that a signal detected on September 22, 1979, by a U.S. VELA monitoring satellite orbiting over the South Atlantic was in fact the flash from a low-yield nuclear explosive test—possibly of a tactical nuclear weapon or of the fission trigger of a thermonuclear device. This event has been attributed by some to nuclear testing by South Africa, and by others to Israel.

Seymour Hersh reports that "according to Israeli officials whose information about other aspects of Dimona's activities has been corroborated," the September 1979 event was indeed an Israeli nuclear weapon test, and was actually the third of a series of tests conducted at that time.[10] The first two tests, Hersh's sources stated, were obscured by storm clouds. The claim that clouds would prevent detection of an atmospheric nuclear detonation by a VELA satellite has been challenged, however, since the satellite is said to rely in part on infra-red sensors that can penetrate cloud cover. Thus this critical matter remains unresolved.[11] Israel's pursuit of the nuclear deterrent option as the basis of national survival has been based primarily on two factors: Israel's lack of territorial strategic depth, which makes it difficult to absorb a conventional attack and respond effectively; and the "preponderance of men and equipment" enjoyed by its Arab neighbors, almost all of whom have been hostile adversaries throughout its history.[12] At the same time, Israel has sought to maintain a margin of qualitative conventional military superiority that would both discourage its foes from resorting to force and ensure victory without the use of nuclear arms in the event of conflict.[13]

In this context, David Ben-Gurion, Israel's first prime minister, formulated Israel's policy of "nuclear ambiguity."[14] It was first enunciated in a 1961 meeting of Shimon Peres, then Ben-Gurion's deputy, and President John F. Kennedy. Questioned about Israel's nuclear capabilities and intentions, Peres responded that "Israel would not be the first country to introduce nuclear weapons in the [Middle East]."[15] A refinement in Israel's defense posture was the "Begin doctrine," which became official policy after Israel's June 7, 1981, air attack on Iraq's plutonium-producing Osiraq research reactor. Israeli Prime Minister Menachem Begin then declared that Israel would block any attempt by adversaries to acquire nuclear weapons.[16]

During the 1980s the strategic balance in the Middle East underwent significant changes. A number of Arab states undertook or accelerated programs to develop or acquire weapons of mass destruction (WMD) as well as delivery systems.[17] By the end of the decade, Saddam Hussein was boasting about Iraq's extensive ballistic missile forces and chemical weapons capabilities by declaring that, if Israel attacked any Iraqi nuclear installations, he would destroy "half of Israel" with chemical weapons. (Iraq had already used chemical weapons in the Iran-Iraq War.)[18] At the same time Syria, Libya, and Iran were expanding their chemical weapons capabilities and a number of Israel's adversaries were also pursuing the development of biological weapons.[19]

While suspicion of Iraq's nuclear weapons program existed prior to the 1991 Gulf War, the scale and range of its efforts were not known. It was subsequently revealed that Iraq had embarked not only on a multifaceted nuclear weapons development program but also, after its invasion of Kuwait, on a "crash program" to develop a single nuclear device by April 1991. The emerging WMD threat was demonstrated during the 1991 Gulf War when Israeli cities and sites in Saudi Arabia were attacked by Iraqi extended-range Scud missiles. Although the attacking Scud missiles carried conventional warheads, it was later disclosed that Iraq had stockpiled chemical and biological warheads for such missiles and it is believed that some of the hidden Scud missiles were so armed.[20] Iraq launched a total of 39 Scud missiles against Israel causing two deaths and hundreds of injuries.[21]

The 1991 Gulf War also demonstrated the difficulties of identifying and striking facilities involved in clandestine proliferation programs. In spite of a massive Coalition air campaign, much of Iraq's nuclear weapons infrastructure remained intact. Several nuclear installations had not been identified by the United States and its partners. In some cases, attacked nuclear-related facilities suffered only slight damage, allowing the Iraqis to remove and hide equipment. It was left to the International Atomic Energy Agency (IAEA) to discover, in a painstaking effort, the magnitude of the Iraqi nuclear program. The case of Iraq raises important questions over the viability of the "Begin doctrine" in the future because potential nuclear infrastructure targets might be too distant, too well-hidden, and too numerous to be destroyed by air attacks.

Middle East Peace. The "tacit collaboration between Israel and the Arab members of the anti-Iraq coalition" prior to and during the Gulf War provided some impetus for the initiation of a peace process in the region, raising the prospect of a possible transition to arms control.[22] The Middle East Peace Conference, which opened in Madrid on October 30, 1991, under the sponsorship of the United States and the Soviet Union, initiated sets of bilateral talks between Israel and its neighbors aimed at comprehensive peace in the region. An additional multilateral component of this process was the establishment of five working groups to address regional issues of common interest, one being the Arms Control and Regional Security (ACRS) working group. However, major Israeli antagonists in the region, such as Iran and Syria, did not participate in the talks.[23] The talks were suspended in early 1995 with few concrete accomplishments. The lack of progress was due in part to Egypt's efforts to mobilize the Non-Aligned Movement to oppose indefinite extension of the NPT at the upcoming NPT Review and Extension Conference unless Israel signed the Treaty (see section on Developments in this chapter).

During 1994, senior Israeli officials reportedly were divided over how to respond to the Clinton Administration's 1993 proposal for a global "Fissile Material Cut-Off" treaty banning further production of plutonium and highly enriched uranium for nuclear weapons and the production of such materials outside IAEA safeguards. The cutoff proposal would permit the five nuclear-weapon states and the three *de facto* nuclear powers (India, Israel, and Pakistan) to retain their existing stocks of unsafeguarded fissile material. Some Israeli officials argued that Israel should not limit its nuclear options, while others believed Israel's inventory of fissile materials could be capped without injuring the country's strategic capabilities.

DEVELOPMENTS

Over the past three years, Israel's presumed nuclear deterrent capabilities have come under renewed scrutiny. In the context of the April 1995 NPT Review and Extension Conference, the Arab states attempted but failed to pressure Israel into renouncing the nuclear option. At the same time the deterioration of the peace process established by the 1993 Oslo accords undermined efforts to resume the regional arms control talks. By signing the Comprehensive Test Ban Treaty (CTBT), however, Israel demonstrated a willingness to participate in what it considers verifiable arms control regimes.

During this period, as ballistic missile threats increased, Israel accelerated the development of active ballistic missile defenses. Deploying missile defenses will require an adaptation of Israel's traditional doctrine of "offensive defense." Israel's postulated threat was amplified by Syria's recent tests of advanced 600-km Scud C missiles, a system capable of striking sites across the Jewish state from deep within Syria—releasing chemical and biological weapons.[24] Iran also posed an increasingly serious threat. In addition to its stockpile of chemical weapons, substantial biological-warfare program, and efforts to acquire nuclear weapons, information surfaced that Iran is developing Shahab missiles, with ranges up to 2,000 km, that would enable Iran to target Israel for the first time (see Iran and Missile Proliferation chapters in this volume). Moreover, Israel continued to face missile threats from Libya, Egypt, Saudi Arabia, and possibly Iraq.

NPT Review Pressures. At the fourth Preparatory Committee (PrepCom) session for the Review and Extension Conference in January 1995, Egypt, as well as Syria, Libya, and Algeria, issued statements indicating that they would consent to an indefinite extension of the NPT only after Israel agreed to accede to the Treaty.[25] The Egyptian position was further refined in February when it reportedly asked Israel to agree to sign the NPT within two years. Israel's response, according to Israeli sources, was embodied in Foreign Minister Shimon Peres's exchange with Egyptian Foreign Minister Amr Mussa: Peres indicated that Israel would agree to a nuclear-weapon-free zone (NWFZ) in the Middle East two years after the conclusion of a comprehensive peace accord among all states in the region, including Iran.[26]

In making these demands, the Arab states were attempting to elicit U.S. pressure on Israel to alter its nuclear policy, in exchange for Arab support of an indefinite extension of the NPT. The Arab states apparently were concerned that once the NPT was extended, the pressure on Israel to acknowledge and terminate its nuclear weapons capability would cease.[27] On the other hand, Israeli experts contended that "It [was] an insult to Israel to ask [it] to sign the NPT because

everybody knows that, given current security problems [in the region], Israel would have to violate it."[28]

Egypt softened its position just prior to the beginning of the NPT Review and Extension Conference in April 1995—reportedly as a result of U.S. pressure—and no longer expressed opposition to an indefinite extension of the NPT.[29] Nevertheless, the issue of Israeli NPT accession simmered throughout the conference, and in the waning hours the Arab states submitted a resolution singling out Israel for failure to sign the NPT and calling for a NWFZ in the Middle East. In order to spare Israel embarrassment, the United States, along with the Russian Federation and the United Kingdom, offered a diluted alternative. This resolution made reference to a section of the draft NPT consensus document calling "on those remaining States not Parties to the Treaty to accede to it, thereby accepting an international legally binding commitment not to acquire nuclear weapons or nuclear explosive devices and to accept IAEA safeguards on all their nuclear activities."[30] (See Appendices A-1 and B on NPT and 1995 NPT Review and Extension Conference.)

Following the conclusion of the NPT Review and Extension Conference, the United States reportedly sought to reengage Israel (along with India and Pakistan) in discussions on halting the production of weapons-grade material, in line with the statement on "Principles and Objectives for Nuclear Non-Proliferation and Disarmament" agreed to at the Extension Conference. Israeli officials indicated, however, that they would not immediately respond to the U.S. proposal.[31] Israel remains reluctant to endorse arms control measures until it is clear that effective verification can be achieved.

Middle East Peace Process. In December 1995, Israeli Prime Minister Shimon Peres (in carrying forward Israel's peace strategy toward the Arabs after Yitzhak Rabin was assassinated) stated: "Give me peace and we will give up the atom. . . . If we achieve regional peace, I think we can make the Middle East free of any nuclear threat."[32] While some observers interpreted the statement as a possible change in Israel's long-standing policy of "nuclear ambiguity," others saw it as a casual remark, "a colloquial reformulation" of Israel's stated willingness to negotiate the establishment of a NWFZ in the Middle East following the achievement of comprehensive peace.[33]

Peres' statement was made against the backdrop of the land-for-peace negotiations then under way between Israel and Syria.[34] In that context, the Israeli government broached the idea of a U.S. security guarantee, promising that the United States would come to Israel's defense in the event of attack. Peres sought such a U.S. commitment as a way of easing Israeli concern over the withdrawal from the Golan Heights, regarded by Syria as part of its territory.[35] While the United States was willing to talk about this issue, it was not willing to provide this security compensation until Israel agreed to withdraw from the Golan Heights.[36] As an alternative show of U.S. support, during a visit in late April 1996 by Prime Minister Peres a month before Israeli elections, U.S. Defense Secretary William Perry signed a "statement of intent" with the Israeli leader reaffirming U.S. backing for Israel's programs to develop missile defenses and emphasizing Israel's need for enhanced early warning and the ability to operate jointly with U.S. forces[37] (see section on Ballistic, Cruise, and Defensive Missiles in this chapter).

Reviving arms control discussions in the ACRS forum, especially about the question of Israel's nuclear posture, proved impossible over the next year-and-a-half. On May 29, 1996, Binyamin Netanyahu, the leader of the right-wing Likud Party, was elected prime minister of Israel. His emergence signaled a hardening of Israeli positions in the peace process, both with respect to implementation of the 1993 Oslo agreement provisions for interim steps toward self-rule in the West Bank and Gaza, and with respect to the negotiations with Syria.[38] Because of a series of suicide bombings in Israeli cities in early 1996, then–Prime Minister Peres had already suspended interim measures under the Oslo agreement delaying, *inter alia*, the redeployment of Israeli troops from the city of Hebron, an event that was supposed to have taken place by March 1996.[39] Negotiations with Syria were also suspended in April as a result of Israeli attacks against the Hezbollah terrorist group in Lebanon in retaliation for its rocket attacks on northern Israel.

Under pressure from the Israeli electorate and the United States, the Netanyahu government eventually signed a Hebron agreement on January 15, 1997.[40] While the redeployment of Israeli troops from Hebron proceeded smoothly, new strains arose in March 1997 causing a stalemate which persisted into 1998.[41]

Arms Control. Israel signed the Comprehensive Nuclear Test Ban Treaty (CTBT) on September 25, 1996, the only one of the three "threshold" non-NPT states to do so. From the Israeli perspective, its adherence to the CTBT and its earlier signing of the Chemical Weapons Convention (CWC) demonstrated Israel's interest in arms control regimes with reliable verification systems not subject to abuse or frivolous requests. According to this view, Israel's arms control credentials and policies were also reflected in the active role it played in the negotiations of the CTBT as a primary participant in the drafting of the accord, in its co-sponsorship of the United Nations resolution that opened the CTBT for signature, and in the fact that it was one of its first signatories.[42]

The potential threats facing Israel received new attention in April 1997 with a report that Syria was mounting warheads armed with deadly nerve gas on its ballistic missiles. According to this report, Syria had obtained precursor materials for this more lethal form of nerve gas from sources in Russia and was producing it with the assistance of Russian weapon experts. Israel's official reaction, as stated by Foreign Minister David Levy, hinted at Israel's nuclear arsenal: "We are following this development and others. . . . Anyone who does this understands that we have capabilities far and above what the other side can even imagine."[43] Syrian President Hafez Assad responded during a news conference with Egyptian President Hosni Mubarak, stating that "those who have nuclear weapons do not have the right to criticize others for whatever weapons they may have. . . . If they want disarmament, let us start with nuclear disarmament, and we Arabs will be willing to get rid of the other weapons."[44]

Ballistic, Cruise, and Defensive Missile Programs. Israel currently deploys two nuclear-capable ballistic missile systems: the Jericho I and Jericho II. Up to 50 Jericho I solid-fuel two-stage missiles with an approximate range of 660 km are thought to be deployed in shelters on mobile launchers, possibly at a facility located midway between Jerusalem and the Mediterranean. The Jericho II solid-fuel, two-stage missile can travel an estimated 1,500 km; commercial satellite photos indicate that the missile base between Jerusalem and the Mediterranean was enlarged between 1989 and 1993 to allow for Jericho II deployment. Furthermore, a Lawrence-Livermore Laboratory study indicates that Israel's Shavit space launch vehicle could be modified to carry 500 kg over 7,800 km, in effect giving it the capability of an intercontinental ballistic missile (ICBM).[45]

The centerpiece of Israel's layered system of strategic missile defense, called *Homa*, is the Arrow II antiballistic missile system. This system's mission is to intercept tactical missiles with capabilities similar to a Scud just as they start reentering the atmosphere after reaching the highest point of their flight trajectory. The program is a joint U.S.–Israeli undertaking begun in 1988 as part of the U.S. Strategic Defense Initiative and now sponsored by the U.S. Ballistic Missile Defense Organization. In August 1996, Israel tested the Arrow II interceptor missile for the third time. In the test, the Arrow II (which has an intercept range of 50 km) successfully tracked and destroyed a modified Arrow I missile with a simulated chemical weapons payload (the target missile was given a radar cross-section and payload design similar to a Scud). A fourth test was conducted in March 1997, and even though the interceptor missile's warhead did not explode, the test was considered a success because the interceptor still destroyed the incoming target. The Arrow II system will achieve initial operational capability in late 1998 when the Israeli Air Force deploys a prototype battery with a significant deployed force planned for the turn of the century.[46]

Another missile interceptor in an earlier stage of development is the Moab, funded in part by the U.S. Ballistic Missile Defense Organization. This missile is the major component of the Israeli Boost-Phase Intercept System (part of *Homa*), whose mission is to intercept Scud-like missiles soon after launch with an air-to-air missile fired from an unmanned aerial vehicle flying at high altitude.[47] Israel is also developing jointly with the United States the Nautilus, a fixed-site high-energy laser capable of shooting down short-range artillery rockets. This system is intended for deployment, in the near term, in Israel's northern regions to help protect against Hezbollah-directed Katyusha rocket attacks on Israel from southern Lebanon. The follow-on mobile version would be the Tactical High-Energy Laser (THEL) system.[48]

Israel's unmanned aerial vehicle (UAV) program has been extended to cover cruise missile development, including land-attack cruise missiles (LACM). Reportedly, Israel has three platforms: the Popeye 1, with a range of 100 km carrying a payload of 360 kg; the Delilah, with a 400-km range and a 450-kg payload; and the Popeye 3, with a 350-km range and a 360-kg payload. The Delilah is said to have been developed with Chinese cooperation, and Israel's armament industries are believed to have extensive ties, including projected STAR cruise missile cooperation with China, India, South Korea, and Turkey.[49] Israeli armaments cooperation with India may be constrained as a result of policy reactions to India's May 1998 nuclear tests.

PROSPECTS

Despite India's and Pakistan's declarations of nuclear weapons in 1998, it is unlikely that Israel will follow suit or change its policy of nuclear ambiguity. Israeli decision-makers will also continue to hold the view, however, that for as long as adversaries in the Middle East region maintain capabilities to mount large-scale military attacks against Israel or threaten Israeli cities with missiles carrying chemical or biological warheads, Israel will need to maintain the nuclear deterrence option.[50] In some respects, one Israeli observer argues, Israel's nuclear posture may have been better understood internationally as a result of the controversy with Egypt prior to and during the course of the 1995 Review and Extension Conference. In his view, the conflict forced "Rabin, Peres and other Israeli Leaders" to articulate for the first time "links between the maintenance of the nuclear capability and the continued threats to

national survival, linked to the military, geographic and demographic asymmetries in the region."[51]

From the Israeli perspective, a substantive discussion of regional arms control issues is inextricably linked to the achievement of a comprehensive Middle East peace settlement. However, such a settlement is unlikely to be achieved any time soon, given (1) the troubled implementation of existing Israeli-Palestinian accords, (2) the difficult negotiations over the final status of Palestinian autonomy that lie ahead, (3) the strong divergence between Israel and Syria over the strategically important Golan Heights, and (4) the bitter enmity of Iran.

If and when the ACRS talks do resume, Israel can be expected to discuss only the near-term, confidence-building measures. In the words of an Israeli specialist, the "negotiations of such measures—let alone the conclusion of agreements and their implementation—can only take place once all the sources of proliferation concern (Iraq, Iran, Libya, etc.) become part of the new regional security and arms control regime."[52]

At the same time, as the chemical, biological, and missile capabilities of Israel's adversaries grow and its cities become more vulnerable to attack, Israel's nuclear deterrent probably will become more prominent in the minds of Israeli planners. The deployment by Israel of effective ballistic missile defenses will only provide partial relief. Indeed, the missile and chemical and biological threat to Israel has grown so serious that some analysts believe it is possible to imagine circumstances short of threatened national annihilation in which Israel might consider escalation to the nuclear level.

Similarly, unless checked in the years ahead, Iran's nuclear program will pose a security threat to Israel of sufficient gravity that Israel may choose to respond to this threat through preventive military action—a choice with unpredictable results. A resurgent nuclear Iraq would pose a similar threat. This could greatly increase the risk of regional conflict and with it the possibility of open-ended escalation.

NOTES

[1]"Revealed: The Secrets of Israel's Nuclear Arsenal," *Sunday Times* (London), October 5, 1986.

[2]In light of what is known about Israel's nuclear infrastructure, it has long been assumed that its weapons use plutonium rather than highly enriched uranium for their cores.

[3]This extrapolation is based on the assumption that the Dimona reactor has been operating at a power level of between 40 and 70 MWt, reportedly reaching the higher capability before Vanunu's arrival in 1977. (See Leonard S. Spector with Jacqueline R. Smith, *Nuclear Ambitions* (Boulder, CO: Westview Press, 1990), pp. 159-160.) Another analysis of the Israeli nuclear program explores the possibility that the unit's power was raised in the late 1970s to 150 MWt, producing, by the end of 1994, 880 kg of plutonium, sufficient for 176 warheads. See David Albright, Frans Berkhout and William Walker, *Plutonium and Highly Enriched Uranium 1996: World Inventories, Capabilities and Policies* (New York: Oxford University Press for Stockholm International Peace Research Institute, 1997), pp. 259, 262.

[4]Seymour M. Hersh, *The Samson Option* (New York: Random House, 1991), pp. 291, 312, 319.

[5]See Harold Hough, "Israel's Nuclear Infrastructure," *Jane's Intelligence Review*, November 1994, p. 508.

[6]See Leonard S. Spector, *The Undeclared Bomb* (Cambridge, MA: Ballinger Publishing Company, 1988), pp. 165-87; Pierre Péan, *Les Deux Bombes* (Paris: Fayard, 1981), chapters V, VII, VIII.

[7]"France Admits It Gave Israel A-Bomb," *Sunday Times* (London), October 12, 1986.

[8]Ibid.; Steven Weissman and Herbert Krosney, *The Islamic Bomb* (New York: Times Books, 1981), p. 114.

[9]See "Israel: The Covert Connection," *Frontline*, PBS Network, May 16, 1989.

[10]See Hersh, *The Samson Option*, op. cit., p. 271.

[11]The issue resurfaced in 1997 when Aziz Pahad, South African deputy foreign minister, declared that his nation detonated a nuclear weapon in the atmosphere in September 1979. When pressed, however, Pahad has stated that he was basing his view only on public understanding of the events, not on official information. See Kathy DeLucas, "Blast From the Past: Scientists Receive Vindication," Press Release, Los Alamos National Laboratory, July 11, 1997; William Scott, "Admission of 1979 Nuclear Test Finally Validates VELA Data," *Aviation Week*, July 21, 1997, p. 33.

[12]Dr. Gerald Steinberg, "The Future of Nuclear Weapons: Israeli Perspectives," paper presented at the Ninth Amaldi Conference on

Security Questions at the End of the Twentieth Century, Geneva, November 21-23, 1996; revised November 25, 1996.

From the Israeli perspective, the utility of this deterrent was demonstrated during the 1973 Arab-Israeli War when in spite of their initial advances in the early days of the conflict, Egyptian troops did not cross the Sinai—a move that would have placed Israeli population centers at risk.

[13]Spector with Smith, *Nuclear Ambitions*, op. cit., p. 157.

[14]At the time Shimon Peres, who had overseen the development of Israel's nuclear program, proposed that Israel follow the French model and declare an independent *force de frappe;* however, Ben-Gurion adopted a cautious approach in line with commitments to U.S. and French leaders and in response to opposition at home. Avner Cohen, "Peres: Peacemaker, Nuclear Pioneer," *Bulletin of the Atomic Scientists*, May/June 1996, p. 16.

[15]See Barbara Opall, "Peres: Keep Nuclear Details Secret," *Defense News*, July 29-August 4, 1996, p. 3.

During 1961-63, President Kennedy insisted on commitments from Ben-Gurion that the activities surrounding the Dimona reactor were for peaceful purposes only. To verify those commitments Kennedy demanded semi-annual, full-access U.S. visits to Dimona. Ben-Gurion, and his successor Levy Eshkol, agreed only to U.S. "periodic visits" which, when implemented, were carried out on an annual basis. (Avner Cohen, "Israel's Nuclear History: The Untold Kennedy-Eshkol Dimona Correspondence," *Journal of Israeli History*, Summer 1995.) The visits lasted from 1964 to 1969 but, given their infrequent and limited nature and Israel's reported deception activities, they proved to be inconclusive. See Spector with Smith, *Nuclear Ambitions*, op. cit., p. 153.

[16]Spector with Smith, *Nuclear Ambitions*, op. cit., pp. 167, 188.

[17]Ibid., p. 168.

[18]"Iraq Threatens to Use Chemical Weapons Against Israeli Attack," *Financial Times*, April 3, 1990; see also "Paper Warns Against Zionist 'Flagrant Threats,'" *INA* (Baghdad), September 18, 1988, in *FBIS-NES*, September 19, 1988, p. 18.

[19]Spector with Smith, *Nuclear Ambitions*, op. cit., p. 168.

[20]Iraq's extensive chemical and biological weapons capabilities were reflected in the fact that, prior to commencement of hostilities in 1991, it had deployed, as part of its active force, about 25 missile warheads and 150-200 bombs filled with biological agents. Similarly, Iraq deployed 50 missile warheads filled with chemical agents. According to some reports, Saddam actually intended to use the chemical and biological weapons (see chapter on Iraq in this volume).

[21]James Bruce, "Israel's Space and Missile Projects," *Jane's Intelligence Review* Vol. 7, No. 8, 1995, p. 352; "BRF-Israel-Missiles," *Associated Press*, January 3, 1997.

[22]Efraim Karsh, Efraim Inbar and Shmuel Sandler, "Arms Control and the New Middle Eastern Environment," *Defense Analysis*, Vol. 12, No. 1, 1996, as published in "Lessons for Arms Control in a Changing Middle East," *Security and Policy Studies No. 26* (Ramat Gan, Israel: The BESA Center for Strategic Studies, Bar-Ilan University, June 1996), p. 40.

[23]For an overview of the ACRS talks see *Arms Control Reporter*, 1992-1996 (Section 453.B).

The ACRS discussions were organized into two subgroups. The first sought to arrive at an acceptable conceptual security framework for the longer-term, while the second explored more concrete confidence-building measures that could be implemented in the short term. Little tangible progress was made during three years of talks. The Arab states used the forum to attack Israel's nuclear capability as an obstacle to peace and to put forward proposals calling on Israel to join the NPT and accept IAEA safeguards. Israel urged that the parties focus on measures designed to "build and nurture mutual confidence between states," such as pre-notification of large-scale military exercises, communication channels and hot lines between military commanders, and a center to coordinate activities and respond to incidents in the Red Sea. Israel's position was outlined in some detail by then Israeli Foreign Minister Shimon Peres on the occasion of the signing of the Chemical Weapons Convention on January 13, 1993. In Israel's view, specific arms control initiatives, such as eliminating weapons of mass destruction from the region, could be undertaken only after comprehensive peace had been achieved in the region. This would involve, first, prohibitions on chemical and biological weapons and missile systems, and then, at the last stage, nuclear weapons. See Steinberg, "The Future of Nuclear Weapons: Israeli Perspectives," op. cit. See also Shai Feld-

man, *Nuclear Weapons and Arms Control in the Middle East* (London: The MIT Press, 1997), p. 253.

[24]Sami Aboudi, "Israel Successfully Test-Fires Anti-Missile Missile," *Reuters*, August 20, 1996; Joshua Brilliant, "Israel Hails New Anti-Missile Missile," *United Press International*, August 20, 1996.

According to some reports, Egypt has recently accelerated its efforts to increase its missile capabilities with North Korean assistance. In addition to procuring equipment and materials from North Korea to expand its existing infrastructure to produce Scud B missiles, Egypt reportedly has reached an agreement with the Stalinist state to acquire mobile launchers for these missiles. Israeli observers are concerned that these offensive weapons would constitute a threat if an Islamic fundamentalist regime emerged in Egypt or if the peace process broke down. "Official to Raise DPRK Launchers to Egypt in Talks With CIA Chief," *Ha'aretz* (Tel Aviv), June 25, 1996, in *FBIS-NES-96-126*, June 28, 1996, p. 21; "Levi on Egyptian Scuds, Dimona Pictures, Sharon 'Crisis,'" *IDF Radio* (Tel Aviv), June 25, 1996, in *FBIS-NES-96-123*, June 26, 1996.

[25]Mark Hibbs, "Last NPT PREPCOM Moves Toward Limited Extension," *Nucleonics Week*, February 2, 1995, p. 6. Also see Kathleen Hart, "Clinton Administration Accelerates Push For NPT Indefinite Extension," *Nuclear Fuel*, April 10, 1995, p. 5; To Sign or Not to Sign: Israel Embattled Over NPT Refusal," *Jane's Defence Weekly*, March 25, 1995.

[26]Egypt also demanded that Israel join a Middle East nuclear-weapons-free zone on the basis of the ACRS talks and agree to international conventions banning production of chemical and biological weapons. See Mark Hibbs, "Israel Counting on NPT Extension to Take Pressure Off Its Program," *Nucleonics Week*, April 20, 1995, p. 5; "Israel: Weapons-Free Zone?" *Nucleonics Week*, March 9, 1995, p. 15.

Another report described Israel's position as insisting that Iraq and Libya become part of a comprehensive lasting peace in the region before Israel makes any nuclear concessions. See "Peres: 'Will Give Up the Atom' if Peace Achieved," *Qol Yisra'el* (Jerusalem), December 22, 1995, in *FBIS-NES-95-247*, December 26, 1996, p. 51.

[27]See Mark Hibbs, "Israel Counting on NPT Extension to Take Pressure Off Its Program," *Nucleonics Week*, April 20, 1995, p. 5.

[28]Hibbs, "Last NPT PREPCOM Moves Toward Limited Extension," op. cit.

[29]Hibbs, "Israel Counting on NPT Extension," op. cit.

[30]Mark Hibbs, "Weapon States Face Pressure on NPT Pledge, Chairman Says," *Nucleonics Week*, May 18, 1995, p. 8; "Russian Federation, the United Kingdom and the United States: Resolution," *Arms Control Reporter* (Section 453.D), 1995, p. 21.

[31]"Israel: Nuclear Option Funded," *Nucleonics Week*, June 1, 1995, p. 15.

For cost of verifying a fissile material cutoff in Israel, India, and Pakistan through the application of IAEA safeguards, see Mark Hibbs, "Fissile Cutoff Verification Snagged on Costs, Intrusion," *Nucleonics Week*, August 17, 1995, p. 8.

[32]"Additional Details on Statements," *Jerusalem Israel Television Channel I*, December 22, 1995, in *FBIS-NES-95-247*, December 26, 1996, p. 51. Also see "Peres: 'Will Give Up the Atom' if Peace Achieved," *Qol Yisra'el*, op. cit.

[33]Cohen, "Peres: Peacemaker, Nuclear Pioneer," op. cit., p. 16.

[34]"Israel-Syria 'Draft Peace Treaty' Detailed," *Al-Manar* (Jerusalem), January 8, 1996, in *FBIS-NES-96-008*, January 11, 1996, p. 9; "'Sources' Cite Points of Framework Agreement," *Ramallah Al-Ayyam*, January 6, 1996, in *FBIS-NES-96-008*, January 11, 1996, p. 9.

[35]Jeff Erlich, "U.S. Expands TMD Links to Israel," *Defense News*, April 29-May 5, 1996, p. 4.

[36]Ibid.; Joshua Brilliant, "Analysts Question U.S.-Israel Alliance," *United Press International*, December 8, 1995; "Controversy Over U.S. Defense Pact Proposal," *Ha'aretz* (Tel Aviv), January 5, 1996, in *FBIS-NES-96-004*, January 5, 1996, p. 27; "U.S. Expected to Recognize Israeli Nuclear Ability in Pact," *Ha'aretz* (Tel Aviv), March 25, 1996, in *FBIS-NES-96-058*, March 25, 1996, p. 46; "Israel-U.S.-Nuclear," *Associated Press*, March 25, 1996; Shai Feldman, "Times Call for Expansion of U.S.-Israeli Defense Cooperation," *Wall Street Journal*, July 10, 1996.

[37]It provided, among other things, for arrangements to improve early warning to Israel of missile launches in the region by reestablishing and strengthening real-time satellite intelligence links with the United States that were in place during the 1991 Gulf War. It

also called for completing development and initial deployment of the Arrow anti-tactical ballistic missile system. See "U.S. Aids Israeli Missile Defense," *Washington Times*, April 29, 1996; David A. Fulghum and Bruce D. Nordwall, "Israel's Missile Defenses Rate U.S. High-Tech Boost," *Aviation Week & Space Technology*, May 6, 1996, p. 23; Jeff Erlich, "Israelis Will Get Missile Warnings From U.S.," *Defense News*, May 6-12, 1996, p. 24; Barbara Opall, "U.S. Pledges Early Warning Aid, Excess Equipment to Israel," *Defense News*, October 21-27, 1996, p. 24.

Israel's link to the U.S. satellite missile warning system became operational in January 1997. See "BRF-Israel-Missiles," *Associated Press*, January 3, 1997.

[38]Netanyahu issued official policy guidelines soon after the elections stating that "retaining Israeli sovereignty over the Golan will be the basis for an arrangement with Syria." Another guideline pledged that Israel would "conduct negotiations with Syria without preconditions." See Serge Schmemann, "Netanyahu Is Ready to Talk to Syria, but Not to Yield," *New York Times*, June 17, 1996. Also see Steven Erlanger, "Netanyahu Airs Differences with Clinton on Peace Issues," *New York Times*, July 10, 1996; Glenn Frankel, "Netanyahu's Statements Disappoint Palestinians," *Washington Post*, July 11, 1996; Thomas W. Lippman, "Netanyahu Tells Congress Democracy Key to Peace," *Washington Post*, July 11, 1996.

[39]Barton Gellman, "Israel, Palestinians Announce Accord," *Washington Post*, January 15, 1997.

[40]Barton Gellman, "Political Realities Forced Netanyahu to Abandon Backers," *Washington Post*, January 17, 1997.

The agreement provided for the redeployment of Israeli troops from four-fifths of Hebron within ten days, a three-stage withdrawal of the Israeli army from designated rural areas to be completed by mid-1988, and the initiation of talks on a final peace agreement which would address such issues as Palestinian sovereignty, final borders, Palestinian refugees, the future of Jerusalem, and of Jewish settlements in the West Bank and Gaza. The deadline for a final agreement was May 1999. See Barton Gellman, "Netanyahu Wins Vote on Hebron," *Washington Post*, January 16, 1997.

[41]In March 1997, Israel started construction of a new settlement in East Jerusalem. From the Palestinian perspective, this was an attempt by Israel to create a *fait accompli* on the ground that would preempt the negotiation of the difficult issues over the nature of Palestinian autonomy that would emerge in a final peace settlement. Consequently, the Israeli-Palestinian dialogue floundered with a new crisis erupting at the end of July 1997 following a suicide bombing in Israel and the resulting imposition of financial and other sanctions by Israel against the Palestinian Authority. Faced with the prospect that the Oslo framework would be completely undone, in August 1997, the Clinton Administration launched a mediation initiative. See William Drozdiak, "Netanyahu Sounds Conciliatory Note," *Washington Post*, August 14, 1997. See also Barton Gellman, "Netanyahu, Arafat Trade Accusations," *Washington Post*, August 3, 1997; Susan Schmidt and Barton Gellman, "Netanyahu Puts Onus of Terrorism on Arafat," *Washington Post*, August 4, 1997; Rebecca Trounson, "U.S. Envoy Returns to Mideast Amid Rising Security Dispute," *Washington Post*, August 10, 1997; "Israel: 'Pessimistic' Mood in Ross Talks; Israel Rejects Minisummit," *Ma'ariv* (Tel Aviv), August 11, 1997, in *FBIS-NES-97-223*, August 11, 1997; Howard Goller, "U.S. Envoy Urges Israelis, PLO to Join Forces Against Militants," *Washington Post*, August 12, 1997; Paul Holmes, "Israel, Palestinians Undertake Renewal of Security Contacts," *Washington Post*, August 13, 1997; Douglas Jehl, "P.L.O. Feels Pinch as Talks Open on Security Issues," *New York Times*, August 18, 1997; Thomas W. Lippman, "Albright Visit Bares U.S.-Israel Division Over Peace Process," *Washington Post*, September 11, 1997; Thomas W. Lippman, "Albright Sees Few Gains in Mideast Trip," *Washington Post*, September 11, 1997.

[42]Dr. Gerald Steinberg, "Deterrence and Middle East Stability: An Israeli Perspective," *Security Dialogue*, Spring 1997; Steinberg, "The Future of Nuclear Weapons: Israeli Perspectives," op. cit. See also Feldman, *Nuclear Weapons and Arms Control in the Middle East*, op. cit., p. 256.

As of mid-1998, Israel had not ratified the Chemical Weapons Convention on the grounds that none of the Arab states suspected of maintaining chemical weapons stockpiles had signed the accord. Similarly, it was refusing to ratify the CTBT until key Middle East countries had done so. See Stephanie Nebehay, "Israel Clashes With Iraq and Iran at UN Arms Talks," *Reuters*, September 4, 1997.

[43]Dafna Linzer, "Israel-Syria," *Associated Press*, April 29, 1997.

[44]"Syria-Israel," *Associated Press*, May 1, 1997. See also Colleen Siegel, "Israel's Netanyahu Warns of Syria, Iran Arms," *Reuters*, May 2, 1997.

[45]See David A Fulghum and Jeffery M. Lenorovitz, "Israeli Missile Base Hidden in Hill," *Aviation Week and Space Technology*, November 8, 1993, p. 29; Steven E. Gray, "Israeli Missile Capabilities: A Few Numbers to Think About," Lawrence Livermore National Laboratories, Z Division, October 7, 1988. Also see "How Far Can Israel's Missiles Fly?" *The Risk Report: Tracking Weapons of Mass Destruction*, June 1995, p. 1.

[46]"Arrow Passes Intercept Test," *Aviation Week & Space Technology*, August 26, 1996, p. 73; Carmella Menashe, "Israel Takes Steps Toward Arrow Missile Deployment," *Defense News*, May 20-26, 1996, p. 33; Sami Aboudi, "Israel Successfully Test-Fires Anti-Missile Missile," *Reuters*, August 20, 1996; Joshua Brilliant, "Israel Hails New Anti-Missile Missile," *United Press International*, August 20, 1996; Steve Rodan, "Arrow Success Launches Debate on Program Path," *Defense News*, August 26-September 1, 1996, p. 4; Barbara Opall, "IAI Starts Production of Arrow Interceptor," *Defense News*, September 2-8, 1996; "Israel's Missile Killer Intercepts Target in Test," *Reuters*, March 11, 1997; Edith M. Lederer, "Israeli Missile," *Associated Press*, August 7, 1997.

The Arrow system will not be able to shield all of Israel's territory because it is designed to intercept missiles launched from distances greater than 300 kilometers. Israel will have to rely on the Patriot system to destroy missiles fired from shorter distances. See "Israel: Arrow Missile to Be Deployed by Late 1998," *Jerusalem Post*, May 15, 1996, in *FBIS-NES-96-095*, May 15, 1996, p. 19.

In early May 1996, Israel launched its Amos-1 communications satellite, which presumably will be an important element of the early warning system of Israel's anti-missile defense shield. A year earlier Israel had launched an Ofeq-3 satellite capable of transmitting high resolution photographs. See James Bruce, "Israel's Amos-1 Launches ABM Early Warning Bid," *Jane's Defence Weekly*, March 6, 1996, p. 23.

[47]"Israel's Moab Scud-Interceptor Detailed," *Jane's International Defence Review*, July 1996, p. 5; "Project Moab Moves Forward," *Jane's International Defence Review*, August 1, 1997, p. 5; Lederer, "Israeli Missile," *Associated Press*, op. cit.

[48]Fulghum and Nordwall, "Israel's Missile Defenses Rate U.S. High-Tech Boost," *Aviation Week & Space Technology*, op. cit., p. 23; "US/Israeli Laser in Desperate Bid Against Hezbollah Rockets," *Jane's Defence Weekly*, July 10, 1996, p. 3; Joseph C. Anselmo, "U.S., Israel Accelerate Laser Rocket Defenses," *Aviation Week & Space Technology*, August 12, 1996, p. 31.

[49]See Missile Chart 2, and its notes.

[50]Steinberg, "The Future of Nuclear Weapons: Israeli Perspectives," op. cit.

[51]Dr. Gerald Steinberg, "Middle East Peace and the NPT Extension Decision," *The Nonproliferation Review*, Vol. 4, No. 1, Fall 1996.

[52]Shai Feldman, Presentation before the Carnegie Endowment Non-Proliferation Conference: *Enhancing the Tools of the Trade*, Washington, D.C., June 9-10, 1997.

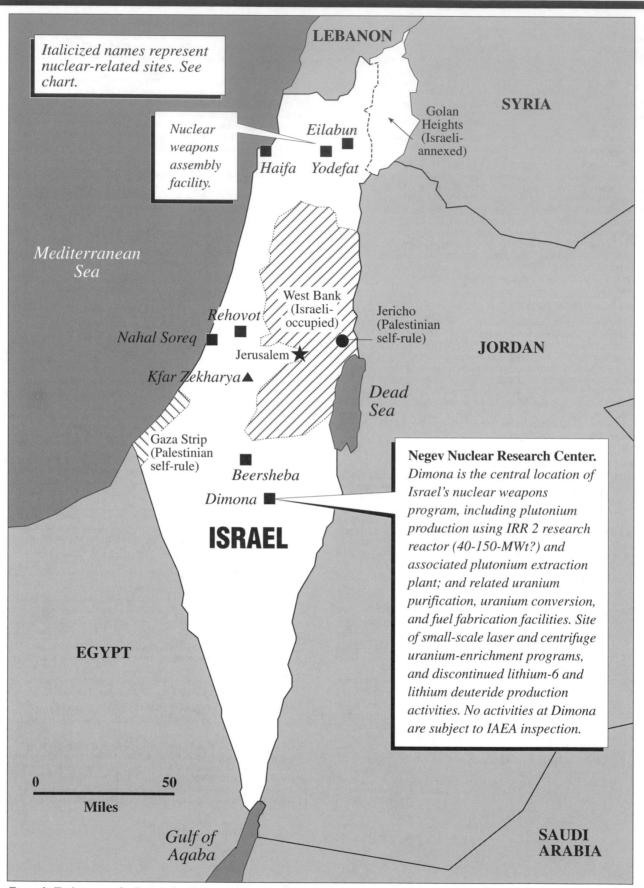

Italicized names represent nuclear-related sites. See chart.

LEBANON

SYRIA

Nuclear weapons assembly facility.

Eilabun

Golan Heights (Israeli-annexed)

Haifa *Yodefat*

Mediterranean Sea

West Bank (Israeli-occupied)

Jericho (Palestinian self-rule)

JORDAN

Rehovot

Nahal Soreq

Jerusalem

Kfar Zekharya ▲

Dead Sea

Gaza Strip (Palestinian self-rule)

Beersheba

Dimona ■

ISRAEL

Negev Nuclear Research Center.
Dimona is the central location of Israel's nuclear weapons program, including plutonium production using IRR 2 research reactor (40-150-MWt?) and associated plutonium extraction plant; and related uranium purification, uranium conversion, and fuel fabrication facilities. Site of small-scale laser and centrifuge uranium-enrichment programs, and discontinued lithium-6 and lithium deuteride production activities. No activities at Dimona are subject to IAEA inspection.

EGYPT

0   50
Miles

Gulf of Aqaba

SAUDI ARABIA

Carnegie Endowment for International Peace, *Tracking Nuclear Proliferation*, 1998

ISRAEL: Nuclear Infrastructure[a]

NAME/LOCATION OF FACILITY	TYPE/STATUS	IAEA SAFEGUARDS[b]
NUCLEAR WEAPONS COMPLEX[c]		
Negev Nuclear Research Center, Dimona	Plutonium production research reactor and plutonium extraction facilities (see below), and other weapons-related infrastructure.	No
Nahal Soreq	Nuclear weapons research and design facility.	No
Yodefat	Nuclear weapons assembly facility.	No
Kfar Zekharya	Nuclear missile base and gravity bomb storage facility.	No
Eilabun	Tactical nuclear weapon storage facility.	No
RESEARCH REACTORS		
IRR 1, Nahal Soreq	Light-water, pool, HEU, 5 MWt; operating.	Yes
IRR 2, Dimona	Heavy-water, natural U, 40-150 MWt; operating.[d]	No
URANIUM ENRICHMENT		
Dimona	Experimental/pilot-scale laser and centrifuge-enrichment programs; operating.	No
REPROCESSING (PLUTONIUM EXTRACTION)		
Dimona	Operating.	No
Nahal Soreq	Pilot-scale; operating.	No
URANIUM PROCESSING		
Negev area, near Beersheba	Uranium phosphate mining; operating.	N/A (Not Applicable)
Haifa	Yellowcake produced in two phosphate plants; operating.	N/A
Southern Israel	Yellowcake produced in phosphate plant; operating.	N/A
Dimona	Uranium purification (UO_2), uranium conversion (UF_6), and fuel fabrication facility; all operating.	No
HEAVY-WATER		
Rehovot	Pilot-scale plant; operating.	No
TRITIUM, LITHIUM DEUTERIDE		
Dimona	Lithium-6 production, allowing the production of both tritium and lithium deuteride; decommissioned.	No

Abbreviations:

HEU	=	highly enriched uranium
LEU	=	low-enriched uranium
nat. U	=	natural uranium
MWe	=	millions of watts of electrical output
MWt	=	millions of watts of thermal output
KWt	=	thousands of watts of thermal output

NOTES (Israel Chart)

[a]The Israel Electric Corporation has expressed a strong interest in importing foreign reactor technology to construct a nuclear power plant, possibly at Shivta in the Negev desert. However, Israel's inquiries in this regard have not been answered because of its unwillingness to sign the NPT or otherwise place its entire nuclear program under international safeguards.

[b]On September 30, 1994, the International Atomic Energy Agency (IAEA) announced that it had "decided to restore technical assistance to Israel and expressed its wish for closer cooperation between the IAEA and Israel in Agency activities in accordance with the Agency's statute and objectives." The IAEA had suspended such assistance following Israel's 1981 attack on Iraq's Osiraq research reactor. See "IAEA Restores Technical Assistance to Israel," *Reuters*, September 30, 1994.

[c]In a 1991 book, Seymour Hersh projected that Israel had a larger nuclear arsenal than earlier estimates of 60-100 devices, and that Israel had also produced thermonuclear weapons. Subsequent reporting has also identified several potential facilities where weapons research, design, and production may take place. See Seymour M. Hersh, *The Samson Option* (New York: Random House, 1991) pp. 291, 312, 319; and Harold Hough, "Israel's Nuclear Infrastructure," *Jane's Intelligence Review*, November 1994, p. 508.

[d]Estimates of the reactor's capacity have varied widely. The original agreement between France and Israel called for an 18 MWt reactor, but changes in the design significantly increased its capability. Subsequent reports have suggested that the reactor operated at about 40 MWt prior to 1977, at which time the power was increased to about 70 MWt. Estimates based on information provided by Mordechai Vanunu (see chapter text for more information on Vanunu) suggest that the reactor has reached a capacity of 150 MWt, but government officials have disputed these estimates, noting that the reactor has probably not exceeded 70 MWt. For a good discussion of the reactor power mystery, see David Albright, Frans Berkhout, and William Walker, *Plutonium and Highly Enriched Uranium 1996: World Inventories, Capabilities and Policies* (New York: Oxford University Press for Stockholm International Peace Research Institute, 1997) pp. 257-264.

Libya

Under its mercurial leader, Colonel Muammar Qadhafi, Libya has sought for nearly 25 years to obtain nuclear arms and other weapons of mass destruction to advance the cause of radical Arab nationalism. Libya first attempted to acquire nuclear weapons in 1970, when it sought to purchase nuclear weapons directly from China and was rebuffed. In the intervening years, Libya invested in nuclear research facilities, with Soviet assistance, but has made little progress toward a nuclear weapons capability. Unconfirmed reports since the early 1990s of continued Libyan attempts to purchase sensitive nuclear technology suggest that Libya has not abandoned its nuclear ambitions. Indeed, in March 1996, CIA Director John M. Deutch testified that Qadhafi reportedly was "trying to recruit nuclear scientists to assist in developing nuclear weapons, although it is doubtful that Tripoli could produce a nuclear weapon without significant foreign technological assistance."[1] Were weapons-grade material to become available on the international black market, however, Libya undoubtedly would attempt to purchase it to accelerate a nuclear weapons program.[2] In the meantime, reflecting a model common among aspiring nuclear proliferants in the Middle East region, Libya is concentrating resources on acquiring other, more easily developed weapons of mass destruction (WMD) and related missile capabilities.

BACKGROUND

Libya ratified the Nuclear Non-Proliferation Treaty (NPT) in 1975 but took until 1980 to negotiate a formal safeguards agreement with the International Atomic Energy Agency (IAEA). Libya currently operates a Soviet-supplied 10-MWt research reactor at Tajoura, but apparently is no longer pursuing plans to build a 440-MWe power reactor near the Gulf of Sidra, originally promised by the Soviet Union in 1977. The Tajoura reactor is subject to IAEA inspection.

Libya's bid to acquire chemical weapons in the late 1980s has been well documented, and Libya is now believed to have a substantial chemical weapons stockpile.[3] In late 1988, Libya finished construction of a chemical production facility at Rabta with extensive foreign technical assistance. The facility produced at least 100 metric tons of blister and nerve agents over a three-year period before it ceased operations as a result of U.S.–led international pressure.[4] Libya also has been seeking to establish a biological warfare capability, but, because of technical shortcomings, this

remains in the "early research and development stage."[5] In 1986, the Reagan Administration imposed a complete trade ban on Libya because of its continued support of international terrorism. In 1992, the United Nations agreed on a whole range of sanctions against Libya because of its continuing involvement in terrorist activities.[6]

DEVELOPMENTS

Over the past two years, Libya has maintained a defiant image on non-proliferation and arms control issues, especially on issues specifically related to the Middle East region and Israel's nuclear capability. At the same time, Tripoli has faced increasing pressures from the United States to suspend or even terminate certain WMD programs—in particular its chemical weapons production capabilities. The United States has progressively tightened its economic sanctions against Libya and has led international efforts to block transfers of arms and sensitive technologies for military purposes to Libya.

At the 1995 NPT Review and Extension Conference, Libya declared that it could not support *any* extension of the NPT—indefinite or limited—unless Israel adhered to the NPT. However, in a last minute reversal, it joined a number of Arab countries in backing the indefinite extension of the NPT.[7] (See Appendix B on 1995 NPT Review and Extension Conference.)

On January 27, 1996, Libya's official news agency restated Colonel Qadhafi's position that the Arab states should manufacture nuclear weapons to counter Israel's nuclear hegemony in the region. It stated: "The Arabs who are threatened by the Israeli nuclear weapons have the right to try in any way possible to possess these weapons so that a balance is achieved, and so that the region is not left at the mercy of the Israelis."[8] Qadhafi has also asserted that the Arab states would be justified in possessing chemical and biological weapons to counter Israel's nuclear capability.[9]

Chemical/Biological Weapons Program. On February 22, 1996, in testimony before the Senate Intelligence Committee, CIA Director John Deutch confirmed reports that Libya was building what he called the "world's largest underground chemical weapons plant" in a mountain at Tarhunah, 40 miles southeast of Tripoli.[10] U.S. intelligence sources indicated at the time that the plant would be completed "late in this decade" and would be capable of producing the ingredients for tons of poison gas daily.[11] Libya maintained that the plant was part of a water-irrigation system.[12]

In early April, Defense Secretary William Perry declared that the United States was determined to prevent Libya from completing construction of the Tarhunah plant. In what appeared to be a reference to the more drastic options under the Clinton Administration's counter-proliferation strategy, Perry said he would not rule out the use of military force to block completion of the plant.[13] However, some Pentagon officials subsequently revealed that it would be another two years before the United States had in its inventory earth-penetrating conventional weapons capable of destroying deeply buried targets like the Tarhunah installation. They alluded to the possibility that the United States might use a modified version of the existing B-61 nuclear warhead, which was projected to be ready by the end of 1996.[14]

In an apparent effort to defuse the controversy over the Tarhunah installation, Secretary Perry issued the following statement on May 7, 1996:

> Preventive action to keep the Libya plant from coming on line is something that can be done first through diplomacy. We have a good period of time in which we can apply that diplomacy, including coercive diplomacy. If that fails, then we can consider military actions. That would not need to be, and I would never recommend, nuclear weapons for that particular application. So any implication that we would use nuclear weapons for that purpose is just wrong.[15]

In any case, tensions over the Tarhunah plant appeared to ease by late 1996 as reports surfaced that Libya had suspended construction.[16]

There were also reports in mid-1997 that Libya had received South African equipment for the manufacture of chemical and biological weapons. According to these reports, after the 1994 national elections in South Africa, several scientists from the South African military's chemical and biological weapons program, called Project Coast, had sold equipment and perhaps had even traveled to Libya to advise in the project.[17]

Nuclear-Weapon-Free Zone. On April 11, 1996, Libya was among 43 African countries that signed the African Nuclear-Weapon-Free-Zone Treaty (ANWFZ). On the same occasion, in signing Protocol I of the treaty, the United States pledged "not to use or threaten to use a nuclear explosive device against [any party to the treaty]." However, on the same day, a senior White House official stated that the protocol "will not limit options available to the United States in response to an attack by an ANWFZ party using weapons of mass destruction."[18] (See Appendix E on Nuclear-Weapon-Free Zones.) This U.S affirmation of its right to use nuclear weapons in response to attacks using any WMD appeared to be directed at Libya's chemical weapons capability, with possible implications for the Tarhunah facility.

The Non-Proliferation Regime. On July 12, 1996, U.S. efforts to block the export of dual-use and military technology to Libya bore fruit in the approval by 33 nations of the Charter of the Wassenaar Arrangement on Export Controls for Conventional Arms and Dual-Use Goods and Technologies (for text of Wassenaar Arrangement, see Appendix H). Moreover, on August 6, 1996, in an effort to place greater pressure on the Libyan economy, President Clinton signed legislation imposing sanctions on foreign companies investing more than $40 million for future petroleum ventures in Iran and Libya, as well as companies exporting items to Libya that enhance its WMD and advanced conventional weapons programs.[19]

On September 10, 1996, Libya, along with Bhutan and India, voted against approval of the Comprehensive Test Ban Treaty (CTBT) by the U.N. General Assembly. Libya supported India's notion that the treaty should provide for nuclear disarmament within a time-bound framework.[20] However, Libya's vote against the CTBT was considered more of an act of defiance and pique—since it had already renounced nuclear weapons by adhering to the NPT and agreeing to its indefinite extension.

During 1997, Libya pursued its efforts to rehabilitate its image in the international community and appeared to have enjoyed some success in that regard. In March 1997, despite strong U.S. objections, the Vatican established full diplomatic relations with Tripoli. Moreover, in October 1997, Russia appeared poised to start talks with Libya on, *inter alia*, cooperating in the overhaul of the Tajoura Nuclear Research Center, location of the Soviet-supplied research reactor.[21]

Ballistic Missiles. In the late 1980s and early 1990s, Libya made several apparently unsuccessful attempts to purchase foreign missiles, such as the Soviet/Russian SS-23 and SS-21, and the Chinese DF-3A, M-9, and M-11. Libya's missile arsenal thus remains relatively limited and antiquated. It currently deploys a number of basic Scud-B missiles that it obtained from the Soviet Union in the mid-1970s. Tripoli continues a program to develop the indigenous al-Fateh missile, with a reported range of 950 km, but so far has "succeeded only in manufacturing liquid-fueled rockets with an approximate range of 200 km."[22] Tripoli may be continuing to cooperate with North Korea in hopes of a future purchase of the Nodong-1 (and related technologies). Libya is not known to have purchased complete Scud Mod. B or Mod. C missile systems.[23]

PROSPECTS

Since an attempted military coup in 1993, the Qadhafi regime has been facing growing dissent. The opposition, though dominated by Islamic fundamentalists, also contains "liberals" and nationalists, as well as army officers who "have brought a professional element to the struggle."[24] In 1996, there were reports that, on at least two occasions, Qadhafi dispatched troops into the northeast region of Libya to crush violent unrest.[25]

Nevertheless, despite this opposition and increasing international isolation, Qadhafi is a survivor who seems likely to remain Libya's leader for some time.

Under his leadership, Libya will continue to pose a threat to the Middle East and African regions and even, potentially, to southern Europe. His desire to expand Libya's WMD capabilities and his demonstrated willingness to use those capabilities are both likely to increase as he comes under greater pressure at home and abroad.[26] Qadhafi's overall strategy is to establish himself as the leader of the Arab world and thereby give Libya prestige among Islamic and other Third World countries, a strategy he has pursued for 30 years.[27] Acquisition of nuclear weapons would give new impetus to his dangerous quest.

NOTES

[1]Testimony of the Director of Central Intelligence John M. Deutch, before the Permanent Subcommittee on Investigations of the Senate Committee on Governmental Affairs, March 20, 1996.

[2]Mark Hibbs, *Nucleonics Week*, August 22, 1991, p. 7, noted in Monterey Institute of International Studies *Eye On Supply*, Spring 1992, p. 40; Bill Gertz, *Washington Times*, February 24, 1992, noted in *Eye On Supply*, Fall 1992, p. 25; R. Jeffrey Smith, *Washington Post*, April 28, 1992, noted in *Eye On Supply*, Winter 1993, p. 37.

[3]Stephen Engelberg with Michael Gordon, "Germans Accused of Helping Libya Build Nerve Gas Plant," *New York Times*, January 1, 1989; "Challenges to Peace in the Middle East," R. James Woolsey, Director of Central Intelligence, address to the Washington Institute for Near East Policy, Wye Plantation, Maryland, September 23, 1994 (revised version).

[4]In 1990, by fabricating a fire, Libya attempted to give the false impression that the facility was seriously damaged. See Office of the Secretary of Defense, *Proliferation: Threat and Response*, April 1996, p. 26.

[5]Ibid., p. 27. Also see James Adams, "South Africa: Libya Said Seeking Secret Biological Weapons," *London Sunday Times*, February 26, 1995.

[6]*Public Papers of the Presidents of the United States: Ronald Reagan, 1996*, Book I, January 1 to June 27, 1986 (Washington, DC: Government Printing Office, 1988), p. 17; David Hoffman, "President Imposes Boycott On Business With Libya; Qaddafi's Isolation Urged," *Washington Post*, January 8, 1996; U.N. Security Council, "Resolution 748 (1992)," S/RES/748, March 31, 1992.

[7]Rebecca Johnson, "Indefinite Extension of the Non-Proliferation Treaty," *ACRONYM No. 7*, September 1995, p. 30. While Libya did not object when the NPT Conference adopted the extension decisions without a vote, it subsequently announced to the Conference that it was "completely and absolutely opposed" to NPT extension "for one or more periods, let alone an indefinite extension." Ibid., p. 31.

[8]"Arabs Must Get Nuclear Bomb to Match Israel—Libya," *Reuters*, January 27, 1996. Also see "Arabs Need Nuclear Bomb, Gaddafi Says," *Reuters*, May 17, 1995.

[9]"Gaddafi Says Arabs Have Right to Germ Warfare Arms," *Reuters*, March 30, 1996; "Gaddafi Tunnels Into Trouble Both Within and Without," *Jane's Defence Weekly*, September 1996, p. 24.

[10]Tim Weiner, "Huge Chemical Arms Plant Near Completion in Libya," *New York Times*, February 25, 1996. Also see John Diamond, "Watching China," *Associated Press*, February 23, 1996.

[11]Weiner, "Huge Chemical Arms Plant," op. cit.; the plant reportedly houses most of Libya's stockpile of chemical weapons.

Subsequently, a Pentagon official indicated that individuals in several countries were assisting in the construction of the plant, "representing commercial interests or in some cases individual interests" by providing expertise or equipment. See Charles Aldinger, "Libya Getting Aid on Chemical Arms—Pentagon," *Reuters*, April 11, 1996. Also see "ZDF Sees Role in Libyan 'Poison-Gas' Plant," *ZDF Television Network* (Mainz), May 1, 1996, in *FBIS-TAC-96-007*, May 1, 1996; "Poison Gas Production Gear Sent to Libya," *Die Welt* (Berlin), August 20, 1996, *FBIS-WEU-96-162*, August 20, 1996; Raymond Bonner, "Germany's Search for Libya Suspect Finds Ties to Its Own Spies," *New York Times*, August 22, 1996; Raymond Bonner, "Germany Charges 3 in Sales to Libya," *International Herald Tribune*, August 22, 1996; "Weekly Faults BND on Libyan CW Plant," *Der Spiegel* (Hamburg), August 26, 1996, in *FBIS-WEU-96-167*, August 27, 1996; "Brussels Bank, Front Company Linked to Libya Smuggling Case," *De Morgen* (Brussels), August 27, 1996, in *FBIS-WEU-96-167*, August 27, 1996.

[12]Weiner, "Huge Chemical Arms Plant," op. cit.; "Libya Denies Weapons-Factory Link," *Washington Times*, February 27, 1996; John Lancaster, "Perry Presses U.S. Charge Against Libya," *Washington Post*, April 4, 1996.

In late May 1996, Egyptian President Hosni Mubarak asserted that, when Egyptian experts toured the Tarhunah facility in late April/early May, they found no evidence of a chemical installation. See John Lancaster, "Egypt Denies Libyan Chemical Arms Site," *Washington Post*, May 30, 1996.

[13]Lancaster, "Perry Presses U.S. Charge Against Libya," op. cit.

[14]Robert Burns, "U.S.–Libya," *Associated Press*, April 23, 1996; Charles Aldinger, "U.S. Lacks Conventional Arms to Destroy Libya Plant," *Reuters*, April 23, 1996. Also see Art Pine, "U.S. Hints It Would Bomb Libyan Facility," *Los Angeles Times*, April 19, 1996; Art Pine, "A-Bomb Against Libya Target Suggested," *Los Angeles Times*, April 24, 1996.

[15]Kenneth Bacon, "Department of Defense Regular Briefing," May 7, 1996.

[16]Bill Gertz, "Libyans Stop Work on Chemical Plant," *Washington Times*, June 24, 1996; Philip Finnegan, "Libya Ceases Work on Chem Factory," *Defense News*, December 16-22, 1996, p. 1.

[17]Peta Thornycroft, "Scientists Said Sell CBW Technology to Libya After 1994," *Johannesburg Mail & Guardian*, February 7, 1997, in *FBIS-TAC-97-007*, February 7, 1997; "Mandela Fears Chemical Arms Sales to Libya 'Tip of Iceberg'," *SAPA* (Johannesburg), February 11, 1997, in *FBIS-TAC-97-007*, February 11, 1997.

[18]"White House Briefing," *Federal News Service*, April 11, 1996. See also George Bunn, "Expanding Nuclear Options: Is the U.S. Negating Its Non-Use Pledges?" *Arms Control Today*, May/June 1996.

[19]Iran and Libya Sanctions Act of 1996, P.L.104-172,50 USC 1701; David E. Sanger, "Congress Curbs Iran Investment From Overseas," *New York Times*, June 20, 1996; Clay Chandler, "U.S. Expects Furor Over Trade Sanctions at Summit," *Washington Post*, June 27, 1996; Rick Atkinson, "Divergent Policies Toward Iran Strain U.S.-German Relations," *Washington Post*, June 27, 1996; Eric Pianin, "Clinton Approves Sanctions for Investors in Iran, Libya," *Washington Post*, August 6, 1996.

For a review of the effect of the sanctions, see "Hearing of the House International Relations Committee: Effect of Sanctions on Iran and Libya," *Federal News Service*, July 23, 1997.

[20]United Nations, "Assembly Adopts Comprehensive Nuclear-Test-Ban Treaty," Press Release GA/9083, September 10, 1996.

[21]"Ties With Vatican, and Other Foreign Policy 'Triumphs' for Libya," *Mideast Mirror*, March 11, 1997; "Russia Ready to Start Talks With Libya on Nuclear Center," *Interfax* (Moscow), October 22, 1997, in *FBIS-SOV-97-295*, October 22, 1997. (In the *Interfax* report the name of the center appeared as "Gazhura.")

[22]*Proliferation: Threat and Response*, 1996, op. cit., p. 28.

[23]Testimony of Joseph S. Bermudez Jr., before the House Committee on Foreign Affairs, Subcommittee on International Security, International Organizations, and Human Rights, February 14, 1993; "Media: Libya Considering Buying Missiles," *Yonhap* (Seoul), May 3, 1996, in *FBIS-EAS-96-087*, May 3, 1996, p. 28.

Most recently, in June 1993, Libya tried to obtain solid rocket fuel chemicals from Russia via Ukraine—a move confirming Libya's continued interest in ballistic missile development. See "Libya: Rocket Racket," *Africa Confidential*, July 16, 1993.

[24]Jonathan Wright, "Tripoli Soccer Shooting Spotlights Dissent," *Washington Times*, July 17, 1996.

[25]James Bruce, "Col. Gaddafi Dispatches Troops to Quell Unrest," *Jane's Defence Weekly*, April 3, 1996, p. 14; Wright, "Tripoli Soccer Shooting," op. cit.; "Gaddafi Tunnels into Trouble," *Jane's*, op. cit.

[26]In 1987, Qadhafi's regime used chemical weapons against Chadian troops and, according to recent reports, is using them against opposition groups in Libya. See *Proliferation: Threat and Response*, 1996, op. cit., p. 25.

[27]*Proliferation: Threat and Response*, 1996, op. cit., p. 25.

Soviet-supplied 10-MWt research reactor, subject to IAEA inspection.

Carnegie Endowment for International Peace, *Tracking Nuclear Proliferation*, 1998

LIBYA: Nuclear Infrastructure

NAME/LOCATION OF FACILITY	TYPE/STATUS	IAEA SAFEGUARDS
RESEARCH REACTORS		
Tajoura	Light-water, HEU, 10 MWt; operating.	Yes
POWER REACTORS		
Gulf of Sidra	Light-water, LEU, 440 MWe; planned.	Planned

Abbreviations:

HEU	=	highly enriched uranium
LEU	=	low-enriched uranium
nat. U	=	natural uranium
MWe	=	millions of watts of electrical output
MWt	=	millions of watts of thermal output
KWt	=	thousands of watts of thermal output

8

LATIN AMERICA

Argentina

Since the initial revelation in 1983 of its capability to produce weapons-usable material and possibly build a nuclear weapon, Argentina has made great strides toward becoming a cooperative member of the non-proliferation regime.[1] The most important landmarks of this evolution occurred in early 1994, when Argentina joined both the Treaty of Tlatelolco and the Nuclear Suppliers Group (NSG), and on February 10, 1995, when it became a party to the Nuclear Non-Proliferation Treaty (NPT).[2] Furthermore, in a sign of the continuing reconciliation with Brazil, its former nuclear rival, Argentina hosted the April 1996 NSG plenary meeting at which Brazil became a member.[3]

BACKGROUND

Nuclear Weapons Program and Policy. More so than other nations, Argentina was able to develop its nuclear program without becoming overly dependent on foreign technology. This trend was established early, with the creation of the National Atomic Energy Commission (CNEA) in 1950, which by 1953 had implemented a research program and had started mining uranium.[4] The first outside assistance to the Argentine nuclear program came in 1958, when it built a U.S.–designed research reactor, the RA-1 at Constituyentes, the plans for which had been supplied pursuant to a nuclear cooperation agreement signed with the United States in 1955. The flurry of activity that surrounded this effort probably catalyzed the establishment of the Brazilian nuclear program in 1953 and marked the beginning of a nuclear rivalry between the two nations that lasted over 30 years.

From the plans for RA-1, Argentina was able to construct three additional research reactors on its own by 1967: the RA-0 at Cordoba, the RA-2 at Constituyentes, and the RA-3 at Ezeiza. By this time, Argentina had also developed the infrastructure to support a nuclear power plant, and in 1968 it purchased a 320-MWe reactor, the Atucha I, from the West German firm Siemens. Concurrently, in its quest for the capability to obtain nuclear weapons–usable material, Argentina built a laboratory-scale reprocessing facility at Ezeiza to extract plutonium from spent reactor fuel; this facility was subsequently closed in 1973 after intermittent operation and the extraction of less than 1 kg of plutonium.[5]

Argentina had thus far rejected International Atomic Energy Agency (IAEA) inspections of its nuclear facilities, and it was only at West German insistence that the Atucha plant was safeguarded. When negotiations on the Treaty of Tlatelolco and the NPT were concluded in 1967-68, Argentina refused to join either; both were perceived as impinging on Argentina's sovereignty and as imposing restrictions on its nuclear program. Argentina claimed at that time that IAEA safeguards did not apply to its indigenously built facilities, particularly the reprocessing lab at Ezeiza, even though evidence existed that an Italian firm had participated in the construction of that facility.[6]

After a military *junta* claimed power in a 1976 coup, efforts were increased to achieve greater nuclear self-sufficiency and progress toward nuclear arms— motivated in part by Brazil's 1975 deal with West Germany to obtain an entire nuclear fuel cycle. In 1978, CNEA began construction of a second reprocessing facility at Ezeiza that had a design capacity of 10-20 kg of plutonium per year; due to economic constraints and political pressure from the United States, construction on the plant was halted in 1990 (see chart). Although Argentina claimed that the facility would be used for mixing reactor fuel, it would not allow IAEA inspection of the plant. Since Argentina had no non-military use for plutonium, the international community suspected the facility was designed to support an undisclosed nuclear weapons program.

In late 1983, just prior to the inauguration of its first democratically elected government in a decade, concrete evidence finally emerged that the Argentine military had taken the first steps toward developing a nuclear weapons capability. At that time, Argentina's departing military *junta* revealed that the country had completed construction of a secret uranium-enrichment plant at Pilcaniyeu, a project that had been initiated in 1978. Military authorities noted that the Pilcaniyeu project was motivated by several factors, including Argentina's desire for independence from developed nations, its goal of nuclear leadership in Latin America, and its nuclear rivalry with Brazil. Although the *junta* claimed (just as it had done with the Ezeiza reprocessing facility) that the facility was intended for peaceful purposes, the secrecy surrounding the plant and the fact that Argentina's nuclear power reactors did not require enriched uranium fuel gave rise to suspicions that it was to be part of a clandestine nuclear weapons development program.[7]

Following the defeat in the Falklands/Malvinas war with the United Kingdom and the inauguration of President Raul Alfonsin in December 1983, a major shift occurred in Argentine nuclear policy. The country's nuclear program, which had been directed by the

Navy, was placed under civilian control, and the new government introduced legislation to legally prohibit development of nuclear weapons. Also, nuclear confidence-building measures with neighboring Brazil were agreed to in November 1985; these included reciprocal visits to all nuclear installations in both countries (even those not subject to IAEA inspection) beginning in 1987 and a series of bilateral nuclear agreements (see below).

Nuclear Exports. Relative self-sufficiency in its nuclear program allowed Argentina to become a large second-tier supplier of nuclear technology and equipment to developing nations. This trend, coupled with Argentina's refusal of non-proliferation norms, confounded efforts by the United States and others to hold several nuclear aspirants, particularly Libya and Iran, at bay.[8]

The restoration of democratic governance in 1983 did little to change the liberal export policy of the Argentine military, especially as it pertained to North Africa. In 1985, Argentina and Algeria concluded an agreement under which Argentina exported a 1-MWt research reactor that became operational in 1989; Algeria was not an NPT member and had no safeguards agreement at the time. Under a second agreement, discussed in 1990 but never concluded, Argentina would have sent an isotopic production reactor and hot cell facility to Algeria.[9]

In 1974, Argentina concluded a deal with Libya to provide Tripoli with equipment for uranium mining and processing. By then, Argentina had already extracted plutonium from spent reactor fuel, but it is unclear if this contract with Libya provided any assistance for this type of activity. In 1982, when Argentina was engaged in the war over the Falkland Islands, Libya provided $100 million in anti-aircraft and air-to-air missiles. In exchange, Argentina possibly provided information or technology for the nuclear weapons program pursued by Libyan leader Colonel Muammar Quadhafi (see also Libya chapter in this volume). According to a May 1983 report, Argentina and Libya continued nuclear cooperation after the Falkland/Malvinas war. Discussions most likely took place on the export of reprocessing and enrichment technologies from Argentina—at the time, Argentina was constructing the reprocessing facility at Ezeiza and the enrichment facility at Pilcaniyeu.[10] Later reports suggested that Argentina was in 1985 prepared to send a hot cell facility to Libya, and only U.S. pressure prevented the sale.[11]

Even though Iran is an NPT member and has concluded IAEA safeguards agreements, it is perceived to be in pursuit of a nuclear weapon (see Iran chapter in this volume). Despite this widely held perception, Argentina has been intimately involved in the development of Iran's nuclear program. Starting in 1987, CNEA joined a consortium that was to complete the Bushehr nuclear power facility; the deal was ultimately suspended in 1995 before the project was finished. In early 1992, Argentina was ready to supply Iran with a fuel fabrication facility and a uranium dioxide conversion plant—facilities that could be used in a program to obtain weapons-grade material—and it was only last-minute pressure, again by the United States, that stopped the shipment.[12] Iran has also targeted Argentina as a potential supplier of hot cell and heavy-water production facilities, but Argentina has refused to export such equipment.[13]

Early in his first term, President Carlos Saúl Menem was able to wrest control of the nuclear complex from the military, which helped stem the flow of nuclear exports. It was not until 1992, however, that Menem was able, by presidential decree, to implement a nuclear export control policy.[14]

Argentina-Brazil Rapprochement. The nuclear competition between Brazil and Argentina had been consistently fueled by mutual distrust since the early 1950s. Both countries pursued civilian and military nuclear programs, but, by the early 1980s, Argentina was thought to be about five years ahead of Brazil in having the capability to produce material suitable for a nuclear weapon.[15] Once the military regimes in both countries had fallen, however, Brazil and Argentina moved toward ending their nuclear rivalry. On July 18, 1991, President Menem and President Fernando Collor de Mello of Brazil signed a bilateral agreement to allow mutual inspections of nuclear installations in their respective countries and to establish the Argentine-Brazilian Accounting and Control Commission (ABACC) to implement the bilateral inspection accord. The accord was the culmination of a bilateral program of confidence-building in the nuclear sphere begun in 1987. A quadripartite agreement to integrate ABACC's bilateral inspection system with that of the IAEA was signed by the two nations, the IAEA, and ABACC in Vienna on December 13, 1991. Exchanges of nuclear material inventories and mutual inspections under the July 1991 bilateral accord began in the fall of 1992 following the inauguration of ABACC. The Argentine Congress approved the Quadripartite Safeguards Agreement on August 5, 1992, but inspections under the agreement were delayed until the Brazilian Congress approved it on February 25, 1994, and it entered into force on March 4, 1994.[16] Under the Quadripartite Agreement, ABACC and the IAEA must establish an initial inventory of all nuclear materials in Argentina as a basis for future inspections. This task is expected to be complicated by the years of unsafeguarded activities at Pilcaniyeu.

In January 1994, Argentina brought into force the Treaty for the Prohibition of Nuclear Weapons in Latin America and the Caribbean (Treaty of Tlatelolco), thus making the commitment not to acquire, manufacture, test, use, or permit the stationing of a nuclear explosive device on its territory and accepting IAEA inspection of all its nuclear activities.[17] Argentina became a party to the NPT on February 10, 1995, signifying its adherence to international non-proliferation norms. (Brazil, however, has yet to ratify the NPT.)

Missile Program. In the late 1970s, during the period of military rule, the Argentine Air Force began work on a single-stage weather rocket called the Condor I; if converted for military use, the Condor I could have served as a short-range tactical missile. Despite the change of government in 1983, missile development by the Air Force continued. In 1984 Argentina concluded an agreement with Iraq and Egypt to develop a 600-mile, two-stage system called the Condor II, with a potential payload of 1,100 pounds. Iraq agreed to fund the project; Egypt would provide technical expertise; and Argentina would construct and test the missiles.[18] Acquisition of key components and technology was done in secret, suggesting that the Condor II was a military system. The Missile Technology Control Regime (MTCR) identified the Condor II project as one of concern, causing Egypt to withdraw from the agreement in September 1989. By March 1990, Argentina had frozen the Condor II project due to lack of funds, and in April, President Menem decided to cancel it.[19] The United States insists, as a requirement for joining the MTCR, that members renounce offensive missiles inherently capable of traveling at least 300 km with a 500-kg payload—criteria that the Condor II project violated. Once the Condor II was scrapped, however, the path was cleared for Argentine membership in the MTCR, and on November 29, 1994, Argentine Foreign Ministry officials announced that Argentina had indeed become a member.

Chemical and Biological Weapons. Argentina has no known chemical or biological weapons programs and is a party to both the Biological Weapons Convention and the Chemical Weapons Convention. In addition, Argentina is a signatory to the 1991 Joint Declaration on the Complete Prohibition of Chemical and Biological Weapons, a regional non-proliferation agreement also known as the Mendoza Accord.

DEVELOPMENTS

Nuclear Weapons Complex. It is believed that the plant at Pilcaniyeu succeeded in producing only small amounts of very low-enriched uranium.[20] No weapons-grade uranium (enriched to 90 percent U-235 or more) is believed to have been produced at the Pilcaniyeu facility, and Argentina has pledged not to produce any in the future. Since Argentina does not possess an operational plutonium-separation (chemical reprocessing) plant, it currently has no source of weapons-grade material.

The conversion of Argentina's nuclear facilities to civilian use continues, guided by the IAEA and ABACC. During 1995, the IAEA's verification of nuclear material and facility design information was "largely completed."[21] ABACC has also successfully implemented its program of ad hoc inspections at nuclear facilities in Argentina, conducting 79 inspections in 1996, and 55 from January to October 1997.[22] The facility of principal concern, the uranium-enrichment plant at Pilcaniyeu, has been under an ABACC ad hoc inspection agreement since 1992, and negotiations are under way to enhance accounting by measuring material in storage.[23]

U.S.–Argentina Cooperation. Another important step on Argentina's path toward full participation in the non-proliferation regime came on February 29, 1996, when then–U.S. Secretary of State Warren Christopher and Argentine Foreign Minister Guido Di Tella signed a new agreement for peaceful nuclear cooperation. On March 18, 1996, President Clinton submitted the agreement to the U.S. Congress for statutory review, and the agreement was brought into force on October 16, 1997. An additional technical agreement was signed during Clinton's mid-October 1997 trip to Argentina; among other things, this agreement, signed with CNEA, will promote the exchange of information and cooperative research and development between both Argentine and U.S. nuclear laboratories.[24] In addition, President Clinton reaffirmed his intent to grant Argentina the status of Major Non-NATO Ally, acknowledging Argentina's participation in U.N. peacekeeping missions; other countries with such status include Israel, South Korea, and Japan. Some concerns have been raised that U.S.–Argentine partnership might affect the military balance in the region, especially considering the recent lifting of a two-decade U.S. ban on advanced weapons sales to the region.[25]

Missile Program. Since scrapping the Condor II project, Argentina has not conducted any further research and development on medium-range ballistic missiles or on an indigenous space launch vehicle. However, in early 1997, Brazil and Argentina began to discuss the joint design and construction of a commercial rocket for low altitude satellite launches.[26] Even though Brazil was required to give up development of its medium-range missiles when it joined the MTCR, it was allowed to maintain its commercial space launch program.

PROSPECTS

Argentina has made remarkable non-proliferation progress since 1983, when it ended the development of its military-nuclear program. Although Argentina was close to having the necessary means to produce weapons-grade fissile material, it never completed the project and has worked toward turning its military-run nuclear facilities into civilian-use facilities. Now, Argentina is a cooperative member of all major elements of the non-proliferation regime. This includes membership in the NSG, which is critical considering Argentina's history of nuclear exports to high-risk nations.

The political climate in Argentina is now viewed as fairly stable. Since 1983, democratic elections have taken place regularly. President Menem is in his second and final term, and the next presidential election is slated for May 1999. Unless there is an economic downturn, the next administration is expected to maintain a strong commitment to non-proliferation. The role of the military in politics and in the Argentine nuclear program is also expected to remain relatively small, especially since CNEA has been drawn away from military control. If economic problems do arise, however, or if regional competitions flare up, the military could re-emerge as a strong political force.

NOTES

[1] There is some question whether the explicit aim of Argentina's military nuclear program was to acquire a nuclear weapon. Other goals, including independence from Western nations, leadership among developing nations and in Latin America, and rivalry with Brazil also motivated the Argentine military to pursue a nuclear program.

[2] Report on Non-Proliferation Policy by the Argentine Republic, June 1995, p. 5; Embassy of Argentina, "Argentina Accesses the Non-Proliferation Nuclear-Weapons Treaty," Press Release, February 10, 1995.

[3] Wyn Bowen and Andrew Koch, "Non-proliferation is embraced by Brazil," *Jane's Intelligence Review*, June 1996, p. 283.

[4] Daniel Poneman, *Nuclear Power in the Developing World* (London: George Allen and Unwin, 1982), pp. 68-72. See also Leonard S. Spector, *Nuclear Proliferation Today* (New York: Vintage Books, 1984), p. 200.

[5] Spector, *Nuclear Proliferation Today*, ibid., p. 203.

[6] Robert Laufer, "Argentina Looks to Reprocessing to Fill Its Own Needs Plus Plutonium Sales," *Nuclear Fuel*, November 8, 1982, p. 3.

[7] For an extensive review of the Argentine nuclear program during the 1980s, see Leonard S. Spector with Jacqueline R. Smith, *Nuclear Ambitions* (Boulder, CO: Westview Press, 1991), pp. 223-41.

[8] For further discussion on Argentina's nuclear exports, see William C. Potter, *International Nuclear Trade and Nonproliferation: The Challenge of the Emerging Suppliers* (Lexington, MA: Lexington Books, 1990), pp. 95-109.

[9] Richard Kessler, "Menem Government Eyes Isotope Production Reactor for Algeria," *Nucleonics Week*, January 4, 1990, p. 11.

[10] Spector, *Nuclear Proliferation Today*, op. cit., p. 157f., and "Brazilian Military Concern Over Argentine Talks with Libya," *Correio Braziliense*, May 24, 1983, translated in *FBIS/NDP*, June 30, 1983, p. 8.

[11] Mark Hibbs, "INVAP Seeks Thai Reactor Sale; Syria Expected to Sue for Supply," *Nucleonics Week*, October 27, 1994, p. 1

[12] Mark Hibbs, "Iran Sought Sensitive Nuclear Supplies from Argentina, China," *Nucleonics Week*, September 24, 1992, p. 2.

[13] Ibid., p. 2.

[14] Gary Marx, "South American Nuclear Threat Fades," *Chicago Tribune*, May 3, 1992; Richard Kessler, "Argentina Unilaterally Adopts Nuclear, Weapons Export Controls," *Nucleonics Week*, April 30, 1992, p. 1.

[15] Spector, *Nuclear Proliferation Today*, op. cit., p. 235.

[16] "Brazil and Argentina Move Toward Safeguards," *Nuclear Engineering International*, September 1991, p. 4; "Brazil's Military May Block Safeguards with Argentina," *Nucleonics Week*, November 28, 1991, p. 8; James Brooke, "Brazil and Argentina Join Up to Open Their Nuclear Sites," *New York Times*, December 13, 1991; Statement by Michael McCurry, "Argentina and Brazil: Ratification of the Quadripartite Safeguards Agreement," U.S. Department of State, March 4, 1994; John R. Redick, Julio C. Carasales, and Paulo S. Wrobel, "Nuclear Rapprochement: Argentina, Brazil, and the Nonproliferation Regime," *Washington Quarterly*, Vol. 18, No. 1, Winter 1995, pp. 107-22; John R. Redick, "Nuclear Weapon Free Zones in a Changing Global Environment," in J.B. Poole and R. Guthrie, eds., *Verification 1994*, (London: VERTIC, 1994).

[17] "Brazil, Argentina and Chile Bring Into Force the Treaty for the Prohibition of Nuclear Weapons in Latin America (The Treaty of Tlatelolco)," Arms Control and Disarmament Agency Press Release, June 3, 1994.

[18] "Nation Joins Missile Technology Control Regime," *Buenos Aires Herald*, November 30. 1994, in *JPRS-TND-93-001*, January 6, 1994, p. 11; U.S. Congress, Office of Technology Assessment, *Technologies Underlying Weapons of Mass Destruction*, OTA-BP-ISC-115, December 1993, p. 224; see also Spector with Smith, *Nuclear Ambitions*, op. cit., p. 229-32.

[19] David B. Ottaway, "Egypt Drops Out of Missile Project," *Washington Post*, September 20, 1989; "Is Condor Kaput?" *U.S. News and World Report*, March 5, 1990, p. 20; "Menem Says Missile Scrapped Over U.S. Concern," *Clarin*, April 25, 1990, translated in *FBIS-LAT*, April 26, 1990, p. 20.

[20] David Albright, Frans Berkhout, and William Walker, *Plutonium and Highly Enriched Uranium 1996: World Inventories, Capabilities and Policies* (New York: Oxford University Press for Stockholm International Peace Research Institute, 1997), p. 371.

[21] International Atomic Energy Agency, *Annual Report for 1995*, p. 45.

[22] Argentine-Brazilian Accounting and Control Commission, *Annual Report 1996*, p. 24, and *ABACC News*, May/October 1997, p. 3.

[23] Argentine-Brazilian Accounting and Control Commission, *Annual Report 1996*, p. 14f.

[24] Department of Energy press release "U.S.–Argentina Implementing Arrangement for Technical Exchange and Cooperation in the Area of Peaceful Uses of Nuclear Energy," October 18, 1997.

[25] Anthony Boadle, "Clinton notifies Congress on Argentina ally status," *Reuters*, October 14, 1997. The change in arms sales policy was announced August 1, 1997. Some U.S. officials have expressed concern that this could spark a regional arms race, especially given unresolved conflicts such as that between Ecuador and Peru. There is also concern that in Chile, which has expressed an interest in a F-16 purchase, democratic reform has not reached the military. See Thomas W. Lippman, "U.S. Ends Ban on Latin Arms Sales," *Washington Post*, August 2, 1997, p. A12.

[26] Wyn Bowen, Tim McCarthy, and Holly Porteous, "Ballistic Missile Shadow Lengthens," *Jane's IDR Extra*, February 1997, p. 5, and "Brazil-Argentina Discuss Building Commercial Rocket," *El Mercurio* (Brazil), March 29, 1997, in *FBIS-LAT-97-091*, April 1, 1997.

Argentina:
Map and Chart

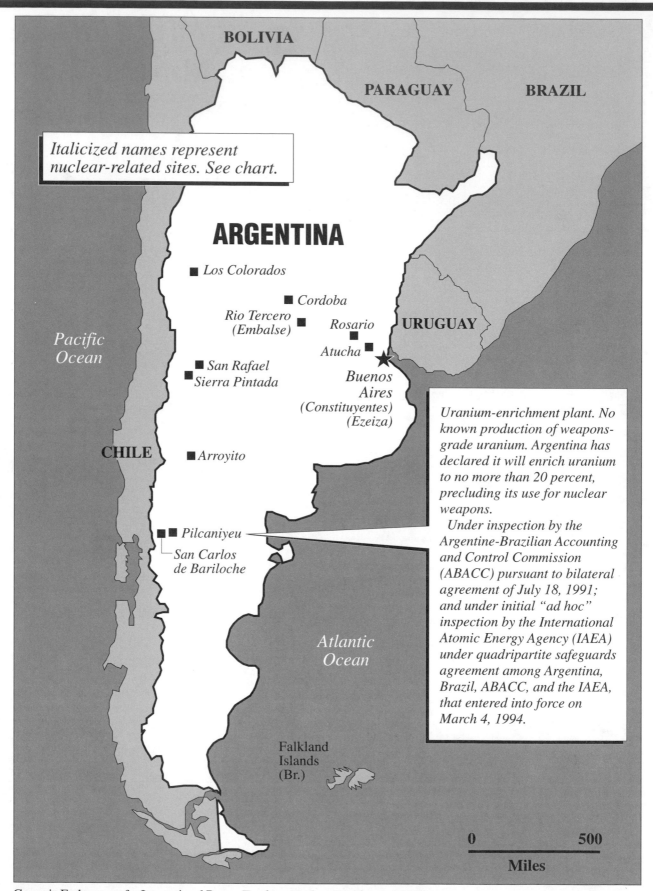

Italicized names represent nuclear-related sites. See chart.

BOLIVIA

PARAGUAY

BRAZIL

ARGENTINA

■ *Los Colorados*

■ *Cordoba*

Rio Tercero ■
(Embalse)

Rosario ■

URUGUAY

Atucha ■

★

*Pacific
Ocean*

■ *San Rafael*
■ *Sierra Pintada*

*Buenos
Aires
(Constituyentes)
(Ezeiza)*

CHILE

■ *Arroyito*

Uranium-enrichment plant. No
known production of weapons-
grade uranium. Argentina has
declared it will enrich uranium
to no more than 20 percent,
precluding its use for nuclear
weapons.
    Under inspection by the
Argentine-Brazilian Accounting
and Control Commission
(ABACC) pursuant to bilateral
agreement of July 18, 1991;
and under initial "ad hoc"
inspection by the International
Atomic Energy Agency (IAEA)
under quadripartite safeguards
agreement among Argentina,
Brazil, ABACC, and the IAEA,
that entered into force on
March 4, 1994.

■■ *Pilcaniyeu*
└ *San Carlos
de Bariloche*

*Atlantic
Ocean*

Falkland
Islands
(Br.)

0   500
_____
              Miles

Carnegie Endowment for International Peace, *Tracking Nuclear Proliferation*, 1998

ARGENTINA: Nuclear Infrastructure

NAME/LOCATION OF FACILITY	TYPE/STATUS	SAFEGUARDS[a]
POWER REACTORS		
Atucha I, Lima	Heavy-water, natural U, 357 MWe; operating.	IAEA/ABACC
Embalse, Cordoba Province.	Heavy-water, natural U, 648 MWe; operating.	IAEA/ABACC
Atucha II, Lima	Heavy-water, natural U, 745 MWe; under construction.[b]	IAEA/ABACC
RESEARCH REACTORS		
RA-0, Cordoba	Light-water, 20% enriched uranium, .01 KWt; operating.	IAEA/ABACC
RA-1, Constituyentes	Light-water, 20% enriched uranium, 40 KWt; operating.	IAEA/ABACC
RA-2, Constituyentes	Light-water, HEU, less than 1 MWt; shut down.	IAEA/ABACC
RA-3, Ezeiza	Light-water, LEU, 4.5 MWt; operating.	IAEA/ABACC
RA-4, Rosario	Light-water, 20% enriched uranium, .001 KWt; operating.	IAEA/ABACC
RA-6, San Carlos de Bariloche	Light-water, HEU, 500 KWt; operating.	IAEA/ABACC
RA-8, Pilcaniyeu	Critical facility; light-water, LEU; not yet operating.[c]	IAEA/ABACC
RA-9, Cordoba	20% enriched uranium, graphite reflector, 20 MWt; planned.[d]	IAEA/ABACC
URANIUM ENRICHMENT		
Pilcaniyeu	Gaseous diffusion method; closed for construction.[e]	IAEA/ABACC
REPROCESSING (PLUTONIUM EXTRACTION)		
Ezeiza	Construction halted, 1990.[f]	N/A (Not Applicable)
URANIUM PROCESSING		
San Rafael	Uranium mining; operating.	N/A
Los Colorados	Uranium mining; operating.	N/A
Sierra Pintada	Uranium mining; operations deferred for financial reasons.	N/A
Cordoba	Uranium purification (UO_2) plant; operating.	IAEA/ABACC
Cordoba	Experimental UO_2 plant; operating.	IAEA/ABACC
Cordoba	Uranium purification (UO_2) plant; shut down.	IAEA/ABACC
Constituyentes	Uranium conversion (UF_6) plant; operating.	IAEA/ABACC
Pilcaniyeu	Uranium conversion (UF_6) facility; operating.	IAEA/ABACC
Ezeiza	Fuel fabrication plant (for Atucha); operating.	IAEA/ABACC
Ezeiza	Fuel fabrication plant (for Embalse); operating.	IAEA/ABACC
Ezeiza	Plutonium fuel fabrication plant; under construction.[g]	IAEA/ABACC
Ezeiza	Enriched Uranium Lab.[h]	IAEA/ABACC
Ezeiza	Triple Altura Lab.[i]	IAEA/ABACC
Constituyentes	Pilot-scale plant to fabricate HEU; operating.	IAEA/ABACC
Constituyentes	Research reactor fuel fabrication plant; operating.	IAEA/ABACC
Constituyentes	Alpha Facility.[j]	IAEA
HEAVY-WATER PRODUCTION		
Arroyito	Production-scale; operating.	IAEA/ABACC
Atucha	Pilot-scale; suspended.[k]	IAEA/ABACC

Abbreviations:

HEU	=	highly enriched uranium
LEU	=	low-enriched uranium
nat. U	=	natural uranium
MWe	=	millions of watts of electrical output
MWt	=	millions of watts of thermal output
KWt	=	thousands of watts of thermal output

NOTES (Argentina Chart)

[a]IAEA and ABACC are conducting parallel inspections at the indicated facilities. At the Pilcaniyeu uranium enrichment plant, the IAEA has been permitted to conduct inspections, following the ratification of the Quadripartite Safeguards Agreement. These inspections are still in the initial or "ad hoc" phase, pending completion of formal IAEA "facility attachments," which by October 1997 had still not been concluded. See *ABACC News*, May/October 1997, pp. 3-4.

[b]Atucha II is expected to begin commercial operation in 1999. See *Nuclear Engineering International: World Nuclear Industry Handbook, 1997*, p. 17.

[c]This is a research and training facility that is currently loading the first batch of fuel according to an ABACC official.

[d]The plans for this facility were conceived in the mid-1980s, when it was to be part of a complex including the 20-MW reactor, three hot cells, and an isotope finishing plant. The plan was shelved in 1987 due to financial reasons, "until sometime next decade." Richard Kessler, "CNEA Shelves Planned & 70-million Isotope Production Complex," *Nucleonics Week*, October 29, 1987, p. 8. RA-9 is listed as "ordered/firmly planned" in the *World Nuclear Industry Handbook 1997*, p. 108, but it is not listed in the IAEA *Annual Report* for 1996.

[e]Mark Hibbs, "Brazil Mulling New Centrifuge Plant to Serve Two Reactors at Angra Site," *Nuclear Fuel*, September 26, 1994, p. 3. Argentina has not produced weapons-grade uranium at the facility and has pledged not to do so in the future. Phase 1 with a 20,000 SWU/year capability is operational and a second phase capable of 100,000 SWU/year is under construction. *World Nuclear Industry Handbook 1997*, p. 120. According to Albright, the main cascade had not been operating as of May 1996 although a small pilot plant was opened in 1993. David Albright, Frans Berkhout and William Walker, *Plutonium and Highly Enriched Uranium 1996: World Inventories,*

Capabilities and Policies (New York: Oxford University Press for Stockholm International Peace Research Institute, 1997), p. 371. Pilcaniyeu was listed as "not in operation at the moment," *ABACC News*, January/April 1997, p. 3.

[f]As of late 1994, the plant was being modified for testing of spent fuel elements and components. Albright, Berkhout, and Walker, *1996 World Inventories*, op. cit., p. 373. ABACC has verified that construction has halted and noted that some parts of the facility were already dismantled. Institute for Science and International Security and Shalheveth Freier Center for Peace, Science, & Technology, "Argentina and Brazil: The Latin American Rapprochement," May 16, 1996, p. 49. At the time the construction was halted, Argentina publicly listed the cause as financial constraints; privately, President Menem hoped to speed relations with several key Western supplier nations, especially the United States, which had been pressuring Argentina to end construction of the reprocessing plant. See John Redick, "Nuclear Illusions: Argentina and Brazil," Henry L. Stimson Center Occasional Paper 25, December 1995, p. 3.

[g]Albright, Berkhout, and Walker, op. cit., p. 183. A small plutonium fuel fabrication plant for Atucha is reportedly under construction.

[h]Listed under "Other Facilities" in the IAEA *Annual Report* for 1996, p. 87.

[i]The Triple Altura Lab, operation since 1992 according to an ABACC official, is a facility used to recover enriched uranium contained in fuel element scraps.

[j]The Alpha Facility undertakes research on MOX fuel rod fabrication and design.

[k]*World Nuclear Industry Handbook 1997*, op. cit., p. 123.

Brazil

In a remarkable turnabout in the fall of 1990, Brazil renounced its secret program to produce weapons-usable material and possibly build a nuclear weapon,[1] and began a series of steps toward binding non-proliferation commitments. A significant milestone on this path came on May 30, 1994, when Brazil brought into force the Treaty for the Prohibition of Nuclear Weapons in Latin America and the Caribbean (Treaty of Tlatelolco), thus assuming obligations not to acquire, manufacture, test, use, or permit the stationing of nuclear weapons or any nuclear explosive device on its territory while accepting IAEA inspection of all its nuclear activities.[2] Even though Brazil has historically refused to sign the Nuclear Non-Proliferation Treaty (NPT) for domestic political reasons, the government of President Fernando Henrique Cardoso has made encouraging moves recently to nudge the Brazilian Congress toward ratification of the accord. Brazil's refusal to sign the NPT has not, however, prevented it from accepting the strictest international supervision of its nuclear activities, which now includes full IAEA safeguards of all nuclear facilities and membership in the Nuclear Suppliers Group.[3]

BACKGROUND

Nuclear Weapons Program. Brazil first demonstrated active interest in pursuing both civilian and military nuclear capabilities in 1953, spurred largely by a developing nuclear rivalry with Argentina, which had shown similar interest since 1950. Brazil first attempted to acquire nuclear equipment and technology in 1953, when its National Research Council sent Admiral Alvaro Alberto to West Germany to purchase experimental ultracentrifuges; this transfer was blocked by U.S. forces occupying Germany at the time. Brazil signed a nuclear cooperation agreement with the United States in 1955, as did Argentina, and, in 1957, the Comissao Nacional de Energia Nuclear (CNEN) began operation of Brazil's first research reactor, which was supplied by the United States under the agreement.

In the early 1960s, Brazil pursued a deal with France for the provision of a natural uranium power reactor, but the negotiations were abandoned in 1964. It was not until 1971 that Brazil acquired its first power plant, the Angra 1 light-water reactor, from the U.S. company Westinghouse. In 1975, West Germany agreed to provide Brazil with ten nuclear power plants and a complete nuclear fuel cycle. Although the German nuclear transfers would be subject to IAEA safeguards, the international community was concerned that Brazil could apply the knowledge gained in its civilian program to a secret military program. After 15 years of cooperation with Germany, Brazil's civilian nuclear sector had little to show but an unfinished reactor and an unsuccessful uranium-enrichment program based on the jet nozzle method. However, during that same period—and as suspected by the international community—the Brazilian military was engaged in a program to acquire the capability to build nuclear weapons.

Begun when the country was under military control and code-named the Solimoes Project, the secret effort included research on nuclear weapons design, the excavation of a 100-meter-deep shaft for underground nuclear tests at a military base near Cachimbo in the Amazon jungle, and the development of three different methods to produce weapons-grade fissile material, none of which were subject to IAEA safeguards. Each military branch pursued a different path. With the cooperation of the Institute for Energy and Nuclear Research (IPEN), the Navy developed ultracentrifuges for uranium enrichment; the Army chose plutonium production reactors. The Air Force undertook research on laser enrichment of uranium, as well as nuclear weapons design and the construction of a nuclear test site.[4] Only the Navy/IPEN project succeeded, and its installations—a laboratory-scale uranium centrifuge plant at IPEN, in São Paulo, and the initial module of an industrial-scale plant at the Brazilian Navy's Aramar Research Center in Ipéro—are capable of producing uranium enriched to the level needed for nuclear weapons. Neither plant is known to have produced such material, however, and Brazil has declared that it intends to produce only low-enriched uranium at the facilities, which cannot be used for nuclear arms.

Underscoring his decision to end Brazil's nuclear weapons program, then-President Fernando Collor de Mello closed the Cachimbo test site on September 17, 1990, and a week later announced at the United Nations that Brazil was rejecting "the idea of any test that implies nuclear explosions, even for peaceful ends."[5]

Brazil-Argentina Rapprochement. The nuclear competition between Brazil and Argentina had been consistently fueled by mutual distrust since the early 1950s. Both countries pursued civilian and military nuclear programs, but by the early 1980s, Argentina was thought to be about five years ahead of Brazil in acquiring the capability to produce material suitable for a nuclear weapon.[6] Once the military regimes in both countries fell, however, Brazil and Argentina moved toward ending their nuclear rivalry. On July 18, 1991, President Collor and President Carlos Saúl Menem of Argentina signed a bilateral agreement to allow mutual inspections of nuclear installations in their respective countries and to establish the Argentine-Brazilian Accounting and Control Commission (ABACC) to implement the bilateral inspection accord. The accord was the culmination of a bilateral program of confidence-building in the nuclear sphere begun in 1987. A quadripartite agreement to integrate ABACC's bilateral inspection system with that of the IAEA was signed by the two nations, the IAEA, and ABACC in Vienna on December 13, 1991. Exchanges of nuclear-materials inventories and mutual inspections under the July 1991 bilateral accord began in the fall of 1992, following the inauguration of ABACC. However, inspections under the Quadripartite Safeguards Agreement were delayed until the Brazilian Congress had approved it on February 25, 1994, and it had entered into force on March 4, 1994. The Argentine Congress had approved the agreement on August 5, 1992.[7]

Under the Quadripartite Agreement, ABACC and the IAEA must establish an initial inventory of all nuclear materials in Brazil as a basis for future inspections. This task will be complicated by the years of unsafeguarded nuclear activities at IPEN and Ipéro, and at other sites—some of which may still remain undisclosed—that contributed to Brazil's nuclear weapons program. It should be noted that the IAEA has no mandate to investigate past weapons-related activities, despite indications that Brazil performed nuclear weapons research in the 1980s. However, once all nuclear materials in Brazil have been inventoried, the IAEA will use inventory checks and inspections to detect potential diversion, or reversion, to military use.

Missile Program. In the 1970s and early 1980s, Brazil developed a series of sounding rockets—some of them modified into short-range surface-to-surface missiles for export to Libya, Saudi Arabia, and Iraq. In the early 1990s, however, Brazil terminated programs to develop more capable missiles, such as the Avibras SS-300 and the Orbita-MB/EE-600 and 1,000, whose ranges (in excess of 300 km) would have placed them in the class of systems that the Missile Technology Control Regime (MTCR) sought to restrict. In 1989-90, reports revealed that the former director of the Brazilian Aerospace Technical Center, Hugo Piva, had taken a team of Brazilian missile scientists and technicians to Iraq to assist in the development of Iraq's missile program. Objections raised by the international community after the 1991 Persian Gulf War resulted in initial export control legislation in Brazil, which set the stage for later adherence to MTCR export guidelines.[8]

Since the 1980s, Brazil has been working on the Satellite Launch Vehicle (VLS) four-stage rocket, designed to place satellites in low earth orbit. The VLS project has been largely dependent on foreign missile technology, however, and the MTCR restricted space launch technology exports to Brazil. To obtain this key missile technology, the Brazilian government on February 11, 1994, announced its decision to comply with the criteria and standards of the MTCR, agreeing to restrict the export of missiles (and key components of missiles) able to carry weapons of mass destruction to distances above the 300-km threshold.[9]

Chemical and Biological Weapons. Brazil has no known chemical or biological weapons programs and is a party to both the Biological Weapons Convention and the Chemical Weapons Convention. In addition, Brazil is a signatory to the 1991 Joint Declaration on the Complete Prohibition of Chemical and Biological Weapons, a regional non-proliferation agreement also known as the Mendoza Accord.

DEVELOPMENTS

Nuclear Weapons Complex. During 1995, the IAEA "largely completed" verification of nuclear material and facility design information in Brazil.[10] ABACC has implemented its program of ad hoc inspections of Brazilian nuclear facilities, conducting 81 inspections in 1996, and 55 between January and October 1997.[11] Since mid-1995, Brazil has taken further steps to establish its non-proliferation credentials by joining the Nuclear Suppliers Group and by ending its nuclear submarine program.

On February 2, 1996, the Minister of the Navy, Admiral Mauro Pereira, announced that the Navy, after 17 years, had suspended plans to build a nuclear-powered submarine, even though $670 million had been invested in the Aramar Research Center to develop enriched uranium to fuel the submarines.[12] Although the facility, which houses about 1,000 ultracentrifuges, has the capability to produce weapons-grade uranium, Brazil has declared that it will not enrich uranium above 20 percent.[13]

Despite the Navy's determination to maintain its centrifuge program at Aramar, the project has suffered a number of recent setbacks. In 1995-96, roughly half the 2,000 employees, including many scientists and researchers, left the center.[14] At the end of 1996, the Brazilian press publicized documents and personal accounts that described several accidents at Aramar involving radioactive material and the contamination of personnel over the previous four years.[15] The Navy claims that these incidents were minor and were below the threshold of the IAEA's International Scale for Nuclear Events.[16]

Another alarming series of reports emerged in June 1997, revealing that the Brazilian Army had made attempts to restart the construction of a 0.5-MWt experimental plutonium reactor in the Guaratiba natural reserve, known as the "Atlantic Project." Apparently, while President Cardoso had been out of the country in November 1996, Vice President Marco Maciel had authorized the project under pressure from Army officials. After the project had been exposed in June, the Army announced it would discontinue it.[17]

As a sign of faith in Brazil's commitment to non-proliferation, the United States initialed with Brazil in March 1996 the text of a new nuclear cooperation agreement to replace an earlier, dormant agreement and allow nuclear commerce for peaceful purposes to proceed between the two countries. This agreement was signed by U.S. Secretary of State Madeleine Albright and Brazilian Foreign Minister Luiz Felipe Lampreia in Brasilia on October 14, 1997. It must now be reviewed by the U.S. Congress for a statutory period before it can enter into force. The United States also supported Brazil's membership in the Nuclear Suppliers Group, which Brazil joined in April 1996, during the Group's plenary session held in Argentina.[18]

Missile Program. Despite agreeing to adhere to MTCR guidelines in 1994, Brazil continued its space launch program into 1995. It discontinued the export of sensitive missile technology but proceeded to import technology for its civilian program—technically a violation of MTCR rules. Most notably, Brazil imported carbon fiber technology for rocket motor casings from Russia in early 1995. The United States—which had been seeking the inclusion of Brazil in the MTCR in order to curb Brazil's missile program—waived sanctions against Brazil relating to the Russian technology deal in May 1995 in return for a pledge by Brazil not to engage in such activities again.[19]

Brazil was admitted to the MTCR in October 1995 and was allowed to maintain its space launch program despite the military capability inherent in space launch vehicles; if converted for military purposes, the VLS, the centerpiece of the Brazilian space program, could launch a 500-kg warhead up to 3,600 km.[20] Brazil currently builds its own satellites but must launch them on foreign rockets.[21] The first flight of the VLS, which has been under development since 1981, was delayed for many years—until early November 1997—by MTCR restrictions, financing problems, and programmatic difficulties. In a serious setback for the Brazilian space launch program, the maiden launch of the VLS on November 2, 1997, was terminated a minute after lift-off due to the failure of one of the engines. Brazilian Space Agency officials stated that the next VLS launch attempt would most likely take place in September 1998.[22]

PROSPECTS

Continued nuclear activities by the military in Brazil, such as the Army's plutonium reactor project uncovered in June 1997, suggest that the military retains some degree of autonomy in its nuclear affairs. Further measures to rectify this situation—NPT ratification, a higher degree of transparency, and clear state control of the nuclear complex—are needed before Brazil can be removed from the list of potential proliferant nations. Despite continuing problems, Brazil has made great strides toward becoming a responsible member of the non-proliferation regime since renouncing its nuclear weapons program. During his 1997 trip to Brazil, President Clinton noted his "appreciation for [Brazil's] historic decision to join the Nuclear Non-Proliferation Treaty and to sign the Comprehensive Test Ban Treaty. In all these actions, Brazil has taken its place as a world leader for peace and security."[23]

In the last ten years, Brazil has also transformed itself from a cash-strapped nation ruled by an authoritarian regime to a country with a strong market economy, democratically elected leadership, and good long-term prospects for further development. Much of this success can be credited to President Cardoso, and, although the Brazilian constitution limits presidents to one term, he successfully pushed through Congress an amendment allowing him to run in the October 1998 presidential contest. As of mid-1998, Cardoso looked to be the clear favorite. In October 1997, however, economic troubles forced him to introduce an austerity package to prevent inflation, which in turn led to increased unemployment. The effect of these measures on Cardoso's popularity remains to be seen, but the economy will probably be one of the defining campaign issues. Even if Cardoso is not re-elected, Brazil is unlikely to retreat from the binding commitments it made in joining the international non-proliferation regime.

NOTES

[1]There has been considerable debate among experts as to whether Brazil had an explicit nuclear weapons program. Some suggest that the government as a whole never endorsed nuclear weapons, but that certain figures within the military advocated a peaceful nuclear-explosion or weapons program. For in-depth discussion, see Leonard S. Spector with Jacqueline R. Smith, *Nuclear Ambitions* (Boulder, CO: Westview Press, 1991), pp. 243-49.

[2]See "Brazil, Argentina and Chile Bring Into Force Treaty for the Prohibition of Nuclear Weapons in Latin America (The Treaty of Tlatelolco)," ACDA Press Release, June 3, 1994.

[3]In June 1997, President Cardoso asked the Congress to approve the NPT, and during President Clinton's October 1997 visit, Cardoso announced his intention to lead Brazil to join both the NPT and CTBT; in part, these announcements were likely made to improve Brazil's bid for a permanent seat on the U.N. Security Council. See "Cardoso Asks Congress to Approve Adherence to NPT," *Brasilia Voz do Brasil*, June 20, 1997 in *FBIS-TAC-97-171*, June 20, 1997; and remarks by President Clinton at the Alvorado Palace, Brasilia, October 14, 1997.

[4]José Casado, "Analyst Views 'Nuclear Explosive Artifacts'," *O Estado De São Paulo*, June 5, 1995, in *FBIS-LAT-95-111*, June 9, 1995, p. 30; Helcio Costa, "CPI Sees Bomb Configuration Project at IEAv," *Gazeta Mercantil*, November 29, 1990 in *JPRS-TND-91-001*, January 4 1991, p. 17.

[5]See James Brooke, "Brazil Uncovers Plan by Military to Build Atom Bomb and Stops It," *New York Times*, October 9, 1990; David Albright, "Brazil Comes in From the Cold," *Arms Control Today*, December 1990, p. 13.

[6]Leonard S. Spector, *Nuclear Proliferation Today* (New York: Vintage Books, 1984), p. 235.

[7]"Brazil and Argentina Move Toward Safeguards," *Nuclear Engineering International*, September 1991, p. 4; Mark Hibbs, "Brazil's Military May Block Safeguards with Argentina," *Nucleonics Week*, November 28, 1991, p. 8; James Brooke, "Brazil and Argentina Join Up to Open Their Nuclear Sites," *New York Times*, December 13, 1991; Statement by Michael McCurry, "Argentina and Brazil: Ratification of the Quadripartite Safeguards Agreement," U.S. Department of State, March 4, 1994; John R. Redick, Julio C. Carasales, and

Paulo S. Wrobel, "Nuclear Rapprochement: Argentina, Brazil, and the Nonproliferation Regime," *Washington Quarterly,* Vol. 18, No. 1, Winter 1995, pp. 107-22; John R. Redick, "Nuclear-Weapon-Free-Zones in a Changing Global Environment," J.B. Poole and R. Guthrie, eds., *Verification 1994,* (London: VERTIC, 1994).

[8]Maria Helena Tachinardi, "Measures to Control Sensitive Exports Announced," *Gazeta Mercantil,* August 10, 1994, p. 5, in *FBIS-LAT-94-162,* August 10, 1994.

[9]Raquel Stenzel, "Government Agrees to Comply With Missile Control Pact,'" *Gazeta Mercantil* (São Paulo) February 12, 1994, in *JPRS-TND-94-006,* March 16, 1994, p. 16.

[10]International Atomic Energy Agency, *Annual Report for 1996,* p. 46.

[11]Argentine-Brazilian Accounting and Control Commission, *Annual Report 1996,* p. 24; and *ABACC News,* May/October 1997, p. 3.

[12]Aramar will now work on the Angra II nuclear power plant and on construction of indigenous conventional submarines. José Tomazela, "Brazilian Minister: Navy Gave Up Nuclear Submarine Plans," *O Estado de São Paulo,* February 7, 1996 in *FBIS-LAT-96-028,* February 9, 1996, p. 12; Philip Finnegan, "Brazil Defers Nuclear Sub Plan," *Defense News,* March 11-17, 1996, p. 4. In an April 1996 interview, however, Admiral Pereira maintained that Brazil needed a nuclear submarine, and that the program was merely postponed due to budgetary and technical reasons. See *Defense News,* April 8-14, 1996, p. 30.

[13]José Tomazela, "Navy Seeks Funds to Launch Nuclear Submarines by 2007," *Agencia Estado,* November 9, 1995 in *FBIS-LAT-95-218,* November 13, 1995, p. 36. In March 1993, Admiral Pinheiro da Silva, director of Aramar, stated that "'because of a political decision' the enrichment of uranium will be limited to 20 percent." Quoted in Jean Krasno, "Brazil's Secret Nuclear Program," *Orbis,* Summer 1994, p. 432.

[14]José Maria Tomazela, "Ipéro Mayor Fears Dismantling of Nuclear Center," *O Estado De São Paulo,* February 14, 1996 in *FBIS-LAT-96-036,* February 22, 1996, p. 50. Also covered in "Brazil's Nuclear Programme Uranium Enrichment Process Perfected," *O Globo,* April 9, 1989, as reported by the *British Broadcasting Corporation,* April 12, 1989.

[15]"Navy Documents Said to Confirm Leaks of Radioactive Material at Base," *Rede Globo Television,* December 30, 1996, in *FBIS-TEN-97-001,* January 23, 1997; Jose Maria Mayrink, "Former Nuclear Plant Employees Report Frequent Past Leaks," *Jornal do Brasil,* January 1, 1997, in *FBIS-TEN-97-001.*

[16]"Navy Communiqué on Radioactive Incidents," *Jornal do Brasil,* December 31, 1996 in *FBIS-TEN-97001.*

[17]"Army Confirms Gas-Graphite Nuclear Reactor Project," *Rio de Janeiro Jornal do Brasil,* June 5, 1997, in *FBIS-LAT-97-156,* June 5, 1997, and "Ministries Term Nuclear Reactor Project 'Peaceful'," *Rio de Janeiro Jornal do Brasil,* June 5, 1997, in *FBIS-TEN-97-007-L,* June 5, 1997.

[18]U.S. Department of State, "U.S.–Brazil Agreement on Peaceful Uses of Nuclear Energy," March 1, 1996. Wyn Bowen and Andrew Koch, "Non-Proliferation is Embraced By Brazil," *Jane's Intelligence Review,* June 1996, p. 283.

[19]R. Jeffrey Smith, "U.S. Waives Objection to Russian Missile Technology Sale to Brazil," *Washington Post,* June 8, 1995.

[20]The Wisconsin Project, *Risk Report,* April 1995, p. 5.

[21]Julio Ottoboni, "Brazil Planning To Expand Satellite Program," *O Estado De São Paulo,* February 10, 1996, in *FBIS-LAT-96-032,* February 15, 1996, p. 30.

[22]John Miller, "Controllers destroy first rocket launched in Brazil," *Reuters,* November 2, 1997.

[23]From a news conference with President Clinton and Brazilian President Cardoso at the Alvorado Palace, Brasilia, October 14, 1997.

Brazil:
Map and Chart

Italicized names represent nuclear-related sites. See chart.

Missile and space launch test facility.

Nuclear test site (dismantled). Part of nuclear-weapons program pursued by Brazil in 1980s until terminated by then-President Fernando Collor de Mello in 1990.

VENEZUELA

COLOMBIA

GUYANA

SURINAME

FR. GUIANA

PERU

BOLIVIA

PARAGUAY

ARGENTINA

URUGUAY

Pacific Ocean

Atlantic Ocean

BRAZIL

Alcantara ▲

Itataia ■

Recife ■

Cachimbo ☀

Lagoa Real ■

Brasilia ★

Belo Horizonte ■

Pocos de Caldas ■

Sao Paulo (IPEN)

Resende ■

Ipero ■

Rio de Janeiro ■

Angra dos Reis

Sao Jose dos Campos

0   500
Miles

Aramar Research Center. *First module of industrial-scale centrifuge uranium-enrichment plant. No known production of weapons-grade uranium. Facility was apparently key component of now-terminated Brazilian nuclear weapons program of 1980s. Brazil has declared it will enrich uranium to no more than 20 percent, precluding its use for nuclear weapons.*

Under inspection by Argentine-Brazilian Accounting and Control Commission (ABACC) pursuant to bilateral agreement of July 18, 1991; and under initial "ad hoc" inspection by the International Atomic Energy Agency (IAEA) under quadripartite safeguards agreement among Argentina, Brazil, ABACC, and the IAEA, that entered into force on March 4, 1994.

Carnegie Endowment for International Peace, *Tracking Nuclear Proliferation*, 1998

BRAZIL: Nuclear Infrastructure

NAME/LOCATION OF FACILITY	TYPE/STATUS	SAFEGUARDS[a]
N U C L E A R W E A P O N S - R E L A T E D S I T E S		
Institute of Advanced Studies, Aerospace Technical Center, São Jose dos Campos	Conducted research on nuclear weapons design.	No
Cachimbo	Planned nuclear weapon test site; dismantled/not operational.	No
P O W E R R E A C T O R S		
Angra I	Light-water, LEU, 626 MWe; operating.[b]	IAEA/ABACC
Angra II	Light-water, LEU, 1,300 MWe; under construction.[c]	IAEA/ABACC (planned)
Angra III	Light-water, LEU, 1,300 MWe; under construction (indefinitely deferred).[d]	N/A (Not Applicable)
R E S E A R C H R E A C T O R S[e]		
IEAR-1, São Paulo	Pool, HEU (20-93% enriched), 2 MWt; operating.[f]	IAEA/ABACC
RIEN-1, Rio de Janeiro	Water, 19.9% enriched uranium, .2 KWt; operating.	IAEA/ABACC
Triga-UMG, Belo Horizonte	Water, 20% enriched uranium, 100 KWt; operating.	IAEA/ABACC
IPEN-Zero Power, São Paulo	Light-water, 4.3% enriched uranium, .1 KWt; operating.	IAEA/ABACC
Renap reactors, Aramar Research Center, Ipéro	Experimental, pressurized-water; designed for nuclear-powered submarine; program suspended.[g]	IAEA/ABACC
Subcritical assembly, Rio de Janeiro	Graphite, nat. U; operating.[h]	IAEA/ABACC
Subcritical assembly, Recife	Light-water, nat. U; operating.	IAEA/ABACC
U R A N I U M E N R I C H M E N T		
Resende[i]	Pilot-scale, jet nozzle method; completed; program canceled.[j]	IAEA/ABACC
Belo Horizonte	Laboratory-scale, jet nozzle method, shut down.	IAEA/ABACC
Aramar Research Center, Isotopic Enrichment Laboratory (LEI), Ipéro	First-stage, industrial-scale plant, ultracentrifuge method; operating. A nearby pilot-plant using carbon-fiber rotor design is under construction.[k]	IAEA/ABACC
Aramar Research Center, Ipéro	Centrifuge production plant; operating.	?[l]
IPEN, São Paulo	Laboratory-scale, ultracentrifuge method; operating.	IAEA/ABACC
Institute of Advanced Studies (IAEv), Aerospace Technical Center, São Jose dos Campos[m]	Laboratory-scale, laser method; not operational.[n]	IAEA/ABACC
R E P R O C E S S I N G (P L U T O N I U M E X T R A C T I O N)		
Resende	Indefinitely postponed.	IAEA/ABACC
IPEN, São Paulo	Laboratory-scale; completed; not known to have operated.[o]	IAEA/ABACC
U R A N I U M P R O C E S S I N G		
Lagoa Real[p]	Uranium mining; under construction.	N/A
Pocos de Caldas	Uranium mining; operating.	N/A
Itataia	Uranium milling; planned.	N/A

237

BRAZIL (cont'd.)

NAME/LOCATION OF FACILITY	TYPE/STATUS	SAFEGUARDS[a]
IPEN, São Paulo	Uranium purification (UO_2) site.	IAEA/ABACC
Aramar Research Center, Ipéro	Laboratory-scale uranium purification (UO_2) facility; operating.	IAEA/ABACC[q]
Resende	Uranium conversion (UF_6) facility; indefinitely postponed.	IAEA/ABACC
IPEN, São Paulo	Pilot-scale uranium conversion (UF_6) facility; operating.	IAEA/ABACC
IPEN, São Paulo	Laboratory-scale uranium conversion (UF_6) facility; not operating.[r]	IAEA/ABACC
Belo Horizonte	Laboratory-scale uranium conversion (UF_6) facility; operating.	IAEA/ABACC
Aramar Research Center, Ipéro	Uranium conversion (UF_6) plant; construction postponed.	IAEA/ABACC[s]
Fuel Elements Factory (FEC), Resende	Fuel fabrication plant; operating.[t]	IAEA/ABACC

Abbreviations:

HEU	=	highly enriched uranium
LEU	=	low-enriched uranium
nat. U	=	natural uranium
MWe	=	millions of watts of electrical output
MWt	=	millions of watts of thermal output
KWt	=	thousands of watts of thermal output

NOTES (Brazil Chart)

[a]IAEA and ABACC are conducting parallel inspections at the indicated facilities. At the IPEN and Aramar Center enrichment plants, the IAEA has been permitted to conduct inspections, following the ratification of the Quadripartite Safeguards Agreement. These inspections are still in the initial or "ad hoc" phase, pending completion of formal IAEA "facility attachments," which as of fall 1997 had not been concluded. Discussions on enhancing safeguards and perimeter control at LEI are also underway. See *ABACC News,* January/April 1997, pp. 3-4; José Maria Tomazela, "IAEA Team Inspects Navy Nuclear Center," *Agencia Estado,* July 7, 1995, in *FBIS-LAT-94-131,* July 8, 1994, p. 40; Mark Hibbs, "Tough Safeguards Negotiations Ahead for Argentine-Brazilian Agreement," *Nuclear Fuel,* September 26, 1994, p. 3.

[b]On August 1, 1997, the Angra nuclear facility was transferred from Furnas to Nuclen, the state-owned project management organization run by Electrobras, a power generation holding company. "Nuclear formally separated in Brazil," *Nuclear Engineering International,* September 1997, p. 6.

[c]Work resumed on the 80 percent complete Angra II in June 1996 and the reactor should be operational by June 1999. Armin Schmid, "Furnas Says Angra-2 Will Be Ready For June 1999 Commercial Operation," *Nucleonics Week,* January 23, 1997, p. 10.

[d]The Brazilian nuclear agency hopes to resume construction of Angra III in 1998. Tania Malheiros, "Angra-3 Construction to Resume Within 2 Years," *Jornal do Brasil,* June 4, 1996 *in FBIS-LAT-96-128,* June 4, 1996.

[e]ABACC lists Brazil as having three research reactors and three critical/subcritical units. The research reactors are IEAR-1, Triga and IPEN-Zero Power and the critical/subcritical units are RIEN-1 and the two subcriticals at Rio de Janeiro and Recife. Institute for Science and International Security and Shalheveth Freier Center for Peace, Science, & Technology, Argentina and Brazil: The Latin American Rapprochement, May 16, 1996, p. 43.

[f]Brazil is planning on boosting the IEAR-1 reactor to 5 MWe. Ronaldo Mota Sardenberg, "Strategic Affairs Secretary Reviews Nuclear Projects," *Correio Brasiliense,* November 7, 1996, in *FBIS-TAC-97-001,* February 4, 1997.

[g]Reports surfaced between 1989 and 1991 of a new series of reactors at the Aramar facility. At that time, the Brazilian Navy reported that the Renap-1, an experimental reactor designed to power a submarine, was under development and expected to be operational by 1995. The Renap-2, a civilian spin-off of Renap-1, was publicized at the time by the Navy as a viable mini-power plant with an output of 60 MWe, but it is unclear if the Renap-2 ever made it past the design phase. Reports in 1996 made clear that the nuclear-powered submarine program at Aramar had suffered long delays due to funding shortages, and that an operational nuclear submarine is not expected until well into the next century. "Brazil's Nuclear Programme Uranium Enrichment Process Perfected," *O Globo,* April 9, 1989, as reported by the British Broadcasting Corporation, April 12, 1989; "Increased Nuclear Fuel Output Justified," *Latin America Regional Reports: Brazil,* June 1, 1989, p. 4; Dean Martins, "Running the SSN Race," *Jane's Defence Weekly,* July 13, 1991, p. 59; "Nuclear Ambitions in South America" *Jane's International Defence Review,* June 1, 1992, p. 517; José Tomazela, "Navy Gives Up on Nuclear Submarine Project," *O Estado De São Paulo,* February 7, 1996, as translated in *FBIS-TAC-96-003,* March 5, 1996, p. 12.

[h]David Albright, Frans Berkhout, and William Walker, *Plutonium and Highly Enriched Uranium 1996: World Inventories, Capabilities and Policies* (New York: Oxford University Press for Stockholm International Peace Research Institute, 1997), p. 377. This facility may have been part of the Brazilian Army's plan for a graphite-based plutonium production reactor. Marco A. Marzo, Senior Planning and Evaluation Officer at ABACC, noted that the Army had constructed a natural uranium/graphite critical unit, but it had never operated. Subcritical assemblies listed in IAEA *Annual Report* for 1996, p. 79. José Casado, "Analyst Views 'Nuclear Explosive Artifacts'," *O Estado De São Paulo,* June 5, 1995, in *FBIS-LAT-95-111,* June 9, 1995, p. 30. The Army's Institute of Space Research was planning to build a reactor in the Rio de Janeiro district of Guaratiba that would have produced electricity and significant quantities of plutonium. Eduardo Oinegue, "Strategic Affairs Official Halts Nuclear Project," *Veja,* January 29, 1992 in *FBIS-LAT-92-022,* February 3, 1992, p. 36.

[i]The Brazilian nuclear industry is exploring the concept of building a centrifuge enrichment plant at Resende, utilizing a type of

centrifuge manufactured in Brazil and now operating at the Aramar Center (see entry below). The projected capacity would be sufficient to supply fuel for the Angra I and II power reactors. The fuel for the reactors is low-enriched uranium, which is not usable for nuclear weapons. See Mark Hibbs, "Brazil Mulling New Centrifuge Plant to Serve Two Reactors at Angra Site," *Nuclear Fuel*, September 26, 1994, p. 3.

[j]In March 1994, Brazil canceled its project to enrich uranium using the German jet nozzle process. Since then, the facilities using this method at Resende and Belo Horizonte have not been operating, and the Belo Horizonte lab has been dismantled. George Vidor, "Jet Nozzle Uranium Enrichment Project Canceled," *O Globo*, Rio de Janeiro, March 19, 1994, in *FBIS-LAT-95-056*, March 23, 1994, p. 48; Hibbs, "Brazil Mulling New Centrifuge," op. cit., p. 3.

INB, Brazil Nuclear Industries, may sell 40 percent of the jet nozzle enrichment equipment as junk. José Casado, "Article Views Efforts to Revive Nuclear Program," *O Estado de São Paulo*, June 4, 1995 in *FBIS-TAC-95-111*, June 9, 1995, p. 29.

[k]Albright, Berkhout, and Walker, *1996 World Inventories*, op. cit., p. 375. LEI currently has about 725 centrifuges, and the Navy plans to install up to 4,000 more in coming years. Eventually, Aramar will produce fuel for Brazil's research reactors. Tania Malheiros, "Aramar Center Manufacturing Equipment to Enrich Uranium," *Jornal do Brasil*, March 19, 1996 in *FBIS-TAC-95-005*, May 8, 1996.

[l]According to Marzo (see note h), if the IAEA asked to visit a centrifuge factory (such as the one at Aramar) inspectors would be refused because there is no nuclear material present at the site. Whether ABACC can inspect these facilities is not clear. ISIS and Shalheveth Freier Center, op. cit., pp. 51-52.

[m]Laser enrichment research and development was performed at IAEv in San Jose dos Campos by the Air Force, and codenamed Sepila. José Casado, "Analyst Views 'Nuclear Explosive Artifacts'," *O Estado De São Paulo*, June 5, 1995, in *FBIS-LAT-95-111*, June 9, 1995, p. 30; Helcio Costa, "CPI Sees Bomb Configuration Project at IAEv," *Gazeta Mercantil*, November 29, 1990 in *JPRS-TND-91-001*, January 4 1991, p. 17. IAEA lists laboratory for laser spectroscopy at San Jose dos Campos under safeguards. *IAEA Annual Report 1996*, p. 84.

[n]Although the project has not been officially canceled, few improvements have been made in the past few years. Marzo, in ISIS

and Shalheveth Freier Center, Latin American Rapprochement, op. cit., p. 25.

[o]This facility was reportedly operated with plutonium simulators because Brazil did not have access to unsafeguarded spent fuel. The lab is reported to have closed in 1989. However, German intelligence indicated that Brazil may have irradiated uranium specimens in reactors and reprocessed a very small amount. Also, plans for a pilot plant (possibly at Resende) never materialized. Albright, Berkhout, and Walker, op. cit., p. 371.

[p]Ivo Ribeiro, "Nuclear Company to Sell Gold Mine in Minas Gerais," *Gazeta Mercantil*, November 6, 1995 in *FBIS-LAT-95-221*.

[q]This facility was commissioned and subsequently inspected by ABACC and IAEA officials in early July 1994. José Maria Tomazela, "IAEA Team Inspects Ipéro Uranium Hexaflouride Plant," *Agencia Estado*, July 29, 1994, in *JPRS-TND-94-016*, August 19, 1994, p. 19.

[r]In its 1996 Annual Report, p. 84, the IAEA listed the facility at Belo Horizonte as safeguarded, but listed the São Paulo facility under "Separate Storage Facilities," suggesting that UF_6 production at the latter has ceased.

[s]Tomazela, "IAEA Team Inspects Ipéro," op. cit., p. 19.; Tania Malheiros, "Navy Confirms Project for Hexaflouride Conversion," *Agencia Estado*, August 4, 1994, in *JPRS-TND-94-016*, August 19, 1994, p. 19.

[t]The Navy plans to supply 35,000 centrifuges, manufactured at its Aramar production plant, for the Resende commercial plant. Brazil has also purchased an "assembly line for the manufacture of uranium powder and pellets" from the German firm Siemens for $12 million. It is to be installed at the Fuel Elements Factory (FEC) in Resende which currently assembles pellets into fuel rods for use in Angra I and Angra II reactors. See José Tomazela, "Navy Seeks Funds to Launch Nuclear Submarines by 2007," *Agencia Estado*, November 9, 1995 in *FBIS-LAT-95-218*, November 13, 1995, p. 36; Tania Malheiros, "Aramar Center Manufacturing Equipment to Enrich Uranium," *Jornal do Brasil*, March 19, 1996 in *FBIS-TAC-95-005*, May 8, 1996; Tania Malheiros, "Country to Spend Millions to Manufacture Nuclear Fuel," *Jornal do Brasil*, October 29, 1995 in *FBIS-TAC-95-006*, December 6, 1995, p. 37. With the plant to convert gaseous uranium into powder at Resende, the government-owned Brazilian Nuclear has contracted to export 30 tons of uranium powder per year for five years, to Siemens. "Brazil: Mastery of Uranium Production Cycle Nears," *Sao Paulo Istoe*, September 3, 1997, in *FBIS-LAT-97-185*, September 3, 1997.

9
SOUTH AFRICA

South Africa

In a surprise announcement on March 24, 1993, President F.W. de Klerk revealed that South Africa had pursued a secret nuclear weapons program in the 1970s and 1980s that had produced a total of six nuclear devices.[1] He made clear, however, that South Africa had destroyed all six devices and the associated weapons infrastructure by 1994 under international inspection. Historically, this was the most dramatic nuclear revelation and renunciation to date.

BACKGROUND

Nuclear Weapons Program. South Africa's first nuclear efforts are believed to have started in the late 1960s as a peaceful nuclear explosions (PNE) program to bolster South Africa's mining industry. Former President de Klerk stated in his 1993 speech to the parliament, however, that in 1974 the government secretly decided to develop nuclear weapons. The project soon expanded with the construction and operation of a pilot-scale uranium-enrichment plant (the "Y-Plant") at Valindaba (now Pelindaba East) and two nuclear test shafts at a site in the Kalahari Desert, completed in 1977.[2]

In mid-1977, a Soviet observation satellite discovered that South Africa was making preparations for an underground nuclear test at the Kalahari site. In response, Washington and Moscow applied substantial diplomatic pressure on Pretoria, which soon abandoned the site and sealed the bore holes. South Africa did not abandon its nuclear weapons program, however, and continued its efforts to enrich uranium to weapons-grade and to perfect the design of a nuclear explosive.[3]

South Africa successfully produced its first dummy nuclear device, without a core of highly enriched uranium (HEU), in August 1977; a smaller version was finished in 1978. Following the production of sufficient HEU, the country's first operational nuclear device was finished in November 1979.[4]

South African officials from that era insist that they never intended to use nuclear weapons in a conflict. Rather, they state, nuclear weapons were to be used as part of a "three-phase nuclear strategy" to deter potential adversaries—especially Soviet-backed forces invading from neighboring states—and to compel Western involvement in a military crisis with such forces, should deterrence fail. Phase I of South Africa's nuclear strategy involved neither confirming nor denying the nation's nuclear capability in order to keep adversaries wary. In phase II, if an attack were immi-

nent, Pretoria would reveal its capability to Western leaders in the hope that they would intervene. If Western nations did not respond, phase III would involve conducting an overt nuclear test to demonstrate to potential enemies South Africa's possession and willingness to use nuclear weapons.[5] In this regard, South Africa's weapons designers took steps to assure that the weapons, similar to the gun-type design used by the United States for the Hiroshima bomb, could be delivered by aircraft. They also went to great lengths to ensure the safety, security, and reliability of the bombs, suggesting that military use had not been entirely ruled out.

The election of F.W. de Klerk as South Africa's president in September 1989 marked the end of the nuclear weapons program. On February 26, 1990, de Klerk issued internal orders to terminate the effort and dismantle all existing weapons. Beginning in July 1990, the uranium-enrichment plant at Pelindaba East was decommissioned, the six devices were dismantled, the hardware and technical documents were destroyed, and Advena, the weapons manufacturing site, was decontaminated and converted for commercial use (after commercialization failed, the buildings were closed). All the HEU was recast and sent back to the Atomic Energy Commission (AEC) for permanent storage by early September 1991, ten days before South Africa signed its safeguards agreement with the IAEA. The entire dismantlement process was completed by 1992, but de Klerk did not reveal the program's existence publicly until his March 1993 address to parliament.[6]

South Africa acceded to the Nuclear Non-Proliferation Treaty (NPT) on July 10, 1991. It then concluded a full-scope safeguards agreement with the International Atomic Energy Agency (IAEA) on September 16, 1991, placing all its nuclear plants and all previously produced enriched uranium under IAEA safeguards. On August 19, 1994, the IAEA confirmed de Klerk's statement that one partial and six complete nuclear devices had been dismantled.[7]

In a historic reform of South Africa's politics, de Klerk ended the country's decades-long policy of racial separation (apartheid) and brought an end to white minority rule. Following nationwide elections open to all races in April 1994, Nelson Mandela became South Africa's president. The Mandela government remains committed to the country's status as a non-nuclear-weapon state under the NPT. The HEU produced during the 1970s and 1980s remains in South Africa, controlled by the AEC and under IAEA inspection. South Africa is estimated to have about 330 kg of weapons-grade uranium and another 55 kg of 80 percent enriched uranium on hand.[8] The Safari reactor has begun to use fuel made out of weapons-grade uranium, despite U.S. objections. The HEU not suitable for use in Safari (less than 60 percent enriched) has been blended down to low-enriched uranium (LEU) for use in the Koeberg reactor fuel elements.

Missile Program. With Israeli assistance, South Africa developed a medium-range ballistic missile (MRBM) during the 1980s under the guise of a space launch vehicle program; South Africa tested this missile in July 1989. In October 1991, the United States imposed missile proliferation sanctions on Armscor, the South African firm developing the MRBM.[9] Following the imposition of sanctions and under heavy U.S. pressure, South Africa announced in June 1993 that it was canceling the project.[10] On October 3, 1994, South Africa signed an agreement with the United States pledging to eliminate its MRBM program and abide by the Missile Technology Control Regime (MTCR).[11] In addition to a ballistic missile capability, South Africa has two unmanned aerial vehicles and is developing a land-attack cruise missile, the Skua, capable of traveling 800 km with a 100-kg payload.[12]

Chemical and Biological Weapons. South Africa initiated secret chemical and biological warfare programs during the 1980s (and abandoned them in 1993) even though it had become a party to the Biological Weapons Convention in 1975.[13] Reports surfaced in February 1995 that apartheid-era chemical weapons specialists were working for Libya and that Libya was seeking the services of South African biological warfare scientists; this revelation raised concerns about a possible "brain drain" of chemical and biological weapons expertise to rogue states.[14]

DEVELOPMENTS

Conversion to Civilian Programs. The United States and South Africa have been discussing converting the Safari reactor from HEU to LEU fuel since June 1994.[15] In August 1995, the U.S. Department of Energy and South Africa's AEC signed an agreement to allow the transfer of American nuclear technology to South Africa to assist in the conversion of the reactor.[16] In late 1995, a South African group of experts decided that, while converting the reactor was technically feasible, it was not practical on economic grounds—a conclusion that U.S. officials dispute.[17] Discussions continue between the two countries on this issue.[18]

With the abandonment of its nuclear weapons program, South Africa began to restructure its nuclear complex program. The semi-commercial Plant-Z was closed on March 31, 1995.[19] The two enrichment plants located at Pelindaba East are slated for dismantlement by the end of March 1999.[20] South Africa has, however, continued research and development of uranium-enrichment technology. In February 1996, the AEC signed a contract with the French nuclear firm Cogema

to jointly develop a uranium-enrichment method called molecular laser isotope separation (MLIS).[21] In 1996, the AEC, with the cooperation of Cogema, decided to construct a demonstration-scale MLIS facility at Pelindaba East.[22] Plans for a new, larger-scale facility were cancelled by the South African Department of Mineral and Energy. Johan Niewenhuis, an AEC official, stated in July 1997, that, in light of the government policy, AEC would construct the new pilot facility inside the Plant-Z shell instead of building a new facility, with the goal of enriching uranium suitable for use in the Koeberg and other reactors.[23] In December 1997, however, AEC announced that the MLIS project had been cancelled due to funding and technical problems.[24]

Non-Proliferation Regime. South Africa played an important role in securing the indefinite extension of the NPT at the May 1995 Extension Conference, where it emerged as the strongest supporter of indefinite extension among the members of the Non-Aligned Movement (NAM). South Africa also favored a strengthened review process and a statement of principles to accompany an indefinite extension.[25] Both proposals were unanimously accepted by the conference.

Although South Africa emerged as a champion of nuclear non-proliferation at the NPT Extension Conference, some concerns have been raised about its nuclear dealings with Iran, a regime that during the apartheid era had good relations with the African National Congress—now the ruling ANC party. In August 1995, South Africa signed a peaceful nuclear cooperation agreement with Iran.[26] In an attempt to reassure the United States, which has led an international nuclear embargo of Iran, the ANC government announced in June 1996 that it had not made any uranium exports to Iran in the last five years.[27] Reports surfaced in 1997, however, that two South African officials (AEC head Waldo Stumpf and then-Minister of Mineral and Energy Affairs Pik Botha) had met in early 1996 with Gholam Reza Aghazadeh, then Iran's oil minister and currently head of its Atomic Energy Organization. At this meeting, Aghazadeh supposedly presented Stumpf with a "shopping list" of items needed to make nuclear weapons. Stumpf denies that the meeting took place, but Botha confirmed the meeting, adding that South Africa turned down the Iranian request for equipment.[28]

When he revealed South Africa's nuclear program in 1993, President de Klerk explicitly stated that South Africa had never conducted a nuclear test or been involved with another country's test and had received no foreign assistance in its nuclear weapons program.[29] A report emerged in 1997, however, citing South Africa's Deputy Foreign Minister Aziz Pahad and former South African chief of staff General Constand Viljoen that Israel had aided South Africa's nuclear weapons program.[30] In return for natural uranium, Israel purportedly supplied tritium for use in boosted fission weapons.[31]

Missile Program. 1994 reports suggested that, about the time when South Africa pledged to adhere to MTCR guidelines in 1993, South African engineers and scientists were offering missile expertise to some Middle East countries.[32] Despite these troubling developments, South Africa was formally admitted to the MTCR in September 1995.[33]

Chemical Weapons. South Africa ratified the Chemical Weapons Convention in September 1995, despite reports that South African scientists had been aiding Libya's quest for biological and chemical weapons.

PROSPECTS

Since 1991, South Africa has made great strides toward becoming a responsible participant in the nuclear non-proliferation regime. It is the first nation to have developed and possessed nuclear weapons and then renounced them. South Africa's accession to the NPT and its constructive participation in the 1995 NPT Extension Conference show it to be a leader among the non-nuclear-weapon states. Despite these positive signs, some concerns remain. Scientists who previously worked on the nuclear-weapon and missile programs constitute a proliferation risk, and reports have indicated that some South African scientists are now in the employ of several Middle East countries. Other reports in fall 1997 suggested that the AEC was secretly selling some of the equipment from Pelindaba to the Chinese; although the transfers appear to have little relevance to China's weapons program, the secretive nature of the deal raises the concern that the AEC operates with too much autonomy.[34] Moreover, even though South Africa has declared its fissile material inventory to the IAEA, it has chosen not to reveal the exact figures to the general public.[35] Until complete transparency is achieved, questions about South Africa's nuclear weapons complex, its continued enrichment activities, and its non-proliferation commitment will remain unanswered.

NOTES

[1]"De Klerk Tells World South Africa Built and Dismantled Six Nuclear Weapons," *Nuclear Fuel,* March 29, 1993, p. 6; Helmoed-Romer Heitman, "South Africa Built Six Nuclear Weapons," *Jane's Defence Weekly,* April 10, 1993, p. 14.

[2]See Mark Hibbs, "South Africa's Secret Nuclear Program: From a PNE to a Deterrent," *Nuclear Fuel,* May 10, 1993, p. 3; Mark Hibbs, "South Africa's Secret Nuclear Program: The Dismantling," *Nuclear Fuel,* May 24, 1993, p. 9; Mark Hibbs, "Pretoria Replicated Hiroshima Bomb in Seven Years, Then Froze Design," *Nucleonics Week,* May 6, 1993, p. 16; David Albright, "South Africa and the Affordable Bomb," *Bulletin of the Atomic Scientists,* July/August 1994, p. 37; Waldo Stumpf, "South Africa's Limited Nuclear Deterrent Programme and the Dismantling Thereof Prior to South Africa's Accession to the Nuclear Non-Proliferation Treaty," speech at the South African Embassy, Washington, D.C., July 23, 1993.

[3]Hibbs, "South Africa: From PNE to a Deterrent," op. cit., p. 3; Albright, "South Africa and the Affordable Bomb," op. cit., p. 37.

[4]See note 3. Although South Africa officially denies ever testing a nuclear device, a U.S. satellite detected a flash over the South Atlantic in September 1979 that was thought to be a nuclear explosive test. A U.S. government expert panel was convened by Frank Press under the Carter Administration and concluded that the flash detected by the satellite most likely was not a nuclear explosion, but rather an anomaly due to the old age of the satellite. Further, they insisted that South Africa did not have enough fissile material at that time to fabricate a complete bomb core. Other military and national laboratory scientists, especially scientists with the Los Alamos National Laboratory, disagreed with the panel findings. For further discussion, see Leonard S. Spector, *Nuclear Proliferation Today* (New York: Vintage Books, 1984), p. 299f. and Appendix G, pp. 453-57.

[5]See Albright, "South Africa and the Affordable Bomb," op. cit., p. 37; Roger Jardine, J.W. de Villers, and Mitchell Reiss, "Why South Africa Gave Up the Bomb," *Foreign Affairs,* November/December 1993; Daryl Howlett and John Simpson, "Nuclearization and Denuclearization in South Africa," *Survival,* Autumn 1993.

[6]Hibbs, "South Africa: The Dismantling," op. cit., May 24, 1993, p. 9; Albright, "South Africa and the Affordable Bomb," op. cit., p. 37; David Albright, "A Curious Conversion," *Bulletin of the Atomic Scientists,* June 1993, p. 6; Jardine, et al., "Why South Africa Gave Up the Bomb," op. cit.; Mark Stansfield, "Kalahari Test Site Explored," *Sunday Star,* March 28,1993, in *JPRS-TND-93-010,* April 16, 1993, p. 7.

[7]"IAEA Confirms All South African Warheads Destroyed," *Reuters,* August 19 1994; Michael Knapik, "South African AEC Head Says Stockpile of HEU Will Be Maintained for Safari," *Nuclear Fuel,* August 16, 1993, p. 5.

[8]David Albright, Frans Berkhout, and William Walker, *Plutonium and Highly Enriched Uranium 1996: World Inventories, Capabilities and Policies* (New York: Oxford University Press for Stockholm International Peace Research Institute, 1997) p. 391.

The authors convincingly rebut the assessment of Peter Hounam and Steve McQuillan in *The Mini-Nuke Conspiracy* (London: Faber and Faber, 1995) that South Africa in fact produced 1,500 kg of weapons-grade uranium.

[9]David Hoffman and R. Jeffrey Smith, "President Waives Sanctions for Israel," *Washington Post,* October 27, 1991.

[10]Fred Bridgland, "South Africa Scraps Missile Plan After US Pressure," *The Daily Telegraph,* July 1, 1993.

[11]"U.S. and South Africa Sign Missile Nonproliferation Agreement," U.S. Department of State Press Release, October 4, 1994.

[12]See the report issued by Humphry Crum Ewing, Robin Ranger, David Bosdet, and David Wiencek, *Cruise Missiles: Precision and Countermeasures,* Bailrigg Memorandum #10, 1995, Center for Defense and International Security Studies.

[13]Paul Taylor, "Toxic S. African Arms Raise Concern," *Washington Post,* February 28, 1995.

[14]James Adams, "Gadaffi Lures South Africa's Top Germ Warfare Scientists," *Sunday Times,* February 26, 1995; Alexandra Zavis, "Mandela Says Chemical Weapons Figures May Be in Libya," *Associated Press,* March 2, 1995; Lynne Duke, "Drug Bust Exposes S. African Arms Probes," *Washington Post,* February 1, 1997.

[15]Ann MacLachan, "Converting Safari-I to LEU Fuel Would Be Too Costly, Study Finds," *Nuclear Fuel,* October 9, 1995, p. 10.

[16]Paisly Dodds, "South Africa-Nuclear," *Associated Press,* August 26, 1995.

[17]MacLachan, "Converting Safari-I to LEU," op. cit., p. 10.

[18]Interview with U.S. official, Washington, D.C., April 1997.

[19]Albright, et al., *1996 World Inventories,* op. cit., p. 383.

[20]"Uranium Enrichment Plants 'Nearly Dismantled' by March 1999," *SAPA* (South Africa), March 20, 1996, in *FBIS-TAC-96-007,* June 17, 1996.

[21]Lynda Loxton, "France, S. Africa Agree on Nuclear Cooperation," *Reuters,* February 29, 1996; Ann MacLachan, "Cogema to Help South Africa's AEC Develop MLIS Enrichment Process," *Nuclear Fuel,* March 11, 1996, p. 4.

[22]"Pilot Plant to Commercialise Uranium Enrichment Process," *Financial Mail* (South Africa), November 1, 1996 in *FBIS-AFR-96-212,* November 1, 1996.

[23]"Atomic Corporation Said Plans New Uranium-Enriching Plant," *Johannesburg Mail & Guardian,* July 11, 1997, in *FBIS-TAC-97-192,* July 11, 1997.

[24]"Atomic Corporation Abandons French Technology Project," *Sunday Independent* (South Africa), December 14, 1997, in *FBIS-AFR-97-348,* December 14, 1997.

[25]Mark Hibbs, "Halfway Through, Indefinite NPT Extension Assured, West Says," *Nucleonics Week,* May 4, 1995, p. 8.

[26]"S. Africa Approves Peaceful Nuclear Ties with Iran," *Reuters,* August 21, 1995.

[27]"Energy Minister—No Uranium Sent to Iran in Last Five Years," *SAPA* (South Africa), February 21, 1996, in *FBIS-TAC-96-007,* June 17, 1996.

[28]Al J. Venter, "Iran's nuclear ambition: innocuous illusion or ominous truth?" *Jane's Intelligence Review,* September 1997, pp. 29-31; "Iran Said To Request Nuclear Weapons Items From AEC Head," *Johannesburg Mail & Guardian,* August 14, 1997, in *FBIS-TAC-97-226,* August 14, 1997; Mark Hibbs, "Blix Told Iran Not to Distort Result of Safeguards Inspections," *Nucleonics Week,* October 16, 1997, p. 15.

[29]The CIA suggested in 1980 that Israel might have aided South Africa in the nuclear explosive test in question. Subsequent reports suggested that Israel had provided aid in constructing the nuclear device and conducting the test. In an April 1997 interview with the Israeli newspaper *Ha'aretz,* Aziz Pahad, a South African deputy foreign minister, said that South Africa had indeed conducted the test. Further investigation revealed that Pahad was not in a position to access such information and had based his statement on the assumption that a test had taken place and that Israel had aided the effort. See Yossi Melman, "South Africa admits: Israel helped us develop nuclear weapon," *Ha'aretz,* April 20, 1997. For a good recounting of the story, see David Albright and Corey Gay, "A Flash From the Past," *The Bulletin of the Atomic Scientists,* November/December 1997, pp. 15-17.

[30]"Israel Reportedly Helped South Africa Develop Nuclear Weapons in the Early 1980s," *Associated Press,* April 20, 1997.

[31]Yosi Melman, "Israel-S. African Nuclear Tie," *Ha'aretz,* April 21, 1997, in *FBIS-NES-97-082.*

[32]Henry Sokolski, "Ending South Africa's Rocket Program: A Nonproliferation Success," unpublished paper, August 27, 1996.

[33]"South Africa Gains Entrance to MTCR," *Armed Force Newswire,* September 15, 1995.

[34]"National Party Condemns Nuclear Technology Sale to China," *SAPA* (South Africa), December 14, 1997, in *FBIS-AFR-97-348,* December 14, 1997; "China-Nuclear" *Associated Press,* December 16, 1997.

[35]For discussion on South Africa's declarations of fissile material stocks, see Albright, et al., *1996 World Inventories,* op. cit., pp. 384-92.

South Africa:
Map and Chart

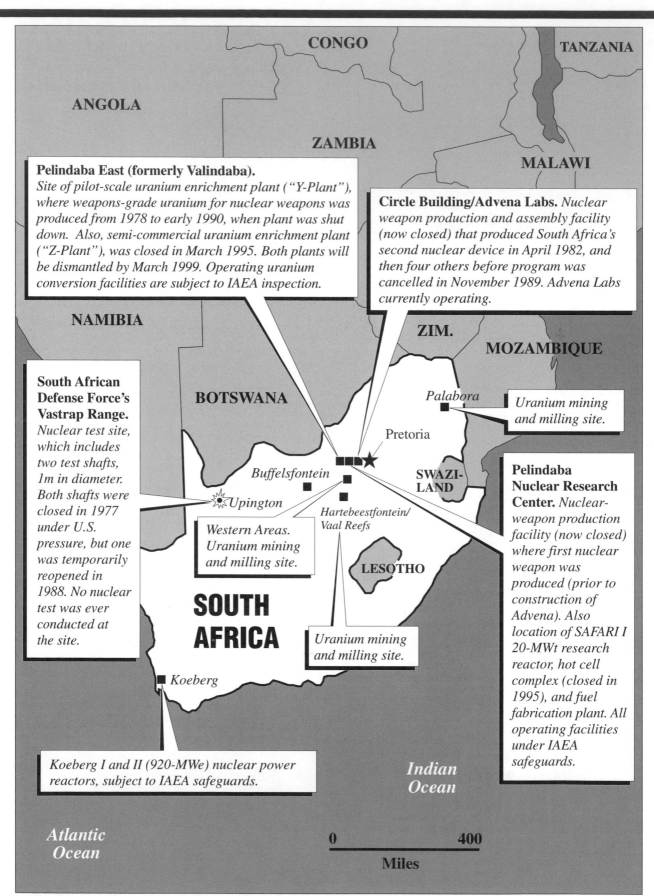

Pelindaba East (formerly Valindaba). *Site of pilot-scale uranium enrichment plant ("Y-Plant"), where weapons-grade uranium for nuclear weapons was produced from 1978 to early 1990, when plant was shut down. Also, semi-commercial uranium enrichment plant ("Z-Plant"), was closed in March 1995. Both plants will be dismantled by March 1999. Operating uranium conversion facilities are subject to IAEA inspection.*

Circle Building/Advena Labs. *Nuclear weapon production and assembly facility (now closed) that produced South Africa's second nuclear device in April 1982, and then four others before program was cancelled in November 1989. Advena Labs currently operating.*

CONGO

TANZANIA

ANGOLA

ZAMBIA

MALAWI

NAMIBIA

ZIM.

MOZAMBIQUE

BOTSWANA

Palabora

South African Defense Force's Vastrap Range. *Nuclear test site, which includes two test shafts, 1m in diameter. Both shafts were closed in 1977 under U.S. pressure, but one was temporarily reopened in 1988. No nuclear test was ever conducted at the site.*

Pretoria

Uranium mining and milling site.

Buffelsfontein

SWAZI-LAND

Upington

Pelindaba Nuclear Research Center. *Nuclear-weapon production facility (now closed) where first nuclear weapon was produced (prior to construction of Advena). Also location of SAFARI I 20-MWt research reactor, hot cell complex (closed in 1995), and fuel fabrication plant. All operating facilities under IAEA safeguards.*

Western Areas. Uranium mining and milling site.

Hartebeestfontein/ Vaal Reefs

LESOTHO

SOUTH AFRICA

Uranium mining and milling site.

Koeberg

Koeberg I and II (920-MWe) nuclear power reactors, subject to IAEA safeguards.

Indian Ocean

Atlantic Ocean

0   400

Miles

Carnegie Endowment for International Peace, *Tracking Nuclear Proliferation*, 1998

SOUTH AFRICA: Nuclear Infrastructure

NAME/LOCATION OF FACILITY	TYPE/STATUS	IAEA SAFEGUARDS
FORMER NUCLEAR-WEAPON (R&D) COMPLEX		
Pelindaba Nuclear Research Center	Nuclear weapons production and assembly facility; closed.[a]	IAEA visited and verified dismantlement.
Building 5000 complex (isolated buildings at Pelindaba)	Dedicated to development and assembly of nuclear explosives; closed.[b]	IAEA visited and verified dismantlement.
Circle Building/Advena Central Labs	Two generations of buildings involved in nuclear weapons production and assembly; closed.[c]	IAEA visited and verified dismantlement.
Upington (Vastrap Range), Kalahari	Nuclear test site; closed.[d]	IAEA visited and verified sealing of shafts.
POWER REACTORS		
Koeberg I	Light-water, LEU, 920 MWe; operating.	Yes
Koeberg II	Light-water, LEU, 920 MWe; operating.	Yes
RESEARCH REACTORS		
Safari-I, Pelindaba	Tank-type, light-water, HEU, 20 MWt; operating.[e]	Yes
URANIUM ENRICHMENT		
Z-Plant Pelindaba East (Formerly Valindaba)	Semi-commercial plant able to produce low-enriched uranium, jet-nozzle ("helikon") method; closed. A molecular laser isotope separation (MLIS) uranium enrichment project was recently canceled.	Yes
MLIS plant Pelindaba East	Demonstration-scale MLIS uranium enrichment plant recently canceled.[f] Nuclear materials present.	Yes
Y-Plant Pelindaba East	Pilot-scale facility for producing weapons-grade uranium, aerodynamic process; closed.[g]	IAEA visited and verified dismantlement.
REPROCESSING (PLUTONIUM EXTRACTION)		
Pelindaba	Hot cell complex; operating.	Yes
URANIUM PROCESSING		
Palabora	Uranium mining; operating.	N/A (Not Applicable)
Hartebeestfontein	Uranium mining; operating.	N/A
Vaal Reefs	Uranium mining; operating.	N/A
Western Areas	Uranium mining; operating.	N/A
Buffelsfontein	Uranium mining; operating.	N/A
Vaal Reefs	Uranium milling (3 mills); operating.	N/A
Pelindaba East	Pilot-scale uranium conversion (UF_6); operating.	Yes
Pelindaba East	Semi-commercial-scale uranium conversion plant (UF_6); operating.	Yes
Pelindaba	MTR fuel fabrication plant; operating.	Yes
Pelindaba	LEU fuel fabrication plant; closed (March 1995).	Yes

Abbreviations:

HEU	=	highly enriched uranium
LEU	=	low-enriched uranium
nat. U	=	natural uranium
MWe	=	millions of watts of electrical output
MWt	=	millions of watts of thermal output
KWt	=	thousands of watts of thermal output

NOTES (South Africa Chart)

[a]South Africa's first nuclear device was produced at this facility.

[b]One criticality experiment was conducted at this facility; it is also the site where the first nuclear weapon was produced.

[c]Five additional nuclear devices were manufactured at the Circle Building between April 1982 and November 1989. When then-President De Klerk canceled the nuclear weapons program, construction of Advena Central Labs had just been completed and equipment was being moved into the facilities. The labs continue to conduct non-nuclear research.

[d]The Kalahari test site, which was never used, was comprised of two shafts 385 m and 216 m in depth, both 1 m in diameter. The shafts were sealed with concrete under IAEA supervision.

[e]The reactor originally ran on 90 percent enriched fuel, but was downgraded to 45 percent enriched fuel following the cutoff of fuel supplies by the United States in 1977. In the early 1990s, South Africa resumed the use of HEU in the reactor, presumably with material from its dismantled nuclear weapons. Ann MacLachlan, "Converting Safari-I to LEU Fuel Would Be Too Costly, Study Finds," *Nuclear Fuel*, October 9, 1995, p. 10.

[f]"Atomic Corporation Abandons French Technology Project," *Sunday Independent* (South Africa), December 14, 1997, in *FBIS-AFR-97-348*, December 14, 1997; "Pilot Plant to Commercialise Uranium Enrichment Process," *Financial Mail* (South Africa), November 1, 1996 in *FBIS-AFR-96-212*, November 1, 1996.

[g]According to South Africa's declaration to the IAEA, the plant generated about 1,500 kg of enriched uranium while active, ranging from low-enriched uranium to weapons-grade HEU. Out of this inventory, 350 kg had been enriched to 90 percent U-235 and above. Each South African nuclear weapon required an estimated 55 kg of weapons-grade uranium.

South African officials have indicated that they would like to keep at least a portion of the weapons-grade HEU to fuel the Safari-I research reactor.

10
MISSILE PROLIFERATION

Missile Proliferation, 1995-97

Ballistic and cruise missiles, and systems that can rapidly be converted into such missiles, are ideal delivery vehicles for weapons of mass destruction. The continued proliferation of such missiles threatens regional security and at some future time may directly threaten the United States.

During the period 1995 through 1997, the missile proliferation threat continued to grow in the Middle East, South Asia, and the Korean Peninsula. Components of missiles dismantled under strategic arms control agreements appeared in Iraq, and the technology for advanced Russian missiles apparently was spreading.

At the same time, the international policy to deal with the threat—the Missile Technology Control Regime, or MTCR (see Appendix G in this volume for a full description of the MTCR)—gained the formal membership of Russia, South Africa, Brazil, and Turkey. But troubling questions emerged as to whether the MTCR might become a "missile supermarket," facilitating the development of missiles among its members. During this period there were only two minor applications of the strongest unilateral U.S. instruments for preventing missile proliferation: sanctions required by a series of laws that went into effect starting in 1990.

The missile proliferation threat has become the driving concern in the development of missile defenses. During the 1995-97 period, the United States accelerated its development of theater ballistic missile defenses and cruise missile defenses. At the same time, the United States initiated a program to deploy homeland defenses on three years notice. Because of the U.S.–Soviet Anti-Ballistic Missile Treaty of 1972 (ABM treaty), the programs for defense against ballistic missile proliferation have become major issues in bilateral U.S.–Russian strategic arms control.

TECHNICAL BACKGROUND

Ballistic and Cruise Missiles. A *ballistic missile* is a guided rocket that is powered during the initial part of its flight and then coasts without power—mostly above the atmosphere—along a ballistic path to its target. A *cruise missile* is an aerodynamic system—indeed, a small airplane with propeller, jet, or rocket propulsion—that is powered all the way to its target.

Ballistic missiles travel at hypersonic speeds, allowing little warning time and making defense difficult. Over the years of the Cold War, ballistic missiles have been considered the most threatening delivery vehicles for nuclear weapons. In the 1988 "War of the Cities" between Iran and Iraq and in the 1991 Gulf War, Scud ballistic missiles came into prominence with conventional (high-explosive) warheads—and with the threat of chemical or biological warheads. As a result, many commentators interpreted the missile proliferation threat to be one of ballistic missiles alone.

But cruise missiles are now recognized as a rapidly growing and particularly dangerous proliferation threat. Cruise missile guidance for attacking distant land targets was previously such an expensive and sophisticated technology that, for most countries, cruise missiles could only be used with terminal homing against ships. The last few years, however, have seen the universal availability of inexpensive satellite navigation—the U.S. Global Positioning System (GPS) and the Russian GLONASS—that will allow cruise missiles to attack land targets with 100-meter accuracy now and 10-meter (or better) accuracy within ten years.

This accuracy greatly exceeds that available from all but the most sophisticated ballistic missiles. For example, the Scud has an accuracy on the order of 1,000 meters, making it ineffective against discrete military targets—except with nuclear, biological, or chemical warheads, which cause damage over wide areas. With cruise missiles' high accuracy—already demonstrated by U.S. Tomahawks—even high-explosive warheads are relatively reliable for destroying their targets.

Moreover, compared to ballistic missiles, cruise missiles are:

- *Cheaper, quicker and easier to build, and increasingly available on world markets.* The Chinese Silkworm—already widely disseminated, produced by a number of regional powers, and relatively easily extended in range—may become the "Scud" of cruise missiles. A proliferator can now acquire a large number of cruise missiles relatively quickly.

- *Easier to launch from planes and ships.* This makes it easier for cruise missiles to reach targets far from the attacker's homeland. The intelligence community has now forecast that Third World sea-launched cruise missiles will be able to reach North America within ten years—at least five years sooner than ballistic missiles.

- *More effective for disseminating chemical and biological agents.* Because a cruise missile can release these agents in a gradual and controlled fashion (as opposed to the wasteful burst of agent or submunitions with a ballistic missile), each cruise missile can adjust its attack to local conditions—creating lethal area coverage some ten times greater than that from a ballistic missile. With chemical and biological agents cheaper and more available than nuclear weapons, and with cruise missiles more affordable than ballistic missiles, cruise missiles with chemical or biological warheads may become more widespread threats than ballistic missiles.

- *Difficult to defend against.* Ballistic missiles (except for the most sophisticated) coast along an observable and predictable path. But cruise missiles can weave around, fly low following the contours of the earth, and attack targets from any direction. They can be small and stealthy. In some cases they need not fly directly over their targets; they can disseminate chemical and biological agents from a distance upwind. All of these factors make cruise missiles difficult to find in flight and, therefore, difficult to shoot down.

Range/Payload Tradeoffs. Knowing about one technical feature of both ballistic and cruise missiles is critical for understanding missile non-proliferation. This feature is the ability to make tradeoffs between range and payload. Iraq demonstrated this tradeoff in 1987 by reducing the 1,000-kg payload of the 300-km-range Scud B and creating the Al Hussein missile with twice the range—enough to reach Tehran.[1] Because the MTCR places special restrictions on missiles "capable" of delivering a 500-kg payload to a range of 300 km, some exporters have tried to ignore the range/payload tradeoff. China, for example, once claimed that its M-11 missile—capable of delivering an 850-kg payload to a range of 280 km—did not have adequate range to be restricted under the MTCR. But a slightly lighter payload (well above 500 kg) would enable the M-11 to travel more than 300 km. In October 1994, China formally recognized the applicability of this tradeoff.[2] In the remainder of this chapter, when only ranges are cited, they apply to the most commonly cited missile payloads.

Routes to Proliferation. There are a variety of ways for states seeking ballistic or cruise missiles to acquire them. They can attempt to import entire missile systems. Or they can try to build them indigenously—usually with imported components and technology. They need not admit that they are building missiles.

Space launch vehicles, scientific research rockets, and large defensive missiles use hardware, technology, and production facilities that are interchangeable with those of ballistic missiles. Various types of unmanned air vehicles—reconnaissance drones, target drones, and remotely piloted vehicles (some with the stated mission of delivering insecticide)—can be converted to cruise missiles, and anti-ship cruise missiles can be converted to land-attack cruise missiles.

Missiles, especially ballistic missiles, are complex machines. For example, the medium-range U.S. Pershing II ballistic missile contained 250,000 parts—each of which needed to work right the first time under high levels of acceleration, vibration, heat, and cold. So the development of missiles is an expensive and time-consuming process, often resulting in an unreliable weapon system.

Moreover, the development of ballistic missiles becomes particularly difficult at a range of about 1,000 km. Above that range, the missile must use two more advanced technologies: staging (firing rockets in series, with the expended rockets reliably jettisoned from the missiles) and more sophisticated re-entry vehicles (to keep the warhead in working order during its fiery descent through the atmosphere).[3] Longer ranges also put a premium on more efficient rocket engines, lighter and stronger materials, more advanced guidance systems, and lighter and more advanced warheads (a considerable challenge when nuclear warheads are at issue).

These technical difficulties, compounded with the export controls of the MTCR and active diplomatic efforts by the United States and other concerned governments, offer hope for restraining missile proliferation.

DANGERS OF MISSILE PROLIFERATION

From the point of view of a proliferator, missiles have certain generic advantages over manned warplanes:

- *Simplicity:* A "pushbutton war" with missiles is much easier for the less technically advanced regional powers than is the development of a trained air force with manned aircraft and a large infrastructure.

- *Survivability:* Airfields have known locations and are large, vulnerable targets from the first minutes of a war. Manned aircraft, which generally operate from airfields, cannot be expected to last long against the United States and its allies. In contrast, hidden or mobile missiles are difficult to find and destroy.

- *Defense Penetration:* Shooting down a ballistic or cruise missile in flight is still a challenge even for the United States, which has until recently emphasized the role for its active defenses of protecting against manned aircraft.

- *High Accuracy*—in the cases of cruise missiles with satellite navigation and of some advanced regional ballistic missile systems. In contrast, the bombing accuracy of manned aircraft depends on equipment and pilot training that can yield variable results.

■ *Geopolitics:* Long-range and sea-launched missiles will diminish the protective effects of distance. They can project the battle to the rear in regional conflicts and someday even to the United States itself.

The use of missiles in regional conflicts has been demonstrated, using conventional high-explosive warheads, since the 1970s.[4] Egypt fired a Scud at Israel at the end of the 1973 war—a mere gesture. But in the 1982 Falklands war, Argentina's French-supplied Exocet cruise missiles sank the British frigate Sheffield. In 1986, after a U.S. air raid, Libya fired three Scuds at the Italian island of Lampadusa, missing the island. But the terror of missiles was demonstrated in 1988, in the Iran-Iraq "War of the Cities," with Baghdad and Tehran receiving repeated Scud strikes over a number of weeks. It is reported that a large number of the inhabitants of Tehran fled the city during these attacks. Starting in 1989, the Soviet-backed government of Afghanistan fired more than 2,000 Scud missiles against rebel forces. And in the 1991 Gulf War, some 88 Iraqi Scuds terrorized Israeli civilians and fell around coalition military bases in Saudi Arabia—without military effect despite a strike on a U.S. barracks at the end of the war that killed 28 soldiers. In contrast, in the Gulf War, the United States used three times as many Tomahawk and air-launched cruise missiles, which—because of their high accuracy—had significant military effects. Scuds were used again in the 1994 Yemen civil war. And in 1995, Serbia used SA-2 air defense missiles in their secondary role as ballistic missiles.[5]

The record to date has been that, with conventional warheads, ballistic missiles cause terror that can affect an adversary's attitude about war continuation; cruise missiles cause significant damage to specific military targets. But missiles are not limited to conventional warheads. After the Gulf War, the United Nations Special Commission (UNSCOM) discovered Iraqi Scud warheads with chemical and biological agents, as well as Iraqi plans for nuclear warheads,[6] for remotely piloted vehicles to deliver biological agents,[7] and for ballistic missiles with ranges up to 3,000 km capable of hitting all of Western Europe.[8]

The world is now seeing the emergence of substantial missile threats in the Middle East, South Asia, and East Asia.

The Middle East. UNSCOM suspects that Iraq is hiding a small number of Scuds. UNSCOM is sure that, after the cease-fire constraints are lifted, Iraq is capable of resuming production of ballistic missiles with ranges greater than the permitted 150 km (perhaps using facilities that it is allowed to retain for surface-to-air SA-2 missiles or for ballistic missiles with ranges below 150 km). The cease-fire terms addressed only Iraqi *ballistic* missiles, leaving their cruise missile industry intact—which has modified Chinese-supplied Silkworm surface-launched anti-ship cruise missiles to enable them to be air-launched as well as modified Polish crop-duster aircraft for the unmanned delivery of biological agents.[9]

Iran—with Chinese and North Korean assistance—is manufacturing an extended-range Scud (the 500-km-range Scud C), acquiring Chinese C-802 cruise missiles to threaten ships in the Gulf, and reportedly is attempting to acquire North Korean Nodong 1,000-km-range missiles (still under development) and to develop the Shahab-3 and Shahab-4 ballistic missiles with ranges up to 2,000 km. Iran was said by U.S. officials in 1996 to have substantial chemical and biological weapons programs.[10]

Libya is attempting to develop the Al Fatah missile with European assistance to supplement its supply of Scuds.[11] Syria possesses an inventory of Soviet-made SS-21 and Scud B ballistic missiles and land- and sea-launched anti-ship cruise missiles. Syria has received 500-km-range Scud Cs and supplies and production equipment for Scuds from Iran and North Korea, and Syria is also developing a production capability for solid-propellant ballistic missiles. It may have chemical warheads for its Scuds.[12] Saudi Arabia has acquired 3,000-km-range CSS-2 ballistic missiles from China—believed to be armed only with conventional warheads—and is now reportedly seeking a follow-on system.[13] Egypt, which possesses chemical weapons, admits to North Korean assistance for the development of Scud Cs.[14] And Israel possesses the Jericho family of ballistic missiles—with reported nuclear warheads and ranges up to 1,500 km—as well as the Shavit space launch vehicle, which can be adapted to a ballistic missile capable of delivering a nuclear-size 500-kg payload to a range of 7,500 km.[15] Israel also has a mature industry capable of producing a variety of cruise missiles and other unmanned air vehicles.

These missile programs threaten regional neighbors, lead to additional missile programs by those neighbors, and encumber the process of reducing regional mass destruction weapons and their delivery systems. The missile programs are also a strategic threat to the rest of the world. The Iranian and Iraqi missiles threaten the world's oil lifeline from the Persian Gulf; cruise missiles with conventional warheads threaten oil shipping, and, with mass destruction warheads, a variety of missiles could threaten key oil facilities. If the United States and its allies tried to intervene in another Middle East crisis, missiles armed with mass destruction weapons could threaten the airfields and ports needed to bring in troops and their supplies.

South Asia. India and Pakistan are engaged in a missile arms race. Currently, India is equipped with the Prithvi ballistic missile, a derivative of the Soviet-supplied SA-2. The Prithvi version that is ready for deployment is capable of delivering a 1,000-kg payload to a range of 150 km. A second version of the system will be able to deliver a 500-kg payload to a range of 250 km.[16] The Prithvi is operational. Although it apparently is not yet deployed, some reports state that deployment could come quickly. A 350-km-range version of the Prithvi has been reported as under development. India has tested the 2,500-km-range Agni, a derivative of its space launch vehicle, and has committed itself to produce the Agni as a ballistic missile; it has not yet approved proposals to develop an intercontinental ballistic missile (ICBM), called the Surya, with targets in Europe and the United States;[17] and it is developing a submarine-launched ballistic missile, the Sagarika, with a 500-kg payload and a 300-km-range. According to press reports purportedly derived from U.S. intelligence, the Sagarika can be operational by the year 2010. India is also developing a family of remotely piloted vehicles, some with Israel's help, that could be adapted as cruise missiles.[18]

Pakistan is said to be equipped with the 850-kg payload, 280-km-range M-11. The status of the M-11 is not clear from public reports.[19] Pakistan has a missile factory, reportedly supplied by China. According to the South Asian press, Pakistan has recently tested an 800-km-range ballistic missile, sometimes called the HATF-3,[20] and is developing a missile with a range up to 1,500-km, called the MK-III or Ghauri.[21]

In 1993, the United States proposed a South Asia Ballistic Missile Initiative to prevent the deployment of Prithvis and M-11s and, later, to deal with other missile issues. Pakistan indicated it was prepared to accept the initiative if India did, but India was lukewarm to the idea at the time. With the 1996 election of a more nationalist government in India, little more has been heard of the U.S. initiative.

Given the direction of events in the region, missiles would contribute to particular dangers in a hotter crisis or a war. As the superpowers learned during the Cold War, an unsophisticated ballistic missile force may not be a stabilizing deterrent but rather a source of crisis instability. That is, given the minimal warning time associated with a ballistic missile attack, the party making the first strike can gain a significant advantage by destroying large numbers of enemy forces before they can either be dispersed against attack or used. South Asia may turn out to be a classic case of ballistic missiles generating the rapid escalation of a crisis into a war. The consequences of such a war are unpredictable. The simplistic expectation—that Pakistan would lose—ignores the possible entry of China as an ally of Pakistan. Indeed, the Chinese threat is increasingly used by India as a justification for its advanced weapons program. But if China entered a South Asian war, the role of Russia—India's traditional friend—would be critical. In this way, the instabilities created by ballistic missile forces could lead to a far wider conflict.

East Asia. For many years, North Korea has been building a single-stage ballistic missile force of 300-km-range Scud Bs and their derivatives: the 500-km-range Scud C and, perhaps in the near future, the 1,000-1,300-km-range Nodong. In 1994, it was revealed that North Korea was developing two-stage ballistic missiles: the Taepo Dong 1 with a range of at least 1,500 km and the Taepo Dong 2 with a range of up to 6,000 km.[22] From North Korean territory, the Scud C can reach all of South Korea; the Nodong would be able to reach most or all of Japan; the Taepo Dong 1 might reach other U.S. staging bases in the region; and the Taepo Dong 2 might reach as far east as Alaska and part of the Hawaiian Island chain. In addition, North Korea possesses ground-, air-, and sea-launched cruise missiles and has demonstrated one with a range of 160 km.[23] All of these systems could be equipped with chemical warheads. Given North Korea's "limited" biological weapons program,[24] these systems might someday be capable of delivering biological agents. If the current freeze on North Korea's nuclear program continues, its development of nuclear warheads for these systems appears unlikely.

South Korea has adapted the U.S. Nike Hercules air defense missile to make the Hyonmu, a 180-km-range ballistic missile. Under a 1979 agreement with the United States, South Korea pledged not to develop missiles with ranges greater than 180 km; it also made an early 1990s decision not to develop space launch vehicles (which have the inherent capability to be adapted as ballistic missiles with ranges of thousands of kilometers). However, South Korea has shown an interest in the Russian S-300 surface-to-air missile, which, if adapted as a ballistic missile, has a greater range and payload potential than the Hyonmu. It also has recently been pressing the United States to set aside the 1979 agreement to allow the development of missiles with ranges up to 300 km as well as space launch vehicles. South Korea also has a program of "scientific" one- and two-stage sounding rockets that could serve as the basis for an upgraded ballistic missile program, and it is developing a cruise missile capability.[25]

China is a nuclear-weapon state with intercontinental as well as shorter-range missiles. In 1996, it engaged in a series of provocative military exercises featuring the firing of M-series ballistic missiles (with ranges of hundreds of kilometers) into the sea near Taiwan. In conjunction with these exercises, a Chinese diplomat made a thinly veiled threat that China could attack Los Angeles if the United States defended Taiwan.[26] During the same period, Israel, Russia, and Ukraine have reportedly discussed—and possibly provided—assistance to China's missile program.

Taiwan has been considering adapting its Sky Bow II air defense missile as a ballistic missile capable of striking targets in eastern China.[27] However, Taiwan, like South Korea, has renounced plans to develop space launch vehicles, which provide longer-range ballistic missile capabilities.

Missiles have clearly contributed to regional tensions in East Asia. In the event of a new Korean War, North Korean Scuds and their derivatives—and possibly North Korean cruise missiles—armed with chemical warheads could contaminate airfields and ports needed by the United States to move troops and supplies. The North Korean concept of war is a rapid take-over of South Korea, before the United States can build up its presence. This concept is perfectly complemented by the use of missiles against the movement of U.S. forces into the Korean Peninsula. In addition, North Korea could use missile threats against Japan to try to impede U.S. staging of forces through Japanese territory. The greater the range of North Korean missiles, the more U.S. staging bases could be threatened or attacked.

North Korean missiles, consequently, present a direct threat to South Korean security. They also create a threat to the security of other regions. North Korea is the most undisciplined exporter of missiles and their technology, with its main customers being Iran and Syria. The Nodong missile or missiles employing its technology, if based in Iran, could be used to strike deeper into Saudi Arabia than can Iran's Scud Bs and Cs, as well as to strike Israel and possibly Egypt.

In the case of China and Taiwan, continued Chinese provocations could lead to Taiwanese development of long-range offensive missiles. Depending on their accuracy, these could have military utility for disrupting a Chinese attack; they would also raise the dangers of crisis instability.

China, like North Korea, is a supplier of missiles and missile technology to other regions. In October 1994, China made a carefully hedged undertaking not to export "ground-to-ground missiles" that exceeded the MTCR's 500-kg/300-km capability. This—and their earlier, carefully hedged agreement to abide by the MTCR "guidelines and parameters"—left open the possibility of exports of other types of missiles as well as missile components and technology. Thus, Chinese missile-related exports continue to be a possible source of instability in the Middle East and South Asia.

Threats to North America. A November 1995 U.S. National Intelligence Estimate (NIE) predicts that, through 2010, there will be no ballistic missile threats to North America from countries other than China and Russia.[28] This prediction was based on a number of assumptions, some stated publicly and some not. The range of North Korea's Taepo Dong 2, reportedly up to 6,000 km, is adequate to reach Alaska and parts of the Hawaiian chain; but the payload on which this range estimate is based has not been made public. A biological weapon payload could be far lighter, and thus less range-limiting, than a nuclear weapon payload. The NIE is known to assume that potential missile exporters will adhere to their MTCR pledges—an assumption that has been questioned with respect to potential exporters such as Russia, Ukraine, China, and Brazil. Public reports of the NIE do not mention India as a possible threat to the United States. However, the absence of an Indian threat is a political, not a technical prediction. The prediction conforms to the received wisdom but is less than certain in light of: India's prolonged hostility after the perceived U.S. tilt toward Pakistan during the India-Pakistan war of 1971 and close cooperation with Pakistan during the 1980-89 Soviet-Afghan war; India's current nationalist government;

and the recent statement by a member of India's Defense Research and Development Organization that the targets for a proposed but not approved Indian intercontinental ballistic missile (ICBM) "will be Europe and the U.S."[29] The NIE does state that India has the capability to convert its space launch vehicles into ICBMs within five years.

The NIE's predictions are also affected by its estimates of the development of sea-launched missiles, which can be fired from the ocean against North America. Reportedly, the NIE predicts that India's Sagarika submarine-launched ballistic missile will be operational by 2010. And it is publicly known that the NIE predicts that a number of potentially hostile nations will possess sea-launched cruise missiles capable of striking North America by 2005.[30]

The U.S. president and secretary of defense have not repeated the NIE predictions of no new missile threats against North America for 15 years. Their statements have limited that reassurance to ten years. The U.S. intelligence community, on the other hand, has recently reaffirmed the key judgments of the 1995 NIE.[31] But, regardless of the precise predictions for an uncertain future, all parties appear to agree on one conclusion: The U.S. homeland may come within range of proliferator missiles after the early years of the next century.

DEALING WITH MISSILE PROLIFERATION

The three most prominent instruments for limiting the dangers of missile proliferation are the MTCR, unilateral and bilateral U.S. measures, and missile defenses.

The Missile Technology Control Regime. The MTCR (more fully described in Appendix G in this volume) is the only international policy to attempt to limit the proliferation of missiles capable of delivering weapons of mass destruction. It consists of an export control policy and associated arrangements among 29 member governments.

Unilateral and Bilateral U.S. Measures. These include legislatively prescribed sanctions and diplomacy. In the two years after the Gulf War, the United States sought diplomatic agreements to limit missiles in the Middle East, with little success. The lack of a regional peace agreement; the nuclear, biological, and chemical weapons in the region; and Israel's dominance in missiles—all were concerns that blocked progress. In South Asia, the 1993 U.S. attempts to promote a South Asia Ballistic Missile Initiative were frustrated by India's publicly stated reluctance. In East Asia, the United States started in 1996 to quietly conduct talks with North Korea to limit its missile program and missile exports.[32] One possible result has been a November 1996 decision by North Korea to cancel a predicted test of its Nodong missile.[33]

U.S. diplomacy on missile proliferation has been coupled with the U.S. veto on MTCR membership. Before Argentina, Hungary, South Africa, and Russia were admitted to the MTCR, they were obliged to renounce ongoing programs inconsistent with the objectives of the regime. Before Brazil was admitted to the MTCR, its president announced that it would not develop ballistic missiles. However, Brazil's ICBM-capable space launch vehicle program—once a target of MTCR export controls—was allowed to continue after Brazil had joined the MTCR. U.S. officials judged that this was justified in view of Brazil's political commitments to all of the non-proliferation regimes. At the end of 1997, the United States was pressing Bulgaria and Slovakia to destroy their 500-km-range Soviet-supplied SS-23 ballistic missiles after the Czech Republic and the former East Germany had destroyed their SS-23s.[34] And the United States was still engaged in diplomatic discussions with South Korea and Ukraine over the conditions for their membership in the MTCR and was considering whether to support membership for the Czech Republic and Poland.

Missile Defenses. The United States now cites the threat of missile proliferation as necessitating the development of systems to shoot down ballistic and cruise missiles in flight. The Patriot defensive missile of the Gulf War is now being supplemented by a family of theater ballistic missile defenses that are under development and may be deployed by regional allies. Additional U.S. development programs are addressing the difficult problem of defense against land-attack cruise missiles.[35]

Because the 1972 Anti-Ballistic Missile Treaty constrains the development of U.S. and Soviet defenses against each other's strategic ballistic missiles, the United States and the successor states of the Soviet Union undertook "demarcation" talks to distinguish defenses against strategic missiles from defenses against theater missiles (the immediate threat from missile proliferators). In September 1997, the parties announced as an agreed demarcation criterion the testing of anti-ballistic missiles against simulated attackers' missiles with a range of 3,500 km.[36] That is, defenses against ballistic missiles with a range under 3,500 km are permitted under the ABM treaty. This demarcation range is somewhat greater than the 3,000-km range of the CSS-2 supplied by China to Saudi Arabia, but it is well under the internationally defined 5,500-km range of an ICBM.

There is no ABM treaty for cruise missiles. Hence defenses against cruise missiles are constrained only by technical and financial—not international treaty-based—limitations.

U.S. missile defenses are only one part of the Clinton Administration's "counterproliferation" program of military measures to prepare for conflicts in which proliferators possess mass destruction weapons.[37] Another part is the counterforce capability to find mobile missiles and destroy them before launch. Still another is passive defense to detect chemical and biological attacks; to employ protective clothing, shelters, and medical measures to limit the damage from such attacks; and to decontaminate facilities after the

attacks. The NATO members have been developing a similar set of counterproliferation programs.[38]

RECENT DEVELOPMENTS

Since the publication of *Tracking Nuclear Proliferation 1995,* there have been a large number of developments with respect to missile proliferation threats, prevention policies, and defenses.

Missile Proliferation Threats. By 1994, the United States and Russia, as described above, had focused their discussions of the ABM treaty on "demarcation" arrangements to permit defenses against ballistic missiles with ranges below 3,500 km. But by 1995, reports were appearing of proliferator efforts to develop missiles with greater ranges.

In 1995 Pakistan accused India of developing an ICBM, which Pakistan called the Surya. The missile was allegedly based on India's PSLV space launch vehicle. In 1997 a writer from India's Defense Research and Development Organization confirmed the Surya proposal, which he said had not yet been approved.[39] It was long known that the two solid-fuel stages of the PSLV could be used to make the world's largest solid-fuel ICBM, with twice the launch weight of the largest U.S. or Russian solid-fuel ICBMs. Engineering calculations suggested that these two stages could deliver a 2-metric-ton payload to a range of 6,000 km—and, differently configured, a nuclear-weapon-size payload to any point in the world. India could also use storable liquid-fuel PSLV stages as the basis for an ICBM.[40]

At the same time, official U.S. descriptions of a projected North Korean missile, the Taepo Dong 2, were attributing to it ever greater ranges. The initial 1994 reports were of a range in excess of 3,000 km—still potentially below the threshold for missile defense. By 1996, the U.S. Department of Defense was describing the range as greater than 4,000 km. Late in 1997, the Defense Department's *Proliferation: Threat and Response* gave the missile's range as 4,000-6,000 km.[41]

Missiles were not only breaking out in range but also in their ability to reach North America. The controversial 1995 National Intelligence Estimate (NIE)—described earlier in this chapter—concluded that no new ballistic missile systems would be able to reach the continental United States from their home countries for at least the next 15 years. But missiles were being liberated from the necessity of being launched from their home countries. India was developing the 300-km-range 500-kg payload Sagarika ballistic missile which, according to reported U.S. projections, could be launched from a submarine by 2010. The same NIE that offered reassurance with respect to ballistic missiles predicted that within ten years the cruise missiles of several nations could be sea-launched against North America.

Cruise missiles were arguably the fastest growing missile proliferation threat. Reports in 1996 carried the long-expected news that foreign anti-ship cruise missiles were being adapted (in this case by China) to attack land targets. The key technical innovation that made this possible was the universally-accessible Global Positioning System, which could reliably guide cruise missiles to within 100 meters of their targets. In 1995, UNSCOM reported that Iraq had experimented with unmanned air vehicles to deliver biological agents.

International sales of cruise missiles might contribute to their rapid spread. By 1995, the French Apache, the British-made but UAE-funded missile called the Al Hakim, and the Russian AS-15 were being discussed for export to the Third World. All three systems come close to, and may well exceed, the Category I parameters of the MTCR.[42]

In addition, missile threats were emerging from systems that were not normally considered offensive. India's Agni medium-range ballistic missile had been adapted from India's SLV-3 space launch vehicle. If India developed the Surya ICBM, it would also be derived from a space launch vehicle.

Defensive surface-to-air missiles were also becoming more widely noted as a source of ballistic missiles. In 1996, a U.N. missile inspector described Iraqi designs using the Russian SA-2 as the second stage of a 2,000-km-range ballistic missile.[43] The same inspector identified the SA-2 as the possible basis for an Iraqi breakout from U.N.–mandated missile limitations. In late 1995, Taiwan was reported to be considering development of a 200-km-range surface-to-surface ballistic missile, the "Sky Halberd," based on the surface-to-air defensive missile, the "Sky Bow II." Press reports have vacillated on whether the project was on or off, but in 1997 a test of the Sky Halberd was predicted in "the near future."[44] With larger surface-to-air missiles being marketed such as the Russian S-300—reportedly to be offered to India in a licensed production deal[45]—the potential contribution of such systems to ballistic missile proliferation appeared to increase.

In 1995, concern about Russia's potential proliferation behavior, previously focused on "loose nukes," spread to include the possibility of "loose missiles" as well. Russian missile guidance equipment had evaded the post–Gulf War embargo on Iraq, with some equipment being found in Iraq and some in transshipment through Jordan. In 1997, extensive U.S. attention was devoted to reports that Russia was aiding Iranian development of ballistic missiles using Russian SS-4 technology. The enormous potential of Russian missile hardware and technology in the hands of proliferators was a major "wild card" in predicting missile threats.

Missile Non-Proliferation Policy. The major development in missile non-proliferation policy was Russia's 1995 achievement of membership in the MTCR. Russian adherence to the MTCR's export limitations had been sought by the MTCR founding governments since before the regime was announced in 1987, but years of negotiation had been necessary. In 1996 and 1997, the increasingly frequent reports of Russia's inability or unwillingness to restrain its missile-related exports, especially with respect to Iran, raised doubts as to the value of its membership in the regime.

The conditions for acceptance as an MTCR member underwent an important change in 1995. Three new non-nuclear-weapon state members accepted since 1993—Argentina, Hungary, and South Africa—had previously possessed or had been developing Category I missiles opposed by the regime. They were obliged to terminate their programs before they could be accepted for MTCR membership. However, in 1995, Brazil was the first nation admitted to membership with an intact program that had previously been opposed by the regime. Although the program was to develop a nominally peaceful space launch vehicle, the same development would give Brazil the rocket hardware for delivering a 500-kg payload to a range of 10,000 km.[46] The president of Brazil had renounced offensive Category I ballistic missiles, but once in the regime, Brazil could gain access to equipment and technology that it had previously been denied, giving it a future option to change its mind about offensive missiles. The U.S. judgment was that Brazilian intentions to pursue a non-proliferation policy were firm enough to override concerns about Brazilian capabilities.

Brazil's membership was followed within a month by a South Korean announcement that it would like to join the regime, and, in so doing, to renounce the 180-km-range limit on its missiles (to which it had agreed bilaterally with the United States in 1979). Instead, South Korea would feel free to build missiles up to the 300-km criterion set by the MTCR. In 1996 negotiations with the United States on possible MTCR membership, South Korea also revived its long-abandoned plan to develop a space launch vehicle, presumably seeking the same MTCR treatment as Brazil. At approximately the same time, the United States was beginning secret talks with North Korea on limiting its missile program and exports. Little is known publicly about the interplay of the conditions for MTCR membership, the revival of South Korean interest in large rocket development, and efforts to bring North Korea's missile enterprise under control. But they were all in play at the same time.

In the same early-1996 time period, Ukraine was staking a claim to even more liberal MTCR membership conditions than Brazil had received and South Korea was seeking. Ukraine, which had bilaterally agreed with the United States in 1994 to "adhere to the MTCR"—i.e., to observe its export restraints without necessarily becoming a member—now wanted to join the regime with no limits on its indigenous offensive missile production other than those imposed by international treaties. Specifically, Ukrainian experts asserted that, if Ukraine joined the regime, it would retain the right to develop ground-launched ballistic and cruise missiles for domestic deployment with ranges up to 500 km (the INF Treaty limit), air-launched cruise missiles with ranges up to 600 km, and sea-launched ballistic and cruise missiles of any range.[47]

Turkey became the most recent member of the MTCR in April 1997. Press reports suggest, however, that Turkey's membership may create more problems for the regime. Reacting to perceived threats from Greece, Iran, and Syria, Turkey is reportedly considering turning to China for medium-range surface-to-surface missile technology[48] and is turning to Israel for coproduction of Popeye air-to-surface and perhaps Arrow surface-to-air missiles.[49]

Government officials and outside specialists were using the term "missile supermarket" to describe what the MTCR—with a relaxed membership policy and liberal trade among members—might become. Misbehaving members, or a careless deal with South Korea or Ukraine that would cause restraint to unravel in many places, could result in a burst of missile proliferation.

Since 1990, U.S. sanctions legislation had reinforced the MTCR's export controls by penalizing transfers that contributed to missile proliferation (see Appendix G on the MTCR in this volume). But no missile sanctions at all were imposed in 1994 and 1995. In 1996 and 1997, the United States imposed missile sanctions twice: against Iranian and North Korean entities. These sanctions had no practical effect because of pre-existing U.S. embargoes against Iran and North Korea.

A widely reported Chinese transfer to Pakistan of M-11 missiles and possibly even complete facilities for their production (the latter completely embargoed under the regime) did not result in U.S. sanctions—reportedly because the missiles were not necessarily operational (not a legal criterion for the imposition of sanctions). The widely reported Chinese transfer of Scud guidance equipment to Iran and the report of China–Saudi Arabia discussions on upgrades of the Saudi IRBMs also failed to trigger sanctions.

Egypt was reported to be receiving Scud components from North Korea, a transfer publicly admitted by President Hosni Mubarak, and was further reported to have acquired North Korean Scud Cs. In neither case did the actions trigger U.S. sanctions against Egypt. To outside observers it appeared that larger issues—the relationship with China and the Middle East peace process—were freezing the implementation of laws designed to prevent missile proliferation.

During 1996, the United States began talks with North Korea to limit its missile program and its missile exports. The November 1996 North Korean decision to cancel a Nodong ballistic missile test may have been related to these talks.

A major decision with respect to the direction of the MTCR was made in the summer of 1995. An ad hoc meeting of MTCR members in Montreaux considered a Canadian proposal for a treaty against missile proliferation and reached a consensus against the idea.[50] The MTCR remains, not a treaty, but an international policy—coordinated by information exchanges and enforced by the efforts of its members.

Missile Defenses. By 1995, the U.S. debate on national missile defense (NMD)—a system to protect U.S. territory from ballistic missile attack—was driven far more by concern with missile proliferation than with Russian strategic capabilities. Thus, the effectiveness of the MTCR in preventing missile proliferation became a key element in the future of the ABM treaty, which places limits on NMD.

The September 1997 theater missile defense (TMD) "demarcation" agreements related to the ABM treaty permit continued development and deployment of several U.S. TMD systems to defend against attack by theater ballistic missiles. These include the upgraded Patriot, the Army MEADS—which is an international project—and the Navy "lower tier" system. All of these missile defense systems have the disadvantage of providing defense only for a small area on the earth's surface.

Wider areas could be defended against theater ballistic missiles by such U.S. systems as the Army THAAD, the Navy "upper tier" system, and the Air Force boost-phase intercept system. The last is a concept for using airborne lasers or interceptor missiles to destroy an attacking missile shortly after launch, before it had achieved enough velocity to reach its target. The demarcation agreements prohibit development, testing, or deployment of space-based TMD interceptors or equivalent components, but the use of space-based tracking to enhance the performance of "wide-area" theater defenses has yet to have its ABM treaty status resolved. The United States, however, has continued testing THAAD and developing elements of the other systems. Moreover, in the last two years, defense against land-attack cruise missiles has grown in the United States from a subject of study and a secondary defense mission to a funded program to develop hardware.

Since 1994, NMD has been a contentious issue in the U.S. Congress. All parties agree that the defense would be designed against a relatively small attack—not against a coordinated strategic attack from Russia. All parties also agree that development of NMD should take place at a rate that would permit an operational system to be deployed in 2003. But the Clinton Administration wants to limit the immediate action to three years of development and only thereafter to address a deployment decision, which would take three more years to implement—the "3 + 3" plan.

Some conservatives in Congress have called for an immediate commitment to NMD deployment, arguing that this could discourage proliferators such as North Korea from developing ballistic missiles that can reach the United States, and that NMD would offer valuable protection against a potential Chinese attack or an unauthorized or accidental Russian attack. Others argue that the nature and timing of a proliferator's ballistic missile threat to North America is not now clear, that the expense of deploying NMD should not be incurred prematurely, and that the effectiveness of NMD can be improved with more development time. Although the ABM treaty allows a limited NMD, the specific concepts advocated by conservatives may not be ABM treaty-compliant. Russia—concerned, among other things, about future U.S. adherence to the ABM treaty—has held up ratification of the START II strategic arms control treaty.

At the time of the last, 1995, edition of this book, strategic arms control and missile proliferation were generally considered to be issues on two separate tracks. Arguably, those tracks have now crossed. Unless the proliferation of long-range missiles is effectively countered, it will hinder traditional arms control methods of achieving strategic stability along with deep nuclear reductions.

NOTES

[1]W. Seth Carus and Joseph S. Bermudez, "Iraq's Al-Husayn Missile Program," Parts I and II, *Jane's Soviet Intelligence Review,* May and June 1990.

[2]Joint Statement of the United States of America and the People's Republic of China on Missile Proliferation, October 4, 1994, distributed by the Office of the Spokesman, U.S. Department of State.

[3]Aaron Karp, *Ballistic Missile Proliferation: The Politics and Technics* (New York: Oxford University Press for the Stockholm International Peace Research Institute, 1996).

[4]Ibid., pp. 44-46.

[5]Duncan Lennox, "Ballistic Missiles," *Jane's Defence Weekly,* April 17, 1996, p. 43.

[6]U.N. Security Council document S/1996/261, April 11, 1996, p. 7.

[7]Barbara Starr, "Iraq Reveals a Startling Range of Toxin Agents," *Jane's Defence Weekly,* November 11, 1995, p. 4.

[8]Stewart Stogel, "Missile Plans by Iraq May Aim at Europe," *Washington Times,* February 16, 1996.

[9]Office of the Secretary of Defense, *Proliferation: Threat and Response,* April 1996, pp. 21-24. Marie Colvin and Uzi Mahnaimi Amman, "Saddam invents germ warfare crop-duster to spray cities," *The Sunday Times* (London), November 9, 1997.

[10]*Proliferation: Threat and Response,* ibid., p. 16. Also see Iran chapter in this volume.

[11]*Proliferation: Threat and Response,* ibid., pp. 27-28.

[12]Office of the Secretary of Defense, *Proliferation: Threat and Response,* November 1997, pp. 38, 40.

[13]See chapter on China in this volume.

[14]Bill Gertz, "Cairo's Missile Buy Violates U.S. Laws," *Washington Times,* June 21, 1996; Editorial, "Turning a Blind Eye," *Defense News,* September 8-14, 1996.

[15]Lennox, "Ballistic Missiles," op. cit., p. 40.

[16]*Proliferation: Threat and Response,* April 1996, op. cit., p. 38.

[17]John Wilson (Indian Defense Research Development Organization), "India's Missile Might," *The Pioneer* (New Delhi), July 13, 1997, p. 1, in *FBIS-TAC-97-195,* July 14, 1997.

[18]"Kalam: Reusable Missiles Under Development," *The Pioneer* (New Delhi), November 28, 1997, in *FBIS-TAC-97-334,* November 30, 1997.

[19]*Proliferation: Threat and Response,* April 1996, op. cit., pp. 38-39.

[20]"Delhi Reports Pakistan Test Fired Medium-Range Missile," Delhi All-India Radio Network (in English), 1135 GMT, July 2, 1997, in *FBIS-TAC-97-183,* July 2, 1997.

[21]C.R. Shamsi, "Scientists Develop 'Ghauri' Missile to Counter 'Prithvi'," Islamabad, Pakistan (in Urdu), August 1, 1997, in *FBIS-NES-97-214,* August 2, 1997.

[22]*Proliferation: Threat and Response,* 1996, op. cit., p. 8, and *Proliferation: Threat and Response,* 1997, op. cit., pp. 5, 8.

[23]Duncan Lennox, "Cruise Missiles," *Jane's Defence Weekly,* May 1, 1996, p. 20.

[24]*Proliferation: Threat and Response,* November 1997, op. cit., pp. 5, 6.

[25]Kyong Yong-won, "Seoul Seeks to Abolish Missile Pact with U.S.," *Choson Ilbo,* July 12, 1995, in *FBIS-EAS-95-133,* July 12, 1995, p. 53; Bill Gertz, "S. Korea counters North's missiles," *Washington Times,* December 2, 1996.

[26]Patrick Tyler, "As China Threatens Taiwan, It Makes Sure U.S. Listens," *New York Times,* January 24, 1996; "Nuclear Warning to US Cited," *Boston Globe,* March 18, 1996.

[27]Lu Chao-lung, "Taipei to Test Surface-to-Surface Missiles," *Chung-Kuo Shih-Pao,* September 11, 1996, in *FBIS-CHI-96-180,* September 17, 1996.

[28]DCI National Intelligence Estimate, President's Summary, "Emerging Missile Threats to North America During the Next 15 Years," PS/NIE 95-19, November 1995, as printed in *Washington Times,* May 14, 1996.

[29]See footnote 17 above.

[30]For critiques of the NIE, see U.S. General Accounting Office, *Foreign Missile Threats: Analytic Soundness of Certain National Intelligence Estimates,* GAO/NSIAD-96-225, August 1996; and "NIE 95-19: Independent Panel Review of 'Emerging Missile Threats to North America During the Next 15 Years;'" enclosure to letter from John H. Moseman, Director of Congressional Affairs, Central Intelligence Agency, to Arlan Specter, Chairman, Senate Select Committee on Intelligence, OCA 96-1908, December 23, 1996.

[31]"CIA Stands by Judgment that Missile Threat Is 15 Years Off," *Defense Daily,* December 5, 1997.

[32]Michael Shields, "U.S. Hails 'Useful' Missile Talks with N. Korea," *Reuters,* April 21, 1996.

[33]"North Korea Seems to Call Off Missile Test—U.S.," *Reuters,* November 7, 1996.

[34]Bill Gertz, "U.S. Asks Bulgaria, Slovakia to Destroy Missiles," *Washington Times,* August 18, 1997.

[35]Counterproliferation Program Review Committee [a U.S. interagency group], *Report on Activities and Programs for Countering Proliferation,* May 1996, pp. 46-49; *Proliferation: Threat and Response,* November 1997, op. cit., pp. 64-65; and K. Scott McMahon, *Pursuit of the Shield: The U.S. Quest for Limited Ballistic Missile Defense* (New York: University Press of America, 1997).

[36]"First Agreed Statement Relating to the Treaty Between the United States of America and the Union of Soviet Socialist Republics on the Limitation of Anti-Ballistic Missile Systems of May 26, 1972," signed September 26, 1997, as reprinted in *Arms Control Today,* September 1997, p. 21.

[37]*Proliferation: Threat and Response,* April 1996, op. cit., pp. 47-62, and *Proliferation: Threat and Response,* November 1997, op. cit., pp. 53-77.

[38]"NATO's Response to Proliferation of Weapons of Mass Destruction," NATO Press Release (95)124, November 29, 1995; Robert Joseph, "Proliferation, Counter-Proliferation and NATO," *Survival,* Spring 1996, pp. 111-130; Ashton B. Carter and David B. Omand, "Countering the Proliferation Risks: Adapting the Alliance to the New Security Environment," *NATO Review,* September 1996, pp. 10-15.

[39]See footnote 17.

[40]"India Eager for Further Development of Agni Missile Program," *International Defense Review,* November 1, 1997, p. 5.

[41]*Proliferation: Threat and Response,* November 1997, op. cit., p. 5.

[42]Dennis M. Gormley and K. Scott McMahon, "Proliferation of Land-Attack Cruise Missiles: Prospects and Policy Implications," in Henry Sokolski, ed., *Fighting Proliferation: New Concerns for the Nineties* (Maxwell Air Base, AL: Air University Press, September 1996), p. 156.

[43]Carnegie Endowment for International Peace, *START II, Missile Non-Proliferation, and Missile Defense,* report of a seminar held February 14, 1996, p. 27. *Proliferation: Threat and Response,* April 1996, op. cit., p. 22.

[44]"Tests Continue on Tien Chi Surface-to-Surface Missiles," *Chung-Kuo Shih-Pao* (Taipei), January 13, 1997, p. 4, in *FBIS-CHI-97-010,* January 13, 1997.

[45]Vivek Raghuvanshi, "India Mulls Russian Air Defense Deal," *Defense News,* February 24–March 2, 1997.

[46]Carnegie Endowment, *START II,* op. cit., p. 24.

[47]Gary Bertsch and Victor Zaborsky, "Bringing Ukraine Into the MTCR: Can U.S. Policy Succeed?" *Arms Control Today,* April 1997, p. 12.

[48]Umit Enginsoy and Brooks Tigner, "Turkey Expands Arms Suppliers, Considers China," *Defense News,* September 15-21, 1997, pp. 1, 48.

[49]"Turkey and Israel to Manufacture Popeye Rockets in 1998," *Deutsche Presse-Agentur,* December 9, 1997.

[50]Carnegie Endowment, *START II,* op. cit., p. 23.

MISSILE Chart 1 (Countries Possessing Ballistic Missiles)[a]

This chart lists the countries (other than the five nuclear powers) that have operational ballistic missiles with range capabilities over 100 kilometers. Although some countries have demonstrated the ability to use surface-to-air missiles in a surface-to-surface role, these systems are not listed unless they are deployed as dedicated ballistic missiles such as China's CSS-8. For China's and Russia's ballistic missiles, see the charts at the ends of their respective chapters.

COUNTRY	SYSTEM	STATUS	RANGE/ PAYLOAD	COUNTRY OF ORIGIN	NOTES
Afghanistan	Scud B	O	300/1000	USSR	
Algeria	Scud-B	O	300/1000	USSR	
Armenia[b]	Scud-B	O	300/1000	Russia	
Azerbaijan	Scud B	O	300/1000	USSR	
Belarus	SS-21	O	70-120/480	USSR	
	Scud-B	O	300/1000	USSR	
Bulgaria[c]	Scud B	O	300/1000	USSR	
	SS-23	O	500/450	USSR	Banned by INF Treaty
Czech Republic[d]	SS-21	O	70-120/480	USSR	
Egypt	Scud-B	O/U	300/1000	USSR	
	Project T	O	450/1000	I/North Korea	
	Scud Mod C[e]	O	500/700	North Korea	
Georgia	Scud B	O	300/1000	USSR	
India	Prithvi-150	O	150/1000	I/USSR	From Russian SA-2
	Prithvi-250	D/T	250/500	I/USSR	From Russian SA-2
	Prithvi 350	D	350/500	I/USSR	From Russian SA-2
	Agni	D/T	2000/1,000 +	I/US/France	From Scout
	Sagarika	D	300/500	I/Russia?	From Prithvi/SA-2
	Surya	D	12,000/?	I	From PSLV
Iran[f]	Mushak-120	O/U?	120/500	I/China?	
	Mushak-160	O/U?	160/190	I/China?	
	Mushak-200	O/U?	200/500	I/China?	
	CSS-8	O	150/190	China	Mod SA-2
	Scud-B[g]	O/U	300/1000	Libya	
	Scud Mod B	O/P	300/1000	North Korea	
	Scud Mod C	O	500/700	North Korea	
	Zelzal-3	D	1000-1500/1000	I/?	
	Tondar 68	D	1000/500	I/China?	Chinese M-18?
	Shahab-3	D	1300/700	I/North Korea	from Nodong?
	Shahab-4	D	2000/1000	I/Russia	from Russian SS-4
Iraq	Ababil-100	P	100-150/300	I	
	Al-Samoud	P	150/?	I	From Scud[h]
	Scud B	Hidden?	300/1000	USSR	
	Al Hussein	Hidden?	600-650/500	I	From Scud
	Al Hijarah	Hidden?	600-650/250?	I	From Scud
Israel	Lance	O/S	130/450	US	MOU
	Jericho I	O	500/500	France	
	Jericho II	O	1500/1000	France/I	
	Jericho III	D	2500/1000	I	
Kazakhstan	SS-21	O	70-120/480	USSR	
	Scud B	O	300/1000	USSR	
Libya[i]	Scud B	O/U	300/1000	USSR	
	Al Fatah (Ittisalt)[j]	D/T	950/500	I/?	

MISSILE Chart 1 (cont'd.)

COUNTRY	SYSTEM	STATUS	RANGE/ PAYLOAD	COUNTRY OF ORIGIN	NOTES
North Korea[k]	Scud Mod B	O/P	300/1000	USSR	
	Scud Mod C	O/P	500/700	I	
	Nodong[l]	D/T	1000/700-1000	I	
	Taepo Dong 1[m]	D	1500+/1000	I	Nodong + Scud
	Taepo Dong 2	D	4000-6000/1000	I	
Pakistan	M-11	S	280/800	China	
	Hatf 1	O	80/500	I/France?	
	Hatf 1A	O	100/500	I/France?	
	Hatf 2[n]	D	280-300/500	I/China?	M-11 derivative?
	Hatf 3	D?	600/500	I/China?	M-9 derivative?
	Ghauri (MK-III)[o]	O/T	1500/500-750	I	Nodong derivative
Poland	SS-21	O	70-120/480	USSR	
	Scud B	O	300/1000	USSR	
Romania[p]	Scud B	O	300/1000	USSR	Unilateral?
Saudi Arabia	CSS-2/ DF-3	O	2650/2150	China	Non-nuclear
Serbia	K-15 Kraijina	D	150/?	I	
	Scud mod[q]	D	400/700	?	
South Korea	Nike-Hercules-1	O	180/300	U.S./I	Mod SAM
	Nike-Hercules-2	D	250/300	U.S./I	Mod SAM
Slovakia	SS-21	O	70-120/480	USSR	
	Scud B	O	300/1000	USSR	
	SS-23[r]	O	500/450	USSR	Banned by INF Treaty
Syria	SS-21	O	70-120/480	USSR	
	Scud B	O	300/1000	USSR	
	Scud Mod C[s]	O	500/700	North Korea	
	M-9	D?	600/950	China?	
Taiwan	Ching Feng	O	130/400	I/Israel?	Green Bee
	Tien Ma	D?	950/500	I/?	Sky Horse
	Sky Spear[t]	D	300/?	I	Mod SAM
UAE	Scud B	O	300/1000	Russia?	
Ukraine	SS-21	O	70-120/480	USSR	MOU
	Scud B	O	300/1000	USSR	
Vietnam	Scud B	O	300/1000	USSR	
Yemen	SS-21	O	70-120/480	USSR	
	Scud B	O/U	300/1000	USSR	
Zaire	Scud Mod B	O	300/1000	North Korea[u]	

Abbreviations:

Status	Country of Origin	Notes
D: Development	I: Indigenous	MTCR: Member of Missile Technology Control Regime
O: Operational		Unilateral: Unilateral Commitment to MTCR
P: Production	?: Uncertain	MOU: Memorandum of Understanding on adherence to MTCR
S: Storage		SAM: Surface-to-air missile
T: Tested		Mod SAM: SAM modified for use as a ballistic missile
U: Used		From SAM: ballistic missile based on SAM technology

Missile Categories and Ranges:

Missile Category	Ranges
SRBM (Short-Range Ballistic Missile)	Up to 1,000 km
MRBM (Medium-Range Ballistic Missile)	1,000–3,000 km
IRBM (Intermediate-Range Ballistic Missile)	3,000–5,500 km
ICBM (Intercontinental Ballistic Missile)	Over 5,500 km

NOTES (Missile Chart 1)

[a]Principal sources for this table: Humphry Crum Ewing, Robin Ranger, and David Bosdet, "Ballistic Missiles: The Approaching Threat," Bailrigg Memorandum 9, 1994, Center for Defense and International Security Studies; Robert Shuey with Craig Cerniello, "Ballistic and Cruise Missile Forces of Foreign Countries," Congressional Research Service, June 5, 1995; Defense Intelligence Agency, "Global Missile Proliferation Threat," presented to the Missile Technology Control Regime Transshipment Seminar, July 15, 1996; Office of the Secretary of Defense, *Proliferation: Threat and Response*, November 1997; "Missile Proliferation" in *The Military Balance 1995/96* (London: Oxford University Press for International Institute of Strategic Studies, 1995) pp. 281-284; *The Military Balance 1997/98* (London: Oxford University Press for International Institute of Strategic Studies, 1997); Duncan Lennox, "Ballistic Missiles," *Jane's Defence Weekly*, April 17, 1996, p. 40; National Intelligence Estimate, November 1995, printed in Bill Gertz, "Intelligence Report Warns of Missile Launches Against U.S.," *Washington Times*, May 14, 1996; "Artillery Rocket, Ballistic Missile, Sounding Rocket, and Space Launch Capabilities of Selected Countries," *Nonproliferation Review*, Spring-Summer 1996, pp. 162-165; and *The Proliferation Primer,* U.S. Senate Committee on Governmental Affairs, January 1998.

[b]Russia shipped eight Scud launchers and twenty-four missiles to Armenia from 1992 to 1995. Nikolai Novichkov, "Russia details illegal deliveries to Armenia," *Jane's Defence Weekly*, April 16, 1997, p. 15.

[c]Vaseil Lyutskanov, "Existence of Eight SS-23 Missile Complexes Viewed," *TRUD*, September 13, 1996 in *FBIS-EEU-96-179*, September 16, 1996.

[d]The Czech Republic dismantled its Scud-B inventory between 1988 and 1991. The last SS-23 and associated launcher and support equipment in the Czech Republic was destroyed by mid-1996. "Czechs Destroy Last Soviet Missiles," *OMRI Daily Digest*, July 26, 1996, p. 4.

[e]According to Admiral William Studeman, Acting Director of CIA, "Pyongyang has provided Scud missiles and production equipment to Egypt." See Senate Committee on Armed Services, *Worldwide Threat to the United States*, January 17, 1995, p. 39. The Defense Intelligence Agency lists Egypt as a recipient of missile-related transfers from North Korea. Egypt reportedly received seven shipments of Scud Mod C-related material, possibly including production equipment, in 1996. Bill Gertz, "Cairo's Missile Buy Violates U.S. Laws," *Washington Times*, June 21, 1996.

[f]The Department of Defense lists a 200-km Zelzal missile and a 150-km Nazeat missile, which may be variations of the Mushak series. Iran has also tried to acquire a complete North Korean Nodong system and the Chinese M-9 and M-11 missiles.

[g]During the Iran-Iraq War, Libya and Syria shipped Soviet-built Scud-Bs to Iran. Department of Defense lists the Libyan-supplied Scuds as still in Iran's inventory.

[h]A recent intelligence report called the Al-Amoud a "scaled down Scud." See "Iraq's Weapons of Mass Destruction Programs," U.S. Government White Paper No. 3050, released February 17, 1998.

[i]The Department of Defense and Defense Intelligence Agency say that Libya's only operational missiles are Scud-Bs acquired from the USSR. However, then-CIA Director John Deutch listed Libya as one of the recipients of North Korean Scud missiles (possibly the Scud Mod B or C). See Senate Select Committee on Intelligence, *Current and Projected National Security Threats to the United States and Its Interests Abroad*, February 22, 1996, p. 9. The DIA also lists Libya as a recipient of missile-related technology from North Korea, but according to a March 1995 CIA report, *The Weapons Proliferation Threat*, Libya possesses only Scud-Bs. Libya has also sought to acquire the North Korean Nodong missile, but is not reported to have made the purchase yet.

[j]According to the Department of Defense, Libya's indigenous missile program has only succeeded in producing missiles with ranges of about 200 km. Libya hopes that the Al Fatah will reach ranges of up to 950 km, but so far it has been successfully tested to only 200 km. A Serbian firm, JPL Systems, is reportedly aiding Libya's Al Fatah missile program. Bill Gertz, "Serbia Is Helping Libya With Ballistic Missiles, CIA Says," *Washington Times*, November 12, 1996.

[k]"North Korea builds and is likely to offer for export earlier Scud-based, short-range ballistic missile systems in the 300, 500, and probably 800-km range. We are talking here about what is known as Scud B, C and D systems." Admiral Studeman, op. cit., p. 18. An 800-km Scud Mod D has not been listed by any other sources.

[l]A December 1995 Defense Intelligence Agency report estimates that the Nodong can carry a 1,000-kg payload to 1,000 km. Defense Intelligence Agency, *North Korea: The Foundations for Military Strength Update 1995*, December 1995, p. 6.
"We assess the Nodong is capable of delivering a 700-kg payload to 1,000 kilometers." Admiral Studeman, op. cit., p. 39. Reportedly, Syria, Libya and Iran are interested in purchasing the Nodong when it is operational.

[m]*Proliferation: Threat and Response*, op. cit., notes that the Taepo Dong 1 has a range of at least 1,500 km. Other sources, including Shuey and Cerniello, and Ewing, Ranger and Bosdet suggest a range of 2,000 km and a payload of 1,000 kg. The CIA believes "it is unlikely Pyongyang could deploy Taepo Dong 1 or Taepo Dong 2 missiles before three to five years." Responses to questions for the record, dated April 3, 1995, from Admiral William Studeman, Acting Director of Central Intelligence, in Senate Select Committee on Intelligence, *Worldwide Intelligence Review*, January 10, 1995, p. 105.

[n]One analysis suggests that Pakistan developed the Hatf 2 based on French sounding rocket engines that it had obtained. See S. Chandrashekar, "An Assessment of Pakistan's Missile Capability," *Jane's Strategic Weapon Systems*, March 1990, p. 4.

[o]Pakistan tested the Ghauri on April 6, 1998, to a distance of 1,100 km. See Andrew Koch and W.P.S. Sidhu, "South Asia goes Ballistic, Then Nuclear," *Jane's Intelligence Review*, June 1988, pp. 36-37.

[p]The United States is assisting Romania in the dismantlement of its Scud missiles and launchers. Prepared statement of Thomas McNamara, Assistant Secretary of State for Political-Military Affairs, Senate Subcommittee on International Economic Policy, Export and Trade Promotion, March 12, 1997.

[q]See the Center for Defense and International Security Studies Web site: www.cdiss.org.

[r]Slovakia's possession of SS-23 missiles has been confirmed by Prime Minister Vladimir Meciar. Nora Sliskova, "Meciar Comments on NATO Referendum, SS-23 Missiles," *PRAVDA*, November 30, 1996, in *FBIS-EEU-96-232*, December 4, 1996.

[s]Admiral Studeman lists a Scud Mod C transfer from North Korea to Syria. Senate Committee on Armed Services, *Worldwide Threat to the United States*, January 17, 1995, p. 39. The Nonproliferation Center's *Weapons Proliferation Threat*, March 1995, states that Syria has both the Soviet-supplied Scud-B and North Korean-supplied Scud Mod-C.

[t]This program was reportedly begun in the fall of 1995 and is based on the Sky Bow II SAM. Lu Chao-lung, "Taipei to Test Surface-to-Surface Missiles," *Chung-Kuo Shih-Pao*, September 11, 1996, in *FBIS-CHI-96-180*, September 17, 1996.

[u]Lennox, op. cit., lists Zaire as a possessor of Scud B variants. North Korea is the only known supplier of such missiles, but this transfer has not been otherwise confirmed.

MISSILE Chart 2 (Countries Possessing or Developing Land-Attack Cruise Missiles)[a]

This chart lists the countries, other than the five nuclear powers, that have land-attack cruise missiles (LACM) in service or under development. Some of these missiles are derived from anti-ship cruise missiles and from unmanned aerial vehicles (UAVs). Many other countries have the ability to convert these types of systems already in their arsenals into land-attack cruise missiles, but are not listed on this chart unless they are known to be actively pursuing such a capability.

COUNTRY	SYSTEM	RANGE & PAYLOAD[b]	STATUS	PROPULSION	COUNTRY OF ORIGIN	NOTES
Argentina	MQ-2	900/40-70	D	Turbojet	I	from UAV
Egypt[c]	AS-5	180/1000	O?	Liquid	USSR	mod. AS
India	Lakshya[d]	500/200	O	Turbojet	Russia?	from UAV
	Lakshya 2[e]	600/450	D	Turbojet	I/Russia?	
Iran[f]	AS-11	50/130	O	Solid	Russia	mod. AS
	AS-9	90/200	O	Liquid	Russia	mod. AS
	Silkworm upgrade[g]	400/500	D	Turbojet	I/China/ North Korea?	
Iraq[h]	AS-4	400/1000	O?	Liquid	USSR	mod. AS
	AS-5	180/1000	O?	Liquid	USSR	mod. AS
	AS-6	300/1000	O?	Liquid	USSR	mod. AS
	Ababil[i]	500/200	O?	Turbojet	I?	
Israel	Popeye 1[j]	100/360	O	Solid	I	
	Delilah	400/450	D	Turbojet	I/China[k]	from UAV
	Popeye 3	350/360[l]	D	Turbojet	I?	
South Korea[m]	?	180+/?	D	?	I?	
South Africa	Skua[n]	800/100	O?	Turbojet	I	from UAV
	MUPSOW	150/400	D	Turbojet	I	
Taiwan[o]	Hsiung Feng 2	80/100	O	Turbojet	I?	mod. AS
	Hsiung Feng 3	300/?	D	Turbojet	I?	
Ukraine[p]	AS-4	400/1000	O?	Liquid	USSR	
	AS-6	300/1000	O?	Liquid	USSR	
	AS-15	3,000/300	O?	Turbofan	USSR	

Abbreviations:

Status	Country of Origin	Notes
D: Development	I: Indigenous	from UAV: LACM based on UAV system
O: Operational		mod. AS: anti-ship cruise missile modified for use as LACM

NOTES (Missile Chart 2)

[a]The information contained in this chart is derived from the sources listed in this note. Due to the uncertain and changing nature of many cruise missile programs, some of the information contained in these sources is contradictory. In these cases, an explanation or best estimation has been given. See Humphry Crum Ewing, Robin Ranger, and David Bosdet, "Ballistic Missiles: The Approaching Threat," Bailrigg Memorandum 9, 1994, Center for Defense and International Security Studies; Robert Shuey with Craig Cerniello, "Ballistic and Cruise Missile Forces of Foreign Countries," Congressional Research Service, June 5, 1995; Office of the Secretary of Defense, *Proliferation: Threat and Response*, November 1997; *The Military Balance 1997/98* (London: Oxford University Press for International Institute of Strategic Studies, 1997); *Strategic Survey 1996/97*, (London: Oxford University Press for International Institute of Strategic Studies, 1996) pp. 23-5; Duncan Lennox and Barbara Starr, "Cruise Missiles," *Jane's Defence Weekly*, May 1, 1996, pp. 19-21; and K.

Scott McMahon and Dennis M. Gormley, *Cruise Missile Proliferation: Threat and Response 1995-1996*, Pacific-Sierra Research Corporation, September 23, 1996.

[b]Range is measured in kilometers and payload in kilograms.

[c]The AS-5 is a Russian anti-ship missile. Ewing, Ranger and Bosdet list Egypt as a possessor of the AS-5, but it is not known conclusively that Egypt has modified the system for use as a LACM. Ewing et al. also note that the United States shipped the Scarab UAV to Egypt, which, if converted, could carry a 130-kg payload as far as 2,500 km.

[d]IISS, *Strategic Survey 1996/97* calls the Lakshya a target drone (UAV) and notes that it is being produced, but had not entered service as yet. The Center for Defense and International Security

Studies (CDISS), notes on its web site that the Lakshya, which it asserts is a LACM, is in service (see http:www.cdiss.org/tabled.htm).

The source of the Lakshya is not entirely clear. CDISS suggests it was developed domestically, but the November 1997 *Proliferation: Threat and Response* suggests that it was aided by foreign technology, perhaps Russian.

[e]The IISS *Strategic Survey* is the only source listing the development of the dedicated LACM Lakshya 2.

[f]The AS-9 and AS-11 are Russian anti-ship missiles that could be converted for use as land-attack missiles. CDISS and Ewing et al., are the only sources listing these missiles in Iran's arsenal. The IISS *Military Balance* notes that Iran is also in possession of the CSS-8, C-801, and C-802.

[g]The exact range and payload of the modified Silkworms are not clear. *Strategic Survey* suggests a 400-km range, while CDISS notes a 450-km range. As well, CDISS suggests that the modified Silkworm is a cooperative effort between North Korea and Iran; China originally sent the Silkworm to Iran in the late 1980s, but Iran may have since acquired the ability to produce and modify it domestically.

[h]CDISS lists the AS-4, AS-5, and AS-6 as both land-attack and anti-ship cruise missiles. It is possible that Iraq has converted the missile for land-attack use, although it is not known if it still possesses this capability.

[i]Although CDISS lists the Ababil LACM (not to be confused with the Ababil-100 ballistic missile) as domestically produced, it is likely that Iraq received foreign assistance for its development. As well, *Strategic Survey* suggests that the Ababil has been in service since approximately 1988, whereas CDISS lists it status as possibly still in development stages as of the end of 1997.

[j]Both CDISS and Shuey and Cerniello suggest that the Popeye 1 has a range of 100 km, while *Strategic Survey* lists the range at 85 km. The payload range varies from 360 to 895 kg.

[k]Lennox and Starr, and McMahon and Gormley assert that the Delilah modification was done with Chinese assistance; no other sources have confirmed this.

[l]*Strategic Survey* is the only publication to list the Popeye 3, and notes that its payload is not accurately known.

[m]The exact specifications of the cruise missile are not known, for it was described only as "long-range" and in violation of a 1979 South Korea-U.S. agreement that limits South Korean surface-to-surface missiles to ranges of less than 180 km. See Bill Gertz, "S.Korea counters North's Missiles," *Washington Times*, December 2, 1996.

[n]*Strategic Survey* calls the Skua a target drone (UAV) that is in service; CDISS suggests that it has been modified for use as a dedicated LACM, but is still in the development stages.

[o]Although the Hsiung Feng 2 is primarily an anti-ship missile, based on the U.S. Harpoon missile, it could be converted for use as a LACM, while the Hsiung Feng 3 is being developed as a dedicated LACM. The range for the Hsiung Feng 2 ranges from 80 to 170 and the payload from 75 to 225. The range for the Hsiung Feng 3 range from 200 to 300 and no payload estimation was listed in any source.

[p]At the time of the dissolution of the Soviet Union, Ukraine had AS-4, -6, and -15 systems in its possession. It is probable that many of the missiles were returned to Russia, and at least the guidance tapes for the AS-15 have been removed, making that particular missile non-operational. Some operational missiles may remain, however.

MISSILE Chart 3 (Countries Possessing Space Launch Vehicle Programs)

This chart lists countries besides the five nuclear powers that have or are developing space launch vehicles. Although space launch vehicles are designed to launch satellites into orbit, they are by definition "ballistic missiles" and some types are adaptable for use as military missiles (i.e., weapon delivery vehicles). Peaceful cooperation in the space technology area can, therefore, have ballistic missile proliferation consequences. Space launcher development may provide knowledge, experience, skills, and sometimes technologies, that can also be applied to offensive ballistic missile programs.

Not all space launch vehicle types are suitable for military missile adaptation. Those whose stages are fueled with liquid hydrogen, such as India's GSLV and Japan's H-II in the table below, would not be suitable for military deployment. Liquid hydrogen is highly volatile and space launchers that rely on it must be fueled under demanding cryogenic conditions very shortly before launch. The types of space launch vehicles that can be most readily adapted to military missile use are those that rely either on solid propellants or on high-density, storable, hypergolic propellants. Apart from the GSLV and H-II, the space launch vehicle types in this table are based on solid propellants, except for Ukraine's, which are all adapted from former Soviet military missiles that used storable liquid propellants.

Sounding rockets, which are used for scientific experiments, can also be employed in the development of smaller space launch vehicles or military missiles but more often provide a newcomer's initial experience with rocket propulsion systems and engineering. Of the non-nuclear-weapon states, Argentina, Brazil, Canada, Germany, India, Indonesia, Italy, Japan, Norway, Pakistan, Poland, Sweden, and Ukraine have sounding rockets.[a]

COUNTRY	SYSTEM	STATUS	RANGE (km)/ PAYLOAD (kg)	MTCR STATUS
Brazil[b]	VLS	D	3500/1000 or 5000/500	Member
India	ASLV[c]	O	4000/1000	
	PSLV[d]	O	8000/1000 or 6000/2000	
	GSLV[e]	D	14000/2500	
Israel	Shavit[f]	O	4500/1100 or 7500/500	MOU
	Next[g]	D	?/300-500	
Japan[h]	M3S-II	O	615/200	Member
	M-5	D	2,000/680	
	H-II	O	8,980/2,200	
	J-1[i]	D	900 kg into orbit	
Spain[j]	Capricornio	D	1,300/500	Member
Ukraine[k]	SL-8 Kosmos	O	1,500/?	MOU
	SL-14 Tsiklon	O	4,000/?	
	SL-16 Zenit	O	1,370/?	

Abbreviations:

Status	MTCR Status
D: Development	MOU: Memorandum of Understanding with the United States on adherence to MTCR
O: Operational	Member of MTCR

NOTES (Missile Chart 3)

[a] Aaron Karp, *Ballistic Missile Proliferation: The Politics and Technics*, (New York: Oxford University Press, 1996), pp. 209-17.

[b] *The Emerging Ballistic Missile Threat to the United States*, report of the Proliferation Study Team commissioned by the Strategic Defense Initiative Organization of the Department of Defense, February 1993, p. 13.

[c] Ibid.

[d] "Artillery Rocket, Ballistic Missile, Sounding Rocket, and Space Launch Capabilities of Selected Countries," *Nonproliferation Review*, Spring-Summer 1996, pp. 162-165. A 1986 DIA unclassified report gave the PSLV the capability of delivering 2,000 kg to 6,000 km, using only the solid fuel stages. *The Emerging Ballistic Missile Threat to the United States* attributes to the PSLV the capability of delivering "at least 5,000-kg payload to intercontinental ranges", see p. 13.

[e] *Nonproliferation Review*, op. cit.

[f] *The Emerging Ballistic Missile Threat to the United States*, citing Steven Gray, "Israeli Missile Capabilities: A Few Numbers to Think About," Lawrence Livermore National Laboratory, October 7, 1988. *Nonproliferation Review*: 7,000/225.

[g] *Nonproliferation Review*: Shavit upgrade.

[h] *The Emerging Ballistic Missile Threat to the United States*, p. 15.

[i] *Aviation Week & Space Technology*, January 8, 1996, p. 118.

[j] Humphry Crum Ewing, Robin Ranger, and David Bosdet, *Ballistic Missiles: The Approaching Threat*, Bailrigg Memorandum 9, 1994, Center for Defense and International Security Studies.

[k] *The Emerging Ballistic Missile Threat to the United States*, p. 15.

11

APPENDICES

Appendix A-1
TREATY ON THE NON-PROLIFERATION OF NUCLEAR WEAPONS

Signed at Washington, London, and Moscow, July 1, 1968

Ratification advised by U.S. Senate March 13, 1969

Ratified by U.S. President November 24, 1969

U.S. ratification deposited at Washington, London, and Moscow March 5, 1970

Proclaimed by U.S. President March 5, 1970

Entered into force March 5, 1970

The States concluding this Treaty, hereinafter referred to as the "Parties to the Treaty,"

Considering the devastation that would be visited upon all mankind by a nuclear war and the consequent need to make every effort to avert the danger of such a war and to take measures to safeguard the security of peoples,

Believing that the proliferation of nuclear weapons would seriously enhance the danger of nuclear war,

In conformity with resolutions of the United Nations General Assembly calling for the conclusion of an agreement on the prevention of wider dissemination of nuclear weapons,

Undertaking to cooperate in facilitating the application of International Atomic Energy Agency safeguards on peaceful nuclear activities,

Expressing their support for research, development and other efforts to further the application, within the framework of the International Atomic Energy Agency safeguards system, of the principle of safeguarding effectively the flow of source and special fissionable materials by use of instruments and other techniques at certain strategic points,

Affirming the principle that the benefits of peaceful applications of nuclear technology, including any technological byproducts which may be derived by nuclear weapon States from the development of nuclear explosive devices, should be available for peaceful purposes to all Parties to the Treaty, whether nuclear-weapon or non-nuclear weapon States,

Convinced that, in furtherance of this principle, all Parties to the Treaty are entitled to participate in the fullest possible exchange of scientific information for, and to contribute alone or in cooperation with other States to, the further development of the applications of atomic energy for peaceful purposes,

Declaring their intention to achieve at the earliest possible date the cessation of the nuclear arms race and to undertake effective measures in the direction of nuclear disarmament,

Urging the cooperation of all States in the attainment of this objective,

Recalling the determination expressed by the Parties to the 1963 Treaty banning nuclear weapon tests in the atmosphere, in outer space and under water in its Preamble to seek to achieve the discontinuance of all test explosions of nuclear weapons for all time and to continue negotiations to this end,

Desiring to further the easing of international tension and the strengthening of trust between States in order to facilitate the cessation of the manufacture of nuclear weapons, the liquidation of all their existing stockpiles, and the elimination from national arsenals of nuclear weapons and the means of their delivery pursuant to a Treaty on general and complete disarmament under strict and effective international control,

Recalling that, in accordance with the Charter of the United Nations, States must refrain in their international relations from the threat or use of force against the territorial integrity or political independence of any State, or in any other manner inconsistent with the Purposes of the United Nations, and that the establishment and maintenance of international peace and security are to be promoted with the least diversion for armaments of the world's human and economic resources,

Have agreed as follows:

ARTICLE I

Each nuclear-weapon State Party to the Treaty undertakes not to transfer to any recipient whatsoever nuclear weapons or other nuclear explosive devices or control over such weapons or explosive devices directly, or indirectly; and not in any way to assist, encourage, or induce any non-nuclear-weapon State to manufacture or otherwise acquire nuclear weapons or other nuclear explosive devices, or control over such weapons or explosive devices.

ARTICLE II

Each non-nuclear-weapon State Party to the Treaty undertakes not to receive the transfer from any transferor whatsoever of nuclear weapons or other nuclear explosive devices or of control over such weapons or explosive devices directly, or indirectly; not to manufacture or otherwise acquire nuclear weapons or other nuclear explosive devices; and not to seek or receive any assistance in the manufacture of nuclear weapons or other nuclear explosive devices.

ARTICLE III

1. Each non-nuclear-weapon State Party to the Treaty undertakes to accept safeguards, as set forth in an agreement to be negotiated and concluded with the International Atomic Energy Agency in accordance with the Statute of the International Atomic Energy Agency and the Agency's safeguards system, for the exclusive purpose of verification of the fulfillment of its obligations assumed under this Treaty with a view to preventing diversion of nuclear energy from peaceful uses to nuclear weapons or other nuclear

explosive devices. Procedures for the safeguards required by this article shall be followed with respect to source or special fissionable material whether it is being produced, processed or used in any principal nuclear facility or is outside any such facility. The safeguards required by this article shall be applied to all source or special fissionable material in all peaceful nuclear activities within the territory of such State, under its jurisdiction, or carried out under its control anywhere.

2. Each State Party to the Treaty undertakes not to provide: (a) source or special fissionable material, or (b) equipment or material especially designed or prepared for the processing, use or production of special fissionable material, to any non-nuclear-weapon State for peaceful purposes, unless the source or special fissionable material shall be subject to the safeguards required by this article.

3. The safeguards required by this article shall be implemented in a manner designed to comply with article IV of this Treaty, and to avoid hampering the economic or technological development of the Parties or international cooperation in the field of peaceful nuclear activities, including the international exchange of nuclear material and equipment for the processing, use or production of nuclear material for peaceful purposes in accordance with the provisions of this article and the principle of safeguarding set forth in the Preamble of the Treaty.

4. Non-nuclear-weapon States Party to the Treaty shall conclude agreements with the International Atomic Energy Agency to meet the requirements of this article either individually or together with other States in accordance with the Statute of the International Atomic Energy Agency. Negotiation of such agreements shall commence within 180 days from the original entry into force of this Treaty. For States depositing their instruments of ratification or accession after the 180-day period, negotiation of such agreements shall commence not later than the date of such deposit. Such agreements shall enter into force not later than eighteen months after the date of initiation of negotiations.

ARTICLE IV

1. Nothing in this Treaty shall be interpreted as affecting the inalienable right of all the Parties to the Treaty to develop research, production and use of nuclear energy for peaceful purposes without discrimination and in conformity with articles I and II of this Treaty.

2. All the Parties to the Treaty undertake to facilitate, and have the right to participate in, the fullest possible exchange of equipment, materials and scientific and technological information for the peaceful uses of nuclear energy. Parties to the Treaty in a position to do so shall also cooperate in contributing alone or together with other States or international organizations to the further development of the applica-

tions of nuclear energy for peaceful purposes, especially in the territories of non-nuclear-weapon States Party to the Treaty, with due consideration for the needs of the developing areas of the world.

ARTICLE V

Each Party to the Treaty undertakes to take appropriate measures to ensure that, in accordance with this Treaty, under appropriate international observation and through appropriate international procedures, potential benefits from any peaceful applications of nuclear explosions will be made available to non-nuclear-weapon States Party to the Treaty on a non-discriminatory basis and that the charge to such Parties for the explosive devices used will be as low as possible and exclude any charge for research and development. Non-nuclear-weapon States Party to the Treaty shall be able to obtain such benefits, pursuant to a special international agreement or agreements, through an appropriate international body with adequate representation of non-nuclear-weapon States. Negotiations on this subject shall commence as soon as possible after the Treaty enters into force. Non-nuclear-weapon States Party to the Treaty so desiring may also obtain such benefits pursuant to bilateral agreements.

ARTICLE VI

Each of the Parties to the Treaty undertakes to pursue negotiations in good faith on effective measures relating to cessation of the nuclear arms race at an early date and to nuclear disarmament, and on a Treaty on general and complete disarmament under strict and effective international control.

ARTICLE VII

Nothing in this Treaty affects the right of any group of States to conclude regional treaties in order to assure the total absence of nuclear weapons in their respective territories.

ARTICLE VIII

1. Any Party to the Treaty may propose amendments to this Treaty. The text of any proposed amendment shall be submitted to the Depositary Governments which shall circulate it to all Parties to the Treaty. Thereupon, if requested to do so by one-third or more of the Parties to the Treaty, the Depositary Governments shall convene a conference, to which they shall invite all the Parties to the Treaty, to consider such an amendment.

2. Any amendment to this Treaty must be approved by a majority of the votes of all the Parties to the Treaty, including the votes of all nuclear-weapon States Party to the Treaty and all other Parties which, on the date the amendment is circulated, are members of the Board of Governors of the International Atomic Energy Agency. The amendment shall enter into force for each Party that deposits its instrument of ratification of the amendment upon

the deposit of such instruments of ratification by a majority of all the Parties, including the instruments of ratification of all nuclear-weapon States Party to the Treaty and all other Parties which, on the date the amendment is circulated, are members of the Board of Governors of the International Atomic Energy Agency. Thereafter, it shall enter into force for any other Party upon the deposit of its instrument of ratification of the amendment.

3. Five years after the entry into force of this Treaty, a conference of Parties to the Treaty shall be held in Geneva, Switzerland, in order to review the operation of this Treaty with a view to assuring that the purposes of the Preamble and the provisions of the Treaty are being realized. At intervals of five years thereafter, a majority of the Parties to the Treaty may obtain, by submitting a proposal to this effect to the Depositary Governments, the convening of further conferences with the same objective of reviewing the operation of the Treaty.

ARTICLE IX

1. This Treaty shall be open to all States for signature. Any State which does not sign the Treaty before its entry into force in accordance with paragraph 3 of this article may accede to it at any time.

2. This Treaty shall be subject to ratification by signatory States. Instruments of ratification and instruments of accession shall be deposited with the Governments of the United States of America, the United Kingdom of Great Britain and Northern Ireland and the Union of Soviet Socialist Republics, which are hereby designated the Depositary Governments.

3. This Treaty shall enter into force after its ratification by the States, the Governments of which are designated Depositaries of the Treaty, and forty other States signatory to this Treaty and the deposit of their instruments of ratification. For the purposes of this Treaty, a nuclear-weapon State is one which has manufactured and exploded a nuclear weapon or other nuclear explosive device prior to January 1, 1967.

4. For States whose instruments of ratification or accession are deposited subsequent to the entry into force of this Treaty, it shall enter into force on the date of the deposit of their instruments of ratification or accession.

5. The Depositary Governments shall promptly inform all signatory and acceding States of the date of each signature, the date of deposit of each instrument of ratification or of accession, the date of the entry into force of this Treaty, and the date of receipt of any requests for convening a conference or other notices.

6. This Treaty shall be registered by the Depositary Governments pursuant to article 102 of the Charter of the United Nations.

ARTICLE X

1. Each Party shall in exercising its national sovereignty have the right to withdraw from the Treaty if it decides that extraordinary events, related to the subject matter of this Treaty, have jeopardized the supreme interests of its country. It shall give notice of such withdrawal to all other Parties to the Treaty and to the United Nations Security Council three months in advance. Such notice shall include a statement of the extraordinary events it regards as having jeopardized its supreme interests.

2. Twenty-five years after the entry into force of the Treaty, a conference shall be convened to decide whether the Treaty shall continue in force indefinitely, or shall be extended for an additional fixed period or periods. This decision shall be taken by a majority of the Parties to the Treaty.

ARTICLE XI

This Treaty, the English, Russian, French, Spanish and Chinese texts of which are equally authentic, shall be deposited in the archives of the Depositary Governments. Duly certified copies of this Treaty shall be transmitted by the Depositary Governments to the Governments of the signatory and acceding States.

IN WITNESS WHEREOF the undersigned, duly authorized, have signed this Treaty.

DONE in triplicate, at the cities of Washington, London and Moscow, this first day of July one thousand nine hundred sixty-eight.

Appendix A-2

DECISIONS AND RESOLUTIONS
Adopted by the 1995 Review and Extension Conference of the Parties to the Treaty on the Non-Proliferation of Nuclear Weapons New York, April 17–May 12, 1995

Decision 1:
STRENGTHENING THE REVIEW PROCESS FOR THE TREATY

1. The Conference of the Parties to the Treaty on the Non-Proliferation of Nuclear Weapons examined the implementation of article VIII, paragraph 3, of the Treaty and agreed to strengthen the review process for the operation of the Treaty with a view to assuring that the purposes of the Preamble and the provisions of the Treaty are being realized.
2. The States party to the Treaty participating in the Conference decided, in accordance with article VIII, paragraph 3, of the Treaty, that Review Conferences should continue to be held every five years and that, accordingly, the next Review Conference should be held in the year 2000.
3. The Conference decided that, beginning in 1997, the Preparatory Committee should hold, normally for a duration of ten working days, a meeting in each of the three years prior to the Review Conference. If necessary, a fourth preparatory meeting may be held in the year of the Conference.
4. The purpose of the Preparatory Committee meetings would be to consider principles, objectives and ways in order to promote the full implementation of the Treaty, as well as its universality, and to make recommendations thereon to the Review Conference. These include those identified in the Decision on Principles and Objectives for Nuclear Non-Proliferation and Disarmament adopted on 11 May 1995. These meetings should also make the procedural preparations for the next Review Conference.

5. The Conference also concluded that the present structure of three Main Committees should continue and the question of an overlap of issues being discussed in more than one Committee should be resolved in the General Committee, which would coordinate the work of the Committees so that the substantive responsibility for the preparation of the report with respect to each specific issue is undertaken in only one Committee.
6. It was also agreed that subsidiary bodies could be established within the respective Main Committees for specific issues relevant to the Treaty, so as to provide for a focused consideration of such issues. The establishment of such subsidiary bodies would be recommended by the Preparatory Committee for each Review Conference in relation to the specific objectives of the Review Conference.
7. The Conference agreed further that Review Conferences should look forward as well as back. They should evaluate the results of the period they are reviewing, including the implementation of undertakings of the States parties under the Treaty, and identify the areas in which, and the means through which, further progress should be sought in the future. Review Conferences should also address specifically what might be done to strengthen the implementation of the Treaty and to achieve its universality.

Decision 2:
PRINCIPLES AND OBJECTIVES FOR NUCLEAR NON-PROLIFERATION AND DISARMAMENT

The Conference of the Parties to the Treaty on the Non-Proliferation of Nuclear Weapons,

Reaffirming the preamble and articles of the Treaty on the Non-Proliferation of Nuclear Weapons,

Welcoming the end of the cold war, the ensuing easing of international tension and the strengthening of trust between States,

Desiring a set of principles and objectives in accordance with which nuclear non-proliferation, nuclear disarma-

ment and international cooperation in the peaceful uses of nuclear energy should be vigorously pursued and progress, achievements and shortcomings evaluated periodically within the review process provided for in article VIII (3) of the Treaty, the enhancement and strengthening of which is welcomed,

Reiterating the ultimate goals of the complete elimination of nuclear weapons and a treaty on general and complete disarmament under strict and effective international control,

The Conference affirms the need to continue to move with determination towards the full realization and effective implementation of the provisions of the Treaty, and accordingly adopts the following principles and objectives:

Universality

1. Universal adherence to the Treaty on the Non-Proliferation of Nuclear Weapons is an urgent priority. All States not yet party to the Treaty are called upon to accede to the Treaty at the earliest date, particularly those States that operate unsafeguarded nuclear facilities. Every effort should be made by all States parties to achieve this objective.

Non-Proliferation

2. The proliferation of nuclear weapons would seriously increase the danger of nuclear war. The Treaty on the Non-Proliferation of Nuclear Weapons has a vital role to play in preventing the proliferation of nuclear weapons. Every effort should be made to implement the Treaty in all its aspects to prevent the proliferation of nuclear weapons and other nuclear explosive devices, without hampering the peaceful uses of nuclear energy by States party to the Treaty.

Nuclear Disarmament

3. Nuclear disarmament is substantially facilitated by the easing of international tension and the strengthening of trust between States which have prevailed following the end of the cold war. The undertakings with regard to nuclear disarmament as set out in the Treaty on the Non-Proliferation of Nuclear Weapons should thus be fulfilled with determination. In this regard, the nuclear-weapon States reaffirm their commitment, as stated in article VI, to pursue in good faith negotiations on effective measures relating to nuclear disarmament.

4. The achievement of the following measures is important in the full realization and effective implementation of article VI, including the programme of action as reflected below:

(a) The completion by the Conference on Disarmament of the negotiations on a universal and internationally and effectively verifiable Comprehensive Nuclear-Ban Treaty no later than 1996. Pending the entry into force of a Comprehensive Test-Ban Treaty, the nuclear-weapon States should exercise utmost restraint;

(b) The immediate commencement and early conclusion of negotiations on a non-discriminatory and universally applicable convention banning the production of fissile material for nuclear weapons or other nuclear explosive devices, in accordance with the statement of the Special Coordinator of the Conference on Disarmament and the mandate contained therein;

(c) The determined pursuit by the nuclear-weapon States of systematic and progressive efforts to reduce nuclear weapons globally, with the ultimate goals of eliminating those weapons, and by all States

of general and complete disarmament under strict and effective international control.

Nuclear-Weapon-Free Zones

5. The conviction that the establishment of internationally recognized nuclear-weapon-free zones, on the basis of arrangements freely arrived at among the States of the region concerned, enhances global and regional peace and security is reaffirmed.

6. The development of nuclear-weapon-free zones, especially in regions of tension, such as in the Middle East, as well as the establishment of zones free of all weapons of mass destruction should be encouraged as a matter of priority, taking into account the specific characteristics of each region. The establishment of additional nuclear-weapon-free zones by the time of the Review Conference in the year 2000 would be welcome.

7. The cooperation of all the nuclear-weapon States and their respect and support for the relevant protocols is necessary for the maximum effectiveness of such nuclear-weapon-free zones and the relevant protocols.

Security Assurances

8. Noting United Nations Security Council resolution 984 (1995), which was adopted unanimously on 11 April 1995, as well as the declarations by the nuclear-weapon States concerning both negative and positive security assurances, further steps should be considered to assure non-nuclear-weapon States party to the Treaty against the use or threat of use of nuclear weapons. These steps could take the form of an internationally legally binding instrument.

Safeguards

9. The International Atomic Energy Agency (IAEA) is the competent authority responsible to verify and assure, in accordance with the statute of the IAEA and the Agency's safeguards system, compliance with its safeguards agreements with States parties undertaken in fulfillment of their obligations under article III (1) of the Treaty, with a view to preventing diversion of nuclear energy from peaceful uses to nuclear weapons or other nuclear explosive devices. Nothing should be done to undermine the authority of the IAEA in this regard. States parties that have concerns regarding non-compliance with the safeguards agreements of the Treaty by the States parties should direct such concerns, along with supporting evidence and information, to the IAEA to consider, investigate, draw conclusions and decide on necessary actions in accordance with its mandate.

10. All States parties required by article III of the Treaty to sign and bring into force comprehensive safeguards agreements and which have not yet done so should do so without delay.

11. IAEA safeguards should be regularly assessed and evaluated. Decisions adopted by its Board of Governors aimed at further strengthening the effectiveness of IAEA safeguards should be supported and implemented and the IAEA's capability to detect undeclared

nuclear activities should be increased. Also States not party to the Treaty on the Non-Proliferation of Nuclear Weapons should be urged to enter into comprehensive safeguards agreements with the IAEA.

12. New supply arrangements for the transfer of source or special fissionable material or equipment or material especially designed or prepared for the processing, use or production of special fissionable material to non-nuclear-weapon States should require, as a necessary precondition, acceptance of IAEA full-scope safeguards and internationally legally binding commitments not to acquire nuclear weapons or other nuclear explosive devices.

13. Nuclear fissile material transferred from military use to peaceful nuclear activities should, as soon as practicable, be placed under IAEA safeguards in the framework of the voluntary safeguards agreements in place with the nuclear-weapon States. Safeguards should be universally applied once the complete elimination of nuclear weapons has been achieved.

Peaceful Uses of Nuclear Energy

14. Particular importance should be attached to ensuring the exercise of the inalienable right of all the parties to the Treaty to develop research, production and use of nuclear energy for peaceful purposes without discrimination and in conformity with articles I, II as well as III of the Treaty.

15. Undertakings to facilitate participation in the fullest possible exchange of equipment, materials and scientific and technological information for the peaceful uses of nuclear energy should be fully implemented.

16. In all activities designed to promote the peaceful uses of nuclear energy, preferential treatment should be given to the non-nuclear-weapon States party to the Treaty, taking the needs of developing countries particularly into account.

17. Transparency in nuclear-related export controls should be promoted within the framework of dialogue and cooperation among all interested States party to the Treaty.

18. All States should, through rigorous national measures and international cooperation, maintain the highest practicable levels of nuclear safety, including in waste management, and observe standards and guidelines in nuclear materials accounting, physical protection and transport of nuclear materials.

19. Every effort should be made to ensure that the IAEA has the financial and human resources necessary in order to meet effectively its responsibilities in the areas of technical cooperation, safeguards and nuclear safety. The IAEA should also be encouraged to intensify its efforts aimed at finding ways and means for funding technical assistance through predictable and assured resources.

20. Attacks or threats of attack on nuclear facilities devoted to peaceful purposes jeopardize nuclear safety and raise serious concerns regarding the application of international law on the use of force in such cases, which could warrant appropriate action in accordance with the provisions of the Charter of the United Nations.

The Conference requests that the President of the Conference bring this decision, the Decision on Strengthening the Review Process for the Treaty and the Decision on the Extension of the Treaty to the attention of the heads of State or Government of all States and seek their full cooperation on these documents and in the furtherance of the goals of the Treaty.

Decision 3:
EXTENSION OF THE TREATY ON THE
NON-PROLIFERATION OF NUCLEAR WEAPONS

The Conference of the Parties to the Treaty on the Non-Proliferation of Nuclear Weapons,

Having convened in New York from 17 April to 12 May 1995, in accordance with article VIII, paragraph 3, and article X, paragraph 2, of the Treaty on the Non-Proliferation of Nuclear Weapons,

Having reviewed the operation of the Treaty and affirming that there is a need for full compliance with the Treaty, its extension and its universal adherence, which are essential to international peace and security and the attainment of the ultimate goals of the complete elimination of nuclear weapons and a treaty on general and complete disarmament under strict and effective international control,

Having reaffirmed article VIII, paragraph 3 of the Treaty and the need for its continued implementation in a strengthened manner and, to this end, emphasizing the Decision on Strengthening the Review Process for the Treaty and the Decision on Principles and Objectives for Nuclear Non-Proliferation and Disarmament also adopted by the Conference,

Having established that the Conference is quorate in accordance with article X, paragraph 2, of the Treaty,

Decides that, as a majority exists among States party to the Treaty for its indefinite extension, in accordance with its article X, paragraph 2, the Treaty shall continue in force indefinitely.

RESOLUTION ON THE MIDDLE EAST

The Conference of the Parties to the Treaty on the Non-Proliferation of Nuclear Weapons,

Reaffirming the purpose and provisions of the Treaty on the Non-Proliferation of Nuclear Weapons,

Recognizing that, pursuant to article VII of the Treaty on the Non-Proliferation of Nuclear Weapons, the establishment of nuclear-weapon-free zones contributes to strengthening the international non-proliferation regime,

Recalling that the Security Council, in its statement of 31 January 1992 [S/23500], affirmed that the proliferation of nuclear and all other weapons of mass destruction constituted a threat to international peace and security,

Recalling also General Assembly resolutions adopted by consensus supporting the establishment of a nuclear-weapon-free zone in the Middle East, the latest of which is resolution 49/71 of 15 December 1994,

Recalling further the relevant resolutions adopted by the General Conference of the International Atomic Energy Agency concerning the application of Agency safeguards in the Middle East, the latest of which is GC(XXXVIII)/RES/21 of 23 September 1994, and noting the danger of nuclear proliferation, especially in areas of tension,

Bearing in mind Security Council resolution 687 (1991) and in particular paragraph 14 thereof,

Noting Security Council resolution 984 (1995) and paragraph 8 of the Decision on Principles and Objectives for Nuclear Non-Proliferation and Disarmament adopted by the Conference on 11 May 1995,

Bearing in mind the other Decisions adopted by the Conference on 11 May 1995,

1. *Endorses* the aims and objectives of the Middle East peace process and recognizes that efforts in this regard, as well as other efforts, contribute to, inter alia, a Middle East zone free of nuclear weapons as well as other weapons of mass destruction;

2. *Notes with satisfaction* that in its report Main Committee III of the Conference (NPT/CONF.1995/MC.III/1) recommended that the Conference "call on those remaining States not parties to the Treaty to accede to it, thereby accepting an international legally binding commitment not to acquire nuclear weapons or nuclear explosive devices and to accept International Atomic Energy Agency safeguards on all their nuclear activities;"

3. *Notes with concern* the continued existence in the Middle East of unsafeguarded nuclear facilities, and reaffirms in this connection the recommendation contained in paragraph VI/3 of the report of Main Committee III urging those non-parties to the Treaty which operate unsafeguarded nuclear facilities to accept full scope International Atomic Energy Agency safeguards;

4. *Reaffirms* the importance of the early realization of universal adherence to the Treaty on the Non-Proliferation of Nuclear Weapons, and calls upon all States of the Middle East that have not yet done so, without exception, to accede to the Treaty as soon as possible and to place their nuclear facilities under full scope International Atomic Energy Agency safeguards;

5. *Calls upon* all States in the Middle East to take practical steps in appropriate forums aimed at making progress towards, inter alia, the establishment of an effectively verifiable Middle East zone free of weapons of mass destruction, nuclear, chemical and biological, and their delivery systems, and to refrain from taking any measures that preclude the achievement of this objective;

6. *Calls upon* all States party to the Treaty on the Non-Proliferation of Nuclear Weapons, and in particular the nuclear-weapon States, to extend their cooperation and to exert their utmost efforts with a view to ensuring the early establishment by regional parties of a Middle East zone free of nuclear and all other weapons of mass destruction and their delivery systems.

1995 NPT REVIEW AND EXTENSION CONFERENCE

The NPT Review and Extension Conference was convened at the United Nations on April 17, 1995, to decide whether to continue the 25-year-old Treaty indefinitely or to extend it for an additional fixed period or periods. While the majority of parties supported indefinite extension from the outset, many Non-Aligned Movement (NAM) members—led by Indonesia and Mexico—advocated limited extension periods tied to concrete disarmament steps.[1] U.S. officials believed that the Treaty would be weakened unless a resounding majority for unconditional, indefinite extension was achieved, and they pressed for an overwhelming consensus in support of that outcome. The proponents of indefinite extension and of a consensus decision ultimately prevailed, but only after several obstacles had been overcome. The adroit leadership of Ambassador Jayantha Dhanapala, President of the Conference, was instrumental in bringing the desired final result.

Preparations for the Conference. The preparatory process for the Conference was launched at the U.N. 1992 General Assembly. Four Preparatory Committee meetings (PrepComs) were held over the next three years, with a mandate to organize the structure of the Review Conference and establish ground rules.[2] At the fourth PrepCom in January 1995, developing nations, led by Indonesia, complained that the lack of progress in the Comprehensive Test Ban Treaty negotiations showed that the nuclear-weapon states were not adhering to their disarmament obligations under the NPT. Other complaints raised were that adequate security assurances against nuclear attack had not been developed, that the proposed cutoff in weapons-grade fissile material production was not moving forward, and that the nuclear-weapon states were blocking access to nuclear technology and equipment for electricity production, fuel fabrication, and reprocessing.[3] In this context, the NAM bloc put the United States, Russia, and other proponents of unlimited NPT extension on notice that the non-aligned countries were likely to support only a series of 25-year extensions, which could be automatically renewed unless a majority of NPT parties voted against extension.

The surprising resistance to indefinite extension of the NPT by NAM members prompted the United States to reevaluate its strategy and make concessions on disarmament and security assurance issues. In a major policy address at the Carnegie Endowment for International Peace on January 30, 1995, then U.S. National Security Advisor Anthony Lake announced that the United States no longer insisted on a provision in a future CTBT that would allow a party to withdraw from the Treaty ten years after it entered into force. He also stated that the United States would extend its existing moratorium on nuclear testing until a CTBT was in place.[4] Lake reiterated the strong U.S. commitment to securing the indefinite and unconditional extension of the NPT, stating that failure to do so would "open a Pandora's Box of nuclear trouble . . . [helping] backlash states . . . that are bent on acquiring the most dangerous of weapons," and that "other countries might seriously reconsider their own decisions to forego the nuclear option." Lake also emphasized U.S. readiness to "work toward a treaty banning the production of fissile materials that go into weapons."

Progress toward the negotiation of a fissile material cutoff treaty followed in March 1995, when member states of the Geneva-based Conference on Disarmament (CD) unanimously established an Ad Hoc Committee with a mandate to negotiate such a treaty.[5] In April, the United States and the other four nuclear-weapon state NPT parties promised further concessions in the form of individual security assurances to the non-nuclear-weapon states. While the United States, the United Kingdom, and the Soviet Union had issued similar security assurances long before— around the time of the signing of the NPT in 1968— the French and Chinese declarations of April 1995 were their first since they signed the NPT in 1992.[6] Each of the five submitted letters to the U.N. Security Council giving both "positive" and "negative" assurances.

France, Russia, the United Kingdom, and the United States offered "positive" assurances in almost identical language, pledging not to use nuclear weapons against non-nuclear-weapon states except in the case of an invasion or attack by such a state in association or alliance with a nuclear-weapon state on the state making the assurance, its allies, or other states toward which it has security commitments. In its letter, China declared that it would not use or threaten to use nuclear weapons against non-nuclear-weapon states or nuclear-weapon-free zones (NWFZs) at any time or under any circumstances.[7]

In extending "negative" assurances in their letters, all five nuclear-weapon states pledged that, if a nuclear attack against a non-nuclear-weapon state did occur, they would bring the matter to the Security Council to ensure appropriate action.[8] In line with these commitments, Security Council Resolution 984 (1995), co-sponsored by the five nuclear-weapon states and adopted unanimously on April 11, 1995, reads as follows:

> 3. [The Security Council recognizes] that, in case of aggression with nuclear weapons or the threat of such aggression against a non-nuclear-weapon State Party to the Treaty on the Non-Proliferation of Nuclear Weapons, any State may bring the matter immediately to the attention of the Security Council to enable the Council to take urgent action to provide assistance, in accordance with the Charter, to the State victim of an act of, or object of a threat of, such aggression; and recognizes also that the nuclear-weapon State perma-

nent members of the Security Council will bring the matter immediately to the attention of the Council and seek Council action to provide, in accordance with the Charter, the necessary assistance to the State victim . . .[9]

Meanwhile, a U.S. diplomatic offensive had been launched under the leadership of U.S. Ambassador Thomas Graham, Jr., to convince countries to support indefinite and unconditional extension of the NPT. Graham's efforts were reinforced by the involvement—especially in the fall of 1994 and early 1995—of the highest political levels of the U.S. government, including the president, vice president, and secretary of state, and senior Department of State officials and U.S. ambassadors overseas.[10]

Emphasis was also placed by the United States on "putting out fires" just before the Review Conference and on avoiding derailments at the end. One nagging problem was posed by statements by Egypt as well as other Arab states that they would support indefinite extension of the NPT only after Israel agreed to accede to the Treaty.[11] Egypt softened its position just prior to the start of the Conference,[12] but other Arab states continued their pressure during the Conference and in the waning hours sponsored a resolution singling out Israel for failure to sign the NPT and calling for a NWFZ in the Middle East. In the end, the Arab states acquiesced to a diluted version offered by the United States, Russia, and the United Kingdom.[13]

Conference President's Strategy. Jayantha Dhanapala, President of the NPT Review and Extension Conference, was confronted with the daunting challenge of not only managing an effective review of the Treaty but also guiding a parallel process that would lead to an extension decision. His strategy for accomplishing his difficult task was to put forward a timetable "with the front-loading of the Conference to ensure that the review aspect was completed by the end of the third week, leaving the final week for the extension decision."[14] While the three main Conference committees met, following past Review Conference precedents, President Dhanapala also created an informal working group to facilitate consultations and decision-making on key issues relating largely to the extension decision. This mechanism, which came to be known as the President's Consultations, reflected a regional and political balance. Group coordinators reported regularly to their constituencies and, in turn, elicited their constituencies' input for the group's deliberations. The forum proved instrumental in negotiating and refining documents central to the extension decision.

One issue that threatened to disrupt the opening of the Conference was a disagreement over Rule of Procedure 28(3), governing how the extension decision would be made by the Conference, mainly whether it would be by open or secret ballot. The NAM bloc—led by Nigeria, Indonesia, and Iran—wanted a secret vote, so that non-aligned or undecided delegations would be protected from the "strong arm" tactics of the United States and others seeking indefinite exten-

sion of the NPT. The Western and Eastern Groups argued that a roll-call vote was the customary practice in United Nations deliberations and was necessary for accountability.[15] In order to commence work on the agenda, the Conference provisionally adopted all the rules of procedure except for Rule 28(3). To break this impasse before an April 26 deadline, President Dhanapala proposed that, once an initial stage of voting by secret ballot yielded a proposal supported by a majority of NPT parties, the Conference should "endorse it with consensus, thereby making the final outcome open and accountable."[16] In Dhanapala's view, a decision by consensus "was the optimum result for the future viability of the Treaty and its capacity to attract universality."[17] When the stalemate continued past April 26, Dhanapala declared that the provisional rules of procedure would continue in force until the question of Rule 28(3) on voting was either resolved or rendered unnecessary. On May 11, the day of the extension decision, the President came up with the ingenious device of accepting, without a vote, that a majority existed among the parties for indefinite extension of the NPT. According to one observer, this approach avoided a divisive vote and "allowed advocates to claim that the Treaty had been indefinitely extended by consensus, while opponents could argue that the decision had merely accepted the legitimacy of the majority decision . . ."[18]

General Debate on NPT Extension. The underlying theme of the plenary statements by the four nuclear-weapon states, as support for indefinite extension, was their commitment to fulfilling their disarmament obligations under Article VI. U.S. Vice President Albert Gore pointed out, for example, that the nuclear-weapon states would be more inclined to make further reductions in their nuclear arsenals if they had the assurance of a permanently extended NPT. In arguing the case against additional fixed periods, he said: "The last thing that we need, as we wrestle with the problem of further constraining nuclear weapons in ways that are irrevocable, is for the Treaty itself to become . . . subject to revocation at regular intervals."[19] Russia, for its part, underlined that "the indefinite extension of the NPT is not a mandate for an indefinite possession by the nuclear powers of their nuclear arsenals. It is a perspective of a progressive movement toward a world free of nuclear weapons."[20] In endorsing indefinite extension, the United Kingdom highlighted its unilateral reductions of nuclear weapons and announced that it had ceased the production of fissile material for explosive purposes.[21] France, speaking on behalf of the 15-nation European Union and six East and Central European states associated with it, also called for indefinite extension of the NPT. Referring to the nuclear-weapon states, French Foreign Minister Alain Juppe said, "We solemnly reaffirm our commitment, in accordance with Article VI [of the NPT], to continue negotiations in good faith on effective measures pertaining to nuclear disarmament, which remains our ultimate goal."[22]

China was the only nuclear-weapon state that declined outright support for the NPT's indefinite extension—despite fierce lobbying efforts by the United States.[23] Instead, the Chinese representative called for "the smooth extension of the NPT," stating that "We hold that the option for extension of one fixed period is not desirable. If the option for indefinite extension is chosen, it is our stand that it must be made clear that such an extension should in no way be interpreted as perpetuating the nuclear-weapon States' prerogative to possess nuclear weapons. And should the option for extension by multiple periods [be] chosen, we hold that each fixed period should not be less than 25 years."[24]

Indonesia strongly advocated a limited extension, representing the views of a large number of developing countries that saw the outcome of this forum as the last chance to push the nuclear-weapon states toward meaningful nuclear disarmament.[25] Indonesian Ambassador Izhar Ibrahim stated that "an indefinite extension would mean the permanent legitimization of nuclear weapons . . . [leading] to a permanent division of the world into nuclear-haves and have-nots." The preferred extension option, from his government's perspective, would be that of additional fixed periods that would constitute "a modality for the advancement of specific disarmament measures as set forth in the Preamble and in Article VI of the NPT. At specified periods the nuclear-weapon states would be obligated to achieve specific agreements leading to the complete elimination of nuclear weapons."[26] Ibrahim did not, however, specify the length of these periods.[27]

Nigeria was the only country to back a single fixed-period extension "to be determined by this Conference."[28] Mexico, once strongly opposed to an indefinite extension, hedged its bets and did not reveal what extension option it would support.[29] Mexican Foreign Minister Jose Angel Gurria proposed a "reinforced review mechanism" to ensure periodic evaluation of the Treaty, and waged approval within a year of a comprehensive test ban treaty and the immediate launch of negotiations to ban fissile materials for military purposes.[30]

In a statement that would prove to be of great significance in setting the stage for an enhanced NPT review process for the future, South African Foreign Minister Alfred Nzo supported, in principle, the indefinite extension of the NPT, provided that the review process called for in Article VIII(3) of the Treaty was upgraded. In his words, this could be accomplished through "the adoption of a set of 'Principles for Nuclear Non-Proliferation and Disarmament,' which would be taken into account when implementation of the Treaty is reviewed. . . . These Principles would not be an amendment of the Treaty; they would rather be a lodestar which would focus attention on the importance of these goals."[31]

NPT Extension Turning Points. South Africa's proposal for indefinite extension, along with a set of "Principles" to serve as a "yardstick" for reviewing the NPT, stirred up a mixed reaction. While U.S., U.K., and French officials characterized the plan as either "constructive" or "interesting," the Russian delegation argued that the principles, if adopted, would be tantamount to setting "conditions" for extending the Treaty.[32] The U.K. and French delegations had reservations about part of the proposal that called for the establishment of "an open-ended Committee which would meet at fixed intervals between Review Conferences, and which would consider specific ways on how to strengthen the Treaty and non-proliferation regime in all its aspects."[33] In their view, this committee would be an NPT disarmament forum competing for its mandate with the Conference on Disarmament.[34] The NAM bloc was deeply divided on how to respond to the South African proposal, with a few states accusing South Africa of "betrayal."[35]

Nevertheless, midway in the Review Conference, momentum started to build for the South African plan as the basis of an agreement. A key contributing factor was the inability of the NAM bloc to reach a common position on the extension decision and the voting procedure.[36] South Africa, Benin, and several other African states reportedly played roles in preventing the emergence of consensus on either a secret vote or a limited NPT extension.[37] Another factor that shifted support to the South African plan was U.S. diplomatic pressure to prevent an alternative Mexican resolution—which also provided for an improved review mechanism (but one linked to specific disarmament measures)—from gaining support.[38]

President Dhanapala gave added impetus to the South African proposal by putting the enhanced review component into a separate draft decision document, "Strengthening of the Review Process of the Treaty." The outline of an enhanced review process had thus emerged by the middle of the third week. President Dhanapala then circulated a draft providing for Review Conferences every five years (as called for in Article VIII of the NPT), and for PrepComs in each of the three years prior to the next Review Conference.[39]

Indonesian Foreign Minister Ali Alatas contributed to the emerging consensus by suggesting "a more explicit linkage" between the draft documents on "Principles" and on "Strengthening the Review Process."[40] His May 8 paper on behalf of the "like-minded" NAM states proposed that PrepComs be lengthened from a week to ten working days and that, in addition to their procedural functions, they should "identify specific objectives to promote the full implementation of the Treaty."[41] The paper also called for specific objectives to be added to the review document as well as to the "Principles" document. After intense debate and negotiations, the President's Consultations worked out a compromise in which the "like-minded" NAM states would drop their demand for a set of objectives in the review document. In return, "Objectives" would be included in the "Principles" document. Moreover, the "extension decision and the review decision would contain explicit references to the agreement on Principles and Objectives."[42] While this compromise represented significant movement toward an agreement on indefinite extension of the NPT, a number of hurdles still had to be overcome during the last days and waning hours of the Conference.

NPT Review. Meanwhile, the three Main Committees reviewed NPT provisions and began preparing drafts of a Final Declaration. Main Committee I, which dealt with non-proliferation and disarmament, found itself mired in controversies over whether U.S. and British nuclear weapons located in other NATO territories violated their Article I obligations, and how much arms control progress by nuclear-weapon states satisfied their Article VI obligations. The NAM bloc states were dissatisfied with the degree of progress achieved toward nuclear arms reduction and disarmament measures.[43] Main Committee I disagreements persisted into the final weekend, as reflected in a 32-page "rolling text" with brackets around key paragraphs.[44]

The review of security assurances, also under the purview of Main Committee I, took place in a special working group behind closed doors. The United States, the United Kingdom, and France were surprised by the skeptical reaction of many non-nuclear-weapon states to the value of the positive and negative security assurances each nuclear-weapon state had already made in U.N. Security Council Resolution 984. Acknowledging the resolution as a first step, the NAM bloc called for "an effective, unconditional, comprehensive, internationally negotiated and legally binding commitment," with an obligation on "the nuclear-weapon states to take action in the event of a threat of use of nuclear weapon[s], to suppress that threat."[45] The nuclear-weapon states rejected new, legally binding commitments, such as an international treaty, on the grounds that binding constraints would free pariah states from fear of retaliation, risking their actual "use of illegally produced chemical or biological weapons in future regional conflicts involving a nuclear power."[46]

Debate in Main Committee II on IAEA safeguards and nuclear-weapon-free zones proved less acrimonious.[47] The review covered enhanced safeguards (e.g., the IAEA's Program 93 + 2), applying full-scope safeguards as a condition of supply, disposition of fissile materials from dismantled nuclear weapons if placed under IAEA inspection, and export restrictions imposed by nuclear supplier groups on certain countries.[48] Iran argued vehemently that the restrictive "trigger lists" and guidelines of the Zangger Committee and the Nuclear Suppliers Group were violations of the "inalienable right" to the peaceful use of nuclear energy under NPT Article IV.[49] Controversy over Iran's proposal persisted through the final stages of the Conference, as did questions relating to the physical protection of nuclear material and the increased use of separated plutonium in "civil" programs.[50]

The core of the debate on nuclear-weapon-free zones (NPT Article VII) consisted of Arab support for the establishment in the Middle East of a zone free of weapons of mass destruction, including nuclear weapons. The Arab bloc sought to insert language explicitly demanding that Israel dismantle its nuclear weapons program and become a party to the NPT. The United States opposed any formulation that would single out Israel. The review process generally supported nuclear-weapon-free zones and reflected a greater readiness by nuclear-weapon states to adhere to the protocols of such treaties.

The mandate of Main Committee III was to review the "peaceful uses" provisions of the NPT, including export controls, international nuclear cooperation, nuclear waste management, and nuclear safety and liability. The biggest controversies in Committee III proved to be over Peaceful Nuclear Explosions (PNEs) and the question of nuclear waste and plutonium shipments between Japan and Europe.[51] China was the leading proponent of a permissive approach to PNEs, desiring an exemption for PNEs in the CTBT. The accommodation finally reached was to record only the factual statements that the IAEA had not received any request for PNE services and that no NPT state party had an active PNE program.[52]

Endgame. At the end of the third week of the Conference, on May 5, three different proposals on extending the NPT were still alive. The first, with 104 co-sponsors and introduced by Canada, called simply for the Treaty to continue in force indefinitely."[53] A second proposal, submitted by Mexico, linked a number of disarmament measures to an indefinite extension of the NPT. The measures included intensification of the CTBT negotiations and the immediate launch of negotiations on a convention banning the production of fissile material for weapons purposes.[54] The third proposal, presented by Indonesia on behalf of eleven "like-minded" NAM countries, called for the Treaty to: "continue in force for rolling fixed periods of 25 years. At the end of each fixed period, a review and extension conference [would] be convened to conduct an effective and comprehensive review of the operation of the Treaty. The Treaty [would] be extended for the next fixed period of 25 years unless the majority of the parties to the Treaty [decided] otherwise at the review and extension conference."[55]

While Canada's proposal reflected the emerging consensus for indefinite extension, Iranian and Arab state proposals presented problems until the end.[56] Iran retreated, reportedly, only after Russian delegates had warned that Iran's reactor deal with Russia was at stake.[57] When the Arab states introduced a draft resolution singling out Israel for failure to sign the NPT and calling for a NWFZ in the Middle East, the United States, the Russian Federation, and the United Kingdom offered a counter-resolution.[58] The final version endorsed the goals of the Middle East peace process, including efforts to establish a Middle East zone free of nuclear weapons and of other weapons of mass destruction.[59] It also called on "all states of the Middle East that have not yet done so, without exception, to accede to the Treaty as soon as possible." (For the full text of the NPT, see Appendix A-1.)

The Middle East resolution became one part of the overall package that was adopted without a vote on May 11, 1995. However, the first part of the package to be adopted consisted of the three decision documents: "Strengthening the Review Process for the Treaty," "Principles and Objectives for Nuclear Non-Proliferation and Disarmament," and "Extension of the Treaty on the Non-Proliferation of Nuclear Weapons." As President Dhanapala explained, the "Extension" document would be legally binding, while the other two decision documents would be politically binding.[60] To emphasize the linkages among the three, he first brought them to the floor together before calling for separate decisions on each in turn. As noted earlier, this ingenious approach avoided a divisive vote by allowing proponents to argue that the NPT had been extended indefinitely by consensus, while opponents could maintain that the decision basically acknowledged that a legitimate majority existed for indefinite extension in accordance with NPT Article X(2). On the other hand, as had been the case in the 1990 Review Conference, the participants failed to achieve formal consensus on the traditional review conference document, primarily because of persisting disagreements in the report of Main Committee I dealing with nuclear disarmament issues.[61] (For full texts of decision documents, see Appendix A-2.)

NOTES

[1]In her detailed review and analysis of the 1995 NPT Review and Extension Conference (extensively referred to in this section), Rebecca Johnson provided a description of the various groupings of states that participated in the PrepComs and the Conference itself. Stemming from the international structure of the Cold War era, states were "grouped according to whether they [identified] with the West, [i.e.,] the Group of Western States and Others; former Eastern European and Soviet countries, [i.e.,] the Group of Eastern European Countries; and those which identified themselves as independent from the Cold War blocs, [i.e.,] the Non-Aligned Movement." See Rebecca Johnson, "Indefinite Extension of the Non-Proliferation Treaty: Risks and Reckonings," *ACRONYM No. 7*, September 1995, p. 7.

[2]Jayantha Dhanapala, "The Outcome of the 1995 Nuclear Non-Proliferation Treaty (NPT) Review and Extension Conference," before the U.N. Conference on Disarmament Issues, June 12-16, 1995; Mark Hibbs, "Last NPT PrepCom Moves Toward Limited Extension," *Nucleonics Week*, February 2, 1995, p. 8.

[3]Barbara Crossette, "Atom Arms Pact Runs Into a Snag," *New York Times*, January 26, 1995; Hibbs, "Last NPT PrepCom," op. cit.

[4]At the same time Mr. Lake noted that the United States would "retain sufficient strategic nuclear forces . . . to deter any future hostile, foreign leadership with access to strategic nuclear forces, from acting against [U.S.] vital interests. . . . In this regard the President considers the maintenance of a safe and reliable nuclear stockpile to be in the supreme national interest of the United States." See Anthony Lake, National Security Advisor, Remarks before the Carnegie Endowment Non-Proliferation Conference, Washington, D.C., January 30, 1995. See also Mark Hibbs, "U.S. Shows Late Flexibility After Fourth PrepCom," *Nucleonics Week*, February 2, 1995, p. 1.

[5]However, the talks came to a standstill in the summer of 1995 and had remained so through early fall 1997 because of the insistence of a small number of CD-member states to link the negotiations to other nuclear disarmament issues. See ACDA, "Fissile Material Production Cutoff (FMCT) Negotiations," Factsheet, March 27, 1997; ACDA, "Conference on Disarmament Will Negotiate a Fissile Material Production Cutoff," Factsheet, March 31, 1995.

President Bill Clinton had first proposed negotiations for an international ban on fissile material production in a 1993 address to the U.N. General Assembly. The agreement would halt the production of highly enriched uranium (HEU) and separated plutonium for use in nuclear explosives or outside of international safeguards. In December 1993, the General Assembly had passed a consensus resolution (48/75L) cosponsored by the United States, calling for the negotiation of a "nondiscriminatory, multilateral and internationally and effectively verifiable treaty banning the production of fissile material for nuclear weapons or other nuclear explosive devices," and called for the IAEA to provide support in creating a verification regime. See ACDA, "Fissile Material Production Cutoff (FMCT) Negotiations," op. cit.; ACDA, "Conference on Disarmament Will Negotiate a Fissile Material Production Cutoff," op. cit.

[6]See ACDA, "Treaty on the Non-Proliferation of Nuclear Weapons: Narrative" and "A Declaration By the President on Security Assurances for Non-Nuclear Weapons States Parties to the Treaty on the Non-Proliferation of Nuclear Weapons," Factsheet, April 5, 1995.

[7]See U.N. Security Council, "U.N. Security Council Adopts Resolution Concerning Response to Nuclear Threat or Aggression Against Non Nuclear States Party to NPT," Press Release SC/6013, April 11, 1995.

In an effort to meet the demand of non-nuclear-weapon states for stronger security assurances, the Clinton Administration's declaration narrowed U.S. options to act in exceptional circumstances, in contrast to the Carter Administration's declaration of 1978. In the words of one specialist, the latter gave the United States the option to "use nuclear weapons against an attacking non-nuclear-weapon state that was simply allied with a nuclear-weapon state—even if the nuclear-armed ally was unaware of the attack. In the 1995 formulation, however, a nuclear-weapon state must be actually involved in the attack for the exception to apply." See George Bunn, "Expanding Nuclear Options: Is the U.S. Negating Its Non-Use Pledges?" *Arms Control Today*, May/June 1996, p. 8.

However, the Clinton Administration's commitment to its "negative" assurance declaration came under scrutiny a year later, immediately after the U.S. signing of the African Nuclear-Weapon-Free-Zone Treaty. (See section on African Nuclear-Weapon-Free-Zone Treaty in Appendix E in this volume.)

[8]In its letter, China "[extended] both positive and negative assurance to include States party to the Treaty and any non-nuclear-weapon State that has entered into any comparable internationally binding commitment not to manufacture or acquire nuclear explosive devices." "U.N. Security Council Adopts Resolution Concerning Response to Nuclear Threat," Press Release, op. cit.

[9]Ibid.

[10]Julia Preston and R. Jeffrey Smith, "The Nuclear Treaty: Product of Global Full-Court Press by U.S.," *Washington Post*, May 14, 1995. The ACDA-led U.S. preparations had begun soon after the conclusion of the 1990 NPT Review Conference. The thrust of those efforts was to win endorsement for indefinite extension from NATO allies, the Group of Seven (G-7) industrial countries, and the Conference on Security and Cooperation in Europe. See Lewis A. Dunn, "High Noon for the NPT," *Arms Control Today*, July/August 1995, p. 5. Also see Kathleen Hart, "Clinton Administration Accelerates Push for NPT Extension," *Nuclear Fuel*, April 10, 1995, p. 5; John D. Holum, "A Treaty for All Time," *Bulletin of the Atomic Scientists*, November/December 1994, p. 19.

[11]Sharon Sade, "No Agreement Reached on Israel's Signing NPT," *Ha'aretz* (Tel Aviv), December 16, 1994, in *FBIS-NES-94-243*, December 19, 1994; "Mubarak on Israeli Visit, NPT, Syrian Track," *Israel Television Channel 1 Network*, December 20, 1994, in *FBIS-NES-94-245*, December 21, 1994, p. 34; Doug Struck, "Israel Continues to Refuse to Sign Anti-Nuclear Treaty," *Baltimore Sun*, January 12, 1995; Statement By H.E. Dr. Nabil Elaraby, Permanent Representative of the Arab Republic of Egypt to the United Nations, to the Fourth Meeting of the Preparatory Committee of the 1995 NPT Review and Extension Conference, New York, January 24, 1995; Thomas W. Lippman and Dana Priest, "Nonproliferation Pact Raising Tension Between U.S. and Egypt," *Washington Post*, January 26, 1995; Crossette, "Atom Arms Pact Runs Into a Snag," op. cit.; Hibbs, "Last NPT PrepCom," op. cit., p. 6.

[12]Mark Hibbs, "Israel Counting on NPT Extension to Take Pressure Off Its Program," *Nucleonics Week*, April 20, 1995, p. 5; Rebecca

Johnson, "Israel's Nuclear Weapons Continue as Stumbling Block (NPT Update #5)," *ACRONYM Consortium and Disarmament Times,* April 21, 1995.

[13]Mark Hibbs, "Weapon States Face Pressure on NPT Pledge, Chairman Says," *Nucleonics Week,* May 18, 1995, p. 8; "Russian Federation, the United Kingdom and the United States: Resolution," *Arms Control Reporter* (Section 453.D), 1995, p. 21.

[14]Dhanapala, "The Outcome of the 1995 NPT Review and Extension Conference," op. cit.; Mark Hibbs, "Failure of Accord on Document Clouds NPT Review Process," *Nucleonics Week,* May 25, 1995, p. 9.

[15]Charles J. Hanley, "U.N.-Nuclear Treaty," *Associated Press,* April 18, 1995; Kathleen Hart, "NPT Conference Opening Marred By Discord Over Voting Rules," *Nucleonics Week,* April 20, 1995, p. 1; Kathleen Hart, "U.S. Fights Nonaligned Maneuver to Make NPT Extension Vote Secret," *Nuclear Fuel,* April 24, 1995, p. 8; Rebecca Johnson, "The Intersessionals: No Agreement Yet on Rule 28 (NPT Update #1)," *ACRONYM Consortium and Disarmament Times,* April 17, 1995; Rebecca Johnson, "The Conference Opens (NPT Update #2)," *ACRONYM Consortium and Disarmament Times,* April 18, 1995.

[16]Rebecca Johnson, "Building Consensus (NPT Update #9)," *ACRONYM Consortium and Disarmament Times,* April 27, 1995.

[17]Dhanapala, "The Outcome of the 1995 NPT Review and Extension Conference," op. cit.; Mark Hibbs, "Outlook on the NPT: Special Report," *Nucleonics Week,* June 29, 1995, p. 1.

[18]Rebecca Johnson, "NPT Treaty Extended Indefinitely Without a Vote (NPT Update #20)," *ACRONYM Consortium and Disarmament Times,* May 12, 1995.

[19]Norman Kempster, "Gore Warns of Regional Arms Races," *Los Angeles Times,* April 20, 1995. Also see R. Jeffrey Smith, "Gore Urges Permanent Extension of Nuclear Pact," *Washington Post,* April 20, 1995.

[20]Sean Howard, Editor, *Nuclear Proliferation News,* No. 23, Wednesday, May 3, 1995, p. 5.

[21]U.K. Foreign Secretary Douglas Hurd also stated: "The reductions in our nuclear forces which I have described mean that even when START II is implemented, British nuclear forces will be considerably less than 10 percent of the total nuclear forces available to the US or Russia. But there is no doubt that a world in which US and Russian nuclear forces were counted in hundreds, rather than thousands, would be the one in which Britain would respond to the challenge of multilateral talks on the global reduction of nuclear arms." Ibid.

[22]Evelyn Leopold, "EU Solidly Behind Nuke Treaty; Mexico Ambivalent," *Reuters,* April 18, 1995. This EU bloc of 21 countries represented almost a quarter of the required total vote in favor of indefinite extension of the NPT.

[23]R. Jeffrey Smith, "U.S. Move to Extend Non-Proliferation Treaty Meets Strong Opposition," *Washington Post,* April 19, 1995.

[24]Howard, *Nuclear Proliferation News,* No. 23, op. cit.

[25]Evelyn Leopold, "Nuclear Powers Are Said To Be Doing Too Little Too Late," *Reuters,* April 18, 1995.

[26]Howard, *Nuclear Proliferation News,* No. 23, op. cit.

[27]Indonesia's proposal had not been formally endorsed by the NAM block. See Smith, "U.S. Move Meets Strong Opposition," op. cit.

[28]Johnson, "Indefinite Extension: Risks and Reckonings," op. cit., p. 14. See also Rebecca Johnson, "The Speeches Begin (NPT Update #3)," *ACRONYM Consortium and Disarmament Times,* April 19, 1995. Nigeria's position was "inconsistent with the majority of legal interpretations, including Nigeria's own, that a single fixed period extension would inevitably result in the termination of the NPT at the end of the period."

[29]Leopold, "EU Solidly Behind Nuke Treaty; Mexico Ambivalent," op. cit.

[30]Ibid.

[31]Howard, *Nuclear Proliferation News,* No. 23, op. cit.

[32]Johnson, "Indefinite Extension: Risks and Reckonings," op. cit.

[33]Howard, *Nuclear Proliferation News,* No. 23, op. cit.

[34]Hibbs, "Outlook on the NPT: Special Report," op. cit., p. 3.

[35]The proposal for an indefinite extension reflected a significant shift in South Africa's position. South Africa earlier had sought to convince other NAM states to back a 25-year rolling extension. Those efforts failed, however, and, after considerable pressure from the United States and others, South Africa decided, less than a month before the Conference, to support indefinite extension. Johnson, "Indefinite Extension: Risks and Reckonings," op. cit., p. 25.

[36]"NAM Ministers Discuss Stand on NPT Extension—No Consensus Reached," *Irna* (Tehran), April 27, 1995, in *FBIS-EAS-95-083,* April 27, 1995. Also see "Indonesia's Alatas Views NAM Stance on NPT," *Radio Republic Indonesia Network,* April 25, 1995, in *FBIS-EAS-95-080,* April 25, 1995; "'Large Number' of NAM Members Oppose NPT Renewal," *Radio Republic Indonesia Network,* April 25, 1995, in *JPRS-TAC-95-013-L,* April 25, 1995; "Nonaligned Countries Review NPT Extension—Egyptian Draft Endorsed," *Arab Republic of Egypt Radio Network,* in *FBIS-EAS-95-081,* April 26, 1995; "NAM Ministers Discuss Stand on NPT Extension—Indonesia's Alatas Views Debate," *Antara* (Jakarta), April 27, 1995, in *FBIS-EAS-95-083,* April 27, 1995.

[37]Hibbs, "Outlook on the NPT," op. cit., p. 3; Johnson, "Indefinite Extension: Risks and Reckonings," op. cit., p. 28; "NAM Ministers Discuss Stand on NPT Extension—No Consensus Reached," *Irna* (Tehran), April 27, 1995, op. cit.

[38]Hibbs, "Outlook on the NPT: Special Report," op. cit., p. 3.

[39]Rebecca Johnson, "Programme of Action (NPT Update #18)," *ACRONYM Consortium and Disarmament Times,* May 10, 1995. See also Johnson, "Indefinite Extension: Risks and Reckonings," op. cit. p. 27; Rebecca Johnson, "Deadlines for Decisions (NPT Update #15)," *ACRONYM Consortium and Disarmament Times,* May 5, 1995.

[40]Dhanapala, "The Outcome of the 1995 NPT Review and Extension Conference," op. cit.

[41]Johnson, "Indefinite Extension: Risks and Reckonings," op. cit., p. 25.

[42]Ibid., p. 27.

[43]Johnson, "Building Consensus (NPT Update #9)," op. cit. See also Rebecca Johnson, "Visions and Divisions (NPT Update #10)," *ACRONYM Consortium and Disarmament Times,* April 28, 1995.

[44]Rebecca Johnson, "The Endgame: Proposals, Principles, and Brackets (NPT Update #16)," *ACRONYM Consortium and Disarmament Times,* May 8, 1995.

[45]Johnson, "Indefinite Extension: Risks and Reckonings," op. cit., p. 40; Dunn, "High Noon for the NPT," op. cit., p. 7.

[46]Dunn, "High Noon for the NPT," op. cit., p. 7. Three distinct proposals that emerged as a result of the discussions were: (1) a protocol to be attached to the NPT—advocated with slight modifications respectively by Mexico, Nigeria, and twelve non-aligned states at the CD; (2) an international convention on the no-first-use of nuclear weapons put forward by China; and (3) a multilateral treaty on negative security assurances based on the unilateral declarations made by the nuclear-weapon states in early April 1995. See Rebecca Johnson, "Security Assurances (NPT Update #14)," *ACRONYM Consortium and Disarmament Times,* May 4, 1995.

[47]Mark Hibbs, "Indefinite NPT Extension Rests on Canadian Draft Effort," *Nuclear Fuel,* May 8, 1995, p. 5.

[48]Rebecca Johnson, "Week Two: Spotlight on Review (NPT Update #11)," *ACRONYM Consortium and Disarmament Times,* May 1, 1995.

[49]Johnson, "Building Consensus," op. cit.; Johnson, "Week Two: Spotlight on Review," op. cit. Iran's objections had been made earlier. At the third PrepCom in September 1994, Iran threatened to withdraw from the NPT on the grounds that the Western embargo violates Article IV of the Treaty, guaranteeing "the inalienable right of all Parties to the Treaty to develop research, production and use of nuclear energy for peaceful purposes" as well as full access to "equipment, materials and scientific and technological information" for such uses. Subsequently Iranian officials toned down the threat of withdrawal and did not renew it at the fourth PrepCom in January 1995. See Mark Hibbs, "Iran May Withdraw From NPT Over Western Trade Barriers," *Nucleonics Week,* September 22, 1994, p. 1; Mark Hibbs, "Western Group Battles Iran at Third PrepCom Session," *Nucleonics Week,* September 22, 1994, p. 9; Mark Hibbs, "It's 'Too Early' for Tehran to Leave NPT, Delegates Say," *Nuclear Fuel,* September 26, 1994, p. 9.

[50]Rebecca Johnson, "The Endgame: Proposals, Principles, and Brackets (NPT Update #16)," *ACRONYM Consortium and Disarmament Times,* May 8, 1995. See also Johnson, "Indefinite Extension: Risks and Reckonings," op. cit., p. 45.

[51]Rebecca Johnson, "Nuclear Power, Access and Limits (NPT Update #12)," *ACRONYM Consortium and Disarmament Times,* May 2, 1995; Johnson, "Indefinite Extension: Risks and Reckonings," op. cit., p. 46.

[52]Johnson, "Indefinite Extension: Risks and Reckonings," op. cit., pp. 46, 49. See also Hibbs, "Indefinite NPT Extension Bid Rests on Canadian Draft Effort," op. cit., p. 6.

[53]1995 Review and Extension Conference of the Parties to the Treaty on the Non-Proliferation of Nuclear Weapons, April 17-May 12 1995, "Extension of the Treaty on Non-Proliferation of Nuclear Weapons," NPT/CONF.1995/L.3, May 5, 1995.

The co-sponsors included the United States, Russia, United Kingdom, France, members of the Organization for Security and Cooperation in Europe, most Central, South American and Caribbean States and a number of African, Asian and Pacific countries. See Rebecca Johnson's, "The Endgame: Proposals, Principles, and Brackets (NPT Update #16)," *ACRONYM Consortium and Disarmament Times,* May 8, 1995 and "Working Towards Agreement (NPT Update #17)," *ACRONYM Consortium and Disarmament Times,* May 9, 1995.

[54]1995 Review and Extension Conference of the Parties to the Treaty on the Non-Proliferation of Nuclear Weapons, April 17-May 12 1995, "Mexico: Draft Resolution," NPT/CONF.1995/L.1/REV.1, May 5, 1995.

[55]The other co-sponsors were North Korea, Iran, Jordan, Malaysia, Mali, Myanmar, Nigeria, Papua New Guinea, Thailand and Zimbabwe. See 1995 Review and Extension Conference of the Parties to the Treaty on the Non-Proliferation of Nuclear Weapons, April 17-May 12 1995, "Extension of the Treaty on Non-Proliferation of Nuclear Weapons," NPT/CONF.1995/L.3, May 5, 1995.

[56]On May 11, when President Dhanapala accepted without a vote that a majority existed for indefinite extension, "by agreement of the sponsors, no action was taken on Mexico's resolution ... or the proposal for 25-year rolling fixed periods co-sponsored ... by Indonesia and [11] other states." See Rebecca Johnson, "NPT Treaty Extended Indefinitely Without a Vote (NPT Update #20)," *ACRONYM Consortium and Disarmament Times,* May 12, 1995.

[57]Mark Hibbs, "Russia, Others Pressed Iran Prior to NPT Extension Vote," *Nuclear Fuel,* May 22, 1995, p. 9.

[58]"Russian Federation, the United Kingdom and the United States: Resolution," *Arms Control Reporter* (Section 453.D), 1995, p. 21; Johnson, "Indefinite Extension: Risks and Reckonings," op. cit., p. 30.

[59]1995 Review and Extension Conference of the Parties to the Treaty on the Non-Proliferation of Nuclear Weapons, April 17-May 12 1995, "Resolution on the Middle East," NPT/CONF.1995/32/RES/1, May 10, 1995.

[60]Dhanapala, "The Outcome of the 1995 NPT Review and Extension Conference," op. cit.; Mark Hibbs, "'NPT Principles 'Politically, Not Legally,' Binding," *Nucleonics Week,* May 11, 1995, p. 14.

[61]Johnson, "NPT Treaty Extended Indefinitely," op. cit. See also R. Jeffrey Smith, "Permanent Nuclear Treaty Extension May Be Approved by Consensus Vote; Most Nations on Record in Support After Effort by U.S. and Allies," *Washington Post,* May 8, 1995; Barbara Crossette, "Treaty Aimed at Halting Spread Of Nuclear Weapons Extended," *New York Times,* May 12, 1995.

The Middle East resolution was adopted without a vote after the Conference, at President Dhanapala's urging, waived a 24-hour rule. This, in combination with a delay in bringing the resolution to the floor, suggested "that it was deemed important to the Arab states to have the decision taken at the same time—though it was not part of the same package—as the extension decisions." See Johnson, "Indefinite Extension: Risks and Reckonings," op. cit., p. 31. Following the adoption of all four proposals without any objections, a number of states made speeches seeking to distance themselves from the extension decisions. Dhanapala, "The Outcome of the 1995 NPT Review and Extension Conference," op. cit.; Mark Hibbs, "Failure of Accord on Document Clouds NPT Review Process," *Nucleonics Week,* May 18, 1995, p. 9.

Appendix C
THE COMPREHENSIVE NUCLEAR TEST BAN TREATY

The two biggest milestones in the development of the nuclear non-proliferation regime between April 1995 and 1998 were the successful extension of the Nuclear Non-Proliferation Treaty (NPT) to an indefinite duration and the completion of the Comprehensive Test Ban Treaty (CTBT) in September 1996. A comprehensive nuclear test ban was prefigured in a pledge embodied in the 1963 Partial Test Ban Treaty and was repeated as a goal in the NPT preamble. The U.N. General Assembly's adoption of the CTBT, on September 10, 1996, paved the way for a permanent ban on nuclear explosive testing to become an integral part of the nuclear non-proliferation regime.[1]

The rationale for the CTBT was that it would "constrain the development and qualitative improvement of nuclear weapons; end the development of advanced new types of nuclear weapons; contribute to the prevention of nuclear proliferation and the process of nuclear disarmament; and strengthen international peace and security."[2] Some opponents doubted that the treaty would totally prevent qualitative improvements of existing nuclear arsenals, or the development of new weapon designs, given the technological capabilities of the established nuclear-weapon states to experiment without fission testing.[3] Other critics objected to the constraints that the treaty might place on the reliability of the U.S. nuclear weapons stockpile, or doubted the verifiability of the treaty in other parts of the globe. Yet others objected to the uncertainties posed by complicated entry-into-force provisions. But it is widely recognized that the CTBT will be, once it comes into force, a major advance in restraining the nuclear arms competition and inhibiting nuclear weapons proliferation.

Background. The Conference on Disarmament (CD) in Geneva negotiated the CTBT over a period of two-and-a-half years.[4] Negotiations began in January 1994 (based on the mandate in the December 1993 U.N. General Assembly consensus resolution 48/70) and concluded in mid-1996. Ambassador Jaap Ramaker of the Netherlands, Chairman of the Nuclear Test Ban Committee, met the deadline to complete CTBT negotiation in time for signature at the outset of the General Assembly's fifty-first session.[5] The key controversies that had to be resolved concerned the scope of the treaty, whether peaceful nuclear explosions (PNEs) would be permitted, the conditions for intrusive verification (e.g., challenge inspections), and the terms of entry into force.

Controversy about the scope of the CTBT centered on whether the nuclear-weapon states would be allowed any nuclear explosive exemptions from the test ban to ensure the safety and reliability of their nuclear stockpiles—i.e., very "low-yield" nuclear tests, or "hydronuclear experiments" (HNE)—and on China's demand that "peaceful nuclear explosions" (PNEs) be allowed for civilian purposes. Initially seeking allowances for experimental low-yield tests, the United States had proposed that a test "which released nuclear energy up to the equivalent of 1.8 kg (4 lb) of TNT explosive power would not be regarded as a violation" of the CTBT.[6] The United Kingdom, France, and Russia wanted any limit on permissible experiments to be set at a higher yield. China officially advocated a ban on any nuclear weapon test explosion but supported an exemption for PNEs.[7]

This controversy began to fade in August 1995, when France and the United States each declared it would support a "true zero yield" CTBT banning any nuclear test explosions and prohibiting hydronuclear experiments. France had been influenced by enormous international criticism of its final series of nuclear tests.[8] The U.S. decision was eased by a JASON report (commissioned by the U.S. Department of Energy), which concluded that sub-kiloton nuclear tests would be of little value in ensuring the reliability of the U.S. nuclear stockpile.[9] Nevertheless, in announcing the U.S. commitment to a true zero-yield test ban, President Bill Clinton explicitly reserved the right to exercise "our supreme national interest rights under a comprehensive test ban to conduct necessary testing if the safety and reliability of our nuclear deterrent could no longer be certified."[10] On September 14, the United Kingdom followed suit, announcing its support for a zero-yield ban. On October 23, in the aftermath of his Hyde Park summit meeting with President Boris Yeltsin, President Clinton announced that Russia had also agreed to seek a zero yield CTBT.

China continued to insist, however, that PNEs be allowed under a CTBT on the grounds that "any disarmament or arms control treaty should not hinder the development and application of science and technology for peaceful purposes. . . . As a populous and developing country with insufficient per capita energy and mineral resources, China cannot abandon forever any promising and potentially useful technology that may be suited to its economic needs."[11] At the 1995 NPT Review and Extension Conference, a large, Australian-led group of states had proposed language for a final conference statement that would prohibit PNEs under a CTBT. Given the strong opposition to PNEs by non-nuclear-weapon states—and apparently not wanting to be held responsible for preventing conclusion of the treaty over this demand—China eventually accepted a face-saving formulation proposed by Canada.[12]

China also objected to a treaty right that would allow any given party to demand inspections—so-called challenge inspections—of activities on another's territory. China recognized that such demands would be based on evidence presented by one or two major powers that possessed sophisticated, global "national technical means" (NTM) of verification, such as near-real-time satellite surveillance. A compromise was eventually reached with China whereby the authorization for on-site (challenge) inspections would require at least 30 votes of the treaty's 51-member executive council.[13]

The issue that dominated the closing stages of the CTBT negotiations concerned the treaty's entry-into-force (EIF) provisions. The issue arose because Russia, China, and the United Kingdom insisted that the 3 nuclear-weapon threshold states—India, Pakistan, and Israel—must become parties to the CTBT before the treaty could take effect. Other nations, including the United States, would have preferred less demanding EIF provisions in order to facilitate early entry into force, and to deny any nation or group of nations the ability to hold its implementation hostage.[14] Chairman Ramaker's compromise formula listed 44 nuclear-capable states (as identified by the IAEA) that were members of the expanded CD (these included the 5 nuclear-weapon states and the 3 threshold states) that would be required to ratify the treaty as a prerequisite for EIF. If the treaty had not entered into force within three years of being opened for signature, Ramaker's formula provided that those states that had already ratified the CTBT could convene a conference to "decide by consensus what measures consistent with international law [could] be undertaken to accelerate the ratification process."[15]

Indian Ambassador Arundhati Ghose formally objected to the EIF provision on June 20, 1996, warning that India was prepared to block a consensus on the treaty text, and thereby prevent its adoption by the CD, unless the provision was made less specific. Ambassador Ghose stated that India "would not accept any language . . . which would affect our sovereign right to decide, in the light of our supreme national interest, whether we should or should not accede to the treaty."[16] India was also opposed to the draft treaty text because it did not contain language definitively prohibiting qualitative improvement of nuclear weapons and committing nuclear-weapon states to a "time-bound" disarmament process.[17] On June 28, at the conclusion of the second part of the 1996 CD session, Chairman Ramaker tabled a draft seeking a consensus. India maintained its opposition on the same grounds as before.[18]

Despite renewed efforts in the CD at the end of July to resolve outstanding differences, the full Nuclear Test Ban Ad Hoc Committee had no choice but to report on August 16 that, due to India's objections, "no consensus" could be reached either on adopting the text of the CTBT or on formally passing it to the CD. In essence, the announcement meant that the CD negotiation had reached a dead end and that no further progress toward opening the treaty for signature could be made in this forum.

On August 22, 1996, Australia moved that the 50th U.N. General Assembly itself consider and adopt the CTBT, opening the treaty for signature at the earliest possible date. The General Assembly adopted the treaty on September 10, by a vote of 158 to 3, with 5 abstentions.[19] The treaty was opened for signature on September 24, 1996, and on that date was signed by 68 nations, including all five nuclear-weapon states.

The earliest the CTBT can enter into force is September 24, 1998. To accomplish this, however, the CTBT requires that the 44 states that were "members of the [CD] as of June 18, 1996, that formally participated in the work of 1996 session of the Conference," and that have research or power reactors identified by the IAEA deposit their instruments of ratification.[20] As of December 31, 1997, 3 of these 44—India, Pakistan, and North Korea—had not yet signed.[21]

Synopsis of the CTBT[22]

Preamble: The preamble notes that the CTBT serves the goals of both non-proliferation and disarmament and reiterates the international commitment to the "ultimate goal" of eliminating nuclear weapons.

Basic Obligations: The treaty parties agree "not to carry out any nuclear weapon test explosion or any other nuclear explosion." This is the "zero yield" formulation which, by not defining a nuclear explosion, seeks to prohibit all nuclear explosions.

Treaty Organization: To implement the treaty provisions, a Comprehensive Test Ban Treaty Organization (CTBTO) has been created in Vienna. The CTBTO includes an Executive Council for decision-making and a Technical Secretariat for implementing the treaty's verification provisions.[23]

Verification: The treaty's extensive monitoring system includes 24-hour-a-day data collection. The International Monitoring System (IMS) will collect four types of data: seismic, radionuclide, hydroacoustic, and infrasound. Information from these sources is compiled at the International Data Center (IDC), a component of the CTBT based in Vienna. The IDC provides preliminary analysis of the information for treaty parties. When completed, the seismic data collection system will consist of about 170 seismic stations, including about 50 primary stations that send their signals to the IDC in real time. The radionuclide detection system consists of about 80 stations that collect airborne particulates and test for the presence of byproducts of nuclear explosions, such as Xenon. This data is relayed to the IDC on a regular basis. The hydroacoustic and infrasound systems will consist of about 70 sensors on land and underwater that detect the sonic signals produced by explosions. These sensors transmit their data in real time to the IDC.

Consultation and Clarification: If a treaty party has questions about "any matter which may cause concern about possible non-compliance," it may request clarification from another party or may request the Executive Council to investigate. In general, the clarifying nation has one or two days to respond.

On-Site Inspections: Any state party may request that the Executive Council conduct an on-site inspection to help clarify ambiguous events. After receiving such a request, the Council must make a decision within 96 hours, with a majority vote of at least 30 of 50 members required to support a challenge inspection. If the Council does order such an inspection, the inspection team must arrive in the suspected nation no less than six days after the inspection request. In making its request for an on-site inspection, a party may present information gathered both from the treaty's data collection network and from that party's own intelligence information (i.e., information based on national technical means).

Confidence-Building Measures: To reduce the possibility of misinterpreting legal chemical explosions, such as mining charges, treaty parties are required to notify (preferably in advance) the Technical Secretariat of chemical blasts using more than 300 metric tons of TNT or equivalent blasting material.

Compliance: If a suspicious event is inadequately clarified through consultations or on-site inspections, the treaty parties may convene in a special session to "ensure compliance" with the treaty and "to redress and remedy" the situation. The session has three options if it determines that a party has violated the treaty:

(1) It can restrict or suspend the party's rights and privileges under the treaty;

(2) It can recommend that "collective measures," such as sanctions, be implemented by the remaining treaty parties; and

(3) It can bring the matter before the United Nations Security Council. This final option may also be implemented by the Executive Council if the situation is urgent.

Entry Into Force: The treaty will enter into force 180 days after 44 specific nations deposit their instruments of ratification with the United Nations. If the treaty has not entered into force by September 24, 1999, the nations that have deposited their instruments of ratification may convene "to consider and decide by consensus what measures consistent with international law may be undertaken to accelerate the ratification process in order to facilitate the early entry into force of this Treaty." The 44 nations required for entry-into-force are: Algeria, Argentina, Australia, Austria, Bangladesh, Belgium, Brazil, Bulgaria, Canada, Chile, China, Colombia, Congo (Democratic Republic), Egypt, Finland, France, Germany, Hungary, India, Indonesia, Iran, Israel, Italy, Japan, Mexico, Netherlands, North Korea, Norway, Pakistan, Peru, Poland, Romania, Russia, Slovakia, South Africa, South Korea, Spain, Sweden, Switzerland, Turkey, Ukraine, United Kingdom, United States, and Vietnam.

Duration: The treaty is of unlimited duration. Any treaty party may withdraw from the pact, giving six-months notice, if treaty-related events "have jeopardized its supreme interests."

Review: Review conferences will be held every ten years (or more frequently if a majority of parties agree) to examine the operation and effectiveness of the treaty and to consider new technological developments.

Peaceful Nuclear Explosions: If any party wishes, the review conference will consider the possibility of amending the treaty to allow peaceful nuclear explo-sions. Effecting such an amendment would first require a consensus decision of the review conference to convene an amendment conference. The amendment conference would then need to agree without objection to amend the treaty.

Prospects for Entry into Force. Two factors are likely to determine when the CTBT will enter into force. One is the timing of the ratification of the treaty by the five nuclear-weapon states. The other is the willingness of the two prominent holdouts—India and Pakistan—to reverse course, and to sign and ratify the treaty. After India's and Pakistan's May 1998 nuclear explosive tests, it may be difficult for either to adhere to the CTBT unconditionally. Two other states—Israel (which is a signatory) and North Korea—might also delay ratification and final adherence.

Quick ratification of the treaty by the five nuclear-weapon states would increase the incentive for other signatories to ratify. Apparently the other four nuclear powers have been looking for U.S. action on the treaty before initiating or accelerating their own ratification processes.[24] After a year of delay, including a prolonged effort to gain U.S. Senate approval of the Chemical Weapons Convention (CWC), President Clinton transmitted the CTBT to the Senate on September 23, 1997.[25] But as in the case of the CWC, ratification of the CTBT is expected to be a difficult and arduous process. While the Clinton Administration expressed optimism that the Senate's consideration of the treaty will proceed expeditiously, a Senate Foreign Relations Committee spokesman indicated that lawmakers "have a lot of concern" about the CTBT and speculated that the treaty would not be considered before the middle of 1998, at the earliest.[26] The May 1998 nuclear tests in South Asia triggered new statements of skepticism and opposition to the CTBT by U.S. senators.

From the U.S. perspective, the treaty's main political benefit was believed to be that by "helping to dispel the charge that five official nuclear weapon states are perpetuating the Cold War double standard between the nuclear haves and have-nots, it [would] create support for U.S. non-proliferation efforts."[27] Its most important direct military effect would be to constrain the development of advanced nuclear weapons by the emerging nuclear powers.[28] While these benefits are generally recognized, and the treaty enjoys widespread support among the American public, it was slated even before the tests in South Asia to face heavy scrutiny in the Senate on the questions of whether it undercuts the reliability of the U.S. nuclear arsenal and whether it is verifiable.[29] Concerns over verification were heightened after preliminary U.S. intelligence assessment mistakenly claimed that a seismic event in the area close to a Russian nuclear test site (Novaya Zemlya) probably had been caused by a nuclear explosion.[30] The consensus now is that it was a natural tremor.

With respect to the question of whether India and Pakistan would be willing to reverse course and sign the treaty, this seems even more unlikely after the May 1998 tests than before. Since the conclusion of the treaty, both countries have restated their essential positions: in the case of India, that it will not sign the CTBT unless the treaty includes a timeframe for complete disarmament and, in the case of Pakistan, that it will not sign the treaty until "its concerns about its neighbor are put to rest."[31] Some believe that India and Pakistan, each having tested a series of nuclear devices, might now be willing to sign the CTBT, but India's cryptic hints that this could occur are hedged by much the same conditions that were rejected during the CTBT negotiations in the first instance.

As noted earlier, if the treaty has not entered into force by September 24, 1999, the nations that have ratified the treaty by then could meet and seek consensus on a set of measures to accelerate the ratification process in order to facilitate the treaty's early entry into force. The treaty does not identify what procedural options would be available to the parties, but those options would likely include bringing the treaty into force provisionally—as was done in the cases of the Conventional Armed Forces in Europe Treaty (CFE) and the General Agreement on Tariffs and Trade (GATT).

NOTES

[1] In the mid-1970s, the United States and the Soviet Union concluded two agreements placing ceilings on the permitted yield of an underground nuclear explosion at 150 kilotons (one kiloton is equivalent to the explosive force of a thousand tons of TNT). The 1974 Threshold Test Ban Treaty set this limit for nuclear weapons tests while the 1976 Peaceful Nuclear Explosions Treaty set this limit for "peaceful nuclear explosions." Rebecca Johnson, "A Comprehensive Test Ban Treaty: Signed but Not Sealed," *ACRONYM No. 10*, May 1997, p. 7. The conclusion of the CTBT was consistent with the Principles and Objectives agreed to at the 1995 NPT Extension and Review Conference, which provided, among other things, for "[t]he completion by the Conference on Disarmament of the negotiations on a universal and internationally and effectively verifiable Comprehensive Nuclear-Test-Ban Treaty no later than 1996."

[2] ACDA, "Comprehensive Test Ban Treaty," Factsheet, September 11, 1996.

[3] Rebecca Johnson, "CTBT: Signed but Not Sealed," op. cit., p. 78.

[4] For reviews and analyses of the CTBT negotiations, see Rebecca Johnson and Sean Howard, "A Comprehensive Test Ban: Disappointing Progress," *ACRONYM No. 3*, September 1994; Rebecca Johnson, "Strengthening the Non-Proliferation Regime," *ACRONYM No. 6*, April 1995; Rebecca Johnson, "Comprehensive Test Ban Treaty: Now or Never," *ACRONYM No. 8*, October 1995; Johnson, "CTBT: Signed but Not Sealed," op. cit.; Rebecca Johnson, "Endgame Issues in Geneva: Can the CD Deliver the CTBT in 1996?" *Arms Control Today*, April 1996; Joseph Cirincione, "The Signing of the Comprehensive Test Ban Treaty" (An Arms Control Association Press Briefing with Spurgeon M. Keeney, Jr., Joseph Cirincione, Richard L. Garwin, Gregory E. van der Vink and John Isaacs), *Arms Control Today*, September 1996; Rebecca Johnson, "The Comprehensive Test Ban Treaty: Hanging in the Balance," *Arms Control Today*, July 1996; "The Comprehensive Test Ban Treaty: Analysis, Summary and Text," *Arms Control Today*, August 1996. Factual statements in this section draw extensively from ACDA, "Comprehensive Test Ban Treaty: Chronology During Clinton Administration," Factsheet, September 10, 1996.

[5] U.N. General Assembly Resolution 50/65 was adopted by consensus on December 12, 1995.

[6] Johnson, "CTBT: Now or Never," op. cit., p. 15. Significantly, this U.S. threshold was also tied to a U.S. proposal that would allow a CTBT party to withdraw from the treaty ten years after it entered into force. This was based on a U.S. Department of Energy assessment that it could only assure the reliability of the nuclear stockpile for a ten-year period (Johnson, "CTBT: Signed but Not Sealed," op. cit., p. 8). However, as noted earlier in Appendix B on the 1995 NPT Review and Extension Conference, U.S. National Security Advisor Anthony Lake announced on January 30, 1995 that the United States would no longer insist on a provision in a future CTBT that would allow a party to withdraw from the treaty ten years after it entered into force. He also stated that the United States would extend its existing moratorium on nuclear testing (effective since September 1992) until a CTBT was in place.

[7] Johnson, "CTBT: Signed but Not Sealed," op. cit.

[8] Newly elected President Jacques Chirac announced that, in September, France would resume nuclear testing and conduct eight tests over the following eight months. In would then be ready to sign a CTBT in the fall of 1996. However, in light of mounting international pressure, on January 29, 1996, President Chirac terminated French nuclear testing in the South Pacific. See ACDA, "CTBT: Chronology During Clinton Administration," op. cit.

[9] Johnson, "CTBT: Signed but Not Sealed," op. cit., p. 9. This JASON report had been commissioned by the U.S. Department of Energy.

[10] As cited in Johnson, "Endgame Issues in Geneva," op. cit., p. 15. U.S. support for a zero-yield CTBT, *inter alia*, is conditioned on: (1) "The conduct of a Science Based Stockpile Stewardship program to ensure a high level of confidence in the safety and reliability of nuclear weapons in the active stockpile, including the conduct of a broad range of effective and continuing experimental programs; (2) The maintenance of modern nuclear laboratory facilities and programs in theoretical and exploratory nuclear technology which will attract, retain, and ensure the continued application of our human scientific resources to those programs on which continued progress in nuclear technology depends; (3) The maintenance of the basic capability to resume nuclear test activities prohibited by the CTBT should the United States cease to be bound to adhere to this treaty." See ACDA, "Comprehensive Test Ban Treaty Safeguards," Factsheet, September 22, 1997.

Under the CTBT, experimental programs may use subcritical tests, although some critics argue that subcritical tests violate the spirit of CTBT. These are chemical explosions designed to determine how the components of a warhead, including plutonium or uranium metal, behave under explosive pressures. The data can be used to refine computer models simulating real nuclear explosions. The United States conducted two such tests in July and September 1997 and planned four more for 1998.

[11] Johnson, "CTBT: Signed but Not Sealed," op. cit., p. 27.

[12] "On the basis of a request by any State Party, the Review Conference shall consider the possibility of permitting the conduct of underground nuclear explosions for peaceful purposes. If the Review Conference decides by consensus that such an explosion may be permitted, it shall commence work without delay, with a view to recommending to State Parties an appropriate amendment to this Treaty that shall preclude any military benefits of such nuclear explosions." Ibid., p. 27.

[13] For resolution see editorial "Hope CTBT will be Signed as Soon as Possible," *Wen Wei Po* (Hong Kong), September 11, 1996, in *FBIS*, Sept. 12, 1996.

[14] Johnson, "The CTBT: Hanging in the Balance," op. cit. p. 3.

[15] Craig Cerniello, "India Blocks Consensus on CTB, Treaty May Still Go to U.N.," *Arms Control Today*, August 1996, p. 31. Also see Johnson, "The CTBT: Hanging in the Balance," op. cit. p. 5. Note that the membership of the CD was expanded on June 17, 1996, when 23 new members were admitted for a total of 61.

[16] Johnson, "CTBT: Signed but Not Sealed," op. cit., p. 16.

[17] Cerniello, "India Blocks Consensus on CTBT," op. cit., p. 31; Johnson, "CTBT: Signed but Not Sealed," op. cit., pp. 15, 22-26.

[18] See Barbara Crossette, "India Warns It Won't Sign Test Ban Pact As It Stands," *New York Times*, June 21, 1996; R. Jeffrey Smith, "Nuclear Test Ban Accord Is Elusive as Deadline Nears," *Washington Post*, June 25, 1996; Barbara Crossette, "Nuclear Test Ban Negotiators To End Talks Without Accord," *New York Times*, June 28, 1996;

Fred Barbash, "Nations Fail To Agree on Nuclear Pact," *Washington Post*, June 28, 1996; Fred Barbash, "Nuclear Test Ban Treaty Faces New Risk of Reopening Old Disputes," *Washington Post*, June 29, 1996.

[19]India, Bhutan and Libya voted against. The five abstentions were: Tanzania, Cuba, Syria, Lebanon, and Mauritius. See Johnson, "CTBT: Signed but Not Sealed," op. cit., p. 18. See also ACDA, "CTBT: Chronology During Clinton Administration," op. cit.

[20]See Article XIV (Entry Into Force) and Annex 2 to the treaty. For CTBT text, see http://www.acda.gov/treaties/ctb.htm (November 9, 1997). Also see ACDA, "Comprehensive Nuclear Test-Ban Treaty Signatories/Ratifiers," Factsheet, http://www.acda.gov/factshee/wmd/nuclear/ctbt/ctbtsigs.htm (November 9, 1997).

[21]ACDA, "Comprehensive Nuclear Test-Ban Treaty Signatories/Ratifiers," ibid.

[22]This is a composite based on "CTB Treaty Executive Summary," *Arms Control Today*, August 1996, pp. 17-30; ACDA, "Comprehensive Test Ban Treaty," op. cit.; ACDA, "Comprehensive Test Ban Treaty," Factsheet, September 22, 1997, http://www.acda.gov/ctbtpage/ctbfs.htm (November 4, 1997).

As of December 31, 1997, 149 states had signed the treaty and 8 had ratified it. Of the countries whose ratification is required for the CTBT to enter into force, only Japan had ratified. See Arms Control and Disarmament Agency Web site, http://www.acda.gov/ctbt.htm; ACDA, "Comprehensive Nuclear Test-Ban Treaty Signatories/Ratifiers," op. cit.

[23]On November 19, 1996, CTBT signatory states met to adopt the Text on the Establishment of a Preparatory Commission for the CTBT Organization. The following day the Preparatory Commission convened to begin the process of developing Rules of Procedure, Financial Regulations, and other necessary measures for the future operation of the organization in implementing the treaty. Since then, the Commission has also begun building the infrastructure for the treaty's International Monitoring System. See ACDA, "CTBT: Chronology During Clinton Administration," Factsheet, September 22, 1997, op. cit.

[24]In Russia CTBT ratification will probably not be considered until late 1998 because of the need to ratify START II and the Open Skies Treaty beforehand.

[25]John F. Harris, "Clinton Tells U.N. He's Ready To Forward Test Ban to Senate," *Washington Post*, September 23, 1997; James Bennet, "Clinton, at U.N., Says He'll Press Senate on Test Ban Pact," *New York Times*, September 23, 1997; Elizabeth Shogren, "Clinton Asks Senate to Ok Nuclear Test Ban; Weapons: President, Using U.N. Appearance to Outline Vision of an Increasingly Integrated World, Also Calls on Other Countries to Ratify Treaty," *Los Angeles Times*, September 23, 1997. ACDA, "Remarks by the President to the 52nd Session of the United Nations General Assembly," http://www.acda.gov/ctbtpage/ctbunga.htm (November 4, 1997).

[26]Harris, "Clinton Tells U.N. He's Ready," op. cit. For an extensive collection of documents relating to the CTBT, including early Congressional testimony, see CTBT section of ACDA Web site, http://www.acda.gov/ctbt.htm; and Web site of the Coalition to Reduce Nuclear Dangers, http://www.clw.org/pub/clw/coalition/ctbindex.htm.

[27]Vincent Dupont and Richard Sokolsky, "On Balance, CTBT Works," *Defense News*, October 13-19, 1997, p. 62.

[28]Ibid.

[29]A nationwide poll taken in September 1997 showed that 70.3 percent of Americans think the U.S. Senate should approve the CTBT. See "Poll Shows Support for Nuclear Test Ban Treaty," *U.S. Newswire*, September 26, 1997.

[30]R. Jeffrey Smith, "U.S. Formally Drops Claim of Possible Nuclear Blast," *Washington Post*, November 4, 1997. Also see Bill Gertz, "Russia Suspected of Nuclear Test; Denies Breaking Word," *Washington Times*, August 18, 1997; Jim Wolf, "U.S. Presses Russia on Seismic Event," *Reuters*, August 28, 1997; "Russia Denies It Carried Out Nuclear Test," *Reuters*, August 28, 1997; Lynn Berry, "Russia—Nuclear," *Associated Press*, August 29, 1997; R. Jeffrey Smith, "U.S. Asks for Assurance on Test Ban After Activity Detected at Russian Site," *Washington Post*, August 29, 1996; John Diamond, "US—Russia Nuclear," *Associated Press*, September 13, 1997; R. Jeffrey Smith, "U.S. Official Acted Hastily In Nuclear Test Accusation," *Washington Post*, October 20, 1997.

According to a July 1997 report of the U.S. National Research Council, the United States lacks the technical means to detect and locate all potential small-scale violations of the CTBT. See Robert Burns, "Nuclear Testing," *Associated Press*, July 3, 1997.

[31]Parminder Brar, "Indian and Pakistani Ambassadors Explain CTBT Positions," *USIS Washington File*, June 12, 1997; "India Says It Won't Trade Security for N-Treaties," *Reuters*, May 31, 1997. Also see Michael Krepon of the Stimson Center, Amb. Prakash Shah, Permanent Representative of India to the U.N., and Munir Akram of the Embassy of Pakistan, remarks from "A Panel on Facilitating the CTBT's Entry-into-Force," at the Carnegie Endowment Non-Proliferation Conference: *Enhancing the Tools of the Trade*, Washington, D.C., June 9-10, 1997; Tahir Ikram, "Japan Advises Pakistan to Sign CTBT Before India," *Reuters*, July 22, 1997; Sonali Verma, "Japan Cautions India, Pakistan Over Nuclear Treaty," *Reuters*, July 25, 1997; "Indian PM, Mubarak Discuss Economy, Nuclear Test Ban," *Reuters*, October 11, 1997.

On the occasion of the first U.S. subcritical test carried out in July 1997, both India and China raised concerns that the test may have violated the spirit, if not the letter, of the CTBT. See Sonali Verma, "India Says Concerned Over U.S. Nuclear Tests," *Reuters*, July 5, 1997; "China Calls for Adherence to Nuclear Test Ban," *Reuters*, July 3, 1997; Mure Dickie, "China Says Keeping Close Eye on U.S. Nuclear Tests," *Reuters*, July 3, 1997.

Appendix D
INTERNATIONAL ATOMIC ENERGY AGENCY SAFEGUARDS

The International Atomic Energy Agency (IAEA) is a key element of the international non-proliferation regime. Founded in 1957, the Vienna-based agency is an independent U.N.–affiliated body with 126 member states. Its mission is to promote the peaceful uses of nuclear energy and to administer a program of on-site inspections, audits, and inventory controls (collectively known as "safeguards") to ensure that nuclear materials subject to its oversight are not used for weapons. Today, the IAEA monitors more than 800 installations in more than 110 nations; its safeguards system has continued to become more sophisticated over time, and it has been a key bulwark against the spread of nuclear arms.

Organization. The IAEA has a 35-member Board of Governors, which meets five times a year and is the main body for formulating the organization's policies. The Board reports through the Director General to the General Conference of all members, which meets annually in September. The IAEA has a staff of more than 2,000.[1] In September 1997, the 41st IAEA General Conference approved the appointment of Dr. Mohamed ElBaradei as Director General as of December 1, 1997.[2]

Safeguards. The basic purpose of IAEA safeguards is to detect, and thereby deter, the diversion of nuclear material to nuclear weapons or other nuclear explosive devices. Effective implementation of IAEA safeguards depends on the capability for timely detection. In essence, the Agency conducts on-site inspections to establish quantities of nuclear material and changes in quantities of nuclear material at nuclear facilities. It accomplishes this by auditing facility records and reports and by verifying declared quantities of nuclear material. Seals and cameras are used to maintain a continuity of knowledge about contained nuclear material when inspectors are not present.

The IAEA is empowered by the Nuclear Non-Proliferation Treaty (NPT) to safeguard all peaceful nuclear activities in non-nuclear-weapon states that are parties to the Treaty. The Agency also monitors individual facilities of non-NPT parties under agreements worked out with these states. Thus, even though India, Israel, and Pakistan are not parties to the NPT and have not otherwise concluded comprehensive safeguards agreements with the IAEA, some nuclear facilities in each of these countries are subject to IAEA monitoring and are thereby legally off-limits to nuclear-weapon activities.

Upgraded Safeguards: Background on Program 93 + 2. Until 1990, it was understood that non-nuclear-weapon-state NPT parties would declare all of their nuclear materials and facilities under their NPT obligations. As a result, the practice of the IAEA was to monitor facilities declared by the inspected country and to not search for possible hidden nuclear installations. After the 1991 Gulf War, however, the discovery that Iraq had violated its NPT obligations by secretly developing a network of undeclared nuclear plants as part of an extensive nuclear weapons program forced a review of the adequacy of IAEA safeguards requirements. As a result, IAEA Director General Hans Blix in 1991 proposed greater IAEA access to information and better physical access to nuclear sites to help ensure that states pledged to comprehensive safeguards were not engaged in clandestine nuclear activities. In 1992, the IAEA's Board of Governors adopted a set of correctives, including:

(1) A reaffirmation of the Agency's original right to conduct "special inspections," i.e., inspections of undeclared sites suspected of housing nuclear activities;

(2) A requirement for the early provision to the IAEA of design information on new and modified installations; and

(3) A reporting scheme under which states would provide the IAEA with information on exports, imports, and production of nuclear material and exports of specified equipment, going beyond information routinely required by their safeguards agreements.[3]

These interim measures served as the springboard for the next set of improvements in the effectiveness and efficiency of the safeguards system.[4] IAEA "Program 93 + 2" was launched in mid-1993 to develop new safeguards measures before the NPT Review and Extension Conference, then two years away. According to a senior IAEA official, the Program 93 + 2 proposals aimed "to broaden the focus of the [IAEA] safeguards system to *undeclared*, clandestine activities" as compared with "the old approach of improving the effectiveness of standard safeguards only on *declared* facilities."[5] In other words, the IAEA would move beyond verification of the *correctness* of a state's declaration with respect to its nuclear material holdings (and its utilization of that material) into the realm of seeking to ascertain the *completeness* of that state's declaration of nuclear activities.

The conceptual basis for strengthened safeguards was that the overall pattern of a state's nuclear activities would have a "signature" (distinctive indications) that would not be apparent from having nuclear material per se. Hidden weapons-related activities might be reflected, for example, in the acquisition or operation of certain specialized equipment or in environmental emissions as an abnormal signature.[6] This new approach would require "access to more information and more access to several kinds of facilities, whether such facilities contain nuclear materials or not."[7]

Making the safeguards system more effective was one goal of Program 93 + 2. Another goal was that it would lead to better use of the IAEA's scarce resources through efficiencies that would result from the strengthening of the system itself. One senior IAEA official saw as a potential early benefit the "simplification of safeguards for existing facilities of the nuclear fuel cycle."[8]

In developing Program 93 + 2, the IAEA invited the direct participation of member states in formulating and testing proposed measures.[9] In June 1995, the IAEA Secretariat advanced two sets of proposed measures for Board consideration under Program 93 + 2. Part 1 consisted of innovations that could be implemented under existing legal authority. Part 2 consisted of measures that probably would require complementary (fresh) legal authority. The Board supported the Secretariat's recommendation to proceed immediately to carry out Part 1 measures, beginning the consultations with member states that were needed to implement the measures successfully. The Board also backed Director General Hans Blix's recommendation that a decision on Part 2 await his next report.[10]

Program 93 + 2: Part 1. During 1996, the IAEA started to implement three categories of measures under Part 1, focusing on broader access to information, increased physical access, and optimal use of the safeguards system.[11] The IAEA requested additional information from states based on their national nuclear accounting systems in order to gain access to certain closed down nuclear facilities and to locations-outside-facilities (LOFs), i.e., installations where nuclear material had never been introduced. This data is intended, in part, to confirm the Agency's right of access to "records of activities carried out before entry-into-force of a safeguards agreement to help ensure that all material has been properly declared."[12] This measure is especially important in the cases of Argentina, Brazil, Belarus, Kazakhstan, and Ukraine, all of which had pre-existing nuclear programs that were partly or wholly outside IAEA safeguards. It should also help the Agency ferret out undisclosed activities.

Another source of data under Part 1 will be location-specific environmental sampling at facilities to which the IAEA has access for design information verification and inspections. This will enhance the Agency's ability to detect undeclared activities at or near declared nuclear sites.[13] Accordingly, the IAEA now takes samples at uranium-enrichment and hot-cell facilities, and it has developed general guidelines for such procedures.[14]

Increased physical access to nuclear facilities will be facilitated through no-notice inspections at strategic points of these facilities.[15] The IAEA has explored different options of implementing such inspections at different types of facilities, including low-enriched uranium fuel-fabrication facilities and research reactors. In the case of the latter, the IAEA's objective is to improve safeguards against the clandestine production of plutonium.

IAEA initiatives for optimal use of the safeguards system have focused on expanding unattended and remote monitoring capabilities. This approach utilizes advanced technologies for the remote transmission of data by satellite and phone lines back to a network of monitoring facilities.

Program 93 + 2: Part 2. In May 1996, IAEA Director General Blix issued his report on measures to be implemented under complementary legal authority[16] for the review of the IAEA Board's designated Committee. The Committee in turn negotiated with member states, including nuclear facility operators, to generate a draft protocol on the measures that depended on complementary legal authority. Nuclear facility operators were often critical of the IAEA's demand for additional physical access to secondary facilities at individual nuclear sites (those beyond "strategic points")—such as workshops, storage areas, and administrative buildings—arguing that this would compromise commercially sensitive information. Moreover, state authorities as well as plant operators were uncomfortable providing information about, and access to, facilities that did not contain nuclear materials.[17] Nevertheless, the negotiations produced a draft model protocol on April 4, 1997, and it was approved as an Additional Protocol by the IAEA Board of Governors on May 15, 1997.[18] Once negotiated with a state, the terms of the Additional Protocol will supplement and supersede the provisions of the existing IAEA safeguards agreement(s) with that party.[19]

The provisions of the Additional Protocol fall into two basic categories. The first category is access to information. It obligates non-nuclear-weapon states to provide the IAEA with a great deal more information—not only on activities involving the production and use of nuclear materials but also on closely related activities not involving nuclear materials per se, as well as on all activities involving nuclear materials—regardless of whether they support nuclear or non-nuclear (e.g., medical) programs. Such information will give the IAEA "a far better understanding of a State's nuclear program, its future direction, and the kinds of nuclear activities the program's infrastructure could support."[20] In this context there is a requirement for each country to submit to the IAEA an "expanded" declaration specifying:

- "[the] location of nuclear fuel cycle-related research and development activities—not involving nuclear material,"

- "operational activities of safeguards relevance at facilities and locations outside facilities where nuclear material is customarily used,"

- "the location, operational status and the estimated annual capacity of uranium mines and concentration plants and thorium concentration plants,"

- "[quantities, intended use, and exports of] source material which has not reached the composition and purity suitable for fuel fabrication or for being isotopically enriched,"

- "quantities, uses and locations of nuclear material exempted from safeguards [pursuant to INFC-IRC/153],"

- "[fuel-cycle development plans for the succeeding ten-year period, including related research and development activities]," and

- "the location of nuclear fuel cycle-related research and development activities not involving nuclear material which are specifically related to enrichment, reprocessing of nuclear fuel or the processing of intermediate or high-level waste containing plutonium, high enriched uranium or uranium-233."[21]

The second category of provisions under Part 2 of Program 93 + 2 deals with "complementary access." Through increased physical access, the IAEA will be better able to resolve questions relating to the correctness and completeness of the information provided in the "expanded" declaration, to provide credible assurance of the absence of undeclared nuclear material and activities, and to verify "the decommissioned status of a facility or location outside facilities where nuclear material was customarily used."[22] One component is the right of the IAEA Secretariat to conduct random short-notice inspections at all nuclear and nuclear-related locations, subject, in some cases, to "managed access" arrangements "to prevent the dissemination of proliferation sensitive information, to meet safety or physical protection requirements, or to protect proprietary or commercially sensitive information."[23] Another component is the right of the IAEA Secretariat to utilize wide-area environmental monitoring techniques in order to assure the absence of undeclared nuclear activities. Related measures are the authority of the IAEA to deploy wide-area environmental techniques once they are proven cost-effective and to utilize all available information in formulating its verification conclusions, including information originating from National Technical Means (i.e., state-provided information based on intelligence collection).

The United States has indicated that "it intends to accept the new measures in the protocol in their entirety except where they involve information or locations of direct national security significance to the United States."[24] The U.S. intention is to make the protocol legally binding and to seek any implementing legislation required.

Implications. Program 93 + 2 has been praised throughout the non-proliferation community as an important reform of IAEA safeguards to enable the Agency to seek out clandestine nuclear activities. Nevertheless, some skepticism over certain aspects of the program was voiced soon after the IAEA Board of Governors approved the Additional Protocol. First, there is concern that, in the interest of achieving efficiencies, the IAEA will ease the safeguards burden on certain existing facilities that have been under traditional safeguards (e.g., spent-fuel pools at reactor sites).[25] A related concern arises from pressure on the IAEA to reduce the intensity of safeguards required on different isotopic grades of stored plutonium. A senior IAEA official has suggested that the degree of proliferation concern is low as it relates to degraded plutonium (such as high-burnup spent fuel), is higher as it relates to low-grade plutonium (such as that contained within separated high-burnup plutonium from light-water reactors), and increases further with high-grade plutonium (e.g., from weapons, in breeder blankets, or in low-burnup spent fuel).[26] In response, critics point to information declassified by the U.S. government indicating that nuclear weapons can be produced from plutonium of virtually any isotopic composition. In the view of some critics, the IAEA may be inclined to ease up on its accountancy procedures for low-grade plutonium as a way of convincing certain nations to join Program 93 + 2.[27]

Even with the Program 93 + 2 reforms, the current IAEA safeguards system will still have some well-recognized limitations. First and most important, key installations including a number of enrichment and reprocessing facilities in countries of proliferation concern, are not under the IAEA system: India, Israel, and Pakistan all remain free to use unsafeguarded installations to manufacture material for nuclear weapons. Only nations that have ratified the Non-Proliferation Treaty (NPT) or for which the Treaty of Tlatelolco is in force have accepted safeguards on all of their nuclear facilities.

A second limitation of the safeguards system is that certain types of facilities, such as fuel fabrication, reprocessing, and enrichment installations, handle nuclear materials in bulk form (as powders, liquids, or gases). Such materials are particularly difficult to safeguard, since measurement techniques are not accurate enough to keep track of 100 percent of these substances as they move through the facilities processing them. This makes it theoretically possible to divert a certain small percentage of material for military purposes without detection—since this could appear to be a normal operating discrepancy. The problem is especially dangerous at fuel-fabrication plants handling plutonium or weapons-grade uranium in powdered form, at reprocessing plants where plutonium is dissolved in various liquids for processing, and at enrichment plants, which use uranium hexafluoride gas as feed. The NPT permits state parties to produce weapons-usable materials provided that these are placed under IAEA safeguards.

Finally, even if IAEA safeguards functioned perfectly, their usefulness might be limited when applied to weapons-grade uranium and plutonium—materials directly usable for nuclear arms. Even if the IAEA reacted instantly to detected diversion, the nation concerned could manufacture nuclear weapons within a matter of weeks if all the non-nuclear components had been prepared in advance, presenting the world community with a *fait accompli*. In such a setting, safeguards would not be able to provide "timely warning" sufficient to allow the international community to react before the nation diverting the material had achieved its objective.

For these reasons, the United States has worked to curtail commerce with nations of proliferation concern involving plutonium, highly enriched uranium, or enrichment and reprocessing facilities—whether or not safeguards would be applied. Virtually all other nuclear supplier nations have adopted the cautious approach of the United States in transferring such items.

It must be stressed, however, that even if safeguards as applied are imperfect, their deterrent value remains strong, since would-be diverters cannot have confidence that their misuse of nuclear materials will go undetected or unpunished.

Indeed, in the event of a safeguards violation, the Agency's Board of Governors has the authority to notify the U.N. Security Council. Security Council members could then pass a resolution imposing economic, political, or military sanctions on the violator—as happened with Iraq in 1991 and as almost occurred with North Korea in June 1994.

NOTES

[1] For details of the structure and work of the IAEA, see "Against the Spread of Nuclear Weapons: IAEA Safeguards in the 1990s," International Atomic Energy Agency, Division of Public Information, December 1993.

[2] IAEA, "General Conference Approves Appointment of Dr. Mohamed ElBaradei as IAEA Director General," PR 97/25, September 29, 1997; Mark Hibbs, "Egypt Has Next Move As IAEA Fails to Agree on Successor to Blix," *Nucleonics Week*, March 27, 1997, p. 4; Mark Hibbs, "Africans Nominate ElBaradei to Succeed Blix As IAEA Head," *Nucleonics Week*, April 24, 1997, p. 6; Mark Hibbs, "IAEA Board Poised to Elect Elbaradei to Succeed Blix," *Nuclear Fuel*, June 2, 1997, p. 2; "IAEA: ElBaradei Election Expected," *Nucleonics Week*, June 5, 1997, p. 16; Mark Hibbs, "Chung Claims IAEA Chief Election Marred by Improper Procedures," *Nucleonics Week*, June 12, 1997, p. 18.

[3] Dirk Schriefer, "New Safeguards Measures: Initial Implementation and Experience," *IAEA Bulletin 38/4*, http://www.iaea.or.at/worldatom/inforesource/bulletin/bull384/scrief.html (February 19, 1997).

The Agency's first attempted special inspection was to be in North Korea in 1992, but Pyongyang refused to comply with the IAEA's request, triggering a crisis that has yet to be fully resolved. However, the IAEA's assertion of this authority has been exercized in Iran. Because an IAEA demand for a special inspection carries the implied accusation that a country may be violating the NPT, Iran, anticipating that the Agency might seek special inspections within its territory, sought to avert the stigma by offering the IAEA the opportunity to visit any location in Iran on request. The Agency made four visits to Iranian sites, in February 1992, November 1993, November 1996, and July 1997, but did not detect any activities in violation of Iran's NPT obligations.

[4] The need to improve the effectiveness and efficiency of the IAEA safeguards regime intensified in the mid-1990s—not only because of the Agency's problems with Iraq and North Korea but also because of South Africa's elimination of its six-weapon nuclear arsenal, the establishment of comprehensive inspection regimes in Argentina and Brazil in cooperation with the Argentine-Brazil Accounting and Control Commission, and the carrying out of special visits to Iran. In addition, the Agency was anticipating that unprecedented challenges might arise from applying safeguards comprehensively in Belarus, Kazakhstan, and Ukraine, all of which had pre-existing nuclear facilities and materials that had been part of the Soviet Union's nuclear-weapon programs. As a nuclear-weapon state, the former Soviet Union was not obliged to have IAEA safeguards on its facilities and materials.

[5] Bruno Pellaud, "Safeguards: The Evolving Picture," *IAEA Bulletin 38/4*, http://www.iaea.or.at/worldatom/inforesource/bulletin/bull384/pellaud.html (May 7, 1997).

[6] Richard Hooper, International Atomic Energy Agency, presentation before the Carnegie Endowment Non-Proliferation Conference: *Enhancing the Tools of the Trade,* Washington, D.C., June 9-10, 1997.

[7] Pellaud, "Safeguards: The Evolving Picture," op. cit.

[8] Ibid.

[9] Schriefer, "New Safeguards Measures," op. cit.

[10] Ibid. Also see IAEA, "Strengthening the Effectiveness and Improving the Efficiency of the Safeguards System: Report by the Director General to the General Conference," GC(40)/17, August 23, 1996, http://www.iaea.or.at/GC/gc40/documents/gc40-17.html (February 19, 1997).

[11] This composite of the IAEA's early experience with Part 1 measures draws heavily from Schriefer, "New Safeguards Measures," op. cit., and IAEA, "Strengthening the Effectiveness: Report by the Director General," op. cit.

[12] ACDA, "International Nuclear Safeguards Strengthened," Factsheet, May 15, 1997, http://www.acda.gov/factshee/wmd/nuclear/npt/nucsafe.htm (July 22, 1997).

[13] Ibid.

[14] Over the course of 1996, more than 400 environmental samples were taken in enrichment plants and hot cells in more than 20 countries. See Schriefer, "New Safeguards Measures," op. cit.

[15] Ibid.

[16] IAEA, "Strengthening the Effectiveness: Report by the Director General," op. cit. Also see Pellaud, "Safeguards: The Evolving Picture," op. cit.

[17] Pellaud, "Safeguards: The Evolving Picture," op. cit.

[18] IAEA, "IAEA Board of Governors Approves Strengthened Measures to Verify Nuclear Weapons Pact," PR 97/9, May 16, 1997, http://www.iaea.or.at/worldatom/inforesource/pressrelease/prn0997.html (May 23, 1997). Also see Thomas W. Lippman, "Nations Agree to Pact Granting Nuclear Inspectors More Access, Information," *Washington Post*, May 15, 1997; Steve Pagani, "Lessons from Iraq Spur Tougher Atomic Inspections," *Reuters*, May 16, 1997; Alison Smale, "Nuclear Access," *Associated Press*, May 16, 1997.

[19] IAEA, "Protocol Additional to the Agreement(s) Between . . . and the International Atomic Energy Agency for the Application of Safeguards," http://www.iaea.or.at/worldatom/inforesource/press-release/protocol.html (May 23, 1997).

[20] ACDA, "International Nuclear Safeguards Strengthened," op. cit. See also Hooper, presentation before the Carnegie Conference, op. cit.

[21] IAEA, "Protocol Additional to the Agreement(s) Between," op. cit.

As defined by the IAEA Statute, "source material" refers to "uranium containing the mixture of isotopes occurring in nature; uranium depleted in the isotope 235; thorium; any of the foregoing in the form of metal, alloy, chemical compound, or concentrate; any other material containing one or more of the foregoing in such concentration as the Board of Governors shall from time to time determine; and such other material as the Board of Governors shall from time to time determine."

INFCIRC/153, the original model safeguards agreement between the IAEA and non-nuclear-weapon states party to the NPT, provides for the exemption from safeguards of limited quantities of certain nuclear materials at the request of a state, including "[one] kilogram in total of special fissionable material." This kilogram may consist of: "plutonium; uranium with an *enrichment* of 0.2 (20%) and above, taken account of by multiplying its weight by its *enrichment*; and uranium with an *enrichment* below 0.2 (20%) and above that of natural uranium, taken account of by multiplying its weight by five times the square of its *enrichment*." See IAEA, "The Structure and Content of Agreements Between the Agency and States Required In Connection With the Treaty on the Non-Proliferation of Nuclear Weapons," INFCIRC/153, June 1992, p. 11.

[22]IAEA, "Protocol Additional to the Agreement(s) Between," op. cit.

[23]Ibid.

[24]ACDA, "International Nuclear Safeguards Strengthened," op. cit.

[25]Paul Leventhal, Nuclear Control Institute, presentation before the Carnegie Endowment Non-Proliferation Conference: *Enhancing the Tools of the Trade*, Washington, D.C., June 9-10, 1997.

Finance remains a problem for the IAEA. In the late 1980s it endured a seven-year period of zero real growth in its budget. This was followed by the dissolution of the Soviet Union and Russia's inability to pay its contribution in 1991, which resulted in a 13 percent budget cut across the range of the Agency's activities in 1992. This state of affairs has coincided with a large increase in the number of facilities requiring safeguarding following the conclusion of new agreements. The amount of material under IAEA safeguards has more than doubled in the last twelve years while there has been only a small increase in the number of inspectors. In 1993, the safeguards budget was increased by 0.8 percent (to $65 million), and by 1996 to $86 million (with an additional $14.5 million in extra-budgetary resources). The IAEA budget for 1998 was approximately $220 million, supplemented by extrabudgetary contributions amounting to about $18 million. See IAEA, "International Atomic Energy Agency: By the Numbers," http://www.iaea.or.at/worldatom/glance/facts (September 15, 1997).

On the other hand, an IAEA official recently noted that, in the context of the ongoing efforts to achieve efficiencies and utilize technological improvements, the annual cost of safeguarding one "significant quantity" of nuclear material has been reduced from US $3,000 in 1980 to $1,000 in 1995. See Pellaud, "Safeguards: The Evolving Picture," op. cit.

[26]Pellaud, "Safeguards: The Evolving Picture," op. cit.

[27]Leventhal, presentation before the Carnegie Conference, op. cit.

Appendix E
NUCLEAR-WEAPON-FREE ZONES

Regional non-proliferation arrangements such as nuclear-weapon-free zones (NWFZs) are increasingly perceived as supplementary elements of the non-proliferation regime. Even though adherence to the Nuclear Non-Proliferation Treaty (NPT) is now nearly universal, NWFZs politically reinforce NPT arrangements; they accommodate regional sensitivities and can be adapted incrementally.[1] From the perspective of the International Atomic Energy Agency (IAEA), NWFZs provide additional verification and assurance to the international community that non-proliferation is working.[2]

The growing role of NWFZs was reflected in the relevant section of the draft review document of the 1995 NPT Review and Extension Conference. It stated:

> The establishment of nuclear-weapon-free zones on the basis of arrangements freely arrived at among the States of the region concerned, particularly in regions afflicted with conflicts, enhances regional and global peace and security and contributes to the ultimate objective of achieving a world entirely free of nuclear weapons ... such zones constitute an important disarmament measure which greatly strengthens the international non-proliferation regime in all its aspects.[3]

During the Cold War, the United States had little enthusiasm for NWFZs. Soviet proposals for the de-nuclearization of Central Europe and other areas failed to meet a set of U.S. criteria: that the zones actually limit the spread of nuclear weapons; that they not interfere with existing security arrangements; that they provide for adequate verification; that the initiative for them originate in the geographical area concerned; and that all states important to the de-nuclearization of the area participate.[4] The United States did support the initiative by Latin American countries to negotiate the Treaty on the Prohibition of Nuclear Weapons in Latin America (the Treaty of Tlatelolco), for example, but shied away from the South Pacific Nuclear-Free-Zone (SPNFZ) Treaty.

With the end of the Cold War, the nuclear-weapon states have been more willing to support NWFZ treaties. The United States and the other weapon states in 1996 signed the relevant protocols to the Treaties of Rarotonga and Pelindaba, establishing nuclear-weapon-free zones in the South Pacific and in Africa.[5]

The Treaty for the Prohibition of Nuclear Weapons in Latin America and the Caribbean. The 1967 Treaty of Tlatelolco, which was stimulated by the Cuban missile crisis, established a nuclear-weapon-free zone in the Latin America and Caribbean region.[6] Parties to the Tlatelolco treaty agree not to test, use, manufacture, produce, or acquire nuclear weapons; nor to receive, store, install, or deploy nuclear weapons on their territory, even if offered by other states. To verify that these pledges are kept, adherents accept "full-scope" International Atomic Energy Agency (IAEA) safeguards (i.e., comprehensive IAEA inspections of all nuclear activities in the host state). The treaty also establishes a regional inspection organization, the Agency for the Prohibition of Nuclear Weapons in Latin America (OPANAL). Tlatelolco originally recognized the authority of both the IAEA and OPANAL, but an amendment of August 1992 designates the IAEA as the sole authority to carry out special inspections of Tlatelolco parties.[7]

The Tlatelolco treaty has two protocols intended to be binding on states outside the region. Protocol I requires that outside nations that still have territories in Latin America respect the treaty's de-nuclearization requirements with respect to those territories. Protocol II prohibits nuclear-weapon states from threatening to use nuclear arms against treaty parties and pledges them to refrain from bringing nuclear weapons into the region. All nations with territories in the region—the United States, the United Kingdom, France, and the Netherlands—have signed and ratified Protocol I. All nuclear-weapon states have ratified Protocol II.

Under its entry-into-force provisions contained in Article 28, the treaty will become fully effective once all eligible states have signed and ratified the treaty and its two protocols and have concluded "bilateral or multilateral" safeguards agreements with the IAEA. However, a follow-on provision states that all signatories have the "right to waive, wholly or in part" these requirements and declare the treaty in force unilaterally. As of July 1997, 32 nations had ratified the accord and waived this provision so that the treaty would become effective for these countries.[8] By July 1997, the amended treaty was in force for Argentina, Barbados, Brazil, Chile, Guyana, Jamaica, Mexico, Paraguay, Peru, Suriname, Uruguay, and Venezuela.[9]

Cuba, which had earlier made approval of the treaty contingent upon U.S. withdrawal from the Guantanamo naval base, signed the treaty on March 25, 1995—the last state in Latin America to do so. In September 1995, the Cuban deputy foreign minister reported that Cuba was "studying ratifying" the Treaty of Tlatelolco.[10]

The South Pacific Nuclear-Free-Zone Treaty. The movement toward a South Pacific Nuclear-Free-Zone (SPNFZ) treaty was fueled by the decision of France to move its nuclear testing to its Pacific Ocean atolls following Algeria's independence. Even before then, however, there was concern about weapons proliferation in the region stemming from the Cold War and about the prospect that the dumping of nuclear waste at sea would eventually contaminate the marine environment.[11]

The SPNFZ treaty (also known as the Treaty of Rarotonga) opened for signature on August 6, 1985, to establish a nuclear-weapon-free zone in the South Pacific—prohibiting the testing, manufacture, and stationing of nuclear weapons in the region as well as the dumping of radioactive wastes at sea.[12] The treaty control system requires all parties to apply full-scope IAEA safeguards in order to verify "the non-diversion of nuclear material from peaceful nuclear activities to nuclear explosive devices."[13] It also provides for mandatory IAEA "special inspections," if they are deemed necessary, to assure compliance.

According to Article 5, each party "remains free to decide for itself whether to allow visits by foreign ships and aircraft to its ports and airfields, transit of its airspace by foreign aircraft, and navigation by foreign ships in its territorial sea"—consistent with the rights under international law for freedom of navigation on the high seas and innocent passage through territorial waters.[14]

The first protocol to the treaty requires the United States, France, and the United Kingdom—three nuclear-weapon states with territories in the zone—to apply the treaty's prohibitions to those territories. Under the second protocol, the five nuclear-weapon states are prohibited from using or threatening to use nuclear explosive devices against signatories of the treaty. The third protocol bans nuclear testing by the five nuclear-weapon states within the zone area.

The United States—not only concerned about the implications for its own freedom of naval movement but also sensitive to French interest in nuclear testing in the region—declined to sign the protocols for ten years. The French decision to resume testing in September of 1995 aroused protests by Pacific islanders and neighboring countries, forcing France to declare, in January 1996, that it would adopt a nuclear testing moratorium.[15] After this change in French policy, the United States and the United Kingdom joined France in signing the three protocols of the treaty on March 25, 1996.[16] Russia and China had become party to Protocols 2 and 3 in 1988 and 1989, respectively, but did not accede to Protocol 1 because neither had any territories within the zone.[17]

The Treaty of Rarotonga is in force for the following states: Australia, Cook Islands, Fiji, Kiribati, Nauru, New Zealand, Niue, Papua New Guinea, Solomon Islands, Tuvalu, Vanuatu, and Western Samoa.[18] Per Article 15, the treaty has been in force since December 11, 1986, the date of the eighth ratification.[19]

The African Nuclear-Weapon-Free-Zone Treaty. The African Nuclear-Weapon-Free-Zone (ANWFZ) Treaty, also known as the Treaty of Pelindaba, had its origins in the first summit of the Organization of African Unity (OAU) in Cairo in July 1964, when participants called for a treaty to ensure that Africa would be free of nuclear weapons.[20] The 32-year quest for a nuclear-free zone culminated in the signing of the Treaty of Pelindaba by more than 40 African nations at a Cairo ceremony on April 11, 1996. When the treaty enters into force, it will prohibit the research, development, manufacture, stockpiling, acquisition, testing, possession, and control or stationing of nuclear weapons—as well as the dumping of radioactive wastes—within the treaty zone.[21]

The verification provisions require all parties to conclude comprehensive safeguards agreements with the IAEA to ensure the peaceful nature of their nuclear activities. The treaty also establishes a regional body, the African Commission on Nuclear Energy, as a complementary mechanism to verify compliance. Under Annex IV of the treaty, the Commission is responsible for implementing complaint procedures. However, if the Commission determines that there is sufficient evidence in a complaint to warrant a "special inspection," it "may request the [IAEA] to conduct such [an] inspection as soon as possible." The Commission may also designate its representatives to accompany the IAEA inspection team.

The treaty goes beyond earlier NWFZ models in a number of ways.[22] First, it calls for "the highest standards of security and effective physical protection of nuclear materials, facilities and equipment."[23] Second, it prohibits "any action aimed at an armed attack by conventional or other means against nuclear installations" in the zone. Third, the treaty calls for the declaration and dismantlement of any clandestine nuclear weapons capabilities that have existed prior to the treaty's entry into force (as was accomplished in the South Africa case).

Under Protocol I, the United States, France, the United Kingdom, the Russian Federation, and China are invited to agree "not to use or threaten to use a nuclear explosive device against" any party to the treaty or against any territory of a Protocol III party within the African nuclear-weapon-free zone. Under Protocol II, the United States, France, the United Kingdom, the Russian Federation, and China are invited to agree "not to test or assist or encourage the testing of any nuclear explosive device anywhere" within the zone. Protocol III is open for signature to states responsible for territories in the zone—specifically Spain and France—obligating them to observe the prohibitions of the treaty with respect to their territories.

China, France, the United Kingdom, and the United States signed the first two protocols to the treaty on the day it was opened for signature on April 11, 1996, in Cairo. France also signed Protocol III covering territories in the region. Both the United States and Britain argued, however, that neither the treaty nor its protocols apply to the military base on the island of Diego Garcia in the Indian Ocean—and thus do not prohibit the possible presence of U.S. nuclear weapons there.[24] Because Russia wanted to examine this U.S./U.K. position, it did not sign Protocols I and II until May 11, 1996.[25]

The treaty will enter into force upon its twenty-eighth ratification; the protocols will also enter into force at that time for those protocol signatories that have deposited their instruments of ratification. As of February 1998, 49 out of the 53 eligible African states had signed the treaty—Botswana, Equatorial Guinea, Madagascar, and Somalia being the non-signatory states. As of that date, Algeria, Gambia, and Mauritius were the only states to have deposited their instruments of ratification; Spain had not yet signed Protocol III.[26]

Shortly after the treaty's protocols had been signed, statements from U.S. officials appeared to contradict the "negative" security assurances embodied in Protocol I. In signing the protocol, the United States pledged "not to use or threaten to use a nuclear explosive device against [any party to the treaty]." In a White House briefing statement on the same day, the U.S. Administration appeared to undercut the intent and meaning of the protocol by stating that it "will not limit options available to the United States in response to an attack by [a treaty] party using weapons of mass destruction."[27] The U.S. position appears to rely on a rule of international law known as the "doctrine of belligerent reprisals." Under this doctrine, the United States could reserve the right to use weapons that are considered illegal (as nuclear weapons would be if used against an ANWFZ party) in response to aggression with illegal weapons against U.S. forces or allies (e.g., chemical or biological weapons) if: (1) the response were proportional to the attack; (2) the U.S. use of nuclear weapons were in direct response to the attack; and (3) the U.S. use of nuclear weapons were necessary to end the attack.[28]

The Southeast Asian Nuclear-Weapon-Free-Zone Treaty. The seven member states of the Association of South East Asian Nations (ASEAN), as well as Burma, Cambodia, and Laos, met in Bangkok on December 15, 1995, to sign the Southeast Asian Nuclear-Weapon-Free-Zone (SEANWFZ) Treaty.[29] The treaty prohibits member countries from manufacturing, possessing, testing, or threatening to use nuclear weapons. SEANWFZ also bans the dumping of nuclear waste in Southeast Asian waters. Individual states may decide whether, in specific instances, to allow the "innocent passage" of nuclear-armed planes and ships of the five nuclear-weapon states through ASEAN territories.[30]

ASEAN also invited the five nuclear-weapon states to sign a protocol to the treaty acknowledging the nuclear-weapon-free zone. The United States and China indicated that they had concerns about signing the protocol, arguing it was too restrictive.[31] In June 1996, U.S. Ambassador Thomas Graham said that the United States was interested in becoming a party to the SEANWFZ Treaty, but that it could not do so unless U.S. security concerns were met. U.S. reservations centered on the treaty's application of a 200-mile exclusive economic zone, which could affect the free passage of nuclear-powered vessels through Southeast Asian waters and interfere with the U.N. Law of the Sea Convention.[32] In July 1996, ASEAN expressed its readiness to reconsider the protocol to the SEANWFZ Treaty in order to accommodate the United States and other established nuclear-weapon states.[33] Later in the year, ASEAN announced that it would negotiate with the five nuclear powers over legal issues and matters pertaining to the exclusive economic zone.[34] At the 1997 PrepCom, the nuclear-weapon states restated their readiness "to work with the signatories of the South East Asian Nuclear-Weapon-Free-Zone Treaty to remove those obstacles currently preventing [them] from signing the Protocol to the Treaty."[35]

The SEANWFZ Treaty came into force on March 27, 1997, after both Cambodia and Singapore deposited their instruments of ratification. As of November 1, 1997, Indonesia and the Philippines were the only two treaty signatories that had not yet ratified the treaty.[36]

Prospects: Other Nuclear-Weapon-Free-Zone Discussions

Several other regional groups have expressed interest in establishing nuclear-weapon-free zones—some of them decades ago—although as of December 1997 none of these had come to fruition.

The Middle East and South Asia. These two geographically and politically distinct regions have been the subject of separate NWFZ proposals. In the case of South Asia, NWFZ proposals date back to the 1960s but have been strongly opposed by India and therefore have never gathered momentum. NWFZ proposals for the Middle East also go back some time but have gathered more interest only in the last few years. Both regions have experienced considerable proliferation, however, and this may now be the most serious technical obstacle to actually designing and implementing a NWFZ. Deep rivalries in both regions also make the prospects politically less promising than in other regions.

Central Europe. Proposals for a Central European nuclear-weapon-free zone were occasionally raised during the Cold War, but a new proposal formulated by Belarus surfaced recently—partly as a reaction to the plans for the enlargement eastward of the North Atlantic Treaty Organization (NATO). Belarus's proposal failed to win broader regional support, particularly among former Warsaw Pact states. NATO has already removed all of its deployed ground-based nuclear forces from Western Europe and, in conjunction with enlargement, has adopted policies that would avoid stationing nuclear weapons in the territory of new members in Central Europe. As a practical matter, Central Europe has been free of nuclear weapons since the withdrawal of Soviet (Russian after the collapse of the USSR) nuclear forces from East Germany and the former Warsaw Pact states—a process that subsequently was extended to Belarus and Ukraine.

Central Asia. Prospects for a formal Central Asian nuclear-weapon-free zone are promising. Led by Kazakhstan and Uzbekistan, discussion has proceeded on a NWFZ proposal, and a meeting to discuss the proposal has been tentatively scheduled to take place in Bishkek, Kyrgyz Republic, in 1998. The Central Asian proposal provides for frequent consultation with the five established nuclear-weapon states, and has a good chance of winning their support.

NOTES

[1] Mark G. McDonough, "Strengthening the Non-Proliferation Regime: Selected Analyses, Findings, and Recommendations," A summary report of the March 1992 Carnegie Endowment Non-Proliferation Conference (Washington, DC: Carnegie Endowment for International Peace, June 1992), p. 8.

Some proponents of NWFZs view them as an alternative to the NPT regime because of the latter's apparent weakness in exposing covert proliferants such as Iraq.

[2] Jan Priest, "The Role of the IAEA in Nuclear-Weapon-Free Zones and Its Relationship with the Brazilian-Argentine Agency for the Accounting and Control of Nuclear Materials," Proceedings from the February 1996 Carnegie Endowment Non-Proliferation Conference (Washington, DC: Carnegie Endowment for International Peace, June 1996), p. 1.

[3] Ibid. See also 1995 Review and Extension Conference of the Parties to the Treaty on the Non-Proliferation of Nuclear Weapons, April 17-May 12, 1995, "Decision 2: Principles and Objectives for Nuclear Non-Proliferation and Disarmament," NPT/CONF.1995/32/DEC.2, May 11, 1995.

At the 1997 PrepCom, in the Chairman's Paper, annexed to the PrepCom Report, Committee participants welcomed "the steps taken to conclude further Nuclear Weapon Free Zone Treaties since 1995 and [reaffirmed] the conviction that the establishment of internationally recognized nuclear-weapon-free zones freely arrived at among the States concerned, enhances global and regional peace and security." See Chairman's Paper, April 17, 1997, http://www.basicint.org.

[4] ACDA, "Treaty for the Prohibition of Nuclear Weapons in Latin America: Narrative," http://www.acda.gov/treaties/latin.htm (February 20, 1997). Also see Zachary S. Davis, "The Spread of Nuclear-Weapon-Free Zones: Building a New Nuclear Bargain," *Arms Control Today,* February 1986, p. 16.

[5] The five states have noted that their signing of these protocols was in line with security assurances they had provided in their national declarations and in U.N. Resolution 984. See Preparatory Committee for the 2000 Review Conference of the Parties to the Treaty on the Non-Proliferation of Nuclear Weapons (PrepCom), First Session, New York 7–18 April 1997. Statement made by H. E. Mrs. Joelle Bourgois, Head of the French Delegation, on behalf of the delegations of France, the People's Republic of China, the Russian Federation, the United Kingdom of Great Britain and Northern Ireland, and the United States of America on Nuclear Non-Proliferation and Disarmament, April 8, 1997. See also ACDA, U.S. Statement by the Honorable Lawrence Scheinman to NPT Preparatory Committee Meeting, April 8, 1997. Both statements are on the BASIC web site (http://www.basicint.org). See also Evelyn Leopold, "Five Nuclear Powers Reaffirm Anti-Nuke Pledges," *Reuters,* April 8, 1997.

[6] The original title of the treaty was Treaty for the Prohibition of Nuclear Weapons in Latin America. As a result of the first amending of the treaty in July 1990, the phrase "and the Caribbean" was added to the title. See ACDA, *Arms Control and Disarmament Agreements: Texts and Histories of Negotiations* (Washington, DC: Government Printing Office, 1982), p. 59; ACDA, "Treaty for the Prohibition of Nuclear Weapons in Latin America: Narrative," op. cit.

The second amending of the treaty in May 1991 modified paragraph 2 of Article 25, in effect, to allow "nonautonomous territories" to become parties to the treaty once they attained their independence. In its original form the paragraph had excluded political entities "part or all of whose territory" was in dispute with "an extra-continental country and one or more Latin American States" prior to the date the treaty was opened for signature. ACDA, "Treaty for the Prohibition of Nuclear Weapons in Latin America: Narrative," op. cit., (the treaty text can be accessed at http://www.acda.gov/treaties.latin2.htm).

[7] ACDA, "Treaty for the Prohibition of Nuclear Weapons in Latin America: Narrative," op. cit.

[8] The treaty is in force for the following nations: Antigua and Barbuda, Argentina, the Bahamas, Barbados, Belize, Bolivia, Brazil, Chile, Colombia, Costa Rica, Dominica, Dominican Republic, Ecuador, El Salvador, Grenada, Guatemala, Guyana, Haiti, Honduras, Jamaica, Mexico, Nicaragua, Panama, Paraguay, Peru, St. Kitts/Nevis, St. Lucia, St. Vincent/Grenadines, Suriname, Trinidad and Tobago, Uruguay, and Venezuela. Communication with the Office of the Secretary General of the Agency for the Prohibition of Nuclear Weapons in Latin America and the Caribbean, September 4, 1997.

[9] ACDA, "Treaty for the Prohibition of Nuclear Weapons in Latin America: Narrative," op. cit.

[10] *Arms Control Reporter, 1995,* p. 452.B.169 and p. 452.B.175.

[11] Priest, "The Role of the IAEA in Nuclear-Weapon-Free Zones," op. cit., p. 3.

[12] See ACDA, "South Pacific Nuclear-Free-Zone Treaty," Factsheet, May 20, 1996, http://www.acda.gov/factsheet/nwfz/spnwfz.htm (February 20, 1997). For text see ACDA, "South Pacific Nuclear-Free-Zone Treaty: Text," http://www.acda.gov/treaties/spnwfz.htm (February 20, 1997).

[13] Priest, "The Role of the IAEA in Nuclear-Weapon-Free Zones," op. cit., p. 3.

[14] ACDA, "SPNFZ Treaty: Text," op. cit. Also see "White House Briefing by Robert Bell," *Federal News Service,* March 22, 1996.

[15] Davis, "The Spread of Nuclear-Weapon-Free Zones," op. cit., pp. 17, 18.

[16] "Nuclear Treaty," *Associated Press,* March 25, 1996.

The United States, France, and Britain announced in October 1995 that they would ratify the protocols of the Treaty of Rarotonga in the first half of 1996, as soon as France completed its nuclear test series in the area. See "Nuclear Free Zone to be Unveiled: France, Britain, U.S. to Sign Off on South Pacific Area," *Washington Times,* October 20, 1995.

[17] See ACDA, "South Pacific Nuclear-Free-Zone Treaty," Factsheet, op. cit.

[18] The Marshall Islands refused to sign the SPNFZ treaty stating that if it became a signatory it would have to continue living with nuclear waste since the treaty bans the transport and disposal of nuclear waste in the region. "Marshall Islands Refuses to Sign Nuclear-Free-Zone Treaty," *FBIS,* March 28, 1996.

Tonga signed the SPNFZ Treaty on August 2, 1996, but has not ratified it. Palau and Micronesia are the only other South Pacific nations not to have signed the treaty. ACDA SPNFZ Factsheet, http://www.acda.gov/factshee/nwfz/spnwfz.htm (December 10, 1997).

The French Polynesian Parliament approved the SPNFZ treaty in July 1996. "French Polynesia: Parliament Approves Nuclear-Free-Zone Treaty," *FBIS,* July 12, 1996.

[19] ACDA, "SPNFZ Treaty Text," op. cit.

[20] The United States has supported the idea of such a treaty since the first United Nations General Assembly resolution on this issue in 1965. It has also made an important contribution to the drafting of the final text of the Treaty and each Protocol. See ACDA, "African Nuclear-Weapon-Free-Zone Treaty," Factsheet, May 1996, http:/www.acda.gov/factsheet/nwfz/whanwfz.htm (February 24, 1997).

[21] For text see ACDA, "The African Nuclear-Weapon-Free Zone Treaty (Treaty of Pelindaba): Text," http://www.acda.gov/treaties/afrinwfz.htm (November 1, 1997). Also see ACDA, "African Nuclear-Weapon-Free-Zone Treaty," Factsheet, op. cit.

[22] Priest, "The Role of the IAEA in Nuclear-Weapon-Free Zones," op. cit., p. 3.

[23] ACDA, "ANWFZ Treaty: Text," op. cit.

[24] *The Arms Control Reporter 1996,* p. 455.B.111.

[25] "Russia, Spain Refuse to Sign Pelindaba Treaty," *FBIS-NES,* April 15, 1996; *The Arms Control Reporter 1996,* p. 455.B.115.

[26] See ACDA, "The African Nuclear-Weapon-Free-Zone Treaty (The Treaty of Pelindaba): Signatories," http://www.acda.gov/treaties/afnwsigs.htm (November 1, 1997).

[27] George Bunn, "Expanding Nuclear Options: Is the U.S. Negating Its Non-Use Pledges?" *Arms Control Today,* May/June 1996, p. 7. See also White House Briefing, *Federal News Service,* April 11, 1996.

In 1978, and again in 1995, the United States provided "negative" security assurances that it would not use nuclear weapons against non-nuclear-weapon states party to the NPT. However, since the 1991 Gulf War the United States appears to have staked out the option to use nuclear weapons to deter the use of WMD. This doctrine was reaffirmed by Secretary of Defense William Perry in his Senate testimony of March 28, 1996: "[As] we stated during the Gulf War, if any country were foolish enough to use chemical weapons against the United States, the response will be 'absolutely overwhelming' and 'devastating' " (William Perry, Prepared Statement, before the Senate Committee on Foreign Relations, March 28, 1996). When asked to clarify, Perry said, "[w]e would not specify in advance what our response to a chemical attack is, except to say that it would be devastating. And we have a wide range of military capabilities to make good on that threat." Senator Pell asked if that range included conventional and nuclear weapons and Perry responded, "The whole range would be considered, that's correct." ("Hearing of the Senate Foreign Relations Committee," *Federal News Service,* March 28, 1996.) Also see Doctrine for Joint Nuclear Operations, Joint Chiefs of Staff Pub 3-12, April 29, 1993; Doctrine for Joint Nuclear Operations, Joint Chiefs of Staff Pub 3-12.1, February 9, 1996.

[28] Discussion with U.S. officials, Spring 1996. See also Bunn, "Expanding Nuclear Options," op. cit., p. 9. George Bunn, a leading expert on security assurances, has criticized the apparent adoption by the United States of this doctrine, *inter alia,* because it makes a "mockery of existing and planned U.S. treaty commitments—which are now or will be legally binding—under a growing number of NWFZ treaties."

[29] ASEAN is currently made up of Indonesia, Malaysia, Singapore, Thailand, Brunei, Vietnam, and the Philippines.

[30] For treaty text, see ASEAN, "Treaty on the Southeast Asia Nuclear-Weapon-Free Zone," http://www.asean.or.id under "Political and Security Cooperation: Basic Political Documents" (May 29, 1997).

[31] Chris Johnson, "ASEAN to Modify Pact to Appease Nuclear States," *Reuters,* December 14, 1995.

[32] Thomas Graham Jr., Special Representative of the President for Arms Control, Non-Proliferation, and Disarmament, "U.S. Wants to Join Southeast Asian Nuclear-Zone Treaty," Press Conference in Kuala Lumpur, June 6, 1996. See also Davis, "The Spread of Nuclear-Weapon-Free Zones," op. cit., p. 17.

[33] "Indonesia's Alatas: ASEAN 'To Reconsider' SEANWFZ Treaty," *FBIS,* July 22, 1996.

[34] "ASEAN Agrees to Submit Proposals to Nuclear Powers," *FBIS,* October 22, 1996.

[35] PrepCom, First Session. Statement made by H. E. Mrs. Joelle Bourgois, op. cit.

In April 1997 the Chinese foreign minister stated that China would support the Southeast Asian NWFZ treaty. "Nuclear Free Zone Treaty Gets Backing from China," *Thailand Times* (Bangkok), April 8, 1997.

[36] "Southeast Asia Becomes a Nuclear-Free Zone," *Jane's Defence Weekly,* April 9, 1997.

Appendix F
NUCLEAR SUPPLIER ORGANIZATIONS[1]

Two informal groups of nuclear supplier states control exports of equipment and materials that can be used to make nuclear weapons and function as components of the non-proliferation regime. The Non-Proliferation Treaty Exporters Committee (also known as the Zangger Committee, after its Swiss former chairman) was set up in the early 1970s to establish guidelines for the export control provisions of Article III(2) of the Nuclear Non-Proliferation Treaty (NPT).[2] In August 1974 the Zangger Committee adopted a set of guidelines and a "trigger list" of export items whose sale would be permitted only to recipients willing to accept International Atomic Energy Agency (IAEA) safeguards. The Zangger guidelines and "trigger list" comprised the first mechanism for uniform regulation of nuclear exports by the principal nuclear supplier states that were NPT parties.

India's nuclear test in 1974 was the catalyst for the formation in January 1976 of the Nuclear Suppliers Group (NSG), which first met in London and was called the London Group. France, not then a party to the NPT, joined the NSG. The NSG adopted guidelines that were similar to those of the Zangger Committee but went beyond the Zangger guidelines in restraining transfers of uranium-enrichment and plutonium-extraction equipment and technology.

In April 1992, in the wake of the Gulf War, the NSG expanded its export control guidelines, which until then had covered only uniquely nuclear items, to cover 65 "dual-use" items as well. In addition, the NSG added the requirement for future exports that recipient states accept IAEA inspection on all of their peaceful nuclear activities. This full-scope or comprehensive safeguards rule effectively precludes nuclear commerce by NSG member states with states such as India, Israel, and Pakistan, which refuse to accept IAEA safeguards on their entire nuclear infrastructure.[3]

The Zangger Committee: Formation. Shortly after the NPT came into force in 1970, a number of nuclear supplier countries began consultations on the standards that should be applied when exporting nuclear fuel and equipment to non-nuclear-weapon states. These consultations were necessary to implement the NPT requirement that exports of nuclear equipment and any special nuclear materials (i.e., enriched uranium or plutonium) produced through their use must be subject to IAEA safeguards in the recipient state. On the basis of these consultations, in August 1974 the governments of Australia, Denmark, Canada, Finland, West Germany, the Netherlands, Norway, the Soviet Union, the United Kingdom, and the United States each wrote the Director General of the IAEA to inform him that they intended to require IAEA safeguards on their nuclear exports. To each letter was attached a memorandum that had been coordinated in advance. The memoranda were identical, and each

included the "trigger list" of special nuclear materials (enriched uranium and plutonium) and items of nuclear equipment that were "especially designed or prepared" (EDP) for the production of these materials. The memoranda declared that these items would be exported only if the recipient agreed to place them under IAEA safeguards; agreed that they would be used only for peaceful purposes; and agreed to retransfer such items only under the same conditions.[4]

Soon afterward, Austria, Czechoslovakia, East Germany, Ireland, Japan, Luxembourg, Poland, and Sweden—all countries with nuclear industrial capacity—were drawn into similar rounds of consultation. Each later sent its own letter to the Director General, referring to and enclosing memoranda identical to those transmitted by the initial group of governments. The Zangger Committee thus encompassed nuclear-supplier states in both Eastern and Western Europe, as well as Japan, which was at that time virtually the only Asian country with nuclear export capabilities.

The Zangger Committee collaboration had great significance for several reasons. It was the first attempt to strictly and uniformly enforce the obligations of Article III(2) of the NPT, requiring safeguards on nuclear exports. It was a cooperative means of dissuading supplier states from allowing their industrial firms to cut corners on safeguards requirements because of competition in the sale of nuclear equipment and fuel-cycle services. It established the principle that nuclear-supplier nations should consult and agree among themselves on procedures to regulate the international market for nuclear materials and equipment in order to prevent nuclear proliferation. Notably absent from the list of actual participants or potential suppliers—as from the list of parties to the NPT—were France, India, and the People's Republic of China.

Zangger Committee: Developments. Due to advances in technology, items on the Zangger trigger list (especially those related to enrichment, reprocessing, and heavy-water production equipment) had to be updated and clarified during the 1980s. Prompted by the discovery that Iraq secretly was pursuing a variety of uranium-enrichment technologies, the Zangger Committee in 1993 added those enrichment technologies to the trigger list (e.g., electro-magnetic isotope separation (EMIS) and chemical or ion exchange techniques) that previously had been omitted.

Changes to the trigger list are integrated into export control legislation and regulations voluntarily by Committee members. At any given time, therefore, the laws and practices of member states may be slightly different, but consultations help achieve a measure of uniformity in actual export practices. Unlike the NSG, the Zangger Committee controls only nuclear-specific EDP items. It does not control dual-use equipment or technology; nor does it call on participants to exercise particular restraint in the supply of sensitive technology and equipment (e.g., items related to plutonium reprocessing and uranium enrichment). The Zangger Committee guidelines also do not require comprehensive IAEA safeguards as a condition of supply; they merely require safeguards on the items supplied and the facilities in which they are used. The Committee has held discussions on introducing the full-scope safeguards requirement as a condition of supply around the year 2000.[5] However, since China opposes this requirement and has now joined the Committee, introducing this requirement may be delayed.[6]

As of December 1997, the members of the Zangger Committee were: Argentina, Australia, Austria, Belgium, Bulgaria, Canada, China, the Czech Republic, Denmark, France, Finland, Germany, Greece, Hungary, Ireland, Italy, Japan, Luxembourg, the Netherlands, Norway, Poland, Portugal, Romania, Russia, Slovakia, South Africa, South Korea, Spain, Sweden, Switzerland, Ukraine, the United Kingdom, and the United States.

The Nuclear Suppliers Group: Formation. Within a year of the transmission of Zangger guidelines to the IAEA Director General, a second series of nuclear supplier state negotiations was begun in November 1974. Convened at the initiative of the United States, this round created the NSG in response to three developments: (1) India's unexpected nuclear test of May 1974, (2) mounting evidence that the pricing actions of the Organization of Petroleum Exporting Countries (OPEC) were stimulating Third World and other non-nuclear states to invest in nuclear power, and (3) growing efforts by France and West Germany to market enrichment and reprocessing facilities to Third World states.

The initial NSG members were Canada, the Federal Republic of Germany, France, Japan, the Soviet Union, the United Kingdom, and the United States. France insisted that the meetings be secret. It soon became known, however, that such meetings were taking place, generating suspicion about the group's purposes. An inaccurate perception arose that the group was an export "cartel." In fact, one of the group's purposes was to foster genuine commercial competition based on quality and prices but untainted by any undercutting of proliferation controls.

NSG members wrestled first with whether, or under what conditions, the most sensitive parts of the nuclear fuel cycle from a weapons proliferation perspective, could be sold to non-nuclear states. The United States strongly urged that the group deny transfers of sensitive technology to new recipients and adopt a commitment that plutonium reprocessing be restricted to facilities under multinational control (rather than in installations under the control of individual states). France had already signed contracts to sell reprocessing plants to Pakistan and South Korea, however, and West Germany had agreed to sell to Brazil technology and facilities for the full fuel cycle (both enrichment

and reprocessing). Hence, France and West Germany objected to any prohibition.

The second key issue area concerned whether full-scope (comprehensive) IAEA safeguards should be made a condition of all nuclear sales to non-nuclear-weapon states. The NSG came close to consensus on requiring full-scope safeguards as a condition of future supply commitments, but the French and the West Germans resisted accepting this as a common requirement. At the time, a full-scope safeguards rule would have blocked new nuclear exports to Argentina, Brazil, India, Israel, Pakistan, and South Africa, since none of these developing countries allowed comprehensive IAEA inspections. The NSG did act to expand safeguards coverage of exports when its members agreed to a trigger list (similar to that of the Zangger Committee) that itemized nuclear technologies and equipment that could be exported only if the recipient agreed to allow the IAEA to apply its safeguards.

On January 27, 1976, the seven original NSG members exchanged letters endorsing a uniform code for conducting international nuclear sales. The major provisions of the agreement required that, before nuclear materials, equipment, or technology are transferred, the recipient state must:

(1) Pledge not to use the transferred materials, equipment, or technology in the manufacture of nuclear explosives of any kind;

(2) Accept, with no provision for termination, international safeguards on all transferred materials and on all facilities employing transferred equipment or technology, including any enrichment, reprocessing, or heavy-water production facility that replicates or otherwise employs transferred technology;

(3) Provide adequate physical security for transferred nuclear facilities and materials to prevent theft and sabotage;

(4) Agree not to retransfer the materials, equipment, or technology to third countries unless they, too, accepted the constraints on use, replication, security, and transfer, and unless the original supplier nation concurred in the transactions;

(5) Employ "restraint" in considering any proposed export of "sensitive" items (relating to uranium enrichment, spent-fuel reprocessing, and heavy-water production); and

(6) Encourage the concept of multilateral (in lieu of national) regional facilities for reprocessing and enrichment.[7]

The industrialized states of both Western and Eastern Europe soon joined the NSG, so that it then included virtually all of the advanced nuclear supplier countries.

The NSG Guidelines went beyond the NPT and the Zangger Committee requirements by imposing safeguards not only on the export of nuclear materials and equipment but also on the export of nuclear technology (e.g., engineering, design, and industrial process information). India had demonstrated the existence of this serious loophole by building its own unsafeguarded replicas of a safeguarded power reactor imported from Canada. The NSG was unable to agree on the application of this principle to reactor technology, however. While the NSG stopped short of absolutely prohibiting the export of sensitive facilities, it raised the consciousness of members about the dangers involved, so that the agreement to "exercise restraint" was meaningful. For subsequent transfers of enrichment plants, NSG members agreed to insist on recipient end-use assurances that only low-enriched uranium (useful for reactors but not for weapons) would be produced.

Nuclear Suppliers Group: Developments. Following the lull in NSG policy-making during the 1980s, the 1991 Gulf War reawakened NSG innovation. At the Hague in March 1991, the NSG decided to adopt the clarified and upgraded specifications on the Zangger Committee trigger list. The exercise, known as "harmonization," was completed in 1992. During 1993, the NSG added another category to its trigger list: uranium conversion plants and equipment—items that are not covered by the Zangger Committee's list.

In Warsaw in March/April 1992, the NSG took a major step forward when its members agreed that, as a condition of supply to any non-nuclear-weapon state, all export contracts involving EDP trigger list items after April 1992 must require that full-scope safeguards be present in the recipient's territory in perpetuity. Updated guidelines on this point were issued by the IAEA in July 1993. The NSG also agreed in 1993 to add to its own trigger list the more specific equipment items and components used for uranium enrichment that had been identified earlier in the Zangger Committee.[8]

In the NSG's Hague meeting of March 1991, members also agreed on the need to expand supplier controls to cover dual-use items that are often used in nuclear activities but that also have legitimate non-nuclear uses. (The original NSG and Zangger Committee rules apply only to "nuclear-unique" equipment and material.) An NSG working group met, under U.S. stewardship, in Brussels in June 1991, in Annapolis in October 1991, and in Interlaken in January 1992—and produced agreement on a list of 65 dual-use items with detailed definitions and a series of guidelines on conditions of transfer. These were formally endorsed by the full plenary meeting of the NSG in Warsaw in April 1992.

The dual-use guidelines—published by the IAEA in July 1992—require exporters not to ship items on the list if they are for use by non-nuclear-weapon states in unsafeguarded nuclear-fuel-cycle facilities or in nuclear explosive activity. They require states not to transfer items on the list "when there is an unacceptable risk of diversion to such an activity, or when the transfers are contrary to the objective of averting the proliferation of nuclear weapons." Suppliers must obtain a written statement from the recipient on the use to which the item will be put and where it will be located, as well as assurances that the item will not be used for proscribed purposes and that no retransfer will take place without the consent of the supplier. Decisions on whether a transfer should proceed are also to be guided by additional criteria, such as the recipient's good or poor non-proliferation credentials.[9]

Although decisions on whether to grant export licenses are left to national discretion, there is a system of consultation among members to ensure uniformity in the implementation of the dual-use guidelines and to guard against commercial disadvantage to a particular state if it denies a transfer request. Members are also encouraged to consult and exchange information on proliferation developments that might be relevant to licensing decisions.[10] Modern communication and electronic bulletin-board technology are now in use among members to expedite information sharing and consultation.[11]

NOTES

[1] This section is adapted from Charles N. Van Doren, "Nuclear Supply and Non-Proliferation: The IAEA Committee on Assurances of Supply," A Report for the Congressional Research Service (Rep. No. 83-202-8), October 1983, pp. 61-64; and Ewen Buchanan, "The Non-Proliferation Regime," unpublished consultant's report for the Carnegie Endowment for International Peace, March 1994.

[2] The Article states: "Each State Party to the Treaty undertakes not to provide: (a) source or special fissionable material, or (b) equipment or material especially designed or prepared for the processing, use or production of special fissionable material, to any non-nuclear-weapon State for peaceful purposes, unless the source or special fissionable material shall be subject to the safeguards required by this article." See ACDA, "Multilateral Nuclear Export Control Regimes," Factsheet, http://www.acda.gov/factshee/expt-con/nuexpcnt.htm (November 1, 1997).

[3] In addition to agreeing to such full-scope safeguards, all nations importing regulated items from NSG member states must promise to furnish adequate physical security for transferred nuclear materials and facilities, pledge not to export nuclear materials and technologies to other nations without the permission of the original exporting nation or without a pledge from the recipient nation to abide by these same rules; and promise not to use any imports to build nuclear explosives. (Similar rules—apart from the full-scope safeguards requirement—apply to exports regulated by the Zangger Committee,

which continues to function, although it has been partially eclipsed by the Nuclear Suppliers Group, whose export controls have in general been more far-reaching.)

[4] The individual letters and the identical memoranda were published by the IAEA in September 1974 in document INFCIRC/209. INFCIRC is the IAEA shorthand for the series of Information Circulars distributed to IAEA members.

[5] Mark Hibbs, "China to Join Zangger Committee, But Not With Full-Scope Safeguards," *Nucleonics Week,* October 2, 1997, p. 1.

[6] China attended the May 1997 Zangger Committee meeting as an observer and, on September 30, 1997, announced that it would join the Committee as a full member. However, China indicated that it was not prepared to reverse its policy of not requiring comprehensive safeguards as a condition of supply, apparently because of its continued civil nuclear trade with India and Pakistan. Hence the Committee's earlier plan to adopt this requirement by the turn of the century may be deferred. Mark Hibbs, "China Attends Zangger Meeting, Might Join Committee After Talks," *Nuclear Fuel,* June 2, 1997, p. 8; Hibbs, "China to Join Zangger Committee," op. cit, p. 1.

[7] These guidelines were published by the IAEA as "Guidelines for Nuclear Transfers," (INFCIRC/254, Part 1).

[8] See INFCIRC/254/Rev.1/Part 1. At the NSG plenary held in Helsinki on April 5-7, 1995, the NSG reviewed the Guidelines for

Nuclear Transfers, and some changes were made, particularly with respect to fuel fabrication items.

[9] Known as "Guidelines for Transfers of Nuclear-Related Dual-Use Equipment, Material and Related Technology" (INFCIRC/254/Rev.1/Part 2).

[10] For further details of the development of the dual-use arrangement and the adoption of full-scope safeguards as a condition of supply, see Carlton E. Thorne, "The Nuclear Suppliers Group: A Major Success Story Gone Unnoticed," *Directors Series on Proliferation,* Lawrence Livermore Laboratory, January 5, 1994, p. 29.

[11] In the early 1990s, the United States suggested a secure computer-based bulletin-board system for information sharing that had been in use unofficially, and on a limited basis, among some NSG parties. (Communication with U.S. State Department official, November 5, 1997.)

Additional References

Carlton E. Thorne, ed., *A Guide to Nuclear Export Controls* (Burke, VA: Proliferation Data Services, 1997 edition); U.S. Congress, Office of Technology Assessment, *Nuclear Proliferation and Safeguards,* pp. 220-21; U.S. Department of State, "Report to the Congress Pursuant to Section 601 of the Nuclear Non-Proliferation Act of 1978," January 1979, pp. 25-27; Charles N. Van Doren, "Nuclear Supply and Non-Proliferation: The IAEA Committee on Assurances of Supply," A Report for the Congressional Research Service (Rep. No. 83-202-8), October 1983, pp. 61-64; U.S. Congress, Office of Technology Assessment, *Proliferation of Weapons of Mass Destruction: Assessing the Risks,* August 1993, pp. 85, 88; Zachary S. Davis, "Non-Proliferation Regimes: Policies to Control the Spread of Nuclear, Chemical and Biological Weapons and Missiles," Congressional Research Service, February 8, 1993; Gary T. Gardner, *Nuclear Nonproliferation: A Primer* (Boulder, CO: Lynne Rienner Publishers, 1994), p. 58; Roland Timerbaev and Lisa Moskowitz, *Inventory of International Nonproliferation Organizations and Regimes* (Monterey, CA: Monterey Institute of International Studies, 1994-1995); ACDA, "Multilateral Nuclear Export Control Regimes," Factsheet, December 17, 1996; Tariq Rauf, James Lamson, Swawna McCartney and Sarah Meek, *Inventory of International Nonproliferation Organizations and Regimes* (Monterey, CA: Monterey Institute of International Studies, 1996-1997).

As of December 1997, the 34 members of the NSG were: Argentina, Australia, Austria, Belgium, Brazil, Bulgaria, Canada, the Czech Republic, Denmark, France, Finland, Germany, Greece, Hungary, Ireland, Italy, Japan, Luxembourg, Netherlands, New Zealand, Norway, Poland, Portugal, Romania, Russia, Slovakia, South Africa, South Korea, Spain, Sweden, Switzerland, Ukraine, the United Kingdom, and the United States.

THE MISSILE TECHNOLOGY CONTROL REGIME

The Missile Technology Control Regime (MTCR) was announced in April 1987 by the group of seven industrialized countries (G-7)—Canada, France, the Federal Republic of Germany, Italy, Japan, the United Kingdom, and the United States. The MTCR consists of an export control policy and the institutional measures to implement it.

The impetus for the MTCR came from U.S. National Security Decision Directive 70, signed by President Ronald Reagan in November 1982. That directive made it U.S. policy to "hinder" the proliferation of nuclear-capable missiles and to seek the cooperation of other supplier nations in doing so. More than four years of negotiations were required to reach agreement on the regime.

Originally, the purpose of the MTCR was to reduce the risk of nuclear proliferation by limiting the spread of ballistic and cruise missiles capable of delivering nuclear weapons. The original export controls focused on rocket and unmanned air vehicle systems capable of delivering a 500-kg payload (considered to be the mass of a relatively unsophisticated nuclear warhead) to a range of 300 km (considered to be a strategic distance in the most compact theaters where nuclear weapons might be used).[1]

In January 1993, the G-7 and 15 additional governments that by then had joined the MTCR announced an expansion of the regime's scope to cover missiles capable of delivering not only nuclear weapons but also chemical and biological agents. New export controls applied to unmanned systems capable of delivering any payload to a range of 300 km and to unmanned systems of any payload or range that were intended for the delivery of nuclear, biological, or chemical (NBC) weapons.

The text of the MTCR appears in a short policy document, the Guidelines, and a longer control list, the Annex.[2]

Functions. The MTCR applies different export control policies to the most sensitive items (Category I) than to other items (Category II), which will generally be approved for export unless they contribute to Category I items. This division of items into two categories enables the regime to target its most stringent restrictions on a limited number of the most dangerous items while still controlling a large number of components with due account taken of their multi-use nature.

Category I consists of complete rocket and unmanned air vehicle systems capable of exceeding the 500-kg/300-km parameters (including ballistic missiles, space launch vehicles, sounding rockets, cruise missiles, reconnaissance drones, and target drones), their major subsystems, and their production facilities and technology. The 500-kg/300-km parameters apply to the inherent capability of a system; that is, they take into account the ability to trade off payload and range.

So Scuds, with the advertised ability to deliver a 1,000-kg payload to a range of 299 km, are included in Category I. As of January 1993, rockets and air vehicles intended for the unmanned delivery of NBC weapons are treated functionally as Category I.

Category II includes lower-level items of hardware and technology, e.g., gyroscopes, which can be used for a variety of purposes. In January 1993, complete unmanned systems capable of delivering any payload to a range of 300 km were added to Category II.

To guide the export decisions on these items, the MTCR prescribes three levels of export control: prohibitions, presumptions of denial, and case-by-case reviews.

Prohibitions apply to the transfer of complete production facilities, or complete production technology for Category I items. It would undermine the purpose of the regime to export production capabilities and create new suppliers of the most sensitive items targeted for non-proliferation.

A *"strong presumption to deny"* transfers applies to all Category I items regardless of purpose. The presumption also applies to unmanned delivery systems of any payload and range, and to Category II items, if the supplier government is persuaded that they are intended for NBC weapons delivery. Transfers of Category I items are to be "rare" and can only be made if the supplier government—not just the recipient—takes responsibility for the end use. The "strong presumption to deny" forms the core of the regime and is the key innovation in the policy laid down by the MTCR.

A *case-by-case review* must be undertaken before any item of equipment or technology on the MTCR Annex can be approved for export. In the case of Category II items, if the item is likely to contribute to a Category I system, its export will probably be denied. If the item could contribute to an NBC delivery system, it can only be exported on the receipt of credible assurances from the recipient's government. In most cases, the Category II item will be approved for export.

The members of the regime cannot veto each other's export decisions. They can, however, support their common objectives by means of information exchanges. A key element of information exchange is intelligence, particularly lists of "projects of concern," i.e., Category I systems targeted by the regime. Another element of information exchange is the diplomatic *démarche*, i.e, the transmission of questions or concerns, usually in regard to a potential or actual export.

The most frequent elements of information exchange are the minutiae of export cases and technical questions that enable export control organizations to avoid unintentionally undercutting each other. The regime includes a "no undercut rule," which obliges members generally to reinforce each other's export denials. This rule is an MTCR innovation that has been copied by some other non-proliferation export control regimes. Because the regime has avoided creating an international institution to administer itself—other than the "point of contact", i.e., clearinghouse service by the Government of France—the information exchange is the glue that holds the regime together.

A function of the regime has always been to encourage all governments of the world to adopt the regime's export control policies—whether or not those governments were "members" of the regime, i.e., admitted by consensus into the regime's information exchanges and decision-making. Recently, this "outreach" function has become more structured, with members jointly approaching non-members. As the objectives of the regime have gained near universal acceptance (with only North Korea among major missile exporters officially remaining aloof), the "outreach" function has gained international weight.

Membership. Between 1989 and 1993, full participation in the regime was awarded to 16 nations that were entitled by treaty arrangements or exceedingly close economic cooperation to many of the items controlled by the regime. These additional 16 members were Australia, Austria, Belgium, Denmark, Finland, Greece, Iceland, Ireland, Luxembourg, the Netherlands, New Zealand, Norway, Portugal, Spain, Sweden, and Switzerland. It was urgent to bring these nations into the regime not only because many of them were missile exporters, but also in order to prevent reexport of items the sharing of which might be required under such treaty arrangements as NATO, the European Union, and the European Space Agency. Under international law, treaties supersede policies such as the MTCR.

Between 1993 and 1995, membership went to five additional nations: Argentina, Brazil, Hungary, Russia, and South Africa. All of these nations had indigenous or export programs targeted by the regime. The conditions for membership therefore included restrictions on these targeted activities. In 1997, Turkey joined the regime, resulting in all NATO members being MTCR members as well. The MTCR now has twenty-nine members.

In 1997 the regime made public the following criteria for membership decisions: Whether a prospective new member would:

(1) Strengthen international non-proliferation efforts,
(2) Demonstrate a sustained and sustainable commitment to non-proliferation,
(3) Have a legally based, effective export control system that puts into effect the MTCR guidelines and procedures, and
(1) Administer and enforce such controls effectively.[3]

In September 1993, the United States formulated a more restrictive public policy toward new members. Because membership must be approved by consensus, this policy has effectively served as a supplement to the criteria just listed. Under this U.S. policy, new members, with the exception of nuclear-weapon states, must renounce "offensive" Category I programs, e.g., the programs of Argentina and South Africa, to develop long-range ballistic missiles. Once accepted into the regime, however, a new member could be considered for Category II assistance that contributed to Category I programs not deemed "offensive," e.g., space launch vehicle development.[4] Brazil was the first nation to benefit from this new policy. However, because the hardware, technology, and facilities for space launch vehicles are interchangeable with those for ballistic missiles, the wisdom of this U.S. policy has been a matter of controversy.

Meanwhile, there is a dispersion of national practices among members with respect to transfers. The United Kingdom, for example, announced in 1989 an Open General Export License that waives the requirement for case-by-case review of dual-use Category II exports to other MTCR members.

The net result of these disparate policies toward trade among partners has been the claim by some governments that membership actually increases their entitlement to missile technology. The regime's partners have explicitly reaffirmed that membership does not involve such an entitlement; nor does it involve any obligation on the part of members to supply missile technology. But the "entitlement" view persists. It increases the desirability of membership in the reckoning of some governments, but it raises questions as to whether the regime is advancing its non-proliferation objectives. Although membership in the MTCR has never guaranteed access to missile technology, questions remain as to the extent to which membership will facilitate such access.

A growing number of non-member governments adhere to the export guidelines of the regime. Israel and Ukraine have officially put MTCR export controls into operation; they are recognized by the U.S. government as "adherents," gaining them advantages under U.S. sanctions laws. Other governments, such as China, Romania, and reportedly the Czech Republic, have made unilateral claims of adherence. China's unusual formulation of adherence—to the "guidelines and parameters" of the regime—has raised questions as to whether China applies MTCR controls only to complete missile systems or also to components and technology, as required by the regime. China's October 1994 agreement to "not export ground-to-ground missiles featuring the primary parameters of the MTCR" left open these questions as well as the question of how China's policy applied to other Category I systems, such as ship-to-ground missiles and space launch vehicles.[5]

Meetings. Policy-making meetings ("plenaries") of all the regime members are held roughly every year. The most recent meetings were in Bonn in October 1995, where Russia and South Africa attended for the first time and Brazil was admitted; in Edinburgh in October 1996; and in Tokyo in November 1997. The next plenary will be held in Budapest in Autumn 1998. These sessions operate by consensus. In conjunction with these policy meetings, there are technical experts' discussions and meetings featuring the sharing of intelligence information.

As the information channeled through the French "point of contact" has grown, the methods for disseminating it have become more structured. Every month or so, the Government of France sponsors a "point of contact meeting" at which Paris embassy representatives of member governments report on any matters they wish to call to the attention of other members. In the last two years, these meetings have been supplemented by occasional "reinforced point of contact" meetings attended by home government representatives and allowing extended discussion of specific issues.

Ad hoc meetings are held intersessionally. The most recent included technical experts' meetings to discuss Annex items, "reinforced contact group" meetings in Paris—with one in June 1996 to discuss the missile programs of four nations—and trans-shipment seminars to discuss means by which proliferators attempt to circumvent export controls. Trans-shipment seminars have been held in Washington in 1996 and in London and Einsiedeln, Switzerland, in 1997. An outreach innovation at the trans-shipment seminars has been the attendance of non-members. The first such seminar included Cyprus, Hong Kong, Jordan, Malta, the Republic of Korea, Singapore, and the United Arab Emirates—all nations that might be exploited by proliferators seeking to launder transfers of controlled items. In addition, the regime sponsored an Asian export control seminar in Tokyo in 1997.

Unilateral U.S. Controls. The United States goes beyond the guidelines of the MTCR in two respects. It has laws requiring the imposition of sanctions for certain transfers contributing to missile proliferation, and it has a "catch-all" regulation which, in specific cases, extends export controls far beyond the items on the MTCR Annex.

The United States is unique in its legal requirement to impose sanctions.[6] U.S. missile sanctions were signed into law in 1990 and have been amended several times since.[7] The legislation punishes U.S. and foreign entities trading (buying, selling, or conspiring to buy or sell) in MTCR-controlled items that contribute to the acquisition, design, development, or production of Category I systems in non-MTCR nations. In the case of companies in MTCR member states (or non-member states recognized in a bilateral agreement with the United States to apply MTCR controls), the sanctions are only applied if the trade was conducted illegally and enforcement action was not taken by the member/ adherent government. To date, sanctions have been imposed on entities only in non-member nations, including China, India, Iran, North Korea, Pakistan, Russia (before it became a member), and Syria.

The penalties imposed by the sanctions legislation depend on whether the transfer was a Category I or a Category II item. For Category I transfers, the sanctioned entities (both buyer and seller) are banned for a minimum of two years from export license approv-

als for any U.S. munitions or dual-use item that requires an export license, and they are banned for the same term from competing for any U.S. government contracts. For Category II transfers, the sanctioned entities are banned for the same minimum term from export license approvals for any U.S. item on the MTCR Annex and are banned from competing for U.S. government contracts for MTCR Annex items. If the United States deems that the penalized transfer has "substantially" contributed to a Category I program, an additional minimum two-year ban may be imposed on all U.S. imports of products from the entities involved. All of these sanctions may be waived on national security grounds, and the import bans may be waived on items needed for U.S. defense purposes.

Two amendments to U.S. sanctions laws are worth noting. The Helms Amendment applies to sanctions against entities in non-market economies (principally China and North Korea). It broadens the sanctions beyond the entities directly involved—to apply to all government electronic, space, and military aircraft activities. A 1994 amendment creates a "rebuttable presumption" that any trade in MTCR items is for use in a Category I system, and therefore subject to sanctions, if the trade is conducted with a nation designated by the secretary of state as a supporter of international terrorism. The effects of these amendments are to raise the penalties for sanctions against China and to expand the number of Chinese exports that are potential triggers of sanctions when made to such nations as Iran and Syria. However, missile non-proliferation sanctions have not been imposed on China since 1993.

The "catch-all" regulation was promulgated in 1991 as the U.S. Enhanced Proliferation Control Initiative (EPCI). The EPCI requires U.S. exporters to seek an export license for any item or service, whether or not on the published export control lists, if the exporter has reason to know or is informed by the U.S. government that the item or service is for a missile project in a non-MTCR member nation that appears on a published list of nations with Category I projects. In contrast to the sanctions laws, the United States is not alone in administering "catch-all" controls. An increasing number of MTCR partners have adopted such controls, and in July 1995 the European Union included "catch-all" controls in its export regulations.[8]

Effectiveness. Because missile proliferation is obviously occurring, it is easy to conclude that the MTCR, and U.S. sanctions to enforce it, are ineffective. However, some missile proliferation has not occurred. The unraveling of the Argentine-Egyptian-Iraqi Condor II program—intended to produce a clone of the U.S. Pershing II ballistic missile—and the termination of South Africa's ballistic missile/space launch vehicle program are noteworthy examples of MTCR and sanctions successes. Other programs have suffered multi-year schedule slippages as a result of MTCR export controls; Brazilian and Indian officials have publicly blamed the MTCR for such problems in their large rocket programs.

Two more sophisticated criticisms of the MTCR are often made. One quotes the second sentence of the Guidelines—"The Guidelines are not designed to impede national space programs or international cooperation in such programs . . . "—to demonstrate that the regime has a huge loophole permitting the proliferation of space launch vehicles, which are interchangeable with ballistic missiles. Although this criticism has been repeated frequently, it fails to take account of the rest of the quoted sentence: " . . . as long as such programs could not contribute to delivery systems for weapons of mass destruction." The criticism also fails to take account of the fact that the MTCR Category I list subjects space launch vehicles to the same "strong presumption to deny" exports as ballistic missiles.

In fact, the quoted sentence from the MTCR Guidelines encourages the sale of space launch services and satellites as opposed to the rockets themselves. This permits all nations to obtain the benefits of space activities without access to potential ballistic missiles.

The other sophisticated criticism, far more frequently made, is that the MTCR can only buy time and cannot prevent missile proliferation altogether. However, the MTCR's export controls not only increase the time required for a missile program but also the cost and unreliability of the program and the international opposition to it. With a missile such as the Pershing II requiring some 250,000 parts, it is not necessary to deny access to all 250,000 in order to damage a missile program substantially.

Even if the MTCR only bought time, that would be a valuable accomplishment. Time allows the preparation of defenses against missiles, and time allows the regime in the proliferator nation to change. A change of regime can be a decisive factor in non-proliferation. The termination of the Condor II program, the South African program, the Category I programs in some Eastern European nations, and the Russian exports that triggered U.S. sanctions all occurred after changes of regimes—after time had been "bought."

Two factors are likely to determine the future effectiveness of the MTCR. One is the willingness of member nations to enforce missile non-proliferation and to persuade non-members to do likewise. The other is the extent to which missile-related trade is restrained within—and not only outside—the growing group of MTCR member nations.

NOTES

[1] For a description of the original regime, see Richard H. Speier, "The Missile Technology Control Regime," in *Chemical Weapons & Missile Proliferation: With Implications for the Asia/Pacific Region*, Trevor Findlay, ed., (Boulder: Lynne Rienner Publishers, 1991), pp. 115-21.

[2] The text of the revised MTCR Guidelines is set out in "The Missile Technology Control Regime," ACDA Fact Sheet, May 17, 1993. The Annex has been revised on average every two years.

[3] Press statement adopted at the Tokyo MTCR Plenary (with appendices), November 6, 1997.

[4] "Fact Sheet: Nonproliferation and Export Control Policy," The White House, Office of the Press Secretary, September 27, 1993.

[5] "Fact Sheet: Joint United States–People's Republic of China Statement on Missile Proliferation," U.S. Department of State, Office of the Spokesman, October 4, 1994.

[6] Japan, however, has a policy of taking proliferation concerns into account in decisions on foreign aid.

[7] See the Arms Export Control Act, Chapter 7, and the Export Administration Act, Section 11B.

[8] "Export Administration 1996 Report on Foreign Policy Export Controls," U.S. Department of Commerce, Bureau of Export Administration, January 1996, section 10.

Appendix H
WASSENAAR ARRANGEMENT: DUAL-USE EXPORT CONTROLS

The Wassenaar Arrangement, established in July 1996, is a voluntary system for coordinating national controls on exports of conventional arms and dual-use technologies that depends on information exchange through a consultative forum. Wassenaar is a multilateral successor to COCOM, the Coordinating Committee on Multilateral Export Controls. COCOM was organized during the Cold War as a Western allied mechanism for restricting strategic military trade with the communist bloc—particularly trade in dual-use technologies that could be imported ostensibly for non-military reasons. After the Cold War and collapse of both the Warsaw Pact and the Soviet Union, the West sought through cooperative security and economic policies to foster political and economic reform in the former communist countries of Eastern Europe and the new states that emerged from the Soviet Union. The promotion of East-West political and security partnership in place of the adversarialism of the previous era required that COCOM, a Western economic warfare institution explicitly targeting the communist East, be dismantled.

This was best done, however, by rebuilding a mechanism for controls against the export of strategic dual-use items to still dangerous countries—a mechanism in which reformed, former communist states could participate as partners. This was the underlying construct for the creation of the Wassenaar Arrangement. Conflict with the countries that were of most urgent non-proliferation attention at the end of the Cold War, especially Iraq and Iran, had a significant impact on the generation of new export control and sanctions policies toward "dual-use" items, and, in turn, influenced the content of the Wassenaar guidelines. In effect, the Wassenaar "dual-use" controls are concerned to a considerable extent with dual-use technologies that can facilitate the proliferation of weapons of mass destruction. To the extent that such proliferation may be related to nuclear weapons capabilities, the Wassenaar arrangement complements (or reinforces) the dual-use controls of the Nuclear Suppliers Group (NSG), which focus on equipment, materials and technologies that are not necessarily intrinsically nuclear but can be used, indeed often are critical, for developing or manufacturing nuclear weapons.[1]

Wassenaar Arrangement Creation. The initiative to control strategic dual-use goods by a multilateral mechanism distinct from COCOM was sponsored by the Bush Administration at a November 1992 meeting of the major Western industrialized states—Canada, France, Germany, Italy, Japan, United Kingdom, and the United States, collectively known as the Group of Seven (or G-7). As a consequence of earlier U.S. efforts and the defining experience of the Gulf War, the G-7 had already agreed to refrain from direct, large-scale sales of military equipment to Iraq and Iran. The new U.S. proposal sought to broaden the scope of the conventional weapons embargo by halting the sale to Iran of dual-use technology that could be used for both military and civilian purposes. This effort was only partially successful, however, with the G-7 agreeing to curtail only those strategic dual-use exports destined for known military end-uses. A number of G-7 countries with important commercial links to Tehran, especially Japan, feared the United States intended to use the dual-use ban to control all aspects of trade with that country.[2]

The initiative was revived by the Clinton Administration in early 1993, when G-7 working groups made some progress in identifying "core lists" of technologies to control because of proliferation concern, although the G-7 continued to fail to agree on a common stand to block Iranian purchases of dual-use goods.[3]

Subsequent Clinton Administration efforts to block the export of conventional arms and dual-use military technology to Iran focused on developing a successor regime to COCOM. The charter for the successor regime, known as the Wassenaar Arrangement on Export Controls for Conventional Arms and Dual-Use Goods and Technologies, was approved by thirty-three nations in the Dutch city of Wassenaar on July 12, 1996. Under the new arrangement, participants have agreed not to export conventional arms to four states—Iran, Iraq, Libya, and North Korea; to share information on military sales to other nations; and to regulate sales of military dual-use items. At the time Russia agreed to join the arrangement as a founding member, the other organizing states agreed that its substantial pre-existing arms sales contracts with Iran would be exempt from the group's export restrictions.[4]

Although the guidelines of the regime do not mention its targets, senior Clinton Administration officials have stated that one key objective of the arrangement, from the U.S. perspective, is "to prevent transfers of arms and sensitive technologies for military purposes to the four pariah countries—Iran, Iraq, Libya, and North Korea."[5]

Guidelines. The Wassenaar regime consists of two sets of guidelines: one on conventional weapons and the other on dual-use items and technologies. The guidelines on conventional arms call for regular information exchanges, consultations, and reviews of arms transfer or export deals. Members agree in principle to exchange information every six months on deliveries of weapons covered by the U.N. Register of Conventional Arms, and are supposed to include details of model and type, together with information on the quantity and the recipient. The guidelines on exports of dual-use items are based on an agreed list of controlled goods. This list is further divided into the Basic List (Tier 1) which includes, for example, telecommunications equipment, and annexes, comprising a Sensitive List (Tier 2), covering supercomputers, and a Very Sensitive List (subset of Tier 2) that includes, among other things, stealth technology. While export of dual-use items is at the discretion of national governments, members have agreed to exchange information twice annually on all denials of export licenses for Tier 1 items; to notify denials of licenses for the export of Tier 2 items within 60 days; and to provide, twice a year, information on licenses to export any Tier 2 items to non-members. Members have also agreed to inform other members, within 60 days, of approval of any license that has been denied by another member during the previous three years.

Member Countries[6]

Argentina	Greece	Romania
Australia	Hungary	Russia
Austria	Ireland	Slovakia
Belgium	Italy	South Korea
Bulgaria	Japan	Spain
Canada	Luxembourg	Sweden
Czech Repub.	The Netherlands	Switzerland
Denmark	New Zealand	Turkey
Finland	Norway	Ukraine
France	Poland	United Kingdom
Germany	Portugal	United States

NOTES

[1]Within the United States, exports of both categories of dual-use items are licensed by the Commerce Department, pursuant to the Export Administration Act. Iran-Iraq Arms Nonproliferation Act of 1992, Division A, title XVI, section 1603, P.L. 102-484, 106 Stat. 2571, 50 U.S.C. Section 1701, note (Oct. 23, 1992).

[2]See Steve Coll, "Technology From West Floods Iran," *Washington Post,* November 10, 1992; Leslie Helm, "Japan Reluctant to Back Embargo on Iran; Tokyo Distances Itself From Policy on Exports to Tehran," *Los Angeles Times,* November 13, 1992.

[3]See "A G-7 Embargo on Iran?" *Mednews,* April 19, 1993; Elaine Sciolino, "U.S. Asks Europe to Ban Arms-Linked Sales to Iran," *New York Times,* June 10, 1993; Kenneth Katzman, *Iran: U.S. Policy and Options,* Congressional Research Service Report 97-231 F, Feb. 11, 1997, p. 8.

[4]See "Initial Elements of the Wassenaar Arrangement on Export Controls for Conventional Arms and Dual-Use Goods and Technologies," adopted by the Plenary, July 11-12, 1996; Philip Finnegan and Theresa Hitchens, "U.S. Fights Dual-Use Technology Flow to Iran," *Defense News,* February 28, 1994, p. 6; "Wassenaar Arrangement on Export Controls for Conventional Arms and Dual-Use Goods and Technologies: Final Declaration," Fact Sheet, December 19, 1995; "Post-COCOM 'Wassenaar Arrangement' Set to Begin New Export Control Role," *Arms Control Today,* December 1995/January 1996; British American Security Information Council, "Wassenaar Arrangement Controversial," *BASIC Reports: Newsletter on International Security Policy,* February 21, 1996; Jeff Erlich, "Future of Multinational Export Control Remains in Question," *Defense News,* July 22-28, 1996, p. 10; Andrew J. Pierre, "The Wassenaar Arrangement," *IISS: Strategic Comments,* August 1996; "Press Briefing by Russian Federation Foreign Ministry Spokesman," *Federal News Service,* September 5, 1996.

[5]See "Address by Under Secretary of State for Arms Control and International Security Affairs Lynn E. Davis," before a meeting sponsored by the Carnegie Endowment Nuclear Non-Proliferation Project, Washington, D.C., January 23, 1996.

[6]As of August 1, 1997, see International Institute of Strategic Studies, *The Military Balance* 1997/98 (London: Oxford University Press for International Institute of Strategic Studies, October 1997), p. 290.

Appendix I
NUCLEAR WEAPONS—A PRIMER

A nuclear weapon is a device in which most or all of the explosive energy is derived from either fission, fusion, or a combination of the two nuclear processes. Nuclear fission is the splitting of the nucleus of an atom into two (or more) parts. Highly enriched uranium and plutonium, when bombarded by neutrons, will release energy and emit additional neutrons while splitting into lighter atoms. In nuclear fusion, light isotopes of hydrogen, usually deuterium and tritium, join at high temperatures and similarly liberate energy and neutrons.

Fission Weapons

Many heavy atomic nuclei are capable of being fissioned; but only a fraction of these are fissile, which means fissionable by neutrons with a wide range of velocities. It is this property of fissile material, principally U^{235} and Pu^{239}, that allows a chain reaction to be achieved in weapons employing the fission process. In a chain reaction, fissile nuclei that have been bombarded by neutrons split and emit two or more neutrons, which in turn induce proximate nuclei to fission and sustain the process. With each successive fission "generation" additional energy is released, and, if the fission of one nucleus induces an average of more than one fission in the following generation, the energy yield of each generation is multiplied. A fission explosion in the range of 1 to 100 Kt, for example, would occur over a few microseconds and involve over fifty generations, with 99.9 percent of the energy released coming in the last seven. The minimum mass of material necessary to sustain a chain reaction is called the critical mass. This value may be lowered by increasing the material's density through compression or by surrounding it with "reflectors" to minimize the escape of neutrons; this makes it difficult to pin down the precise amount of uranium or plutonium required for a bomb.

Two basic nuclear-weapon-design approaches that are used to achieve a supercritical mass (i.e., exceeding the critical level) are the implosion technique and the gun assembly technique. In the implosion technique, a peripheral charge of chemical high explosive is uniformly detonated to compress a subcritical mass of plutonium or highly enriched uranium into a supercritical configuration. In the gun assembly technique, two (or more) subcritical masses of highly enriched uranium (plutonium cannot be used) are propelled together by a conventional explosion, resulting in a supercritical mass. In both cases, a tamper may be used to keep the material from exploding before enough generations of a chain reaction have occurred, and this tamper often doubles as a reflector to reduce the escape of neutrons.

Fusion Weapons

Fusion of light atomic nuclei requires a high density of fusion material and extraordinary heat, both of which are provided by a fission explosion in a "thermonuclear" or "hydrogen" bomb. Lithium 6 deuteride is the most widely used thermonuclear material, serving as a source of both deuterium and tritium, the atoms whose nuclei merge, in a fusion weapon.

In a "boosted" weapon, fusion material is introduced directly into (or next to) the core of fissile material, improving the efficiency of a fission weapon and thus increasing the yield of a given quantity of highly enriched uranium or plutonium. Although energy is released in the fusion reaction of a boosted weapon, the primary contribution of the fusion material to the explosion is that it provides additional neutrons for the fission process and therefore allows a more rapidly multiplying chain reaction to occur.

Other thermonuclear weapons are designed to capitalize on the energy released in a "secondary" fusion reaction triggered by a "primary" fission explosion. In such devices, fusion material is kept physically separate from a fissile or boosted fissile core that compresses and ignites it. Additional "stages" of fusion or fission material may be included to augment the weapon's yield, with each layer being triggered by ones closer to the core. For example, the hydrogen bomb includes a third stage or "blanket" of natural uranium, a widely available fissionable but not fissile material, that is fissioned by fast neutrons from the primary and secondary fission and fusion reactions. Hence, the energy released in the explosion of such a device stems from three sources—a fission chain reaction, the first stage; "burning" of the thermonuclear fuel, the second stage; and the fission of the U^{238} blanket, the third stage—with, very roughly, half the total energy stemming from fission and the other half from fusion.

Notes

This Appendix is adapted from Thomas B. Cochran, William M. Arkin, and Milton M. Hoenig, *U.S. Nuclear Forces and Capabilities* (Cambridge, MA: Ballinger Publishing Company, 1984), Chapter 2.

Additional References

1992: Robert Serber, Richard Rhodes, *The Los Alamos Primer* (Berkeley, CA: University of California Press, 1992). **1993:** U.S. Congress, Office of Technology Assessment, *Technologies Underlying Weapons of Mass Destruction* (Washington, DC: Government Printing Office, December 1993); David Albright, Frans Berkhout, and William Walker, *World Inventory of Plutonium and Highly Enriched Uranium—1992* (New York, NY: Oxford University Press, 1993). **1994:** Gary T. Gardner, *Nuclear Nonproliferation: A Primer* (Boulder, CO: Lynne Rienner Publishers, 1994).

Appendix J
MANUFACTURING NUCLEAR WEAPONS

Overview. A state seeking to manufacture nuclear arms must complete a number of essential, often extremely demanding steps. Detecting whether a non-nuclear-weapon state is attempting to develop nuclear weapons, or assessing technically how far it may have progressed in such an effort, relies on information about these steps. The aspiring state must:

- Develop a design for its nuclear device or obtain such a design from another state;

- Produce the fissile material for the core of the device or obtain it from an external source and then machine the fissile material to fabricate the nuclear parts of the weapon;

- Fabricate, or obtain from outside, the non-nuclear parts of the device, including the high-explosive elements and triggering components that will detonate the nuclear core;

- Verify the reliability of these various elements individually and as a system; and

- Assemble all of these elements into a deliverable nuclear armament, commonly referred to as "weaponization."

Design. It is generally accepted today that designing an early-generation atomic bomb—drawing a blueprint—is within the capabilities of most contemporary states. Indeed, a number of American college students have come up with plausible designs based on unclassified information. But developing a reliable, militarily acceptable weapon would take a technical team with special facilities and financial support—and is not a project that could be carried out by an individual in a home workshop.

Several states are believed to have received nuclear-weapons design information or assistance from other states. During the 1950s, the Soviet Union, then a close ally, supplied China with a wide range of nuclear know-how and equipment, and tentatively made a commitment to supply an actual atomic weapon, although it finally decided not to send the weapon. France and Israel are believed to have collaborated on the design of French nuclear weapons in the late 1950s and early 1960s, and Israel may have had access to information from a number of French nuclear tests. Chinese sources allegedly provided Pakistan with the design of the nuclear device used in its fourth nuclear explosive test—a device launched on a ballistic missile. India apparently designed and manufactured the plutonium-based implosion device that it detonated in 1974 without outside assistance, and South Africa also apparently designed its uranium-based "gun-type" nuclear weapons without foreign aid.

Acquiring Fissile Materials. The major technical barrier to making a nuclear device is obtaining the necessary fissile material, i.e., weapons-grade uranium or plutonium, for the weapon's core.

Amounts Required: How much fissile material would be needed for a nuclear weapon depends on the technical capabilities of the country involved and the size of the weapon it sought to produce. International Atomic Energy Agency (IAEA) regulations assume that 25 kg of weapons-grade uranium or 8 kg of plutonium are the minimum amounts that would constitute a "critical mass" (that could spontaneously fission) with a yield up to about 20 Kt (equivalent to the explosive force of 20,000 tons of TNT), roughly the size of the Nagasaki bomb. However, by utilizing more sophisticated designs that rely on high compression of the core material, neutron reflecting "tampers," or both, a state could build such a weapon with considerably less fissile material. According to one recent estimate, a country possessing a "low technical capability" could build a 20-Kt device with only 6 kg of plutonium or 16 kg of weapons-grade uranium. A state with a "high technological capability" could potentially build such a device with as little as 5 kg of weapons-grade uranium or 3 kg of plutonium; a 1-Kt device, which would require considerable sophistication to manufacture, might need only about half these amounts.[1]

Highly Enriched Uranium: To make a weapon from uranium, the U^{235} "isotope" of uranium is used. The number represents the 235 protons and neutrons in the nucleus of this uranium isotope, and denotes its atomic weight.[2] Since natural uranium consists of less than 1 percent U^{235}, and because nuclear weapons must have U^{235} material that is highly concentrated (normally 90 percent or more U^{235}), natural uranium must be "enriched"[3] at an enrichment plant to achieve this concentration. Uranium enrichment is a highly complex process, typically consumes large quantities of electricity, and requires considerable equipment and investment. For this reason, the uranium enrichment route was generally considered a less likely path to proliferation than the plutonium option. However, Argentina, Brazil, Iraq, South Africa, and Pakistan all selected uranium enrichment as their preferred route for acquiring nuclear arms or the potential to manufacture them, and all developed independent uranium enrichment capabilities.[4] India and Israel, although they have relied on the production of plutonium for their nuclear weapons capabilities, have also conducted research on uranium enrichment. India is known to have two experimental enrichment plants. The status of Israel's enrichment program is not publicly known.

Enriched uranium can also be used as a fuel in nuclear power reactors, research reactors, or naval propulsion reactors. The power reactors used in the United States and most other countries (called "light-water reactors") use low-enriched uranium fuel, i.e., uranium that has been enriched from 3 percent to 5 percent uranium-235.[5] Thus a country can have entirely legitimate, non-weapons-related reasons for developing uranium enrichment technology even though the same technology can be used to upgrade uranium to the high enrichment level useful for nuclear weapons. On the other hand, developing a sizable independent uranium-enrichment capability is economically justifiable only for nations with large domestic nuclear power programs or significant potential export markets.

Because highly enriched uranium is sometimes used to fuel research reactors, a nation can have legitimate reasons for obtaining quantities of this material, despite its usefulness in nuclear explosives. In recent years, the United States and France have developed lower enriched uranium fuels that can be used in lieu of highly enriched material in most of these reactors, considerably reducing the proliferation risks posed by fuel from these research facilities.[6]

Several methods have been developed for enriching uranium. All ultimately rely on differentiating among the isotopes of uranium and isolating material with increased concentrations of U^{235}. Two principal techniques are in use today: the gaseous diffusion method, in which uranium hexafluoride gas is forced through a selectively porous barrier, and the ultra-centrifuge or gas centrifuge method, in which uranium hexafluoride gas is swirled in a cylinder rotating at extremely high speeds. Electromagnetic isotope separation (EMIS) using uranium tetrachloride is an inefficient, but less complex, method that was abandoned in the 1950s. In the 1980s, however, Iraq unexpectedly revived this option as part of its nuclear weapons program. Considerable research and development has been conducted on two additional enrichment techniques—the chemical method and laser isotope separation—but neither is used in commercial production of enriched uranium or for weapons-manufacturing purposes.

Producing highly enriched uranium entails many steps apart from the enrichment process itself, and many other installations and capabilities are necessary. Nations wishing to obtain highly enriched uranium, without international restrictions prohibiting its use for nuclear explosives, would have to develop enrichment technology independently, or obtain it illegally, since virtually all nuclear exporter states are unwilling to sell nuclear equipment and materials unless recipients pledge not to use them for nuclear explosives and agree to place them under the inspection system of the International Atomic Energy Agency (see Appendix D on IAEA Safeguards in this volume).

For illustrative purposes, the basic nuclear resources and facilities that would be needed to produce weapons-grade uranium indigenously include:

- Uranium deposits;

- Uranium mine;

- Uranium mill (for processing uranium ore usually containing less than 1 percent uranium into uranium oxide concentrate, or yellow-cake);

- Conversion plant (for purifying yellowcake and converting it into uranium hexafluoride (UF_6), or uranium tetrachloride (UCl_4) the material processed in the enrichment plant);

- Enrichment plant (for enriching the uranium hexafluoride gas or uranium tetrachloride in the isotope U^{235}); and

- Capability for converting the enriched uranium hexafluoride gas or uranium tetrachloride into solid uranium oxide or metal.[7]

Plutonium: To obtain plutonium on its own, a country needs a nuclear reactor that can irradiate uranium, converting part of it into plutonium. This can be one designed specifically to maximize plutonium production (a "production reactor"), or it can be a large research reactor, or a power reactor for producing electricity. Uranium fuel, usually in the form of uranium-filled tubes (fuel rods) made of zirconium alloy (zircaloy) or aluminum, is placed in the reactor. For most production and power reactors and many large research reactors, the fuel itself is either natural or low-enriched uranium, which is not usable for nuclear weapons at this point. As the reactor operates, the uranium fuel is partly transformed into plutonium. This is amalgamated in the fuel rods with unused uranium and highly radioactive waste products, however, and must then be extracted.

To do this, "spent" fuel rods are taken to a reprocessing plant, where they are dissolved in nitric acid and the plutonium is separated from the solution in a series of chemical processing steps. Since the spent fuel rods are highly radioactive, heavy lead casks must be used to transport them. In addition, the rooms at the reprocessing plant where the chemical extraction of the plutonium occurs must have thick walls, lead shielding, and special ventilation to contain radiation hazards.

Although detailed information about reprocessing was declassified by France and the United States in the 1950s and is generally available, it is still a complex procedure from an engineering point of view. Indeed, almost every nation that tried to develop nuclear-weapons via the plutonium route—India, Iraq, Israel, and Pakistan—has sought outside help from the advanced nuclear-supplier countries, although North Korea apparently succeeded in constructing a reprocessing facility at Yongbyon without such foreign assistance.

Like enrichment facilities, however, reprocessing plants can also be used for legitimate civilian purposes, because plutonium can be used as fuel in nuclear power reactors. Indeed, through the 1970s, it was generally assumed that as the use of nuclear power grew and worldwide uranium resources were depleted, plutonium extracted from spent fuel would have to be "recycled" as a substitute fuel in conventional power reactors.

In addition, research and development is under way in a number of nations on a new generation of reactors known as breeder reactors, most notably in France, Japan, Russia, and India. Breeder reactors use mixed plutonium-uranium fuel surrounded with a "blanket" of natural uranium; as the reactor operates, slightly more plutonium is created in the core and the blanket together than is consumed in the core, thereby "breeding" new fuel.

Like plutonium recycling, the economic advantages of breeders depend on natural uranium's becoming scarce and expensive. However, over the past two decades, new uranium reserves have been discovered; nuclear power has reached only a fraction of its expected growth levels; and reprocessing spent fuel to extract plutonium (a critical step in the manufacture of plutonium-based fuels) has proven far more expensive and complex than anticipated. Moreover, concern over the proliferation risks of wide scale-use of plutonium as a fuel has grown. These factors in the late 1970s led the United States to abandon its plans to recycle plutonium in light-water reactors, and, in the early 1980s, to abandon its breeder reactor development program. Germany has abandoned its breeder reactor program and is phasing out its recycling of plutonium. Great Britain, too, has frozen its development of breeder reactors, although it is continuing to reprocess spent fuel on a commercial basis for itself and several advanced nations.

The principal proponents of the use of plutonium for civilian purposes are France, Japan, and Russia, all of which are continuing to develop the breeder reactor option and are moving forward with sizable plutonium recycling programs. Belgium and Switzerland, although they do not have breeder reactor programs, are using increasing amounts of recycled plutonium in light-water reactors. Broadly speaking, the proponents of nuclear energy in these countries have maintained support for the civil use of plutonium by arguing that, although it may not be economical, it represents an advanced technology that will pay off in the future and reduce dependence on foreign sources of energy.

A new factor that will affect the economics of civil plutonium use is that many hundreds of tons of low-enriched uranium produced by blending down weapons-grade uranium from dismantled Russian warheads will soon be added to the international power-reactor fuel market. This will keep prices of this material low and should reduce the attractiveness of high-cost plutonium fuel cycles.

Whatever the thrust of their domestic nuclear programs, the advanced nuclear-supplier countries are strongly discouraging plutonium use by states of proliferation concern.

The longstanding view that plutonium is a legitimate and anticipated part of civilian nuclear programs, however, allowed India and North Korea to justify their reprocessing programs—even though such efforts provided these nations with a nuclear-weapons capability.

Like the production of enriched uranium, the production of plutonium entails many steps, and many installations and capabilities besides the reactor and reprocessing plant are needed. For illustrative pur-

poses, the following facilities and resources would be required for an independent plutonium production capability (assuming the use of a research or power reactor, moderated by either heavy-water or graphite, and employing natural uranium fuel):

- Uranium deposits;
- Uranium mine;
- Uranium mill (for processing uranium ore containing less than 1 percent uranium into uranium oxide concentrate, or yellowcake);
- Uranium purification plant (to further improve the yellowcake into reactor-grade uranium dioxide);
- Fuel fabrication plant (to manufacture the fuel elements placed in the reactor), including a capability to fabricate zircaloy or aluminum tubing;
- Research or power reactor moderated by heavy-water or graphite;
- Heavy-water production plant or a reactor-grade graphite production plant; and
- Reprocessing plant.

In contrast to heavy-water and graphite moderated reactors, which use natural uranium as fuel, a light-water moderated reactor would necessitate use of low-enriched uranium, implying that an enrichment capability may be available. If so, highly enriched uranium could, in theory, be produced, obviating the need for plutonium as a weapons material. (It is also possible that a state might import fuel for a light-water reactor under IAEA inspection and, after using the material to produce electricity, reprocess it to extract plutonium. Although IAEA rules would require the country involved to place any such plutonium under IAEA monitoring, the state might one day abrogate its IAEA obligations and seize that material for use in nuclear arms.)

Acquisition of Fissile Material from Abroad: Although, historically, every state that has developed nuclear weapons has also built an indigenous capability to produce fissile material for this purpose, the weakening of controls over such material in the former Soviet Union has increased the possibility of its becoming available on an international black market. As discussed in the Russia chapter in this volume, during 1994, the smuggling of plutonium and weapons-usable enriched uranium, apparently of Russian origin, was observed for the first time. The widespread availability of clandestine supplies of weapons-usable nuclear materials could greatly accelerate the pace at which emerging nuclear powers could develop nuclear arms and could simultaneously undermine the inspection and auditing system of the International Atomic Energy Agency.

Testing. It is generally assumed that, by rigorously testing the non-nuclear elements of a nuclear device and performing computer simulations, a state could build a reliable first-generation fission weapon without having to conduct a full-scale nuclear explosive test.

The greatest confidence could be achieved with a uranium-based, gun-type weapon (plutonium cannot be used in this design). The United States, for example, was so confident that the gun-type Hiroshima bomb would work as designed that it did not need to conduct a test of the device before it was used against Japan. (The Trinity test was of the more complex implosion-type bomb, the type that was later used against Nagasaki.) As noted above, South Africa employed the gun-type design and is not known to have conducted a nuclear test. Although a full-scale nuclear detonation may not be essential to develop a reliable nuclear weapon, of the three current *de facto* nuclear powers, India in 1974, and both India and Pakistan in May 1998, conducted such tests, while Israel received assistance from more advanced countries, which may be deemed the equivalent of such experimental proof of design.

Since Israel is thought to have "boosted" fission weapons but is not known to have conducted a nuclear test, building reliable versions of such weapons without testing appears possible. To build multi-stage hydrogen bombs, which are far more complex, nuclear testing would be required.

There has been speculation that an ambiguous signal detected on September 22, 1979, by a U.S. satellite overflying the South Atlantic may have been the flash from a nuclear test and, if the event was indeed a test, that it was conducted by Israel or South Africa. Uncertainties about the event have never been resolved, however, and, in addition to the five established nuclear powers, India was the only country known to have detonated a nuclear device before 1998.

Non-Nuclear Components, Assembly, Delivery. Finally, the manufacture of nuclear weapons requires the design and fabrication of: specially designed high-explosive components to compress the fissile-material core of the device; high-speed electronic firing circuits, or "triggering packages" to set off the high explosives uniformly at precisely the correct instant; and, in most designs, an "initiator"—an intense source of neutrons to initiate the nuclear chain reaction in the core. Developing all of these components necessitates considerable technical skill and, though less demanding than producing fissile material, can nonetheless be quite challenging. Iraq's effort to develop these elements of nuclear weapons, for example, is known to have suffered considerable setbacks and had not succeeded prior to the 1991 Gulf War, despite several years of effort.

Assembly of the completed components of nuclear weapons and delivery by aircraft are relatively less demanding. To produce nuclear warheads for ballistic missiles, however, additional steps are necessary, such as the development of reentry vehicles, the miniaturization and/or reconfiguration of nuclear weapons to fit into missile nose cones, and certifying the weapons to withstand the rigors of blast-off, extremely high altitudes, and re-entry.

NOTES

[1]Thomas B. Cochran and Christopher B. Paine, *The Amount of Plutonium and Highly-Enriched Uranium Needed for Pure Fission Nuclear Weapons* (Washington, DC: Natural Resources Defense Council, 1994).

[2]Isotopes of the same element behave the same way chemically but have slightly different atomic weights and may have quite different physical properties.

[3]Technically, a weapon could be made of uranium enriched to more than 20 percent, but it would be very cumbersome. As a practical matter, material enriched to more than 90 percent is preferred. The Hiroshima bomb used uranium enriched to 80-85 percent, however, and South Africa's first nuclear device used material enriched to 80 percent for the first device and 90 percent for the remaining 5 nuclear weapons.

[4]For details and the current status of these efforts, some of which have been terminated, see the individual country sections in the main body of this volume.

[5]Technically, low-enriched uranium is defined as uranium enriched to less than 20 percent in the isotope U^{235}. Such material cannot be used as the core of a nuclear explosive device.

[6]Large research reactors can, however, be used to produce plutonium (discussed earlier in Plutonium section of this appendix).

[7]The conversion of uranium hexafluoride into uranium oxide or metal is often associated with a yellowcake-to-hexafluoride conversion plant.

atomic bomb A bomb whose energy comes from the fission of uranium or plutonium.

beryllium A highly toxic steel-gray metal, possessing a low neutron absorption cross-section and high melting point, which can be used in nuclear reactors as a moderator, reflector, or cladding material. In nuclear weapons, beryllium surrounds the fissile material and reflects neutrons back into the nuclear reaction, considerably reducing the amount of fissile material required. Beryllium is also used in guidance systems and other parts for aircraft, missiles or space vehicles.

blanket A layer of fertile nuclear material, such as uranium-238 or thorium-232, placed around the fuel core of a reactor. During operation of the reactor, material in the blanket absorbs neutrons and decays, with products forming new fissionable material.

breeder reactor A nuclear reactor that produces somewhat more fissile material than it consumes. The fissile material is produced both in the reactor's core and when neutrons are captured in fertile material placed around the core (blanket). This process is known as breeding. Breeder reactors have not yet reached commercialization, although active research and development programs are being pursued by a number of countries.

CANDU (Canadian deuterium-uranium reactor.) The most widely used type of heavy-water reactor. The CANDU reactor uses natural uranium as a fuel and heavy water as a moderator and a coolant.

centrifuge See ultracentrifuge.

chain reaction The continuing process of nuclear fissioning in which the neutrons released from a fission trigger at least one other nuclear fission. In a nuclear weapon, an extremely rapid, multiplying chain reaction causes the explosive release of energy. In a reactor, the pace of the chain reaction is controlled to produce heat (in a power reactor) or large quantities of neutrons (in a research or production reactor).

chemical processing Chemical treatment of nuclear materials, usually in irradiated fuel, to separate specific usable constituents. Chemical re-processing may be carried out with spent (irradiated) fuel to separate fissionable materials and other usable radioactive byproducts from the residual fuel. A different kind of chemical processing may occur in preparation for uranium enrichment; natural uranium feed-stock is processed chemically to convert it to gaseous form for enrichment operations.

coolant A substance circulated through a nuclear reactor to remove or transfer heat. The most common coolants are water and heavy water.

core The central portion of a nuclear reactor containing the fuel elements and, usually, the moderator. Also the central portion of nuclear weapon containing highly enriched uranium or plutonium.

critical mass The minimum amount of concentrated fissionable material required to sustain a chain reaction. The exact mass of fissionable material needed to sustain a chain reaction varies according to the concentration (purity) and chemical form of the material, the particular fissionable isotope present, its geometrical properties, and its density. When pure fissionable materials are compressed by high explosives in implosion-type atomic weapons, the critical mass needed for a nuclear explosion is reduced.

depleted uranium Uranium having a smaller percentage of uranium-235 than the 0.7 percent found in natural uranium. It is a by-product of the uranium enrichment process, during which uranium-235 is culled from one batch of uranium, thereby depleting it, and then added to another batch to increase its concentration of uranium-235.

enrichment The process of increasing the concentration of one isotope of a given element (in the case of uranium, increasing the concentration of uranium-235).

feed stock Material introduced into a facility for processing.

fertile material Nuclear material composed of atoms that readily absorb neutrons and decay into other elements, producing fissionable materials. One such element is uranium-238, which decays into plutonium-239 after it absorbs a neutron. Fertile material alone cannot sustain a fission chain reaction.

fission The process by which a neutron strikes a nucleus and splits it into fragments. During the process of nuclear fission, several neutrons are emitted at high speed, and heat and radiation are released.

fissile material A fissionable material that is especially amenable to fission and therefore readily usable for the core of a nuclear weapon. Uranium-235 and plutonium-239 are examples of fissile materials.

fissionable material Material whose atoms are easily split when struck by neutrons, and that can easily sustain either a controlled or explosive chain reaction, depending on concentration and other conditions of use; also commonly referred to as a "fissile" material.

fusion The formation of a heavier nucleus from two lighter ones (such as hydrogen isotopes), with the attendant release of energy (as in a hydrogen bomb).

gas centrifuge process A method of isotope separation in which heavy gaseous atoms or molecules are separated from light ones by centrifugal force. See ultracentrifuge.

gaseous diffusion A method of isotope separation based on the fact that gas atoms or molecules with different masses will diffuse through a porous barrier (or membrane) at different rates. The method is used to separate uranium-235 from uranium-238. It requires large gaseous diffusion plants and significant amounts of electric power.

gas-graphite reactor A nuclear reactor in which a gas is the coolant and graphite is the moderator.

heavy water Water containing significantly more than the natural proportion (1 in 6,500) of heavy hydrogen (deuterium) atoms to ordinary hydrogen atoms. (Hydrogen atoms have one proton, deuterium atoms have one proton and one neutron.) Heavy water is used as a moderator in some reactors because it slows down neutrons effectively and does not absorb them (unlike light, or normal, water) making it possible to fission natural uranium and sustain a chain reaction.

heavy-water reactor A reactor that uses heavy water as its moderator and that typically uses natural uranium as fuel. See CANDU.

highly enriched uranium Uranium in which the percentage of uranium-235 nuclei has been increased from the natural level of 0.7 percent to some level greater than 20 percent, usually around 90 percent.

hot cells Lead-shielded rooms with remote handling equipment for examining and processing radioactive materials. In particular, hot cells are used for reprocessing spent reactor fuel.

hydrogen bomb A nuclear weapon that derives its energy largely from fusion. Also known as a thermonuclear bomb.

isotope A form of any element that is identical chemically but different in physical properties from other isotopes of the same element. Isotopes of an element have the same number of protons in the nucleus and therefore the same atomic number, but they have differing numbers of neutrons in the nucleus and therefore different atomic weights. Radioactive elements may have some isotopes that are readily fissionable and others that are not.

kilogram (kg) A metric weight equivalent to 2.2 pounds.

kiloton (Kt) The energy of a nuclear explosion that is equivalent to an explosion of 1,000 tons of TNT.

laser enrichment method A still experimental process of uranium enrichment in which a finely tuned, high-power laser is used to differentially excite molecules of various nuclear isotopes. This differential excitation makes it possible, for example, to separate uranium-235 from uranium-238.

light water Ordinary water (H_2O), as distinguished from heavy water (D_2O).

light-water reactor A reactor that uses ordinary water as moderator and coolant and low-enriched uranium as fuel.

low-enriched uranium Uranium in which the percentage of uranium-235 nuclei has been increased from the natural level of 0.7 percent to less than 20 percent, usually 3 to 6 percent. With the increased level of fissile material, low-enriched uranium can sustain a chain reaction when immersed in light-water and is used as fuel in lightwater reactors.

medium-enriched uranium Uranium in which the percentage of uranium-235 nuclei has been increased from the natural level of 0.7 percent to between 20 and 50 percent. (Potentially usable for nuclear weapons, but very large quantities are needed.)

megawatt (Mw) One million watts. Used in reference to a nuclear power plant, one million watts of electricity (Mwe); used in reference to a research or production reactor, one million watts of thermal energy (MWt).

metric tonne One thousand kg. A metric weight equivalent to 2,200 pounds or 1.1 tons.

milling A process in the uranium fuel cycle by which ore containing only a very small percentage of uranium oxide (U_3O_8) is converted into material containing a high percentage (80 percent) of U_3O_8, often referred to as yellowcake.

moderator A component (usually water, heavy water, or graphite) of some nuclear reactors that slows neutrons, thereby increasing their efficiency in splitting fissionable atoms dispersed in low-enriched or natural uranium fuel, to release energy on a controlled basis.

natural uranium Uranium as found in nature, containing 0.7 percent of uranium-235, 99.3 percent of uranium-238, and a trace of uranium-234.

neutron An uncharged elementary particle, with a mass slightly greater than that of a proton, found in the nucleus of every atom heavier than hydrogen.

nuclear energy The energy liberated by a nuclear reaction (fission or fusion) or by spontaneous radioactivity.

nuclear fuel Basic chain-reacting material, including both fissile and fertile materials. Commonly used nuclear fuels are natural uranium, and low-enriched uranium; high-enriched uranium and plutonium are used in some reactors.

nuclear fuel cycle The set of chemical and physical operations needed to prepare nuclear material for use in reactors and to dispose of or recycle the material after its removal from the reactor. Existing fuel cycles begin with uranium as the natural resource and create plutonium as a by-product. Some future fuel cycles may rely on thorium and produce the fissionable isotope uranium-233.

nuclear fuel element A rod, tube, plate, or other mechanical shape or form into which nuclear fuel is fabricated for use in a reactor.

nuclear fuel fabrication plant A facility where the nuclear material (e.g., enriched or natural uranium) is fabricated into fuel elements to be inserted into a reactor.

nuclear power plant Any device or assembly that converts nuclear energy into useful power. In a nuclear electric power plant, heat produced by a reactor is used to produce steam to drive a turbine that in turn drives an electricity generator.

nuclear reactor A mechanism fueled by fissionable materials in a controlled nuclear chain reaction that releases heat, which can be used for civil purposes to generate electricity. Since reactors also produce fissionable material (e.g., plutonium) in the irradiated fuel, they may be used as a source of fissile material for weapons. Nuclear reactors fall into three general categories: power reactors, production reactors (for weapons), and research reactors.

nuclear waste The radioactive by-products formed by fission and other nuclear processes in a reactor. Most nuclear waste is initially contained spent fuel. If this material is reprocessed, new categories of waste result.

nuclear weapons A collective term for atomic bombs and hydrogen bombs. Weapons based on a nuclear explosion. Generally used throughout the text to mean atomic bombs, only, unless used with reference to nuclear-weapon states, (all five of which have both atomic and hydrogen weapons).

plutonium-239 (Pu^{239}) A fissile isotope occurring naturally in only minute quantities, which is manufactured artificially when uranium-238, through irradiation, captures an extra neutron. It is one of the two materials that have been used for the core of nuclear weapons, the other being highly enriched uranium.

plutonium-240 (Pu^{240}) A fissile isotope produced in reactors when a plutonium-239 atom absorbs a neutron instead of fissioning. Its presence complicates the construction of nuclear explosives because of its high rate of spontaneous fission.

power reactor A reactor designed to produce electricity as distinguished from reactors used primarily for research or for producing radiation or fissionable materials.

production reactor A reactor designed primarily for large-scale production of plutonium-239 by neutron irradiation of uranium-238.

radioactivity The spontaneous disintegration of an unstable atomic nucleus, resulting in the emission of subatomic particles.

radioisotope A radioactive isotope.

recycle To reuse the remaining uranium and plutonium found in spent fuel after they have been separated at a reprocessing plant from unwanted radioactive waste products also in the spent fuel.

reprocessing Chemical treatment of spent reactor fuel to separate the plutonium and uranium from the unwanted radioactive waste by-products and (under present plans) from each other.

research reactor A reactor primarily designed to supply neutrons for experimental purposes. It may also be used for training, materials testing, and production of radioisotopes.

spent fuel Fuel elements that have been removed from the reactor after use because they contain too little fissile material and too high a concentration of unwanted radioactive by-products to sustain reactor operation. Spent fuel is both thermally and radioactively hot.

strategic In modern military usage, the term "strategic" usually implies a war-prosecuting plan, campaign, or combat capability that could be rapidly decisive in defeating an opponent. In this book on proliferation, "strategic" usually refers to those weapons—*long*-range offensive nuclear arms, whether missiles or bomber aircraft—that are deployed for nuclear deterrence or retaliation, and to corresponding, strategically capable defensive weapons. Although the term "strategic" is usually associated with *long*-range weapons and operations, in regions consisting of heavily armed small states (e.g., the Middle East), even *shorter*-range offensive systems may be considered strategic if they are nuclear-equipped and capable of striking deep into an opponent's heartland with potentially crippling effects.

tactical In modern military usage, the term "tactical" usually refers to military operations with *shorter*-range weapon systems, on the battlefield, between the frontlines of opposing military forces, and to corresponding defensive systems. Tactical weapons and operations may decide the outcome of a battle, but normally do not determine the outcome of a war. In his book on proliferation, "tactical" usually refers to *shorter*-range (non-strategic) missiles and aircraft, and corresponding (non-strategic) defensive systems. Weapons systems that a major power may consider tactical for its operations may, however, be considered strategic by small states in their relations with hostile neighbors.

thermonuclear bomb A hydrogen bomb.

thorium-232 A fertile material.

tritium The heaviest hydrogen isotope, containing one proton and two neutrons in the nucleus, produced most effectively by bombarding lithium-6 with neutrons. In a fission weapon, tritium produces excess neutrons, which set off additional reactions in the weapon's fissile material. In this way, tritium can either reduce the amount of fissile material required, or multiply (i.e., boost) the weapon's destructive power as much as five times. In fusion reactions, tritium and deuterium, another hydrogen isotope, bond at very high temperatures, releasing approximately 14 million electron-volts of energy per set of neutrons.

ultracentrifuge A rapidly rotating cylinder that can be used for enrichment of uranium. The spinning cylinder concentrates the heavier isotope (U-238) of uranium hexafluoride gas along the cylinder's walls, while the lighter isotope (U-235) concentrates at the center of the cylinder, where it can be drawn off separately.

uranium A radioactive element with the atomic number 92 and, as found in natural ores, an average atomic weight of 238. The two principal natural isotopes are uranium-235 (0.7 percent of natural uranium), which is fissionable, and uranium-238 (99.3 percent of natural uranium), which is fertile.

uranium-233 (U^{233}) A fissionable isotope bred in fertile thorium-232. Like plutonium-239 it is theoretically an excellent material for nuclear weapons, but is not known to have been used for this purpose. Can be used as reactor fuel.

uranium-235 (U^{235}) The only naturally occurring fissionable isotope. Natural uranium contains 0.7 percent U^{235}; light-water reactors use about 3 percent and weapons grade, highly enriched uranium normally consists of 93 percent of this isotope.

uranium-238 (U^{238}) A fertile material. Natural uranium is composed of approximately 99.3 percent U^{238}.

uranium dioxide (UO$_2$) Purified uranium. The form of natural uranium used in heavy water reactors. Also the form of uranium that remains after the fluorine is removed from enriched uranium hexafluoride (UF$_6$). Produced as a powder, uranium dioxide is, in turn, fabricated into fuel elements.

uranium oxide (U$_3$O$_8$) The most common oxide of uranium found in typical ores. U$_3$O$_8$ is extracted from the ore during the milling process. The ore typically contains only 0.1 percent U$_3$O$_8$; yellowcake, the product of the milling process, contains about 80 percent U$_3$O$_8$.

uranium hexafluoride (UF$_6$) A volatile compound of uranium and fluorine. UF$_6$ is a solid at atmospheric pressure and room temperature, but can be transformed into gas by heating. UF$_6$ gas (alone, or in combination with hydrogen or helium) is the feed stock in all uranium enrichment processes and is sometimes produced as an intermediate product in the process of purifying yellowcake to produce uranium oxide.

vessel The part of a reactor that contains the nuclear fuel.

weapons-grade Nuclear material of the type most suitable for nuclear weapons, i.e., uranium enriched to 93 percent U^{235} or plutonium that is primarily Pu^{239}.

weapons-usable Fissionable material that is weapons-grade or, though less than ideal for weapons, can still be used to make a nuclear explosive.

yellowcake A concentrate produced during the milling process that contains about 80 percent uranium oxide (U$_3$O$_8$). In preparation for uranium enrichment, the yellowcake is converted to uranium hexafluoride gas (UF$_6$). In the preparation of natural uranium reactor fuel, yellowcake is processed into purified uranium dioxide. Sometimes uranium hexafluoride is produced as an intermediate step in the purification process.

yield The total energy released in a nuclear explosion. It is usually expressed in equivalent tons of TNT (the quantity of TNT required to produce a corresponding amount of energy).

zirconium A grayish-white lustrous metal which is commonly used in an alloy form (i.e., zircaloy) to encase fuel rods in nuclear reactors.

References

1979: Anthony V. Nero, Jr., *A Guidebook to Nuclear Reactors* (Berkeley: University of California Press, 1979). **1984:** Thomas B.Cochran, William Arkin, Robert S. Norris, and Milton Hoenig, *Nuclear Weapons Databook, Volume 2: U.S. Nuclear Warhead Production* (Cambridge, MA: Ballinger Publishing Co, 1984); *Nuclear Power in an Age of Uncertainty* (Washington, DC: Office of Technology Assessment, 1984). **1993:** U.S. Congress, Office of Technology Assessment. *Technologies Underlying Weapons of Mass Destruction* (Washington, D.C.: U.S. Government Printing Office, December 1993); David Albright, Frans Berkhout, and William Walker, *World Inventory of Plutonium and Highly Enriched Uranium, 1992* (Oxford, England: Oxford University Press, 1993).

About the Authors and Contributors

Tracking Nuclear Proliferation: A Guide in Maps and Charts, 1998, was prepared by the Non-Proliferation Project of the Carnegie Endowment for International Peace.

The book was produced under the direction of **Rodney W. Jones**, Senior Advisor to the Carnegie Endowment's START II Ratification Project. A specialist on the spread of nuclear weapons and strategic nuclear arms control, and the author or editor of six other books on nuclear weapons spread and regional arms transfer, Dr. Jones served on INF and START Treaty affairs in the U.S. Arms Control and Disarmament Agency from 1989 through 1994, and was advisor to the U.S. START delegation and member and working group chair of the U.S. Joint Compliance and Inspection Commission delegation. He is President of Policy Architects International, a consulting firm in Reston, Virginia, and active in the defense and arms control community.

Mark G. McDonough, primary co-author of this book, as well as of its 1995 predecessor, authored the Gulf and Middle East chapters and prepared the International Nuclear Non-Proliferation Regime chapter and associated appendices. He also reviewed and commented on the other chapters, and made important contributions to planning and quality control throughout the present book. A consultant to the Non-Proliferation Project, Mr. McDonough has worked on defense and proliferation issues since the mid-1980s, providing support to the U.S. Departments of Energy and Defense and contributing to numerous publications.

Richard Speier, consultant to the Non-Proliferation Project and an internationally recognized expert on the problems of missile proliferation and the MTCR, authored the chapter on Missile Proliferation and the appendix on the MTCR. Dr. Speier served on non-proliferation staffs in the Arms Control and Disarmament Agency from 1973 to 1982 and in the Office of the Secretary of Defense from 1982 to 1994 before becoming an independent consultant in the Washington, D.C., area.

Gregory Webb, Deputy Director of the Nuclear Non-Proliferation Project, served at the Endowment from 1995 through 1997. He was a managing editor of *Nuclear Successor States of the Soviet Union*, nos. 4 and 5, co-produced with the Monterey Institute of International Studies. Mr. Webb contributed to the planning for the present book and prepared preliminary drafts of the chapters on Belarus, Kazakhstan, Ukraine, and North Korea.

Toby F. Dalton, Junior Fellow in 1997 and now Project Associate with the Non-Proliferation Project, was a managing editor of *Nuclear Successor States of the Soviet Union*, No. 5, prepared the final updates of the chapters on Argentina, Brazil, and South Africa; did extensive work on all the maps and charts; and shouldered major administrative tasks in formatting, pre-editorial review, and compilation of the book's many parts.

Gregory D. Koblentz, Junior Fellow on the Non-Proliferation Project from mid-1996 to mid-1997, contributed research support and preliminary draft materials for the chapters on Argentina, Brazil, North Korea, India, Pakistan, and South Africa; prepared initial drafts of the missile charts; and helped in the fall of 1997 by reviewing several draft chapters on Asia.

David Merrill, an independent graphic design artist, created and updated all the maps for this version of *Tracking Nuclear Proliferation*.

CARNEGIE ENDOWMENT FOR INTERNATIONAL PEACE

The Carnegie Endowment for International Peace was established in 1910 in Washington, D.C., with a gift from Andrew Carnegie. As a tax-exempt, 501(c)(3) non-profit organization, the Endowment conducts programs of research, discussion, publication, and education in international affairs and U.S. foreign policy. The Endowment publishes the quarterly magazine, *Foreign Policy*.

Carnegie's senior associates—whose backgrounds include government, journalism, law, academia, and public affairs—bring to their work substantial first-hand experience in foreign policy. Through writing, public and media appearances, study groups, and conferences, Carnegie associates seek to invigorate and extend both expert and public discussion on a wide range of international issues, including worldwide migration, nuclear non-proliferation, regional conflicts, multilateralism, democracy-building, and the use of force. The Endowment also engages in and encourages projects designed to foster innovative contributions in international affairs.

In 1993, the Carnegie Endowment committed its resources to the establishment of a public policy research center in Moscow designed to promote intellectual collaboration among scholars and specialists in the United States, Russia, and other post-Soviet states. Together with the Endowment's associates in Washington, the center's staff of Russian and American specialists conduct programs on a broad range of major policy issues ranging from economic reform to civil-military relations. The Carnegie Moscow Center holds seminars, workshops, and study groups at which international participants from academia, government, journalism, the private sector, and non-governmental institutions gather to exchange views. It also provides a forum for prominent international figures to present their views to informed Moscow audiences. Associates of the center also host seminars in Kiev on an equally broad set of topics.

The Endowment normally does not take institutional positions on public policy issues. It supports its activities primarily from its own resources, supplemented by non-governmental, philanthropic grants.

ABOUT THE NON-PROLIFERATION PROJECT

The Non-Proliferation Project at the Carnegie Endowment for International Peace serves as an independent source of information and analysis on nuclear affairs and conducts a wide array of professional and public-education activities promoting international efforts to curb the spread of nuclear arms.

To promote increased communication and interaction among non-proliferation specialists, the Project organizes frequent press briefings and seminars, distributes Proliferation Policy Briefs and e-mails a Proliferation News Service to selected experts. The annual Carnegie Endowment International Non-Proliferation Conference, organized and hosted by the Project, is widely regarded as one of the premier events in the field.

In Washington, the Project's ongoing program of research, analysis, and commentary includes two major survey publications: *Tracking Nuclear Proliferation*, and *Nuclear Successor States of the Soviet Union: Nuclear Weapon and Sensitive Export Status Report*, a semi-annual report on nuclear controls and disarmament in the former Soviet Union (prepared in cooperation with the Monterey Institute of International Studies).

Through the Carnegie Moscow Center, the Project conducts a series of activities promoting debate on non-proliferation policies and internal nuclear control measures in the former Soviet Union. Managed by Program Associate Alexander Pikayev, these efforts include regular seminars with key Russian experts and officials at the Carnegie Moscow Center, major conferences, and publication of two Russian-language periodicals on non-proliferation: the Russian edition of *Nuclear Successor States of the Soviet Union* and *Nuclear Proliferation—A Periodic Compilation of Materials and Documents*. The Project also maintains an extensive Web site (www.ceip.org). For copies of its latest reports, contact the Project by e-mail (nnp@ceip.org) or at the Carnegie Washington numbers or address below.

The Project is directed by Joseph Cirincione, Senior Associate at the Carnegie Endowment.

The work of the Non-Proliferation Project is supported by grants from the Carnegie Corporation of New York, the Ford Foundation, the Henry P. Kendall Foundation, the John Merck Fund, the Ploughshares Fund, the Prospect Hill Foundation, the Rockefeller Foundation, and the W. Alton Jones Foundation.

Carnegie Endowment for International Peace
1779 Massachusetts Ave., N.W
Washington, D.C. 20036
Tel: 202-483-7600   Fax: 202-483-1840
e-mail: carnegie@ccip.org   Web Page: www.ceip.org

Carnegie Moscow Center
Ul. Tverskaya 16/2, 7th Floor
Moscow 103009
Tel: 7-095-935-8904   Fax: 7-095- 935-8906
e-mail: info@carnegie.ru   Web Page: www.carnegie.ru

JAPAN'S NUCLEAR FUTURE:

THE PLUTONIUM DEBATE AND EAST ASIAN SECURITY

SELIG S. HARRISON, EDITOR

The Japanese decision to build independent plutonium reprocessing capabilities is officially explained in terms of national energy security and environmental priorities. In a 1971 resolution known as the Three Non-Nuclear Principles, the Japanese Diet pledged that Japan "will not manufacture or possess nuclear weapons." But neighboring East Asian countries, eyeing Japan's plutonium stockpiles and the sophisticated rocketry in its space program, are suspicious of Japanese intentions.

This book presents the views of a leading Japanese proponent of the reprocessing policy, Atsuyuki Suzuki, Professor of Nuclear Engineering at Tokyo University; a leading critic, Jinzaburo Takagi, Director of the Citizens Nuclear Information Center, and Taewoo Kim, Senior Researcher of the Peace Studies Research Institute in Seoul, who warns that the Japanese nuclear program could lead South Korea, or a unified Korea, to pursue comparable reprocessing capabilities.

Assessing the possibility of a nuclear-armed Japan, Selig S. Harrison, former Director of the Carnegie Endowment Project on Japan's Role in International Security Affairs and Northeast Asia Bureau Chief of the Washington Post, analyzes the domestic debate in Japan over nuclear policy and the factors that will determine whether or not Japan will become a nuclear-weapons power.

"*Japan's Nuclear Future* is unique because it provides the international community with unprecedented access to a range of sophisticated Asian views on the possibility that Japan may convert its nuclear-energy programme to a nuclear-weapons programme. . . . The book is important because Harrison pulls no punches. He reviews both the political and technical possibilities for a nuclear-armed Japan—an uncomfortable subject in polite Japanes company. . . . Others have analysed the unconvincing rationales offered by Japanese officials for the country's commitment to a plutonium-based energy. But no one has spoken with such an authentic voice or as accessibly to the international policy community. Moreover, no one has been as ambitiously comprehensive in offering policy options to enhance nuclear safety in the region."

—*Survival*

ISBN: 0-87003-065-5 $12.95

To order, call Carnegie's distributor, Brookings Institution Press, 1-800-275-1447 toll-free, or 202-797-6258. Fax 202-797-6004. When ordering, please refer to code CA08.

STRATEGIC GEOGRAPHY AND THE CHANGING MIDDLE EAST

GEOFFREY KEMP AND ROBERT E. HARKAVY

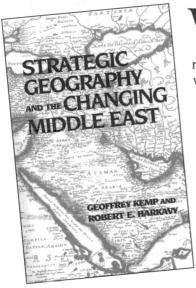

With the breakup of the Soviet Union and growing links between the Middle East and the Caucasus as well as Central and South Asia, a new strategic map of the region is emerging with far-reaching implications for the United States and other major powers with interests in the region.

Geoffrey Kemp and Robert Harkavy argue that increasing demand for Persian Gulf and Caspian Basin energy, especially from the booming Asian economies, ensures that the Middle East will remain a global strategic prize and source of continued rivalry. At the same time, radical changes in conventional military technology and the proliferation of weapons of mass destruction, along with the specter of megaterrorism, present ominous future possibilities—in relation to both warfare scenarios involving the Arab-Israel, Iran-Iraq, and India-Pakistan conflicts and the potential need for interventions by the United States.

The authors likewise signal the region's positive potential. The Middle East has the capacity to move toward a more constructive and peaceful future. Intra-regional proposals already exist for joint infrastructure projects, shared oil and gas pipelines, and improved transportation and communication grids linking the region to Europe; these could usher in a new era of prosperity and cooperation.

A wealth of information is made very accessible through the use of 36 maps detailing the region's history, geography, energy resources, military conflict zones and basing infrastructure, as well as roads and rail and water routes.

"Kemp and Harkavy have written a definitive book on the 21st century Middle East. This book should become a point of departure for understanding the region's strategic significance in the post-Soviet era—including the growing capacity of Middle East actors to conduct megaterrorism against Western powers."

—Graham T. Allison, Harvard University

"Debates about America's security interests and the prospects for peace in the post–Cold War world usually focus on Asia and Europe. Harkavy and Kemp have written a terrific book that shifts the focus to what they call the 'greater Middle East.' They show convincingly that there is real potential for trouble in this region and that the United States, rightly or wrongly, is likely to be in the middle of it."

—John Mearsheimer, University of Chicago

491 pp   Cloth: $52.95 (0-87003-022-1)   Paper: $22.95 (0-87003-023-x)

Published in cooperation with Brookings Institution Press

**To order, please call Brookings Institution Press,
toll-free at 1-800-275-1447, or call 202-797-6258. Fax: 202-797-6004.
When ordering, please refer to code CA08.**

A CARNEGIE ENDOWMENT BOOK

RUSSIA IN THE WORLD ARMS TRADE

ANDREW J. PIERRE AND DMITRI V. TRENIN, EDITORS

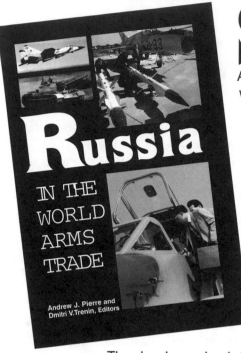

Since the early 1990s, Russia's once colossal defense-industrial complex has been in upheaval. Parts of the arms industry have collapsed, and hopes for conversion from military to civilian production have proven largely illusory. An aggressive arms-sales policy—seen as a panacea—has met with mixed results. Turmoil in domestic politics has deterred much-needed changes in the defense industry's organization, operations, and decision-making as well as in establishing effective controls over the export of arms and sensitive technologies.

Eight prominent Russian experts contribute to this unique Russian-American analysis of the state of Russia's arms industry and national export controls and the strategic implications of Russian arms sales to China and clients in the Middle East.

The authors examine these and other issues posed by Russia's participation in the world arms trade. They also weigh the chances of Russian-American discord over arms exports to "rogue states" as well as the possibilities for arms cooperation, discuss the prospects for Russia's expanded participation in multilateral arms restraint and international norm-setting, and offer policy proposals.

The book evolved from discussions of the Russian-American Working Group on Conventional Arms Proliferation convened by the Moscow Center of the Carnegie Endowment for International Peace and chaired by the co-editors.

Andrew J. Pierre, a former Senior Associate at the Carnegie Endowment for International Peace, is with the School of Advanced International Studies of Johns Hopkins University. **Dmitri V. Trenin** is Deputy Director of the Carnegie Moscow Center and Co-Chair of the Center's Foreign and Security Policy Project.

"Russia in the World Arms Trade is the first book-length attempt by Russian authors to tie together the strategic, political, and commercial aspects of Russia's arms exports. It provides highly useful insights into the current condition of Russia's armaments industry and the drive for arms sales. The book offers a well-informed and insightful view of the Russian debate on this formerly completely taboo subject."

—**Sergei Rogov,** Director of the Institute for USA and
Canadian Studies, the Russian Academy of Sciences

$14.95 in paper (ISBN 0-87003-083-3)

To order, call Carnegie's distributor, Brookings Institution Press,
1-800-275-1447 toll-free, or 202-797-6258. Fax 202-797-6004.
When ordering, please refer to code CA08.